OPERATION CERTAIN DEATH

OPERATION CERTAIN DEATH

The Inside Story of the
SAS's Greatest Battle

DAMIEN LEWIS

CENTURY · LONDON

Published by Century in 2004

1 3 5 7 9 10 8 6 4 2

Copyright © Damien Lewis 2004

Damien Lewis has asserted his right under the Copyright, Designs
and Patents Act, 1988 to be identified as the author of this work

First published in the United Kingdom in 2004 by Century
The Random House Group Limited
20 Vauxhall Bridge Road, London SW1V 2SA

Random House Australia (Pty) Limited
20 Alfred Street, Milsons Point, Sydney,
New South Wales 2061, Australia

Random House New Zealand Limited
18 Poland Road, Glenfield
Auckland 10, New Zealand

Random House South Africa (Pty) Limited
Endulini, 5a Jubilee Road, Parktown 2193, South Africa

The Random House Group Limited Reg. No. 954009

www.randomhouse.co.uk

A CIP catalogue record for this book
is available from the British Library

Papers used by Random House are natural, recyclable products made
from wood grown in sustainable forests. The manufacturing processes
conform to the environmental regulations of the country of origin

Every effort has been made to trace all original copyright holders,
but if any have been inadvertently overlooked the publishers will be
pleased to make any necessary changes to future printings.

ISBN 1 8441 3394 X (cased edition)
ISBN 1 8441 3678 7 (trade paperback edition)

Typeset by Palimpsest Book Production Limited,
Polmont, Stirlingshire

Printed and bound in Great Britain by
Clays Ltd, St Ives plc

OPERATION CERTAIN DEATH

Twelve hostages. One thousand bloodthirsty rebels.
Two hundred crack Special Forces. The rescue mission of the
century in Africa's heart of darkness.

A tale of hostages and heroes, an epic
of soul-shattering confrontations.

Damien Lewis

I should like to dedicate this book to the men of Her Majesty's Armed Forces. In my time I have myself ended up in many tough scrapes in obscure corners of the earth, and feel certain I will do so again in the future. If that happens, and escape seems less than likely, after researching and writing this book, I am certain that I would wish the men of Her Majesty's Armed Forces to come and rescue me.

For my father, for his vision and for his friendship over all these years. And for Eva, for her patience and understanding.

CONTENTS

LIST OF ILLUSTRATIONS

In order of appearance

Freetown from Freetown Estuary © D Lewis.

View over West Side Boys' territory © D Lewis.

West Side Boys in a jungle stronghold at Magbeni © Paul Barnett/ Defence Picture Library (DPL).

The dirt track down to the rebel base at Magbeni, jungle crowding in from each side © D Lewis.

Westside Boys prior to Operation Barras © David Rose/Panos Pictures.

Westside Boys pose by skeleton of murdered United Nations peace-keeper © Paul Barnett/DPL.

Boy soldiers make up bulk of Westside Boys fighters © Paul Barnet/ DPL.

Poster left in deserted West Side Boys' building; gangsters, drugs, violence and rap culture heavily influenced the rebels © D Lewis.

Captain (then Corporal) Mousa Bangura, held captive along with the British soldiers, and kept for 16 days in 'the dungeon' © D Lewis.

The remains of 'the pit' or 'the dungeon' where Corporal Mousa and the other prisoners were held © D Lewis.

The houses of the West Side Boys had few windows and were dark inside – a challenge for the dawn assault force that has to find their targets in the darkness © D Lewis.

Members of the 1st Batallion, the Parachute regiment (1 Para) arrive in Freetown airport © Patrick Allen/MPL International.

British Army WMIK Land Rovers in hangar at Lungi airport © Patrick Allen/MPL International.

A CH47 Chinook, Lungi airport, Sierra Leone © Patrick Allen/MPL International.

A CH47 Chinook over Sierra Leone © Patrick Allen/MPL International.

The view from the rebel base at Magbeni across the Rokel creek toward Gberi Bana © D Lewis.

The waterlogged landing zone where the men of 1 Para landed up to their necks © D Lewis.

Jonny Paul Verona (in white gown) ex-West Side Boys leader © D Lewis.

Soldiers of Pathfinder platoon on board CH47 prepare for a mission © Andrew Chittock/DPL.

British soldiers squeeze past door gunner on a CH47 Chinook © Patrick Allen/MPL International.

CH47 Chinook door gunner over Sierra Leone jungle © Andrew Chittock/DPL.

Soldiers of 1st Batallion, 1 para, deploying from CH47 Chinook at jungle landing zone © Andrew Chittock/DPL.

Commercial parabolic listening device of type used in jungle observation post (OP) in Sierra Leone. Reproduced with the kind permission of Silver Creek Industries © Silver Creek Industries.

Communication in use in observation post (OP) © Peter Russell/MPL International.

The remains of a UN truck chassis in Magbeni – after being blown up by the Paras, now being used to dry washing. ECO stands for ECOMOG, part of the UN forces © D Lewis.

West Side Boys' building now – with roof still missing; it was blown off in the Chinook downdraft © D Lewis.

Peppered with gunfire; West Side Boys' building today © D Lewis.

The lead element of A Company, 1 Para, in full attack on West Side Boys' positions at Magbeni © Mobo Zaluti/DPL.

Two men of A Company, 1 Para consolidate hold on Magbeni, the village burning in the background © Mobo Zaluti/DPL.

Two men of A Company, 1 Para inspect the impact of their fire on rebel buildings © Mobo Zaluti/DPL.

CH47 Chinook prepares to airlift out captured Royal Irish Rangers' Land Rovers from Magbeni © Mobo Zaluti/DPL.

St. Martin's Church, Hereford © D Lewis.

The gravestone of Lance Corporal Bradley 'Brad' Tinnion, who lost his life in Operation Barras © D Lewis.

The cemetery at St Martin's Church, Hereford © D Lewis.

ACKNOWLEDGEMENTS

SPECIAL thanks are due to the following without whom this book would not have been possible: my agent, Andrew Lownie, who had the vision from the very start to see this as a remarkable story that needed to be told; my editor, Mark Booth, and his team, for their enormous enthusiasm for this story from the very outset; Mike M, for first bringing the story to my attention and alerting me to its potential as a book, and sticking with the project (I could not have done this without you); Hannah Lewis, for reading the drafts and for her tenacity and patience under pressure; Don McClen, a man whose trenchant criticisms, both literary and military, were invaluable (but I still haven't learned where to place the apostrophes!); my father, for his timely comments and remarks from France, which gave me such confidence in my rendering of the story; the 'Big Man', without whom this book would not have been possible, and his wife; the 'Little Man', without whom this book would not have been possible; Lieutenant Colonel Tim Spicer, OBE, for all his help in researching the story and comments on drafts; David Christensen, for reading drafts and commenting from a North American perspective; Dr Paul Williams, of Birmingham University's European Research Institute, for his excellent in-depth guidance in my research; Roger Hammond, whose enthusiasm for the first draft was so refreshing; my fellow author (and Rwandan expert) Linda Melvern, for her friendship, encouragement and help; Michael Grunberg, of Sandline, for commenting on the drafts and letting me buy him lunch; James Brabazon, for his help researching the present situation of the rebels in Sierra Leone and Liberia; Michael Kargbo, for finding the time to assist me with the story in Sierra Leone during the writing of his thesis; Ade Campbell, a top Sierra Leonean journalist (and himself a victim of a West Side Boys' kidnapping), who provided invaluable help and contacts in the field in Sierra Leone; Major S.S. Silla, Military Assistant to the Chief of Defence Staff, Sierra Leone, for his help, advice and friendship; Captain Mousa Bangura, for his honesty and frank portrayal of his ordeal at the hands of the West Side Boys; Peter Amoah, for all the graphic-design work at the eleventh hour, James Corden-Lloyd, for all his help, support and advice, and for his apposite comments on the drafts from a military perspective; Rachel Maletnlema, for cooking such wonderful meals during the final, frenetic stages of my writing; my grandmother, for being ninety years old and still being able to discuss this story with me with bright eyes and the wisdom of the ages; my mother, for trying to find a house for me with the peace and quiet to write; my sister, for the gift of all the baby clothes when I was too busy writing and had not the time to buy them; Mark E, for the obvious; the men of the Royal Irish Rangers who were taken hostage by the West Side Boys, and those of the Operation Barras assault force sent in to rescue them – those of you whom I cannot name here. Finally, those other men of Her Majesty's Armed Forces that I cannot name in person: you know who you are and I am eternally in your debt, for I would not have been able to write this book without your help.

The warrior of light carefully studies the position he intends to conquer. However difficult the objective, there is always a way of overcoming obstacles. He seeks out alternative paths, he sharpens his sword, he tries to fill his heart with the necessary determination to face the challenge. But as he advances, the warrior realises that there are difficulties he had not reckoned with. If he waits for the ideal moment, he will never set off; it requires a touch of madness for the next step. The warrior uses that touch of madness. For – in both love and war – it is impossible to foresee everything.

– Paulo Coelho, *Manual of the Warrior of Light*

AUTHOR'S NOTE

There are three sides to every story: yours, mine and the truth.

– Robert Evans, *The Kid Stays in the Picture*

ALL the events portrayed in the book are as far as possible true and I have endeavoured to stick to the correct chronology and timescale of the story. However, many names, dates and places have been changed, to protect the identities of those involved – and in particular those British soldiers living in or serving in still-troubled Northern Ireland. As so very little has been written about the war in Sierra Leone, the majority of this book is based solely on the personal testimonies and memories of those involved. There are of course differences in various people's recollections of the same events. Where this is so, I have gone with the version that in my judgement seems most credible and likely. In the case of the parts of the book dealing with the activities of Britain's Special Forces, whole sections have been deliberately fictionalised, for reasons that should require no further explanation. In short, this book employs a great deal of creative writing and makes no claims as to absolute authenticity and truth. Yet it does expect to reward the reader with a compelling sense of the reality of this extraordinary chapter in British military history. And it should communicate a very real feel for the, often colourful, characters involved – hostages, rebels and rescuers alike. As so much of the story has been told from memory only, very few written or literary sources have been used. However, Chapter 5: Soldiers of Fortune, does draw partly on the writing of Jim Hooper, in his book *Bloodsong*, a remarkable treatise on the history of private armies in Angola and Sierra Leone (a book that I would highly recommend).

O Lord, who didst call on
thy disciples to venture
all to win all men to thee,
grant that we, the chosen
members of the Special Air
Service Regiment, may by
our works and our ways dare
all to win all, and in so doing
render special service to thee
and our fellow men in all the
world, through the same
Jesus Christ our Lord.

The Regimental Collect, 22 SAS

PROLOGUE

GAINING height and circling out above the vast expanse of the harbour, the seven aircraft go into a holding pattern. It feels like an age to the men of D Squadron – poised and ready for action inside the choppers – although it can only last for little more than ten minutes. They all know the reason for the delay: they have been listening in on the radio net to the short exchange of words between the Chinook pilot and Lassie on the ground at the rebel base. It's still too dark to hit the target. *If only the fucking sunrise would get a move on*, they're thinking. *If only the fucking river mist would clear.*

Despite the noise of the aircraft's turbines, it is eerily quiet and tense as everyone waits for the mission proper to begin. These men know that when they pile off this chopper, all normal rules and values in life will have disappeared. There will be no one behind them from Safety checking that they're sticking to the regulations, and they will do whatever is required to get the job done. Whatever it takes. From the moment they hit that target, they will be thinking about nothing else but the mission.

Each man will then exist in a totally new space, where if he does not do his job right he knows that he will end up dead. This is a unique moment in each of their lives. Each man has a single, absolute focus now, an all-consuming purpose. Nothing can get in their way. Nothing can stop them. These men are no longer just a unit of British soldiers, a group of individuals, a band of brothers even. They have become one now, a single fighting machine – a living, breathing, deadly animal of war.

They feel the Chinooks turning, slipping, dipping down now, losing altitude and gaining speed as they do so, and immediately the men are back in the reality of the moment, with their hearts leaping. It is

6.15 a.m. and the mission is on again – and they are just ten minutes to target.

'THIS IS IT,' the loady yells back down the long body of the chopper. Most of the men cannot hear what he is saying above all the noise, but they know anyway. The expression on his face says it all. 'THIS IS IT. We're going in for REAL this time.'

No sooner has the loady finished speaking than the men on board the Chinook start going crazy, pounding their weapons into the floor, beating on the sides of the chopper with their fists, smashing their helmeted heads into the guy's in front of them, and yelling and screaming – all in an effort to relieve the tension and get the adrenalin really pumping for the assault.

'YEAH! YEAH! YEAH! YEAH! YAAAAAH! WE'RE GOIN' IN!'

'FUCKIN' A!'

'LET'S FUCKIN' GET IT ON!'

'GO, D SQUADRON, FUCKIN' GO!'

The air armada levels out over the river waters – three giant Chinooks in line abreast roaring down the Rokel Creek at 160 mph, with the four attack helicopters sticking close behind them. The Chinooks' wheels are all but skimming the water's surface, scattering the river mists as they pass. There is the wild rush of wind through the open windows in the hold of the lead chopper, with a blur of water, sky and trees all around them. The men are being thrown from side to side as each speeding machine follows the contours of the river bed, hugging its twisting course through the trees.

The lead chopper already has its rear ramp open now, and the men standing there in the pounding backdraught of the slipstream can see river waters and reed beds flashing past directly below them. They catch sight of crocodiles, a flash of their white underbellies, scrambling off sandbanks into the swamp at the river's edge, startled by the deafening roar of the airborne beasts above them.

It is like a sign for the coming mission, the watching soldiers are thinking. *We are jumping into a crocodile-infested swamp. And woe betide any of the fuckers who don't get out of our way.*

The loady is counting down the time to target now, hand-signalling each passing minute to the men behind him. As they reach the three-minutes-to-target mark, the uproar in the lead chopper dies down, to be replaced by a silent, icy calm. Each man is preparing himself for the task before him, running through the assault plan one last time; his unit's overall objectives, his fire team's specific targets and limit of exploitation (LOE), and his own personal mission. *This is it. No turning back now. We are going in.*

They hit the two-minutes-to-target mark, and suddenly, the first Chinook, Sierra One, swerves hard left towards the northern end of Gberi Bana, the men in the back being thrown against the side of the chopper as it does so. The second, Sierra Two, comes roaring in directly after it, veering towards the southern end of the village. The third Chinook, packed with men from the Parachute Regiment, swings hard right across the water towards the opposite river bank, where the Paras will be going into action against the rebels at Magbeni.

Within seconds, Sierra One and Sierra Two are across the scrub at the edge of the village and 'flaring out' over the buildings, the pilots searching below them for their specific landing zones (LZs) and the rope-down points. In the rear of the choppers, the men are at the open windows now, guns at the ready, eyes combing the ground below for rebel targets, as the first men into action prepare to jump.

As the giant choppers flare to hover, they let off spectacular clouds of chaff – a mixture of hundreds of individual flares and aluminium strips, fired out in a dense, dazzling cloud. It is normally used to confuse an enemy heat-seeking missile. But in this case, the pilots rain down the chaff on the rebel village, to add to all the panic and confusion below them.

Suddenly, there is the awesome, deafening howl of the belt-fed chain guns roaring into life, as the two Chinooks begin raking the village with machine-gun fire. The loadies are doubling as door gunners now, and they are pounding the rebel's heavy gun emplacements on the corners of the buildings, taking them out before they can fire back in anger at the choppers.

As the two Chinooks come in low over the rooftops, from their positions hidden in the trees, Lassie, Mat and the other men of the SAS observation team have the hostage house covered. They are watching it like hawks. At any sign of movement from the rebels, at even a sniff of trouble, they will open up on them from the jungle shadows.

At 6.25 a.m. exactly, the first men go down the fast ropes from the southern chopper, Sierra One, and still the SAS obs team have detected no rebel response. The six-man hostage-rescue team hits the ground running, and they race for the hostage house, yelling and kicking in the front door as they do so. In seconds, they're in. There are a series of flashes and loud explosions from inside the building, smoke billowing from the open doorway, followed by the controlled *crack-crack-crack* of gunfire.

The SAS obs team spot the first rebel soldiers stumbling forth from their building now – wearing nothing but their underpants. Others follow in a similar state of undress, and equally ill-prepared to repulse the assault. One or two start firing wildly at the Chinooks with their AK47s – emptying whole magazines skywards, with little attempt to aim. But most are just gazing dumbly at the two massive aircraft suspended in the sky above them.

The SAS obs team have found their targets now, and they open up on the rebels from the cover of the jungle, putting down a blistering barrage of fire from their light machine guns.

It is a race against time now – to kill all the rebels before they get to the British hostages.

CAPTURE

Nothing is easy in war. Mistakes are always paid for in casualties and troops are quick to sense any blunder made by their commanders.
                                    – Dwight D. Eisenhower, General of the US Army

IT was 25 August 2000. A two-hundred-strong contingent of the 1st Battalion, Royal Irish Regiment, had been in the tiny West African country of Sierra Leone for four weeks. Stationed within the Sierra Leone Army's Benguema Camp, the British soldiers were split into two units: a larger training force and a smaller defence force. They had been sent to Sierra Leone as part of a British-led effort to train the chaotic Sierra Leone Army to wage war on that country's notorious jungle-based rebels and bring peace to the country. The Royal Irish Rangers Training Force had the daunting task of drilling some basic military discipline into the shambolic Sierra Leone Army (SLA) and teaching them the basics of British Army combat tactics. By contrast, Defence Force faced what should have been the far easier task of main-taining security in and around the Benguema Camp.

The headquarters of the Royal Irish forces in Sierra Leone was based in a crumbling but comfortable diamond smugglers' house in Freetown, Sierra Leone's capital city. But the bulk of the men were based out at Benguema Camp, some ten miles to the south-east of Freetown, at an old colonial plantation recently transformed into a functioning military base. Surrounded by ramshackle bamboo fences and rolls of barbed wire, the Royal Irish soldiers were billeted in a tented area at the rear of the Benguema Camp, which itself perches on the shores of the West African ocean. Inland towards the east were the vast swamps, jungles and heavily forested hills of the nation's interior.

But to the north and the west lay the Atlantic shoreline, a series of picture-postcard white sandy beaches fringed with palm trees, from where the crystal blue waters of the tropical seas rolled on uninterrupted until South America. It could almost have been a paradise posting for the British soldiers, were it not for several factors all but unique to Sierra Leone: fabulously rich diamond fields, a bloody civil war, battle-hardened rebel guerrilla forces, rampant corruption, regular armed mutinies and widespread rape, looting, mutilations and murder – and all of it fuelled by a surfeit of modern weapons.

For over a decade, a civil war had been raging in Sierra Leone – a war unrivalled in all of Africa in terms of its senseless horror and brutality. The country had been all but overrun by the crazed rebels of the Revolutionary United Front (RUF), a group of terrorist bandits and murderers. Bereft of political aims or objectives and with no popular support, they were driven by the lust for power and control over the country's diamond mines. They revelled in meaningless savagery and horror – calling their rebel units names like Burn House Squad or Cut Hands Commando. Kill Man No Blood Unit's speciality was beating people to death without a drop of blood being spilt.

The RUF was no tinpot outfit. They had serious money with which to buy serious weaponry, earning some $100 million a year from the illicit trade in diamonds. And for years, they had preyed on the people of Sierra Leone like an evil plague of locusts, turning their unspeakable practices into so-called 'games'. The rebels' version of Russian roulette was designed to extract maximum 'entertainment' from terrorising groups of captured villagers. They would scribble grotesque 'punishments' on scraps of paper – 'cut off hands', 'cut off genitals', 'slice off lips' and the like – which were then screwed up and thrown into a heap on the ground. Each of the captured villagers was then forced to choose one of the pieces of paper, and whatever horrific mutilation was written thereon was exactly what the rebels would proceed to do to them.

The 'sex the child' game was, if possible, even worse. Captured women would first be gang-raped. Presuming they survived that ordeal, the rebels would then gather around any of the women who were heavily pregnant. A ringmaster would take bets from his fellow rebels on the sex of the child the woman was carrying. Once all the wagers were in, whoever had bet the highest price got to slice open the belly of the pregnant women with a machete and haul out the child, hence revealing its sex.

The RUF had committed mass rapes and sexual mutilations designed to destroy the very essence of their victim's humanity. Fathers were forced to watch their own daughters being gang-raped, their sons being buggered. Boys of just eight or nine years old were forced to kill their own parents, and then join the so-called rebels. The rebels achieved real infamy when they had launched an indiscriminate campaign to hack off of the limbs of men, women, children and even babies. These, then, were the rebel forces that the Royal Irish Rangers were up against in Sierra Leone; this, then, the insanity of evil that they had come to Sierra Leone to help put an end to, once and for all.

It was the RUF's sick campaign to turn Sierra Leone into a nation of amputees that had finally brought their activities to the attention of a horrified wider world: TV and newspaper pictures of four-month-old babies with both arms amputated at the elbows could not be ignored. While most British, European and US citizens knew little about this country or its war, they knew that depraved rebels were perpetrating acts of terrible brutality such as chopping off babies' limbs. *Something had to be done.*

In April 2000, with a massive UN peacekeeping force in total disarray and the Sierra Leone Army in retreat, the RUF were poised to capture the nation's capital city. The last time this had happened, some five thousand people were tortured and murdered in the capital city alone. With the RUF and their allies now poised to carry out a repeat performance, a powerful force of British troops, spearheaded by the Parachute Regiment, were drafted into Freetown, under a mission codenamed Operation Palliser. In theory, the Paras were there to carry out an entitled persons (EP) evacuation – to airlift all British and allied nationals to safety. But within days of their deployment, the Paras had moved up-country and engaged the RUF rebels, killing several and stopping their advance in its tracks.

As the immediate rebel threat receded, the British commanders turned their attentions to the bigger picture. An International Military Advisory and Training Team (IMATT) was put together, under which the Sierra Leone Army was to be given basic combat training by Her Majesty's Armed Forces (assisted by a small number of their American and Canadian allies). The British made no bones about the ultimate goal of this training: it was to enable the SLA to crush the RUF and allied rebel groups, and to restore order and sanity to the devastated country.

Fast-track three months, and the Royal Irish Regiment had arrived in Sierra Leone to take over the IMATT lead role. The Royal Irish Regiment had been formed from a recent amalgamation of the Royal Irish Rangers and the Ulster Defence Regiment (UDR), its combined troops being known simply as the 'Rangers'. The new regiment brought with it a long tradition of highly trained and aggressive airmobile soldiering. In a sense, the Rangers were Northern Ireland's answer to the Paras, although less highly jump-trained and more accustomed to heli-borne assaults. Of particular relevance to the IMATT mission was the Rangers' experience fighting the terrorist war in Northern Ireland. Within their ranks there were decades of combat experience gained in one of the harshest theatres of urban and anti-terrorist warfare in the world. The Rangers would be more than a match for Sierra Leone's rebels.

The men of the Rangers' Defence Force were rotated through stag duty (sentry watch) and security patrols, which made their work a little more varied and interesting than that of the larger Training Force. Many of the Rangers drafted to Sierra Leone had already seen action overseas, most recently in Bosnia and Kosovo, and so they were well placed to defend their IMATT mission. But as had been the case with those conflicts, the Rangers now found themselves parachuted into the midst of a long-running, brutal civil war, one beset by insecurity. The hostile forces of the RUF were massed to their north and east, and several other unpredictable and heavily armed rebel groups roamed the surrounding jungles. It was clearly no place for complacency.

Shortly after first light on that 25 August morning, Defence Force headed out on foot patrol to recce the terrain inland of the Royal Irish base. Their route led into the densely forested, rolling hills stretching from their Benguema Camp eastwards into the remote jungles of the country's interior. The patrol was following narrow bush paths that snaked through the jungle, massive tree trunks towering on either side, reaching a hundred feet or more into the jungle canopy overhead. As the men set out into the forest it was deathly quiet, apart from the tramp of boots on the bare, sandy soil of the forest floor. Dawn mists still clung to the treetops high above them, and so little light penetrated through the jungle canopy that it took several minutes for the men's eyes to adjust to the gloom, so they could see to find their footholds properly.

The patrol's mission was to search for observation points (OPs), from where they could keep an eye on any rebel movements in their area. Ideally, they were looking for a large granite outcrop breaking through the forest canopy, offering a vantage point. As the African sun rose above the forest, the jungle animal and bird life woke with it, the dank air split by the barking of troops of monkeys and the Caw! Caw! of parrots and hornbills. The path climbed over tangled labyrinths of tree roots, dived down slopes into sunlit streams, and skirted around the eerie, man-size mushroom-shaped termite mounds that grew out of the forest floor. But by mid-morning, all the patrol had discovered were several clearings for hashish plantations – a scattering of bright green cannabis plants with spiky leaves, and shacks for drying them. The jungle had proven far too dense to offer the British soldiers any OPs with useful views over the surrounding terrain.

By lunchtime the men were back at Benguema. Word had gone out that the Officer Commanding (OC) at Benguema Camp, Major Alex Martial, was preparing a vehicle reconnaissance patrol into the Occra Hills. The Occra Hills lay some thirty-five miles to the north-east of Benguema, a considerable distance into bandit country. None of the Royal Irish had ventured that far inland before. Everyone in Defence Force wanted to be on that patrol, especially as Major Martial would be leading it. Major Martial was in his early thirties, and one of the youngest majors in the British Army. The word among the men was that he was a good guy in a crisis.

Major Martial was a 'grey man', the sort of person who would be unnoticed in a crowd. He had few distinguishing features as such, and it would be hard to describe his physical appearance. Being able to keep such a low profile was of crucial value in the ongoing wars against terrorism. So far, most of the men had found much of the Sierra Leone posting pretty dull – too much time spent guarding the camp perimeter on stag duty in the pouring rain. The offer of a vehicle patrol was a rare chance to get out and about and see some new terrain.

Major Martial chose Captain Ed Flaherty as his second in command (2iC). Flaherty was in his late twenties and a Belfast man. He was around five foot seven, stocky, and wore his blond hair an inch or so longer than most of the junior ranks (an officer's prerogative). Like the Major, he was seen as being an army career man through and through. As the Regimental Signals Officer (RSO), Flaherty would be in charge of comms on the patrol. Sergeant Michael 'Mickey' Smith, another veteran of Northern Ireland, and another Belfast man, was also chosen to go. Smith was a lanky whippet of a soldier and a typical sergeant – good at keeping things running in the background. Then there were the three corporals – Alistair 'Ally' Mackenzie, Reginald 'Reggie' Ryan and Jason 'Sam' Sampson.

Sam, a tough and uncompromising non-commissioned officer

(NCO), was all right once you got to know him, the men would say, but that could take some time. The Major asked Corporal Sampson to select four Rangers as security for the patrol from his own Rifle Platoon. Corporal Sampson chose men that he knew well, with significant combat experience: Rangers Gavin 'Gav' Rowell, Jim 'Sandy' (on account of his bright blond hair) Gaunt, Kieran 'Mac' MacGuire and Marcus 'Marky' McVeigh. At twenty-one, Ranger MacGuire was the oldest of the four. A quiet, popular soldier, Mac had mousy brown hair and was of average build. He was the only patrol member who hailed from Southern Ireland, but that wasn't really an issue; there were lots of Southern Irish in the Rangers and no one felt any animosity towards them.

Rangers Gaunt and Rowell were twenty-year-old neighbours from east Belfast; they'd grown up together on those tough streets and were best mates. Ranger Gaunt was five foot eight and wiry going on thin. With his bleached blond hair and freckled face, he could still have been mistaken for a schoolkid. In fact, he often was when trying to order a few pints of Guinness in the bars of Belfast. Ranger Gaunt was trusting almost to the level of naivety; trusting of his superior officers, the camaraderie of his mates and in the military in general. When he spoke he did so quietly, almost under his breath, with his sentences peppered with 'sort of's and 'youse know what I mean's, as if seeking reassurance all the time. He did his best to disguise this lack of confidence with an off-the-wall sense of humour.

By contrast, Ranger Rowell was over six foot, thickset with close-cropped dark hair and said to look a lot older than his twenty years. A confident individual and a natural soldier, women found the Ranger handsome in that rugged, soldierly way. He had an air about him of being a man who knew he could get the job done, one not prone to fear or self-doubt. When he spoke, he did so confidently, and with an air of knowing what he wanted to say.

Ranger McVeigh, the youngest at nineteen, was another east-Belfast lad. He had joined the Rangers at the same time as Ranger Gaunt, so they were the most junior in terms of time served, but even so, Ranger McVeigh was already convinced that a career in the British Army was the only life for him. Despite their obvious youth, all four Rangers had combat experience, both from Northern Ireland and recent tours in the Balkans. Ranger Rowell, the most experienced of the four, had also served for seven months in Macedonia, so he had spent nearly a year on combat duty before being posted to Sierra Leone. For most of these young men, joining the British Army was a welcome ticket out of Belfast, and one of the few ways to escape from the Troubles that had blighted so much of life in Northern Ireland.

Settling down in the shade of a tree for a chow down of spam (again), Ranger Gaunt glanced around the base. To his right, there was the coiled razor-wire camp perimeter, with the dirt track on the far side. To his left, there was a series of khaki tents in which the Rangers slept, with the old colonial-style red-brick plantation house in the background, where the officers were billeted. As he looked around, the Ranger spotted a group of his mates preparing some Sierra Leone Army (SLA) soldiers for ambush training. God, what a shower the SLA looked, slouching about in their ragtag uniforms, the Ranger thought to himself. At least with Defence Force it felt like they were doing some real soldiering. According to his mates, the SLA recruits were usually half pissed on some locally brewed hooch. Which meant that it was all but impossible to get them up and out for PT early in the morning. The SLA had a long way to go before they'd be ready to patrol the jungles of Sierra Leone, he thought to himself, let alone the streets of Northern Ireland.

As he began cleaning his SA80 assault rifle in preparation for the patrol, the Ranger thanked his lucky stars that he'd been put on Defence Force. He was getting out and about that afternoon, not overseeing some gang-fuck of an SLA training exercise. It was no wonder the SLA had proven so incapable of defeating the rebels, he reminded himself, slamming the breech back into his SA80. He began preparing the rest of his kit for the patrol, checking on his grenades, flak jacket and spare magazines. Now, where was his flaming jungle hat? Oh, there it was. He'd been sitting on it while cleaning his weapon. The five-thousand-strong Sierra Leone Army might outnumber the rebels some three to one, but they remained a bunch of complete incompetents, that was for sure.

There were only one or two exceptions that Ranger Gaunt had come across during his time in Sierra Leone. One of them was the SLA's Corporal Mousa Bangura, a damn fine soldier if ever there was one. Formerly a militia member, 'Corporal Mousa', as he was known to the British soldiers, had gone on to join the Sierra Leone Army, and had then been one of the first to benefit from the British-led IMATT training. In November 1999, he'd been seconded to a platoon-sized unit of British Special Forces, based at a small military camp at Hastings, on the outskirts of Freetown. They were running recce and combat missions up-country, the forty-odd men being taken in via chopper and dropped on to target, and then extracted by chopper once the mission was complete. Though Corporal Mousa was never actually allowed to go on one of these missions, he had learned an awful lot from the three months he had spent working with the British soldiers.

Ranger Gaunt was relieved to discover that Corporal Mousa would be accompanying them on the patrol. He was a tough soldier and a smart one too. He knew how the rebels and the militia and the British forces tended to think and operate, often from first-hand experience. While Corporal Mousa had felt very much like a boy who'd suddenly met the real men when liaising with the British Special Forces troops, he felt more the Rangers' equal, which was a good feeling. His role on the patrol would be to act as a guide, translator and adviser to Major Martial.

Corporal Mousa's opposite number in Benguema was Captain Flaherty, and he had given the Sierra Leonean liaison officer prior warning of the patrol's intentions. Two days earlier, Captain Flaherty had approached Corporal Mousa to discuss the intended route of the patrol. The destination was Masiaka, extending the normal range of the Rangers' previous patrols. To date, these had reached only as far as Mabontoso, a village on the outskirts of Freetown. Beyond Mabontoso was bandit country – a large swathe of terrain controlled by a notorious rebel group called the West Side Boys. As Corporal Mousa had already passed along the road to Masiaka with other British Army units, he wasn't overly concerned. The rebels were unlikely to cause any trouble as long as the British patrol stuck to the main road passing through their territory.

All in, it was a twelve-man patrol then, made up of the eleven British soldiers and the one Sierra Leonean. But with two officers and five NCOs, it was very top heavy. The British members were armed with the British Army standard-issue SA80 assault rifle. As usual, Corporal Mousa chose to take with him the far more reliable and larger-calibre AK47 assault rifle. The patrol would be using three vehicles, all in drab military olive green: a WMIK, an open-backed Land-Rover fitted with a weapons-mount installation kit, including a chunky 50-calibre machine gun and a 7.62mm general purpose machine gun (GPMG), a standard Land-Rover, and a signals Land-Rover bristling with radio antennae. Ranger McVeigh had been chosen for the patrol in part because he was one of the few men who knew how to operate the 50-cal: it was an older design of gun which had to be manually calibrated in order to fire on automatic.

After they'd finished their lunch of spam sandwiches, the Major outlined the mission to the assembled men. 'OK. Listen up, lads. We'll be heading up towards the front line, passing through the Occra Hills, to pay a liaison visit to the UN base at JordBat2 – Masiaka. There's little likelihood of any trouble, but stay alert. If there is a contact, you are to follow standard drill: return fire and drive out of the contact if at all possible. If we cannot get the vehicles out and need to go out on foot, form a base fire line and fire and manoeuvre out of the situation in the normal way. I want to stress that we are to avoid contact if at all possible. That's all, men.'

JordBat2 was the neighbouring UN peacekeeping base at the town of Masiaka, where a Jordanian battalion held nominal control over a large swathe of territory. The Jordanians were part of the 13,000-strong United Nations Mission in Sierra Leone (UNAMSIL), a multinational peacekeeping force that had been made to look hopelessly foolish and incompetent by the rebel forces in recent months. More than a thousand UN troops had been taken hostage en masse and had scores of their vehicles stolen, while the rebels had wrought havoc across the country. Four British UN officers had been captured along with the hundreds of other UN forces, but they had managed to make their own getaway.

Rouge elements within the Jordanian UN contingent were widely suspected of having done a deal with the West Side Boys – whereby they would not interfere with the rebel's road-piracy activities, if the rebels didn't threaten their men. This went totally against the Jordanians' UN peacekeeping mandate, one of keeping the peace and ensuring safe passage of people and vehicles up and down the highway to Freetown.

Masiaka is situated on the most crucial road in the country's transport system – the main route heading north and east into the country's interior. The British patrol's route to Masiaka lay along this tarmac road, which snaked through the rolling jungle. The drive was expected to take around an hour, and en route the patrol would have to pass through a series of UN checkpoints, and two roadblocks manned by the West Side Boys. The rebels called themselves the West Side Boys to signify that they held the territory to the west of Freetown, as opposed to the Sierra Leone government territory to the east. They had taken the inspiration for their name from a rap song by the US gangster rapper Tupac Shakur. They were renowned for looting and pillaging the civilian cars and buses and aid vehicles that passed through their territory. Many Sierra Leoneans suspected the Jordanian peacekeepers of having an even more dubious pact with the West Side Boys. They accused them of buying up the loot that the rebels seized on the highway, and doing deals with the rebels to purchase any diamonds that fell into their hands. Whatever the exact nature of the shady Jordanian–West Side Boys relationship, it would end up costing the Royal Irish Rangers dear.

The thousand-strong West Side Boys – who styled themselves the 'West Side Niggas' – espoused no coherent political ideology. They had fought alongside the larger RUF rebel group during past battles, seizing power and presiding over months of anarchy and murder in the country. Their men and boy soldiers were renowned for dressing up in women's wigs before combat, and being permanently drunk and high on drugs. Supposedly allied to the Sierra Leonean government, the Boys had recently fought a series of battles against the forces of the UN and the SLA. The only thing you could be certain about with the West Side Boys was that you could never be certain whose side they were really on. In short, they were famously violent, unpredictable and trigger-happy.

Ten miles north-west of the Royal Irish base at Benguema was the Freetown Amputee Camp, housing several hundred victims of the violence in Sierra Leone. The camp 'chairman', Lamin Jarka, was a former bank employee and one of the victims of the West Side Boys. One afternoon in January 1989, the Boys had come for his daughter Hannah, who was just fourteen. Lamin Jarka had fought them off while she escaped through a back window. When he was finally overpowered, he was ordered to go and stand outside in a line with other captives. At the front was a teenage rebel with the name 'Commander Cut Hands'. Cut Hands stood beside the stump of a tree and proceeded to chop off the hands of each man in turn with an axe. Those who resisted were shot. It was three days before Lamin Jarka received any medical treatment. But his daughter had been saved from the rebels.

This horrific story was far from unusual. A couple of days after the Rangers' arrival in Sierra Leone, an escaped West Side Boys prisoner had been brought to their Benguema base. Under questioning by the British troops, it turned out that he was an SLA soldier who had been captured in one of their roadblocks. He had been dragged from his vehicle and taken to a nearby hut, then stripped naked and buggered. Just at that moment, another vehicle had appeared out on the road, and the West Side Boys had rushed off to loot it. The SLA soldier had grabbed his chance and escaped through the thatched roof of the hut. If he hadn't done so, he was certain the rebels would have killed him.

But despite such reports, Major Martial's heavily armed patrol didn't think they had too much to fear from the West Side Boys. Several times in recent months the British military had shown its teeth against the RUF rebels in Sierra Leone, and each time the RUF had come off very badly. Hopefully, word had got around by now that British forces were not to be messed with. In any case, in all of the Royal Irish Rangers' intelligence briefings to date, the West Side Boys had been identified as 'friendlies'. Presumably, intelligence knew what they were talking about, and so the West Side Boys must have somehow allied themselves to the British forces in Sierra Leone. It was a strange alliance, to be sure, but hardly unheard of in the shifting miasma of allegiances in Sierra Leone's civil war. So, Major Martial's patrol would head up for a lunchtime chat with the Jordanians, check that everything was all right, and then return. Simple.

Prior to departure, Major Martial established the order of driving to be maintained throughout the patrol: the standard Land-Rover leading, followed by the WMIK and then the signals vehicle. In theory, the WMIK would be able to use its heavy machine guns to cover either the vehicle in front or to the rear if they got into trouble. Major Martial and his driver, along with Rangers Rowell and Gaunt, manned the lead vehicle. The WMIK carried Corporal Sampson and Rangers MacGuire and McVeigh. The signals vehicle to the rear had Captain Flaherty, Sergeant Smith and Corporals Ryan, Mackenzie and Mousa on board. But just as the convoy was about to pull out of Benguema, Defence Force's Company Sergeant Major (CSM) Head ordered the Major's driver out of the lead vehicle and jumped in himself.

'No ways are you taking this patrol out and leaving the bloody CSM behind, sir,' he announced. 'I hope you don't mind, sir, but you're safe now with Sergeant Major Head at the wheel.'

The Major smiled wryly to himself and decided to go with the flow. The CSM was in his mid-thirties, and one of the oldest and most experienced soldiers in the Benguema Camp. He was held in awe by most of the junior ranks and, the Major surmised, would be an asset to have on the patrol. As the CSM had elbowed Major Martial's driver out, the two Rangers in the rear of the Land-Rover had looked at each other and groaned. Oh fuck, they were both thinking, why him? The CSM, or 'Scouser' as he was known to the junior ranks, was a big man, over six foot, and built like the proverbial brick shithouse. Originally from Liverpool, where the Rangers did a lot of their recruiting, he was a hard man, with a reputation for merciless piss-taking and 'slabbering' – tongue-lashing the new recruits – on the parade ground. No one would ever have chosen to have Scouser as their CSM, but one way or another he'd be bound to get the job done.

'Get those bloody gates open,' the Sergeant Major bellowed, as he gunned the lead vehicle towards the base exit, 'and let's get this fookin' show on the road.'

'Here we go then, Gav,' Ranger Gaunt muttered to his mate, with a grimace, 'the charge of the flamin' Light Brigade, if you know what I mean.'

'Aye, Sandy. The charge of the flamin' Macho Brigade, more like it,' Ranger Rowell replied, grinning.

'Sorry? Did you two frobbers have something to say back there?' the CSM roared, shouting to make himself heard above the racket of the vehicle, as its tyres hummed on the damp road surface. 'Fookin' speak up then, lads. Share it with the OC and us, why don't you?'

'Nothing, sir,' the two Rangers muttered. 'Just welcoming youse aboard, like, sir.'

'Nice to hear it, lads!' the CSM replied, grinning back at them in the driver's mirror. 'Nothing like 'aving a couple of keen, fresh-faced fookin' Rangers to take out on a nice little jolly like this, is there, sir?'

The Major raised his eyebrows at the CSM in an 'if you say so, Sergeant' type of expression, and went back to reading his map.

The patrol pulled out of the Benguema base at around 11.30 a.m., and half an hour later, it was approaching a West Side Boys checkpoint. At first sight, the rebels looked to be about as crazed as their reputation would have them: young guys sporting pink shades, shower caps and singlets, with strings of machine-gun ammo slung around their torsos. Nearly all of them had bullets on chains hung around their necks, and strange tattoos on their arms and shoulders. Later, the patrol would learn that the West Side Boys believed that these were powerful voodoo charms – which made them invulnerable to gunfire and invincible on the battlefield. As the Boys peered into the back of the leading Land-Rover with roving, bloodshot eyes, the air around the checkpoint was thick with the sweet, sickly smell of cannabis smoke.

'They sure look a sort of fucked-up bunch,' remarked Ranger Gaunt under his breath, as their vehicle pulled away from the checkpoint.

'Aye, youse could say that,' replied Ranger Rowell. 'Youse smell all that weed they were smokin'? They looked doped to the bloody eyeballs, if youse know what I mean.'

'No, Gav, I don't know what youse mean,' replied a grinning Ranger Gaunt, deliberately raising his voice so the two men in the front could hear him. 'How do youse know what weed smells like, anyways? Youse sort of partial to the odd puff, now is it?'

'Sure, I never touch the flamin' stuff, Sandy,' retorted Ranger Rowell. 'Youse was the one I clocked checking out those plants in the jungle this morning. Looked like youse reckoned they were dead on –'

'Will you two fookers quit bitching in the back like a couple of girls and keep your eyes on the fookin' road,' the CSM barked from the front of the vehicle, interrupting the Rangers' verbal spat. 'I don't much like the look of that bunch of bastards back there. Weed or no weed, I wouldn't trust those fookers as far as I could throw them.'

That first checkpoint marked the patrol's entry into the West Side Boys' territory. Half an hour later, the patrol members breathed a sigh of relief at the approach of the second, marking their exit from the rebels' domain. But just as they were driving up to the roadblock, things suddenly got very tense, as several short bursts of gunfire erupted from the surrounding jungle. The firing sounded close, a couple of hundred yards away or so. A group of the rebels came racing over to the British vehicles, shouting and gesticulating wildly in an effort to ascertain if the Royal Irish patrol was the source of the firing. Rangers Rowell and Gaunt felt their grip tighten around their weapons. But after a few more seconds' chaos and confusion, it turned out to be a Jordanian UN patrol loosing off a few volleys to signal their safe return to base.

The British vehicles passed through this second checkpoint and arrived without further incident at Masiaka, the first major town inland of the Freetown Peninsula. But other than small groups of rebels hanging about and the odd Jordanian UN soldier, Masiaka was now a deserted and battle-scarred place, a blasted ghost town. In the very centre, the colonial grandeur of the Railway Hotel had been reduced to a blackened ruin. Pushing on through the eerie, empty streets – where stray dogs scavenged among the old refuse – the British vehicles finally arrived at the Jordanian peacekeepers' base at around 12.30 p.m. As they did so, the Jordanian soldiers were just breaking for lunchtime prayers.

The British soldiers were welcomed by Jordanian troops with traditional Arabic sweet mint tea served in tiny glasses. Then they were invited to lunch – the Major, Captain Flaherty and the CSM being served in an officers' mess in a tent to one side, with the Rangers and the NCOs squatting outside with the Jordanian soldiers. They were presented with a dish of local goat curry, with rice, yogurt and cucumber, served on a huge communal platter on the floor. The idea seemed to be that everyone squatted around the platter, scooped up some of the goat curry and rice and crammed it into their mouths. Which was all very well, the Rangers thought to themselves, but it did make you wonder where the soldier opposite you had last had his hands, and whether he'd washed them recently. Over lunch the Jordanians had little of interest to report to the British officers about security in their area.

It was a stiflingly hot and humid afternoon as the patrol set off to return to base. In the rear of the Land-Rovers each of the patrol members could feel his back running with sweat. They were keen to have the return journey over with as soon as possible and get out of the baking hot vehicles. But around one-third of the way back to base, the convoy pulled up at the first UN checkpoint, at Mansumana village. Major Martial got out of the lead Land-Rover and had a quick chat with the Jordanian troops manning the checkpoint, while the rest of his men stayed in the roasting vehicles.

Shortly after the checkpoint was a left-hand turning leading on to a narrow dirt road the Jordanian soldiers told him. The track led down into Magbeni village, on the banks of the Rokel Creek, a large river flowing into the Freetown Estuary. En route were several small settlements whose inhabitants were suffering terribly as a result of food shortages and lack of access to medicines. As far as the Jordanians knew, it was safe territory inhabited only by civilians, and perhaps the British patrol might like to check the area out? If access could be provided to the area for the aid agencies, they could do an awful lot to relieve the suffering of the people.

Thanking the Jordanian for his help, Major Martial returned to the lead Land-Rover and spread out his map over the bonnet, pondering the route ahead. He knew what he was about to propose was risky, but so far the patrol had been more or less uneventful and the rebels had seemed friendly enough. Defence Force had already paid several visits by vehicle to local villages controlled by the Kamajors – a group of traditional hunter-warriors allied to the Sierra Leone government, and none of these visits had suffered any incidents. In fact Snake, one of the local Kamajor leaders, had started paying regular liaison visits to the British base at Benguema. But the area Major Martial was now considering visiting was not Kamajor territory: it was the heartland of the area controlled by the West Side Boys. Should he trust the Jordanian troops advice, and take a detour down to the village, or continue back to his base?

Making a snap decision, the Major jumped back into the lead vehicle and gave his driver the order to take the next left-hand turn off the main road. It was part of the Major's job to open up areas affected by the civil war to the aid agencies, so help could be brought to remote villages. He had seen at first-hand the terrible conditions in which people were being forced to live. If he could assess the needs in the area identified by the Jordanian major, then he could file a report to the aid agencies, and shortly food and medicines would get to the people. As a spin-off, this was also a good opportunity to gather some intelligence on the West Side Boys' area and activities. After all, they were rebel forces whose actions might impact on British military security.

In the back of the lead jeep, the two Rangers had no idea exactly why they were deviating from the main route. They just presumed that it was a routine detour, that perhaps an order had come in from HQ to go in and check out this area. Within minutes, the patrol found itself driving on a narrow, heavily rutted track into completely unfamiliar territory. It became increasingly claustrophobic, the jungle crowding in from either side and the branches blocking out the sky above them. As the vehicles ploughed on through the flood waters that had filled up the giant potholes, their speed dropped to no more than 10 mph. It was the rainy season in Sierra Leone, and this dirt road was now impassable to all but the hardiest four-wheel-drive vehicles.

As soon as the patrol had turned off the main road, Corporal Mousa had an uneasy feeling. Why were they deviating from their route? He held his tongue for the first ten minutes or so, until they reached a tiny settlement called Layah. There was little sign of life in the village, and the patrol passed through without stopping. Corporal Mousa was even more concerned now. He was well aware that with every turn of their wheels the patrol was heading deeper and deeper into West Side Boys' territory. Not only that, but the road led down to the rebels' hidden jungle headquarters.

'Where are we going, sa?' he finally ventured to Captain Flaherty.

'I don't know, Corporal,' the British captain replied. 'The OC's obviously chosen to take a detour for some reason.'

'Well, can we have radio contact to the OC, to ask him where we're heading, sa? This is the Occra Hills area, the West Side Boys' territory. I know it well, sa. It is infested by the West Side Boys, sa.'

'Are you afraid, Corporal?' Captain Flaherty joked.

'Not really, sa. But the West Side Boys are very unpredictable, sa. Very. We should at least know where we're going.'

'I'm sure the OC knows what he is up to,' Flaherty said, trying to reassure Corporal Mousa.

Last radio contact with HQ had been back at the Jordanian base at Masiaka, giving a situation report (sitrep) that the patrol was leaving JordBat2 for the return journey to Benguema. As they were now making an unscheduled detour, Captain Flaherty gave the order that they should try to make radio contact with HQ again, to report the change of route. But it was proving impossible to do so in the midst of the dense jungle. At the approach of Macabi, the second deserted village on the track, a worried Corporal Mousa broke the silence again.

'I'm really not comfortable with this, sa. The West Side Boys are very unpredictable. I don't think we should be going into their area.'

'Come on, Corporal, you have to admit, you are feeling afraid now, aren't you?' Captain Flaherty remarked, still trying to make light of things.

'No, sa. I just think we should check where we are going.'

'Well, I guess the OC knows what he's up to, eh?'

After some thirty minutes driving, the patrol passed through Warreh, a third deserted village, and a very worried Corporal Mousa was tempted to voice his concerns again. He was not about to challenge the decision of a superior officer, and he was somewhat in awe of the British military. These were the men who had come to his country to train their army to fight properly, and to give them enough backbone to take the war to the rebels. Yet even so, Mousa was gripped by a growing sense of foreboding, and his fear overcame his deference to the British captain.

'Sa, I think we must find out why were are going to this place, we really must.'

'Mousa, I'd swear you're looking really afraid now, eh?' Captain Flaherty replied, still ribbing the Sierra Leonean corporal.

'I'm not afraid, sa. But I'm not comfortable. Why are we really going to this place? Can you ask the Major? Really. I'm worried, sa.'

But before the Captain was able to reply, the convoy quite suddenly emerged from the dark jungle shade into the dazzling brightness of a village clearing. Almost immediately, a crowd of around 150 heavily armed men came swarming out of the shadows.

'What the hell's going on?' Ranger Rowell exclaimed, as the lead

Land-Rover ground to a halt, its progress brought to a stop by the seething mass of people up ahead.

One man cradling a GPMG stepped out in front of the Land-Rover, completely blocking its way.

'This is de WEST SIDE NIGGAS' AREA!' the big rebel machine-gunner yelled out, cocking his weapon as he did so. 'What de FUCK you doing in dis our area?' he snarled, his eyes bulging with fury. To either side of him, other rebel fighters fanned out, levelling their shoulder-held rocket-propelled grenade launchers (RPGs) at the vehicles, taking aim on the driver's cab.

In response, Rangers Rowell and Gaunt immediately cocked their weapons, slipping a round into their assault rifle's chamber. Ranger Rowell, who was in a better position than Ranger Gaunt, took aim with his SA80 at the man with the GPMG blocking their way.

'Shall I take him down, sir?' Ranger Rowell asked, requesting permission to fire. 'Then we can get the hell on our way.'

'No. Hold your fire,' Major Martial replied. 'Keep your weapons down for now, lads. Let me get out and try to talk the situation down first. I'm sure it's just a misunderstanding. For now, hang back and keep a low profile.'

With their guns at their sides, Major Martial and Sergeant Major Head made their way the fifteen yards or so across to the group of rebels at the front of the convoy. Rangers Rowell and Gaunt moved around to the rear of the Land-Rover, as the Major clearly wanted to adopt a non-aggressive approach, similar to the peacekeeping missions they'd been on in Kosovo. The rest of the men remained in their vehicles. As Major Martial began speaking to the West Side Boys' obvious leader, the crowd pushed in closer. It was made up of a mixture of men and boys, the youngest no more than eight or nine years old, and all of them were armed: they carried a mixture of AK47 assault rifles, self-loading rifles (SLRs), GPMGs and RPGs.

Glancing around them, the British soldiers could see that they were already pretty much trapped. They had been driving far too close together, that much was clear now. There should have been at least a hundred metres between each of the three vehicles. If there had been, the lead vehicle would have driven into the rebel crowd, but the two Land-Rovers following would have been able to stop in time. From their position to the rear they could then have put down accurate covering fire with their heavy machine guns to aid the lead Land-Rover, or beat a retreat to seek reinforcements.

But as things stood now, all three vehicles were trapped. There was no escape route forward as the track led further into the rebel village. And the Land-Rovers were now all but surrounded by the rebel fighters, which prevented them from turning around and heading back the way they had come. Just then, a group of the rebels came roaring up out of the village on a 'cut-off', an open-backed army truck. They slammed the cut-off across the track to the rear of the signals Land-Rover, just to make sure there was no chance for the British soldiers to make a getaway.

The cut-off, a Bedford lorry in military olive green, was mounted with a Soviet-era twin 14.5mm ZPU-2 heavy machine gun. It was obvious to the British soldiers that they were getting to be outgunned, as well as outnumbered and outmanoeuvred. From its markings they could see that the truck must have been captured from the SLA, which suggested that the West Side Boys might make a habit of seizing military vehicles. It was starting to look increasingly like a planned ambush. The big rebel machine-gunner who had first stepped into the road started yelling at the Major now. It was hard for the Major to understand him, as the rebels were speaking in Creole, a form of pidgin English, and few if any spoke proper English. 'You come into de CENTRE of dis our area with NO FUCKING PERMISSION!' he bawled. 'You tink you can just DRIVE in here like this this? You no know who WE ARE? We are *de West Side Niggas*. Dis be our fucking area. You cannot do dis ting!'

'Listen, guys, we're just on a routine military patrol,' the Major tried to reason with the rebels. 'We're British Army. British Army. We're working with the Sierra Leonean Army. We're training the SLA. That's all. Just a routine patrol.'

'NO!' The rebel leader cut in, getting himself eyeball to eyeball with the Major. 'NOT "just a routine patrol". You no know who de HELL WE BE? Me be the Colonel SAVAGE and dis is de SAVAGE GROUP! You tink you go into dis de centre of OUR AREA? Who de HELL-HELL you tink you are? We know why you done come here. You done come to ATTACK de West Side! And you go pay pay de heavy price for doing so!'

The self-styled 'Colonel Savage' was a striking individual, sporting a goatee beard, wraparound shades and a T-shirt with the US rap star Tupac Shakur emblazoned across the front of it. It was all topped off with a red beret. And just in case anyone was in any doubt as to who was in control here, Savage carried a Browning pistol in a holster at his side. Following the example of their leader, the rest of the rebel crowd started to jostle the Major, pressing close around him.

To the rear of the convoy, Captain Flaherty and the signals NCOs had their radio sets on permanent 'SEND, SEND, SEND' – keeping the radio frequency open in the hope that their HQ was receiving them, and would be able to hear what was happening. By now, the noise of the crowd was deafening, so headquarters should have no doubt as to what had befallen the patrol.

Then Colonel Savage strode across to the second vehicle, the WMIK, and shoved his pistol through the open window. With the muzzle of the gun thrust up against Corporal Sampson's temple, he began screaming for him to get down from the vehicle.

'Get out of de car! GET OUT! NOW! Out! Or I de bloody shoot you!'

'Stay in the vehicle, Sam,' CSM Head barked over. 'Don't get down. Stay the fook inside.'

'You stay inside, I go blow blow you fucking head off!' Savage snarled at Sam, his face so close that the Corporal could smell the stench of his stale sweat and rotting breath.

Savage's words were punctuated by the distinctive clunk-clunk! of a round being chambered, as the rebel on the twin 14.5mm heavy machine gun levelled his gun at the rear Land-Rover and started yelling over at his commander.

'Permission to open fire, sa!' As he was speaking in Creole, only Corporal Mousa could understand exactly what he was saying.

Colonel Savage ignored his gunner's request, and brought the press-ure to bear on his trigger finger. Corporal Sampson could see the knuckles of Savage's finger tensing around the trigger of his pistol. Convinced that the rebel colonel was about to put a bullet in his brain, Sam slowly opened the door and got down from the vehicle. As he did so, Savage ordered one of his men into the driver's seat. More of the West Side Boys started swarming on to the rear of the WMIK, Ranger McVeigh finding himself surrounded by hostile faces contorted into masks of hate and fury. There was a jostling and shoving for a few seconds more, as the men tried to retain control of their vehicle, and then the rebels put their guns up to the Rangers' heads. Ranger McVeigh just had time to disable the 50-cal HMG before he and Ranger MacGuire were grabbed by a sea of hands and hauled off the vehicle. As neither had personal firearms, they were now effectively unarmed and defenceless as they were swallowed up by the seething mob.

At the front of the convoy, Rangers Gaunt and Rowell found the mob closing in on them, too.

'There's no feckin' way youse fuckers are getting my weapon,' Ranger Rowell threatened, bringing his SA80 to bear on the crowd and trying at the same time to cover the Major and the CSM.

'Yeh. Fuck 'em, eh, Gav?' added Ranger Gaunt, nervously, following suit. 'What d'youse reckon our chances are of escape? Just about feckin' zero, eh?'

'Meybe. But we'll be taking some of the fuckers with us, that's for sure,' replied Ranger Rowell, in a murderous voice.

The two Rangers could see that they really were outnumbered and outgunned. If the shooting started off, they'd have to grab the Major and make a run for it. They tried to keep the crowd covered with their weapons, while at the same time searching out of the corner of their eye for the most likely escape route. There was a wall of thick jungle barely ten yards away. A quick dash and they could be in among the trees. They'd have to run and fight for a few hundred yards as the Boys would be bound to pursue them. But then the rebels might give up the chase, as they would have already captured the patrol vehicles. There was still a chance they might make it out of there yet.

Just as they were weighing up their options, the rebel soldier who'd taken the wheel at the WMIK Land-Rover gunned its engine, floored the accelerator, and it went careering past the other vehicles, veering wildly into the jungle. A bunch of the rebels were hanging off the sides, shouting and whooping and jeering over at the British soldiers. None of them knew it at the time, but late afternoon was the worst possible moment to cross the West Side Boys. By this time each day, they would have worked themselves up into an alcohol- and drug-fuelled frenzy.

Rangers Gaunt and Rowell were joined by Captain Flaherty now, who'd walked the forty yards or so up to the front from the signals Land-Rover at the rear. He brought with him news that the men from his vehicle were already being disarmed by the rebels. It was probably best if they also handed over their weapons, the Captain advised the two young soldiers. This was deeply disturbing news for the two Rangers, who could see very little of what was going on with the other vehicles, due to the density of the surrounding mob. They had little realised just how bad things were getting for the patrol. As they fought with their better instincts to keep a hold of their SA80s until the last possible moment, they heard a familiar voice behind them. It was Sergeant Major Head, who'd come over from his position with Major

Martial at the front of the convoy. They immediately noticed that the CSM was without his SA80.

'Sorry, lads. But you'd all do best to hand over your weapons,' the CSM told them, with obvious difficulty. 'Most of the lads have been disarmed already. Best you do the same.'

The CSM was seen as a real hard man by the junior ranks, a real soldier's soldier. If even he had been disarmed, then there seemed little point in not following suit.

To the rear of the convoy a terrified Corporal Mousa caught sight of a crowd of some fifty more rebels coming tearing down the road behind them on foot, weapons at the ready. They raced up to the rear Land-Rover and ripped open the back door, grabbing the weapons off the soldiers who were still inside the vehicles. As they did so, one of the rebels recognised Corporal Mousa.

'Oh, look who we have here,' one of them crowed in Creole, jabbing his AK47 into Corporal Mousa's ribs. 'It's Corporal Bangura! So it was you who brought these Brittonians here. You've been helping them in their plans to attack us. But now you're in our trap. How much have they paid you? You must have been paid one hell of a lot to do this. Get down from the vehicle, Corporal. Now it's payback time.'

'Hey! Mousa! We de saw you pass-pass,' another yelled excitedly. 'We allow you go through de bush so we go ambush you here. How you feel now, Mousa, bringing dem your whiteboy friend-friend into dis our trap?'

Shortly, all twelve members of the patrol had been disarmed.

What followed next was a frightening mêlée of mob justice, as the crowd closed in around the British soldiers, shoving and slapping them and jeering. Gleeful rebels snatched hand grenades, compasses, watches – and even the wedding rings off the bewildered patrol members' fingers. Drug-crazed faces leered in at the British soldiers, as a rebel fist went Crack! into the side of a head without warning, and a young Ranger was sent reeling. Claw-like hands yanked the patrol member's hair sharply backwards, as a fist went Smack! into the soldier's solar plexus. Down went the Ranger on to the deck, as a rebel boot went slamming into his ribcage. The rebels were getting down and dirty now, and the crowd was working itself up into a frenzied orgy of violence.

Eventually, Colonel Savage stepped in to stop the beating. He ordered the British soldiers to line up in the centre of the clearing instead, where they were shoved roughly to the ground, and forced to keep kneeling with their heads bowed. As they did so, the men were convinced that this was the prelude to their execution. But Major Martial just kept stubbornly refusing to kneel – goading Colonel Savage into a blind fury.

'You fucking kneel!' he began screaming. 'FUCKING KNEEL! Fucking kneel when I de tell you! Fucking British whiteboy army officer! Fucking kneel.'

'We're just a British Army patrol,' the Major began, still trying to reason with the Colonel. 'All we were doing was paying a friendly, liaison visit . . .'

But the Major's last words were lost in a torrent of abuse as Savage and half a dozen of his men began laying into him, trying to punch and rifle-butt him to the ground.

'Look, sir,' interrupted the CSM, pulling the Major down on to his knees, 'just fookin' kneel down, sir. Then we'll get to speak to them properly later, when they've calmed themselves.'

With all the eleven British soldiers and Corporal Mousa on their knees in the middle of the village clearing, things started to get wilder and more chaotic still. The West Side Boys had taken the WMIK Land-Rover and scrawled *WEST SIDE ONE* along both sides of the vehicle in white paint. They were screaming up and down the track now, hanging off the sides of it, and chanting: 'West Side One, British Army None! West Side One, British Army None! West Side One, British Army None!'

The crowd were really whooping it up to the chanting now, dancing and cavorting around with their guns. Every now and then, one of the fighters loosed off a burst of AK47 fire into the air. Over everything hung the cloying smell of ganga smoke, mixing with the acrid tang of cordite from all the gunfire. Eventually, one of the more drugged-up of the rebels strode over and grabbed one of the young Rangers by his hair. He bent down and stared into the Ranger's eyes – so he could feast on the fear he could see written on the young British soldier's face. Then the wired rebel soldier threw back his head until it was at an unnatural angle, drew his lips back, rolled his eyes up into his sockets and bared his teeth in an agonised grin.

'We gonna STUFF de whiteboy, den KILL him and COOK him,' he snarled, in a weird high-pitched half-scream, rolling his head from side to side, 'and then we de go EAT HIM ALL UP.'

'YAAAHHH! De motherfucking, Aids-ridden, WEST SIDE NIGGAS!' the rest of the Boys behind him started chanting. 'De motherfucking,

Aids-ridden, WEST SIDE NIGGAS! De arse-kicking, Aids-ridden, WEST SIDE NIGGAS.'

'Yaaaah . . . WE BE DE SAVAGE-SAVAGE GROUP! And we de STILL RULE!'

Just in case the Ranger and the rest of the patrol hadn't understood exactly what the crazed rebel had meant by 'STUFF de whiteboy', a couple of the others started a little charade of their own in the background. One bent over the bonnet of the nearby signals Land-Rover, while his rebel mate came up behind him and started to thrust backwards and forwards. All the crowd were laughing and wailing in delight, as the rebel soldier bending over the bonnet began a series of rhythmic, high-pitched yelps, in time with the other's shafting movements.

'Eehh! Eehh! Eehh! Eehh! Eehh! Eehh! Eehh . . .'

Just as the rebels' sick charade was ending, Corporal Mousa was separated from the British soldiers and marched down to the river bank. He was stripped naked – the rebels ripping his Republic of Sierra Leone Military Forces (RSLMF) uniform off him and laughing and jeering as they did so. And then they began to give Corporal Mousa a savage beating – with rifle butts, boots and sticks. All the time they were berating him for being 'a slave to the Brittonians, the colonial masters, the source of all the chaos in the country'. The savage assault went on for thirty minutes or more, until the Corporal was unconscious.

Back up at the village clearing the West Side Boys were still partying on down with the terrified patrol members kneeling in front of them – and looking like they would keep doing so until sundown. But then, a helicopter suddenly came swooping in low over the rooftops of the village. At the first sound of the beat of its rotor blades the rebel mob panicked, and the British patrol members were able to catch a glimpse of the chopper as it flashed overhead. It was a large helicopter – a Soviet-era Hind or a British Sea King – and as it was painted white it had to be a UN chopper, as opposed to British military. Which meant that it was probably just a routine UN flight, the British soldiers reasoned, rather than a patrol sent out to look for them.

But the West Side Boys were immediately spooked – convinced that the chopper was out searching for the captured British patrol – and they rushed the men in under the cover of the nearest hut. At last, the British soldiers were able to breathe a small sigh of relief. The chance flight of the chopper seemed to have taken a little of the edge off the terrifying situation, the West Side Boys seeming very concerned that the search for the lost patrol had already begun. They began jabbering away at each other in their own language and then yelling over at the British soldiers in broken English.

'You call in de chop-chop helicopter? Not de fucking smart idea,' Savage was shouting. 'Now you go see what happens! Fucking whiteboy British Army!'

2

TRAINING'S OFF

An army may be likened to water: water leaves dry the high places and seeks the hollows; an army turns from strength and attacks weakness. The flow of water is regulated by the shape of the ground. Victory is gained by acting according to the state of the enemy.
— Sun Tzu, *The Art of War*, c. 500 BC

AT the same time that the Royal Irish soldiers were being taken captive in the Sierra Leonean jungles, D Squadron of the 22nd Special Air Services Regiment (22 SAS) were on training exercises over three thousand miles away on the other side of Africa. In north Kenya, at a place called Nanyuki Showground, the British military have a permanent base where they have been carrying out military exercises for many years. The Nanyuki base is situated south of the vast and sparsely populated lands of the nomadic Samburu tribe. The baking hot Sahelian bush is an ideal training location for British soldiers acclimatising to desert operating environments. Kenya also boasts the second highest mountain in Africa, Mount Kenya, ideal for high-altitude and mountain training, and a huge diversity of riverine and coastal environments. There would be more than enough terrain for D Squadron to get its teeth into over the coming days.

Nanyuki town itself is listed in many guidebooks to Africa as a great place for tourists: 'A pretty and prosperous town, a base for expeditions to and around Mount Kenya' (*Lonely Planet*). The magical mountain is so close that it seems to dominate the town, and there is rarely a mention of the British military presence. But many a tourist has been shocked on arriving in Nanyuki to discover that the locals are able to swear at foreigners ('*muzungus*') just as well as the proverbial British trooper. Walking down the main drag in Nanyuki like the Pied Piper with a bunch of Kenyan kids singing, '*Muzungu, muzungu*, how are you?' might be fun for a while. But when one of those kids turns round and offers a mouthful of filth in a thick Geordie accent – 'fuck off, like' – well, that can prove distinctly unnerving. Not quite the authentic African cultural experience that most tourists have come for.

As for the men of D Squadron, Nanyuki wasn't exactly their idea of a peachy location either. They reckoned the town had been ruined by the 'green army' (the regular military). Decades of drunken squaddies in town had done little to endear the locals to the British Army. Talk about 'hearts and minds', the SAS men thought to themselves, the green army just didn't get it. To be fair to them, it wasn't their job to, either, as they were basically a fighting force only. But no doubt about it, Nanyuki could do with an intensive programme of hearts and minds if the locals were to be brought back on side. As they rarely had to deploy in uniforms anyway, the men of D Squadron made a point of only ever wearing civvies in town in an effort to keep a low profile.

In fact, D Squadron had at first been scheduled to go to Australia on special joint exercises with the Aussie SAS (SASR), and the men had been looking forward to getting into some serious training (and drinking) with their Antipodean colleagues. Formulated on exactly similar lines to the British SAS – a regiment with three 'sabre' squadrons, a training squadron and a headquarters – the Aussie SAS has operated alongside British Special Forces in several theatres (including Borneo, Vietnam, Cambodia, Somalia, East Timor and during Operation Desert Fox in Kuwait). Together with the New Zealand SAS (1st NZ SAS Group), these three Special Forces Regiments share a pedigree going back to the famous exploits of the British Long Range Desert Group (LRDG) and the Australian Allied Intelligence Bureau (AAIB) during the Second World War.

To complete the picture, US (and to a lesser extent Canadian) Special Forces (SEALs and Delta Force) were on yearly exchange programmes with their British counterparts. While US soldiers would be fully integrated into British Special Forces training programmes – such as D Squadron's Nanyuki deployment – they weren't strictly speaking supposed to be deployed alongside them on *actual missions*. But the Aussie SAS in particular had argued that to maximise the effectiveness of these allied Special Forces when operating together in the same territory, Special Forces on placements with British units should be allowed to go into action on British Special Forces missions, and vice versa. This was now becoming more and more the norm.

There were usually a dozen-odd Kiwis serving as actual members of the British SAS, and D Squadron had its fair share of them (traditionally, the Aussies normally served with the Special Boat Service – SBS). They worked well alongside each other, the nationals of these allied countries, there being a strong collective ethos among the men: one of peerless military professionalism, a can-do attitude coupled with lateral thinking, an evil sense of humour and an enormous capacity for drinking beer. This time around, however, D Squadron had been out of luck. For some reason, Australia had been cancelled, and so they had been slated for Kenya instead.

Nanyuki Showground is exactly what it sounds like: a giant showground used for local Kenyan agricultural and cultural shows. Every year, for three or four months during the English summer, the British military take over the place – whereupon it's transformed into a vast khaki-tented base camp, with a few hard-standing buildings for the officers. From there, the various sections of Her Majesty's Armed Forces can head out to take advantage of Kenya's rich abundance of terrain: the baking deserts of Archer's Post (known to the soldiers as 'Archer's Toast' or 'Archer's Roast', for obvious reasons); the Sahelian bush lands of the Dondol; or the endless expanse of classic safari terrain at Mpala Farm in the rolling foothills of Mount Kenya.

Four squadrons (A, B, D and G) make up 22 SAS, and each squadron consists of four troops: Mountain, Boat, Mobility and Air. Each troop comprises of approximately a dozen men. In addition to the fifty-odd men of D Squadron, there were also several SBS guys going through the Kenya training alongside their SAS colleagues. The SBS is the smaller, sister Special Forces unit to the SAS – its speciality being marine and water-borne operations. Historically, there has been intense rivalry between the two Special Forces outfits. But after the Falklands War, where there were a number of unfortunate blue-on-blue (friendly fire) incidents between the two units, closer integration between the SAS and SBS had been made the order of the day. Increasingly, the two outfits were being melded together under a new, combined identity – that of UK Special Forces (UKSF).

Well, even if it wasn't quite Australia, Kenya was nevertheless a magnificent and stunning country. And before they got down to the training proper, the men of D Squadron were still determined to have a damn good time of things. Camped down at Lake Baringo (a bird-watching Mecca of Kenya) for a few days' R'n'R, the men of Boat Troop had got right into some first-class survival and adventure training

– namely crocodile jumping and hippo chasing. So far, no one had had their legs bitten off by a hungry croc or been sat on by an angry hippo, but they'd come pretty close.

Late one night, the men had gone out goading the hippos with torches – and suddenly they'd had a whole herd of thirty-odd very angry hippopotamuses (that's a lot of hippos) stampeding through their tented camp. It was a miracle that no one was crushed. (It is a fact now well understood by the men of Boat Troop that these huge animals may be very large and very chubby, but they can move exceedingly quickly when upset. After the charge of the hippos, the men could well appreciate why more people are killed every year in Africa by pissed-off hippopotamuses than by any other wild animal.)

While Boat Troop were learning about the nocturnal behaviour of angry hippos, the other three troops were taking advantage of some somewhat less life-threatening forms of R'n'R. There'd been offers of wildlife safaris, but the take-up hadn't been that high, because, as one of D Squadron's old Kenyan hands had put it: 'Once you've seen one ball of fur you've seen 'em all.' Likewise, the offer of helping to construct some new tourist paths up Mount Kenya hadn't been met with an overwhelming response either. Even in their down time, the men of the squadron craved action. So, the men of Mountain Troop had been out climbing Devil's Rock, in the middle of Lake Naivasha. The other most popular pastime over the past few days had proved to be deep-sea fishing – for barracuda, sharks and blue marlin – down at Malindi and Mombasa on the Kenyan coast. This had the added advantage that the fishing trips were run out of the legendary Hemingway's Hotel, right on the beach front – a great place for a few sundowners after a hard day on the high seas.

But all good things have to come to an end, and by 25 August – the day of the Royal Irish patrol's capture by the West Side Boys – all four D Squadron troops had been dispersed across the country to their various training locations. Mountain Troop were preparing for a difficult ascent of snow-capped Mount Kenya. Having prepped in the aptly named Mountain View Hotel at the base of the massive peak, they had driven to the meteorological station to set up base camp, in preparation for the main assault. They weren't expecting to get much sleep, either: they had their ice axes, crampons and bergens ready, and were waiting for the final signal to begin the pre-dawn climb. Back at Nanyuki, meanwhile, Air Troop were scheduled to take yet another dawn C-130 Hercules flight from the military airstrip on the base, heading out for a day's practice jumping over the clear Kenyan airspace.

Some hundred miles to north of them, Mobility Troop were deep in Samburu country, carrying out extended exercises with fully loaded 'Pinkies' (desert-adapted Land-Rovers). They'd been practising desert-driving techniques, using sand ladders and the Turfer Winch, a beast of a machine if ever there was one. Whenever a vehicle got bogged down in the dunes, the men would bury the winch in the sand on pickets (huge iron sand anchors), attach a cable to the front of the Land-Rover and winch it out by hand. They had been rehearsing vehicle fire and manoeuvre techniques. The Pinkies worked in tandem, with one vehicle remaining stationary and putting down covering fire, as the sister vehicle advanced ahead of it, and so on. Some 350 miles to the south of them, Boat Troop were awaiting another day's fun and games off the Kenyan coast at Mombasa, practising sea exercises and amphibious assaults.

At around 3.30 a.m. on the morning of 26 August 2000, barely twelve hours into the Royal Irish hostage crisis, Mountain Troop were just about to start their pre-dawn ascent of Mount Kenya when a radio call came through ordering them to abort and return to base. At the same time, the commanders of Mobility Troop received similar orders to abandon their night exercises and head back to Nanyuki, while Boat Troop were also told to pack up their gear and begin the long drive back to base. At Nanyuki itself, Air Troop's C-130 Hercules flight had already been cancelled, and the men were allowed to sleep on for a few hours more, undisturbed. There seemed little point in waking the men of Air Troop, as it would take their three sister troops several hours to return to base.

After packing all their gear, Boat Troop set off at around 5 a.m. on the long drive back to Nanyuki. They were travelling in two Pinkies and an AKMAK (a new French-designed six-wheel-drive truck). With the Land-Rovers leading, the AKMAK followed piled high with Boat Troop's kit. The Kenyan roads were atrocious – eroded, potholed and subjected to chaotic driving by the locals. An hour or so into Boat Troop's journey on the Mombasa–Nairobi road, an oil tanker swerved to avoid a crater. Hopelessly overloaded in any case, the truck slewed out of control and shed its load, a huge gout of oil gushing across the tarmac. The first Boat Troop vehicle managed to get through the glistening oil slick without losing control, but the heavily laden AKMAK lost traction halfway across and went into a horrible spin. As the vehicle plunged into a ditch at the edge of the road, it rolled over once, and came to a standstill lying on one side, its wheels still spinning slowly in the air.

The men from Mountain and Mobility Troops had only just arrived back at Nanyuki, and were trying to get some shut-eye, when they were woken by the camp clerk. He seemed highly agitated, and wanted an address and phone number for one of Boat Troop's family back in Hereford. Immediately, the men of D Squadron knew that something was wrong; the camp clerk didn't wake up troopers to ask for a squadron member's family details in the middle of exercises unless something untoward had happened. Cursing under their breaths, they got up and wandered sleepily around the base, trying to find out what on earth was going on. Eventually, they were told that two members of Boat Troop had just been killed in a road accident south of Nairobi – although no names were being given out as yet. No one would be getting any more sleep that morning.

An hour later, Peter Cutgood, the D Squadron OC, gathered the men together in the officers' mess. The squadron's mood was dark and sombre.

'As you all know, there's been a dreadful accident,' he began. 'Two of the men of Boat Troop – Corporal Martin Halls and Trooper Adrian Powell – are dead. I'll be giving you more details of what happened later – when the rest of the troop finally get back to base. This is obviously a tragic incident, and I understand there was no way in which it could have been avoided.' He paused for a second before continuing. 'At the same time, and as you've probably realised, the shit has hit the proverbial fan back at Hereford. We're being pulled off training and warned off for a possible hostage-rescue operation in Sierra Leone. That's about all I can tell you at the moment – as I don't know a great deal more myself. Obviously, I'll let you know more as and when I can.'

A little over six foot, with short dark hair, Peter 'Pete' Cutgood was seen as a good officer and he was universally liked within the squadron. He was still a Rupert, of course, and 'once a Rupert always a Rupert' as the saying went. But the men called him just 'Pete' or 'the Boss', and he was seen as being down to earth and accessible. He was also damn good at getting the job done. For his part, the OC used to maintain that he was running the best unit in the SAS, and D Squadron did have the reputation of being a crack outfit (though none of the three other SAS squadrons agreed, of course). D Squadron's standing was certainly helped by the fact that the Director of Special Forces Brigadier Simon Chadwell, was an ex-D Squadron man himself. To the men of the squadron it just seemed that, somehow, they kept on getting the peachiest jobs.

It was at times like this – after two unexpected and senseless deaths – that a good OC could really help pull the unit's spirit back together. Pete Cutgood definitely fell into that 'good officer' group, as far as the men were concerned. The wonderfully named Captain Dan Temper was another strong contender for the good-officer camp. The Rupert in charge of Air Troop, Captain Temper was six foot four, with swept-back blond hair, he was every woman's fantasy come true of an SAS officer. A female author who wrote Jilly Cooper-style romance novels had actually approached him once and asked if she could base one of her characters upon him. The only problem with the Captain was that he did have to be brought down to earth once in a while. Recently, he'd gone to a nightclub with the rest of Air Troop, and one of the veterans had had to wrestle him to the floor, just to demonstrate to Captain Temper that he wasn't completely invincible.

As the morning dragged on at the Nanyuki base, further details of the accident began to emerge. A third member of the AKMAK's passengers had suffered a broken collarbone, but other than that the rest of the troop were uninjured. After the accident, the AKMAK had been recovered using a truck out of the British Army permanent base in Nairobi. The remainder of Boat Troop had then continued their long drive back to Nanyuki using the two surviving vehicles. The two dead men were known as 'Martie' and 'Adie' to the rest of the men of the squadron. Adie had only just passed SAS selection, but Martie was an old hand with five or six years under his belt. Both had been popular soldiers in what was an unusually popular troop with the rest of the men of D Squadron.

When the Boat Troop Land-Rovers arrived back at base, it became clear just how hard the surviving members of the troop were taking the two deaths. In particular, Davie, the AKMAK driver, looked completely taken apart. He was beside himself, seeming to think that all fingers of blame were pointing at him. But everyone was blaming the Kenyan truck driver who'd taken his overloaded death trap of an oil tanker out on the road in the first place. Apparently, the Kenyan truck driver had survived his accident largely unscathed, but had then failed to warn the approaching British convoy of the oil slick.

Boat Troop's paramedic, Brad Tinnion, was also very cut up about the whole incident. He'd tried to administer first aid at the scene, but there had been nothing that he could do for either Martie or Adie, which had made it even more upsetting for him. He did his best to comfort Davie, telling him that the accident wasn't his fault. But Davie seemed inconsolable. When Boat Troop finally got back to the Nanyuki base, Brad was the first to step out of the vehicles. As he did so, none of the men from the other three troops could quite believe that he'd just been in a serious road accident. Brad Tinnion had got down from the lead vehicle looking barely the worse for wear. The only thing that had given it away was the look in his eyes.

A lot of the men in D Squadron used to joke that Brad was wasted on the military. He had sun-bleached hair, was boyishly handsome and always managed to look a million dollars. The others would tease Brad that rather than joining the SAS, he should've been a male model. Bradley 'Brad' Tinnion hailed from Harrogate, in Yorkshire. He had enlisted in the Royal Artillery when he was just sixteen, and become a bombardier by the time he passed selection, and so took the rank of Trooper in the SAS. He was an army career man, and a brilliant soldier, a real natural. But more than that, he was a dashing individual, with a natural flare and style. He could wear anything and look good in it, even if it was just a beach towel. Sometimes, this irked his mates. While they'd come back from the ranges with their arses hanging out of their trousers and their collars ripped off, Brad would always be looking immaculate.

As soon as the squadron had been 'warned off' for the Sierra Leone operation, a planning team of the head sheds (the officers and NCOs) had flown back to Hereford to prepare the ground. But that didn't mean a thing in the experience of the men of D Squadron: an operation could get right through to the deployment stage or further and still be called off. But whatever the Sierra Leone mission might turn out to be, it had better bloody well happen, the soldiers were telling themselves. As far as they were concerned, two of their number – two good men who had dared all to win all – were already dead as a result of it.

Big Gracie, as the men from D Squadron affectionately called her, ran things down at the Sportsman's – the only bar in Nanyuki worth drinking in, as far as they were concerned. It was to the Sportman's that they all retired that evening to hold an impromptu beery wake for Martie and Adie. Of course, they all knew that they did a dangerous job: at any moment they could be thrown into a potentially fatal combat situation, and for many that was one of the attractions of being in the Regiment. But everyone was thinking the same thing about the two deaths: *what a senseless way to have been killed – in a fucking road accident.*

'*Jambo*, love,' 'Cockney' Jimmy said, using the traditional Kenyan word to greet Big Gracie as he was the first into the bar. 'Been a while, eh? You're lookin' gorgeous as ever, love. You 'eard the fakin' news? Fakin' tragic, that's what it is, fakin' tragic.'

'My best *muzungu* soldier boy!' Big Gracie called over, breaking into a wide grin, She came across the bar and tousled Jimmy's hair affectionately. Fine, sandy hair, worn long for a soldier – a habit Jimmy had got into in Northern Ireland, when he'd been on covert ops, posing as a down-and-out in Belfast. Big Gracie was a giant of a Samburu woman – like many of that tribe – being well over six foot. She towered over Cockney Jimmy, who was a short, barrel-chested bloke.

'You know I don't like to hear you having bad news,' Big Gracie continued, gently. 'Why don't you have a beer and tell Big Gracie all about it.'

'What, an' get it off me chest, like? Fakin' nice one, Big Gracie, don't mind if I do. Line up the Tuskers, will you, love? I'm gettin' 'em in for everyone, like.'

Tusker was the favoured Kenyan lager among the men of the squadron. They soon had Big Gracie lining up several bottles to each man – so they could give their two dead comrades the sort of send-off that they knew they would have wanted. Cockney Jimmy was renowned for being a big drinker, and he could put away thirty or forty bottles of Tusker and still be standing. And he liked it so much in the Sportsman's bar he never seemed to want to leave. Brought up in the East End of London, he used to joke that half the families in his street had been black, so he felt right at home when in Africa. He'd been through Nanyuki two or three times on training before, and Big Gracie and he had become well acquainted.

'*Ahsante*, Big Gracie,' Jimmy remarked, using the traditional Kenyan 'thank you', as he took his first beer and downed it in one. 'Give us another, love. We've got a lot of fakin' sorrows to drown, that we 'ave.'

For as long as anyone could remember Big Gracie had always been there, running the Sportsman's. Several of the men from D Squadron were on their third or fourth visit to Nanyuki, and over that time they'd witnessed the bar go from a couple of old tin shacks to a set of swanky (for Africa, anyway) apartment-like buildings with a swimming pool. It was always full of 'night fighters' of course – local ladies of the night – but where was there a bar in Africa that wasn't? In any case, they weren't the aggressive, hangdog sort of hookers you'd meet in many parts of the world (like some countries in Eastern Europe the men could mention). Sure, the African girls would be keen as mustard to drag one or other of the guys off at the end of a night's partying – after all, that was how they earned their living. But most of the time they seemed happy just to tuck into some Tuskers with the British soldiers, get down on the dance floor and have a good time. In fact, that was one of the only complaints that the men had against their OC, Pete Cutgood: he could be a bit of a moraliser when it came to the men enjoying themselves. Especially if they were hanging around with night fighters and the like.

As more and more Tuskers were sunk, Billy 'the Big Scottish Monster' ('Nessie' to his mates back at home in Aberdeen) – a gnarled giant of a man, and a typically dour Scot – found himself accosted by two of the local girls. Whenever he'd got several beers inside him, the Scottish Monster found himself relaxing a little and growing unusually talkative. With one of the ladies on each arm, the Scottish Monster had begun regaling them with tales of yore, his booming laughter now joining the general uproar in the Sportsman's. Billy was having the time of his life, too. He was married with a wife and three little girls back home, and fiercely faithful. But he could still have a damn good drink and a laugh with the girls.

But then Pete Cutgood had sidled over to have words with him. It soon turned out that one of the Boat Troop lads had pulled a wind-up on the OC – by telling him that the Scottish Monster had been shagging one, if not both, of the night fighters. The OC was definitely not amused. Pretty quickly, Billy had clocked what was going on and decided to play along. He could see Cockney Jimmy leering drunkenly from ear to ear at the other end of the bar, and giving him a wink and a wobbly thumbs up. No trouble guessing who had pulled the wind-up on the OC this time, then, Billy thought to himself. Boy, that laddie could put away the beers, especially when it was two of their own troop whom they were drinking their farewells to.

Cockney Jimmy was a real practical joker, with a sharp cockney wit, and a lot of the men reckoned he went a bit too far at times. Having left school at fifteen, he acted as if he didn't have two brain cells to rub together. However, long years in D Squadron had proved him to be one of the sharpest men in the Regiment, a good man to have on your team. He and the Scottish Monster went back a long way, having been together in Boat Troop for seven years or more.

'Erm . . . Billy, can I have a minute?' the OC asked, for a second time, clearing his throat to signal that he needed a serious word.

'Sure, laddie.' The Scottish Monster called everyone 'laddie', regardless of age or rank.

'Erm . . . Look, I've had word that you've been seeing one of the local . . . erm . . . ladies.'

'Aye, and if I have, what of it, laddie?'

'Well, erm, it's a bit of a delicate matter . . .'

'Nothing delicate about her, laddie. Built like a real Big Mamma she is. Fookin' looovely . . .'

'I think you know that's not exactly what I mean. It's not really very, well, erm . . . wise, is it? Gives us a bad image and all that when we're abroad, don't you think?'

'No, actually, sir, I don't think.'

'All I'm asking, Billy, is that you give the local ladies a wide berth from now on.'

'Listen, sir, she's no fookin' lady. And can I ask ye something, sir?'

'What?'

'D'ye *wank*, sir?'

'Sorry?'

'D'ye wank? You know, pull your plonker? Fookin' five-knuckle shuffle? Do ye, sir? Wank, like?'

'Well . . . erm . . . it's not something I've ever been asked before . . .'

'Well, it's a pretty simple question, sir. Just a "yes" or a "no" really.'

'It's not something I want to discuss, Billy.'

'Fair enough, laddie. But I've never met a man who does ne wank. So, let's say for argument's sake that ye do, eh? And when ye do, ye don't always think o' your good lady wife, now do ye? No, ye don't. Sometimes, ye think o' girls like . . . well, like say *Charity* here, don't ye? So, what's the fookin' difference between thinking about it – which is what y'do – and putting some flesh on those thoughts? Eh?'

'Well . . . now you put it like that, I suppose I've never really, erm, thought about it like that before . . .'

'Aye. So, you get my point, don't you, laddie? Fancy a beer, do ye?'

'Well . . . why not, eh? You say her name's, erm, *Charity*?'

'Aye. Fookin' ironical, eh? A night fighter called Charity. Charity?'

This is the OC. OC, meet Charity. I'm just gettin' some more beers. Gracie! Four Tuskers, loovie. And while ye're at it, laddie, this is her friend, Faith. Oh, and Hope's just over there talking to Cockney Jimmy.'

'Is that so? Where's Prudence, then, Billy?' the OC asked, playing along with the joke. 'Serving behind the bar, is she?'

'Nooo, laddie. That's Big Gracie. Surely ye recognise her after all these years?'

As the Tuskers flowed in the Sportsman's and the night fighters took to the dance floor, several of the younger guys joined them – gyrating and shaking to the pulsating beat of the pumping Zairean *quasa-quasa* music. With each and every beer, the dancing girls – several of whom were really quite beautiful, white teeth flashing, skins smooth like ebony – were looking ever more tempting.

When the men of D Squadron had first started visiting the Sportsman's, Big Gracie had been a heavy girl, all of twenty stone or more. But over the years she'd shed the pounds, and was now as thin and wiry as any Samburu who'd wandered the bush with her cattle for the last ten years. Big Gracie was worried that she might be ill, and she had one piece of advice that she never failed to impart to any of D Squadron's new boys: however many beers they'd drunk, they were not to shag any of the girls. Wanking over them – that was fine. But positively no shagging. HIV and Aids was big in Africa, and Big Gracie didn't want any of her favourite customers catching the virus.

The following morning, the OC decided that the squadron needed to shake down and get their minds off the accident. Hanging around Nanyuki would be a disaster as far as morale was concerned. So the complete squadron – fifty-odd men nursing some very serious hang-overs – headed down to the ranges at Mpala Farm for some live-firing exercises. This would also prove useful preparation for whatever might lie in store for them in Sierra Leone. Over a two-day period, each man put several thousand rounds down the ranges, using Minimis FN C9 light machine guns (a 5.56mm belt-fed weapon, popular with the squadron), 50-cal heavy machine guns, Barrat 50-cal sniper rifles and the new Diemaco C7 assault rifles (a Canadian version of the US M16-A2 5.56mm assault rifle, with a re-engineered barrel, reputed to be more reliable and accurate than the standard M16). There were also a lot of 61 and 81mm mortar shells thrown down the ranges, as well as several hundred 40mm grenades from the men's M204 grenade launchers.

At the end of the forty-eight hours of live firing the squadron was feeling a lot more positive. They had one final afternoon's target practice left, before heading back to Nanyuki. One of the Ruperts, Mitch, had put out an electrical pop-up target, but it was stubbornly refusing to pop up when requested. Mitch was seen as a crazy bastard (even by D Squadron's standards), and the most likeable Rupert in the whole squadron, if not in the entire Regiment. Being as mad as a hatter and totally unconcerned for his own safety, Mitch headed off down to the far end of the range to sort things out.

'I'll operate the bitch manually, if need be,' he'd remarked over his shoulder, with a grin. 'I'm usually good with me hands, especially where the bitches are concerned.'

'Fakin' nice one, Mitch!' Cockney Jimmy shouted after him, as he disappeared down the range. 'Dozy faker,' he added under his breath, 'you're gonna get some.' Jimmy had immediately sniffed the opportunity for a great wind-up.

''Ere, lads, listen up,' Jimmy said, calling the other men of Boat Troop around him. He could always rely on the boys of Boat Troop – *the Brave and the Fearless* – for a good crack at the Ruperts. ''Ere's what we do, right. Once that daft bastard gets down the far end of the fakin' range, we open up over 'is 'ead wiv everything we've got, all right? Let the fakin' Rupert 'ave it good 'n' proper, like, know what I mean?'

'You're a crazy fooker, Jimmy lad,' the Big Scottish Monster responded, wondering why he hadn't spotted the opportunity for the wind-up himself. 'But how d'ye reckon he'll handle it?'

'Mitch? 'E'll be all right, mate,' Jimmy replied, with a grin. ''E's crazier than the rest of us put together, like.'

'No mortars or any big stuff, though, right, Jimmy mate?' the Kiwi asked. Kiwi Mike was one of the younger men in Boat Troop. He was a quiet bloke and a good, solid soldier, universally liked and respected by the others. A New Zealander, he'd been with the troop some time now. He was less cynical than his fellow British soldiers, and had a refreshingly open and generous view of the world and his fellow men. If ever you needed someone to help move house, saw up a fallen tree into logs, or go on a hunting trip, Kiwi Mike was your man. Few of the D Squadron boys knew that his real name was Mike, as he had always been known just as 'the Kiwi'.

'Na, mate. Hit 'im wiv anything you like. Couple of 81mm mortar rounds should do the trick, like . . .' Jimmy answered Kiwi Mike, keeping as straight-faced as he could manage. 'You dozy Kiwi fucker. Course it's only fakin' small arms, mate, what did you fakin' think? We don't really want to splatter 'is brains all across the fakin' sand, do we? Come on, lads, 'e's almost there, make sure you've got one up the spout and let's give 'im a surprise 'e'll never forget.'

Sure enough, just as Mitch was trying to prop up the target by hand, the men of Boat Troop – led by Brad Tinnion, Kiwi Mike, Billy the Scot and Cockney Jimmy – opened up on him with everything they'd got, sending bullets whining over his head and slapping into the sand-bank behind him. Mitch went sprawling on to the dirt, where he was forced to keep so low to avoid the incoming that he couldn't even reach his radio set to call the bastards off. When the men finally stopped firing – on the insistence of the Big Scottish Monster, who was Boat Troop's 2iC – he staggered out shaking like a nervous wreck and having pissed his trousers, to the total amusement of the men watching. It had been a damn good wind-up, one of the best. But ten minutes later, Mitch was back on form – bragging on about how he had just survived a full-on SAS ambush.

'Call yourself the fuckin' SAS? Britain's finest?' he mocked. 'Bunch of fuckin' wasters if you ask me. How many of you was there opened up on me? Half a dozen, was it? All the fuckin' hardware you could have asked for. An' still you couldn't take me out. What are you? A fuckin' SAS troop on an ambush mission, or the Women's Institute organising a fuckin' village tea party? If you're going to do it, at least do it right. If you're gonna ambush someone, you don't fuck around: you gotta mallet him good and proper. You're a fuckin' shower, that's what I say.'

'Still, 'ad a little fakin' accident, eh, mate?' Jimmy retorted, nodding at the wet patch spreading out across Mitch's crotch. 'Even my little un's learned not to do that, and she's not even knee-'igh to a fakin' grasshopper yet, mate.'

'Still did a wee peepee in yer pants, didn't ye, laddie?' the Scottish Monster added, grinning.

'So? Big fuckin' deal. When did that ever stop the fuckin' enemy?' Mitch came back at them, mockingly. 'Sort of: "Yeh, well, boss we made the enemy piss themselves, like, but missed every one of 'em." That'd put you right in the OC's good books, wouldn't it, lads? Where was the fuckin' mortar you could have used to finish me off with then, eh? Plenty of 81mms I can see lyin' around here. Put one of them down the range and I'd have been toast. But lost your bottle, did you, lads?'

'Right. What did I say, mate?' the Kiwi said, directing his comment at Jimmy. 'Put a couple of mortars down the range then, shall we, mate?'

'Wouldn't waste a fakin' mortar on that ugly bastard even if I was paid to,' Jimmy retorted. 'Fell out of the ugly tree an' 'it all the fakin' branches on the way down, that fakin Mitch did, innit. Good mortar round would be wasted on the fucker.'

'Not every day you get to survive a full-on SAS ambush, now is it, lads?' Mitch boasted, as he turned his back on the rest of Boat Troop and headed for one of the vehicles, getting in the final word. There was no doubt about it, D Squadron were back on form, bitching and piss-taking as good as ever.

The following day, 29 August, six men from Boat Troop headed back to the UK to be pall-bearers at Martie's and Adie's funerals, and to begin preparations for the Sierra Leone op (whatever it might turn out to be). They flew back as unobtrusively as possible – dressed in civvies, BA from Nairobi direct to London Heathrow. On arrival at Hereford, preparations for the funerals were already well underway. But no one seemed to have any sense of whether the Sierra Leonean mission was going to get the go-ahead or not. By lunchtime on 30 August, all of D Squadron had arrived back at their base. The funeral of the two dead soldiers took place that afternoon in St Martin's Church, Hereford, and all members of the Regiment present at the time turned up in their best dress uniform. Several of Martie's and Adie's close friends read tributes about the soldiers – 'two good men who had died in their line of duty'. Then there was the traditional fly past, the gun salute and the playing of the last post.

The official wake was to be held later that day at the Regimental HQ at Creddon Hill, and all the men were looking forward to getting well lashed again. But the wake had hardly got going before word went round that D Squadron were to prepare for rapid deployment to Sierra Leone. Whatever the mission was, it was obviously looking more like a goer. The six men who had flown back early from Kenya were to be sent out more or less immediately, as an advance party. This would give the majority of the squadron twenty-four hours or so with their families, before they followed on. That much the men had gleaned from the gossip that was going around and, not surprisingly, Martie and Adie's wake fizzled out pretty quickly.

There is intense rivalry between all four SAS squadrons as to which one gets the 'best' missions (best most usually being defined by the chance of getting some action). And apparently, B Squadron were pissed as hell that they hadn't been given the Sierra Leone gig. Which was something to be thankful for, as far as D Squadron were concerned. Anything to piss off their mates in the other three squadrons. As G Squadron were on counter-terrorism (CT) duties and A were off somewhere obscure on an operation, neither of them could have gone to Sierra Leone, even if they had wanted to. That had left B Squadron as the only other contenders.

But as Macedonia was thought to be on the brink of blowing, B Squadron were said to be on standby for that job (only, as everyone in the Regiment knew, there was little hope of getting any fun out of that one). So the Regiment's CO was adamant that D Squadron should get the Sierra Leone mission. He had other reasons too. D Squadron had just got back from Africa, and so would be acclimatised to the operating conditions in Sierra Leone. In addition to which they'd also just completed a very useful two-day live-firing exercise.

But in truth, the men of D Squadron believed that the CO was just giving them the nod because they were his old squadron. Still, deployment didn't mean that they were definitely going into action, although it was a big step closer to doing so. There was no guaranteeing that Sierra Leone would actually get the go-ahead, even once they were out there on the ground. Mostly, the men were worried that they'd end up kicking their heels in some obscure back end of beyond in Africa for the next few weeks, with nothing to do but sit around and smoke themselves silly. That was the worse scenario of all, especially as they could have been spending some of that time catching up with their families.

The men were used to being stood down at the last minute on an operation, so they tried not to get too excited about Sierra Leone. In fact, the squadron had been far more pumped up at the prospect of the Stansted op, earlier that year. In February, a hijacked Ariana Airways plane had been refused permission to land in both Russia and Germany, before entering British airspace. D Squadron had themselves been on CT duties at the time, and they had watched the hijack drama unfold live on Sky TV. Running short on fuel, the aircraft had eventually been allowed to put down at Stansted, by which time the men of the squadron had known that they would soon be dealing with it. Sure enough, four hours later they had been blue lighting it down the motorway to London. When they had arrived at the airport, the Antonov A222 aircraft had already been isolated out on the main runway. There were 156 passengers on board, being held hostage by nine hijackers armed with knives, guns and grenades.

For three days – in what became Britain's longest airport siege – the men of the squadron had prepared and rehearsed for the aircraft assault. Despite the hijackers' claims that they were asylum seekers who had been forced to hijack the aircraft to escape from Afghanistan's Taliban regime, the men had become increasingly convinced that they would be sent in to assault the plane. Then, following a daring escape by the Antonov's pilot and aircrew – via a cockpit window – the hijackers had just lost it, and taken things out on one of the hostages. The body of a man had been thrown out of the aircraft on to the tarmac. As he had lain there not moving, the British hostage-negotiating team had presumed that the unidentified male passenger was dead. In fact, it turned out that he was still alive, but he had been badly beaten and was taken off the runway in an ambulance.

That had been the catalyst for the men of D Squadron to go in. Suddenly, they had been stood to in all their black CT gear, with gas masks on and their hearts pumping and the engines of their Range Rovers running. They had even got the fuses in the plastic explosives ready to take the doors off the plane. But then, at the eleventh hour, the specialist police negotiators had reached a deal with the hijackers, and D Squadron had been stood down. As one of the men had commented at the time, the hijackers had never known just how close they'd come to the Black Death hitting them.

With the wake for Martie and Adie now all but over, the men of D Squadron headed for the mess anteroom for a formal briefing on the Sierra Leone operation by Brigadier Simon Chadwell. As they listened to their CO outlining the plan for Operation Barras – the mission's code name – it quickly became clear that this op was a very rare thing indeed: *it was a peach job, the absolute dog's bollocks, the business.*

D Squadron had been recalled from Kenya because a group of rebels calling themselves the West Side Boys were holding eleven British soldiers from the Royal Irish Regiment hostage in their jungle base in Sierra Leone. The rebels were heavily armed, and were making impossible demands as their terms for releasing the hostages. Hence D Squadron were to deploy to Sierra Leone as soon as possible, in preparation for a hostage-rescue operation. If Operation Barras was to get the green light, the men of D Squadron were to take no half measures, the CO stressed. If at all possible, the West Side Boys were to be totally eliminated as an effective fighting force.

'If this mission gets the go-ahead – and I have every reason to believe it will – I want you to be in no doubt about one thing,' the CO had said, as he rounded off his briefing. 'You are going into that rebel base to teach those people a lesson they will never forget. And I have every confidence that that is exactly what you will do.'

This sort of job happened only once or twice, if ever, in an SAS soldier's lifetime. Enough said. Suddenly, everyone wanted in on the mission.

3

TAKEN HOSTAGE

I have seen much war in my life and I hate it profoundly. But there are worse things than war; and all of them come in defeat.
         – Ernest Hemingway, *Men at War*, Random House Inc

THE eleven Royal Irish Rangers had just fallen into the hands of some of the most brutal rebels in Sierra Leone. Before joining the West Side Boys, Colonel Savage and the five-hundred-odd thugs and boy soldiers of his Savage Group had been part of the infamous RUF rebels. They had spent two years living and fighting in the bush with the RUF, and, bar their guns, their bases had looked like the camps of some long-forgotten medieval army. Scraggy fighters in rags were surrounded by even scraggier camp followers: young women they had abducted as sex slaves, older women who'd been taken as cooks and porters, and young children who'd been forced to become RUF 'recruits'. Colonel Savage himself had been renowned for giving orders and directing his battles from a camp armchair – surrounded by scores of bodyguards, and with a battery-powered ghetto blaster blaring out bad rap music at a deafening volume.

But back in February 2000, Colonel Savage had managed a bad falling-out with the RUF high command. So the rebels had turned on the Colonel and his Savage Group, determined to wipe them out. But then the United Nations had come riding to their rescue. The UN had proceeded to broker a deal between the RUF and the Savage group, in which the Colonel and his men would disarm in return for free passage to a UN demobilisation camp in Freetown. Colonel Savage had had little choice but to accept the deal: surrounded by a hostile RUF baying for his blood, and running low on ammunition, his days had clearly been numbered.

While the main body of the Savage Group had been trucked some 250 miles across Sierra Leone under a UN escort, Colonel Savage and his young wife and family had been plucked by UN helicopter and flown to safety. On arrival at Freetown, the motley bunch of five hundred rebels had been dumped at the UN demob camp, near the international airport at Lungi. But few had stayed there long. In the ensuing days Colonel Savage had reformed his Savage Group, and come over to join the West Side Boys.

The group were put in charge of road piracy and general looting for the West Side Boys, and they also did a good number in kidnapping too. And one thing that Colonel Savage hadn't forgotten from his days with the RUF was his pathological hatred for all things British, and in particular the British military.

Some twenty minutes after the surprise overflight of the UN chopper, Colonel Savage ordered the British soldiers to start marching down towards the Rokel Creek, which was visible from the village clearing. Half a dozen guards from the Savage Group went with them. At first, the British soldiers feared that they were being taken into the jungle to be shot, and that their bodies would be thrown into the river as the easiest way to be rid of them. From where they had been captured, the Rokel Creek flowed down to the Freetown Delta and then out to sea. As the river was infested with crocodiles, it would be unlikely for anyone to ever find the British soldiers' bodies.

'Looks like we've got no choice but to stay calm and quiet, lads, and do as they say,' the Major whispered around the frightened British soldiers, as they prepared to depart into the jungle. He was starting to recover from the shock of capture, and was taking control of his men again. 'Just keep your spirits up, all right? I'm sure they just want to know who we are and why we're here, lads. Once that's clear, they'll let us go.'

As they were marched through the jungle, the more experienced patrol members were already going into automatic survival mode. Major Martial tried to strike up a conversation with the guards. In simple English, he asked where he and the men were being taken. He was told that they were going to meet one 'Foday Kallay', the West Side Boys' leader. A little under a year ago, Foday Kallay had himself been a rebel officer with the RUF, commanding the 'Born Naked Squad', a unit with a horrible reputation of stripping their victims naked before torturing and killing them. A power-hungry opportunist, he had come over to join the West Side Boys less than a year ago when the leadership position became vacant. Foday Kallay had brought most of the Born Naked Squad with him.

But none of the British soldiers had heard much about Foday Kallay's past history. All they knew was that they were going to meet the West Side Boys' leader. Talking did seem to calm the rebel guards down, and after a few minutes they began asking the Major about his favourite football team. It turned out that all of the rebels were Manchester United fans, and, in an instant the whole patrol became avid Man U supporters too. At the same time as he was trying to break the ice with the guards, Major Martial passed a whispered order down the line of march from his position at the front.

'If you see a chance, we'll do these guys and make a run for it,' the order reached Rangers Gaunt and Rowell at the back. 'They're unarmed this end. What's it look like back there?'

'It's a no-go, sir', Ranger Rowell was forced to pass back a whispered reply. 'There's four of 'em here, all with AKs.'

After fifteen minutes or so of trekking, they were led into a clearing on the banks of the Rokel Creek itself. It was a wide muddy brown river, some thousand yards across, with jungle crowding in from either side. August was the height of the rainy season in Sierra Leone, and the river was swollen and the current strong. Since the Royal Irish Rangers' arrival, every day without fail there had been a torrential downpour, usually lasting from mid-morning through to lunchtime. It wasn't like English rain, either. This was no drizzle or mizzle or Scottish mist. This was raining cats and dogs, bucketing down, a veritable opening of the heavens. Standing on the river bank, it was steaming hot, the humidity being around 90 per cent and the air saturated with moisture.

On arrival at the river bank, the dazed British soldiers caught sight of Corporal Mousa. He was lying naked on the muddy ground and had obviously been badly beaten. The way the rebels were treating their fellow Sierra Leonean soldier was a huge shock to the younger British soldiers – more so even than their own rough treatment. None of the men could look at Corporal Mousa directly, they were so embarrassed and ashamed at what had been done to him.

Corporal Mousa managed a few words with the British patrol members, and he was able to let them know they were being taken across river to Gberi Bana, the West Side Boys' headquarters. Two dugout canoes were being prepared for their crossing. The men climbed gingerly into the dugouts – six patrol members to each plus their two escorts, loaded down to the gunwales. With one of their escort paddling in each, they crept slowly across the Rokel Creek, the water slurping at the canoes' sides. It seemed to take for ever, but in reality it was only twenty minutes or so before they nudged their way into the mud of the far bank. From here, they could see nothing of the rebel HQ up ahead of them, as it was obscured by tall reeds.

After wading through the sucking mud at the river's edge, the patrol members were marched up into the village. From what they could see, Gberi Bana consisted of twenty or so single-storey houses of a grey, mud-stained concrete, roofed over with rusting sheets of galvanised iron, and a collection of scraggy mud huts thatched with dried grass. The clearing for the village itself had been hacked out of the pristine jungle, and it was surrounded on three sides by a wall of ragged forest, the fourth, southern side opening out on to the reed swamps and the river. From one edge of the village clearing to the other was no more than a thousand yards or so, and in several places the bush was doing its best to reclaim the village.

The soldiers' route took them up a dirt track that ran through the centre of Gberi Bana, cutting a swathe through the tall, emerald-green 'elephant grass' that grew to shoulder-height throughout the rest of the village. By the river's edge, the track was littered with what looked like seashells. But as there was no sea around for many miles, these must have been fresh-water oysters or something. And there were thick wads of fibrous coconut husks lying on the ground, which squelched with a rotten wetness under the boots of the passing soldiers. Tall coconut palms grew all along the river bank, their palm fronds drooping in the hot and humid air.

As the men made their way up into the village, they could see that everyone had come out to gawp at them. There were men and women slouched in doorways and kids on rusty bikes, and all of them had guns. Even the mangy village curs had stopped their doggy doings to stare at the British soldiers. Few if any of the West Side Boys had any semblance of uniforms: mostly, they wore combat trousers and T-shirts. Apart from the guns they carried, there was nothing much else to distinguish them as combatants from the normal African villager. The women of the village wore colourful African kangas, a thin piece of cotton wrapped around the body like a dress, and flip-flops. Most of the kids were dressed in a pair of ragged shorts, if they were lucky, and went barefoot.

Halfway through the village at the central clearing a reception party was awaiting the patrol members. It consisted of Foday Kallay, the rebel leader, and Colonel Changa Bulanga, his deputy (*changa bulanga* is a Creole term for a shotgun – so the equivalent in English would be Colonel Shotgun). But as neither of the two top West Side Boys' leaders had had any education, they couldn't speak English and were unable to introduce themselves to the British soldiers. Instead, they spoke to Corporal Mousa in pidgin English (Creole).

'Aha, so dese dem be the whiteboy Brittonians?' said a grinning Foday Kallay. 'Na Corporal Mousa, isn't it?' he added, recognising Mousa. 'All right, Corporal. So, you do know what we dem say in West Side? We say: "He who inflicts the worst fear and terror is de King." So an here I be de king, OK? And dese the British soldiers dey now be my men. OK? Y'unnerstand? When you driving here, my men dey keep telling me by radio: "De whiteboy dem comin! De whiteboy dem comin!" So you go bring de whiteboys into my trap, Mousa. Is a good day, na don't you think?'

Corporal Mousa nodded and said nothing. There was no way he was going to risk translating any of this for the British soldiers. He knew that the West Side Boys' leader believed that he had led the British patrol to his HQ, with hostile intent. If he tried translating anything for his British colleagues, Kallay was likely to put a bullet in his brain.

Kallay then turned to Colonel Changa Bulanga. 'So, go take them to dat Cambodia's house and keep dem there for now-now.'

The patrol members were marched up to the top end of the village, to an unremarkable, slab-sided single-storey concrete house. The walls were crumbling and pockmarked, and covered in graffiti. *MAKA VELT THE DON WEST SIDE* was the graffiti scrawled in black marker pen across the front doorway, whatever than might mean. Presumably, it did mean *something*; perhaps it was a hybrid of the pidgin English that the rebels spoke, and their own tribal language. Somehow, the fact that the British soldiers could read it, yet not quite understand it, made it all the more disquieting.

The twelve men were lined up before a veranda at the front of the house and told to wait for one 'Colonel Cambodia'. On the wall next to the front door was scrawled *COL JUNGLE DEFENDER* – presumably the war name of another of the rebel leaders.

After a few minutes, Colonel Cambodia came shuffling out of the building, looking groggy. He'd obviously been having an afternoon nap. He was in his mid-thirties, around five foot seven, slim and lean-looking. He wore the standard-issue combats and T-shirt and had no insignia or other signs of rank. Rubbing his eyes clear of the fog of recent sleep, he blinked in surprise at the group of white men lined up outside his door. Turning to his men, he launched into a series of grumpy questions, obviously trying to find out who on earth these British soldiers were and why they'd been brought to him. In response, the rebel guards shuffled around uncomfortably, and stared at the ground or into the nearby bush. Finally, the rebel machine-gunner who had first stepped out in front of the British convoy began a long speech, accompanied by a lot of gesticulations. The Colonel nodded and grunted a lot, fired off a few more questions and then turned to face the British soldiers.

'Welcome, welcome,' he said, with a bemused grin. 'It seems you have come to visit with us. Here, the British Army are always welcome, of course. You must make yourselves at home, my friends. You are not our prisoners. We just need to keep you here while we find out what you were doing in our area. Once I have spoken with our leader, Foday Kallay, it should all start to get clearer and then it will all be sorted out very quickly. Come. Come,' he added, gesturing to his veranda. 'Make yourselves at home. My home is your home.'

From what the British soldiers could tell, Colonel Cambodia seemed genuinely surprised to see them and concerned to sort out why it was that they had strayed into his area of operations. Compared to their experiences across the river with Colonel Savage, Cambodia seemed to be remarkably, refreshingly sane. He even spoke good English, compared to the pidgin language that some of the rebel leaders and most of their rank and file seemed to manage. Making his apologies, the Colonel ordered his men to search the patrol members once more. But the Boys had little enthusiasm for their task this time around: they knew that the Royal Irish soldiers had already had any valuables stolen off them by the mob. Still, they took away the men's flak jackets, their webbing, their water bottles, ammunition and emergency rations. Finally, each man's British military ID was also confiscated.

Once the search was completed, the patrol members were allowed to sit down on the veranda and have a smoke, to try to calm their nerves. And boy, did they need it. There was a bit of forced laughter, as one or two of the men tried to crack a joke. But the jokes weren't really that funny, and anyway, their minds were elsewhere. *How the fuck did we end up here?* they were thinking to themselves. *What the hell's going to happen to us now? What do these bastards really want with us?* Each of the British soldiers was trying to work out just how bad their predicament *really* was. *How far away are the nearest British or UN troops (not that the UN can be relied upon to be much help)? How long before British forces realise that we've been captured? What're the chances that they'll be able to rescue us?*

With their vehicles now lying across the other side of the river, the patrol members knew that there was little chance of a quick getaway. Any escape would have to be made on foot through the jungle. And they had to presume that the Boys knew the jungle around there far better than any of them did. There was nothing to be done but to wait and see what happened. Maybe Colonel Cambodia was telling them the truth? Maybe, despite appearances otherwise, they weren't the rebels' prisoners after all? Maybe, once the rebel leader had checked that they were just a normal British Army patrol, they would let them all go?

The hardest thing that first hour in the rebel base was the sitting around doing nothing. Time just seemed to drag and drag, especially as all the British soldiers had had their watches stolen off them by the rebel mob. They reckoned they'd been captured around about 2 p.m., so it must be mid to late afternoon by now. But Colonel Cambodia was still acting as if the British soldiers were more his guests than his prisoners, and most of them still believed that they would be released as soon as Foday Kallay was alerted to the situation. Sergeant Smith took stock of the soldiers' cigarette supplies. In all the chaos and confusion of their capture, only one soldier had by chance brought a packet with him. Sergeant Smith took control of these sixteen precious, remaining smokes: they would clearly need to be rationed out very carefully now, until they got the hell out of there.

As the afternoon dragged on, Colonel Cambodia sent a couple of his boy soldiers to gather coconuts for the British soldiers. The boys propped their AK47s against the trunk of the nearest palm tree, shinned up it with a machete clasped in their teeth, and, holding on to the trunk with one hand, they used the other to hack the coconuts down. They came back with half a dozen or so, covered in a thick, fibrous husk. The boy soldiers sat down in front of the patrol members, gripped their machetes between their toes with the blades facing upwards, and smashed the coconut down on to the blade repeatedly, ripping and tearing sideways as they did so in order to split off the tough, fibrous husk. Once de-husked, the shell of the first coconut was smashed open by one blow from the machete – and the grinning boy soldier held up half a fresh coconut brimming with coconut milk.

For a second, the British soldiers had to pinch themselves, to see if they weren't dreaming. Here they were, just having been taken captive by a clearly crazed group of rebels, yet they were sitting out on a sun-washed veranda being handed fresh coconuts by smiling boys. If it hadn't been for the fact that even the eight- and nine-year-olds were carrying AK47s, they could have been forgiven for thinking for one moment that they were in some idyllic tropical paradise. More than likely, these boy soldiers had been forced to join the rebels, and had carried out scores of horrific atrocities themselves. Yet here they were, acting just like any other kids in Africa might – fascinated by these strange foreign 'guests' and pleased as punch to be able to show them a few local tricks with a coconut and a machete.

After about an hour or so, Major Martial decided to chance his arm and ask Colonel Cambodia for a tour of the rebel village. To his surprise, the Colonel readily agreed. Like he was some sort of tour guide and they were a party of Western tourists, Cambodia proudly showed the men around his camp. At first sight it did look pretty much like any other African village, but Cambodia was careful to demonstrate otherwise. He pointed out the heavy machine-gun nests on the corners of the buildings, the 61mm mortar emplacements and the anti-personnel landmines located around the village perimeter. There were several GPMGs and DshKas (a Soviet-era heavy machine gun) lying around, and scores of RPGs.

Situated on the north bank of the Rokel Creek, Gberi Bana was the more heavily fortified of the West Side Boys' positions, housing their top commanders and some two hundred fighters or so. There were some thirty or forty women in Gberi Bana, as a number of the rebel commanders had their 'wives' living with them, and about the same number of young children (younger than the eight- to fourteen-year-old rebel boy soldiers). Across the river at Magbeni, the village on the southern river bank, the majority of the West Side Boys' soldiers – some four hundred or so men and boys – were positioned.

Perhaps Cambodia had agreed to the Major's request to show him and his men around the base in the hope that it would act as a warning to them not to try to escape. But the four Rangers had little idea why their OC had requested this morale-bashing tour of their captors' camp. They were going into shock now, and they could only think that it was to kill time, and to help break the ice between them and their captors. Yet in the hours directly after the ambush of his convoy, the Major's 'conduct after capture' training was starting to kick into gear.

It had drilled into him the importance of getting early intelligence of any enemy defences, ones that might stand in the way of any escape or rescue attempt. As he was being shown around the camp, the Major was making detailed mental notes of all the rebel weapons positions and fortifications.

Just as the tour was coming to an end, a tiny light aircraft hove into view flying high above the village. The men reckoned it must have been around 5 p.m., three hours after headquarters would have lost radio contact with them. They figured their patrol was bound to have been reported missing by now, and they were fully expecting Cambodia to rush them in under the cover of the nearest veranda, so that the aircraft couldn't spot them. But instead, the rebel colonel craned his head skywards watching the plane for a few seconds, and then started waving.

'Come on,' he urged, grinning at the patrol members, 'give the plane a wave.'

The British soldiers needed no second urging, and they started waving skywards for all they were worth. The tiny plane looked like it was a Cessna, a single-engined aircraft, of a type that the soldiers knew had been used for aerial surveillance by British and allied forces in Sierra Leone before. If the plane was on a search mission it was bound to have spotted them now, and British military command would have a very accurate fix on their location. For some bizarre reason, while the West Side Boys seemed terrified of helicopters, planes just didn't appear to worry them at all.

As they were making their way back to Colonel Cambodia's house, Captain Flaherty and Corporal Sampson stumbled upon a tangle of struggling bodies in the long grass. They were almost on top of them, before they heard the stifled cries and saw the thrashing, naked limbs. Three of the rebels had a young girl pinned down on the ground, and were in the process of raping her. One of them had a dirty rag pulled tight across her mouth, which was half strangling her and stopping her from crying out. The two British soldiers had looked over at Colonel Cambodia, hoping he would intervene. But the rebel colonel had hardly turned a hair, as if this were just another everyday occurrence in Gberi Bana. He skirted around the struggling bodies without a word, leading the British soldiers on up the hill towards his house. As they left the rape scene behind them, the girl's stifled cries faded into the background *thrum, thrum, thrum* of the jungle insects.

Back at Colonel Cambodia's house, there was a welcome distraction that took the West Side Boys' focus off the British soldiers. A lone prisoner was frogmarched into the camp. He was a young, local man who was bleeding from a nasty head wound, and he looked dazed and confused. As he stumbled across the clearing in front of Cambodia's house, he didn't even seem to notice the British soldiers sat out on the veranda. Several of the rebels wandered off to amuse themselves with their new plaything, and the patrol members were left alone with Cambodia and a couple of the youngest of the guards.

Just then, the British soldiers caught the faint, rhythmic throb of a helicopter to the south-west of the rebel village. The aircraft was circling over what must have been the last known location of the patrol, the UN/West Side Boys' checkpoint, around ten miles or so distant from the rebel village. As the noise of the chopper became more and more intrusive – it was clearly following a search pattern and moving closer towards them – Cambodia became increasingly agitated. Finally, he jumped up from his wicker chair and stalked off down to the southern end of the village, without a word to the British soldiers. Fifteen minutes later he was back again, looking as if he had got the answers he was looking for.

'Those helicopters are out searching for you,' he remarked, irritably, pointing in the direction of the distant aircraft. 'But we have told them they have to give up. Your Regiment has already sent a patrol up as far as our first checkpoint. We told your officers that we are holding you and to call off the helicopter search. We told them that if they send in any helicopters to attack us or to try a rescue, then we will be forced to kill you. This is not what we want. *Definitely not.* We just want to find out what you were doing coming into our area, if it was for peaceful reasons only. Our commander is still suspicious that you came here to attack us.'

'Absolutely not, Colonel. We didn't come here to attack you, I can assure you of that,' Major Martial replied. 'You're right on one point though. The choppers will be out looking for us. But we did not come here to attack you. Far from it. All we wanted to do was explain to your commanders what the British military are doing at Benguema – the training programmes – and invite your men to join in. In the same way that we are working with the SLA, we were seeking to start training your own forces.'

This was the cover story that the Major had told the patrol members to use, if any of the rebels asked them why they had driven down into the West Side Boys' area. It was a reasonably convincing scenario, and as none of the junior ranks had any idea why they *had* come, it would have to do for now. Cambodia grunted a response – which seemed to indicate that he accepted the story – and went back to watching the distant helicopters.

By the time the helicopters had called off their search, it was around 6 p.m. and the sun was fast sinking towards the forested horizon. After the initial shock of capture, the men began taking more note of their surroundings. It had been intensely hot and humid in the village that afternoon, and even in the shade of Camdodia's veranda the men had found themselves sweating heavily. The conditions were made even worse by the claustrophobic atmosphere of the jungle crowding in on them. Without the rebels there to keep the forest at bay, it would clearly soon overtake Gberi Bana, turning the village back into tangled bush once again. As the steamy heat of the afternoon abated, and dusk settled over the village, the men realised that they were starving hungry and parched with thirst. All they'd had to drink was the little water they'd been carrying in their water bottles, and – apart from the coconuts – they'd had no food since their somewhat dubious lunch with the Jordanian UN soldiers.

As dusk settled over Gberi Bana, the only light emanating from the village came from the odd cooking fire or lantern. With the jungle night noises now crowding in from the surrounding forest, a grim mood settled over the hostages sat out on the darkened veranda. There seemed little chance of them getting out of there that day, or any time soon. Although there appeared to be no formal guard or sentry system, the British soldiers noticed that there were always a handful of rebel soldiers hanging around them with guns. To make matters worse, four of the rebels then came up from the southern end of the village and ordered Corporal Mousa to leave with them. Major Martial asked Cambodia what was happening. He was told that Mousa, as a Sierra Leonean, was to be held separately from the British soldiers.

'But Corporal Mousa is a member of my patrol,' the Major had objected, 'under my command. He should stay with us. As the commanding officer of the patrol, he's my responsibility. It is not appropriate to separate him from my other men.'

'But, Major, those are my orders,' Cambodia had retorted. 'There's nothing I can do about it.'

The eleven British soldiers watched as Mousa was led away around the side of the house, where there was a trapdoor in the ground. It seemed to lead down into some sort of bunker, and Mousa was shoved roughly underground, the door being slammed shut above him. This, it turned out, was the 'dungeon'. It was a hole dug in the ground, about four feet deep and ten square, and roofed over with logs, corrugated iron and then soil on top. With the trapdoor shut, it was pitch black inside, and it was half filled with stagnant, putrid water. Into it slithered and crawled all manner of life from the nearby jungle. It was too shallow to stand, but if the prisoner lay down he would drown. It would be freezing cold at night and boiling hot and fetid by day, as the corrugated iron heated up under the tropical sun. Mousa would be sharing the pit with the other, unidentified prisoner who had been brought into camp that afternoon.

Mousa had been separated from the rest of the patrol members because the rebels didn't want him translating for the British soldiers. Cambodia had realised that if he was discussing what to do with his captives, and Mousa overheard him, then he would be able to pass this information on to the others. Mousa's fate was another blow to the group's morale. Not only were they worried for his well-being, but, with each passing hour, their status as captives seemed to be getting more and more well established. In Mousa's treatment lay a clear, if unspoken, warning: step out of line, boys, and you will end up joining your friend in the pit.

Around 8 p.m., Cambodia came to have another word with the men. He told the British soldiers that he would be able to do no more for them until he'd spoken to his commander-in-chief, Foday Kallay. Unfortunately, Kallay wasn't there at that moment and so he'd have to try to speak with him the following day. Then, Cambodia assured the British soldiers, they'd soon be on their way.

In fact, Foday Kallay had spent the whole day in his house down in the southern end of the village. He'd had a busy time of it too. Shortly after the arrival of the British patrol in his camp, Kallay had started receiving reports of sustained helicopter activity in the region where the men had been captured. Once the Royal Irish HQ had lost contact with the patrol, a Royal Navy Lynx helicopter had been scrambled from HMS *Argyll*, anchored off Freetown harbour. The pilots, Lieutenant Commander Al Jones and Lieutenant Cunningham, had flown many missions over the jungles of Sierra Leone already. Their knowledge of the terrain around the West Side Boys' base allowed them to make repeated, probing flights over the last known location of the patrol. These flights had forced Foday Kallay into contacting British forces by radio to admit to taking the Royal Irish patrol hostage. In return for giving the British details of the British soldiers' whereabouts and condition, Kallay had demanded that the helicopter search cease.

Once it had become clear that Foday Kallay was not going to see them that day, the British soldiers were herded inside Cambodia's house. Four rooms led off a wide central hallway, and the men were placed in the front, right-hand room. Its walls were covered in a flaking, mottled brown plaster that was covered in unidentifiable stains (but which left little to the imagination). The floor was bare, uneven concrete. There was one shuttered window and a single bed. The mattress had seen far better days. It was bleak and musty-smelling.

A little later, Cambodia managed to rustle up some plates of boiled rice for the British soldiers. Handing them around, he apologised for not having anything better to offer them. He even promised to provide some brown sauce next time to go with the rice, which brought a wry smile to the soldiers' faces.

'HP feckin' Sauce,' one of the Rangers quipped, under his breath. 'Perhaps youse could get us some feckin' Marmite while yer at it.'

As the door to their room was slammed shut, they heard a key turning in the lock. The men had no idea who would be sleeping in the other three rooms in the house, although presumably one of them was Cambodia's and the others were for the guards. The patrol members were so hungry that they wolfed down the rice in no time. There wasn't that much of it, but it was better than nothing. That first night, eight men bedded down on the concrete floor of the room side by side like sardines, with three crammed on the bed. All they had to sleep in was their uniforms. But however uncomfortable it was, it was as nothing compared to the pit.

And back out in the dungeon, poor Corporal Mousa's ordeal was only just beginning. As soon as the British soldiers had been herded inside Cambodia's house, Mousa was hauled out of the pit. Waiting for him was the Colonel Contobie, the so-called Camp Commandant, Changa Bulanga and Colonel Mines (as in landmines). They had been ordered by Foday Kallay to 'initiate' Mousa. First, Changa Bulanga ordered the Sierra Leonean corporal to be 'tabay' – tied so tightly they he could not move. Mousa was bound so severely hand and foot that the ropes cut into the skin. Then his arms and legs were forced up behind his back until they felt as if they were coming out of their sockets, and tied together.

Tabay is also called handbagging, because once tied in this way, the victim's hands and legs can be used to carry him about, like the handle of a handbag, causing yet more agony. As Mousa lay there screaming with the pain of being handbagged, Colonel Mines ordered his Small Boys Unit (SBU), a force of some fifteen eight- to fourteen-year-olds, to initiate him. They fetched sticks, rifles, lengths of electric cable and anything else they could lay their hands on, and a savage free-for-all began, as they beat Mousa unconscious for the second time that day. Eventually, the Colonel Contobie took out his pistol and pistol-whipped the unconscious Mousa so badly that he cut open his skull.

Changa Bulanga then ordered Mousa to be put back in the pit. They carried him over there handbag fashion and threw him down the trapdoor head first. Mousa came to lying on his side with his head under water. It was a few seconds before he realised where he was and that he was drowning; he had already gasped some of the stagnant water into his lungs. Choking and fighting to get free of the foul water, he somehow managed to get himself up on to his knees and press his head and back against the earthen wall of the dungeon. In that position, he was able to cough out the water and grab a few precious lungfuls of air. But the respite was short-lived.

Changa Bulanga and the rest of them came to take a look at him. Putting their heads down and peering through the trapdoor, they were clearly surprised to see that Mousa was still alive. Glancing up at them, Mousa noticed the fresh-looking plasters the men were wearing over their temples. He knew what this signified: the rebels would make a small incision in the vein that runs just under the skin at the temples, take a mixture of heroin and crack cocaine and rub it directly into the vein. It provided a direct-line injection of the hard drugs right into the brain's bloodstream – the plaster ensuring that all the drugs were absorbed.

'Oh look, de someone has done de bad things to de army officer man, eh?' Changa Bulanga said. 'He be de Corporal, but de man be all dirty now-now. Let us give him de good clean, eh?'

'You do mean de dick bath, na good idea?' a grinning Colonel Mines responded.

'Eh-eh. Washing him wid de hot shower,' Colonel Contobie added, unzipping his flies as he did so.

As Mousa crouched against the wall in the dark, he felt the three rebel commanders start to urinate through the trapdoor on to his head. As the warm liquid splashed all over his wounds, Mousa tried to keep his mouth and eyes closed. But the urea in the urine started burning into the wounds on his skull. Up above him, he could hear the three commanders laughing away to each other as they finished pissing on him. Then the trapdoor slammed shut again and he heard their boots stomping away, and Corporal Mousa was left down there in the complete blackness.

Back in their room, Major Martial ensuring that the one bed was reserved for whichever soldier needed it most, regardless of rank. Normal divisions between the officers and men were already starting to break down under such conditions. Increasingly, the men would find rank and power structures becoming more fluid and fragmented. The eleven men would find themselves changing from being a rigidly hierarchical British Army unit to a group of captives sharing a common and ever more desperate situation. They would need to rely on the group pulling together more or less as equals, if they were to get through the ordeal that lay ahead of them.

For now at least, the captured patrol members had been blessed with one stroke of good fortune. The Boys had failed to confiscate the military maps that several of the senior ranks – Major Martial, CSM Head, Sergeant Smith and Corporal Sampson – had been carrying with them when captured. In fact, as was often the case in rural Africa, the rebels who had searched them hadn't seemed to appreciate quite what the maps were. They had seen the chance to search the British soldiers as an opportunity for some looting, and the maps had been totally uninteresting. They were pieces of folded paper with strange coloured patterns on them: they couldn't eat them or wear them or sell them or fight with them. None of the West Side Boys seemed to carry a map; they relied on their instinctive bush sense and knowledge of the local terrain to plan all of their military operations.

At Major Martial's urging, the men gathered round and spread out the four Ordnance Survey maps on the floor. Fablon-coated for waterproofing, the maps gave off a faint other-worldly glow in the fluorescent green light of the soldiers' cyalumes. Just like the 'useless' maps, the cyalumes had appeared like lengths of boring plastic tubing to the West Side Boys, and so they hadn't bothered confiscating them, either. As none of the hostages knew just how long they'd get to keep hold of the maps, they did their best to memorise them. There was a lot of hushed discussion of the possible options for escape. Only two routes looked possible. The first was a fairly known quantity, an overland slog some thirty-five miles through the jungles back to the Royal Irish base. The second was the wild card. Presuming they could steal a couple of canoes, it was the forty-mile boat journey down the uncharted waters of the Rokel Creek to the Freetown Estuary, which was in friendly hands. As the idea of escape became more concrete in the soldiers' minds, it lifted their spirits considerably.

'Listen, lads,' the Major whispered. 'You'll have heard the door being locked shut from the outside. We have to presume there's one of those bastards on guard out there too. So our only hope is to look for a chance to do one of the sods, and make a break for it. Now, remember our grid reference, in case we don't all make it out; it's four-six-two-four. Got it? Four-six-two-four. It's not that far as the crow flies back to base. A night's march through the jungle, that's all. It's just a stroll in the park, really. Don't worry, we'll be breaking out of here pretty bloody smartly, you mark my words.'

'Youse know what, sir,' Sergeant Major Head mused out loud, 'I've been trying to think of a title for my bloody book. And you've just given it to me, sir: *Four-Six-Two-Four*. Got the right ring to it, hasn't it? I bagsy that title, OK, lads? And, sir, don't be breaking us out of here too fookin' smartly, like, not before I've got something to write about. Always fancied myself as a writer I 'ave. What d'you reckon, lads? Can you shitbags hold on in here long enough to make me a good story, like? Bloody better had, or you'll 'ave Sergeant Major Head to answer to. Bloody damn sight more scary than these dope-smoking bastards.'

A ripple of exhausted laughter went round the room as the CSM finished speaking.

'Not if I get there first,' Captain Flaherty retorted, from his side of the room. 'Fancy I'd be a damn sight better writer than you would, Sergeant, wouldn't you agree?'

'Wouldn't be feckin' hard,' Rangers Rowell muttered, under his breath.

'WHAT the hell is that supposed to mean?' the CSM hissed. 'Bloody Ranger there thinks he's fookin Bill Shakespeare himself. Well, you can piss off the lot of you, 'cause it's me that thought of it first. I can see it now. "*Two-Six-Two-Four* – the true story of how CSM Head saved a group of British soldiers from a bunch of dope-smoking bastards in Africa." Best-seller. Got to be.'

Gradually, the junior ranks drifted off into a fitful slumber. The four Rangers in particular had gone into shock now, and were withdrawing from their surroundings, seeking the forgetfulness of an exhausted sleep. But as they tried to do so, they kept being jerked awake, on account of the wildlife that seemed to share the room with them. At first, there was the noise of animals – *they had to be rats* – scuttling across the roof beams above them. Then the big tropical spiders emerged from the thatch to catch the insects that had emerged from the forest with the coming of night. And lastly, closer to home, cockroaches the size of mice went scuttling across the floor and over the prostrate forms of the British soldiers – occasionally scrabbling right across one or another of the men's faces.

While the junior ranks tried to get some sleep, Major Martial, Sergeant Major Head and Captain Flaherty stayed up half the night to make meticulous, written notes of all the defences and weaponry that they'd seen around the village that afternoon. The Major sketched out a map of the river, with the location of the rebel base, giving the direction of north and showing any contours and vegetation (in particular, the extent of the jungle). The CSM identified specific mortar emplacements and machine-gun nests that he had spotted during that afternoon's walkabout – in particular, the three heavy machine guns positioned on the corners of the roofs of the main buildings. And Captain Flaherty had identified the rebels' communications headquarters – a building they marked as the 'radio shack' on the map – which was situated halfway down the hill from Cambodia's house towards the river. Finally, the Major marked an X at Cambodia's house itself, noting that this was the 'location of the hostages'.

In the coming days, Major Martial would try to ensure that this detailed map of the West Side Boys' HQ would be smuggled out to British forces. If any of his men were released by the rebels, he would try to ensure they carried the map out with them, hidden on their person somehow. Or if not, he would seek other ways to get the map out. He would remain vigilant and await an opportunity. Sooner or later, one would present itself, of that he felt certain. The intelligence the map provided could prove vital if there was to be an attempt to rescue the captured soldiers.

And unbeknown to the hostages, a massive military machine had already swung into gear in the UK to attempt that very rescue.

4

RESCUE MISSION

The warrior of light knows that silence precedes an important battle. He listens intently to that silence; somewhere, something is happening. He has walked through the forest at night and knows that it is precisely when the animals are silent that danger is near.

– Paulo Coelho, *Manual of the Warrior of Light*

PRIOR to the Sierra Leonean hostage crisis and Operation Barras, Operation Nimrod, the 1980 Iranian Embassy siege in London, was the single biggest British Special Forces' hostage-rescue mission since the Second World War. It has rightly gone down in British military legend. The central-London embassy had been seized by an obscure group of Iranian terrorists, who had taken its occupants hostage. Members of B Squadron's on-call Pagoda Troop (a twenty-five-man special-projects alert team within the SAS, consisting of a sniper group and an assault group) had driven down from Hereford and prepared to assault the building and rescue the hostages. When the police negotiations had finally broken down, the men from B Squadron had been sent in, the whole operation being broadcast live on British TV. All the hostages in the embassy were rescued, all the terrorists bar one were killed, and there were no SAS casualties. Operation Nimrod was an extraordinarily high-profile success story for the SAS.

Compared to Operation Nimrod, the plan that was now being drawn up for Operation Barras was unprecedented in terms of scale and logistical complexity, speed and secrecy. Nothing of this size or scope had been tried by the Regiment before, and Sierra Leone was to lead the way for Special Forces operations during the forthcoming conflicts in Afghanistan and Iraq (Gulf War Two). Operation Barras would eventually require some 250 men (aircrews included) to go into action. Some fifty members of D Squadron would be joined by two dozen of their colleagues from the SBS, and for the first time ever, the men of SAS and the SBS would fight alongside each other as integrated UKSF Fire Teams. They would be augmented by some 150 men from the 1st Battalion of the Parachute Regiment – and again, UKSF had never operated so closely with the Paras before. Together, these two-hundred-odd crack troops would be deployed as a combined assault force, and they would require seven helicopters and their aircrews to go into action with them.

The success of Operation Barras would rely on all three services of the British military working together: the Army, in the form of SAS, the Parachute Regiment and Army AH7 Lynx attack helicopters; the Navy, in the form of the SBS, RFA ship *Sir Percival* and HMS *Argyll* along with her Lynx helicopter; and the RAF in the form of C-130 Hercules transport aircraft and three giant CH47 Chinook transport helicopters. It would also require the support of the SLA, and forces deployed under the United Nations. And most importantly for the success of the op, a huge body of men and equipment would have to be shipped out to Sierra Leone in a matter of days, in complete secrecy. Operation Barras was to be a covert exercise on every level, and mission concealment was of paramount importance.

The name for the Sierra Leone mission – *Operation Barras* – doesn't actually mean anything. British operation code names have almost always been chosen at random. But past Special Forces mission names have often reflected the nature of the operation: like Operation Nimrod (a skilful or enthusiastic hunter), or Sandy Wanderer (the Oman Desert exercise), or Operation Mikado (the term for a Japanese Emperor, the aborted SAS Argentine operation during the Falklands War). Such names as *Operation Barras* are now chosen at random using a computer program, for operational security (opsec) issues. Bland and meaningless operational codenames give no clue to the enemy as to the possible nature of the mission. Yet at the same time, they are hardly an inspiration to the soldiers tasked to carry out the mission, often at great risk to their own lives.

Like Operation Palliser three months before it – the Paras' intervention to stop the rebels seizing the Sierra Leonean capital – Operation Barras was to be coordinated from Permanent Joint Headquarters (PJHQ), the British military's operational nerve centre in Northwood, north London. Brigadier Andrew Stewart, one of the Northwood high command, knew that you couldn't resolve a situation like the hostage crisis with laser-guided bombs from 30,000 feet. It would require a steady nerve and good men on the ground. And whatever else happened, the media had to be kept out of the picture. Hence security for the mission was to be extremely tight. No one – not even the families of the Royal Irish soldiers and very few if any Sierra Leonean Army top brass – were to get so much as a sniff of the fact that the assault force was being sent in-country.

But by now the British and international media were crawling all over the story of the Sierra Leone hostage crisis. If any Special Forces were seen entering Sierra Leone, this would alert the press – and hence in turn the West Side Boys – to the fact that a major hostage-rescue operation was underway. A tri-service command centre (Army, Navy, Air Force) was established in Freetown, and a plan was drawn up to sneak the men and machines into Sierra Leone under the cover of ongoing British military activity. D Squadron were to fly from the UK to Dakar, in Senegal, and thence on to the British Army's Waterloo Camp, situated several miles to the south-east of Freetown. Waterloo was a simple, tented camp, with some small firing ranges out the back. Its single biggest advantage was that it was situated in the middle of nowhere, and as far as possible from the international press corps now working out of the Sierra Leonean capital.

On 31 August, six days into the hostage crisis, the six-man SAS advance party left Hereford for Sierra Leone. There was barely enough time for Brad Tinnion to say goodbye to his long-time partner and childhood sweetheart, Anna Homsi, at their house in the tiny village of Sutton St Nicholas, before heading for the motorway and the airport. Anna was seven months pregnant with their first child, and they already knew it was going to be a baby girl. Brad was looking forward to getting back home again to be there at the birth. It was a golden rule among British Special Forces that when the men went off on an operation they weren't supposed to tell their wives anything about where they were going or why. But the wives were generally a pretty smart bunch of ladies, and they'd normally be able to work out where their husbands were most likely heading. With the hostage crisis now hitting the headlines, few of them had any doubts this time: they knew that their husbands were going to Sierra Leone.

In any case, the men of D Squadron felt they had to trust their wives; after all, it was highly unlikely that they'd married a spy, they told themselves. And with this operation in particular, it was in the back of all of their minds that there was a very real risk that they might not make it back again. They weren't just popping out to buy a bag of sprouts, they kept telling themselves. Because of this, they made sure they said their goodbyes differently, with more feeling, so as to ensure that it would mean something. Of course the wives in turn noticed this, and realised that their husbands were acting differently because they were afraid they might not come back alive. The nights of 31 August and 1 September were a time for many a difficult and emotional parting back in Hereford.

Before departing for Sierra Leone the six-man advance party had not even had the time to unpack and repack their kit properly after the training exercises in Kenya. At least that made things easy: as the operating environments in Kenya and Sierra Leone were pretty much the same, headquarters decided just to ship out the squadron's entire Kenya kit lock, stock and barrel to Sierra Leone (with a bit of tweaking here and there and a top-up on the weapons and ammunition fronts). As the West Side Boys' headquarters were known to be based around the Rokel Creek, a sizeable river, it was decided that the SBS would be deployed alongside the men of D Squadron. No one yet had a clear sense of exactly how the assault itself would take place – but the one thing they were all pretty certain of was that it would involve a riverine approach to the target. Having the SBS boys along could prove very useful.

The whole of the Sierra Leone deployment was made all the easier by one major stroke of good fortune. Three months ago, under Operation Palliser, the British military had established a ground-breaking air bridge to Africa – via which the Paras had flown out to Sierra Leone and stopped the RUF rebels from seizing Freetown. As Op Palliser was still in effect ongoing, most of the infrastructure needed to get the Operation Barras assault force in-country was already up and running. Which was most convenient, as far as the Operation Barras planners were concerned.

The six-man D Squadron advance party followed the same route into the country that the Paras had done before them. Dressed in civvies, they flew into Senegal's Prince Leopold International Airport, in Dakar, the staging post for their deployment to Sierra Leone. They were billeted in an old hangar – a hot, dusty and cavernous building in a forgotten corner of the military section of the airport. After the basic logistics had been sorted out in preparation for the arrival of the rest of the squadron, the advance party found they had nothing to do but sling their beds and hang out. It was even worse when the rest of the squadron turned up the following day; hordes of blokes hanging about with absolutely nothing to do but fiddle with their kit (or anything else that came to hand). Dakar was blisteringly, suffocatingly hot, the only wind being the seasonal *harmattan* that blew in off the vast Sahara Desert. But that's just how it was, the men told themselves: you did find your-self in some very strange places with the Regiment.

There was a small contingent of French troops permanently based at the airport, and they were keen to show their fellow NATO soldiers how Senegal was the party capital of West Africa. They invited the men from D Squadron for a night out on the town, giving graphic descriptions of partying until dawn in some of Dakar's wilder bars and nightclubs. But the men were under strict orders not to let themselves be seen and, regret-fully, they had to decline. Pete, the squadron OC, had warned them that there was a strong international press presence in Dakar. The last thing they needed was a story breaking about the SAS being on their way to Sierra Leone to spring the Royal Irish hostages, and beat some sense into the West Side Boys at the same time.

Pete and the other head sheds had their hands full getting communi-cations up and running with Sierra Leone and working on the next stage of operational planning. At first, they planned to send the men into Sierra Leone in dribs and drabs, so as not to attract any unwanted attention. But, pretty quickly, the OC realised that his men were getting roasted alive and going stir-crazy stuck in the old airport hangar. And so, some twenty-four hours after they had arrived, the OC just thought: *To hell with it, let's get the whole of the squadron in-country.* In order to disguise the fact that they were SAS, the OC ordered his men to dress in the 'green army' uniforms that they'd brought with them. In this way, anyone who might catch sight of them on arrival in Freetown would almost certainly conclude that they were just regular British Army.

On the morning of 2 September, nine days into the hostage crisis, D Squadron lined up to board their C-130 Hercules aircraft out of Dakar. While the whole squadron could fit on to one aircraft, they'd needed a total of three to carry all the gear that had been shipped out from Hereford. It was a huge mountain of kit, consisting of comms equipment, piles of weapons and ammunition, the SBS inflatables and their engines, plus tents and personal gear. The only things they hadn't brought with them were vehicles, as they knew that these were already in-country. So the men had piled the kit high and lashed it down in the centre of the Hercs, and then squeezed on board down either side of the aircraft. After a two-hour, six-hundred-mile flight from Senegal to Sierra Leone, the three aircraft touched down at Lungi Airport. Here, there was a reception party waiting for them, consisting of a couple of standard British Army Land-Rovers and two four-ton army trucks. All going to plan, the convoy would look like a regular rotation of British troops going into the British garrison in Freetown.

From Lungi, it was a short drive down to the Sierra Leone River estuary, where the trucks were loaded on to an ancient army ferry for the journey across to the capital. The ferry was a roll-on roll-off affair, and it basically consisted of a flat chunk of metal with a tiny one-man boathouse on one side. As the river estuary was ten miles or more across, the ferry was clearly going to take its time to reach Freetown, so the men got out on deck for a jolly boat trip, sunning themselves in their shades. From across the far side of the estuary, Freetown did look pretty stunning – a low-rise city fringed by palm trees and dazzlingly white sandy beaches. From a distance, it could have been any tropical paradise. But the closer they got, the clearer it became that a lot of the city was made up of tin shacks and shanty towns. As the ferry drew into the docks, the stench hit them too, the tangy smell of the sea now mixed with the stink of rotting vegetables and raw sewage.

The convoy trundled off the ferry and drove up into Freetown itself, and the first thing that struck the men was how friendly everyone seemed, the locals waving and grinning at the passing trucks. British soldiers seemed mighty popular here in Sierra Leone. Freetown turned out to possess a crumbling colonial splendour, which gave a sense of how grand and imposing this outpost of the British Empire must once have been. But as the convoy crawled through the outskirts of the city, the road was pockmarked by craters and the scars of recent battle. The burned-out hulks of derelict cars, trucks and buses littered the route, and few of the buildings seemed to have escaped the ravages of the fighting. Their route took the men up through the fringes of Freetown, where the worst, most poverty-stricken shanty lands were. Up close like this, it was clear that there was nothing much to come back here on holiday for.

Suddenly, as the convoy rounded a bend in the road, the lead Land-Rover swerved to avoid a drunk who had stumbled into the road and collapsed. But the four-tonners weren't so nimble, and one of the trucks went trundling over the prostate figure with a sickening lurch. But the convoy couldn't stop and take the risk of the men being seen, or the whole mission could be compromised. Their orders were clear:

once they had hit the ground in Sierra Leone they were on immediate standby to go. The last thing they needed at this moment was to be forced to a halt to deal with a drunk injured in a road accident. Instead, a radio message went out from one of the lead vehicles, reporting the accident to the regular British forces in town.

'Looks like we're fakin' one-nil up before the operation's even started, lads,' Cockney Jimmy remarked, as the convoy drove away from the scene.

It was a sick joke, of course. All part of the process that the men of D Squadron were now going through to harden themselves for what they had ultimately come to Sierra Leone to do – *and that was to kill people*. None of the men had any illusions as to what they were here for. They had come as killers, and it wouldn't do them any good to get too close to the locals just yet. If the mission got the green light, they would be going into action very shortly now, and the West Side Boys would be getting their come-uppance. Hearts and minds were all well and good, but that only came after the real fighting had started and the key battles had been won. *Grab them by the balls first, and their hearts and minds would follow.*

It was late afternoon by the time the men reached Waterloo Camp, a clutch of khaki tents set out in the middle of nowhere. The camp was situated on a wide expanse of flat scrubland; but barely half a mile inland, the mist-shrouded, jungle-clad hills of the Freetown Peninsula dominated the skyline. When the first Europeans landed on these shores, they named the country Sierra Leone – Lion Mountain – after these hills. They mistook the rolling thunder of the tropical thunderstorms in the hills for the roaring of lions. Somewhere, just beyond those forested crags, the West Side Boys had their base. Somewhere, where the Rokel Creek snaked between rolling hillsides, a thousand rebel soldiers were playing the hostage game. Somewhere, just beyond those rugged peaks, eleven British soldiers were being held to ransom. It all felt so tantalisingly close to the men now arriving at Waterloo Camp.

Waterloo Camp had long been used as a base for British and allied military operations. There was a fence of sorts around it, but not a secure one, and a field kitchen with a mess tent attached. Out the back of the camp was a small firing range. The khazis, situated near the ranges, consisted of a couple of long drops and a row of 'desert roses' (a pipe that you had to urinate into, leading into the latrines). The camp was pretty basic, and whichever unit of the British military had been occupying it up until now had moved out to make way for the Op Barras assault force. First, the men went about pitching their four accommodation tents – one to each troop. Then they set to erecting the larger, twelve-yard-square working tents: a general store, an ammunition store, a medical tent and an operational headquarters (or 'ops tent').

Even before they'd finished making camp, updates and intel started coming into the ops tent. From now on, this would be the nerve centre of the whole mission, the epicentre of the squadron's collective will-power and cunning. From here the assault on Gberi Bana would be mapped, strategised, reworked and coordinated, nurtured by a growing body of intelligence – most of which was coming in from JFHQ Freetown.

Over the past few days, the British intelligence people at JFHQ Freetown had been on overdrive, gathering information on the West Side Boys. They had succeeded in 'turning' two of Foday Kallay's senior rebel commanders – persuading them to help the British forces. These two men were now providing a stream of highly accurate – and disturbing – intelligence. With each of their clandestine visits to JFHQ Freetown, an ever more detailed picture was being drawn up of Foday Kallay's power-crazed plans, and the overall intentions of the West Side Boys.

Kallay had declared to his men that the capture of the British hostages was the start of a new mission for the West Side Boys – codenamed 'Operation Kill British'. The aim of Operation Kill British was – as the name indicated – to kill some British soldiers. Kallay argued that if enough of them could be killed, *and in horrible enough ways*, then the British Army would be forced to abandon Sierra Leone. This was Kallay's grand plan – to 'do a Somalia' on British forces. Once Operation Kill British was successful, he would launch Operation Kill All Your Family. In stage one of Operation Kill All Your Family, the West Side Boys would capture the Benguema Camp.

Upon seizing Benguema and its well-stocked ammunition dump and armoury, Kallay believed he would then have enough well-armed men for stage two of Operation Kill All Your Family, the capture of Freetown itself. Once Freetown was under his control, Kallay would declare himself President, with his commanders taking up lucrative posts as his ministers. Kallay had called this mission Operation Kill All Your Family because the ultimate aim was to capture and kill all the people in Sierra Leone's government *and their families*.

For now, the British hostages were the key to the success of his plans. He would use them as bargaining chips to get food rations,

radio sets, medical supplies and vehicles off the British – all the logistical requirements for a full-scale assault on Benguema and Freetown.
Once he had forced the British to hand over all these things, the hostages
would then become his insurance policy. Kallay believed that there was
no way in which the British forces would attack his bases, if in doing
so the hostages' lives would be threatened. In the meantime, Kallay
had told his men that he aimed to turn the 'whiteboy Brittonians' into
'proper Africans'. He would feed them only African food – boiled
plantains and cassava leaves.

All of this intelligence and more was being fed across to the assault
planners in the ops tent at Waterloo Camp, so they could bring themselves up to speed on the enemy forces that they faced. A detailed
profile of Foday Kallay had been drawn up. He came from a military
family, his father being an NCO in the Sierra Leone Army. He had
enlisted himself, becoming a young officer with a glowing career ahead
of him. He was handsome and athletic, and such a good football player
that he was a regular in the army football team. But then the wheels
had begun to come off the wagon. He was involved in a bad road
accident that damaged his spine and he only partially recovered. When
he came out of hospital he walked with a pronounced limp. His army
career was over.

Bad luck followed bad luck, and Foday Kallay had finally gone
into the bush to join the RUF. There he had thrived, becoming an
officer in the Born Naked Squad. With his conventional army career
plans thwarted by injury, he decided to use the rebel movement to
further his own ambitions. And like most of the RUF, he had become
increasingly dependent on hard drugs. Over time, the combination of
drugs, alcohol and horror had warped his mind, and turned him into
a sadistic killer.

In May 2000, he had seized his chance, leaving the RUF and declaring
himself leader of the West Side Boys – taking most of the RUF Born
Naked Squad with him. As the new rebel leader, Kallay instigated a
new *esprit de corps* for the West Side Boys – one inspired by his time
with the RUF. He aimed to give the West Side Boys the aura of a secret
society, an exclusive killing club. None of the rebels was allowed to
utter even one word about these secret practices to a non-West Sider.
The basic thread that ran throughout all of this was a worship of death
and of blood. The two rebel officers had told the British intelligence
boys that Foday Kallay was only ever happy when surrounded by those
who urged him to kill, kill, kill.

On joining the West Side Boys, every recruit would have to take an oath of allegiance and secrecy, which would be sealed by drinking a beaker of human blood. The best blood for the initiation ceremony was seen as being the blood of a virgin woman. At night, the rebels' Revolutionary Reverend – part voodoo priest, part Christian visionary, part shamanic soothsayer – would kill a white chicken and bathe the new recruit in the chicken's blood. This would make them 'fearless in battle'. Then the new recruit would have to squat down in a big vat over a fire, and be half boiled alive in 'medicine' – the Revolutionary Reverend's own secret concoction. This was the chief ceremony that was supposed to make the new recruit 'bulletproof'.

In this way, the new rebel recruits were brainwashed to have a sense of invincibility and fearlessness. And it often worked. In battles with the Nigerian UN peacekeeping troops, new West Side recruits had literally stormed positions and captured the Nigerians with their bare hands. But these men were not destined to live long. When a bullet did eventually find them, it was always put down to the 'medicine' not having been applied religiously enough. No one ever questioned whether the medicine actually worked. As far as Kallay was concerned, it was crucial to have a revolutionary reverend on hand at all times – and men from the Limba tribe made the best. They could predict which operations would be successful and which would fail.

Kallay introduced a series of new passwords for the West Side Boys, to strengthen the sense of death and blood worship around the rebel camps. On catching sight of an unrecognised soldier coming into the base, the rebel guard was supposed to call out a series of questions. If the person challenged did not know the right answer, then he had not been initiated into the West Side Boys, which meant that capture and death were sure to follow.

'What makes the grass grow?' the challenger would shout out.

'Blood. Blood. Blood,' would come back the answer.

'Who is the commander?' the challenger would then call out.

'Evil, evil Foday Kallay, the jungle big boss.'

The intelligence that had been gleaned from the two rebel commanders was of immense value to the British commanders at JFHQ Freetown. Any attempt to reach a negotiated deal to end the hostage crisis would clearly run up against Kallay's power-crazed plans. In addition to which, any British team sent in to negotiate would be doing so in the face of Kallay's Operation Kill British. They would literally be walking into the lion's den. At the same time it was vital to open negotiations, as there was no way that British forces were ready to launch the assault on the rebels yet. Further intelligence needed to be gathered on the rebel bases: their positions, layout, armaments, rebel numbers, state of alertness and morale. More men and equipment needed to be shipped out from the UK. And the options for the assault itself needed to be drawn up and evaluated. By opening negotiations – risky though it might prove – they could at least buy some time.

For the assault planners at Waterloo, certain conclusions could be drawn from the rebel commanders' intel: little tactical sophistication could be expected of an enemy that relied on a revolutionary reverend to predict the success of operations. An enemy that believed it was bulletproof would have few concerns about taking cover. Likewise, men who were used to trying to overrun their enemy and catch them with their bare hands would have little fear of running into a field of fire. And finally, when faced with an enemy such as the West Side Boys, it was clear that no member of the British assault force should ever allow himself to fall into their hands alive.

Such were the evaluations now being made by the SAS and SBS officers and senior NCOs in the Waterloo ops tent. But the main focus of the rest of the men's lives was rather more mundane, and centred around the cookhouse tent. Already, the cookhouse tent was acquiring that familiar mixture of smells that the men knew so well and loved: damp canvas, sweaty male bodies, stewed tea and frying food. Long wooden benches and tables, spilt sugar, the stacks of collapsible wooden chairs; it could have been any cookhouse tent in any British Army camp anywhere in the world. This would be D Squadron's home from home for as long as it took to get the job done.

A couple of young chefs had been brought over from the Royal Irish base at Benguema to do the catering, and they were trying to fire up the cookhouse stoves and get a brew on and a feed going for the newly arrived troops. But all the two chefs seemed to have to cook with was a pile of fairly ancient-looking British Army ten-man ration packs (rat packs). There was no fresh food as far as the men could see, which was typical. The ten-man rat packs were pretty much universally despised by the men of D Squadron. The boiled sweets and the chocolate were all right, and the bacon grill and meat curry ready meals were generally considered to be edible. But as for the 'babies' heads' (steak-and-kidney puddings – for obvious reasons), 'cheese possessed' (processed cheese – 'you had to be possessed to eat it') and 'truncheon meat' (luncheon meat – 'you could knock someone out with it') – you had to be starving or crazy or preferably both to want to eat any of those.

The chefs did a pretty good job, all things considered, rustling up a huge fry-up and a giant canteen of tea – enough to get the squadron fed and watered before they crashed out for a night's well-earned kip. There was even the bonus of some real fried eggs. But the bulk of the meal was made up of boiled 'growlers' (tinned pork sausages that resembled swollen frankfurters). The men had a standing joke about growlers. The sausages were packed into tins vertically, surrounded by a thick, white grease. It was said that you could pull the central sausage out leaving the others where they were, and then shag the tin. If you were really messed up, you could slide the central sausage back in again when you'd finished, and give the tin to one of your mates to eat. Hence the Regimental saying that was treated as gospel: 'Never eat from an open tin.'

Several of the men were just having a laugh over this around a table in the cookhouse tent, when one of the Royal Irish chefs came over to have a word.

'How're youse doing?' he asked, a little nervously. 'I mean, sir. I mean, is the food all right, sir?'

Cockney Jimmy had thrown his beret down on the table, cap badge up. It was a habit he'd got into over the years, especially as it seemed to have such a positive effect on his pulling power with the girls. He reckoned he needed all the help he could get, too: he was a short, stocky bloke with a face to match. He was proud of his working-class roots and did his best to sound like it too. The winged dagger of the SAS was universally recognised by British soldiers, and the chef had clearly just clocked exactly who it was that he had been cooking fry-ups for. It wasn't just any bunch of hairy-arsed blokes. *It was the feckin' Regiment.* It's generally recognised in the British military that the winged dagger SAS cap badge demands the respect of most ranks – although a lot of regular army officers resent this greatly. The Royal Irish chef had obviously decided to err on the side of caution and address all of the men of the squadron as 'sir'.

'Anything wrong with the eggs, sir?' the chef tried again. He was a particularly ugly specimen, this chef, even for a British soldier. Young and anaemic, he had a bad case of acne – looking like he'd spent far too long slaving over hot pans of fat preparing fry-ups for British squaddies.

'Yeah. They're not fakin' white enough, mate.' It was Cockney Jimmy, replying to the question about the eggs.

'Uh . . . sorry? Youse mean not yellow . . .'

'Na, mate. Read my lips: not white enough. You call that egg white? Looks more like fakin' piss-in-the-snow-yellow to me, mate.'

'Uh . . . there's not much I can do about it . . . Youse can take yer pick from this lot or I can fry youse some more . . .'

'It's all right mate. I'm just taking the fakin' piss, innit?' said Jimmy, his face lighting up with a grin. 'Pullin' your plonker, like. You're all right. You're doing a fakin' good job on the scoff, too, what wiv ten-man rat packs being all you got to feed us wiv. Luverly. Perfick nosh. Just pulling your plonker, mate, that's all. Any chance of some more growlers?'

'Yes, sir, coming right up, sir.'

'Luverly. And, er, mate? No need for all that "sir" shite around 'ere, is there? We're all in this crap-heap of a camp together, innit? So between us, we're all just mates or lads or whatever, all right?'

'Yes, sir, I mean . . . mate,' the chef spluttered, as he retreated in confusion back out to the kitchen.

'Fuck me,' said Jimmy, under his breath, nodding in the direction of the retreating chef. 'Looks like cheffy there fell out of the ugly tree, innit?'

'Aye' said Big Scottish Monster with a grin, his mouth full of a half-chewed growler.

'D'you 'ave to talk with your fakin' mouth full, mate?' Jimmy snorted, in mock disgust. 'Get more manners in a fakin' pigsty than you do round 'ere, like.'

That first night, a massive tropical storm blew up. Raging in off the ocean, it crashed into the British camp sometime in the small hours of the morning. The cookhouse tent was the worst affected, its cavernous structure channelling the powerful onshore winds, whereupon it threatened to rip out its guy ropes and take off like a giant khaki kite. At intervals, the black night would be torn asunder by fork lightning – the whole scene of the British soldiers trying to rope down the massive mess tent momentarily lit up in stark relief. There were flashlights winking in the darkness, as voices strained above the howl of the wind and the men struggled to keep hold of the mess tent and stop it from flying away into the inky black night.

'Cop 'old of this, and 'elp anchor 'er down, me shipmates,' one of the men would yell, as a newcomer came stumbling over to help. 'Aye aye, Cap'n' and 'Thar she blows' came back the sleepy replies. With the big canvas monster of the cookhouse tent rocking and swaying in the wind and lashing rain like this, there *was* something akin to being in a boat on the high seas about it all. After what seemed like an eternity the storm finally passed on, leaving a soaked and blasted camp behind it. It was now 4 a.m., which left just enough time to pick up the pieces, salvage what they could, and try to grab some kip before the coming African dawn, which by the looks of the horizon wasn't that far off. But first things first, it was time for a brew.

There was a definite sense of purpose and mission to the cookhouse tent by now, and the men were getting attached to it already – each man finding his own favourite place to sit and stop for a fag and a quiet think, each troop graduating to a particular table, that sort of thing. Like any good cookhouse tent, you could pop in and get a brew at any time of the day or night. It'd be hot and stinky most of the time, but then there'd be a big belt of rain, and it'd take the heat and sweatiness out of the atmosphere. This was a far better environment in which to throw around ideas for the coming assault – however crazy they might at first seem – without the danger of having them shot down in flames in the more formal atmosphere of the ops tent. Try them out on your mates over a cup of tea first. If the idea was seen as having legs, you could always then shuffle off to the ops tent and put it to one of the officers.

'Shiver me timbers, if the fookin' thing wasn't about to get hulled out to fookin' Liberia, laddies,' the Big Scottish Monster remarked, jerking his head in the direction of the damp canvas ceiling above them.

'You don't reckon it was a bad omen, mate?' the Kiwi ventured. 'I mean, doesn't look very much like this place exactly welcomes us, does it, mate?'

'You're 'avin a fakin' nonsense, aren't you, Kiwi mate?' Jimmy butted in, slurping his tea. 'That was a flamin' tradishnul African welcome, that was.'

'Yeah? Well, they can keep their fookin' welcomes if ye ask me, laddie,' the Monster grunted. 'Noothin' like a fookin' hurricane, is there, laddie, to make ye feel at home.'

'Call than an 'urricane?' Jimmy snorted. 'Only fakin' 'urricane round here, mate, is gonna be D Squadron when we go into Gberi fakin' Bana, that's what.'

'Too right, laddie. Fookin' loovely, that's what we'll be, fookin loovely,' the Monster said, while at the same time being somewhat disappointed at having found something they both could agree on.

Mates of old, Jimmy and the Monster liked nothing better than a good solid row.

''Urricane, mate, thunder and fakin' lightnin', a whirlwind, mate – that's what this squadron's gonna be – and those fuckers'll never know what hit them,' Jimmy continued, now jumping to his feet and starting to swing his arms about. He was a real performer, and Kiwi and the Monster knew what was coming next. 'For I will strike down with GREAT vengeance upon THEE . . .' Jimmy began at the top of his voice, quoting a line from the Bible. It was about the only one that he knew, and he'd actually memorised it while watching a video of *Pulp Fiction* – some fifteen times over – when, a few years back, they'd been stuck waiting for a mission to get green-lit in the Gulf. It was still one of his favourite movies of all time.

'Sit doon and finish you're fookin' tea, laddie,' the dour Scottish Monster grunted, pulling Jimmy back down on his chair. 'There'll be plenty o' time for that later – that's if this fookin' mission ever gets the fookin' go-ahead.'

5

SOLDIERS OF FORTUNE

You have to stop the violence before you can start the peace negotiations. Sometimes the only way to stop it is to go in with a bigger bunch of guys and guns than the bad guys have. Executive Outcomes did that in Sierra Leone. They literally stopped the war.
    – Canadian Brigadier General Ian Douglas

IN 1995, five years before the Sierra Leone hostage crisis, another military force had been sent to that country to sort out the rebels. That time it had been Executive Outcomes (EO). EO had been asked by Sierra Leone's leaders to mount a counter-attack against the RUF rebels, who had been ravaging the countryside and were poised to seize the capital. In an extraordinarily effective operation, fewer than two hundred Anglo-South African mercenaries had succeeded in routing the rebels. Five years later, some of the key figures in EO's short but highly effective military campaign would end up playing a vital role in the mission to rescue the British hostages. Chief among them would be 'Fearless' Fred Marafono, a giant Fijian veteran of the SAS, and Neall Ellis, his ace helicopter gunship pilot, plus a group of traditional Sierra Leonean hunter-warriors, called the Kamajors, who had long been the traditional enemies of Sierra Leone's rebels and therefore the natural allies of British forces in the region.

Back in 1995, EO – a South African-based outfit with strong links to the UK – was unarguably the world's most famous (or infamous) mercenary outfit – or Private Military Company (PMC) as these operatives are far happier to be known. Its adversaries in Sierra Leone, Foday Sankoh's RUF, were Africa's most brutal and mindless rebels, and by the mid-nineties their strength was reaching its zenith. As the

RUF's armed strength grew, so did its ferocity and cruelty. Rural villagers had born the brunt of their attacks, but the RUF had also started targeting Western companies and aid workers. In February 1995, they took seventeen Westerners hostage, including several Italian nuns. And they executed one Irish priest, just to make sure that everyone knew that they meant business.

As five hundred or so RUF rebels had advanced towards Freetown, the 12,000-strong RSLMF – the nation's army – appeared incapable of stopping them. This was hardly surprising. Captain Valentine Strasser, at that time Sierra Leone's military leader, had press-ganged hundreds of teenage boys and street kids into uniform, giving them an AK47 and some tattered combats and little or no training. With wages of just $20 a month along with a couple of bags of rice, many of the new recruits were forced to indulge in their own share of looting and terrorising civilians – for which they became known as 'sobels', soldiers by day and rebels by night. They had little incentive to take on the advancing rebels, and the scene was set for an RUF takeover of Freetown, with the untold horrors that would accompany it.

Sierra Leone's rulers faced two choices: the first, to do a runner with all the diamonds and cash that they had creamed off during their years in power; the second, to contract in some outside muscle to take on the RUF. Captain Strasser chose the latter option, and in late January 1995 a force from Jersey-based Gurkha Security Guards was flown into the country. It comprised some fifty Gurkha mercenaries, under the leadership of the legendary Canadian-born Captain Robert Mackenzie. Captain Mackenzie came highly recommended. He had served as a Paratrooper with the 101st Airborne, qualifying for a Purple Heart in Vietnam, and had been invalided out of the US Army on 100 per cent disability. Within the year, he had gone on to train for and pass the then Rhodesian SAS selection course, becoming one of the most highly decorated soldiers in that African war. He brought with him to Sierra Leone one ex-Gurkha officer and British Sergeant Andrew Myres.

However, their time in Sierra Leone was to prove tragically short-lived. On 24 February, Captain Mackenzie led Sergeant Myres and five Gurkhas, along with a platoon of RSLMF troops, on a scouting mission into the Malal Hills. While searching for a suitable training and live-firing site, Mackenzie stumbled into a surprise contact with a unit of the RUF rebels. Wounded in the initial exchange of fire, Mackenzie found his Sierra Leonean military escort promptly deserting him, as he, Myres and his

Gurkha soldiers tried to repulse the rebels. They fought on until their ammunition was exhausted and they were finally overwhelmed and killed. The RUF then went on to cook and eat Mackenzie, believing that in so doing they would gain the courage and heroism of this great white warrior.

With their commanding officers having been killed and eaten by the rebels, Gurkha Security Guards promptly pulled out of Sierra Leone. As news of the disaster reached the wider military community, Captain Strasser feared that no one else would agree to step in and help. Who in their right minds would want to risk getting killed and eaten by the rebels? It was at this stage that Tony Buckingham, a British soldier-cum-industrialist, intervened. Buckingham had retired from the military and taken up the chairmanship of an oil company with extensive operations in Africa. He had recently witnessed Executive Outcomes deploy a mixed group of South Africans and British soldiers – all ex-Special Forces or related units – to the war-torn African nation of Angola, quickly retaking the oilfields and bringing that country's rebels to heel.

To Tony Buckingham, the solution to the problems posed by the RUF rebels in Sierra Leone was simple: the country needed Executive Outcomes. In November 1994, Buckingham set up a meeting between the Sierra Leonean government and EO. By May 1995 – and with rebel gunfire echoing on the outskirts of Freetown – a deal was agreed for EO to provide military support and training. The contract was to cost no more than $2 million a month, in return for which EO was to provide personnel and equipment to enable the RUF to be dealt with once and for all.

Two weeks later, several dozen black and white EO mercenaries had been installed in the Cockerill Military Headquarters (CMHQ) in Freetown. Mostly, these men were veterans of crack (some would argue, notorious) units within the South African Defence Force (SADF) – in particular the 32nd 'Buffalo' Battalion (a Special Forces unit, which used a lot of foreign fighters), the Koevoet (the South-West Africa Police counter-insurgency unit) and the Reconnaissance (Recce) Commandos (another SADF Special Forces unit). In order to maintain absolute operational secrecy over the Sierra Leone mission, these men were not even informed of their destination until they were in the air in two chartered Boeing 727s, and on their way to Freetown.

EO also recruited several British and allied ex-Special Forces – including Fearless Fred Marafono. Fred Marafono had served with unique distinction as a sergeant major in the SAS, where he had become a legend in his own time. EO brought him on to the force as a last-minute measure, to give them some wider combat experience. Fred was a thickset Pacific Islander, with a big mop of unruly black hair and a wide grin to match. He put great store in bone-crushing handshakes, which were almost a ritual with him. Now all of fifty-nine years old, age had not dimmed Fearless Fred's appetite for action. EO set up the highly effective Air Wing in Sierra Leone, operating several Soviet bloc Mi-17 Hip and Mi-24 Hind helicopter gunships. When not soldiering on the ground, Fred would serve as a door gunner in one or other of these choppers.

Invariably, Fred's pilot was his good mate Neall Ellis. In his early fifties, bespectacled Neall had the demeanour and bearing of a country doctor going slightly to seed, but his appearance belied his reputation. He had a long track record as a gunship pilot in wars in Angola and elsewhere. The Air Wing's air logistics man, one Murdo MacLeod, was a somewhat eccentric Scottish pilot now well past the fifty mark. Murdo had flown Harriers in the Falklands War with distinction and gone on to become an RAF Squadron Leader. These men were fiercely proud of their British heritage, and they would rarely go into combat without first having a good cup of Commonwealth tea.

Shortly after arrival in Sierra Leone, the men of the EO Air Wing sat listening to an introductory briefing. It was a bleak picture. Sierra Leone was potentially a wealthy country, possessing great mineral riches, including 25 per cent of the world's known reserves of rutile – the ore which when refined went to make up the titanium armour cages of the Soviet gunships that Neall and Fred operated. It had massive bauxite deposits (the principal ore of aluminium) and enough diamonds to support a gem trade amounting to some 250,000 carats a year (one carat equals 200mg). And as if that wasn't enough, it also had significant gold, platinum and oil reserves. Sierra Leone should have been an affluent country.

Historically, the first European visitors were the Portuguese, who gave the country its name. Britain built up strong links with the country, and in 1787, 356 'Black poor' – the freed British slaves of African origin – went to establish a colony there. In 1792, 1,200 freed slaves from America followed and founded Freetown. Sierra Leone became a Crown colony in 1808 under British rule, and it was thus one of the first modern political states in Africa. The Creoles, as the freed slaves came to be known, adopted much of the British lifestyle and built up a flourishing business trading on the West African coast.

In 1827, the country's first university was founded, the Fourah Bay College, one of the first in Africa – though health and education services were still largely provided by missionaries. By 1938, diamonds had become the nation's largest export earner and, along with iron, made the country rich. At independence in 1961, Sierra Leone was one of the most affluent nations in the region – being known as the 'Switzerland of West Africa'. It was an exporter of rice, cocoa and one-fifth of the world's ginger. Independence from the UK was marked by a period of high expectations and optimism: the nation's currency, the leone, was on a par with the US dollar.

Now, less than forty years later, there were over two thousand leones to the US dollar, and this tiny, fertile country was unable to feed itself. It had recently earned the dubious distinction of being the poorest country in the world, coming bottom – 174th out of 174 countries – of the United Nations' 'quality of life' index. Rebel atrocities, civil war, and human-rights abuses – the country was beset by such problems. And for the last half-decade or so, the people of Sierra Leone had even gone as far as asking the old colonial power, Britain, to reoccupy the country to sort out its unimaginable ills. How had this happened?

Since independence, the country had suffered under the ruinous leadership of a series of increasingly corrupt regimes. And for the last six years it had borne the added burden of the excesses of Foday Sankoh's RUF. The brutalities and predations visited on the men, women and children of Sierra Leone by the RUF had earned them the chilling title of 'Africa's Khmer Rouge'. Certainly, their activities had done much to turn the country into a Cambodia-like horror show. Yet the rebels were now poised to launch an assault on the capital Freetown itself. Until the RUF were defeated, Sierra Leone would remain bankrupt and ungovernable. EO's task was thus simple: to defeat Foday Sankoh's RUF, recapture the mineral- and diamond-rich territory lost to the rebels and re-establish peace and the rule of law in the country.

EO began their preparations by commandeering several transport and fighting vehicles from the Sierra Leonean Army. They took a number of BMP-1s (a Soviet bloc light-armoured vehicle, mounted with a 30mm cannon) and a couple of Bedford trucks, and they imported several long-wheel-base Land-Rovers – and then modified the vehicles with extra machine guns, grenade launchers and armour. For air transport, EO purchased two Soviet-built Mi-17 transport helicopters, at a cost of around $1 million each. They also took possession of a sleek and powerful Mi-24 helicopter gunship (a Soviet-built machine on lease to the Sierra Leone regime). In case of significant numbers of casualties requiring casualty evacuations (casevacs), EO purchased two Hawker Siddeley Andovers, and they also brought in a tiny, Cessna light aircraft to conduct airborne recce and surveillance operations.

Three weeks of boot camp saw EO trying to put a unit of RSLMF soldiers through basic PT and combat training, at an army camp at Waterloo, several miles south-east of Freetown. But it was like trying to make a silk purse out of the proverbial sow's ear. The RSLMF soldiers were high on drugs or the local hooch the whole time, and there seemed to be no way of breaking them of this habit. EO quickly realised that it was their men that were going to end up doing all of the real combat missions. Meanwhile, covert EO recce teams had been inserted into the jungle, and the RUF forces had been identified massing at nearby Moyamba, for a final push on Freetown. EO drew up plans for a pre-emptive strike by their modified armoured convoy, with the Mi-24 gunship flying in close support.

Less than a month after their arrival in Sierra Leone, EO launched a blistering dawn assault on the RUF Moyamba base. On arrival over the target, the Mi-24 gunship let fly with a salvo of eight 57mm air-to-surface rockets, four from each of the stubby wing pods to either side of the aircraft. The chopper banked sharply right and left again, taking evasive action, and then levelled out on target as the nose gunner let rip with a series of short bursts from the Gatling gun. As the side gunners in the rear of the Mi-24 were not strapped in (unlike in NATO gunships), they were hanging on for grim life as the pilot threw the chopper through these 2G manoeuvres.

From the rear of the chopper the aircrew could hear the reassuring low-pitched, throaty roar of the Gatling gun as it started up. The four-barrelled, 12.7mm machine gun has a cyclic rate of fire of over four thousand rounds a minute, and they could feel the kickback the weapon made, almost as if the pilot had eased back slightly on the chopper's throttle. Circling above the jungle canopy, the gunship began hunting for more targets, as sitreps started coming in over the radio of the conflict raging below them.

The RUF had been taken by complete surprise, but once they were over the initial shock, they grouped together in platoon-sized groups, and mounted a spirited defence. It was a large enemy base and the EO assault force was heavily outnumbered. The EO-crewed Mi-24 gunship made repeated attack runs – but while the dense jungle obscured the target, the rebels could obviously see the chopper, and heavy ground fire kept arcing up towards it. It was hit several times, and if it hadn't been for the titanium cockpit armour, the aircraft might well have gone down. But as the day wore on and the rebels began passing around the hooch and the drugs, the battle began to turn in EO's favour. The more inebriated and drugged out the rebels became, the more their defence lost cohesion and resolve.

One of EO's best commanders on the ground was one Simon Witherspoon, a former member of the SADF's crack Recce Commandos. Around lunchtime, he found his twelve-man unit caught in a small defile on a hillside and all but surrounded by the rebels. Whichever way his men probed, they met heavy gunfire. After a couple of hours of this, they were almost out of ammunition, and all attempts at air evacuation had failed. A typical hot extraction by Mi-17 was out of the question as the two sides were almost in sight of each other, and the chopper would almost certainly have been shot down. Instead, and despite the obvious risks from friendly fire, Witherspoon decided he had no choice but to talk the Mi-24 down to attack the rebel forces that surrounded him.

The Mi-24's cockpit radio crackled into life, with Witherspoon saying that he had the gunship visual. Gradually, Witherspoon coaxed the chopper in towards his besieged unit, until it was hovering almost directly above him. He then asked the pilot if he could see a small crossroads, to his front at eleven o'clock. Once the pilot had got that, Witherspoon gave him his own unit's location, in a clump of bushes on the far side of the crossroads. The main body of the RUF were in a patch of dense bush some 150 metres to the north, Witherspoon explained. Armed with that information, the gunship pilot put the four-barrelled Gatling gun on to automatic and rolled the chopper on to target, putting several hundred rounds into the bush ahead of him. That seemed to break the RUF's spirit, and shortly thereafter, the main body of the EO ground-attack force swept into Moyamba, completely routing the rebels.

That evening, EO took stock of its damage: one EO soldier had lost an eye to an RPG fragment and three Sierra Leonean soldiers had received minor shrapnel wounds. In subsequent radio intercepts, EO learned that over thirty RUF had been killed and many more wounded. The RUF retreated to their base in the Malal Hills – where, barely six weeks earlier, Captain Mackenzie and his men had been ambushed and eaten. The operation was hailed as a major victory, halting the RUF advance on Freetown in its tracks. EO's employers were ecstatic, and when news of the victory was broadcast on Sierra Leonean radio, the inhabitants of Freetown went wild. At local street parties, EO's troops were mobbed like returning heroes. But to them it had been a relatively minor operation. The bulk of the work, they knew, was still to be done.

One of the main teething problems with the operation had been the amount of spent ordinance that the Mi-24 Gatling gun spewed out – and at more than four thousand rounds a minute of 12.77mm, that was a lot of brass. It meant a good deal of hot gun casings rained down on anyone below – not too clever if the Mi-24 was hovering over its own forces, as was often the case. In the heat of the tropics, none of the men would wear helmets, and several ounces of metal dropping from over a hundred metres would crack a man's skull open. Assault profiles and attack runs were reviewed, so they could be applied more exactingly in future, to avoid any such unwelcome cases of friendly fire. With such teething problems behind them, the EO aircrews were in action again by the end of the week, extending their reach further into RUF territory.

With the air ops now in full swing, it was time to embark on stage two of the EO grand plan – a series of carefully choreographed ground strikes, designed to drive the RUF back into the remote jungles and finish them as a fighting force. EO's key strategic objective was to retake the rich Kono diamond fields, thus depriving the rebels of any cash-generating capability. As the RUF would be bound to defend them vigorously, EO allowed for a three-week campaign. Once Kono town itself was reached, a vicious house-to-house clearance operation was envisaged.

In fact, EO's forces took the diamond fields in just three days. A force of some 150-odd EO soldiers with Fred Marafono leading the combat operations, accompanied by two companies of SLA troops, defeated the RUF with an ease that belied the rebels' fearsome reputation. Basic military discipline, classic combat expertise and professional soldiering had won the day. But as the rebels had retreated, they had left behind the severed heads of villagers mounted on poles, as a gruesome warning to the advancing forces.

After capturing Kono town, the EO–RSLMF forces began to fan out into the surrounding countryside to clear it of the rebels. Fred Marafono worked closely with RSLMF Captain Silla on these search-and-destroy missions – consulting him over the local terrain and likely rebel numbers. Soon, the ex-SAS soldier was showing the SLA captain how to live off the land, cooking and eating the giant African snails (about the size of a man's fist) that are found all over the forested region of Sierra Leone.

It was in the days of these clearance operations that the EO assault force was to face its toughest challenge yet. Tellingly, it would not be a spate of chilling, mind-numbing atrocities. One morning in mid-June 1995, they heard a series of distant shots coming from the direction of the village of Wordu, about ten miles to the south of Kono town. Wordu was a typical rural settlement, populated by farmers who cared little about wider Sierra Leonean politics or power. Over the past two weeks, EO's foot patrols had regularly passed through Wordu, dispensing basic medical care and gathering information as they did so. This was a typical 'hearts and minds' operation, one that the mercenaries were now attempting to run in all the areas they controlled.

Upon hearing the distant shots, a dozen EO operatives had jumped into their two Land-Rovers and roared off towards Wordu. By the time they had reached the village, a huge plume of smoke could be seen rising into the still morning air. Large birds of prey were wheeling above, picking off the insects thrown up in the flames and hot air. Dismounting and preparing to fight their way into whatever mayhem lay ahead of them, the men advanced cautiously on foot into the village. But it soon became clear that the rebels had already done their dirty work and departed. Scores of huts were still blazing and the acrid stench of scorched flesh hung in the bitter, smoky air. As mud walls collapsed inwards under the intense heat, the men could see that the village huts were full of charred human remains.

EO launched an immediate follow-up operation, tracking the RUF rebels into the bush and killing several. From two captives the EO operatives then extracted the full story of the raid on the village. The previous evening, several score RUF had arrived in Wordu and overnight it had been turned into a living hell. The so-called rebels had spent the night raping the females, regardless of their age. Seven-year-old girls had been gang-raped in front of their fathers, who were forced at gunpoint to watch. Adolescent boys had been forced to rape their own mothers. Women and girls who had been raped had then had burning stakes rammed up their vaginas. After that, the village boys had been ordered to shoot their own parents, or face death themselves. Horribly traumatised, they would make for perfect RUF forced recruits.

The RUF had then turned to the one, particularly gruesome speciality that had made them infamous internationally – amputation as torture. Villagers had had their hands, noses, lips and ears sliced off by machete and many had had their eyes gouged out. As the night of torture had reached its final crescendo, the RUF had herded the surviving villagers into their huts and set alight the flimsy mud and thatch buildings. The final body count was 265 men, women and children. The only survivors that the EO patrol discovered were two babies of not more than a few months old, found lying beneath their mothers' charred bodies. It seemed that even as their huts had turned into raging infernos around them, the mothers had fought to shield their tiny infants from the flames.

From the two rebel captives, EO learned that this force of rapists and child killers had been sent out from an RUF base at Gandorhum, twenty miles to the south. Back in Kono that evening, EO prepared for an assault on their base. Three days after the massacre at Wordu, they were ready. Fearless Fred Marafono would lead a ground force towards Gandorhum, while a mortar team would be dropped atop a high rock outcrop within range of the RUF base. The mortar team would then open up with an 81mm and 120mm mortar barrage.

That night, from the vantage point of their rock outcrop, the mortar team swept the jungle in the direction of the rebel camp with night-vision goggles (NVGs). A crude circle of white-heat sources was visible – campfires beneath the double canopy jungle – exactly where their intel had reported that the rebel base should be. Once the range and distance had been calculated, the first 120mm round was dropped down a waiting mortar tube. Watching the flash of the first exploding shell in the NVGs, a slight adjustment was made – and then the mortar teams were ordered to fire at will, using a mixture of white phosphorous (WP), an incendiary shell, and heavy explosives (HE).

As many of the shells hit like airbursts, detonating in the jungle canopy, the peace of the sleeping RUF camp was shattered from all directions. Confused and injured rebels stumbled about in panic, trying both to locate their attackers and to make their getaway. At that moment, the heavens opened, an intense tropical rain beating down on the forest and adding a surreal edge to the scene. Then, just as suddenly as it had started, the fearsome mortar bombardment came to an abrupt end. In the eerie quiet that followed, all that could be heard around the RUF camp were the cries of the wounded rebels, amid the hiss of rain hitting burning WP shells. The EO mortar team then spent an uncomfortable remainder of the night, as their exposed outcrop was lashed by the tropical thunderstorm. But it was all made more than worthwhile by the knowledge that they had hit hard those responsible for the Wordu massacre.

At first light the mortar team started putting down harassing fire on the rebel base, while Fred Marafono closed in with the main force overland. For the next twenty-four hours they maintained sporadic fire, varying the time and duration of the mortar barrage, just to keep the rebels guessing. By the time the mortar team were finally extracted at dawn the following morning, Fred's ground forces had completely overrun the rebel positions. The EO attack had accounted for as many as forty RUF dead, with many more wounded. And by now EO believed that the rebels should be receiving their message loud and clear: a repeat of anything like the massacre at Wordu would be swiftly and bloodily avenged.

The action at Gandorhum had proved the crucial role that intelligence played in EO's military strategy. It gave them a unique, almost supernatural advantage as far as the rebels saw things. To the rebel soldiers camped out in the jungle darkness, EO's mortar assault had come like magic out of the night sky – like the avenging wrath of some white man's god. As the rebels didn't even know about – let alone understand – aerial intelligence-gathering operations, or the technology of NVGs, the attack had seemed little short of miraculous. How had the mercenaries found them in the first place? How had they pinpointed their camp? How had they targeted them in a remote stretch of jungle in the darkness? How had they called in fire so accurately at night? Where had the bombs even come from, as there had been no aircraft roaring across that night sky above them? For the RUF there were no answers to such questions, and not surprisingly their morale was facing imminent collapse.

EO's intelligence strategy in and around Kono was based around a classic 'hearts and minds' operation, involving regular rural foot-patrols-cum-mobile-clinics. Through such measures, EO quickly attracted the support of Chief Sam Hinga Norman, a tribal leader and former officer in the colonial British West African Force (BWAF). During the Second World War, the British had recruited several Sierra Leonean BWAF units, which had gone on to distinguish themselves in combat in India and Burma. Sandhurst-trained Chief Norman had been posted with the British Army to the Rhine, and his military experience and acumen were now to make him a vital ally. Even more importantly, Chief Norman commanded the absolute loyalty of the Kamajors.

The Kamajors were the traditional warrior class, ubiquitous to all tribes across Sierra Leone. 'Kamajor' is a word that in the language of the Mende, one of the largest tribes in Sierra Leone, means the 'hunters'. With an intimate knowledge of the jungle, the Kamajors were both the defenders of their villages and the guardians of tribal tradition. They were also absolute adherents to voodoo, a magical-religious belief system that has its birthplace in West Africa. And the Kamajors were the arch enemies of the RUF rebels. The warriors were rooted in the traditions of respect for the forest, its animal inhabitants and for all fellow human beings: to them, the RUF's senseless cruelty and brutality betrayed a deep and residing evil.

Beneath the shadowed jungle canopy and guided by their ancestral spirits, the Kamajors had no equal. They could move as silently as a gentle breath of wind stirring the dank jungle air, melt in an instant into the cavernous shade of a forest giant, and remain motionless as that tree for as long as it took for the enemy to pass. And then, armed only with a rusty, home-made shotgun or a machete, they would pounce from the rear with the ferocity of a forest leopard. While the RUF were terrified of EO's helicopter gunships, these at least they could hear and see and run from. By contrast, the Kamajors were the terror of the unknown. The terror of bloodshot eyes in the forest shadows, of horrible stranglings beneath the bending trees, of a blade thrust deep between the ribs by the hand of a dark and powerful magic.

Chief Norman quickly established a highly effective Kamajor intelligence network, to transmit information back to EO's headquarters. Soon, EO was using the Kamajors as people-hunters, sending them into the jungle to track down specific RUF bases. They went on to set up specially trained Kamajor Hunter Force units. By now, Fred Marafono was acting largely as the Chief's bodyguard. The bond between EO and the Kamajors was to become all but unbreakable after he saved Chief Norman from almost certain death at the hands of the RUF. Fearless Fred was subsequently made an honorary chief of the Kono area, a rare privilege indeed for a foreigner.

But soon EO were facing unexpected problems: there was growing international concern about the presence of 'mercenaries' in Sierra Leone. In particular, the US Clinton administration seemed keenly opposed to EO's operations. In order to reach out to their critics, EO went on a charm offensive, sharing regular intelligence and strategic planning briefings with the major foreign powers in Freetown. Not surprisingly, liaisons with the British proved closest of all. The British High Commission served as EO's primary conduit for outgoing

information, and soon EO was briefing visiting Foreign Office officials. Their reports were in turn going right to the top of the
Conservative British government. But despite this, critics continued to
agitate for EO to be forced out of the country.

It was at this stage that EO had its single biggest intelligence break-
through. Mamma Sankoh, the wife of RUF leader Foday Sankoh, was
arrested while trying to sell diamonds illegally. Mamma Sankoh was the
obese 'voodoo high priestess' of the RUF rebels – her spells supposedly
promising them invincibility on the battlefield. But EO got her into their
custody, threw her in an isolation cell, and cut down her food rations
to the bare minimum. And sure enough, within forty-eight hours,
Mamma S's greed had prevailed and she was ready to talk. As suspected,
she wielded immense power within the RUF, possessing a detailed
knowledge of rebel operations.

Her interrogation provided a detailed database on all the key RUF
players, down to the individual RUF murderers and rapists, as well as
detailed plans of all the RUF bases, allowing EO to draw up a complete
Order of Battle. The rebels were soon to pay dearly for their high
priestess's gluttony. Armed with this information, EO's Air Wing went
into overdrive, recce flights confirming Mamma Sankoh's information
about RUF base locations with pinpoint accuracy. Once they had an
accurate fix, an attack plan was drawn up in Freetown, with input
from all players. In this way, EO's airmobile strike force began snuffing
out the remaining RUF bases, one by one.

By January 1996, just eight months into their contract, EO had
achieved its key mission objectives in Sierra Leone. The main diamond
fields were back in government hands and Freetown was secure. The
country was more peaceful than it had been for many years. The RUF
were still carrying out sporadic attacks in isolated areas, but they had
been badly mauled. The rebel terror tactics had been minimised and
the UN was starting to prepare for democratic elections. Foday Sankoh
boycotted the elections of course, but they went ahead in any case,
and Ahmed Tejan Kabbah was elected the new President of Sierra
Leone. Kabbah, an ex-United Nations diplomat, was a firm believer
in democracy, civil rule and the power of law.

In March 1996, President Kabbah called a meeting with Michael
Grunberg, one of EO's executives. He revealed that he was under serious
pressure from foreign powers to terminate EO's contract. Grunberg
offered Kabbah one month of EO's services free of charge, so he could
see for himself how useful they were to his country. If, in late April,

Kabbah decided to cancel the contract, there would be no fee. If he decided to continue, EO would then work on a month-by-month basis, as before. Kabbah was worried that a group of SLA officers and the RUF rebels were plotting to unite and remove him from power. EO advised Kabbah that the only way to secure the new democratic regime was to finish Foday Sankoh and the RUF once and for all. That being done, the military would come to heel. And so President Kabbah agreed to one final search-and-destroy mission.

EO's aircraft took to the skies again, and eventually, Foday Sankoh's new HQ was located deep in the Kambui Hills, to the south-east of the country. Having surrounded the base, EO launched a blistering assault using 105mm howitzers, ground forces and choppers. Within three days, hundreds of demoralised rebels had surrendered. In light of the total obliteration of his last significant base, Sankoh was forced to sue for peace. Two weeks later, on 30 November 1996, a ceasefire was signed between the RUF leader and the President of Sierra Leone. Following this peace deal, EO pleaded with President Kabbah to be allowed to retain a rapid-reaction capability, or at least an intelligence unit, in his country. They wanted to retain their lucrative contract; but even more importantly, they were committed to getting the job done in Sierra Leone.

In their last, highly confidential report to Kabbah and allied powers, EO warned that two things would happen if they were forced to leave the country. The first, that there would be a coup attempt by power-hungry elements of the military. The second, that the RUF rebels would emerge from the jungle resurgent again. But despite such warnings, Kabbah terminated EO's contract and they withdrew from the country.

Less than a hundred days later, all EO's warnings and worse came to pass. On 25 May 1997, SLA Major Johnny Paul Koroma seized power in a military coup, forcing President Kabbah to flee the country. Major Koroma then set up the Armed Forces Revolutionary Council (AFRC) to rule the country. Consisting of an alliance of renegade army officers and rebel groups that included the RUF, the AFRC truly was a coalition of the mindless and evil. And in seizing power, Major Koroma had been backed by a new and powerful faction of army deserters and renegades.

They were calling themselves the *West Side Boys*.

6

THE NIGHTMARE BEGINS

This is the first teaching of the Knights: you will erase everything you had written in the book of your life up until now: restlessness, uncertainty, lies. And in the place of all this you will write the word 'courage'. By beginning the journey with that word and continuing with faith in God, you will arrive wherever you need to arrive.

– From the breviary of a medieval knight

ON the first morning of the Royal Irish patrol's captivity, it became a longer waiting game. Colonel Cambodia explained to the British soldiers that, by now, their commanding officer, Lieutenant Colonel Simon Fordham, knew exactly where the hostages were being held. Foday Kallay had told him as much during recent radio negotiations with the British forces. Lieutenant Colonel Fordham had sent a unit of Royal Irish soldiers up as far as the West Side Boys' first checkpoint, in an attempt to establish direct negotiations with them. Just as he had promised, things were moving forward at last, Colonel Cambodia tried to reassure the captured soldiers. But unfortunately, his leader Foday Kallay still wasn't available to see them.

'He is not free to see you yet. But soon, soon. And you know you should not have come into our area like this,' Colonel Cambodia told the British soldiers, somewhat resentfully. 'You should have contacted us first, explained what you wanted and then we would have given our permission. And you know Foday Kallay will want you to give him some answers.'

The British soldiers spent the morning sitting out on Cambodia's veranda, trying to kill time. Apart from the clearing in front of Cambodia's place, their vision of the rest of the village was limited.

To the left-hand side and straight ahead, there lay a wall of jungle, with the pit more or less directly in front of them, sixty yards or so away. To the far left, about eighty yards away, there was one, dilapidated mud hut, on a dirt track that petered out at the edge of the forest. To the right they had a view of the buildings leading down the track into the southern half of the village, towards the 'radio shack', Foday Kallay's house and the river.

The village of Gberi Bana was roughly divided into an upper and a lower area. The lower area consisted of a U-shaped dirt track looping up from the higher, western end of the river bank and back down again to the lower, eastern end. The track was lined with a motley collection of circular mud huts, and the occasional, more substantial concrete block house. The upper end of the village consisted of a second dirt track heading north for a couple of hundred yards up to Cambodia's house. In the lower part of the village, at the junction of the two tracks, there were half a dozen concrete-block houses painted a dirty off-white, clustered around a central clearing. This was the headquarters of Foday Kallay and his coterie of political high command.

By contrast, the upper end of the village, where the hostages were being held, was the hang-out for most of the West Side Boys' Rambos and psychos – the apolitical, gun-toting, macho men. And as there was precious little other activity to distract the rebels' attention, the hostages were still the star attraction in the village. With two hundred rebels hanging around Gberi Bana, all of whom had time on their hands, it felt to the British soldiers very much as if they were exhibits in a zoo.

The soldiers' biggest immediate concern that morning was that their supply of tabs was rapidly running out. Few of the patrol members had smoked prior to their capture. But now, every one of them had taken up the habit – apart from the Major and Corporal Mackenzie. A couple of the Rangers joked that they'd only recently given up, and 'what a bloody time to be starting again, when there were no feckin' tabs to be had'. Major Martial kept trying to reassure his men that it wasn't a problem really, because they'd soon be out of there. It was just a matter of time before Colonel Cambodia got to speak with Kallay, and then they'd be on their way. The Rangers suspected that he was just saying this to try to keep their morale up, but they chose to half believe him anyway, rather than face the dire truth of their situation.

'Not a moment too soon, sir, that'll be,' Ranger Gaunt remarked, 'getting out of this place, if youse know what I mean. I sort of promised me ma at New Year's that I'd give up the tabs, then. She'll kill me if she knows I've started again.'

'Well, who's fookin' telling, lad?' the CSM butted in. 'Hardly likely to parachute into Gberi fookin' Bana, now is she, your ma, like?'

'Don't you worry, lad,' Major Martial continued, turning to Ranger Gaunt. 'Once we're back in Benguema, I'll make a personal point of keeping an eye on you on your mum's behalf. Catch you smoking one bloody tab, lad, and then you'll be in real trouble.'

As the soldiers watched village life unfold around them, what they saw wasn't encouraging. By mid-afternoon that first day, the West Side Boys were working themselves up into a drug- and alcohol-fuelled frenzy. There were huge cannabis joints being passed among groups of men sat around in tattered, outlandish uniforms. There were kids with guns as tall as they were, being sent off into the jungle to harvest more hash plants. They'd return with their weapon clutched in one hand and a bunch of bright green, star-shaped leaves in the other. The cannabis was washed down with copious quantities of the locally brewed hooch. Some of the British soldiers had also caught the whiff of people 'cooking up' a hit of either heroin or crack cocaine.

Back at Benguema, the British soldiers had heard some pretty lurid stories about what the rebels would get up to, when drugged up to their eyeballs like this. Apparently, their speciality was 'the monkey jump game'. Dressed in monkey skins, they would hide up the trees in nearby villages. Unsuspecting kids would pass beneath the branches, and the 'monkey men' would jump down on them, snarling and whooping like half-humans half-monkeys. The terrified children would be rooted to the spot, and the rebels would grab them and drag them back to the rebel base, where they would be brutalised and forced to 'join' the West Side Boys.

Life in the rebel base that first full day seemed to be defined by a complete lack of anything remotely resembling military discipline or routine. As far as the hostages could see, the rebel soldiers never saluted their so-called officers, or acknowledged their rank in any way. As they spoke to each other in their own, local language, the hostages couldn't, of course, tell how they addressed their officers. But somehow, it just didn't sound like it was with a respectful 'sir'. Neither had they seen any of the rebels cleaning their weapons. In fact, one of the rebel 'officers' had an old Hechler & Koch G3 assault rifle which he had to stamp on first in order to make it work.

The British Army standard-issue SA80 assault rifle had never been renowned for its reliability or ease of maintenance. Which made the British soldiers wonder how long their captured assault rifles were likely to survive in the hands of the rebels. They gave them a few days, a week at the most. One of their SA80s had been taken by Foday Kallay's bodyguard. The soldiers had spotted him posing around the village, sporting one of their flak jackets and toting the British assault rifle. In fact, he came to fetch Ranger Gaunt that first day, so that the Ranger could show him how to operate the weapon. Down at the southern end of the village, a group of curious rebels had gathered round to watch the Ranger's weapons demonstration. Weapons. The West Side Boys had an endless fascination with weapons.

Ranger Gaunt found Corporal Mousa down there with the rebels. This day, he had been lucky. They had taken him out of the pit for a short while, so he could speak with Foday Kallay. He was looking to be in a bad way, and the Ranger managed to slip him half a lighted cigarette. *Poor bastard*, the Ranger had thought to himself, *at this rate they're going to kill him.* But the Ranger wasn't happy when he realised that the rebels wanted him to show them how to use the SA80.

'I'm not allowed to show youse, under British Army rules, like,' the Ranger protested, nervously.

'We de kill-kill you, whiteboy, if you don't go show us, na true,' the rebels began threatening him.

'But youse don't understand,' the Ranger persisted. 'It's against British Army rule. I'm not allowed to do so.'

'You go tell dis fuck whiteboy he be dead man him if he no go show us now-now,' the rebel responded angrily, speaking to Corporal Mousa. 'Or if no kill-kill him, you go show us how to use de weapon.'

'But I no know how to use de ting,' Mousa protested. No one had ever shown Mousa how to use the SA80, as he always carried an AK47.

'But de whiteboys dey be your friend friend,' the rebel soldier persisted. 'Dey must go show you how to fire de ting.'

Eventually, the argument was settled when Ranger Gaunt realised he might well be shot if he didn't give them the lesson in how to use the SA80. As he started to show them how to operate and maintain the weapon, it quickly became clear that the rebels were only interested in one thing: how to cock, aim and shoot the assault rifle. When the Ranger started explaining how to strip it down and clean it, the rebels acted like they didn't know what on earth he was on about and quickly lost interest. Which was all good, as far as the Ranger was concerned, because it would guarantee that the weapon would be unserviceable in next to no time.

Having rounded off the SA80 'training session', Ranger Gaunt was marched the three hundred yards or so back up to the northern end of the village. As he trudged up the village track, threading its way through the tall elephant grass, he began to curse his bad luck. If only he'd been put on Training Force, he thought to himself, morosely. If he had, this nightmare wouldn't be happening to him. Trouble was, he was a damn good shot with an assault rifle, one of the Rangers' best. Which meant he always got chosen for the more combat-oriented tasks.

He had found the SLA's shambolic performance on the training exercises embarrassing, and he had been glad not to be working with them. But now, he'd give anything to be back there, putting the raw SLA recruits through their paces – however pissed up on the hooch and useless as soldiers they might prove to be. Ranger Gaunt cast his mind back to a story he'd been told of one of the more ridiculous SLA training escapades: he had a deep, nostalgic longing to be there with his mates right now, cussing and bitching, but trying to get the training job done.

Several dozen SLA soldiers had been split into two groups by the Rangers: a larger Ambush Force and a smaller Attack Force. Ambush Force had been placed in the dense bush to either side of a dirt track running north out of Benguema. They had camouflaged their positions and been briefed to keep prone and motionless and alert for 'the enemy' – Attack Force, being led by some of the Rangers' more experienced soldiers. Ambush Force were briefed that the enemy would be advancing along the track towards their positions, whereupon they should open fire and eliminate them. However, intel was never infallible, the SLA soldiers were warned, so Ambush Force would have to stay alert for attack from all directions. That, at least, had been the plan. Three hours and several plastic bottles of gin into the stakeout later, most of Ambush Force had crawled under a bush to get out of the blazing sun and promptly fallen asleep.

As the hot afternoon had dragged on, a two-man security team had been sent up ahead of Ambush Force. Lacking radios, the men were supposed to pull on a string of vines stretching back to their commander once the enemy had been spotted, giving them an early warning to prepare the ambush more effectively. But suddenly, the crack of an assault rifle had torn the men of Ambush Force out of their hooch-induced stupor, and within seconds all hell had broken loose. Ambush Force had opened fire in the direction of the gunshots, up the track ahead of them, just as their two-man security team had come charging back down the trail towards them.

It turned out that the two soldiers of the security team had popped their heads up at just the wrong moment. Attack Force had spotted them and opened fire. Beating a hasty retreat, the two men had fled back down the track towards their own men. But Ambush Force had reacted to those first shots by opening fire without warning, and so the two-man security team had run into their indiscriminate barrage of fire. By opening fire, Ambush Force had also given away their carefully camouflaged positions. Attack Force had proceeded to outflank Ambush Force, coming in to attack them from behind, cutting the men to pieces as they did so. By the time Attack Force withdrew, Ambush Force had three dead and a dozen wounded. As the survivors had stood around looking at their injured and dying men, and wondering what on earth to do, Ranger Gaunt's mates had emerged from the bush, shaking their head in disbelief.

'What the feck'r youse doin' standing around like a bunch of feckin' pussies watching yer own men die?' one of the Rangers had yelled. 'You've just had the feckin' shite kicked out of youse by the enemy, man, now the least youse can feckin' do is look after yer wounded. Feckin' get to it. NOW!'

Of course, the whole exercise had been carried out using blanks, and no one was really dead or injured. But if it had been a real contact, it would have been a complete shambles, of that the Rangers were certain. But what Ranger Gaunt wouldn't have given now to have been chosen for Training Force, and to have missed out on Defence Force's fateful vehicle patrol.

That evening passed quickly enough for the hostages. One of their guards had a small, short-wave radio set, which he tuned to the BBC World Service, and the British soldiers were allowed to sit out on Cambodia's veranda with their captors and listen to news from home. It was hard for the men to pay attention, when the events being reported seemed so far from their present, all-consuming worries. But suddenly, an item came on that made them all sit up and take notice. *Early reports are coming in of several British soldiers being taken hostage in Sierra Leone,* the newscaster's voice intoned. *Details are still sketchy, but there are believed to be around a dozen soldiers being held hostage by a rebel militia calling themselves the West Side Boys.*

Each subsequent time the BBC reporter made mention of *a Sierra Leonean rebel group calling themselves the 'West Side Boys'*, the faces of the listening rebels would lighten and they'd nudge each other in the ribs and have a good laugh together. *That's US*, they were obviously thinking. *Fuckin' A! Us on the BBC*. At the end of the report, they got up and strutted around the clearing outside Cambodia's house, puffed up by their own sense of self-importance. From now on, the BBC Africa Service in particular would start running regular reports on the hostage story. And ironically, this would prove to be one of the best ways for the hostages to receive news about their own fate. Not surprisingly, the rebels would also be glued to these radio reports.

The eleven men bedded down for their second night in captivity in a gloomy mood. The BBC report had made their situation seem all the more real to them: they were growing ever more convinced that they weren't getting out of there any time soon now.

But sometime in the small hours of the morning, they were woken by terrible cries coming from just outside their door. A heavy, brittle silence descended on the room, as the soldiers lay there in the darkness listening to the screams. Each man knew that the others were also awake, and occasionally would catch a glimpse of white, fearful eyes in the darkness. At first, Major Martial tried to pass whispered reassurances around his men that it was just someone who was sick with malaria making all the noise. As there was clearly more than one person making the chilling cries, the Major said that Cambodia must have gathered their sick and wounded together, so that they could all be treated in one place. But none of his men really believed the Major: this time it was all too clear what was happening.

The rebels had begun torturing people in the darkness of the corridor just outside their room. Whether they were doing this just for the enjoyment, or more to terrify the British soldiers, wasn't obvious yet. But the victims were clearly receiving a savage beating and worse. Between the horrible thuds of a blunt object impacting on human flesh, they could hear the gleeful cries of 'Cut him! Ya, cut him!' followed by blood-curdling screams. Whoever the victims were, the rebels were clearly using their machetes to slice them up. Lying there listening to all this, it felt like they were in a horror movie, only this time it was all too real. Finally, through all the screaming, they recognised the voice of Corporal Mousa, also coming from the corridor just outside their room. He sounded terrified, but he was still trying to talk the Boys down.

Tonight it's Mousa's turn, each of the hostages was thinking. *He's one of ours. Who the fuck's it going to be next time?*

As the men lay there, unable to sleep, their imaginations started running riot, with horrible images of what the rebels might have in store for them running through their minds. All but one of the hostages were from Ireland (the CSM being from Liverpool, a city with a close historical tie to the Rangers). Of those ten, nine lived in Belfast. Over the years, they'd all had family or friends lost in the Troubles. So they were painfully aware of what rebels and terrorists were capable of doing to those who were their enemies.

Those men knew Belfast like the back of their hands – the streets that were 'friendly' and those that were very, very hostile (controlled by the IRA and their sympathisers). Each man had known that terrifying moment when, on a dreary Sunday afternoon, his mind had wondered for a moment and he'd taken a wrong turn. Suddenly, he'd found himself on the *west* side of Belfast – the wrong side of the city for a serving member of Her Majesty's Armed Forces. Suddenly, a hated British soldier was driving into the heart of the Troubles, alone and unarmed. Nine of the patrol members had fought as soldiers on the front line of that Northern Irish war against terror – a war that had been raging for thirty years or more in Belfast and the Ardoyne. A war that had claimed the lives of more than three hundred British servicemen (both soldiers and police).

So feared was the brutality inflicted by the IRA that most British soldiers would try to ensure they were never taken alive. A captured British soldier would be beaten, humiliated, and forced to talk if at all possible – being made to divulge not only information about British military operations, but also about their personal, family background. If the soldier's family lived in Ireland and could be got at, then they would in turn be targeted by the terrorists. Eventually, the captured soldier would be taken out into a field and kicked into a coma by a pack of thugs, before being shot in the back of the head. His body would then be dumped out of a fast-moving car on some isolated back lane in rural Ireland, for some farmer to discover early the next morning.

And so, ever since joining the British Army, the Rangers had had to keep their identity as soldiers in Her Majesty's Armed Forces absolutely secret. As the 1st Batallion Royal Irish Regiment was billeted in Canterbury, in south-east England, that made things a lot easier for the men. They only ever wore their uniforms when away from Belfast, on duty in Mainland Britain. When back in Belfast they stuck to civvies.

Few knew that they were soldiers with the Royal Irish Rangers, a regiment with a long record of successful operations against the IRA. The threat of IRA violence, cruelty and brutality – it was something that they had lived with all their lives.

And as for foreign hostage scenarios? Well, most of the young lads had read the *Bravo Two Zero* books of this world. They knew that nasty things happened to British soldiers held hostage in dark places far, far from home. Could they really expect any better here in Sierra Leone, from the West Side Boys? If anything, Sierra Leone's rebels had an even worse reputation for unspeakable brutality and unimaginable violence than did the Irish or Iraqi terrorists. The West Side Boys hacked off ears, lips and limbs just for the fun of it, and they raped and killed and murdered for kicks. They used brutalised children as their foot soldiers, and drink and drugs as their fuel on the battlefield.

In the still, deadly hours of that long, hot night of torture in Gberi Bana, it was all too easy for the young British soldiers' imaginations to start playing tricks on them. The innocent actions of a rebel going to cut some coconuts with his machete became the drugged-up posturings of a maniac out to mutilate, maim and disfigure one of the British captives. The boy soldiers de-husking a coconut with his machete became the depraved child killer practising what he might do to the British soldiers' faces. No one got much sleep that second night in captivity.

The next morning, the Major again asked that Corporal Mousa be brought to join the rest of his men. It was day three now, and he was worried for the Sierra Leonean corporal's survival. When Corporal Mousa was finally taken out of the pit and led over to them – naked and unable to stand unsupported – he looked like a dead man walking. He was covered in blood and filth and barely conscious. As soon as Major Martial caught sight of the Corporal, he could contain himself no longer.

'Colonel Cambodia! How can you do this to your own brother soldier?' he demanded, unable to disguise his indignation and disgust. 'This is not the way to treat another human being. This is a human-rights abuse. It is against the Geneva Convention, and the rules of war. This is not how you should treat your prisoners.'

A heated argument followed, and soon Colonel Changa Bulanga and the Camp Commandant had joined in. As the rebel leaders worked themselves up into a towering rage, they ordered the Small Boys Unit to strip the British soldiers down to their boxer shorts. There was a short tussle as one or two of the men tried to keep their combats on them, but that just provoked a hail of savage blows. Once all the British soldiers were stripped to their underwear, they were ordered to parade through the village. They were forced to run all around the circumference of Gberi Bana as if doing PT, with the SBU goading them on. The whole village turned out to watch, and laugh and jeer at them. The message of the exercise was clear: criticise us, and you will be punished. And in Corporal Mousa's treatment, the British soldiers had a horrible demonstration of just how cruel and inhuman that punishment could be.

Once the parading was over and the British soldiers were allowed to dress again, Major Martial pleaded for Mousa to be allowed to stay with him and his men for a few hours' rest. Finally, Colonel Cambodia relented. After he'd had time to recover a little, Mousa explained to the British men the events of the night before. There were two prisoners being held in the pit, Mousa and another man named 'Killer'. Killer was a West Side Boy who had gone AWOL for a month or so. The day before, he had been recaptured and brought back to the camp. The British soldiers had seen him led across the village clearing and placed in the pit. Unfortunately for Killer, the rebel leaders were linking his recapture with the arrival of the British patrol, and accusing him of being in league with the British forces.

The previous night, the West Side Boys had taken Mousa and Killer out of the pit and marched them over to the corridor outside the British soldiers' room. There, they had proceeded to torture Killer close to death with their machetes, slicing off parts of his anatomy, while having the odd go at Mousa at the same time. Mousa had then been made to walk into the jungle, helping along Killer, who was by now barely alive. The rebels had quickly put an end to Killer's misery with a couple of bullets to the back of the head.

And then they had made as if they were going to kill Mousa, too. But they had told him that they feared he had some heavy voodoo protecting him. They suspected he might be 'bulletproof', because he had survived for so long as a soldier in Sierra Leone. So, they had decided that they would have to drown Mousa in the Rokel Creek, instead of shooting him. And as they couldn't be bothered to walk all the way down to the river that night, they told Mousa they'd have to wait for another opportunity to kill him. Hearing Corporal Mousa's story, British hostages had their worst fears about the West Side Boys confirmed.

Needless to say, none of the men had felt like venturing out of their room to relieve themselves during the previous night's torture, and so they'd just had to hold it in until morning. In fact, for the last couple of days, they'd had so little water to drink that they'd been peeing a lot less than normal. And on the tiny rice rations that Cambodia was giving them, it felt like they might go a week or more in Gberi Bana without needing a crap. On the rare occasions when they had needed to take a leak, the Colonel had sent one of the guards as an escort, usually a young kid called 'Movement', who must have been about twelve years old. Cambodia was taking no chances that one of them might try to make a break for it and get away.

Cambodia had also been using Movement to fetch the hostages' supplies of drinking water. That's if you could call it drinking water. The first few bottles that Movement had brought up from the Rokel Creek had been full of a brown, turbid liquid. Despite their better instincts, the men knew that they would have to drink it, as there was no other alternative. The rebels hardly ever seemed to drink themselves – apart from their afternoon alcohol binges. And they couldn't quite figure out why these white soldiers kept asking for more water all the time. But the Major knew that if they drank the river water just as it was, then they would have big problems: it probably carried amoebic dysentery, cholera, or worse. Luckily, one of the soldiers had discovered a tinfoil strip of Puritabs (water-purifying tablets) in the pocket of his combat trousers. So the men had used these to purify the first few bottles of water. But now, the Puritabs were all finished.

'Colonel, I'm afraid we can't drink the river water like it is,' the Major remarked to Colonel Cambodia, who was sat out on the veranda having a lunchtime doze in his wicker chair. 'It's kind of your men to fetch it for us, but we will need to sterilise it first.'

'Why can't you?' Cambodia snorted. After the night's fun and games with the torture of the prisoners, there was a dark, evil atmosphere around the house now. 'I do. So do the rest of my men. Why are *you* so special?'

'We're not special, Colonel,' the Major explained, patiently, as if talking to a child. 'We're just not used to it, that's all.'

'Well, what do you suggest? You don't want to die of thirst, do you?'

'No, Colonel. Not really. But you see in all the kit you took off us, there are some Puritabs. Little white pills. We use them to sterilise our water, to make it safe for us to drink.'

'*Puritabs*? I've never heard of them. If they're pills, how do I know they're not drugs?' the Colonel demanded, suspiciously. 'Maybe they are some dangerous British pill that you will use to drug us? I've heard about the Americans doing such things in Cambodia and Vietnam. How can I be sure that they're not, eh?'

'Well, I can assure you, Colonel, that they're just for sterilising water,' the Major replied. 'In fact, if you read the writing on the packet that's what it'll tell you.'

Sure, Colonel, youse think they're drugs. So why don't youse feckin' well go try them, as youse seem to be the experts on drugs around here, one of the listening Rangers felt like saying. *You're welcome to try grinding up a couple of Puritabs and snorting them. Or putting one or two in one of your feckin' joints and smoking them. Or even sticking a handful up your feckin' rectum if you like. Be my flamin' guest.*

Eventually, a grumbling Cambodia wandered off to search through the British soldiers' kit for the Puritabs. He returned a little while later with a white plastic bottle full of the water-purifying pills. After dropping one of the Puritabs in each bottle and letting it stand for a few minutes, the water was effectively sterilised. It still looked and tasted revolting. But at least drinking it wouldn't end up killing the British soldiers.

A little later, the leader of the West Side Boys finally put in an appearance. Foday Kallay turned out to be a small, insignificant-looking man, wearing a dirty white vest stretched over a pot belly bulging out over a pair of polka-dot Lycra cycling shorts. He sauntered up to Cambodia's house with a bunch of bodyguards and other assorted hangers-on in tow. It quickly became clear that the self-styled Brigadier General Kallay had zero charisma, and there was something distinctly effeminate about him, too. If they hadn't been alerted to the fact by Cambodia, none of the British soldiers would ever have believed that this was the infamous rebel force's leader.

Kallay launched into a stumbling, rambling speech in Creole, in which he attempted to reassure the captured British soldiers that they would not be held for long. He had started negotiations with the British Army for their safe release, he told them. He only wanted to work out why they were in his area, and once he'd got some satisfactory answers, the men would be going free. Whatever the truth of the matter, Kallay's speech was something of a bombshell for the junior ranks. They had been hanging on to Major Martial's promise that as soon as the rebel leader got directly involved, then they would all be released more or less immediately. That hope had now been shattered. It was clear that Kallay wasn't going to let them go that easily. He seemed to be revelling in the sense of power and importance that the British soldiers' presence in the camp was bringing him. Lord knows, Kallay had little else going for him.

Shortly after Kallay had put in his appearance, the hostages had another visitor, this time as unexpected as it would prove welcome. After their depressing meeting with the rebel leader, they needed something to lift their spirits. Sony was a quietly spoken Sierra Leonean man in his mid-twenties and he introduced himself to the British soldiers in almost faultless English. In fact, his accent was so pukka that the men wondered whether he might have been educated in England. He was dressed more smartly than any of the other rebels, wearing a clean basketball top and pair of blue jeans. And whereas the rest of the Boys wore either army-style boots or flip-flops, Sony wore trainers. Sony's was definitely not the image of a typical rebel soldier, and during this first visit, he spent a lot of time trying to reassure the men that everything was going to be all right.

'Don't worry, we're making arrangements to get you out of here as quickly as possible,' he told the soldiers. 'You'll be out of here in a few days' time, you see if you aren't.'

The captives didn't really believe what Sony was telling them. Why should they have? There was no evidence to back up what he was saying. But it did serve to boost their morale a little. At least one of the rebels did seem to be on their side. Foday Kallay was making a series of demands conditional on their release, Sony went on to explain. Among other things, he wanted the release of the West Side Boys officers who were being held in Freetown jail on charges of murder and a series of other human-rights abuses. And he was demanding negotiations with the Sierra Leonean government, seeking a place for the rebels in the leadership of the country.

All of these things could be worked out, Sony reassured the hostages, and then they would be free to leave. They shouldn't worry. It wasn't going to take too long. Sony stressed that he was taking personal responsibility for getting them out of there as quickly as possible. As he seemed so capable and self-confident, this did lift the British soldiers' spirits a little. Finally, he asked Captain Flaherty if he would come and help get the radios on the patrol's captured signals Land-Rover working again. If they could get the radios operational, Sony explained, Foday Kallay and his cohorts would be able to communicate directly with the Royal Irish Regiment's Freetown HQ, so speeding up the hostage negotiations.

Sony had made it pretty clear to the hostages that Foday Kallay's chief aim in the hostage negotiations was to try to secure a place for himself in the Sierra Leonean government. He was even suggesting that he should replace Ahmed Tejan Kabbah, Sierra Leone's democratically elected President. This was not as far-fetched as it might at first have seemed, Sony explained. During the 1997 rebel takeover of the country, Army Captain Johnny Paul Koroma (J.P. for short), the ex-leader of the West Side Boys, had declared himself President. Now, Sony explained, Foday Kallay seemed to believe that it was time for him to follow in J.P.'s footsteps. And the British hostages, Kallay seemed to think, were to be his ticket to that destiny.

Over the next few days, the men would notice several things about Sony that set him apart from the other rebels. He never carried a gun, and neither did he seem to drink or do drugs. And, regardless of their rank, the rest of the rebels seemed to treat him with great respect. Whoever Sony was – and the hostages really weren't quite sure yet – he would play an increasingly important part in their fortunes, assuming the role of a trusted source of information and encouragement for the British soldiers. Over the coming days, it would become clear that Sony was some sort of informal 'ambassador' for the West Side Boys. Eventually, he would turn out to be the one true ally that the British soldiers had in the rebel camp.

Sony came from the southern end of the village, reinforcing the impression that he played some sort of political role within the West Side Boys' set-up. Up at the northern end of the camp, where the hostages were being held, all the tooled-up Rambo types and apolitical lunatics seemed to congregate. That afternoon, as they were sat out on Cambodia's veranda, the hostages noticed the oddest individual yet up at their end of camp. He came crawling out of a room at the back of Cambodia's house, squinting up at the sun like he hadn't seen daylight for an age. He was a fully grown man – in fact a seeming giant among the West Side Boys, being a good couple of inches over six foot. He was muscular and athletic-looking, too. But all he was wearing was a pair of dirty Y-fronts, which was a little underdressed, even for one of the West Side Boys. And because he had a chain attached to his leg, he was only able to get so far out of the house before it brought him to a stumbling halt.

Initially, the hostages presumed that he was just another prisoner. But the more they watched, the more they realised that there was something decidedly odd about this one. For a start, once he got out the front of the house, he just sort of crouched down on his haunches and mumbled and cackled away to himself, as an inane grin spread across his face. Pretty quickly it became clear that he was either mentally retarded or insane – both qualities that seemed to be very much in vogue in Gberi Bana. But in the big man's case, he was clearly too far out left field even for the West Side Boys. So they had chained him up and stuck him in a room out the back of Cambodia's place, like a dog in a kennel.

He was obviously being kept there as some sort of plaything, Rangers Rowell and Gaunt realised. And as both of them had seen *Pulp Fiction*, the man in the Y-fronts was promptly nicknamed 'the Gimp' (the name for that cult movie's male sex slave, who is kept chained up in a basement). As the afternoon wore on, a couple of Cambodia's boy soldiers noticed the two Rangers' interest in the Gimp. Loving an attentive audience, they started dragging him around by his chain, and taunting him with their AK47s, as if they were about to shoot him. The Gimp clearly knew that the weapons were dangerous, as he kept trying to break free and crawl back into the house to escape the gun muzzles pointed at him.

Once he'd managed to get back inside, the boy soldiers put down a bowl of dirty food just outside the door to Cambodia's house and then hid, in an effort to try to lure the Gimp out again. Eventually, thinking it was safe to come out, the Gimp first sniffed at and then grabbed the food, whereupon his tormentors fell upon him and beat him across the back with their rifle butts. Seeing this giant of a man being beaten and humiliated and treated worse than an animal was enough to turn the two Rangers' stomachs.

But what made it even worse was that the rebels seemed to expect the Rangers to actually be enjoying the grim spectacle. They kept looking over at them, grinning and gesticulating at the Gimp, as if to say: 'Look! Look! Look what we're doing! And guess what we're about to do *next*! Isn't it *fun*?!' The Rangers' instinctive reaction was to look away, and they were tempted to try retreating into the comparative privacy of their own room. They felt that their interest in proceedings was simply making things worse for the Gimp. But at the same time, they knew that if they showed the slightest revulsion or anger at the West Side Boys' antics, then they could easily end up being the subject of the rebels' twisted attentions instead.

Finally, the two rebels forced the Gimp back into the house at gunpoint and then followed him in there themselves. The Rangers caught a brief flash of the petrified look on the simple man's face as he was hounded back into the shadows of his room. Whereupon the door slammed shut and a series of muffled, rhythmic grunts and groans started coming from inside the room. Remembering their first day in Gberi Bana, when the hostages had stumbled across the two rebels raping a woman, they had little doubt now as to what the two boy soldiers were doing to the Gimp, in the darkened room out the back of Cambodia's house.

'Dirty feckin' motherfuckers,' one of the Rangers had muttered under his breath. 'The sick, perverted, nasty, dirty wee motherfuckin' bastards. Sick, sick savages, the whole lot of them.'

The Rangers felt that the more outspoken and extreme the expletives were that they could find to condemn the West Side Boys' behaviour, the more they could block out the filth and depravity of it all from their own minds. But for how long could they remain there, in this sick, crazed place, before the rot started to seep into their own souls, too? How long would it be before it started to corrupt them, to pollute them, to drive any sense of right and wrong, of the ways of civilised being, from their own minds? Clearly, the rebels had little concept of the norms of decent human behaviour, of morality, of the ways in which it was acceptable to treat another human being. Whether they'd had any innate, instinctive human warmth and kindness beaten and abused out of them when they were younger, the Rangers didn't know. But they couldn't think of any other reason to explain how these young boys were able to behave as they did.

That evening, as they sat out on the veranda, Colonel Cambodia and Dennis, one of the older rebel guards, tried to lure the British soldiers into a political discussion. Sony had already warned the men to be wary of Dennis. He had scars all over his body from where some of his fellow rebels had given him a savage beating. They had done this, Sony had explained, in order to punish him. Apparently, he'd walked into a local village and just gone completely psycho, opening up with his weapon on everything: men, women, children, babies, the lot. He hadn't been given clearance to do this from any of his commanders, and he hadn't even been bothered to take any prisoners, which might have proved useful. Hence the punishment beating.

Dennis and Cambodia started banging on about all the injustices of the recently signed Lome peace accord – under which the rebels had agreed to stop fighting and accept the rule of the UN- and British-backed democratic government. Dennis in particular was vitriolic in his condemnation of the 'mercenaries, Jews and Western stooges' who had brokered that ceasefire deal. As the rebels' arguments became more and more heated, the hostages' only interest was getting away from them into the comparative safety of their room.

But a clearly frustrated Dennis was becoming increasingly aggressive, as the British soldiers held their silence and refused to be drawn into this political argument. The more the men repeated that they were just British soldiers, and that they didn't know much about such political matters, the angrier Dennis seemed to get. Eventually, he started accusing them of ignoring him, 'just because he was a black man – a West Side *Nigga*'. It was a while since the hostages had heard the rebels refer to themselves in that way – the last time being upon their capture by the Savage group – and it sent a shiver up each man's spine.

Finally, Cambodia dragged an irate Dennis away, whereupon the British soldiers were allowed to retire to their room. Corporal Mousa, however, was separated from them once more and returned to the dungeon. Once inside, there was a general venting of pent-up anger by the British soldiers, about how much more punishment Mousa could take. Then one of the Rangers commented on 'what a feckin' psycho Dennis the feckin' Menace was'. And of course, the nickname stuck. Dennis the Menace he would be known as from now on.

A little while later Cambodia brought the exhausted soldiers their one daily meal of rice. They were just about to wolf it down, when Cambodia cleared his throat a little theatrically from the doorway where he was standing.

'I'm sorry that I have so few condiments for you,' he announced, somewhat self-consciously. Then with a quick flourish he produced a small, squarish bottle from behind his back. 'But I do have some of this,' he added proudly, plonking the bottle down and backing out of the room. It was instantly recognisable to the British soldiers.

'Will youse take a look at that,' piped up Ranger Gaunt, snatching the bottle. 'Friggin HP Sauce! Now where the bleedin' hell did he get HP Sauce from, in the middle of the feckin' jungle, if youse know what I mean?'

A ripple of spontaneous laughter went round the room. The black mood that had settled over the men that day lifted a little. Funny what a bottle of brown sauce could do in the midst of a crisis.

'Would you feckin' well believe it?' piped up Ranger Rowell. 'From some messed-up flamin' commie politics about feckin' niggers and Jews and shite this afternoon to HP Sauce this evening. Fucked up, that's what it is, to be sure.'

'Mad – the whole lot of them. Now I'll be taking care of that, so I will,' Sergeant Smith remarked, grabbing the sauce bottle off the young Ranger. 'Just in case youse all go gettin' any ideas to finish the whole bloody lot at one sitting. Plates my way now, and I'll dole youse all out a ration, then.'

After the crazed aggression and violence of their capture by Colonel Savage, the British soldiers felt like Colonel Cambodia was a comparatively sane figure. If they were to look to anyone for their protection and well-being, it would have to be him. Thankfully, they'd not seen Savage again since that first day, as he stayed on the other side of the river, carrying out his road-piracy activities. But it was puzzling for the British soldiers to try to work out the comparative roles of the rebel leaders. There was no easily defined hierarchy, as there was in the British military. Colonel Cambodia had certainly taken over from Colonel Savage as being in charge of the hostages. And Cambodia seemed to run things up at his end of the village.

But the big cheese in Gberi Bana was supposed to be Foday Kallay, the overall rebel commander, and he seemed like an ineffectual frontman with few leadership qualities. In theory, he commanded all the territory under the West Side Boys' control: Gberi Bana and Magbeni, their two main bases that straddled the Rokel Creek; a fifteen-mile stretch of the river itself as it wound through the rebels' territory; the seven miles of dirt track stretching out to the Masiaka–Freetown highway, where Colonel Savage and his five-hundred-strong Savage group was based; and several miles of that highway itself, stretching as far as Masiaka town (which seemed to be half under rebel control and half under the UN). All in all, it was a shifting area of territory, consisting of some 150 square miles of jungle, within which there were a few scattered villages. And Kallay extended his unpredictable and chaotic rule over this area with the thousand-odd rebel fighters under his command.

Once the British soldiers had finished their feast of boiled rice and HP Sauce, Movement came to lock them in their room for the night. But just as he was about to do so, he spotted one of the soldiers' cyalumes – the young, twelve-year-old's eyes lighting up at its gentle, fluorescent green glow. Clearly fascinated, Movement asked the men if he could come in and see what it was. He was just a kid really, spellbound by a new toy, and almost trying to make friends. In his simplest English, one of the Rangers explained that it was a light stick – a plastic tube filled with a special liquid. A chemical reaction in the liquid produced the eerie, emerald glow that Movement found so mesmerising. Nothing magical about it at all. No ju-ju or voodoo or any of that nonsense. Just science. The Ranger gave Movement one of the 'miraculous' cyalumes – showing him how to operate it – and the young rebel soldier left, pleased as punch.

As the door closed behind him, the men settled down to sleep, fearing that another night's torture and screams lay ahead of them. What would they dream of tonight? they wondered. It wasn't as if they were starved of stimuli or characters to populate their nightmares. There was Colonel Cambodia. Colonel Savage. A boy soldier called Movement. *Dennis the Menace.* Kid rebels with bikes, drugs and guns. Horrific machete tortures. *The Gimp.* Summary night-time executions. Hooch, heroin and weed binges. *The dreaded pit.* And to top it all now, a bottle of flamin' HP Sauce. And here the British soldiers were, caught right in the middle of it all.

Welcome to Gberi Bana, the soldiers told themselves, *and the wonderful world of the West Side Boys.*

7

GET THE BRITS

No living enemy had beaten us. The battalion was unbeaten yet, but they could not have much chance, with no ammunition, no rest and with no positions from which to fight. No body of men could have fought more tenaciously than the officers and men of the 1st [sic] Parachute Brigade at Arnham Bridge.

– Major General John Frost, *A Drop Too Many*,
Pen & Sword Books Ltd

THE West Side Boys came into being in 1997, and their rank and file consisted of renegade soldiers from the SLA and a good number of ex-RUF rebels. Upon seizing power, the AFRC had thrown open the Freetown jails, and the West Side Boys' ranks had been swollen by several hundred prison inmates: rapists, murderers, thieves and various other assorted villains. One of those inmates had been Johnny Paul Koroma himself, who declared himself Chairman of the AFRC and leader of the West Side Boys. Four Ukrainian mercenaries had also thrown their lot in with the revolutionaries. The AFRC's brand of mob rule had then taken over, and dark months of anarchy and mayhem followed. As the human-rights group Amnesty International noted: 'The rule of law completely collapsed and violence engulfed the country.' There were few who were willing to stand and fight against this evil.

Among those who did, were some of the so-called mercenaries of Executive Outcomes. Although EO had been forced out of Sierra Leone, a number of its men had refused to abandon the nation – Fearless Fred Marafono and Neall Ellis among them. Somehow, the tiny country had got under their skins, and they just couldn't turn their backs and leave. In order to escape further criticism for allowing the now ex-EO operatives – *'those mercenaries'* – to remain in his country, President Kabbah decided to offer the men Sierra Leonean citizenship. By definition, a mercenary is 'a professional soldier paid to fight for an army other than that of his or her own country'. Clearly, once the men became Sierra Leonean citizens, they couldn't be dismissed as being 'mercenaries' any more.

As the AFRC had seized power in Freetown, Fearless Fred Marafono, Neall Ellis and the other men of the Air Wing had raced for their gunships and flown out to combat what they had presumed was a RUF assault on the capital. Instead, they had encountered the forces of the AFRC intent on a full-blooded military-rebel takeover, one in which President Kabbah had already been forced to flee the country. On learning the grim facts of the situation, the ex-EO men had returned to base, collected all of their ground crews and flown out to join President Kabbah in exile in neighbouring Guinea. Several months later, Fearless Fred, Neall Ellis and the others were to play a key role in returning President Kabbah to power, this time aided by yet another mercenary outfit, Colonel Tim Spicer's London-based Sandline International.

Lieutenant Colonel Tim Spicer, OBE, ex-Scots Guards and a Falklands War hero, was already a confidant of Kabbah's, due to his past dealings in Sierra Leone (Lifeguard Security Services, Sandline's sister company, provided security for diamond-mining operations). At meetings in Guinea with the deposed President, Spicer negotiated a $10 million contract to ship out arms and men to help the legitimate, democratically elected leader of Sierra Leone return to power. Sandline proceeded to launch Operation Python, in which it threw together a coalition of the willing similar to that assembled two years earlier by Executive Outcomes: a dozen or so mercenaries, Neall Ellis and Fred Marafono's Air Wing choppers, and the all-important Kamajors. They would join forces with the soldiers of ECOMOG – West Africa's own peacekeeping troops – who had drawn up a plan to retake the capital, codenamed Operation Sand Storm.

Operation Python's Air Wing began ferrying thirty tons of Sandline-supplied weapons across to the Kamajors. As they did so, their Mi-17s were being continuously shot at, and a considerable bounty was put on Neall Ellis's and Fred Marafono's heads, dead or alive. British military support was not long in coming: air mechanics on the guardship HMS *Cornwall*, anchored off the coast, provided regular servicing for the Air Wing's choppers, which by now had all but flown themselves into the ground. And Sandline was able to put two teams of military advisers in-country. One, based at Lungi Airport, north of Freetown, drew up the assault plan for the retaking of the capital, working with the ECOMOG forces. The other, led by an ex-commander of the US Delta Force Special Forces, was inserted up-country to work with the Kamajors.

Sandline was eventually forced to withdraw from Sierra Leone due to lack of funds (less than half the contracted $10 million was ever paid). Yet for the coalition of West Side Boys, RUF and renegade military rulers in Freetown – already badly mauled by Operation Python – the writing was on the wall. The Nigerian forces of ECOMOG, together with the fearsome Kamajors – backed up by Sandline's military advice and staff planning – retook the capital and returned President Kabbah to power. With the AFRC defeated, the RUF and the West Side Boys retreated into their jungle bases to lick their wounds. From there, they launched 'Operation No Living Thing' – a name that leaves little to the imagination in terms of the havoc and terror that they wreaked across the interior of the country.

As Sandline had withdrawn from Sierra Leone, Fearless Fred and Neall Ellis had been given their third Mi-17 helicopter in lieu of their payment. Gradually, the Air Wing was building up a fleet of battle-worn Soviet choppers. Operation Python may have driven the AFRC out of Freetown and forced the rebels back into the jungles, but somehow Fred and Neall had a feeling that the peace so earned would prove short-lived. And whatever the next few months might hold, the Air Wing knew it was always good to have a few ageing Soviet gunships to hand.

By now, Fred, Neall and others in the Air Wing had undergone a true conversation on the road to Damascus – the one-time mercenaries becoming all but volunteer fighters on behalf of a free and democratic Sierra Leone. Together, these men had spent decades fighting in many theatres around the world, at first for their respective governments and then for money. Now, they had found a greater cause – a driving reason for doing what they were doing other than just military professionalism, the buzz of war or financial gain. Many of their fellow freelance warriors didn't approve of Fred and Neall's new-found mission in life: the men of the Air Wing, they said, had 'gone native'. Some even refused to work with them. So be it: the Air Wing would battle on regardless.

Three years later, in the spring of 2000, a UN-brokered ceasefire seemed to have brought a lasting peace to the country, one policed by the forces of the UN. In January 1999, the forces of the AFRC (the RUF and the West Side Boys foremost among them) had again tried to invade Freetown, bringing yet more murder and mayhem with them. But this time the AFRC's military adventure had been only partially successful, and it had ended in the signing of the UN ceasefire deal. And for twelve, miraculous months afterwards there had been peace in Sierra Leone. But in the first days of May 2000, the RUF broke that ceasefire and launched yet another assault on Freetown. Just days before they were predicted to overrun the capital, a British military force, spearheaded by the Paras, was sent out to Sierra Leone to stop them.

Upon their arrival, just about the only part of the Sierra Leonean armed forces that still appeared to be functioning properly was Fearless Fred and Neall Ellis's Air Wing. By now, that consisted of a couple of barely serviceable Mi-17s and one Mi-24 gunship. Five years into their time in Sierra Leone, Fearless Fred and Nellis (as he was now known to the locals) had earned a fierce loyalty among the citizens of Freetown. Many of the gunship crews had not even been paid for the past two years of, often intensive, air operations.

Some 13,000 UN peacekeepers had been drafted into the country, as part of the UN's peace deal with the rebels. The United Nations Mission to Sierra Leone (UNAMSIL) had a yearly budget of some $500–600 million dollars to play with. Yet despite their enormous numbers and massive funding, the UN was now looking increasingly incapable of stopping a few hundred rebels from seizing the capital. In the face of RUF attacks and armed provocations, the Indian and Jordanian blue helmets dithered and prevaricated, and the SLA had begun to desert their posts. The inhabitants of Freetown – terrified of facing a repeat of past rebel takeovers of the capital – were poised to turn on the UN peacekeepers, who appeared unable or unwilling to protect them.

As the RUF pressed home its psychological advantage and made a grab for the capital, the Air Wing's operations had become increasingly frenetic – Nellis and Fearless Fred averaging three of four missions a day in the Mi-24 gunship. Twice, they went up six times in one day, even using NVGs to target rebel position after dark. During five weeks in April and May, they clocked up some ninety combat missions. As Lieutenant Colonel Rob Symonds, British Military Liaison Officer in Sierra Leone at the time, commented admiringly: 'Pilots in the majority of the world's air forces don't achieve a fraction of that figure during the course of their entire careers.'

Yet despite their efforts, the RUF's inexorable advance on Freetown continued. With 13,000 impotent UN soldiers standing by, members of the SLA began deserting their posts and abandoning their uniforms en masse. The RUF sensed victory. But then, they made their fatal mistake. Maybe they had just become too sure of themselves, because instead of simply bypassing the UN peacekeeping bases as they advanced towards the capital, they started attacking them. As they did so, rebel leader Foday Sankoh began cranking up the radio propaganda, accusing the British in particular of being the root cause of all Sierra Leone's troubles.

The British and their UN allies had occupied his country, Sankoh ranted. It was a 'foreign takeover' of Sierra Leone. Now they were keeping the RUF from their place as the nation's true rulers. Foday Sankoh, not Ahmed Kabbah, was the country's rightful President. Among the crimes that Sankoh was accusing the British of, he listed colonialism, exploitation of his nation's resources, and the sending in of the 'British' mercenary companies Executive Outcomes and Sandline.

Of the 13,000-strong UN peacekeeping forces in Sierra Leone, only fifteen were British servicemen. But there were also some seventy-odd British soldiers in-country carrying out the IMATT training programme with the SLA. Now, word went out that the rebels were planning to 'do a Somalia' on the British soldiers – referring to the infamous 1993 Black Hawk Down incident, where seventy-odd crack US Special Forces (Rangers and Delta Force operators) were wounded, and eighteen lost their lives to militia forces. At the time, US forces had intervened in war-torn Somalia to back up Operation Restore Hope, a well-intentioned United Nations aid effort to feed that nation's starving people. However, their mission had soon got way out of hand, and the angry Somali people had turned on the US soldiers.

As several US helicopters had been shot down by Somali militia, pictures were broadcast live on CNN showing the naked bodies of dead US servicemen paraded through the streets of Mogadishu by jubilant Somalis. Not surprisingly, that event had shocked the American public to the core, and forced the withdrawal of all US forces from Somalia. The UN had followed shortly thereafter, plunging that country back into years of lawless rule which have still not been brought to an end. Somalia remains a so-called 'failed state' and ever since then, the US military had been reluctant to set foot in Africa.

Foday Sankoh, it seemed, was now seeking a similar cataclysmic victory over British forces in Sierra Leone. His was a victory designed to so revolt the British people that they would force their government to withdraw all their forces from his country (after which, the days of the UN in Sierra Leone would also be numbered). Then, and only then, his glorious RUF would be left free to rule their country.

In 1993 in Somalia, the militia of the Habr Gdir clan that had routed the US military were reported to have received arms and training from Osama bin Laden's al-Qaeda network. Likewise, in Sierra Leone, Foday Sankoh was known to have Islamic extremist backing. In 1980, Sankoh had travelled to the US to meet with radical black Muslim groups. Fired up with extremist ideology he had gone on to Libya, where he had been trained and armed by Colonel Gaddafi – going on to launch the RUF's reign of terror in the early nineties. As early as 1993, Sankoh had been accused of direct dealings with al-Qaeda itself. Al-Qaeda operatives had been looking to buy up Sierra Leone's illicit 'conflict diamonds' (diamonds produced illegally from war zones) – as an untraceable source of funds in a world increasingly intent on freezing terrorists' bank accounts. The RUF would provide them with the perfect means to do so.

In 1998, directly following the horrific al-Qaeda bombings of US embassies in Kenya and Tanzania, Abdullah Ahmed Abdullah, a senior al-Qaeda financial operative, pitched up in Liberia, Sierra Leone's western neighbour. He met with several of Foday Sankoh's closest RUF lieu-tenants. In March 1999, the same al-Qaeda operative returned to Liberia, and crossed over the border into RUF-held Sierra Leone, spending several days touring the diamond fields as a guest of Foday Sankoh. Hundreds of thousands of dollars' worth of RUF diamonds subsequently passed into the hands of al-Qaeda, with arms shipments to Foday Sankoh's RUF routed via Liberia in return. Subsequently, Ahmed Rhalfan Ghalilani and Fazul Abdullah Mohammed, two al-Qaeda operatives on the FBI's most wanted list of terrorists, also sought refuge in this part of the world from US law enforcement agencies. Sankoh's desire to try to 'do a Somalia' on British forces in Sierra Leone was doubtless fulled by the encouragement he recieved from his al-Qaeda friends.

On 1 May – just as the Air Wing's Mi-24 was battling in the skies over the Freetown Peninsula – the RUF struck, in what appears to have been a well-coordinated, concerted assault. Over a two-day period, several hundred UN peacekeepers were attacked by the RUF, including half a dozen British soldiers. By the evening of 2 May, approaching one thousand UN peacekeepers had been taken hostage and several dozen had already been executed. In the ensuing carnage and terror, rebel soldiers ran riot and scores of UN troops were stripped naked and tortured, sexually abused and buggered.

In the rebel stronghold of Kailahun, the RUF surrounded and laid siege to some 500 Indian peacekeepers in their UN base. One British soldier, Major A. Harrison of the Paras, was captured by the RUF and held hostage, along with fourteen other UN troops. In Makeni, some 120 miles to the west, the RUF surrounded a Kenyan base of some seventy-odd troops, seeking to get their hands on the handful of British officers that the Kenyan soldiers were sheltering. Inside the base were Para Major Phil Ashby, Royal Navy Lieutenant Commander Paul Rowland and Major Andy Samsonoff of the Light Infantry. Major Dave Lingard, a signals officer from the New Zealand Army, was also with them, and as the RUF were unable to distinguish between a Kiwi and a Brit, he was seen as being an equally worthy target for the rebels who had vowed to spill British blood.

The RUF had well and truly overstepped the mark now. As of yet, no British soldiers had been killed. But at least one, Major Harrison, had fallen directly into their hands. He had been beaten and tortured and threatened with execution, and few doubted what the rebels now had in store for him. Several others were also facing clear and present danger. The British forces were well aware of Foday Sankoh's power-crazed intentions in Sierra Leone. 'The word has gone out within the RUF to get some Brits,' a senior British military officer told journalists, in a May 2000 briefing in Freetown. 'They want to make Sierra Leone into the next Somalia.'

And there were very serious international implications in the events now unfolding in Sierra Leone: if a rebel group with known links to Colonel Gaddafi and al-Qaeda could be seen to defy the world community – by defeating the British military and the UN – the impact could be felt all across Africa and beyond. It was a chilling scenario. With a nod from Washington, a massive British military machine started to swing into action, with Foday Sankoh's RUF in its sights.

On 3 May, just forty-eight hours after the RUF hostage-taking, the British mission code-named Operation Palliser was born. Op Palliser would share similar aims to those of Executive Outcomes and Sandline before it: to bring security to Sierra Leone by putting an end to the RUF. Once directed to do so by General Sir Charles Guthrie, then Chief of Defence Staff (and a former SAS man himself), PJHQ in Northwood began assembling a task force for the operation. When informed of the planned British military intervention, the US backed the British deployment, even giving permission for US military personnel on exchange programmes with the British military to participate in Operation Palliser with their host units.

Under Op Palliser all units were to be deployed as part of the Joint Rapid Reaction Force (JRRF). Creating this new rapid reaction capability had been the core priority of the 1998 Strategic Defence Review. It was designed to enable British forces to respond to the changing face of conflict in a post-Cold War world, where more numerous and rapid British military deployments were envisaged. Across the UK's three armed services, units were now held at one of five levels of readiness. At Level R1, Spearhead elements would be on twenty-four-hour standby, or less. At the top of that level were the SAS and the SBS. Level R2 units were on a five-day turn-around, R3 elements on an eight-day call-out, and so on and so forth. It was all Level R1 units that were to be deployed to Sierra Leone, and some of these men would be in the air just eight hours after first being told to muster for Operation Palliser. Over the next two weeks, the mission would build to a force of more than 4,500 British troops, with helicopters and fixed-wing aircraft in support, and seven Royal Naval ships and Royal Fleet Auxiliaries lying off Freetown.

The deployment was spearheaded by an RAF airlift of four-hundred-odd men from the Parachute Regiment, along with a few dozen Special Forces troops. A larger force of some eight hundred Royal Marines, part of the Amphibious Ready Group (ARG), then followed on by sea from their anchorage at the French port of Marseilles. The ARG deployment to Sierra Leone would be spearheaded by the helicopter-carrier ship HMS *Ocean*, with HMS *Illustrious* bringing Harrier attack aircraft in support. Op Palliser would end up being the most complex British defence deployment in Africa since the Suez debacle of 1956, and a test case of the rapid-response capability now possible from all three British services.

On the morning of 5 May, companies from 1 and 2 Para were warned off for an immediate overseas deployment. It was at first characterised as a non-combatant evacuation operation (NEO) – in other words a mission to evacuate all British and allied citizens out of Freetown. But when planning teams from 1 and 2 Para were called together for a preliminary orders group (OG), they were left in no doubt as to the real nature of the mission before them. Following a successful evacuation of British and allied citizens, the Paras were tasked with dragging Sierra Leone back from the brink of yet another chapter of rebel-induced chaos and terror. In addition to this, one British soldier had been taken hostage, beaten and tortured by the rebels. He was a fellow Para, and was now being threatened with execution. Three other British soldiers were also in serious danger of being captured. So the Paras already had a score to settle in Sierra Leone.

At the same time as the Paras were being warned off, pilots and aircrew from 7 Squadron RAF received their own warning order for an anticipated rapid deployment to West Africa. Eight hours later, four giant CH47 Chinook helicopters – one of which had been recalled from special exercises in Scotland – took off from RAF Odiham on a staggered dispatch, carrying several Special Forces and significant numbers of the Paras' Spearhead Lead Element (SLE). The first two Chinooks would take just sixty hours to make the epic journey to Freetown, routed via Portugal, Gibraltar, Tenerife and Senegal. But the second pair of giant helicopters would do even better than that: quickly overtaking their colleagues, they would fly almost non-stop making their final destination in an incredible thirty-seven hours. With one stretch of the journey lying across some eight hundred miles of open ocean, internal long-range fuel tanks had to be fitted to the aircraft.

On landing safely at Lungi Airport, to the north of Freetown, the ninety-man British advance party had to secure the area so that the bulk of the British airborne forces could land. Which was easier said than done. The airport was in complete chaos. In the general panic induced by the collapse of the UN, all international flights had ceased and air-traffic control was now non-existent. Of even greater concern, the RUF were already reported to be in SAM7 (a Soviet bloc surface-to-air missile) striking distance of the airport, and the scores of British transport aircraft that were supposed to be landing there over the next forty-eight hours. Once the Paras had dug in along a security perimeter, a British team of Military Air Management System (MAMS) set about getting air-traffic control up and running again. After that, RAF C-130 Hercules transport aircraft could start to ferry the main body of the Paras into the airport.

As media interest in the British deployment was anticipated to be high, Lieutenant Colonel Tony Cramp, an army media liaison officer, was one of the first to receive the order to deploy. At 10 a.m. on 5 May, he was told to prepare for immediate departure for Sierra Leone, as part of the JFHQ Freetown. Under the command of Brigadier David Richards, JFHQ Freetown would take control of Operation Palliser on the ground in Sierra Leone. The JFHQ command team left RAF Northolt that same day, at 6 p.m. Some forty-eight hours later, they were settling into the British High Commission in Freetown, where they were just starting to realise how serious the whole situation had become. The RUF were preparing for their final push on the capital – a city whose two million inhabitants were on the brink of panic. Intelligence reports had the rebels advancing on two fronts, the first, barely thirty miles to the north-east of the capital, and the second, just south of Rogberi Junction.

It was immediately clear to the newly arrived British officers that the Air Wing's lone Mi-24 gunship and its Mi-17s were about the only part of the Sierra Leonean armed forces that still seemed to be functioning properly. Whatever action the British military might now be planning against the RUF, the Air Wing made it clear that it wanted in. The British ground forces could count on all possible combat and intelligence support from the Air Wing. And if the British needed use of their Mi-17 choppers to insert SAS recce teams up-country to get an eye on RUF troop movements, then the Air Wing was at their disposal.

Back in the UK, 5 May had fallen on the last weekend of Easter leave, not the best of times to call in the main bulk of the men of 1 and 2 Para. However, ever since Operation Agricola – the Para's mission to Kosovo, in 1999 – the men had been held on short notice to deploy. Within twenty-four hours of the initial warning for Sierra Leone going out, four hundred British soldiers had flown in from France, Greece, Spain and Scotland or driven up from London, Wales and the West Country, to be with their units. At 6 p.m. on 6 May, the order came through to assemble on several coaches and make 'best possible speed' to their departure point. Speeding down the motorway in their coaches, these men were soon to become part of an air bridge to Africa – the first of its kind in British military history.

Meanwhile, some three thousand miles away, a forward mounting base (FMB) was being set up in a military section of the Prince Leopold International Airport in Dakar. Senegal lies some six hundred miles to the north of Sierra Leone – making it the nearest West African country to Britain. Intense diplomatic negotiations over the previous twenty-four hours had secured the use of the airport as a command, control and transit point for Operation Palliser. Five RAF C-130 Hercules transport planes now started ferrying the British forces out of the UK to Senegal. This not only included the four hundred men of the Paras, but all their kit too, including Land-Rovers, 105mm howitzers and 81mm mortars. After a short stopover in Senegal, the Paras were ferried into Sierra Leone. At 9.15 on the morning of Sunday

7 May, the first Hercs touched down at Lungi Airport, carrying 102 troops from C Company, 1 Para.

Para Major Harrison, the direct prisoner of the RUF, and the three British soldiers being held under siege at the Kenyan UN base heard news of this massive airlift with mixed emotions. If the Paras were going into action, these men knew that they had suddenly become even choicer targets. And the RUF reacted angrily to the news of the arrival of the British forces. In Makeni, they gave the seventy-odd besieged Kenyan UN soldiers a grim ultimatum: either they would hand over the British soldiers sheltering in their base, or face the consequences. Just in case the Kenyans had any doubts what those consequences might be, the rebels kept up an incessant drumming, chanting vigil outside the base all night long, as they pursued an orgy of rape and violence across the town. The screams of the rebel victims would end in a burst of gunfire, whereupon a severed limb would be tossed over the wall of the UN base. The Kenyans had proved to be brave, resourceful troops. But there was no doubt about it: it was definitely time for the British soldiers to be getting the hell out of there.

On the night of 5 May, the three British soldiers and their fellow Kiwi made a break for it. At 3 a.m., faces blackened by charcoal, the unarmed men climbed over the outer wall and silently stole across towards the lines of the besieging RUF forces. Miraculously, they managed to pass through the rebel positions undetected, and so began a week-long exercise to escape and evade the enemy. At first moving only at night, the four soldiers travelled through dense jungle-clad hills, avoiding RUF checkpoints. But by the end of fifth day, with no food or clean water, they had little choice but to walk into the nearest village and ask for help. As luck would have it, the village turned out to be a Kamajor stronghold. After standing guard over the four exhausted soldiers all night long, the Kamajors took them on the last leg of their journey to safe territory.

At the same time as the four escapees were making their bid for freedom, Major Harrison was still being held hostage by the RUF, along with the fourteen other UN troops. As a Para he knew he had to make a run for it – for as soon as his parent regiment went on the offensive, he was a dead man. On the morning of 11 May, in a daring and audacious move, Major Harrison and two colleagues told their rebel guards that they had the RUF commanding officer's permission to go for a wash at the nearby UN base (where five hundred Indian peacekeepers were still being held under siege by the RUF). This was pure front and bluster, but it seemed to pay off. Stepping out of the storeroom in which they'd been held hostage and forcing themselves not to look back, the three men marched off into town.

In a piece of outstanding and selfless bravery Major Harrison then went directly to the local rebel commander's house, instead of heading for the comparative safety of the UN base. There, in an extraordinary escalation of the bluff, Major Harrison convinced the RUF officer that all of his fellow hostages had been granted permission by the RUF high command to go for a wash at the UN base. When the RUF leaders discovered that their only British prisoner had walked, taking the fourteen other UN hostages with him, they were not best pleased. An enraged Foday Sankoh ordered his forces to recapture the men. But inside the besieged UN base, there were a hundred battle-hardened Indian Army Gurkhas, men who were fiercely loyal to the British. No amount of RUF threats or firepower would succeed in forcing them to hand back the British Major. For now, at least, he was safely out of harm's way.

With all four of the British soldiers having now escaped his clutches, Foday Sankoh was forced to shelve any immediate plans to 'do a Somalia' on the British. But he still had nearly two thousand UN peacekeepers either held under siege or taken hostage by men under his command, and UNAMSIL was imploding on a massive scale. It was shaping up to be one of the biggest UN debacles in history, and he, Foday Sankoh, was responsible. Sensing victory in his grasp, it was time to concentrate on taking the capital. And all that now stood between his forces and Freetown were the hopelessly ineffectual UN peacekeeping troops, and a few hundred pesky British paratroopers.

Two days earlier, a complete battalion of five hundred Zambian UN peacekeepers had been sent to relieve the besieged Kenyan forces still trapped in Makeni. Hopelessly ill-prepared and badly briefed (they didn't even have any usable maps), the whole convoy had itself blundered into a trap and been taken hostage by the RUF. Just one Zambian soldier had escaped. Sankoh now ordered his men to dress up in the Zambian UN uniforms, take the captured Zambian UN armoured personnel carriers (APCs) and trucks, and advance to take Freetown. With RUF rebels now sporting the distinctive United Nations blue helmets, several UN checkpoints were taken in this way, the peace-keepers either captured or gunned down by soldiers whom they had presumed were fellow UN soldiers. Just two days after Major Harrison and the other British hostages had escaped to safety, the advance party of rebels arrived at the British-held outskirts of Freetown. Their first objective was Lungi: if they could take the international airport, the British air bridge to Sierra Leone would be shut down.

But while Sankoh had been busy, so had the British. Once the main body of the Paras had flown in by Hercules to Lungi Airport, 1 Para's D Company (around 120 men) had been ferried by Chinook to the Aberdeen area of Freetown. Here, the distinctive Mammy Yoko Hotel had been chosen as the evacuation point (EP) for all British and allied foreign nationals who might wish to leave the country. Of course, once the Paras could be seen calmly patrolling the streets on foot around the hotel, the number of those seeking evacuation fell drastically. Still, at the hotel gates members of the British High Commission worked alongside the Paras' evacuation handling cell (EHC) to check those eligible for airlift out of the country. Over two hundred entitled persons were processed that first day. Meanwhile, 2 Para's D Company had advanced overland to secure the Targrin ferry point on the southern end of the Freetown Peninsula, just in case the airport was shut down and the evacuees had to go out by sea.

Back at Lungi, 1 Para's B Company were pushed out to the northern side of the airport (the most likely avenue of attack), mortars were bedded in to form an inner cordon, and C Company were sent out to provide a mobile patrol capability for areas of heightened threat. By 9 May, regular patrols across the city of Freetown had calmed the situation to almost normal levels. At the Freetown amputee camp – a place of abject horror that housed hundreds of mostly child victims – the British soldiers out on patrol saw the first direct evidence of the rebel atrocities that they'd heard so much about. The sight of so many despairing child amputees was almost too much to bear, especially for those with families. There were no mosquito nets, no fresh food and no sleeping or washing facilities available to the British troops for the first two weeks of Operation Palliser. But it would clearly all be more than worth it if only they could get the chance to give the RUF a taste of their own medicine.

Once Lungi and Freetown had been made secure, the Paras started pushing inland in mobile vehicle patrols, probing the terrain for enemy resistance. On 17 May, with the Pathfinder Platoon pushing eastwards in several WMIK Land-Rovers, SAS intelligence reports identified a large body of RUF heading towards the Paras' positions. That afternoon, the

Paras detected signs of a rebel presence up ahead of the village of Lungi Lol, about thirty miles east of the capital. The Pathfinder Platoon advanced to the village, and a battle group dug in on forward positions alongside the road leading east. That evening, they had a major stroke of luck: a rebel defector walked into camp with crucial intelligence for the British forces. The RUF were planning to attack their positions that night, he told them, using the cover of darkness to mask a full-frontal assault.

Sure enough, at around 3 a.m. the men of the battle group were told to stand-to: a force of around two hundred RUF had been spotted, silently creeping towards their positions. A minute later the Paras initiated the action by firing parachute flares – the dead of night suddenly rendered into the stark iridescence of burning phosphor flares. Around 150 rebel troops were caught out in the open, frozen in the harsh white light, about eighty yards from the Paras' positions. Until then the RUF had been shrouded in darkness, using their natural night vision to feel their way towards the British positions. Now, they were startled and blinded by the sudden burst of near daylight.

The Paras opened up with everything they'd got – SA80 assault rifles, 7.62mm GPMGs, 81mm mortars, and the 50-cal heavy machine guns mounted on the Land-Rovers. In seconds, the eerie night-time scene had been turned into a killing field. Pinned down and hopelessly exposed, the RUF were cut down in droves. As the rebels tried to take cover and retreat, the Paras went after them in a series of hot pursuits, killing and wounding several more of the enemy. At break of day, it was clear that the RUF had been seriously blooded. The battle scene was littered with rebel bodies. Officially, four RUF rebels were killed. Unofficially, the rebel death toll was said to be some forty killed or mortally wounded.

The Paras had spoken the only language that Foday Sankoh and his rebel forces seemed to understand, that of brute force. For the next eleven days, the Paras put out regular patrols on the streets of Freetown, while at the same time probing the terrain deeper into the interior of the country. Several patrols went up the rivers to the east of Lungi Peninsula, in inflatable boats. But no more rebel forces were detected. By the time the Paras were relieved by the men of 42nd Commando Royal Marines, on 24 May, no further contacts with the RUF had been reported. Foday Sankoh's rebels appeared to have well and truly gone to ground.

With the airport open for business again, UN-chartered heavy-lift

Antonov AN124–100s (larger than Boeing 747s) started ferrying in Indian UN reinforcements. This time, the Indian military weren't messing around, flying in two battalions of crack troops fresh out of the Kashmir conflict and three disassembled Indian Air Force (IAF) Mi-24 gunships. In one corner of the airstrip, IAF technicians quickly began work on reassembling the Mi-24s. If Indian UN troops were going to be kidnapped, tortured and killed, then the Indian high command was determined to retaliate in kind. The whole credibility of the UN was at stake.

Just over a month later, those Indian gunships were to more than prove their worth. On 10 July, Operation Khukhri was launched, a daring, combined mission between the RAF and the IAF to rescue the largest group of UN hostages still being held under rebel siege. A pair of C-47 Chinooks flew in a British assault force to the besieged UN base, with close air support from the IAF Mi-24s. As the Chinooks lifted free scores of UN hostages, an Indian column led by the Gurkhas fought its way out of the base, breaking through the rebel cordon that surrounded it.

Having painted their white UN APCs camouflage colours and improvised extra armour with planks of wood, the Indian column fought a running battle with the RUF for the next sixty miles until it reached safety. When the day's action was over, the Indians had suffered one fatality and several wounded. But they had inflicted far heavier losses on the RUF – including the capture of their brigade HQ at Pendembu, long regarded as one of the rebel's key strongholds. And among those men who had been airlifted out of the UN base was Major Harrison. And so, the RUF had lost their last British captive.

Once Foday Sankoh had got the measure of British forces, it seemed that he had decided taking Freetown might not be such a good idea after all. Now, with British help, the UN had started playing hardball too. In addition to the Air Wing's Mi-24, there were three more of the hated Mi-24 gunships in the country intent on hunting down his forces. It was time to go to ground.

For ten years, Sankoh had commanded the RUF rebel forces. He was the chief architect of the insanity of evil that they had wreaked on the civilian population of the country. A bearded, smiling figure in his fifties, Sankoh's was the archetypal image of a benign African elder. But rarely have appearances been more misleading. Bereft of political or ideological beliefs, Sankoh was renowned for being cruel, venal and power-hungry, and he had wrought his rebel movement in his own image.

This is a quote from one of Sankoh's speeches to a group of kidnapped children: 'There is no fairness and transparency in the system in Sierra Leone . . . No one in government is listening. Thus the time for talking is past. Violence is now the only option. Your people have been abducted for guerrilla training to regain their birthright.'

Sankoh knew that he had lost this battle with the British and the UN, but that the war was far from over. He would regroup his forces in the jungle, and capture more forced recruits. He would seek further support from his Liberian and Libyan allies and funds from his terrorist friends. He would be patient. He would be vigilant. He would use all his cunning. And he would await another opportunity to strike against the British and the UN. Surely, it could only be a matter of time?

And as for the British, the big gamble of their military intervention in Sierra Leone seemed to be paying off. Foday Sankoh had been put right back where he belonged – deep in his jungle lair. And with British help, UNAMSIL seemed to be getting back on track again. The British military's political masters were now keen to take the credit, and there were pats on the back all round at Westminster and Whitehall. Sure, with the British military intervention now morphing into an expanded IMATT training operation, there were cries of 'mission creep' from the Tories. But for now at least, Tony Blair could bask in the glory of a job well done. And nothing, but nothing, would be allowed to stand in the way of all this success.

Foday Kallay and his West Side Boys had shared power with Foday Sankoh and his RUF during the glory days of the AFRC. Sankoh was the stronger rebel leader, with some five thousand men and boys under his control, as opposed to the West Side Boys' thousand-odd fighters. But both of them were now deeply unhappy with the UN-British 'takeover of Sierra Leone'.

Following the RUF's example, the West Side Boys now began shooting up vehicles passing along the main Freetown–Masiaka highway. Their first victim was Sam Willy, a Sierra Leonean businessman. Kallay found a bag of uncut diamonds and 15 million leones ($2,500) on his person: the businessman was executed by a bullet to the head and Kallay pocketed the loot. Aid convoys operating under the UN taking food and medical aid into the country's interior were the next targets.

Within weeks, the West Side Boys had captured a fleet of ten four-wheel-drive jeeps and aid trucks, which were parked up at Magbeni. They abducted four aid workers, and tortured and raped several others. Then, on 21 July, they ambushed a food-aid convoy and took hostage four relief workers with the Christian Health Association of Sierra Leone (CHASL).

On 28 July, UNAMSIL reacted by providing the first armed escorts to food aid convoys passing through the West Side Boys' territory, to guard against such road piracy. Despite this, the UN Office for the Coordination of Humanitarian Affairs (OCHA) reported 'continuing concern among humanitarian agencies about access and security for aid workers in the area'. The West Side Boys made it clear that they were angry and resentful at the UN-brokered, British-backed peace deal now being implemented in Sierra Leone: they were threatening to execute the four CHASL hostages to 'get revenge on the UN'.

The UN was swift to react. Just two weeks after Op Khukhri, the three IAF Mi-24 gunships were in action again. This time, they turned their wrath on the West Side Boys. In Operation Thunderbolt, they hosed down a number of the rebels' positions along the Freetown–Masiaka–Lungi highway. British Special Forces carried out a key role, calling in the gunships to their targets. In the follow-up ground assault one Guinean UN peacekeeper was killed, but the West Side Boys suffered far greater casualties. In New York, UN Secretary-General Kofi Annan spoke of a 'pre-emptive strike' against the West Side Boys. 'We are going to remain vigilant. Anyone who attempts to attack peacekeepers should know that there is a price to pay.'

A few days after Op Thunderbolt, journalists were taken to witness the surrender of twenty-eight demoralised West Side Boys. Among those who gave themselves up were several women, some with children as young as two years old. The rebels handed over weapons including light machine guns, SLRs and AK47s. The leader of the group, Colonel Danny 'Hard Guy' Sandy, told the assembled press that many more of the rebels wanted to surrender. The Jordanian UN peacekeepers in nominal control of the area appeared to agree. 'I believe they are nice people. I believe they mean what they tell me,' the Jordanian UN Commander told the BBC. 'Really, I am very optimistic. More are coming.'

Unfortunately, such optimism proved ill-founded. The main body of the West Side Boys reacted with angry defiance to the UN attacks. Immediately following the surrender of the twenty-eight rebels, Foday Kallay had thirty of his fighters executed on suspicion of wanting to do likewise. Just days after Operation Thunderbolt, the West Side Boys rebuilt their roadblocks along that same highway, and restarted their road-piracy activities. Two government buses were the first victims of the rebels. They ambushed and looted the vehicles, and sent the survivors back to Freetown with a message for the UN and the British: the West Side Boys were still in control of the highway and very much in possession of all their territory. And woe betide anyone who tried to demonstrate otherwise.

Just two weeks later, Major Martial's patrol of Royal Irish Rangers drove down into the rebels' headquarters, and were taken hostage. With eleven British soldiers in his custody, Foday Kallay began issuing his demands – the single most important of which was the revocation of the Lome Agreement, the treaty under which UN and British forces had been drafted into Sierra Leone. Kallay was seeking a 'presidential' role for himself in a new rebel-based government, and using the British hostages as his leverage to do so. Of course his real motive by now was to launch Operation Kill British, to force the British military out of Sierra Leone. And this was to be followed up by Operation Kill All Your Family, which would see Foday Kallay seize the seat of government in Sierra Leone and execute all the ministers and their families.

As press interest in the story of the hostage-taking mushroomed, there was growing controversy over just how exactly the Royal Irish patrol had come to be captured. What on earth had they been doing in the heart of the West Side Boys' territory? It seemed particularly inexplicable, especially as this was not the first time that the West Side Boys had seized and threatened to kill British hostages.

On 19 August 1999, five unarmed British soldiers with what was then UNOMSIL (the United Nations Observer Mission to Sierra Leone), along with Pasco Temple, a journalist with Star Radio, and Ade Campbell, a top Sierra Leonean TV journalist, had been taken captive in Magbeni. They had been invited there to witness the rebels handing over a group of child soldiers to the UN. The twenty-odd Nigerian security force that had accompanied them had also been captured. At that time, the West Side Boys had issued demands and a deal had been struck. Ten days after their capture, the men had been released. But the rebels had refused to let the Nigerian soldiers go free, as they had wanted to kill them all. Only the refusal of the other hostages to leave without the Nigerians had eventually forced the West Side Boys to let them go.

Speaking to the press in Freetown about the capture of the Royal

Irish Rangers patrol, Brigadier Gordon Hughes, overall Commander of British Force in Sierra Leone, maintained that the Rangers were simply on a routine mission, coordinating security with the Jordanian peacekeepers at Masiaka town. 'The British patrol had completed their mission in the area on Friday the 25th,' he said, 'and on their way back to Benguema they were stopped and detained.' But then, the Deputy Commander of UNAMSIL, Nigerian Brigadier General Mohammed A. Garba, started publicly criticising the British forces. 'This is one thing I want to categorically deny,' Brigadier General Garba had said, referring to the British account of the patrol. 'At the rate at which things are going, the British may . . . shift the blame on to the UN troops deployed in that area . . . The British did not say to the UN peacekeepers at Masiaka that they were going into the West Side Boys' rebel positions, which I would describe as very dangerous.'

In fact, relations between the British forces and the UN were showing signs of great strain. UN officers were privately claiming that the Royal Irish patrol had been on a 'Rambo-style' mission, deep inside enemy territory. Brigadier General Garba had even gone so far as denying that the British soldiers had ever visited the Jordanian UN base, which had been the whole *raison d'être* of the Royal Irish patrol. The UN had then added insult to injury by ruling out the use of force should the British hostages have to be rescued. 'UNAMSIL's position in Sierra Leone is for peace,' a spokesman had said. 'We are not going to use force. We believe by the efforts of UNAMSIL, and the British themselves, the twelve soldiers being held will be released very soon.'

The RUF now began hinting at their own interest in the British hostages. At a meeting on 30 August – five days after the British patrol's capture – to hand back some captured UN vehicles, RUF 'Brigadier General' Morris Kallon used the hostage crisis as an opportunity to push their own, anti-British agenda. 'As far as we are concerned, the British deserve the abduction by the West Side Boys because the British do not want to see peace in Sierra Leone,' he had told reporters. 'If they are really determined to see peace, they should not have been training soldiers and sending in weapons. This time around,' the RUF leader had continued, with a broad smile, 'we are ready to work with the government and the people of Sierra Leone in the interests of peace.'

As the hostage crisis dragged from days into weeks, the West Side Boys started hearing rumours of a massive British rescue operation in the offing. And so a worried Foday Kallay began to prepare the ground for taking the British hostages further into the remote jungles – to areas where the British assault forces would never find them. In order to do so, he would need the help of his more powerful rebel allies, Foday Sankoh and his RUF, who controlled the territory of the remote jungle interior. For the British force commanders and their political taskmasters, this was the ultimate nightmare scenario. Any chance that the British hostages might fall into the hands of a joint West Side Boys–RUF alliance had to be avoided at all costs.

For if that happened, there were worse things than death that could happen to the British soldiers.

8

DANCES WITH DEATH

If we take the generally accepted definition of bravery as being a quality which knows no fear, I have never seen a brave man. All men are frightened. The more intelligent they are, the more they are frightened. The courageous man is the man who forces himself, in spite of his fear, to carry on.

– General George S. Patton Jr, *War As I Knew It*

ON the morning of day four of the hostage crisis, Corporal Mousa was taken out of the dungeon to see Foday Kallay. But first things first – he was given yet another beating, just for good measure. He had reached the stage now where he no longer felt the pain: they were blows upon blows and injuries upon injuries, and his body's pain management system just seemed to have reached shutdown. He was thrown on to the floor of the veranda at Kallay's feet, 'handbagged', naked and stinking. He had been given no food or water since he arrived in the rebel camp, and was starting to hallucinate from the hunger and dehydration.

'Mousa, we de know you help de Brittonians and you de be de traitor,' Kallay said, ordering Mousa's binds to be slackened a little, so he could talk. 'Now, I de go kill-kill you. Dat is for sure. Only way to save yourself to na tell me de truth. You have been wid de whiteboy Brittonians for so-so long now, over a year. You de travel with dem whiteboys everywhere, like best friend-friend. But you de never think about come to de West Side area, to my kingdom, na true? Tell me why de British come. You tell me de truth, maybe I na go kill-kill you. But if you de lie to me, I go kill-kill you in de next hour come.'

Mousa lay there at the feet of Kallay racking his brains for some lie convincing enough to save his life. There was no way a paranoid Foday Kallay was going to believe the truth – that they just stumbled down the road to Magbeni largely by accident – but Mousa could think of no lie that would work. Finally, he decided to give the rebel leader a blow-by-blow account of what had happened on the day of their capture, hoping that would be enough to save his life.

'You wanna know why we de come, sa. OK. Dis is de story,' Mousa began, speaking to Kallay in Creole. 'First de Jordanian man, he invite us to come visit de camp at Masiaka. We de go there for lunchtime, den we coming back on de main road again. But suddenly de Major took now now de road down to West Side. I no go know why. Me, I de be in de last car, and I no know why de Major do this. You think I de wanna come to West Side? I de know it be de last thin I do in my life, cause maybe the West Side go kill me. Why would I else wanna come?'

As Mousa was narrating his story, Foday Kallay had got on his radio set and was checking his story with all the main rebel checkpoints – both out on the main Masiaka–Freetown road, and on the dirt track heading down towards Magbeni. 'He say dey do come past your place de go visit Jordanian. Na true?' All of Kallay's radio calls confirmed that the story Mousa was telling him was true.

'But why-why you de come, Mousa? What de *reason*?' Kallay persisted.

'Honestly, sa, I no know,' Mousa continued. 'Honestly, you can de imagine if I knew de Major wan come come right into West Side – my God if dey de give me de whole world I not come to dis place. It could cost me my life, sa. It was jus accident, sa. No plan, sa. Why would I de come, sa – I know it cause my death death.'

'OK,' said Kallay, sitting for a while in silence, thinking. Mousa knew that his life hung in the balance now, depending on whether Kallay believed the story or not. Finally, Kallay ordered Mousa's binds to be slackened off a little and for him to be put back into the dungeon. At least it seemed as if he wasn't going to kill him just yet. As he lay back in the pitch black of the pit, Mousa heard the British soldiers being let out of their room for the day. He could overhear just about everything that happened over at Cambodia's place, because the pit was so close. The first thing the Major did was enquire after his welfare. Despite his condition, Mousa felt a little encouraged. At least the Major was still doing his best to look out for him.

'Good morning, Colonel,' the Major said, greeting Cambodia. 'I am very worried about Corporal Mousa still. Tell me, what is his condition?'

'He's fine. You shouldn't worry yourself so,' Colonel Cambodia reassured the Major. 'He is like our brother. So how can we treat him too badly?'

'Whenever you are able to, Colonel, I should like to see Corporal Mousa and to talk with him. After all,' the Major added. 'he is one of my men and I am responsible for him, whatever may happen.'

Just before lunchtime, Mousa was taken out of the pit again and brought down to Kallay once more.

'Mousa, I de think go kill-kill you at any any time still,' Kallay began. 'You tell me you de come by accident. I no convince by dat. Still, my situation it be dis. I wanna President Kabbah to resign de government. After, I wan de West Side Boys in de government with me as de actin President. Now, you de be an educated man, an officer in de army. Now, you de go tell me dis. I want de whiteboys, dem be part of my plan for to make Kabbah resign. If you wann live, you de go tell me how I de do dis thing.'

'Well, if you go kill me, or de British men, it no go help you plans.' Mousa replied, thinking fast. 'It go gain you nothing, nothing. All that happen then is de world see de West Side as de killers. My advice be you go negotiate. *Negotiate.* You go want President Kabbah go resign and you go be head of de government, you negotiate wid de British for to get dis thing. Right now you have de best negotiating chip in me and de British soldier men.'

'All right,' said Kallay, looking pleased. 'But how now I de best go negotiate?'

'You de use de British Major. No negotiate yourself, as de Major can speak for you, na true?' Mousa replied. 'You go explain de Major what exactly you wanna do with de government and all dese things. Then de Major get de message out to de British and then to de whole world what Foday Kallay and dem West Side dey want. Na true?'

'Na true, Corporal!' Kallay enthused, patting Mousa on the head like a clever dog. 'I no de thought to use de Major like dat. Is a very fine-fine idea. Oh yes. De brilliant. Good man. Dis Mousa he de be a good man for now . . .'

Kallay immediately rushed off to have words with Major Martial and explain the negotiation strategy that Corporal Mousa had outlined. Within the hour, he had given orders for all the radio communications kit to be stripped out of the Land-Rovers and brought across river from Magbeni to Gberi Bana. The Major had advised Kallay that if he was to be directly involved in the negotiations, they'd need the British radio sets on their side of the river to communicate effectively with Benguema Camp.

Now that Foday Kallay had realised that Corporal Mousa could be useful, the beatings started to decrease and his binds were left permanently less tight – they had cut deep into his skin, leaving raw-red gashes. But any of the rebel leaders was still free to come over and drag Mousa from the pit for a small beating – usually using his Small Boys Unit to lend a hand. Still, Mousa felt convinced that as long as he could remain useful to Kallay, no one would be able to kill him.

Unfortunately, Mousa's proposal had one shortcoming. The West Side Boys' leaders had little patience and were highly unpredictable and volatile – especially when the afternoon drugs kicked in. Kallay seemed to believe that as soon as the Major had got on the case with the British, things would be sorted out and that his demands would be put into effect. Instead, word had come back via the Major that Kallay's set of demands would be looked into and considered as the negotiations progressed.

Around mid-afternoon, another of the West Side Boys' leaders, 'Colonel GS', came stomping up to Cambodia's house. The Colonel's war name, GS, stood for General Staff, as in Chief of the General Staff. Each of the rebel leaders had adopted his own war name, the more bloodthirsty-sounding the better. In addition to Colonels Savage, Changa Bulanga, Cambodia, Mines and GS, there was also a Colonel Terminator, and a Colonel Blood in the village.

Colonel GS was bigger and scruffier than Colonel Cambodia, and all he ever seemed to wear was a pair of shorts and a vest, Foday Kallay-slob style. The hostages had seen him around a bit, but he'd always been aloof and unfriendly. As far as they could ascertain, GS seemed to be on a lower rung of the West Side Boys power ladder than Cambodia, and was somewhat jealous of him. Whenever Cambodia wasn't around, GS liked to try to throw his weight about. Today, he was in an even worse mood than normal.

Colonel GS ordered all eleven British soldiers to line up outside Cambodia's house. As they did so, he started ranting on and on about 'all de British lies and cheating' and being 'tricked by de British'. Why were the negotiations taking so long? he demanded. The time had come to show the British that the West Side Niggas were serious. Walking down the line of men, he jabbed each of them hard in the chest, spitting out a number from one to eleven as he did so, between clenched teeth. The hostages were clearly being numbered off, but for what reason they were as yet uncertain.

'KNEEL,' he yelled at them, once he'd completed the numbering exercise. 'Go get DOWN on your knees. You de know what de numbers are for for, na true? That is de order in which we go start KILL-KILL YOU. ONE for each dem hour de deadline no go met for our demands.'

What deadline? the terrified British soldiers were thinking. *And which fucking demands? And who the hell was going to be first to be shot, then? Did this crazed bastard intend to start killing them with number 1, or number 11?*

'You tink you de whiteboy British can just PLAY wid us!' he ranted. 'Yaaah . . . Our demands no be important? Dey can be just ignored?! That de needs of DE BLACK MAN are not true? De WEST SIDE NIGGAS do not matter? Well . . . Now I go start killing one by one, one by one, unless dem whiteboy Brittonian commanders start listening to us. I will go take ONE of you for EACH hour they go refuse us. And I go shoot-shoot de man in de head. Yaaah . . . But you no go know which number I go start with, eh? Eh?' he swung about from one end of the line of the kneeling British soldiers to the other, grinning maliciously. 'So . . . Will I be go start wid number one or number eleven? Number one or eleven? WHERE shall I go start?'

After leaving a few seconds to let his words sink in, the rebel colonel spun around and barked an order at the boy soldier at his side. 'Movement, go na fetch my gun.'

Movement scuttled off, and the Colonel slumped down into the wicker chair on Cambodia's veranda. As Colonel GS had been going about setting up his little killing game, Major Martial had been glancing all about him, searching frantically for Colonel Cambodia. Cambodia appeared almost sane in comparison to Colonel GS, but he was nowhere to be seen. A minute later, Movement came hurrying back with an ancient, but well-used AK47. Colonel GS cocked it, patted it lovingly and laid it down at his side.

As the British soldiers knelt there with their heads bowed, believing they were about to be executed, they found themselves starting to pray. '*Our Father who art in Heaven, hallowed be Thy name, Thy kingdom come, Thy will be done, on Earth as it is in Heaven . . .*' Somehow, that familiar mantra that each knew so intimately – having being brought up in deeply religious, if troubled, communities – was a great comfort to these eleven men who thought they were about to die. But Colonel GS – sensing somehow the men's prayers and deciding to use this against them – began to goad the hostages again.

'So, you go saying your *prayers* now now?' he demanded, sneeringly. 'Which of you go be *religious*? Which of you go tink about de GOD, now you stare de death in de face? Eh? You go tell me, Major, which of dese your men is actually *stupid* enough to believe that dere is a God?'

'We all are, Colonel,' the Major replied, evenly. 'Every man under my command believes there is a God.'

'Yaaah . . . But which of him *really* do tink dat, Major?' GS demanded again, with an evil laugh. 'Which of you whiteboys really believe it enough to admit it and *die*.'

Slowly and deliberately, Major Martial raised his hand. '*I do*, Colonel.'

There was a moment's deathly silence, as both the British soldiers and the watching rebels held their breaths, waiting to see what would happen next. And then Captain Flaherty followed suit, slowly raising his arm in the air. He was joined in turn by Sergeant Smith, and within the space of a few seconds, all the British soldiers had raised their hands. *Fuck it*, they thought. The Major had always said it would be all of them or none of them. *They'd stick together, even if this was the very end.*

'So it be time-time to say de *prayers*, then, whiteboys,' GS sneered in response. 'You go have less than one hour left. We go see if dis your God can save you now now. Tink about it. *One hour*. And den I go start de shooting.'

A grim silence settled over the group, as Colonel GS turned away from the men and stared off into space, his hands twitching nervously. He kept glancing at his wristwatch, as if to make a show of the fact that time was ticking by, and that someone's death sentence was drawing closer and closer by the second. After half an hour or so of this, Major Martial decided the time had come to chance his arm. Things were looking pretty desperate in any case, so there was little left to lose.

'Excuse me, Colonel,' he began, breaking the heavy silence, 'but listen, we have a tradition in England that a man who's about to die is granted a last request. If you're agreeable, I'd ask you to share a last drink with us. In the spirit of peace and all that, because when we came here in the first place we came in the spirit of peace and we meant you no harm . . .'

Colonel GS sat up straight and turned and stared rigidly at the

Major. The hostages barely dared breathe. They were half expecting him to grab his AK and shoot their CO outright. Instead, an evil grin began to spread across the Colonel's face.

'You go have a last request, Major? Why not? I *like* dis your idea,' the Colonel purred. 'A dying man's last drink. We no let no one say that de West Side Boys deny de British whiteboy soldiers their last request. Movement, go na fetch some drinks. De English men dey want to go get drunk with us before we go kill dem.'

Movement dashed off into Colonel Cambodia's house and returned with a couple of plastic jerrycans and an armful of Cellophane-wrapped bright orange alcopops. The jerrycans turned out to be full of palm wine, a drink which the British troops had already come across during their posting to Sierra Leone. Palm wine is made by draining the sap of a palm tree into a plastic container, and then fermenting it in the tropical heat for a few days. The end result is a slimy, milky-white liquid generally full of dead insects. It is mildly alcoholic and tastes sour-sweet and nauseating.

'Drink!' Colonel GS ordered, thrusting the jerrycan of palm wine at the Major. 'Drink,' he ordered again, with a grin.

With no time to fish out the flies, Major Martial took a long pull on the sludgy liquid. He passed the jerrycan on to the next in line, Sergeant Smith. 'Try some,' he remarked. 'It's delicious. Not quite Guinness, but not bad all the same.'

The palm wine went quickly down the line. Then the rebels started on the alcopops. These were the revolting, locally brewed hooch that the hostages had seen the West Side Boys drinking on a more or less daily basis. Each carton was marked 'Rum', 'Gin' or 'Whisky'. But they all contained the same, noxious liquid, which had a burning, gut-wrenching effect when swallowed.

Ten minutes passed. Then half an hour. More and more alcopops were passed around and the hostages drank whatever came their way. Partly they did so in order to give themselves some Dutch courage, as they were all supposedly about to die. But it was more about showing willing to the rebel colonel. Perhaps by forging some sort of drinking brotherhood with him, the hostages could parley for their lives. *Did Colonel GS really have the authority to execute them?* the men were wondering. Things were chaotic and anarchic in the rebel camp, but would GS really act without any orders? Or had he been told to do this by Kallay and Cambodia, as a way to terrorise the British soldiers? *If they kill us now, they've lost their only bargaining chip with the*

British forces, the men were thinking. *Surely even they can see that would be a stupid move.*

As the boozing continued, the atmosphere seemed to calm a little, a crowd of twenty-odd young rebels gathering to join in the drink-and-drugs binge. A couple of the younger West Side Boys started chopping up blocks of cannabis, and soon, everyone was being passed a joint. The hostages also noticed a couple of the rebel soldiers sprinkling a white powder on to strips of tinfoil. A lighter held beneath the foil was used to heat up the powder, the smoke it gave off being inhaled via a rolled-up scrap of paper. It was heroin or crack cocaine.

Eventually, the hour deadline came and went without anyone having been shot. By now, Cambodia had returned, and Colonel GS had invited him to join in his 'dying man's last drink party'. 'Colonel Cambodia!' he had greeted his fellow rebel commander with an exuberant wave, the drink already beginning to take effect. 'Come join us. It is an English tradition. We are having a last drink with de whiteboy British soldiers, before we go kill them.'

As time wore on and the drugs-and-alcohol high started to really kick in, the hostages noticed Movement quietly remove Colonel GS's AK47 from the veranda and put it back in his room. GS was in a drunken discussion with Cambodia, and he didn't even seem to notice. Despite all of the rebel colonel's threats, it looked as if the eleven British hostages weren't about to be executed that day, after all.

By now, the crowd of West Side Boys that had gathered to join the party was some thirty or more strong – and they were having a great laugh at how the British soldiers were sharing their booze with them. The hostages were trying hard to look like they were genuinely enjoying themselves, and racking their brains for topics of conversation they might strike up with their captors. But the choices were fairly limited. The only safe bet seemed to be football. But there was only so much time you could spend talking about Manchester United. And Colonel Cambodia kept steering the drunken discussion around so they could discuss his warped ideas on politics. *Thank God feckin' Dennis the Menace is nowhere to be seen*, the hostages were thinking. They were learning to be thankful for small mercies.

The only thing to do was to keep humouring Cambodia, whatever he said, and always to agree with him. Man U were the best football team in the world. *Sure they are, Colonel, sure they are. The greatest.* But Sierra Leoneans could play better football. *You bet.* The country just needed better facilities to train with. *Of course, then they'd be world class*. It was the fault of the British colonialists that the country remained so poor and underdeveloped and had no football facilities. *Well, you couldn't say fairer than that, now could you. For sure, the British had made a lot of feckin' mistakes in the past. Just look at Ireland.* That was why the country needed a strong man like Kallay as its leader, to stand up to the foreign powers who just exploited the country and never developed it. *For sure, Kallay was yer man.* Then they'd train a Sierra Leonean football team that could beat Man United! They'd have a football team that would be world-beaters, that could win the World Cup even. *Like we said, world class. To be sure, they'd be unbeatable, so they would.*

What a warped situation it was, sitting there drinking the West Side Boys' booze as if they were all best of buddies. The rebels kept asking the British soldiers if they liked the drink, and they in turn kept enthusing about the alcopops and the palm wine, although it was the shittiest hooch they'd ever tasted in their lives. A couple of the Boys even tried to pass the British soldiers the odd joint. But having no idea exactly what the smokes contained, the men declined. It was somewhat worrying to refuse the rebels' offer of drugs, in case it offended or provoked the young hotheads. But the hostages needn't have worried. The rebels seemed happy to accept the fact that the British soldiers only ever smoked straights, and didn't seem to do drugs.

Steering the drunken conversation back to the safety of football, Ranger Gaunt brought up the subject of the village football pitch. The hostages had noticed it during their camp walkabout on the day of their arrival. It was a large patch of cleared forest to the west of the village, with a couple of sagging goalposts at either end. It was hopelessly overgrown with long bush grass and clearly hadn't been played on for ages. Why didn't any of them ever get a match together? the Ranger wondered. Would the West Side Boys fancy a kickaround with the British soldiers even? Sure, they had enough men for a full team, the Ranger enthused, especially if they would let Mousa play on the British side. And what a great excuse that would be for getting Mousa away from the horrors of the pit, the Ranger thought to himself.

'Yo! A football match. Na true – is a good idea,' one of the drunken rebels enthused. 'But no one has go play there-there for a veeery long time.'

'Sure, it's just yer grass that's a problem there,' the Ranger slurred back at him. 'Can't youse get it cut? Then we can get a game together, so we can.'

(*Above*) The capital city, Freetown, as seen from the Targrin Ferry on the Freetown Estuary, the route taken by British troops as they arrive in Sierra Leone. (*Below*) View over the territory of the West Side Boys rebels, where the eleven British and one Sierra Leonean soldier were held hostage for 17 days – until the combined SAS/SBS assault force rescued them.

(*Above*) West Side Boys rebels pictured in their jungle stronghold at Magbeni, where the British military patrol was ambushed and taken captive. Heavily armed, violent and unpredictable, the rebels were an enemy to be reckoned with, especially as they used voodoo to make themselves 'invulnerable' to bullets in battle.

(*Left*) The dirt track leading down to the rebel base at Magbeni, with jungle crowding in from either side – the route taken by the Royal Irish Rangers' military patrol that was captured.

(*Above*) Heavily armed West Side Boys rebels pictured prior to the attack on their base by SAS/SBS assault forces. (*Below*) West Side Boys pose by the skeleton and rotten uniform of a murdered United Nations peacekeeper. In the centre is a woman. The daily cocktail of drugs (cocaine, heroin and cannabis) and locally-brewed alcohol made the heavily-armed rebels notoriously volatile and dangerous.

(*Right*) Boy soldiers made up the bulk of the West Side Boys fighters. Drugged-up, brutalised and brainwashed, they made for fearless fighters on the battlefield.

(*Left*) Posters decorating the walls of the West Side Boys' buildings at their Gberi Bana base; gangster culture, drugs, violence and rap lyrics heavily influenced the rebels.

(*Above*) Captain (then Corporal) Mousa Bangura, held captive along with the eleven British soldiers of the Royal Irish Regiment, and kept for 16 days in the terrible 'dungeon', or 'pit'. (*Right*) The houses of the West Side Boys rebels at their Gberi Bana base had few windows and were dark inside – presenting a challenge for the SAS/SBS dawn assault force. They had to find their targets in the darkness and locate and rescue the British hostages. (*Below*) The remains of the 'pit', or 'dungeon' in the rebel base, a waterlogged hole in the ground where Corporal Mousa and the other prisoners were held captive. The pit was "hell on earth".

(*Above*) Members of the 1st Batallion, the Parachute Regiment (1 Para), prepare to disembark Lungi Airport for operations in Sierra Leone.(*Below*) British army 'WMIK' (Weapons Mounted Installation Kit) Land Rovers in hangar at Lungi Airport, Sierra Leone, prior to deployment in country. The WMIKs are armed with a 50 Calibre Browning Heavy Machine Gun (HMG) and a 7.62 mm General Purpose Machine Gun (GPMG).

(*Above*) British forces prepare to board a CH47 (HC2) Chinook helicopter from 7 Squadron RAF, at Lungi Airport, Sierra Leone, prior to deployment in country.

(*Right*) A CH47 (HC2) Chinook flown by aircrew from 7 Squadron RAF going low over the jungles of Sierra Leone. The pilots used such low-altitude flying tactics to minimise risk of the aircraft being shot down by rebel ground fire.

(*Above*) The view from the rebel base at Magbeni across the Rokel Creek to Gberi Bana, the rebels' headquarters, where the eleven British soldiers were held hostage.

(*Left*) The waterlogged landing zone (LZ) at the rebel base of Magbeni. When the heavily-laden men of 1 Para jumped from their hovering Chinook helicopter to attack the rebel base, many sunk into the swamp up to their necks.

(*Above*) Johnny Paul Koroma, (in white gown and cap), the ex-leader of the West Side Boys rebels, tried to negotiate the release of the British hostages ... and failed.

'Yaah! You British soldiers are *strong*. We go give you machetes and you go cut-cut it,' replied the grinning rebel. 'Then we all go have de football game. Is a good idea.'

Somewhere in the back of the drunken Ranger's mind he was wondering whether they should agree to cut the grass: if they could get their hands on some machetes, it might be a good thing. Turn on their captives, slice a few of them up, and make a run for it. It would be the Great Escape all over again, and all down to Ranger Gaunt's quick thinking. But then he had an image in his drunken mind of the eleven of them slaving under a blazing hot sun, cutting the football-pitch grass, with a bunch of hung-over rebel thugs standing guard with AK47s. No. Perhaps it wasn't such a good idea after all. Maybe he'd change the subject.

But what to talk about other than football? Beer and women, they were pretty safe bets too. Only trouble was, the rebels' idea of how to treat their women seemed to involve kidnapping teenage girls from the nearby villages, raping and forcibly 'marrying' them. So, it was difficult to know how to broach the subject of women. And as far as beer went, none of the rebels had so much as supped a decent pint in their lives. So that was pretty much a non-starter, too.

'If we're all going to play football, like, maybe we should all sort of be cutting the grass,' Ranger Gaunt ventured, 'to even out the workload, if youse know what I mean. And if we're going to be beating youse all at football, we'll need some beers to celebrate with afterwards, so we shall. Youse know anywhere we can get some good Guinness around these parts?'

The hostages were allowed to turn in early, around 8 p.m. Back in their room, the eleven men struggled to make their alcohol-befuddled minds take stock of what had just happened to them. But there was no way in which they could make any sense out of it. All they could think was that either Colonel GS had been bluffing, or that Major Martial's condemned man's last request had somehow managed to break the Colonel's murderous mood. But none of them could work out how the Major had been so sure that his ruse would work. It wasn't as if he'd been able to warn his men about what he was about to do, either. His request to Colonel GS for a dying man's last drink had just come completely out of the blue.

'Jezus, but that was a blinding move, sir,' Ranger Gaunt ventured, with an uncertain grin. He didn't know quite what else to say. He couldn't exactly come out with: *Thank fuck for saving my life, sir.*

Somehow, it would sound all wrong. 'But how did youse sort of know how yer man was going to react, sir?'

'Well . . . it was a bit of a gamble,' the Major replied, with a grin. 'But I couldn't see we had much choice, lad. It did seem to do the trick, though.'

'Bit of a gamble be fooked,' said the CSM, shaking his head. 'Stroke of fookin' genius, that's what it was, sir.'

As the noise of drunken revelry continued out on the veranda, the men tried to shake off the effects of the alcohol binge, and work on their escape plans. It was clear that they could be killed at any moment now, just on a whim. Concentrating on the idea of escape also gave the four Rangers in particular something positive to think about. And Lord knows they needed it. As they settled down to sleep, the hostages heard guards being placed outside their door as usual. But the rebels seemed too drunk and drugged up to start any fun and games with their machetes that night.

It was the night of day four by now, and with every day that passed, the men were getting weaker and weaker, which would make escape increasingly difficult. All they were getting to eat was the one plate of rice each evening. The previous night they had been lucky as there was a piece of blackened cassava to go with the rice – a tropical root vegetable that had been roasted over an open fire which felt and tasted like a lump of wood. And tonight there had been the leaves of a green plant pounded into a slimy, spicy paste. But it was never enough and there was little if any protein. Admittedly, the West Side Boys didn't seem to be faring much better; there just wasn't enough food to go round. But the British soldiers were on average bigger than their captors, and they could feel their muscles starting to waste away. A few more days of this, and they wouldn't have the strength to escape, even if a golden opportunity did present itself.

It wasn't until late on the morning of day five – a Tuesday – that most of the Boys surfaced from their drug- and alcohol-induced stupor. The British soldiers had no idea what time the rebel drinkers had finally got to bed. But Cambodia was slouched in his wicker chair out on the veranda, nursing what was obviously a major hangover. For some reason, last night's cocktail of palm wine, alcopops, hashish and crack cocaine (or whatever the white powder was) hadn't seemed to agree with him that well. For that matter, the hostages didn't exactly feel on top of the world, either.

Ranger MacGuire was struck by how bizarre the situation was

becoming. From execution time to an all-night drinking party in the space of a few hours. And now here they all were, hostages sitting around with their captors, and all of them suffering from stonking great hangovers. He thought about how the conversation would have developed, were he back home in Southern Ireland after an all-night drinking party there – and they weren't exactly rare where he came from.

'You'll not be feeling too good, then, Colonel Cambodia?' Ranger MacGuire imagined as his opening gambit, in his broad Southern Irish brogue. 'Ah, to be sure, the feckin' poteen around here's not a touch on what we have back at home, now is it there, Colonel? Sure, you'd best be getting a good Irish breakfast down you, some fried black puddin' and the like, then. Now let me tell you a thing, my brother knows this wee shebeen down Colnakarny way that serves the best poteen this side of Dublin, and to be sure you'll be needin' to come over and visit, so. He's sure to make you mighty welcome . . .'

But he guessed the Southern Irish hail-fellow-well-met approach wouldn't go down too well with Colonel Cambodia this hung-over morning. When the Colonel did momentarily rouse himself from his stupor and bark some orders to his men, he was looking and sounding very grumpy indeed. No, the Ranger told himself, the Colonel didn't seem as if he'd be overly receptive to a dose of Irish bonhomie. Eventually, Cambodia shook himself half awake and turned to speak to the British soldiers.

'Major, we will need you this afternoon for the hostage negotiations,' he said, in a flat, disinterested voice.

'Of course, Colonel,' the Major responded. 'You're having a face-to-face meeting, I take it, rather than radio negotiations?'

'Would I be asking you if I wasn't?' the Colonel snapped. The conversation was clearly not going to progress very far. 'We need you to do some direct talking for us. Kallay will brief you.'

The British soldiers left the Colonel to his own devices, and pretty soon he dozed off again. Not surprisingly, that afternoon's face-to-face hostage negotiation meeting was now foremost in their minds. If anyone could restart the stalled negotiations, Major Martial could. Around mid-afternoon the Major was told to get ready to go, and Captain Flaherty was ordered to go with him. The two officers set off, leaving the other men to spend an anxious afternoon on Cambodia's veranda, imagining all sorts of outcomes to the meeting.

After crossing back over the Rokel Creek, the Major and Captain

Flaherty were driven by Foday Kallay to the nearest UN–rebel check-point out on the main road. This was the site of the ongoing hostage-negotiation meetings. They were riding in the front cab of a 'technical' – a battered Toyota pickup, with a GPMG mounted on the open truck-back. Kallay and the British officers were in the front, and there were several guards clustered around the GPMG in the rear.

The trouble was that Kallay was such a bad driver and his men were so stoned that they kept falling out the back of the pickup – which was clearly a source of great hilarity to all concerned. Each time one of them did so, the technical would screech to a halt, the fallen rebel would pick himself up and dust himself down, amid peals of laughter, and then clamber back on board. And then they'd be off again, Kallay exhorting his men to hold on tight in the back there, as he slewed around bends and kangarooed over craters in the dirt road.

The two British officers couldn't help breaking into a bemused grin at the antics of the men in the back of the pickup. But Kallay warned them to show some respect, or he would order his men to kill the white soldiers and eat them. Over the coming days, the threat of being 'cooked and eaten' would be repeated so many times that it would begin to get a little predictable. It was one of the rebels' favourites. Somehow, they knew that cannibalism wasn't all too common back in Cork, Belfast or Liverpool – and so the prospect was a peculiarly unpleasant one for the British soldiers.

One of the rebel leaders, Colonel Mines, had a particularly nasty reputation for cannibalism. Only that morning, one of the Rangers had asked Sony why the West Side Boys kept banging on about cannibalism. *Was it really true that they ate people?* Unfortunately, it was, Sony had explained, the rebels believing that by eating someone they would take on that dead man's spirit and courage. Colonel Mines was renowned for cutting out the internal organs of his enemies and eating them. Usually he did so while the organs were still raw and warm, and as the wounded man lay dying on the battlefield. The young rebels who boasted to the British soldiers about eating their enemies, described how cooked human flesh tasted just like barbecued pork, only less fatty and more tender.

By late afternoon, Major Martial and Captain Flaherty had returned from the hostage meeting, but with little news to report. They had been taken to the UN–West Side Boys' checkpoint, out on the Benguema–Masiaka road. The CO of the Royal Irish Regiment, Lieutenant Colonel Simon Fordham, had been at the meeting, as had a number of other senior Royal Irish officers. The British side of the negotiations was being handled by two specialist hostage negotiators from the Metropolitan Police, who had flown out from London. Major Martial filled his men in on the details.

'The two Met officers had a couple of other men with them, but I'm not sure exactly who they were. They didn't introduce themselves as such, just first names, and they were dressed in civvies. So, probably Special Forces types is my guess. Anyhow, it's a high-level negotiating team, lads, you mark my words. These guys are specialists, experts, flown out from London, so they're pulling out all the stops to get us out of here. Of course, Kallay was there, and Cambodia, and a load of their goons all tooled up with weapons. But the British team were making a show of being unarmed. Taking the non-confrontational approach, like we used in Kosovo.'

The Major left it unsaid that the men of the British negotiating team were brave indeed, to walk into the West Side Boys' territory with no weapons. But all his men really wanted to know was what terms had been discussed for their release. *What deal is being negotiated, and what is the timescale?* the Rangers were thinking. *When are we getting the hell out of here?*

'Well, the Captain and I weren't actually allowed to say that much,' the Major continued, picking up on the Rangers' obvious concern. 'It was more like we'd been taken along as a proof-of-life exercise. And in terms of the actual negotiations, I'm afraid it's not really that simple, lads. The West Side Boys are still after getting a renegotiation of this Lome peace accord and, as you know, that's no easy thing. It'd involve the Sierra Leonean government agreeing to play ball, and I just don't think they're going to do that. If they did, it would mean giving in to the demands of a terrorist group. They just can't do that.'

'So basically, sir, you're saying we're fooked?' CSM Head interrupted. ''Cause that's what it sounds like to me.'

'No, Sergeant Major, I am not,' the Major replied, somewhat irritably. 'But what I am saying is that we may need to brush up on our escape plans a little. We can't *rely* on the negotiators getting us out of here, that's all. And even if we *could*, we should still be ready to take any escape opportunity that presents itself. That's just standard operating procedure in a situation like this, plain and simple.'

'But are youse saying there's nothing these bastards sort of want that they can't easily be given, sir – so as to help get us out of here?' Ranger Gaunt asked, in bewilderment. 'I mean, like engines or boats or even flamin' guns, sir? I thought they was after all that sort of shite, sir, if you know what I mean?'

'They are, lad. And they'll be getting it, don't you worry,' the Major reassured the Ranger. 'Now they've said they want a satphone, too. That's their most recent demand. Apparently, it's Cambodia's idea, and they want to use it so they can talk to the BBC, put their side of the story across if you like. They'll be getting all of that in the next few days.'

'So, won't that sort of get us somewhere, sir?' the Ranger pressed. 'I mean, sure as hell we'll be getting something in return, sir.'

'Sure as hell we will, Ranger,' the Major replied. 'We're talking about some hostage releases in exchange. But we don't *rely* on it, that's all I'm saying. If there's ever a chance to escape, lad, we take it. We're British soldiers, remember. Escape and evade – that's our training. I don't trust these bastards as far as I can throw them, that's all.'

'Aye. Youse can say that again, sir,' Ranger Rowell growled.

'And one other thing,' the Major continued, lowering his voice to a whisper, 'on the issue of escape, or rather *rescue*. Now don't go getting your hopes up too much, but there is some good news. Don't ask me how, but we managed to pass the map of this place across to our side – the one we drew up showing all the rebel defences, the terrain of the village and our position. It's now in the hands of the British negotiating team. If there is to be any rescue attempt, it'll be damn useful to them, you mark my words.'

The Major's news managed to lift the men's spirits a little: getting the map smuggled out was a small but significant victory over their captors. But his biggest concern now was one that Major Martial didn't feel able to share with the rest of his men, for fear of a collapse in their morale – which so far was holding up remarkably well. As far as he could tell, the West Side Boys' demand for a satphone signalled a change of strategy on their part. It meant that they were seeking to escalate the situation, by publicising their demands internationally. And you could bet your bottom dollar that they weren't going to be talking to the BBC about their demands for boats, engines and guns. The satphone was so they could put their crazed political demands out on the BBC. *Release Colonel Bomblast and our other glorious rebel leaders from prison! Put them into parliament! And Foday Kallay for President!* That sort of propagandist shite. Oh, and down with the imperial, colonialistic warmongering British invaders at the same time.

This was not a good scenario. It meant that the West Side Boys' leaders were digging their heels in. It meant that the political dimension, the real stumbling block to any successful hostage negotiations, wasn't going to go away. And it meant that far from being a purely military matter – one to be patiently negotiated away between Her Majesty's Armed Forces and the West Side Boys – it was now no longer contained in that way. Once the satphone was delivered – and as long as the West Side Boys could work our how to operate it – they'd have a direct line to the international media. And that meant a direct line to the British public and thence to the British government. It was either a very clever or a very stupid move by the West Side Boys, and the Major just wasn't quite sure which. Either way, it was worrying news.

But if the satphone *was* delivered to the rebels – and the Major had every reason to believe that it would be – then that would mean that at least some of his men would be getting released in return. Which meant he had to prepare them for that eventuality. By now, the men had established a de facto 'Chinese parliament' for collective decision-making. Generally, when they were put in their dingy room each night, the men would gather in the best circle they could make in such cramped conditions, and an open discussion would be held over any issues at hand. It might be options for escape, the best tactics for keeping their morale up or, as in this case, hostage releases. In this way, everyone could get to have their say.

At first, the Rangers had found it strange to be sitting around and openly discussing such things with their CO, something that in normal circumstances would never have happened in the British Army. Information was normally given out on a need-to-know basis only. The main job of the junior ranks was to be on guard, that being the chief task of a member of Rifle Platoon when on duty. The way the commanding officers saw it, the junior ranks should be alert at all times, no matter what information they had to hand. And too much sensitive information was seen as being dangerous; the less the junior ranks knew about overall British military strategy and objectives in the region, the better. What they didn't know they couldn't tell.

But now things were very different. As dusk fell over the village of Gberi Bana, the Major called his men together for one of these 'heads up' sessions. The aim of the negotiating team was to get all the patrol members released unharmed, the Major explained. But at the same time, they'd want to reach a settlement that didn't make too many concessions to their rebel captors. And there was no guaranteeing that the patrol members would be released all together. In fact, it was far more likely that they'd be released in dribs and drabs, as the British negotiators pressed for more concessions from the West Side Boys and they in turn sought more concessions from the British. That was the name of the game. So if the satphone was given over to the rebels, some, *but not all*, of them would very likely be going free. It was best to decide now who would be the first men to be released.

'It seems to me that as I got you into this bloody mess in the first place,' the Major continued, 'it's my job to get you out again. So, I'll be staying until the very last man. But, if these bastards offer, say, two or three of us to go free, we need to be sure who the first ones are going to be. It seems to me that it should be our priority to get the junior ranks out first. But I'd like to hear what the rest of you have to say.'

'Bloody A, sir,' replied Ranger Gaunt, enthusiastically. 'Sounds dead on to me, like.'

'Don't want to stay here a second longer than I have to with these bastards,' another added.

'Just give me the nod and I'm gone, sir,' said a third.

'Typical fookin' reaction I'd expect from you fookers,' the CSM growled. 'Any chance to get out of here and you'll be like rats up a bloody drainpipe.'

'Well, seeing as how you're enjoying it so much, Sarge, wouldn't want to deprive youse of the crack of staying, then,' one of the Rangers retorted.

'Got yer book to write an' all, Sarge.'

'Aye, Sarge. Think of all the chapters. You know – every day youse stay here is another few pages, sure it is.'

'Ah, piss off, the bleedin' lot of you. Fookin' tell you what, lads, no problem guessing what parts you'll all be playing when I get to write it, now is there? Buggered off at the first bloody opportunity, they did.'

'I take it that's settled, then,' the Major interjected, bringing them all back to the subject in hand. 'Junior ranks first and then as follows. But I don't want you getting your hopes up too much. They'll not be releasing many of us for that satphone, of that much we can be certain. And who knows where the negotiations will go after that. But like I said, whatever happens, I'll be the last man out. None of you would be in this mess if it wasn't for my decision back there on the road.'

There was a moment's awkward silence, broken finally by Sergeant Smith. 'Look, sir. Respectfully and all that sort of stuff, but that's nonsense.' The Sergeant was quiet and serious most of the time, and considered a man of few words. But when he did speak up, all the men took notice. 'None of us blame you for what happened. We're all responsible. We're all in this together and we're going to have to make sure we get through this together. At least, that's the way I see things.'

'Thanks, Sergeant,' the Major replied, quietly. 'And get through it we will, of that I am absolutely bloody certain.'

And so it had been decided, the junior ranks would be the first to go free. It is a long-standing British military tradition that in such circumstances, the lowest ranks (invariably also the youngest) should be released first. That tradition is partly steeped in the military's sense of honour and fairness, and of the officers' role and responsibility as the leader of his men. But there is also a very practical side to it. In a situation such as this, if all the officers left first, the command and control structure, and hence the morale of the remaining troops, would almost certainly collapse. If the junior ranks were left behind, they would rightly feel abandoned and would probably crack under the strain. Put bluntly, there was no way that the four Rangers would have the ability, experience or training to stand their own against the West Side Boys' leaders.

Later that evening, the hostages sat around on Cambodia's veranda listening to the BBC World Service, and another report came on the radio about the Sierra Leone hostage crisis. 'The hostage negotiations are said to be well underway,' intoned the BBC reporter's voice, 'and hopes are now high for all the hostages to be released.' *Well, that's feckin' news to us*, the British soldiers were thinking to themselves. As the Major had made clear, the best they could hope would be for one or two of them to be released in return for the satphone. The West Side Boys would hold on to the majority of them, as bargaining chips to secure their main demands. And as all the men knew, there was little, if any, hope of the British forces meeting those demands.

Around 10 p.m. the eleven men were put back in their room and locked in for the night. But before they dropped off to sleep, they discussed whether the BBC might be being deliberately fed a line. The British negotiating team would be well aware how much attention the rebel leaders would be paying to the BBC reports. The Met negotiators would know that they had to keep a sense of momentum going, a feeling of moving forward, a belief that all was close to being resolved. And the BBC was certain to be seen a useful asset in helping them communicate that message. The trouble was, from where the hostages were sitting, the BBC's report sounded way off the mark. Hopes were high for all of them to be released? As far as the hostages were concerned, nothing could be further from the truth.

Unless they were rescued, the only way that they could see themselves getting out of there anytime soon would be in body bags.

9

THIS MEANS WAR

In the intervals between battles, the warrior rests. But he does not commit the capital sin of Sloth, because he knows where that can lead – to the warm monotony of Sunday afternoons when time simply passes. The warrior calls this 'the peace of the cemetery'. A warrior rests and laughs. But he is always alert.

– Paulo Coelho, *Manual of the Warrior of Light*

THE first thing Cockney Jimmy decided to do, once he had some time on his hands at Waterloo Camp, was to check out the stores tent. Ducking through the canvas doorway, his eyes lit up when he spotted a pile of MREs lying in one corner. These are US Army 'meals ready to eat'. But British soldiers have long known them as 'meals rejected by Ethiopians'. Which isn't exactly fair, because the US ration packs are no worse than British ones, and a damn sight better than the Germans', which seemed to contain nothing but chunks of boiled sausage meat congealed in fat, with names like 'fatwurst' or 'lardfurter'. But there it was, the name had stuck, and Meals Rejected by Ethiopians it was.

Certainly, Jimmy's joy at seeing the MREs had nothing to do with their culinary attributes. *Oh no. Bugger that.* Jimmy wasn't interested in eating them. Only, with a little bit of British ingenuity plus a big dollop of SAS lateral thinking, Jimmy and his mates had discovered what you could turn them into. *Bombs.* The MREs made very passable bombs. Now they could have some real fun with the Shakyboats, as the SAS men called their SBS colleagues (rivals, more like). The CB-MRE-B (Coke-bottle meals-ready-to-eat bomb), the lads had called it, the first time they'd made their historic discovery.

It was really the late, great Yokel who'd made the discovery, although they'd all claimed the credit for it afterwards. Brian was the Yokel's real name, though he never let on unless he had to, and his thick Somerset accent had been the cause of much hilarity among the Regiment. At the time, the Yokel – a fellow Boat Troop member – had been Jimmy's best mate, but he'd since been invalided out of the Regiment. Jimmy cast his mind back to the time they had first deployed that experimental CB-MRE-B. It had been something of a life-changing experience for him and the other lads.

They'd been on a combined training op in the US, hosted by the US Special Forces (SEALs and Delta Force). Their base had been out in some remote back end of beyond, and boredom had soon started to get the better of the British soldiers. One afternoon, the Yokel had found himself alone in Boat Troop's tent messing about with a box of MREs. Logic was telling him that there had to be some way to get one hell of a lot of fun out of these self-heating meals. There just had to be. They were a simple enough concept: rip open the foil wrapping of a vacuum-packed ration of chilli con carne or Homey Pie, add some cold water, leave to infuse for five minutes or so, and bingo! You had a steaming hot meal. You were then supposed to plunge in a spoon and start eating, only that part was best avoided.

The British Army didn't bother with such niceties, thank God. You either heated your food up over a standard stove, or, in situations where opsec precluded it, you ate your food cold. No big deal. With the self-heating meals, there was obviously some sort of serious chemical reaction that went down between the water and the food, the Yokel figured. God only knew what the stuff did to your stomach. Anyway, the self-heating process gave off a gas that smelled to the Yokel like a badly drained silage pit. Not nice. But a chemical reaction that produced gases also produced heat and pressure, that sort of thing, the Yokel reasoned. *Yeah.* Gases given off meant *pressure*, and pressure meant maybe the opportunity for an *explosion*. What would happen, the Yokel wondered, if the self-heating happened inside some sort of closed container, rather than an open foil bag? *Aha! Now, there was a thought.*

He cast his eye around the tent. Among the discarded socks and other assorted bits of kit, the Yokel spotted an almost empty plastic Coke bottle. Coke? Water? What's the difference, the Yokel mused. Hardly able to contain his excitement, he grabbed the bottle and ripped the top off a self-heating pack of Homey Pie. What the heck did they put in Homey Pie? he wondered, as he used his fingers to stuff the contents of the ration pack down through the neck of the Coke bottle. Approximately one-third of the Homey Pie ended up scattered all around him in the tent, but what the heck, no new invention was ever perfect, was it?

The Yokel lifted up the bottle to take a look. Through the weirdly distorting prism of the curved plastic side, he could see that interesting things were happening inside. The Homey Pie mix had hit the Coke, whereupon it fizzed and popped and gurgled for a few seconds, before wisps of gas started to snake up from the gloopy mixture in the bottom of the bottle. Fuckin' A! Quick, on with the fuckin' lid, the Yokel told himself.

A frantic scrabble around the floor and a few seconds of mad panic thinking he'd lost the lid, and the Yokel finally had it on and screwed down tight. Then he stuck his head out of the front flap of the tent to choose his victim. Aha! Just across the way, there was fuckin' Air Troop's tent. Of the four troops in D Squadron he obviously wasn't going to attack his own. And of the other three, Air Troop made the perfect target. Captain Dan Temper's Air Troop; thought they were a cut above the rest, that's what they did. Bunch of elitist bastards was what the Yokel thought of the Air Troop lads. *They'd do nicely*.

The Yokel crept carefully across the clearing, and as he approached Air Troop's tent, he could hear the sound of muffled conversation coming from inside. Taking great care not to make any noise, he carefully placed the bottle on the grass right next to the tent. Fuckin' 'ell, the Yokel thought to himself as he did so, the plastic was already starting to get too hot to handle.

Back inside his own tent and hardly able to contain his excitement, the Yokel kept a careful lookout. He checked his watch. He'd need to know the exact time from deployment to detonation for future reference purposes. A minute passed. Then another. Surely the bottle must be about to blow? The Yokel was certain he could see the sides bulging out under the pressure from within. What, he wondered, was Air Troop's reaction going to be? Would they come piling out of their tent, MP5 machine guns at the ready, about to take out whichever terrorist bastards had managed to infiltrate and bomb the US camp? He bloody well hoped so.

Suddenly, there was an almighty explosion and shards of plastic Coke bottle went flying in all directions, closely followed by gloops of steaming hot Coke 'n' Homey Pie – most of it, it had to be said, splattering all over the side of Air Troop's tent. Fuckin A! the Yokel roared inside his head. FUCKIN' A. RESULT.

In a split second, men were piling out the front flap of Air Troop's tent, and springing to their feet in combat-ready poses. There was a mixture of shock, anger and raw aggression written across their faces. And yes, a couple of them had even remembered to grab their MP5s. The Yokel wasn't going to take any prisoners – he just knew he was going to rip the piss out of them mercilessly after it was all over.

The minds of the ambushed men were racing. Who the fuck could have managed to attack them here, in the middle of the US base? The American camp was like Fort Knox, only without the gold bullion. But as they scanned around them, there was no obvious sign of a contact or any other sort of trouble. And then one of the lads noticed the Yokel, head stuck out of his tent watching them – and it was obvious that the Yokel bastard was pissing himself laughing.

'What the fuck . . . ?!' a couple of the Air Troop lads started.

But all they got in reply was increased hilarity from the Yokel, who was laughing fit to burst.

'Fuck you, Yokel, you childish fuckin' git!' one of them yelled across, half in anger, half in relief. 'You could've given us all an fuckin' heart attack.'

'Yeh. Fuck you, you fuckin' carrot cruncher.'

'What's the fuckin' crack, you big, thick Yokel bastard?'

'Well . . . I cain't read and I cain't write, but that don't really matter,' the Yokel started to sing, ''cause I come from Zummerzet and I can drive a tratter.'

It was the Yokel's signature tune, and they'd heard it a thousand times before. That big, thick Yokel bastard had obviously set them up, *but how?* They spun round to inspect the damage to their tent. All they could find were globs of a thick, gloopy substance plastered all over it. The smell test proved it to be . . . fuckin' Homey Pie. What the fuck was Homey Pie doing splattered all over their tent? Best they work out what, and pretty smartish too, otherwise they'd look even more stupid than they did already. One of the men then spotted the circular, black base of a Coke bottle lying exactly where the Yokel had placed it. There was a rosette of shattered plastic still adhering to the surface of it. First, an almighty bang, then Homey Pie splattered every-where, and now a shattered Coke bottle. *What the fuck did it all mean?* Well, it had to be a fuckin' home-made bomb of some sorts, that much was clear.

'Thick as pigshit and twice as smelly, that's what they say about you Dorset folks, isn't it, mate?' an Air Troop lad yelled over.

'Dorset-born, Dorset-bred, strong in the arm, thick in the 'ead, innit, Yokel, you dozy fucker?'

'Better watch your bloody back, you dumb Worzel bastard. We'll be having some real fun and games with you from now on, like.'

'Fuckin' A. War is fuckin' declared, mate, make no mistake about it.'

''Tis Zummerzet where I come from, not Dorset,' the Yokel threw back at them, grinning. 'Get it right, won't you? Come on then, my zonners, bring it on, bring it on. Let's see what you airborne men'r made of.'

The men of Air Troop knew that however good their insults had been, the laugh was on them this time. OK. It was time to go to war. Time to grab a few Coke bottles and some MREs and do some bomb-building of their own.

'Crafty fucker, that Yokel,' one of them commented, as they ducked back inside their tent. 'Never have believed he spent all his childhood skiving off school and driving a fuckin' tractor.'

For several days thence, the men of D Squadron had waged total, relentless war on each other. But eventually, it had all boiled down to how many times they could roll back from the camp bar pissed as farts, launch a CB-MRE-B attack on the rival troop's tent, and still find it hilariously, uproariously funny. A surprisingly large number of times as it turned out, especially with the amounts of beer Cockney Jimmy, the Scottish Monster and the Yokel managed to put away together. But like all good things, the war did finally have to come to an end. And once all the troops had sussed out the technology, then they had a case of MAD (mutually assured destruction) on their hands. At which stage there was only one thing for it. It was time to go to war against the Americans.

There were numerous advantages to this. For one thing, the Americans didn't have the bomb yet. It was such a rare delight for the men of D Squadron, for once to feel technologically superior to their American allies. Sure, the Americans had heard the odd explosion drifting over from the British side of the camp. And sure, one or two had been curious, even asking their British buddies what the hell was going on over there. But they'd yet to suss the *technology*. And for another thing, the British would have the advantage of surprise. The Americans just weren't expecting to be attacked. It would be Pearl Harbor all over again, only this time with the added advantage of modern technology.

Once again, it was the Yokel, Jimmy and their mates from the Brave and the Fearless – Boat Troop – who were to spearhead the new attack.

And on the first few occasions they did so, it proved even funnier than it had done attacking their own men. Somehow, the Americans just didn't get it. They just didn't find being woken in the middle of the night by a bunch of drunken Brits blowing them up with a Coke-bottle MRE bomb the remotest bit funny. In fact, they found it distinctly enraging. And the angrier the Americans got, the funnier it all became to the D Squadron lads.

It wasn't long before an international incident was in the offing, and the Yokel and Jimmy found themselves hauled before the squadron OC. Over the years that they'd served together, Cockney Jimmy – usually a mouthy bugger at the best of times – had learned that when in the Yokel's company and in trouble, it was best to let him do the talking. Whichever way he cut it, he was always bound to have a good story up his sleeve.

'Now, don't you worry, Cockney, me old bugger,' the Yokel had confided, as they strolled across to the OC's tent. 'I got it all squared away in me 'ead, like. You let me do the talkin', you.'

'Now, I've been having some unusual complaints from your American colleagues,' the OC began, somewhat bemusedly, after greeting the two men. 'They're saying that you keep trying to blow them up. Your two names in particular keep coming up and they say you're both quite mad. It's not good for opsec, either, all these explosions going off. So, tell me, lads, just what exactly has been gong on?'

'We 'aven't been jus' *tryin'* to blow them up. We *'ave* been blowin' them up, you,' the Yokel began, launching into an outraged defence of his CB-MRE-B campaign. Whenever he was put on the spot by his OC, the Yokel would adopt the strongest possible rural accent. Largely, that meant attaching a 'you' to the end of each and every phrase. It was a deliberate defence mechanism he used whenever faced with 'posh wankers' as he called the officers, regardless of how they spoke.

'We was just spuddling about, OC, and we thought we'd 'ave a little test of base security, you,' the Yokel continued. 'Couple of 'armless 'ome-made explosions, s'all t'was, you. But 'fernal security on this base leaves summat to be desired, OC. Bain't never seen nothing like it, you. Give us 'Ereford any day. Least a man feels safer 'n houses back there, you.'

'Are you trying to tell me that you've been deliberately probing the American base's security, is that it?' the OC said, sceptically.

'Cain't never be too careful, OC. Not with 'fernal terrorists an' all around and about every which way. Just 'cause we're SF don't mean we can get up on our pedalstool, on our 'igh 'orse, like, does it, you?

'Cause you never know before 'til after, do you, OC? You never know before 'til after. We bain't no more unvulnerable than the next sod, are we, you? One moment you're just spuddling about, the next –'

'Look, lads, I strongly suspect you're just having a laugh on our American cousins,' the OC cut in, before the Yokel could launch into an even longer justification of what they'd been up to. 'And I sort of know where you're coming from here. They do often seem to have a certain sense-of-humour failure, don't they? But best if it stops, eh? After all, we are their guests and they are out closest allies. Not too sensible to keep blowing them up, now is it?'

'Fair 'nough, OC. Cain't say fairer 'n that, can he?' said the Yokel, turning to Jimmy for approval.

'Na, mate,' Jimmy nodded in agreement. He'd let the Yokel do all the talking, and so far he'd done a sterling job of it. 'Reckon we'd better stop tryin' to blow the fakin' Septics up then, innit, sir.'

'Sorry? Septics? Oh yes. Yank – Septic Tank. Course it is. Silly of me not to remember,' the OC muttered. 'Well – good on you, lads, anyway. Oh, and if you do have any more worries about base security,' he added, raising one eyebrow, 'you'd best bring them to me first, eh?'

'Right. 'Tis time to go bloody covert,' the Yokel remarked, as the two men made their way back to Boat Troop's tent. 'Covert *and* chemical.'

'What you fakin' on about, mate?' Jimmy asked.

'No point talkin' 'bout it, is there? I'll bloody show you,' the Yokel replied, with a grin. 'Oh. Sorry. Forgot to put a "you" on the end of that. 'I'll bloody show you, *you*. 'Tis time for the CB-MRE-B Mark II.'

Back at their tent, the Yokel started to build another Coke-bottle bomb. The only difference was that this time, once he'd stuffed some chilli con carne into the bottle, he proceeded to urinate on to it. Once he'd finished relieving himself, he held up the fizzing, yellowish-brown concoction for general Boat Troop appraisal.

'Good 'nuff for a country job, as we say down my way,' the Yokel remarked, staring at the evil-looking, frothy liquid.

'You aren't fakin' serious, mate?' Jimmy asked, grinning. 'That's fakin' disgustin'. Only a dirty Yokel pigshit farmin' type like you could ever 'ave thought of anything so fakin' 'orrible.'

''Tis a proper job, that is,' the Yokel replied, indignantly. 'Like I said, *covert and chemical*. That'll teach those septic Yank fuckers to go grassing us up.'

'If you're going to use fakin' cockney rhyming slang, at least use it fakin' properly,' Jimmy interjected, shaking his head. 'It's fakin' Yank

– Septic Tank – Septic. You just call 'em Septics, all right? Anyway, we did tell the OC we'd stop, innit?'

'Slowly, slowly, catchy monkey,' the Yokel replied, grinning. 'Wrong 'tis to grass on your fellow soldier, just over a couple of innocent pranks. Everyone knows that, even the septic tanks. Anyways, like I said, chemical and *covert*. Cain't say it was us 'til they catch us at it, can they?'

Once the new bomb had been successfully tested out the back of the camp, the Yokel put his plan to Cockney Jimmy, the Scottish Monster and the rest of the troop. There was a patch of bush close by the American side of the camp that they'd spotted earlier. That night, after a good session at the bar of course, they'd set up an OP in those bushes. Once their American cousins were safely tucked up in bed, they'd launch a covert CB-MRE-B Mark II attack. They'd leave the bottle bomb – now chemically weaponised – outside the nearest tent, retreat back to their OP, and await the results. The Americans would never know what hit them, or who was responsible.

'Who d'ye want to hit with it, then, laddie?' the Scottish Monster asked, somewhat sceptically. 'The SEALs or the DF boys?'

'Delta. Gotta be. I'm sure they're the buggers who grassed us up to the OC. Get more laughs from a bunch of Somerset best-pedigree growlers, than you would with that lot of up-tight fuckers.'

'Mate, what the shite's a Somerset best-pedigree growler when it's at home, mate?' the Kiwi asked.

'What the 'ell for d'you have to put "mate" on the start and end of every sentence for, Kiwi?' the Yokel asked, incredulously. 'Anyways, 'tis a pig. Now, I know you don't 'ave many of 'em in New Zealand. More sheep 'n people so I've 'eard. Sounds like bloody paradise to me, so it does. Spent 'alf my adolescence shaggin' 'em, sheep I mean, not pigs. But growlers is pigs, Kiwi, pigs what maketh bacon. You know, 'tis the stuff I catch you stuffin' down your fat Antipodean gullet every morning.'

Later, after a good few beers, the men of Boat Troop went into action. Only trouble was, they were so drunk that they didn't have a hope in hell of keeping covert. In fact, they were so pissed that they didn't even realise they were too pissed to keep quiet – and went ahead with the attack anyway. Dead on cue, the SAS's version of the dirty bomb went off, and half a dozen Delta men came tumbling out of their dripping tent, torn from sleep by the shock of the explosion. Of course, it didn't take them long to work out that it was the mad

Brits at their 'fucked-up shite' again. But what the Delta guys couldn't for the life of them figure out was how the Brits seemed never to tire of the same joke.

This time, however, the *smell* was different. *Where were the fucking Limey bastards who had done this?* They weren't usually hard to spot. Often as not, they'd find the so-called crack British soldiers rolling around on the grass nearby like a bunch of schoolkids, laughing fit to burst and often too drunk to stand. Pumped up with adrenalin and aggression, the Delta boys were in no mood to mess around. Hell, they took their job seriously and they needed their kip. Sometimes, they just couldn't believe that these guys really were the SAS, supposedly Britain's finest. It didn't take them long to work out where the Boat Troop OP was. The noise of the troop's drunken hilarity carried clearly across to them on the still night air. A couple of the Delta boys stomped across to have it out with them.

'Guess yu still finding it funny, huh?' one of them drawled, as they approached the bushes where the Boat Troop boys were doing a very bad job of hiding. 'Jus' gets funnier every time, don't it, Brit?'

The only response the Delta trooper got was a chorus of barely suppressed sniggers from the bushes.

'Go away,' the Yokel finally managed to slur back at them. 'We're in a secret OP. You're not s'posed to be able to see us.'

'Fuckin' so-called professional soldiers or what?' the other Delta man fumed, turning and shaking his head at his mate. 'Fuckin' Britain's best. Shi-ite. C'mon, Larry, let's sack it.'

'Hold on there just a second, Dwayne,' the other Delta man said, approaching closer to the bushes. 'Y'all know, you Brits – like, this just ain't funny no more. An', like, y'know, we ain't gonna go on takin' this shit from y'all no more.'

At this, the men in the bushes erupted into spasms of strangled laughter. Finally, Cockney Jimmy managed a choking reply.

'It ain't shit,' he choked. 'It's piss, mate. It's the CB-MRE-B Mk II. Awesome bit of kit, innit, mate? Chemically weaponised an' all, it is. Bit of a mouthful I admit, the name. But fakin' awesome all the same, mate.'

'I ain't no fuckin' mate of y'all, Brit,' the Delta man growled, threateningly, kicking some dirt in the general direction of the uproar coming from the bushes. 'Fuckin' disgustin', that's what y'all are.'

'C'mon, Larry, best we leave these fuckin' idyuts to sort their own shite out,' Dwayne said. Probably had the whole place booby-trapped with shit bombs or something, for all he knew. 'Ain't nothing we can do 'bout it tonight. They just ain't *normal*.'

So that was how the CB-MRE-B Marks I and II had been discovered and first deployed. A few days later, the Yokel, Jimmy, the Scottish Monster, the Kiwi, and some of the other lads had been invited to a wedding reception off the US base. All the men were doing beers and the barbie outside in the garden, and the fresh-faced American girls in frilly summer frocks were chatting politely indoors. Then, quite suddenly, there was a bout of hysterical screaming from inside the house. The D Squadron lads had raced in only to find the source of the disturbance was, of course, one of their own. In the living room, they discovered that a young girl had fainted, and was now on the sofa being revived and comforted by two of her girlfriends. And propped up in the corner of the kitchen behind them was the Big Scottish Monster, with blood pouring out of his nostrils and all down the front of his white shirt.

'Fookin' awesome, laddies,' the Monster had roared, as they appeared at the kitchen doorway. 'Fookin' snortin' fookin' Vladimir vodka, *comrades*. Come and fookin' try some.'

With that, he'd slopped a shot of vodka into a glass, and proceeded to slurp the whole lot up his big bloody Scottish nose. At this, the Yokel, Cockney Jimmy, the Kiwi and the other D Squadron lads had collapsed in a heap of laughter, as the Monster had carried on with his outrageous antics.

'Shi-ite. You guys are fuckin' crazy,' one of the American soldiers had interrupted, clearly appalled, and directing his anger towards the Scottish Monster. 'You can't do that at someone's *wedding* party. It's real *fucked up*. And Jesus, you're *worse*,' he continued, turning on the Yokel and the rest of the D Squadron lads. 'You're actually finding it *funny*.'

After that, a stiff report had gone back to D Squadron's boss from the American base commander. He was not best pleased.

But Jimmy had never forgotten what a crack they'd had with those Coke-bottle bombs. Now, stuffing a couple of the US ration packs inside a plastic carrier bag he'd found kicking around the floor of the stores tent, he emerged through the low doorway trying not to look too pleased with himself. He had a quick check around Waterloo Camp, to make sure that he wasn't being watched – he didn't want any of the other troops to clock what he was up to. No telling whom he might choose as his first victim.

By rights, it should be the Shakyboats. But part of him said that that was just too damn predictable. It was what the other lads would expect of him – to start a war with the SBS. And if there was one thing Jimmy didn't like, it was doing the expected. Maybe he should have a go at Air Troop again – revive the old enmity as it were? They'd been getting a bit above themselves again recently. That Captain Dan bloody Temper in particular. God's gift he thought he was. But just then Jimmy was hit by a blinding flash of inspiration. *Hold on a minute*, he thought. *What about the fakin' Paras?* They were scheduled to arrive in Waterloo Camp any time now, fresh on the scene. Then it'd be Special Forces against the green army. That decided it, then. Once the Paras had arrived and had a few hours to settle in, they would be his target.

What a crack that would be – to put a rocket up some of those young lads.

LOTTERY OF FREEDOM

I am constantly surprised by the number of people who come up to me and ask that Britain recolonise Sierra Leone.
– Brigadier David Richards, Commander of British Forces in Sierra Leone

DAY six of the hostage crisis was a Wednesday, and Captain Flaherty and Major Martial were dragged off to a second face-to-face hostage-negotiation meeting. Around 5 p.m., they returned with news that the West Side Boys had been given the satphone that they had demanded. At first there had been some confusion, as the satphone appeared to be broken. Luckily, the Met negotiators had brought a spare with them, and the West Side Boys had left happily with that one.

Both Foday Kallay and Cambodia had been over the moon at getting the satphone, Captain Flaherty explained. In fact, the two rebel leaders were so pleased at the end of the hostage-negotiation meeting, that they had driven across to visit the nearby Jordanian UN base. As they had tucked into a pleasant lunch with the Jordanian officers, they had left the British officers sitting outside in the vehicle. On the return journey to Gberi Bana, the rebel leaders had agreed that five hostages could go free. Major Martial had tried to push his advantage, and convince the rebel leaders to let all of them go free. But Cambodia, in particular, was adamant that it was five only, and that five in return for a satphone was a damn good deal.

Cambodia had left it up to the hostages themselves to choose which five would go. And Major Martial had immediately argued that Corporal Mousa should be among the five to be released.

'Look, Colonel, I think the priority has to be to get Corporal Mousa released,' he had told him. 'He's in a very bad condition. You keep him in the pit much longer and he's a dead man. Let him be released among the five men, Colonel. Let us get him to see a doctor and then to hospital. That's my main request.'

'Aaah, you should just forget about him, Major. Why do you always worry so about Mousa?' Colonel Cambodia had replied. 'All that we are doing is between us and you. You just need to forget about him.'

'Sorry, Colonel, but it's no deal,' the Major had responded. 'Corporal Mousa is one of the men under my command and I am responsible for him. I have to know that he is OK. And I believe he is very unwell and should be among the first men to go free.'

'Well, Major, you should stop all this worrying.' Cambodia had insisted. 'He's our brother. We'll treat him like a brother. And we have our own doctor here. We'll get him looked at by our doctor in the hospital house. Don't worry. But I'm afraid, Major, Mousa has to stay. Any of your other men can go free, but not him.'

As soon as Major Martial had delivered his news, that five of them were being released, the four Rangers had felt their hearts leap. There were four of them. That meant freedom! Fucking FREEDOM at long last! The Rangers jumped to their feet, all but delirious with joy and relief at the news. Fuckin A! They were getting out of there! Fuck the West Side Boys! Fuck Cambodia and Savage and the whole stinking lot of bastards. Fuck the pit. Fuck the whole insane, murderous bunch of rapists and child-killing motherfucking bastards! They were going FREE! They were getting OUT of there. They were heading HOME. After the four of them, the next most junior rank would be one of the Corporals – either Mackenzie, Ryan or Sampson (whoever had served the shortest time).

'So which of the Corporals gets to go, too, sir?' Ranger Gaunt asked excitedly, as the four of them scrabbled to get their kit together. But they were all stopped dead in their tracks by Major Martial's reply.

'Hang on a minute, lads. Take it easy. You'd best stop what you're doing,' the Major said, quietly, evenly. With a sick, sinking feeling in their stomachs, the four Rangers turned to face him. 'Look. There's been a change of plan,' he continued. 'I'm sorry, but there's five married men here. Men with wives and kids and families back at home. And these bastards have said that only five can go. So, I've decided it's best that it's the five married men. Sorry, lads. But you'll be staying. It's a tough call, and I don't like having to make it, but there it is.'

The Rangers just couldn't believe their ears. Despite all their previous discussions, the Chinese parliament, the Major's insistence that the junior ranks should go out first, despite all the promises, he had changed his bloody mind. They had *trusted* the Major. Just a few days earlier they had sat around and made a deal together as to who should go free: *the most junior ranks first.* He couldn't just fuck with their heads like this.

'What the feck! No way, sir, is that fair . . .'

'Sir, youse it was who said it was the juniors . . .'

'We've all of us got families, sir . . .'

'I'm as good as engaged to my girl, back in Belfast, sir. What about her . . .?'

'Quit bitching the lot of you!' the CSM growled, butting in. 'You're a fookin' shower. You heard what the Major said. Hostages you may be, but you're still soldiers in the fookin' British Army. Don't you ever forget that. And what the OC says, goes.'

The four Rangers were well aware that under the Major's new set of criteria, the CSM, being one of the married men, would now be one of the five to go free – along with Captain Flaherty, and Corporals Sampson, Mackenzie and Ryan. You could cut the atmosphere with a knife, as the young Rangers' animosity and anger boiled and seethed just below the surface. A brittle silence descended on the room, with everyone avoiding eye contact. Tension crackled like an electric charge around the walls, as everyone waited to see if the four Rangers would, in effect, continue to defy their commanding officer and speak their minds. After what seemed like an age, the Major finally broke the silence.

'Look, lads, I know this is tough. No one wants to stay in this shithole. But they've said five and there's the five married men. And I have my reasons, you'll just have to trust me on that. So, that's an order. You'll be staying. There's no time to piss around now. Before these bastards change their minds again. Captain Flaherty, Sergeant Major Head and Corporals Sampson, Mackenzie and Ryan – get your things together. You'll be leaving.'

The four Rangers slumped back down on the floor in a stunned silence. They were devastated. They felt tears of anger burning at their eyes, but they'd not sink as low as showing their emotions openly in front of the others. After a few seconds' silence, they turned to face the wall, ostensibly to unpack their meagre kit again, but really so they'd not have to watch as the other five men prepared to leave. They were completely torn up inside and they felt that they had been betrayed.

Fuck, you, sir. FUCK YOU, FUCK YOU, FUCK YOU, their angry, confused young voices were screaming inside their heads. *Fuckin' look after your own, youse bastard. Fuckin' A. 'The married men.' Why not just fucking come out and say it straight, like you mean it, SIR? It's the fucking 'officer class', isn't it, sir? 'You little fucking Ranger SCUM. Pieces of SHITE. You really think you're getting out first?' That's what you're really fucking thinking, isn't it, SIR? Let the la-di-da fucking officer class go free. You're all the same. Stick to your own, you bastards.*

Over the last six days of captivity, the Rangers had put their whole belief and trust in the Major. They'd put their lives in his hands, hanging on his every word. None of them would have credited it before, but the Major had started to assume heroic status in their eyes. Prior to their capture, he'd just been the 'grey man'. One of those quietly competent officers who chose to blend into the background. He didn't exude charisma. He didn't stand out as an obvious leader among men. But there was no doubt about it now, the Major was good in a crisis. *Damn good.* In fact, he'd risen to the occasion. When the going had got tough, the Major really had got going. Major Martial was the most resilient and capable of the lot of them.

More importantly, he'd solicited their trust. He'd convinced them that they could and would make it out of there alive. That they'd get to see their grey, rain-lashed streets of Belfast again. Their fussy, over-protective mothers. Those crude, childlike murals in east Belfast put up by the Loyalists – men in black balaclavas with Armalite rifles, striking heroic poses. And their counterparts in west Belfast – same dreadful colour schemes, same heavy-handed symbolism – only this time, put up by the Provos.

God knows how they missed it all now. Down a pint of Guinness. Eat a bad curry. Laugh with their mates. Drink, fight, fuck and puke. Shout, scream and cry at the match on a big screen in the local. God, how they missed all those things that now made a young soldier's life seem so worth living. They'd never take it for granted again. Not any of it – never, ever again. If only they could be given another chance. Set free. Sent home. They'd savour the whole, gorgeous, wonderful gift of life and thank God for every single bloody second. And never set foot in Africa again.

And it had been the Major who'd got them to believe that they really could have it all again. He'd built them up as a team, making team decisions on how to survive the bloody nightmare that their lives had suddenly become. He'd shown them that with teamwork, and the grim, piss-taking humour that the Royal Irish Rangers were so renowned for, they could make it through. He'd led from the front, by example. He'd shown them how they'd watch each other's backs. How they'd hold out for each other. How they'd make deals and pacts and stick together, no matter what the fucking murderous bastards outside their door might be trying to do to break them. They were still British Army. *Still the best.* No one was going to fuck with their heads and take that away from them. But where was all that trust and team-work now?

Perhaps the Major had underestimated the effect his change of mind would have on the four Rangers. From the very first, the Major had reconciled himself to lasting out the hostage crisis to the very end. Like every good commanding officer, he had decided that he would go down with his ship if need be. Perhaps the Major's own internal strength had clouded his judgement about the other hostages – especially the four young Rangers. After all, two of them were still in their teens. Perhaps the Major had viewed the Rangers' ability to cope through the prism of his own sense of duty and calling. Perhaps, because he was willing to face death or worse at the hands of their captors, he had come to believe that every last man of them was willing to do the same. But in that he had badly misjudged the four Rangers.

Quickly, the five almost-free men gathered their kit together. They gave their maps and anything else that might be of use to those left behind. And then, with barely a backward glance, they were gone. There were a couple of sheepish, 'Hang on in there, lads,' and that sort of thing, but that was all. What else could they say? Was it just the Rangers' imagination, or did one or two of the five have their heads hung really low? The Major may have given his orders, they were thinking to them-selves, but there was nothing to stop any one of them volunteering to remain behind. Abso-fucking-lutely nothing. Burn in shame, the Rangers thought bitterly, as the five left the room. Burn in shame.

The six remaining hostages trudged out to Cambodia's veranda, to watch the others file down the hill to the river. There, a canoe was waiting to carry them away to safety. Major Martial accompanied the five men right down to the riverside. These were men that he had led into the rebel trap in the first place. He was determined to do his duty and see them as far as possible away to safety.

'Maybe he's sort of got his reasons, like . . .' Ranger Gaunt ventured at last, breaking the dark silence that had settled over the men slumped on Cambodia's veranda.

'Who? The Major? Like fuck he has,' one of the others spat out, beneath his breath.

'I dunno. But he's been dead on so far.'

'Oh aye. Youse know – just like yer man was when he took us down to have a nice wee chat with this murderous bunch of fuckers in the first place.'

'OK, then he's a fucking cunt, if you'd like,' Ranger Gaunt snapped back, almost in tears.

As the four Rangers vented their bitterness and bile, Sergeant Smith could think of little to say to stop them. He was sitting a little way apart, and as an NCO, Smith was painfully aware of how the Rangers must be seeing things. The senior ranks getting to go free, while the four of them were forced to stay behind. After a few minutes, Major Martial hove into view again, striding back up to Cambodia's house. But he was clearly in a fair hurry and he wasn't alone: two of the other hostages were coming with him.

'What the feck's it now?' one of the Rangers exclaimed.

'Who is it? Is it the RSO?' Ranger Gaunt asked the others. 'It looks like the RSO. And Corporal Mackenzie.'

'What the feck's Flaherty and the Corporal coming back for? Changed their minds now, have they?'

'Or meybe they've just come back to scrounge some smokes for the ride, like.'

Once he'd reached Cambodia's veranda, Major Martial launched into a hurried explanation of what had happened. It turned out that Cambodia had been down at the riverside, to oversee the hostage releases. And just as Corporal Mackenzie and Captain Flaherty were about to get into the dugout canoe, he'd stopped them. Because they were the signallers, Cambodia had argued that they would have to stay behind, so as to help with the ongoing hostage negotiations (which were still taking place by radio and soon, also, by the new satphone). So they had been prevented from leaving.

As Captain Flaherty had trudged up the hill to Cambodia's house, he had looked to the four Rangers like the saddest man on the planet. It must have been a nightmare, they realised, to have been so close to getting out, and to have been stopped right at the riverside. By contrast, Corporal Mackenzie didn't seem to be showing any visible signs of the ordeal he'd just been through. But maybe that was just his survival mechanism kicking in. Maybe when the shit really started, the Corporal just shut down all visible signs of engaging with the outside world.

The four young Rangers suddenly realised that there were now two spare places on the canoe. Surely, each of them was immediately thinking to himself, surely they'd be able to wangle one of those two tickets to freedom for themselves. *They bloody well had to.* By rights, the two most junior Rangers were Gaunt and McVeigh. They were convinced that now that the Major would be forced to revert to plan A – the junior ranks out first. But it seemed that Major Martial had a different plan in mind.

'Quickly, before the bloody boat leaves,' the Major urged, 'you four Rangers and you, Sergeant Smith, get your names scribbled down on to a scrap of paper. The first two names pulled out of a hat get to go.'

There was no time for any more bitching now. While the Major kept Cambodia busy in conversation, lest he change his mind about the two remaining hostage releases, Captain Flaherty pulled himself together enough to make the draw. Frantically, the men scribbled their names down, screwed up the scraps of paper, and dropped them into one of their remaining jungle hats. But just as Captain Flaherty went to pick out the first name, Sergeant Smith stopped him.

'Hold it there a minute, sir,' Smith said quietly. 'Youse best take my name out. I'm thinkin' I'll be staying.'

'You *what*, Mickey?' Flaherty responded, turning to stare at the Sergeant. 'You want your name *out*? You sure?'

'For sure I'm sure. Like I said, I'm thinkin' I'll be staying.'

'Your call, Mickey,' Flaherty said, as he turned and searched through the scraps of paper. 'There, "Mickey Smith". Your name's gone. Glad to have you staying with us, Sergeant.'

'Aye. A real pleasure, sir,' Sergeant Smith replied, with a forced grin.

Oh, thank fuck for that, the four Rangers were thinking, their minds racing. With Mickey out, that increased all their chances still further. Four Rangers and two places on the canoe now. It was a fifty-fifty chance. Each Ranger told himself that he was a lucky, lucky son of a bitch, and that he was bound to get one of the two tickets out of there. *Mickey – you're a true mate*, they were thinking. *Jesus, Mickey, you've got balls to do that. You're a fucking HERO. Come on, Flaherty. Make the draw. You know which names you're going to choose.*

'OK. First one – McVeigh,' Flaherty announced, as the Rangers crowded round him. There was an audible groan from Rangers Gaunt, Rowell and MacGuire. 'And second, Ranger MacGuire.'

'Oh feck, why us? *Why us?*' Ranger Gaunt groaned, under his breath, before quickly correcting himself. 'Sorry, youse two. Feckin' good on youse both, then.'

'Yeh. Feckin' A, Mac, Marky,' Ranger Rowell added, with a grimace. 'What d'you know, Jim, but life's a son of a bitch, so it is.'

'Sure, you'll be OK,' the two lucky men said, backslapping their fellow Rangers that they were leaving behind. 'You'll see, lads. We'll have youse out of here in no time, so we will.'

'Come on. Get your kit together and double quick down to the river,' the Major interrupted. 'Don't you lucky bastards go missing that ferry now, whatever you do.'

'Fucking A, sir,' the two Rangers responded, 'we'll not be tarrying. See youse all around, then.'

As the two Rangers hurried off down to join their colleagues at the riverside, six British soldiers were left sitting on Cambodia's veranda: Major Martial, Captain Flaherty, Corporal Mackenzie, Sergeant Smith and Rangers Rowell and Gaunt. And, of course, there was Corporal Mousa.

The six men watched from the veranda as the canoe nosed out unsteadily into the Rokel Creek. As it was gripped by the fierce current it disappeared into the gathering dusk, and the remaining hostages felt a strange mixture of conflicting emotions. On the one hand, they were completely devastated. They were the ones who were being left behind. On the other hand, if five had been released in exchange for only a satphone, surely it wouldn't take very much more to get the rest of them out? Maybe this meant that the West Side Boys had finally seen sense and had dropped their political demands. If that was true, they could all be getting out of there in the next few days.

Whatever the truth of the matter, Rangers Gaunt and Rowell were too exhausted by the day's events to feel angry or let down any more. It had been a horrible, roller-coaster ride of elation, hope, betrayal and disappointment. And when all was said and done, they knew that they'd have to pull together again now as a smaller, more intimate team. It was the only way that they would be able to get through the days ahead. And the Major was certain to have had his reasons, of that they felt sure. Maybe he'd needed one of the NCOs to be released, as a way to get more information out to their potential rescuers. Certainly, someone like Captain Flaherty had seen far more of the rebel set-up – right from their signals capabilities, their defences and their troop strength – than any of the Rangers had done. In his

role as RSO, he'd travelled to and fro across the river several times
to go to the hostage meetings, giving him a good sense of the lie of
the land in the rebel bases on both sides of the river. The four Rangers
had only ever been across the river once, on the day of their capture,
and they'd hardly been in a fit state then to take note of their
surroundings.

No doubt about it, getting a man like the Captain out would have
been a great bonus to any British rescue party. And the same went
for one or two of the other NCOs. Perhaps that was why the Major
had done what he had done.

In any case, Sergeant Smith's selfless act of removing himself from
the final release lottery had set an example for the rest of them to
follow. Quiet, lanky Mickey Smith, a man who never complained.
Dark hair cropped short, going grey around the edges. A methodical
man, who was good at admin, stores, that sort of thing. *Mickey*. The
man who kept everything running in the background, giving logic
and a sense of rules and order to a chaotic, bad, mad, crazed situation. Mickey Smith was no different now from how he had been that
morning, before the lottery over the hostage releases. There was
nothing to mark him out as an exceptional man. But there was no
doubt about it: he was the real, unsung hero of the story.

As evening descended over the village, the hostages sat huddled
over the West Side Boys' tiny short-wave radio set, waiting for news
from the BBC World Service that the hostages had reached safety. But
as they listened, a report came on that none of them had been
expecting. The BBC announced that they had one of the leaders of
the West Side Boys on a live link-up from Sierra Leone. The rebels
must have got the satphone working, and were doing a live interview
with the BBC. In seconds, the six hostages could hear the voice of
Colonel Cambodia coming over the radio at them.

'Yaah. It is good to speak to the BBC directly, so we can make our
position clear and communicate our demands . . .' Cambodia began.

The rest of his words were lost in uproar, as the whole camp just
started going wild at hearing one of their own leaders on the BBC. A
couple of the Boys swept up the radio set from the veranda and started
dancing around the clearing with it glued to their ears, chanting and
whooping it up to the broadcast. There was no way that they could
actually be listening to what their glorious Colonel was saying, amid
all the racket; but it was clearly more than enough for them to know
he was speaking on the BBC.

'Jesus, it'd be nice to know what the fecker's saying, like,' remarked Ranger Gaunt, morosely.

'Yer man's too much of a fuckwit to make much sense anyway,' Ranger Rowell replied. 'Meybe it's best we don't hear – it'd probably fry our feckin' brains.'

'Ranger Gaunt's right – it'd still be good to know,' muttered the Major, shaking his head at the dancing rebels.

Finally, the uproar in the village died down enough to hear the broadcast as it continued. The West Side Boys had taken the British soldiers hostage as a way to communicate their grievances to the Sierra Leonean government, Cambodia was saying. They would hold them until all their demands were met.

'They have to release all the AFRC prisoners, including our wives and children, and our brothers,' Cambodia was saying, excitedly. 'Because we need a new government. In fact, the AFRC has a new leader now. No more Johnny Paul Koroma, because he has betrayed us. Now we have got another AFRC representative as a leader here, and he is Brigadier General F. Kallay. Now the government is against us, although we are the strong forces in this country, but due to the activity or the negligence of the politicians, they don't want to recognise us. We took over the government from Kabbah in 1997. And we can take it over again.'

'Brigadier General F. Kallay my arse,' Ranger Rowell muttered, as the village erupted in uproar again, marking the end of Cambodia's interview. 'Youse know what the F stands for? Fuckwit. Brigadier General Fuckwit Kallay.'

'Well, what the feck was Cambodia on about, anyways?' Ranger Gaunt asked, nervously. 'What's the feckin' AFRC when it's at home? And who's yer man Corona – this feckin J.P. fella, then?'

'The Armed Forces Revolutionary Council, lad,' the Major answered. 'Sort of unholy alliance of the RUF rebels, the West Side Boys and renegade SLA officers. Back in '97, they toppled the democratic government and ruled for several months. Well, if you can call it "ruled". Pure anarchy and bloodshed, more like. J.P. Koroma – *Ko-ro-ma* – was an SLA officer who headed up the AFRC. Which made him sort of honorary leader of this lot, too. The West Side Boys were in theory loyal to Koroma, before Kallay came on the scene, that is.'

'So, what, like, does it sort of *mean*, sir?' the Ranger replied, perplexedly. 'I mean, what do the feckers actually want? In return for us getting freed, then?'

'Oh, not much,' continued the Major. 'Just the freeing of all their criminals and bloody terrorists from the jails and the bringing back of the AFRC to power by the sounds of it, and probably Foday Kallay for President while they're at it. It's pie in the sky, lad. It'll never happen.'

'So where the feck does that leave us, then, sir?' the Ranger asked, quietly.

'Well, that's what all these hostage negotiations are about, lad. Get these bastards to drop their demands down to something more realistic. It's all a process of negotiation, trial and error, give and take, and seeing what's possible practically speaking.'

'So in the end they just sort of get a couple of Mars bars and a Cadbury's Cream Egg, like, sir?'

'You got it. Something like that, lad, yes.'

With Cambodia's broadcast having finished, a group of the Boys came dancing and singing their way over to the hostages, clapping them around the shoulders with broad grins. They were clearly ecstatic about the BBC broadcast, and the British-supplied satphone that had enabled it. At last the rebel rank and file felt that they could see some concrete progress coming out of the taking of the British hostages. Their leader was speaking directly to the BBC, on their behalf, on behalf of the West Side Boys. No matter what he was saying, he was speaking to the BBC. That was enough. For once, the British hostages were flavour of the evening.

'Yaaah, British soldiers! You hear the Colonel speaking on the BBC?' one of rebels was crying. 'You hear him? Very gooood, very goood. The West Side Boys on the BBC!'

'Yaah. Thank you, British, thank you for the special radio,' another joined in, enthusiastically. 'Now, you see things start to happen. Not long now, not long.'

'British soldiers, we will promote you,' another of the rebels began singing. 'British soldiers, we will promote you. We promote you for the special radio and the speaking on the BBC.'

'Yaah. Yaaah. We promote you all to Lieutenant Colonel, to Lieutenant Colonel.'

'Yaah. Lieutenant Colonel. All you British soldiers, now you are Lieutenant Colonel. No more Ranger or Major. All Lieutenant Colonel.'

'Is a very big thing, the West Side Boys promote their prisoners. First time ever. Is a very big thing.'

'Well, cheers, guys,' Ranger Gaunt replied. 'Youse know, I always

wanted to be a flamin' Lieutenant Colonel when I grew up, like. Never sort of thought I'd make it. But dead on, guys, dead on.'

'So, we're all the same rank now, is it?' Ranger Rowell remarked, wryly. 'How d'you like that, sir? We're all Lieutenant Colonels now, by the sounds of things.'

'No standing on rank here, lad,' replied a grinning Major, joining in with the humour of the moment. 'Anyways, I always fancied a bit of fast-track promotion myself.'

Congratulating the six hostages on their 'promotion', the crowd slowly dispersed – all the while chatting away excitedly among themselves about the broadcast. All that the hostages hoped for from their 'promotion' was a little improvement in their treatment, and perhaps some more cigarettes, water and food.

By now, dusk had given way to the warm, muggy blackness of a tropical night – their seventh in captivity. As the crowd had dispersed and the men continued listening to the BBC's Africa Service, the Rangers stole a couple of glances over at Sergeant Smith. Quiet man, grey man, just like Major Martial. He was sitting there across the veranda glued to the radio, acting as if nothing unusual had happened. *You're a flamin' hero, Mickey*, they were thinking to themselves. *A flamin' hero.*

The quiet, level tones of the BBC reporters' news-speak droned on in the background, as each of the men sat there on the darkened veranda. But suddenly, there was the zzzt-zzzt-zzzt of interference crackling over the radio. The static was so powerful that the broadcast was rendered all but inaudible. It lasted just a few seconds, and then the BBC signal came back on as normal. A couple of the hostages glanced over at each other in the darkness, but none of them said a word. They knew that each of them was thinking the same thing. *That had sounded like close-quarter interference, the sort you might expect from British Army radio sets.*

As soon as they were locked in their room for the night, Captain Flaherty, the RSO, broached the subject that was now foremost in all their minds.

'You heard that interference, I take it,' he whispered to the others, 'interrupting the BBC? Close quarter it was, short but powerful bursts of radio static. I'd wager that's just the sort of interference high-frequency radio comms would make. Especially if it's being used in the jungle somewhere nearby. D'you get what I'm saying?'

'Youse mean, sort of like Special Forces would use?' Ranger Gaunt ventured, hardly being able to conceal his excitement as he did so. 'If they were out there, in the jungle, keeping watch, like, if you know what I mean.'

'Aye, Sandy. He means like the SAS might use,' Ranger Rowell answered, speaking on the Captain's behalf. 'Isn't that your drift, sir?'

'That it is, lad,' Captain Flaherty confirmed. 'There's no guaranteeing it, of course. But I'd be at a loss to think what else could be causing it. It's not as if there's heaps of high-frequency comms around Gberi Bana to produce that sort of interference.'

'I'm inclined to agree, Captain,' Major Martial commented. 'It just might be the case that some of our boys are out there in the jungle, keeping watch. And if they are, then that's certainly a comforting thought, isn't it, lads?'

This was indeed a reassuring thought for the hostages, because it meant that if the West Side Boys did start killing them, at least the SAS could radio word back to British headquarters. And that in turn was bound to mean that something would be called in – an emergency air strike with a ground assault most probably – in an attempt to rescue those who were still alive. The men hoped and prayed that Captain Flaherty was right, and that the SAS were out there, radio sets at the ready, standing by in the jungle shadows.

Despite the morale boost this gave the men, it was still a sombre night. There had been no news on the BBC of the five freed hostages. Had they really got away to safety? the men wondered. Or had the West Side Boys played a trick on them somehow? They talked a little more, but mostly they were lost in their own thoughts. Images of five friends lying murdered in the forest, of floating corpses flashing white in the moonlit waters of the Rokel Creek, kept flitting through their minds.

Unbeknown to the British soldiers an unusual delegation had set out from Freetown to visit the West Side Boys that evening. It consisted of the mothers of the rebel leaders, and they were on a mission to persuade their wayward sons to release the British hostages. The delegation came bearing traditional gifts of milk, sugar and bread, and the whole initiative had been organised by Major Johnny Paul Koroma himself.

Having presided over the months of AFRC murderous rule back in 1997 – with himself as Chairman, Foday Sankoh of the RUF as his right-hand man, and the West Side Boys as his fighting force – J.P. Koroma had since realised that the writing was on the wall for the rebels in Sierra Leone. With the arrival of British forces, the whole game plan had changed, and J.P. was keen to ingratiate himself with the new powers in Sierra Leone. He knew that if he could persuade the West Side Boys to release the British hostages, it would be an enormous feather in his cap. For some days now, he had been working hard behind the scenes to achieve that aim.

Until recently, J.P. had been the nominal leader of the West Side Boys. For that reason, the British had taken him to some of the face-to-face hostage-negotiation meetings – to try to build bridges with the rebels. On his own initiative, J.P. had then sent Colonel Tamba Bremma and General Lion – two ex-AFRC members – to speak with Foday Kallay and bargain for the British soldiers' release. But Kallay had the men arrested, intending to kill them both the next day. That night, Bremma had managed to bribe a guard to cut his binds, and then he had escaped by swimming down the Rokel Creek to safety. As a long-time Navy man he knew what he was doing. But Foday Kallay had had his colleague, General Lion, executed.

But J.P. Koroma had still not given up. He had then sent a letter to Foday Kallay, via the Jordanian UN peacekeepers, seeking permission to send in the visiting delegation of mothers. '*The continuing holding ransom of people coming to Sierra Leone to assist in the peace process does not augur well. I therefore ask that, the earlier the better, you free the British soldiers.*' J.P. also urged the West Side Boys to leave the bush and disarm. Via the Jordanians, word had come back that the rebels were happy to receive the delegation of mothers. The rebels had been isolated in the bush for months now, and they hadn't seen their relatives for a long time.

In any case, the day before the release of the five British hostages, a number of the relatives of the West Side Boys' leaders had spoken on a local radio talk show. They had called on the rebels to release their British captives. 'I am not happy about their behaviour and holding these British people,' a relative of one of the rebel leaders had said. 'These British people are here to assist us, and it is high time these rebels stop the fighting and come out of the bush, and they should come on board so we can try to develop this nation.' The following evening, the delegation of mums had set out to talk directly with their sons: Foday Kallay, Colonel Cambodia, Colonel GS and the others rebel leaders.

After handing over their gifts, they had pleaded with their sons to release the six remaining British hostages, for their own good. Sierra

Leone was facing a new dawn, they told their boys. With the arrival of the British, peace was coming at long last. The power of the RUF was finished, the foreign soldiers would see to that. The 'day of the rebels' was over. The West Side Boys had to come out of the jungle and play their part in rebuilding the country. They had been in the bush far too long, and had forgotten how to live properly and decently.

Just look at their surroundings. Living in the jungle like this. They should come out of the forest, come back to Freetown, and start paying attention to their lives and their families again. Sierra Leone was moving on, and they were in danger of being left behind. If the rebels released the remaining hostages now, J.P. had assured the mothers that no harm would come to their sons. On that, the British had given their word. If they didn't, the Lord only knew what would happen to them.

But the pleas of the mothers had fallen on deaf ears. Later that evening, the delegation of mothers returned to Freetown with discouraging news. The West Side Boys were angry at the British and the UN for what they were doing in Sierra Leone. They had no right to come to the country and take it over like this. They had even attacked the West Side Boys' bases, and for no reasons. The rebels did not trust them any more and would not release the British hostages, until all their demands were met. As for J.P. Koroma himself, he should realise that he was no longer the leader of the West Side Boys and had no power over them. Brigadier General Foday Kallay was their leader now, and he and his deputies would decide exactly what would happen to the hostages and when. Hadn't J.P. heard the West Side Boys leaders on the radio, speaking on the BBC? Didn't he pay attention to such things? They had the world as their audience now, and as long as they kept hold of the British hostages, the world was listening. So why give them up? It was a stupid idea. The mothers and old people should stick to what they did best; rocking babies on their laps, dozing on their porches in the mid-afternoon sun, and pottering around in their gardens.

In traditional African society, the elders of a tribe are normally treated with immense respect and deference – far more so than is generally the case in the West. The trouble was that in the land of the West Side Boys, all such norms had long since broken down. The mothers had tried. They had done what they could do. But they had been disrespected and sent away with only insults to show for their efforts. That same evening Foday Kallay's father – who was himself a regimental sergeant major (RSM) in the SLA – had even made a radio call to his son, pleading for him to see sense and release the hostages. But Kallay's only reaction had been to tell him that the British soldiers would be released over his dead body. 'I am disowning you, old man,' Kallay had told him. 'You are no longer my father.'

The rebel leader had given the delegation of mothers a letter to take back to J.P., with a copy for the British High Commission. In it, there were demands for a new government to be set up with Foday Kallay as a 'senior member'. Foday Kallay also declared himself the new Chairman of the AFRC: the letter was signed *Brigadier General Foday Kallay, leader of the West Side Boys and the AFRC.*

This letter was the biggest 'fuck you' Foday Kallay could possibly have sent to the British forces. As everyone knew, the AFRC's mission was to bring down the Sierra Leonean government – the very regime that the British were in Sierra Leone to keep in power. And Kallay had now made it clear that he would use the British hostages as bargaining chips to help him achieve that aim. By declaring himself the new AFRC leader, Kallay was putting himself directly in the British firing line.

In short, Foday Kallay's letter was a declaration of war.

VIRGIN WARRIORS

Every soldier knows that there are only two kinds of plans: plans that might work and plans that won't work. The art of war is to take a plan that might work and then drive it to success.
                    – General Wesley K. Clark, *Winning Modern Wars*

IN Waterloo Camp the ops tent was getting into full swing now. Comms were up and running with JFHQ based in the British High Commission in Freetown, and PJHQ in Northwood. Updates on the situation in the West Side Boys' territory were coming in thick and fast, as were reports on the latest state of play with the hostage negotiations. Supplementary intelligence – high-resolution satellite photographs of the West Side Boys' headquarters, threat assessments on the rebels' firepower and the state of their morale – was also being made available to the assault force. It was a vast amount of data to process, and several laptop computers had been set up in the ops tent for that purpose. From the outside, the ops tent looked just like any old knackered khaki army tent. On the inside, with its rows of laptops and banks of communication equipment, it looked more like a high-tech flight deck.

There was still the traditional cork noticeboard, with scraps of paper pinned up on it with mission updates for all to read. But the men were discouraged from hanging around too much. Otherwise, the place would get full of blokes spilling their brews or dropping their scoff on the computers. The men had learned that if they mooched about the ops tent too long, then they'd be bound to get landed with a job to get them out of the way – shifting ammo around or the like. So it was best to keep a low profile and hang out somewhere safe, like the cookhouse tent. Different-level briefings were going on all the time, with the troop head sheds getting called off to the ops tent to see the OC, and then returning to brief each of their troops in turn. Which gave each man the chance to feed his own ideas into the planning process, via the troop head shed back up the chain of command.

One of the first priorities in the ops tent was to get some accurate, detailed plans of the West Side Boys' bases drawn up. Working with satellite images, D Squadron command was able to study the layout of the area carefully, identifying where the enemy had their heavy machine guns, vehicles and other weapons positioned. Using these detailed plans, the men were then able to build a life-size mock-up of Gberi Bana village out the back of the camp, complete with all satellite-visible fortifications. D Squadron and the SBS would use this mock-up village for intensive training purposes, rehearsing the assault over and over again, to prepare for all eventualities.

Two of D Squadron's number – Gerry Birt and Tigger – had been seconded to the negotiating team. Both men were skilled in hostage-negotiation tactics, and Tigger had already been in-country for some weeks now, working on other Special Forces operations. Unlike most Special Forces around the world, the members of UKSF are highly trained in aspects of hostage negotiation and other delicate psychological operations (so-called 'psyops', all part of their CT). There was no middle ground with CT work. You could give a man some pointers and teach him some tricks of the trade, but at the end of the day you were either a born natural or you weren't. First and foremost, you had to have the gift of the gab; you had to be able to talk to the enemy and get them to trust you, which was no small thing. Only a few of the men were able to operate in this high-intensity hostage-negotiation role where so much was at stake, while at the same time being able to think straight and keep their cool.

That was one of the major differences between UK Special Forces and, say, the Americans. In the US military, they would invariably get their CT negotiators from the FBI or State Department. The US Special Forces were seen as fire platforms, as the best combat monsters in the whole US Army. Which was fine, as far as it went. But you would never pass SAS selection on those criteria alone. You had to have real brains these days, as well as brawn, to get through SAS selection, and nowhere more so than with CT work. It was all very well unleashing a Rottweiler, the men of D Squadron would argue, but when you unleashed the Regimental Rottweiler you needed to have a damn good chance of getting your stick back.

No soldier would ever get into the Regiment unless he was a particular type of individual. Cockney Jimmy, the Big Scottish Monster, the Kiwi – whoever it was, they all shared one factor in common: each was a specific type of person with a peculiar type of intelligence. Each was a self-starter, a lateral thinker, a total believer in the maxim that anything was possible with a few elastic bands and a ball of string – as long as you thought about it hard enough and long enough. The Regiment had a can-do attitude that was second to none in the world of Special Forces. In that sense, it was unique.

On top of their regular troop-specific combat, survival and infiltration training, each soldier was taught at least two, specific disciplines that suited his own particular abilities. It might be advanced medicine (the paramedics), explosives (the demolition boys), communications (the sparks), tracking (the recce boys), forward air control (FAC) or sniper work. And each man would also take a language skill. Over and above this, each member of the Regiment was encouraged to develop his own peculiar qualities, to discover the set of natural, instinctive skills that he was born with. So, for example, those who just happened to be the best talkers and listeners – the types who were always popular down the boozer – they would be encouraged to develop CT and hostage-negotiation skills. And for those like the Scottish Monster, who weren't the world's greatest talkers, there was always explosives to be played around with.

From day one of arrival in country, a nightly sitrep was being held at Waterloo Camp – where the OC presented all the latest information and developments on the hostage crisis. And while they weren't encouraged to hang around there, the men were free to go into the ops tent at any time and consult the maps and the data coming into the base. The OC encouraged each man in his unit to make their own suggestions as to how the assault could better be effected, regardless of their rank.

The West Side Boys' HQ was situated in deep jungle, seven miles away from the nearest main road, the Masiaka–Freetown highway. The base straddled a significant river, the Rokel Creek, which was some one-thousand yards across at this point. From here, the Rokel Creek flowed down some forty miles or so into the Freetown Estuary and harbour. Only one narrow track led into the rebels' territory from the highway, ending at their first base, Magbeni, on the southern river bank. Across the other side of the Rokel Creek, on the northern bank, was the rebels' second base, Gberi Bana. This was where the British hostages were being held. Gberi Bana was not accessible by vehicle, the only routes in being via the river or the jungle. This left three options open for the assault: walking into target, flying into target, or going in by boat. None of these had yet been ruled out.

Three different assault plans were drawn up covering each avenue of approach, and they were graded according to the likelihood of success. This was a hostage-rescue operation first and foremost, so the priority had to be springing the eleven British (and one Sierra Leonean) hostages, without getting any of them killed. The key factors the assault planners were seeking were therefore stealth and surprise. This favoured a staggered assault: getting up as close as possible to the base at night undetected and then going in hard at first light. The easiest and most logical way of doing that was the riverine approach: get the men taken in upriver by inflatables during the hours of darkness, and then launch a dawn assault with a combined force attacking on foot from the jungle, and from the Rokel Creek by boat.

That, then, was plan A, the main assault plan. It put a great deal of responsibility on Boat Troop and the SBS, as they would be tasked with getting the assault force upriver, theirs being the expertise of operating on the water. All the men knew that the best-laid plans were bound to fail in one aspect or another once they were put into action. The trick was to have enough of a plan to know what you were doing, while remaining flexible at the same time. But plan A had a lot going for it, and the men knew that it could work.

Plan B was the overland assault, which would involve the men being driven in as near as possible to target, and then trekking in the last few miles through the forest. As with plan A, the assault force would then lay up in the jungle near the rebel bases overnight, and move up to launch a dawn assault. Plan B was definitely a possibility, although it lacked the ease of access of a riverine approach. Lugging in all their weapons and ammo by foot through the jungle wasn't the easiest of ways to launch an assault. But it was plan C that was clearly the total non-starter. The option of an airborne assault had nothing going for it: it was completely lacking in either stealth or surprise. It scored zero points. Plan C would only ever be considered if all else failed, and heaven forbid that that became necessary.

It was at this stage that the Paras were first written into the assault plans. Clearly, with some one thousand or so rebels located at two separate bases straddling a major river, some seventy-odd Special Forces would be unable to handle this job on their own. If the men of the SAS and SBS went in alone, they would be outnumbered ten to one.

And however good they were, those were suicidal odds. In addition to which, there were the lives of the hostages to consider. If the assault force concentrated their efforts on rescuing the hostages from Gberi Bana village alone, the rebels were known to have several weapons systems at Magbeni capable of putting down devastating fire across the river. There was the 50-cal and the GPMG heavy machine guns on the captured Royal Irish WMIK Land-Rover, and several 51mm and 81mm mortars. Clearly, without a suppression force going in and simultaneously attacking Magbeni, the assault force hitting Gberi Bana would be left highly vulnerable.

A lot of the D Squadron boys had at first argued that it should be their fellow SAS soldiers from B Squadron going into action on the southern river bank. The SAS had never operated closely with the Paras before, and so they remained an unknown quantity. With B Squadron, at least the men would know where they stood. Yet there were stronger arguments that went against it. First and foremost, B Squadron could muster no more than fifty men, and the plan for the southern assault required a force approaching a hundred or more. Secondly, under Operation Palliser, 1 Para had led the recent assault against the RUF rebels, and so they were already combat-experienced in Sierra Leone. And thirdly, it could be argued that the southern assault didn't really require the particular skills of Special Forces. As there were no hostages to be rescued there, it was purely a seek-and-destroy mission, and that was something at which the Paras excelled.

When explained like this it did made sense to the men of D Squadron to use the men of the Parachute Regiment to assault Magbeni. Even with them involved, it would still be an SAS operation, with their OC, Pete Cutgood, in overall command. The Paras would simply be tasked with taking out the southern river bank, nothing more. They would be involved in operational planning only as far as their side of the river was concerned. And when all was said and done, it would also be a great chance for many of the young lads of 1 Para to see some action for the first time.

With planning now well underway, the men of D Squadron tried to kill time as best they could. Some of the blokes unpacked and repacked their gear time and time again; others checked and rechecked and then checked again the comms equipment to be used on the assault; and the paramedics went over their medical kits until they had everything just right. But mostly, they were just taking it easy.

The men had had everything shipped out from the UK in terms of life's little luxuries, and so they went about building themselves their own version of the Hilton out the back of Waterloo Camp. There were deckchairs, lilos, a ghetto blaster and a couple of short-wave radios, and soon the men were out there in their flip-flops and boxers sunbathing, or lounging around and reading their favourite novels. The only downer was that the Scottish Monster had brought along just one ZZ Top tape with him, and he kept playing it over and over again. But that problem was solved when one of the blokes managed to get hold of the tape and sabotage it.

Some of the blokes had become chess addicts, as a result of count-less missions spent killing time waiting for a green light that never came. So they piled up the empty ammo cases, to make seats and a makeshift table between them, and were playing endless rounds of chess on those tiny, foldable travel chess sets. And of course there was porn. Especially with the Shakyboats: somehow, they always seemed to get their hands on the best porn mags (*Hustler*, *Buttman* and the like), which was probably down to the Navy in them.

Ever since hearing of the Sierra Leone op, none of the men had been anticipating that much was going to happen. They had been in this situation too many times before, and then at the last minute the mission had been cancelled. The squadron had come a hair's breadth away from going into action during the Stansted Airport hijacking, earlier that year. The general consensus was that Sierra Leone was far less likely to happen than Stansted had been. Moreover, the men knew that the hostage-release negotiations were still underway. It was far more likely that they were going to get a negotiated end to the hostage crisis. In which case, the Regiment would have been called in more as a contingency measure than anything else. And then they would all just have to fly home again.

Back in the UK Major Lowe, of A Company, 1 Para and his twenty-two-year-old 2iC, Captain Danny Matthews, had received their first briefing on a potential hostage-rescue operation in Sierra Leone. They were tasked with identifying a force of between 120 and 140 men at 1 Para's Aldershot barracks who could go into action immediately alongside a Special Forces team. At this stage, the Paras' specific mission tasking was to 'find and fix' the enemy. No assault options had been ruled out, the Paras officers were told. There would be WMIK Land-Rovers, quad bikes, Pinzgauers (all-wheel-drive trucks) and inflatable boats available for the attack. And three Chinook

CH47s were in country for an airborne assault. As the Paras began preparing for their deployment, the men declined the offer of an issue of new jungle boots; the short duration of the intended mission went against the hassle of breaking in the new footwear.

Operational secrecy (opsec) was seen as being paramount. A cover story was told to the 120-odd Bayonets (as the Paras call their fighting troops): the unit was preparing to go on exercises in a tropical overseas environment. As an overland assault on the West Side Boys' positions was still possible, 1 Para's parent unit, the 16th Air Assault Brigade, shipped several WMIKs and Pinzgauer trucks across to them. So, while the men waited for further news of the deployment, they were able to put in some practice with the vehicles. There was also a scrabble to update tropical inoculations and start on the Lariam (an anti-malarial drug). As the men of 1 Para speculated on where they might be going 'on exercises', the most likely destination was seen as being Belize, a regular haunt of the Parachute Regiment.

On 1 September, the Paras moved forward to the operational mounting centre (OMC) at South Cerney, in Gloucestershire. Suspicions that they weren't simply going on 'exercises' were raised when all mobile phones were taken off the men and isolation enforced. By the time the head sheds had begun to thoroughly check next-of-kin details and identity discs ('dog tags'), the men of 1 Para suspected that there was a serious mission in the offing. Ten of the 120 Bayonets were only two weeks out of training, and there was a palpable buzz of excitement around the base. Major Lowe and Captain Matthews had been told that Op Barras could take place any time now, and so they had decided to take their men into Sierra Leone battle ready. By the time ammunition, explosives and weapons were being broken down and handed out to the men, each of them knew that this was now a combat mission. As the hostage crisis had already been on the news before isolation was enforced, many of the Paras had their suspicions that they were off to Sierra Leone.

The initial operation briefing took place in the departure area. An intelligence officer from PJHQ began outlining the nature of the mission. He explained that they were being deployed to Sierra Leone, and outlined the nature of the terrain and the enemy target. The West Side Boys were similar to the other main rebel group in Sierra Leone, the RUF, with whom the Paras had already crossed swords during Op Palliser. Like the RUF, they were not expected to be a pushover. They were battle-hardened and well armed, possessing a significant arsenal of weaponry, including 60/81mm mortars, medium machine guns, RPGs, grenades, anti-personnel mines and AK47s. They were well dug in at their jungle headquarters, and during the last month they had already survived two UN attacks designed to deny them of their territory. There were around a thousand, loosely grouped into five battalions, with some pretty colourful names: the 'Gulf Battalion', the 'Savage Group', and so on.

Then the briefing moved on to the nature of the Paras' specific mission. There were eleven soldiers of the Royal Irish Regiment being held hostage by the West Side Boys. The Paras were to deploy alongside UKSF, in a mission to rescue the hostages and deny the rebels their base. The rebel headquarters straddled the Rokel Creek, with the hostages being held on the northern bank, at Gberi Bana. The main body of the rebels was on the opposite, southern river bank, at Magbeni. While the Special Forces would be dealing with the hostage rescue itself, the Paras would concentrate on what they did best – taking out the enemy firepower on the southern river bank.

Here the rebels kept their vehicles and most of their heavy weapons. Critically, the distance between Magbeni and Gberi Bana was just under a mile, and so it was well within range of the rebels' heavy weapons. The Paras would need to get into Magbeni and silence the rebels before they had a chance to use their weapons against the hostage-rescue force on the northern river bank. They would be going into action outnumbered some five to one.

Shit, the Bayonets were now thinking, *some 'exercise' this is turning out to be.* They were up against a heavily defended rebel camp, and they were outnumbered and pretty much outgunned. And to cap it all, they were going in alongside the SAS *and* the SBS, which was certainly something to live up to. If they messed up their side of the assault, it wouldn't just be them who got hit. It would be the men of the Regiment, and the British hostages they were going in to rescue. As the majority of the SAS are recruited from the Paras, many of the men now assembled at South Cerney had their own, private hopes of joining that elite group of soldiers. And as every man in that room now knew, this operation would be a crucial proving ground for them. There were plenty of questions in the young soldiers' minds. What would be their assault approach (by air, overland or by river)? What air power would they have in support? Any helicopter gunships? Any fixed-wing attack aircraft? But all of that could come later.

On the evening of 2 September, the head sheds held their final planning session on the mission before them. An ISIS communications system had been provided to the unit, giving them a secret and direct coded communications link between Africa and PJHQ in the UK. Upon arrival at the forward mounting base, at Senegal's military airport, the Paras got down to some serious operational planning, using computerised systems to walk them through a virtual-reality mock-up of the target village. This system, compiled with the aid of ultra high-resolution satellite images, gave the head sheds an excellent feel for the nature of the terrain on the ground. Two possible landing zones were identified in the event of an airborne assault, and the road from Laia Junction was scoped out as an overland assault route.

Of the two LZs, LZ1 had surprise in its favour, being in the middle of the rebel village itself. But it would require a force of at least two Chinook loads (around a hundred men) to be put down at the same time – to ensure enough combat power survived the insertion to take out the rebel base. LZ2 – being on the western side of Magbeni and separated from the village by a strip of jungle – looked more promising, as the assault force would be shielded from the rebels as they put down. But the suitability of the terrain there was unknown. Whichever LZ they went for, a second, blocking force of Paras would need to be dropped on to the road leading out of Magbeni, to stop any rebel reinforcement being driven in from Laia Junction.

While the village roofs were known to be corrugated iron, the thickness of the walls was an unknown, and the assault force would need to ascertain if they could fire through them with their SA80 assault rifles and light machine guns. In case they could not, the Paras would be taking with them 66mm light anti-armour weapons (LAWs). As the assault force would need to sweep through the village coordinating firepower and mortar support, a restricted fire line (RFL) would be imposed. Basically, any troops this side of the RFL would be friendlies; any on the far side would be the enemy. While no fire would be put down this side of the RFL, terrain on the far side would be subjected to intense mortar bombardments and heavy machine-gun fire. And as the Paras advanced through Magbeni, the RFL would move with them.

The 120 Paras of A Company were broken down into three forty-man platoons. An M-Unit radio communications system provided secure comms up to platoon level, enabling all parts of the assault force to be in direct radio contact with each other – critical with such a tight battle space and speed of assault. An air-landing airborne-refuelling platform (ALARP – basically a tanker of avgas with a unit of Paras as protection) would be flown to a forward position prior to the assault, to keep the choppers refuelled and flying. And a mobile reserve force of a dozen Bayonets with two WMIK Land-Rovers would be stationed out past the Laia Junction, in case of any emergencies.

So much for the planning phase. The main body of the Paras finally pitched up at Waterloo Camp on 5 September, four days after D Squadron's arrival and twelve days into the hostage crisis. They arrived carrying with them only their basic personal and assault kit. At first they had looked over at D Squadron's section of camp – a bunch of blokes in boxer shorts and shades lounging about on deckchairs – and had thought to themselves: 'Who's that bunch of fat old blokes loafing about over there?' Then word had got out that *they were the Regiment*. They were the boys who would be doing the hostage rescue, the mission that the Paras had come here to support. Well, they hadn't looked much like the crack SAS assault force that the young soldiers had been expecting. They'd looked more like a bunch of hairy-arsed blokes taking it easy on the Costa del Sol. Still, you could never tell . . .

The Paras set themselves up at the rear of the base, forming their own camp under canvas. From now on, everyone would be using the same facilities – the cookhouse tent, the khazis – but the men of the Paras and of the Regiment would keep pretty much to themselves. Out at the rear of the camp, the Para officers began putting their Bayonets through their paces, mapping out their objectives and running through possible attack routes again and again. Because their mission briefing had given them the task to 'defeat' the enemy, as opposed to 'destroy' them, the plan for the assault on Magbeni was designed to give the rebels a 'Golden Bridge' of escape. Moving in fast from the west, the Para attack force aimed to sweep the rebels east out of the village. Once they had done so, the rebels would be prevented from putting down any fire across the river on to Gberi Bana village, because it would then be out of range. Which would mean that they were not longer a danger to the hostage-rescue mission.

As speed and mobility were crucial to the success of the attack, minimum equipment would be taken in on the assault: weapons, ammunition, water and point-of-injury medical aid only. By now, the Paras' rehearsals were concentrating on a sequential landing at LZ2, the western drop zone shielded from the rebel village by the jungle. An initial force of some fifty-odd Paras would be flown in by Chinook to secure the LZ, the second half of the Para assault force coming in closely behind it. Once both forces were on the ground, they would attack Magbeni and clear it of rebels. They would destroy any captured heavy weapons, vehicles and ammunition dumps, and attempt to locate and secure the three Royal Irish Rangers Land-Rovers. All being well, these would be extracted at the end of their mission by Chinook.

To the young men of the Parachute Regiment now present in Waterloo Camp, this sort of fighting combat was exactly what they had trained for: to go into a target and clear out the enemy. Even so, this was a daunting mission. So much could easily go wrong. If the first Chinook went down or was just disabled on the first drop, half the assault force could be taken out in one go. If the second Chinook was even slightly delayed – due to being hit by ground fire or the LZ becoming too hot to land – it would have the same effect. With the best will in the world, fifty Paras would have their work cut out holding off the rebels indefinitely – especially as their numbers could be reinforced to some seven hundred or more. But if they failed to do so, the results didn't bear thinking about. There was no doubt about it, for their first ever mission going in alongside the men of the Special Forces, this was going to be a tough one.

And to the D Squadron boys, a number of the newly arrived Paras had seemed decidedly young and green around the gills. Some looked to be no more than seventeen or eighteen years old. Which was a worry, as the men of D Squadron were relying on the Paras to seriously kick arse on the southern side of the river. If the Paras screwed up their part of the mission, or bottled it, then they, D Squadron, would end up getting it in the neck. Seeing as the Paras were young guns, they'd be up for a fight, that much was certain. But as for combat experience, well, the men of the D Squadron just hoped that the Paras had a few veteran soldiers in their ranks, and some bloody good officers to lead them.

Cockney Jimmy had watched the arrival of the Paras with a good deal of concern; many of them clearly lacked combat experience. But shite, everyone had to start somewhere. It was a fuckin' good opportunity for the young lads to get their hands dirty, Jimmy had told himself. Anyway, the Paras were here now and they would be going into action alongside each other, so he may as well have some fun and games with them in the meantime. As far as Jimmy was concerned, this was a golden opportunity to put his CB-MRE-B campaign into operation. There was great scope for a major inter-regimental war now. The 22nd Regiment SAS versus the 1st Parachute Regiment. Some of those young lads would never know what hit them, that much was for sure. *And what a bleedin' laugh that would be.*

Arriving back at his troop's tent, Jimmy ducked inside, stooping low to get past his Union Jack towel that was hung up to dry in the middle. Brushing aside his mosquito net, he plonked himself down on his foldable camp bed. It was time to start work on the finer points of his attack plan. He was thinking about hitting the first young lads when they went out to the khazis, out the back of the camp. The khazis were in an isolated position, set apart from the rest of the camp and facing the Occra Hills. That was a wicked idea.

But just as he was about to start building his first CB-MRE-B, he began having second thoughts. This was no training exercise with the Yanks, a voice in his head was warning him. They were here on a deadly serious combat mission. If Op Barras went ahead, a lot of people were going to end up getting killed, of that he was certain – though hopefully all of them would be the enemy. The Regiment tolerated a lot of horseplay from the men, but maybe his bombing campaign would be going a little too far. After all, rebel territory wasn't that far away.

Both the West Side Boys and the RUF had been operational around Waterloo Camp in recent months. And there were a hundred-odd jumpy young Paras just arrived in the camp. His prank bombs might even be mistaken for real ones, and if that happened someone could easily end up getting shot. Jimmy may have been crazy, but he wasn't *that* crazy. Just as he was coming to terms with the fact that maybe his bombing campaign wasn't such a good idea after all, word went out that the men of D Squadron were wanted in the ops tent, double quick. The OC was about to hold an important briefing.

Somewhere, something seemed to have blown up, as it were.

THE SIEGE OF THE GIMP

Convince your enemy that he will gain very little by attacking you. This will diminish his enthusiasm.

— a Chinese proverb

SHORTLY after dawn on day seven of the hostage crisis, Sony – the West Side Boys' informal ambassador – came across to speak to the remaining captives. As always, he was quiet and eloquent and had a sane, measured bearing. He asked for Captain Flaherty to go with him and lend a hand with the radio communications, so they could progress the ongoing hostage negotiations. But maybe because he could see how depressed Rangers Gaunt and Rowell looked, Sony paused before leaving to have an encouraging word with them.

'Don't worry so,' he reassured them. 'You've not been forgotten. You'll be out of here by tomorrow. I'm doing everything I can to secure your release. So don't despair. Keep your hopes up, all right?'

The two Rangers tried to find some reassurance in Sony's words. But it wasn't easy. After the release of the five others, their spirits had taken a real nosedive. They were experiencing the bitter disappointment of being left behind in the rebel village, and it wasn't proving easy.

As the days dragged by, Sony was becoming an increasingly important lifeline for the hostages – a vital source of information about the camp and the outside world. But as to just exactly who Sony was, the men were none the wiser. While they had been able to pigeonhole everyone else in the village – boy soldier, psycho hard man, rebel commander – Sony defied any easy definition. He remained the unknown quantity, the enigma.

He seemed clever and well educated. He never carried a gun and he clearly wasn't a military man as such. He didn't seem to be one of their high political ranks, either. Yet at the same time he could act like he was at one with the rebels and pass unnoticed among them. In fact, it was hard to describe just how the rest of the West Side Boys related to Sony. In his own, quiet way, he behaved like he was a cut above the rest, or something, yet he was still able to walk around the camp wherever he wanted without being molested, and see Foday Kallay whenever he chose. Sony, like the Major, had something of the grey man about him. But for the six British hostages, he was their beacon of hope in an otherwise dark and fearful situation.

That evening, even the Gimp must have decided that he had had enough of things in Gberi Bana. One of the boy rebels had been taunting him out the front of Cambodia's place, and the Gimp had finally cracked, wrestling his AK47 off him and stumbling back inside the house. As the rebel soldier had rushed in after him, a series of gunshots had split the air – bullets ricocheting down the central hall of Cambodia's house and out across the veranda where the hostages were sitting. As madness descended into farce, a large group of West Side Boys gathered outside, attracted by all the shouting and the gunfire. They started dancing about and whooping it up, clearly finding the Gimp going wild with a sub-machine gun inside Cambodia's house the most amusing thing to have happened in Gberi Bana this side of Christmas.

'Fuck this for a game of soldiers,' Major Martial finally exploded, with uncharacteristic vehemence. 'The bloody loonies have really taken over the asylum this time. I'm going to find Cambodia and have it out with him,' he snapped, as he strode off into the darkness.

By now, the older rebels were trying to find out exactly which of the youngsters had allowed the Gimp to grab his gun. They then ordered this young boy back into the house to disarm the Gimp. From being the tormenter, this boy soldier had suddenly become the tormented, as the rest of the rebels turned their guns on him and forced him back into the building. He started pleading with them, begging them not to send him in there, fawning on the ground. He was obviously terrified now, and close to tears. But the more distraught he became, the funnier the rest of the rebels seemed to find it. Just then, Major Martial emerged from the shadows with Cambodia in tow.

'I don't know if you've noticed, Colonel, but there's a flaming Gimp inside your house running amok with a gun, and we're not keen to stay around and get shot at,' the Major was saying. 'Where can we move to where we'll be out of range – just until you've dealt with all this?'

'Oh . . . Don't worry . . . It's nothing much to worry about,' said Cambodia, waving his arms vaguely in the direction of all the chaos and grinning. 'Why not stay for the fun? No? You don't want to? Well, if you like, you can go down to the end of the track. There is a hut, over there, by the forest. You wait there, and we will deal with the big man.'

'Thank you, Colonel. Come on, lads,' said the Major, turning to his men. '*We* are getting out of here.'

They needed no second urging. They followed the Major up a track heading north-east for a hundred yards or so, which ended in a small hut at the forest's edge. As they did so, they could hear more firing and uproar and hilarity behind them, as the rebels continued to force the young boy soldier into the house to disarm the Gimp, and the boy tried to resist.

'Couldn't organise a flamin' piss-up in a brewery,' the Major muttered to himself, as they strode away from the chaotic scene.

By the time they reached the forest's edge, the sound of the siege of the Gimp had faded away behind them, and the six British soldiers were enveloped in the rhythmic, deafening chirrup-chirrup and whirr-whirr of a myriad jungle insects doing their night-time thing. It was a magnificent sound, and somehow strangely calming. Barely a hundred yards away, the West Side Boys could be up to the most insane, addled madness imaginable, and yet the great, immutable forest took absolutely zero notice of them. Just as the Major was about to congratulate the wall of darkened trees before him on their wonderful, solid, unshakeable sanity, he was struck by a sudden realisation: if he wasn't mistaken, Cambodia had forgotten to send any guards with them. For the first time since their capture, the six British soldiers were gathered together without a single gun-toting West Side lunatic anywhere to be seen.

'Hang on a minute, lads. Shh,' he hissed, bringing the men to a halt in the darkness. 'Am I dreaming things, or are we guardless?'

The men stood stock still and listened. As they did so, their eyes became accustomed to the darkness, as their natural night vision kicked in. All around them, towering against the brilliant, starlit sky, were the massive stumps of broken trees. The smell of damp earth and charcoal was in their nostrils. There had recently been a burning here. On the rare occasions that the West Side Boys bothered to cultivate anything, they practised slash-and-burn farming. This patch of forest had recently been cut, the loose wood and branches being left to dry under a hot, tropical sun, and then set alight. There was no movement that any of them could detect on the path behind them. And the forest was just fifteen yards away to their front. They could still hear fragments of the uproar over at Cambodia's house drifting across to them. But as far as they could tell, the West Side Boys had forgotten them, and they were completely alone.

'This is it!' the Major whispered, excitedly. 'Come on, lads. Let's go for it. Now. Into the forest.'

'What, sir, youse mean . . . *escape* . . . ?' Ranger Gaunt asked, hesitantly.

'Of course I mean *escape*,' the Major urged. 'Escape and evade. You've all seen the maps. It's one night's walk back to the base from here, that's all. Come on, we can make it. These bunch of idiots won't even realise we're gone, let alone organise themselves to follow.'

'Sir, I . . . I don't sort of think it's a good idea, sir,' Ranger Gaunt ventured, uncertainly. In normal circumstances, none of the soldiers would ever have dreamed of challenging their OC. But these were far from normal circumstances. 'Surely, those bastards know the forest round here far better than we do, don't you reckon, sir?'

'Aye. I'm with Sandy, sir,' Ranger Rowell chipped in. 'And, I mean, we've no compass and no torch, it's pitch black under them trees, there's no paths that we know of, and we've no machete or nothing. Sir, I don't think we'd get so far before they found us, sir. And to my mind this way takes us sort of aways from British Forces, further into the jungle.'

'I know it does,' the Major replied, exasperatedly. '*Exactly*. They won't think of looking for us in this direction. We can work our way round through the edge of the forest, back to the other side of the village, and set off from there. Then it's a night's march and we're back to our base. Look, lads, I know it's nowhere near bloody perfect. But we aren't going to get perfect, are we? It's a case of making the best of any opportunity that presents itself. And right now we've got no guards and the bloody great jungle just a few feet away from us. Turn this down, lads, and we probably won't be getting a second chance. Not one as good as this, anyway.'

'But what about the feckin' river, sir?' insisted Ranger Rowell. 'Isn't the river lying between us and the British base, sir?'

'If need be we swim it, lad,' said the Major. 'We can all swim, can't we? And none of those crazy bastards seem able to. We swim the river and beast it back to base, lad. *C'mon*, lads, what d'you say?'

There was a few seconds' silence, broken at last by Ranger Gaunt. 'I . . . I'm sorry, sir, but I . . . I just don't think I'm flamin' well psyched up for it, sir. And I don't sort of think the others are, either. I mean, I know *I'm* not, anyways. One moment there's the Gimp loosing off with a flamin' AK, and the next we're supposed to be haring off into the jungle and escaping. Sorry, sir. I can't be doing it, like.'

'I'm with yer man, sir,' Ranger Rowell added. 'Sure, it's a great opportunity, the best yet, but I just don't think we'd make it. There'll be other chances, sure there will be, sir, and better ones, too.'

'Well, it's a group decision, lads,' the Major conceded, disappointedly. 'Always has been. It's all of us or none of us, that's for sure. We all have to want to go. Anyway, perhaps you're right. Perhaps we would be biting off more than we could chew.'

'Looks like we'll be sort of staying at this feckin' holiday camp a wee bit longer, then, eh, sir,' Ranger Gaunt quipped, trying to make light of things.

'Aye. And youse thought Belfast was a shitehole, Sandy,' added Ranger Rowell, under his breath.

Whenever they had discussed their options for escape, the Major had always made it clear that it had to be all of them or none of them. Any partial escape attempt would almost certainly result in the killing of the hostages who'd been left behind. One or two of the more senior ranks had tried to argue for a unilateral escape attempt: for one man to slip away into the river at dusk to seek help from the British forces downstream. But what would that have gained them? British forces knew exactly where the hostages were being held. No. The Major was adamant. The only option was for all the hostages to escape together, or not at all.

Of course, that meant all of the *British* hostages. Corporal Mousa was another matter. The Sierra Leonean Corporal was being kept permanently isolated from the others, most of the time in the dreaded pit. Each morning, Major Martial would insist on going walkabout in the village, largely in an attempt to check up on Mousa. One of the guards would be sent with him, but the Major always found some excuse to have a quick word with the Corporal. And it was clear that after several days in the pit, Corporal Mousa was in a very bad way. But with all the will in the world, there was no way that they could include Corporal Mousa in their escape plans. He was being held separately and under guard. If they got the chance to break out, he was being left behind: none of the British soldiers liked it, but that's just the way it was.

After half an hour or so, the siege of the Gimp finally came to an end: one of the rebels had finally grabbed the AK47 off him. The six hostages trudged back to Cambodia's house, and took up their positions on the veranda again. The Gimp had been punished horribly but not killed. It was more the boy soldier who'd let the Gimp grab his gun who was blamed and he was badly beaten by the older rebels. But the siege of the Gimp had reinforced in the minds of all the hostages the level of insanity that gripped the West Side Boys' village, and hence they need to escape. It was not so long since the Major had changed his mind over the five men to be released, but already the Rangers had forgiven him. There had been no single event that had redeemed the Major in their eyes. It was more a cumulation of little things: the way the Major braved the rebels' wrath by keeping contact with Corporal Mousa; the way he stood up to Cambodia and protected his men from the siege of the Gimp; the way he accepted the junior ranks' resistance to his escape plans without complaint; the way in which he maintained group solidarity and loyalty as the key to their survival; and the way in which he continually encouraged and boosted their morale.

No man was perfect, and the Major had made some mistakes along the way. But to the Rangers, his behaviour and bearing ever since their capture marked the Major out as a true hero. A man of fortitude, courage and principle. A man who led by example. A man whose behaviour they all could aspire to follow. A man whose self-sacrifice proved more than anything else the deep loyalty he felt towards his fellow soldiers. They respected the Major, they looked up to him, and they looked to his leadership in this deeply challenging time. They believed that with the Major's help, they could get through this living nightmare. With Major Martial by their side.

Day eight of the hostage crisis was a Friday, and very early that morning, Cambodia ordered the six British soldiers to move down to the Camp Commandant's house at the southern end of the village. No reason was given, and as the six men had got used to being at Cambodia's place it was not a happy move. They'd also heard the rumours about the Camp Commandant, that he was the craziest of the lot of them. Sony had told them that before joining the West Side Boys, the Camp Commandant had actually been an inmate in the Freetown asylum for the clinically insane. He was supposed to have recovered now, Sony added. But none of the hostages had been convinced. They'd seen the Camp Commandant around and about. He was a small, skinny, scruffy man with a nervous, twitching energy, and a mass of wild fuzzy hair above mad, bulging eyes. The Camp Commandant looked far from sane.

While he called himself the Camp Commandant, the British soldiers had no idea if that meant that he was supposed to be in charge of things in Gberi Bana, or if that was just his *nom de guerre*. The Camp Commandant was supposed to be some sort of second in command to the rebel leader, Foday Kallay. But whether that meant he was superior in rank to Colonel Cambodia, none of the British soldiers could tell. In short, over a week into their incarceration in Gberi Bana, the hostages were no nearer to fathoming the rebels' command and control structure than they had been on their arrival.

The Camp Commandant's house was situated on the junction of the two tracks that led through the village. It was of a similar construction and layout to Cambodia's, only it had been painted more recently, so it was a slightly less dirty shade of white. The British soldiers were put in a smaller room with no bed, and Assan, one of the Camp Commandant's boy soldiers, a lad of no more than nine years in age, showed them what was what in the house. He was particularly proud of a latrine of sorts that they had out the back. It was just a shallow hole dug in the ground with a hammered flat oil drum providing a crude cover behind which to squat. A grinning Assan showed them where a little yellow plastic watering can (minus rose) was kept to one side of the latrine, and mimed how they should use it for cleaning themselves.

That first morning, the six hostages sat out on the Camp Commandant's veranda and watched the sun creep its way skywards, lifting itself lazily out of the mist-laden waters of the Rokel Creek, which snaked away into the forest below them. The West Side Boys were rarely awake at this time, and so the village at dawn would offer a little space and a few precious moments of peace and solitude to the British soldiers. As the rising sun lit up the river mists below them in magical shades of pink and turquoise, for a moment it almost seemed as if Sierra Leone was a beautiful land, a captivating tropical paradise . . . What a pity that this country had been inherited by such a bunch of murderous bastards, the men thought to themselves. In a different time, under a different set of circumstances, they could even have imagined enjoying a few days' holiday here. But for now, the view did little to compensate for the company.

Once the Camp Commandant was awake, the hostages got a small taster of his madness. They spotted him wandering about the lower part of the village, shouting and gesticulating wildly into the air. Lord only knew what he was on about. Eventually, his wife came over and started hollering: 'Calm down fresh,' trying to grab his arms and pin them to his sides. 'Calm down fresh, calm down fresh,' she kept repeating. 'Calm down fresh' is what you would say in Creole slang to someone who's very angry, to cool them down. And after the British soldiers overheard that, the name just stuck: the Camp Commandant became 'Calm Down Fresh'. Calm Down Fresh was clearly very prone to 'going off on one', as the Rangers put it. He was soon to become the British soldiers' single greatest tormenter.

Calm Down Fresh's wife clearly held a lot of power over him, as, it seemed, did Foday Kallay's wife over her husband. The difference was that in Calm Down Fresh's case, he was the lunatic and his wife was the only voice of sanity that he'd listen to. In Foday Kallay's case, she was the lunatic, and he seemed all too inclined to listen to her demented ramblings. Kallay's wife was a big, fat woman, who styled herself as the Voodoo Queen of the West Side Boys (rather like Foday Sankoh's wife, Mamma Sankoh, had done with the RUF). She was a complete psychopath, who regularly demanded of her husband the arbitrary murder or horrible torture of one or another of the prisoners in the camp. She carried her own AK47, and there were terrible rumours about what she had got up to with it: shooting off prisoners' testicles as a prelude to their execution, that sort of thing. It was not a nice thought for the soldiers – being Calm Down Fresh's house guests, and having Mr and Mrs Kallay as their next-door neighbours.

At first, the British hostages' daily routine changed little with the move. But from the veranda out the front of Calm Down Fresh's house there was a more interesting view, with a lot more going on. The Camp Commandant's house overlooked the central village clearing, with the two dirt tracks stretching down to the river, and the one leading north towards Cambodia's. Directly in front was the West Side Boys' hospital house, where the rebels housed their wounded. On one of the Major's walkabouts he had managed to get a quick look inside the hospital house, and it was clear that the rebels had almost zero medicines and no medical facilities. To the rear of Calm Down Fresh's house was the overgrown village football pitch.

The boy soldier Assan was now their main guard. He was basically all right – just another brutalised kid who really wanted to make friends, rather like Movement had been before him. But over the next few days, the men would witness the savage beatings that Calm Down Fresh would visit on Assan – and as they did so, they would start to better understand just what made these young boys into the killers they had become. Assan should have been at school, dreaming of his future, and messing about on a bicycle with his mates in his spare time. He was just a kid. He should have been fishing in the river, building tree houses in the forest and collecting coconuts from the palm trees in his home village to take to his mother. Instead, he was sitting out on a veranda in a rebel base clutching an AK47 almost as tall as he was, keeping guard over a group of British hostages.

Fairly quickly, Assan started treating the British soldiers more like his friends than his prisoners. And one morning, he told them something of his short life story, a typical tale for a rebel boy soldier in Sierra Leone. Kidnapped from his family by the West Side Boys at eight years old, Assan had been brought to Gberi Bana, given a gun and told he was a rebel soldier. He'd had some pretty nasty experiences at the hands of the older rebels, but he didn't go into those in great detail. He did talk about his family, though, and in particular his mother, and about how he longed to see her again. His parents had been fairly wealthy inhabitants of Freetown, but he couldn't think of how to get away from the rebels and get back to his home again. Assan was himself a victim – yet he was destined to victimise other innocents as long as he stayed there in that rebel village.

But just as Assan had finished telling his story, Calm Down Fresh had come storming out on to the veranda. A guilty Assan had started waving his gun at the prisoners, in a pathetic attempt to assume the proper posture of a guard. But this sad charade would get him nowhere with Calm Down Fresh. The Camp Commandant must have overheard him telling the British soldiers his life story. He stormed over to the boy and cracked him as hard as he could around the head with his fist. As Assan keeled over, dropping his gun, Calm Down Fresh started booting him in the ribs, the boy soldier letting out an agonised groan each time that he did so. All the while that he was kicking him, Calm Down Fresh was screaming at Assan in their own language. The hostages couldn't understand a word, of course, but they had a good idea what the evil bastard was on about.

'I hear you go talk wid de fucking whiteboys again,' KICK! 'I go beat you so hard yo go wish you be dead.' KICK! 'And then I go trow-trow you in de river for de snap-snap crocodiles to eat, you little bastard.' KICK! KICK! 'How many times I go have to tell you dat they go be prisoners,' KICK! 'and you go be de fucking guard.' KICK! KICK! 'Get dat into you thick head, you no be a fucking kid no more,' KICK! 'you no have de family no more,' KICK! 'you now be de West Side Nigga, and dat be de great honour and de privilege, one dat you no be even worthy of.' KICK! KICK! KICK! 'And you don't go fucking forget it ever-ever.' KICK! KICK!

After he'd finished beating the living daylights out of the young boy soldier, Calm Down Fresh spun round on his heel and went to storm off the veranda. But he hesitated for a second, and then turned back again, to face the British soldiers.

'So you go see, Major,' he spat out, 'dat is what happen to de little boy soldier when he go stop being de guard and be start being you friend-friend. Yah! A small-small warning when he go starts *liking* you too much. Now, you go see if you can protect *him* as well as you go protect de rest of you men!'

'Feckin' evil bastards,' Ranger Rowell muttered, as soon as Calm Down Fresh was out of earshot. 'But what's his beef with you, sir?'

'I reckon he's sort of envious of you, sir,' Ranger Gaunt butted in. 'I reckon he's just jealous, 'cause youse aren't a fucked-up lunatic like he is, if youse know what I mean, sir.'

'You might have a point there, lad,' the Major replied. 'Whatever his problem is, it's poor bloody Assan I'm worried about.'

Assan was lying in a cowed heap on the floor in a corner of the veranda, his arms curled protectively over his head. The poor kid was crying and wheezing, and trying to suck in lungfuls of air through his painful, heaving ribcage. Calm Down Fresh had put over a dozen, hard kicks into the boy's chest. But the physical pain was bearable: it was the total humiliation and degradation that Assan must have found the most difficult to deal with. He was lying there now a broken heap in front of the white men that he'd started to befriend, and to whom he'd just been telling his sad little life story. Assan tried to sit up, hugging his bruised ribs as he did so, and the six British hostages could see that his dark cheeks were streaked with tears.

Shite. That poor fucking kid, they were thinking to themselves. *Jesus, what a life, what a nightmare of a childhood. It's not even a fucking childhood. It's no life at all.*

That afternoon, the hostages' spirits lifted a little when they heard confirmation on the BBC that the five of them who had been released had reached safety. Morale improved still further when Cambodia came over with news that a stack of British Army ratpacks had arrived for them. A patrol of the Royal Irish Rangers had handed over the ratpacks to the rebels at their checkpoint, out on the Freetown–Masiaka highway. Cambodia asked what the British soldiers wanted out of the rations, and they all went for the chocolate and the biscuits. When the dozen or so ratpacks were finally brought over, a gleeful Sergeant Smith took control of the supplies.

But it soon became clear that the rebels had rifled through all the ratpacks, and that the chocolate and biscuits had gone. It was little things like that which made the hostages really hate and despise their captors. But the Sergeant's face lit up with joy when he discovered a tiny, Hexy stove (a tiny, collapsible metal burner, which uses solid, paraffin-based fuel) in the bottom of one of the ratpacks, complete with several fuel blocks. This meant they could start making their own meals and brews, which was no small thing in their present, undernourished condition. Sergeant Smith assumed immediate cooking duty, and that first night he rustled up a giant feast of corned beef hash with mustard and brown sauce. Food had never tasted so good to the hostages.

As day eight came and went, and day nine dawned, and nothing seemed to have changed in the lives and fortunes of the six British hostages, the men began losing track of time. The days were starting to merge into one. As neither the CO nor Captain Flaherty were being taken along to the hostage negotiations any more, the only source of news was the BBC World Service. But for the last day or so, there had been no further reports of any kind on their story. The men began sinking into a hopeless depression, fuelled by the fear that they were being left to rot in that rebel village, their plight forgotten by the outside world.

It was at this time – when the hostages were at their lowest ebb – that they received their greatest morale boost yet. Sometime around midnight on what they believed was the night of day ten, there was a faint tap, tap, tapping at the window of their room. Major Martial was the first to wake up, and as he looked over towards the source of the noise, he saw a piece of paper being poked through the gap between the shutters of their window. Jumping to his feet, he grabbed hold of it and eased it inside. He pulled out his mini Maglite (the rebels had not yet got around to taking the Major's tiny, black metal torch off him), carefully unfolded the scrap of paper and began scanning its contents. After reading the note several times over, just to make certain he wasn't dreaming, the Major let out a long, low whistle under his breath.

'Well, lads,' he whispered, looking up at them with a grin, 'it seems we've not been forgotten. We're not alone. It's a note and it reads: *"You're doing Stirling work. You'll be seeing the boys soon."'*

'What does that mean, sir, *sterling work*, sir?' asked Ranger Gaunt, excitedly.

'Stirling. You know, lad, *Stirling*. Spelt S-T-I-R-L-I-N-G. Like Stirling Lines, you know, the SAS base in Hereford,' the Major said under his breath. 'The note's from the Regiment. Has to be. It means they're out there in the jungle somewhere. We thought they might be. Here's the proof.'

'Who the heck put it through, sir, d'you think – I mean the note, I mean through the window?' the wide-eyed Ranger asked. 'D'youse think it was . . . one of *them*?' The way he had said the 'them' – his voice laced with a deep respect, approaching awe – it was clear that he'd meant the SAS. 'How d'youse think they all sort of got through the camp without being seen, then?'

'I don't know, lad,' the Major responded. 'But I doubt if it was one of *them*, as you put it. It'd be too risky for *them* to do it. They probably used one of the locals. Maybe a Kamajor – they're legendary in these parts for being able to slip through the jungle unnoticed, that sort of thing. Or a local villager, someone who's known around the camp and wouldn't arouse any suspicions.'

'Or meybe it was flamin' Sony, sir?' the Ranger ventured.

'Could be, lad. But I'll bet he's not telling. We'll probably never know,' the Major continued, 'but what we can be sure of is that it's genuine. It's written in such a way that it wouldn't do too much harm if it fell into the wrong hands. But it's the way they've spelled Stirling – that's the clincher. None of these bastards would know about that sort of thing.'

'It's grand, that is, sir. No – it's bloody better than grand. It's a flamin' miracle,' said Ranger Gaunt, grinning from ear to ear. 'When d'youse sort of think they'll be coming for us then, sir?'

'Well, lad, it's obviously meant to be a morale booster for us, that's for sure.'

'Like a kind of hang-on-in-there note, sir?'

'That's it. I reckon it means they must be in there on the ground, preparing for an attack,' the Major continued. 'It can only be a matter of days now, that's my guess. So, keep your spirits up, lads, all right?'

The episode with the note was an extraordinary high point for the hostages. Short of outright rescue, it was the biggest morale booster they could possibly have hoped for. An excited discussion followed – all be it in muted tones – about how the SAS rescue force might be coming for them. They were clearly out there somewhere in the jungle, keeping watch. The Major suggested to his men that they should try to get out and about and be seen more. That could help make the SAS's observation tasks easier, he reasoned.

There was also discussion about how the assault force was likely to attack and how their captors might respond. The rebels had already warned the hostages that if any British or UN helicopters came over Gberi Bana or Magbeni, then they'd start killing them. So, the hostages' main worry was whether the SAS rescue party would get to them quickly enough, before their rebel captors came to kill them. The Major gave orders for defensive measures to be taken in such event. If the assault force did come in, the best they could do was to barricade the door, to try to buy themselves some time.

'You'll need to make damn sure you let them know you're British Army, lads,' the Major added, in a whisper.

'Just how do we do that, sir?' Ranger Gaunt asked.

'You bloody bawl at the top of your voice: "British Army! British Army! British Army!" that's how, lad,' the Major answered, grinning. 'And then you keep your bloody heads down.'

'Should we try to make some sort of makeshift weapons, sir? Just in case, like.'

'With what, lad?' the Major replied. 'Four walls and no bed? Right now all we can hope for is to keep the door closed long enough to prevent the bastards getting in. How're your muscles, Ranger? Feeling strong? I reckon we can manage that, don't you?'

Sometime in the early hours of the morning, the men were torn from fitful sleep by the sound of gunfire. Crack-crack! Crack-crack! Two sets of two shots in quick succession. Six pairs of worried eyes peered at each other in the darkness. There was a huge commotion developing just outside their room, with people shouting and yelling and what sounded like a struggle. Without saying a word, the Major crept across to the window to investigate. Part of him was worried that whoever had delivered the note to them had somehow been discovered, perhaps while returning with a further message. If that was the case, it would not be good news.

Peering out through the thin crack between the wooden shutters, he could just make out a large crowd of rebels milling around. Bizarrely, it looked as if one of the rebel officers had been tied up by a group of the West Side Boys. As the Major tried to see what was happening, he noticed the officer was wearing a distinctive red beret, so it had to be that evil bastard Colonel Savage. Other than that, the Major couldn't make out much of what was happening. But whatever *was* going on, it didn't look like it could be anything to do with the British hostages, or their visitor who'd come with the note. The Major hoped that his men could just remain safely in their room, keeping out of the way of any trouble for the rest of the night.

The next morning, Sony appeared and told them the story of the night's strange events. Woken by the gunshots, some of the rebels had discovered that Calm Down Fresh had gone completely AWOL. Apparently, he'd tried to shoot Assan, but had missed, so was giving him a pistol-whipping instead. Some of the rebels had then grabbed Calm Down Fresh and tied him up, to stop him causing any more trouble. It was Calm Down Fresh that the Major had seen from the window, not Colonel Savage, Sony explained. Finally – and for reasons that Sony was at a loss to explain – the rebels had decided to settle matters by 'promoting' Calm Down Fresh. So the mad bastard was now a 'Lieutenant Colonel'. It was nothing to do with the British soldiers, Sony reassured them.

At least, that was Sony's version of events, and it was all the British hostages had to go on. But the reality – as Corporal Mousa knew – was very different. The previous night, six new prisoners – bound hand and foot – had been thrown into the dungeon alongside him. To Corporal Mousa's astonishment, one of them was instantly recognisable as Colonel Savage. With him were three of his infamous sub-commanders – Mr Die, the Cobra and Mr Murder. From the ensuing conversation between the six men, Mousa pieced together the full story of what had happened. It seemed that Foday Kallay had become paranoid that Colonel Savage and his men had done a treacherous deal with the British to over-throw him and release the hostages. The previous night, an enraged Kallay had decided to act, and had ordered Colonel Savage to be arrested and thrown in the dungeon, along with five of his lieutenants.

Once someone had been consigned to the dungeon, they rarely came out alive. It was practically a death sentence, and Colonel Savage and his five deputies had no doubt as to the seriousness of the situation. Just to show that he wasn't messing around, Kallay had taken two of Savage's men and had them executed on the spot – hence the four gunshots that the British soldiers had heard in the night.

So why had Sony lied to the British hostages, telling them a completely made-up story? Probably because he was trying to protect them from knowing the worst. The fact that their very presence in the rebel camp had caused such a deep split in the West Side Boys was a dangerous development. It meant that the rebel group was now more unstable and volatile than the British hostages could ever have imagined. And it meant that there were now disgruntled forces inside the West Side Boys – the five hundred men of the Savage Group – who had every reason to want the British soldiers dead.

Especially if Foday Kallay did go ahead and execute Colonel Savage.

1 3

RIVERINE ASSAULT

Country in which there are precipitous cliffs with torrents running
between them, deep natural hollows, confined places, tangled jungle
thickets, quagmires and crevasses, should be left with all possible speed
and not approached.

– Sun Tzu, *The Art of War, c.* 500 BC

COCKNEY Jimmy had abandoned his Coke-bottle bombing campaign,
and headed instead for the cookhouse tent, where the men of the assault
force were gathering to hear Pete Cutgood's briefing. It was only four
days after their arrival in Sierra Leone, but already five of the hostages
had been set free by the West Side Boys. In return, the rebels had been
given nothing more than a satphone. After some rest and recovery, two
of the five released hostages had agreed to come over to Waterloo
Camp, to give the men of D Squadron a face-to-face briefing. Now
would be the best time to raise any questions that the men might have,
the squadron OC explained, while the hostages' experiences were still
fresh in their minds.

Straight after their release, the five Royal Irish soldiers had been
flown out to the Royal Fleet Auxiliary ship, *Sir Percival*, anchored off
Freetown harbour – for a shave and a wash, a feed and a change of
uniform. There was a permanent press corps hanging around the gates
of Benguema, the Royal Irish Rangers' base camp, so there was no
way in which the five men could have been taken there. But in order
to satisfy the hunger of the world's media for news of the hostages,
Brigadier Gordon Hughes, Commander of British Forces in Sierra
Leone, had held an impromptu press conference in Freetown. 'The five
men were naturally tired,' the Brigadier had told the assembled media,

'and they have been taken to a place where they can recover and get some rest. They were medically checked and are fit and well. We have plans to continue talks with the West Side Boys today.'

Lieutenant Colonel Tony Cramp, the British military spokesman, had then taken questions from the press, which had largely focused on whether any deal had been done to secure the hostage releases. 'We have done no deal with the West Side Boys,' the Lieutenant Colonel had maintained. While negotiations were continuing in 'a calm and positive manner', there was no timeframe for the remaining hostages' release. When asked what would now happen to the five freed men, the Lieutenant Colonel had stressed that the British Army had set procedures for such situations. The men would be put through the normal debriefing cycle, 'involving taking them through their story and answering questions to give us information on their ordeal'.

Their release had been wonderful news for the hostages, of course, but it had seemed like bad news to the men of D Squadron. As far as they were concerned, five hostages released so early and so easily could only mean one thing – that the rebels were more likely to cave in and release the rest of them. In which case, Operation Barras would be over and they'd all be going home. But nothing was certain in this game, and in the meantime they had to get on with the job in hand. The men had high expectations for the hostage debriefing. One of the most useful pieces of intelligence that D Squadron had yet received from any quarter had come from the hostages themselves.

A couple of days earlier, a hand-drawn map of the village of Gberi Bana and all its key defences had been smuggled out by one of the hostages. Gerry Birt, the SAS man on the British hostage-negotiation team, had told the rest of the men of D Squadron the full story. At one of the face-to-face negotiation meetings, the Royal Irish patrol's Captain Flaherty had used the opportunity of shaking hands with one of the Met officers to pass on the map concealed in the palm of his hand. He'd rolled the piece of paper up into a tube and stuffed it inside a Biro lid, so as to make it as small and unobtrusive as possible.

Where he'd kept the Biro lid hidden until then didn't bear thinking about, Gerry Birt had added. It was probably in one of his bodily orifices, and there were no prizes for guessing which one. Either way, the map constituted a priceless piece of information, and had contributed a vital part to the intelligence jigsaw that D Squadron was now piecing together. It showed details of the West Side Boys' fortifications that even the satellite photos had been unable to pick up – for example, machine-gun emplacements located under palm trees.

Paying particular attention to the hostage debriefing would be Captain Dan Temper, whose Air Troop was earmarked to undertake the actual hostage rescue itself. He hoped to learn a great deal from observing exactly how the two men spoke, and reacted, to questioning. Were they alert and responsive, or did they seem dazed and confused? How far had their minds deteriorated during captivity? How good was their morale? Such observations would provide vital clues to help him plan his part of the assault, as they would demonstrate the likely state of mind of the six remaining British captives. Would the six men be mobile and responsive to his commands, or would they just have shut down? Might they even try to resist their own rescue? Was there any sense in which they might have 'bonded' with their captors – the so-called 'Stockholm syndrome'? In short, how would the remaining hostages react to the arrival of his six-man rescue team at their door?

The first of the released hostages to speak was Corporal Sampson. As Sam stood up and proceeded to give a short, succinct account of what had happened, the men of D Squadron were struck by how calm and reassured the Corporal appeared. He spoke in a relaxed, deliberate way, as he took the men through a potted history of the hostage crisis, from the day of his capture to the day of his release. He showed a deep concern for the fate of the six fellow soldiers that he'd left behind him in Gberi Bana, but was honest about being glad to be out himself. In particular, he painted a clear picture of the rebels' anarchic command and control structure, and their generally appalling state of vigilance. In short, it was an impressive performance – especially considering what the Corporal had just been through – and he hadn't seemed at all fazed by the crowd.

CSM Head had little to add to what the Corporal had already told them. His briefing was over pretty quickly, after which they were to see little more of him.

But after the formal presentation, Corporal Sampson stayed around the camp and had a brew with the men. Soon he was swinging the talk with them almost as if nothing had happened. Occasionally, one or other of the D Squadron men would steer the conversation around to cover something he needed to clarify about the state of play in Gberi Bana. But other than that, the Corporal just seemed to fit in really well. He wasn't a sycophant or anything; he wasn't in awe of the Regiment; he just wanted to lend a helping hand with getting the job done. The men asked him about all the 'vital intangibles' that could only ever be gleaned from human-intelligence (humint) sources. At what time of day was the rebels' morale the lowest? When did they do their drinks and their drugs? What effect did this have on their state of vigilance, and for how long did it last? They covered all the 'usual specifics' too: how high were the windows in the buildings? Any glass? What were the doors and roofs made of? What was the strength and thickness of the walls? No matter how sophisticated satellite spying systems might be, they would rarely pick up this sort of detail.

According to Corporal Sampson, the West Side Boys lounged about on the stoops of their houses most of the day, doing bugger all; they never cleaned or maintained their weapons; they really didn't believe they were going to be attacked; and, in the unlikely event that they were, they claimed that they would kick the British soldiers' arses. In short, the West Side Boys seemed to think that they were invincible. In part, Sam put this down to the bizarre voodoo tattoos and the weird charms that they all wore – 'sacred' bullets on a rusty chain around their necks, animal teeth and chicken bones on a dirty bracelet, and even tufts of human hair dangling on a string. Mamma Kallay, the rebels' voodoo queen, had told her young fighters that these would 'make the gunshots flow off them like water'. As a result, the young rebels did seem to believe that they were bulletproof.

The most galling thing about his whole hostage experience, Corporal Sampson added, was that the West Side Boys had stolen his wedding ring.

'Don't ye worry about that, laddie,' the Big Scottish Monster had reassured him, with a growl. 'Aye, we'll be getting your fookin' wedding ring back if that's the last thing we do. So, the fookers reckon they'll whip us arses, do they? They doon't know they're fookin' born, laddie.'

'Hurricane, Sam. Thunder and fakin' lightning, mate,' Cockney Jimmy cut in, enthusiastically, jumping to his feet as he did so. 'Fakin' whirlwind, mate. That's what's gonna hit those fuckers when we go in. For I will strike down with GREAT –'

'Shoot the fook up, Jimmy, laddie,' the Scottish Monster roared, pulling him back down on to his seat. 'Time a-fookin'-nough for that later. Now, Sam me laddie, tell us again about that GPMG they have on the roof of the fookin' Camp Commandant's house, will ye? How often do they actually have it manned, then?'

Once Corporal Sampson had got the measure of the men of

D Squadron, he began to open up with them some more. He told Jimmy, the Scottish Monster and the others about some of the worst things that had happened to them. There'd been the mock executions and beatings that they had suffered, of course, but that wasn't the worst. Far more difficult was the way the West Side Boys had treated Corporal Mousa and some of the other prisoners – the machete tortures and the unbearable days and nights locked in the pit. A few more days of such treatment, Corporal Sampson added, and Mousa was a goner.

Sam remained around Waterloo Camp to help guide the men through their assault rehearsals – pointing out the exact location of the rebels' gun emplacements that the assault force would have to take on. Out the back of the camp, D Squadron had marked out a life-size replica of Gberi Bana village. With more time and resources they'd actually have constructed a full-size mock-up of the village (rather like a film set). But at Waterloo Camp, they had made do with a ground plan marked off with white incident tape. It was still good enough to enable D Squadron to run through the whole assault plan in real time: from each man's initial entry point into the village, to the door they were going through or the gun emplacement they were tasked to take out.

Each troop had been broken down into two six-man fire teams, each fire team being tasked with a specific set of targets. Within each fire team, each man had a specific task and limit of exploitation (LOE) – basically the territory that his fire team should occupy in the assault. It was a golden rule in the Regiment that you never crossed your LOE. If you did, you'd be straying into another fire team's territory, and then you'd be highly likely to get mistaken for the enemy and wiped out. Each man had to keep the overall assault plan clear in his mind with a good sense of how his fire team fitted into it, while at the same time remaining clear on his own LOE and those of the fire teams around him. It was one hell of a lot to remember and remain conscious of, especially when in the thick of combat and under fire.

This is where repeated rehearsals – running through the assault time and time and time again – helped drill the details and the routine into each man's head. Eventually, movement, awareness, synchronicity and timing all became part of a ritual, a dance, an instinctive course of action learned over countless hours of assault practice. There could never be too many of these trial runs, and as new intelligence became available, it was factored into the rehearsal process. Liken it to a ballet troupe learning a new dance routine, or an orchestra learning a new symphony: every person needed to know their own part, while the group as a whole needed to function in perfect harmony. One dancer out of step, one musician out of tune, and the whole performance would be ruined. Likewise, the men of D Squadron and their SBS colleagues were learning a newly choreographed dance of combat, the score of a new symphony of war.

But at the same time as memorising the assault plan, each man needed to remain highly flexible: he might get retasked at any time, as a fellow fire team got bogged down in the firefight. He might receive an emergency call on his radio headset, and right then, right at that moment, the lives of those men might depend on him knowing exactly where to find their fire team. In short, each man had to keep the big picture in his head, remain focused on his task and his LOE, and yet remain flexible, all at the same time.

In practice, the men of D Squadron would carry out only one or two rehearsals where they went through the whole assault with every man involved. Then, they'd break it down into individual fire teams, and practise until they had it sorted. Each fire team had a team leader, a 2iC and four others – and they would practise and practise until everyone on the team was happy with the result. Over time, having sat through many sets of assault orders and countless rehearsals, the men would have learned to recognise what was most pertinent to their team and what was not. That was part of the skill. Each man would tend to be most focused when he knew that a particular element of the overall mission might affect his own life directly. The smaller details – the specific door or window each man would choose to go in through – would be down to each individual fire team to work out among themselves.

In terms of the assault on Gberi Bana, the village was broken down into two areas of attack. Area 1 comprised the southern end of the village, consisting of the buildings and clearings around Calm Down Fresh's house. Area 2 comprised the northern end of the village, covering the buildings and clearing around Colonel Cambodia's house. Each area had its own overall commander: Area 2's commander was a South African called Bill; Area 1 fell under Captain Dan Temper's command. Where Areas 1 and 2 butted up against each other in the centre of the village, there was the greatest danger of having a blue-on-blue ('friendly fire') incident. This would be guarded against by each fire team sticking rigidly to their LOE, as outlined in the overall assault plan.

Once each fire team was satisfied that they had fully rehearsed their role, there would be one dummy run using all the kit that the assault force would be going in with. It was crucial that each man carried exactly the same kit in the dummy run as he intended to take on the assault itself. Each man would then know exactly what it felt like moving with all that weight and bulk, and exactly what he was and wasn't capable of: he'd know that his water bottle either was or wasn't going to snag on that doorpost; he'd know that he either was or wasn't too bulky to get through the target entry window; he'd know that he either was or was not carrying the right weapon with the right range for the principal targets of his fire team on the ground. He'd know at what speed he could cover a stretch of open ground that had to be crossed. He'd know whether he was able to crawl into that ditch and take cover. Practice was everything.

At this stage of proceedings, the rehearsals were no longer a laughing matter. No one was joking or larking about any more. This was deadly serious. If the dummy run was not done with approaching the speed and aggression of the real thing, it was next to useless. It had to be as close as you could get to the actual assault itself. And by now, the men rehearsing the assault would be able to see every building and every machine-gun nest and every enemy in their mind's eye, as if they were real. This *was* the target village; this taped-off mock-up was Gberi Bana; that marked-off area was the hostage house; those piles of kit were the rebel machine-gun nests; and those dummy targets were the West Side Boys.

The dummy run was also each man's final opportunity to familiarise himself with where the other men in the assault force would be; not just those in his own fire team, but all of them. So when he turned that corner he would expect to see so-and-so's fire team racing for that machine-gun emplacement; when he burst through that doorway, he would expect to see so-and-so over there, against that far wall; when he crossed the village track heading down towards the river (upstream end, north side), he would expect to see so-and-so kicking down that door. And because he expected to see these men in those places, he wouldn't mistake them for the rebels and shoot them in the head.

Everyone had to be completely happy with the rehearsals. If anyone remained unclear about anything, then they would all have to go through the whole thing again. And again, and again. Until it was done. Inwardly, the men might be groaning: *Oh, fuck me, not again.* But outwardly, no one actually showed it or said anything. If any man was actually that dumb or incompetent to deserve another's open resentment, then they wouldn't be in the Regiment in the first place. So each man respected the other's need to run through it one more time, knowing that ultimately it might teach him something. That ultimately, it could just save his life. By the time that he had reached this stage of the game, there was so much on each man's mind, so much stored up in his head, that there was no room for fear any more; fear had been crowded out, terror reduced to a drill, the dread of death being replaced by a set of moves, a process. Now, there was no space to be scared any more – there was only the mission.

The day following Corporal Sampson's briefing, word came through that the hostage negotiations were beginning to deteriorate. More worryingly still, there was credible intelligence being received that the rebels were planning to move the hostages, taking them further into the jungle. That would almost certainly mean moving them into the territory of Foday Sankoh's RUF rebels, which was as good as signing the British soldiers' death warrant. Once the six men had been taken to their new hiding places, it would likely be all but impossible for the forces now assembled at Waterloo Camp to find them. And if they then had to take on the forces of the RUF (as well as the West Side Boys), they were talking about some six thousand battle-hardened rebels. This was not good news.

As a result, it was decided to send in two observation teams immediately, to set up hidden OPs in the jungles on the outskirts of the rebels' base. From there, they were to keep a careful eye on the increasingly erratic behaviour of the rebels towards the six remaining hostages, watching in particular for any attempts to move them. They would be reporting any significant developments back to Waterloo Camp by coded radio transmissions. If the rebels did start to move the hostages, then the obs teams were to split up, sending some of their number to track them through the jungle. And if the rebels started executing the British captives, that would be the catalyst for them to call in an air strike and an emergency assault.

It was no secret among the men of D Squadron that the Green Slime had succeeded in recruiting a 'local element' in the rebel camp. He was now feeding intel back to Green Slime in JFHQ Freetown. By the quality of the intel that this local element was providing, it had to be someone within the West Side Boys set-up itself – not just a local villager or one of the Kamajors, although they were certainly helping too. Indeed, the local element – whose code name was 'Ibrahim' – was actually someone very close to Foday Kallay himself. He had visited the British High Commission on several occasions, helping the British assault planners draw up an order of battle of all the West Side Boys' units, from the top commanders down to the foot troops.

Using the local element's first-hand experience – he had been a rebel commander for many years but had grown tired of all the senseless killing – the British assault planners were able to map out all of the West Side Boys' positions, not just those at Gberi Bana and Magbeni. There was a major combat camp at Laia Junction, on the main Freetown – Masiaka highway, which Foday Kallay had set up as part of Operation Kill British. It was situated so as to stop any advance by British troops along the main road down to his HQ. On the dirt track leading off the main road down to Magbeni, there was an ambush camp, situated so as to thwart any attempt to drive into the rebel HQ undetected. Once they had been mapped out at JFHQ, it was obvious that any overland assault by vehicle would have to fight its way through stiff resistance to get to the rebel HQ – by which time it would be game over for the hostages.

It was from Ibrahim that reports were now coming in of the rebels threatening to execute the remaining six hostages, or move them deeper into the jungles. After the successful hostage-release deal over the satphone, the rebels' position seemed to be hardening. Not only that, but they were getting into a take, take, take mentality. For example, the rebels had asked for boat engines, and the British had given them some outboard motors. But the rebels had given nothing in return. And Foday Kallay had now presented a whole new shopping list of weaponry and vehicles that the British negotiators were supposed to deliver to the rebels' Gberi Bana base, before any further progress in the hostage negotiations could be made.

D Squadron had been getting a daily briefing on the hostage-negotiation meetings, from their two guys on the British team, and things were clearly going downhill fast. While the four British negotiators had been adopting a non-confrontational approach, going to these meetings unarmed, Foday Kallay had started turning up with a massive entourage of 'bodyguards'. They were tooled up with all sorts of weapons and gear that made the supposedly conciliatory hostage talks look more like a scene from some *Mad Max* film. Kallay himself had taken to sporting a white shell suit and dark shades, which made him look more like some sort of gangster rapper than the leader of a rebel army. To cap it all, the rebels kept turning up deliberately late – sometimes by as much as two or three hours. The hostage-negotiation meetings were becoming increasingly unproductive, tense and confrontational. Something had to give.

To make matters worse, the local element had passed on intelligence that some of the rebel leaders were now pressing for a more aggressive approach – even for a second round of British hostage taking. The men of D Squadron didn't know exactly who this local element was – it wasn't their need to know – but they hadn't been ordered to avoid any specific West Side Boys' casualties. A couple of the men had raised this at one of the daily briefings. Shouldn't they be aware who this local element was, so that they could avoid shooting the poor bastard? After all, just going in and wasting the local element wasn't really acceptable. But they had been told that it wasn't something that they need worry about. Which either meant that the spy would be killed in the assault, which seemed unlikely, or that he was to be warned off the night before the attack so he could make his getaway.

'There's always one of 'em with 'arf a brain cell, in't there?' Jimmy had remarked, after the briefing.

'What d'you mean, mate?' the Kiwi asked.

'Well, it's obvious, innit?' Jimmy grunted through his tea. 'One of 'em – the one wiv 'arf a brain cell, that is – 'as clocked the fact that they're gonna get their fakin' 'eads kicked in, know what I mean?'

'You mean the local element, right, mate?' the Kiwi queried. It had taken him a good many months to get his head around how these Brits spoke. So many weird accents and bizarre expressions. His mum would have called it quaint. But give him NZ any day. All you had back there was North Island and South Island accents, which were hardly that different anyway, and the Maori. In bloody Britain you'd have thought there were a hundred different tribes or something, the way they all spoke. Four years in the Regiment, and he still hadn't got it completely sorted.

'Aye. The local element, laddie,' the Scottish Monster confirmed. 'The local element has realised he is ne going to be able to rely on this fookin' voodoo shite to save him. Not with the Regiment breathing down his neck, like.'

'What d'you reckon to this voodoo stuff then, eh, mate?' the Kiwi ventured. 'Heap powerful big magic is it, mate?'

'You're 'avin a fakin' nonsense, aren't you, Kiwi?' snorted Jimmy, incredulously. 'Fakin' voodoo, me old cobber? It's a fakin' load of shite, mate. Fakin' bullets running off 'em like water? Got more fakin' magic in a packet of Rich Tea biscuits, Kiwi, you mark my words.'

With that, Jimmy grabbed a handful of biscuits off the table in front of them and shoved a load in the Kiwi's direction.

''Ere you go, Kiwi. Get a load of 'em down your fat New Zealand neck,' he said, with a wink, rubbing his hands together in excitement. ''Ow old are you, Kiwi? Twenty-seven? Twenty-eight? Right, you scoff twenty-eight fakin' Rich Teas, or whatever your age is, mate – I only need to scoff twenty-one, like – then you runs twenty-one or twenty-eight or whatever number it fakin' is times around the fakin' cookhouse tent, mate – 'as to be the cookhouse tent, mind – singing out loud the Regiment's own fuckin' ongo-bongo voodoo spell, like. Out loud, mind, loud as you can, Kiwi, all right? Tell you what, I know all the words, so you just follow me and do what I do, all right? That's heap big fuck-off voodoo British Army style, mate. Come on,' he shouted, jumping to his feet and dancing from one foot to another. 'Let's try it.'

The other men just looked at each other and rolled their eyes in exasperation. For a while now, they'd all known that Jimmy was cracked. But this, well, this just took the biscuit, as it were.

'You fink I'm off my bleedin' rocker, innit?' Jimmy remarked, frowning. 'Well, you can just sit there and tiddlywink your fakin' tea and munch your fakin' biscuits – but don't ever say I didn't make the fakin' offer, all right.' With that, he set off with a handful of Rich Teas biscuits in one hand on a run around the cookhouse tent, wurbling a mouthful of chewed biscuit, spewing gibberish as he did so.

'You Brits are crazy,' the Kiwi remarked, shaking his head. 'How did you ever manage to get it together to win the war, eh, mate?'

'Dunno, laddie,' the Scottish Monster observed morosely, staring into his tea. 'Reckon we'll just have to do the same as we always do, and leave it all to the fookin' Kiwis, eh?'

'Just like the rugby, you mean, mate?'

'Now just ye fookin' watch yer step, laddie,' the Big Scottish Monster roared, in mock anger. 'There's two fookin' things we don't ever talk about in the Regiment. One's religion, the other's fookin' rugby. Has ne one ever told ye that before, laddie?'

But much that they'd like to have done, the men of Boat Troop couldn't sit around all evening chewing the fat, as there was work to be done. Once it was well and truly dark, they'd be going upriver along with some of the Shakyboats, to insert the two obs teams into the jungle around the West Side Boys' base. They'd be heading across the Freetown Estuary and then up the Rokel Creek. One four-man SAS team was supposed to set up an OP on the southern bank of the Rokel Creek, where the main body of the West Side Boys were based. The other six-man SAS team would set up an OP on the northern bank at Gberi Bana, near where the hostages were being held.

The Big Scottish Monster spread out a couple of maps on the table. Green Slime had come up with some ancient charts of the Freetown Estuary, which covered a good part of the Rokel Creek as well. But they looked like they'd been drawn up during colonial times, and God only knew how much the river had changed since then. It would have been best to have got some local knowledge in on the act, say one of the Kamajors who knew the river well. But there was little time for that.

'Go and fetch that crazy fooker, will ye, Kiwi laddie?' the Monster asked, nodding in the direction of Jimmy, who was still jogging around the perimeter of the cookhouse tent, singing gibberish. 'We need to have a fookin' heads up on this fookin' river infil.'

'Sure, mate,' the Kiwi replied, unwrapping his lanky form from the bench and stepping out to fetch Jimmy. 'Hey! Jimmy! Over here, mate. The Big Scot wants a heads up on the infil, mate.'

'Fakin' luverly. Perfick timing, Monster me old mate,' gasped Jimmy, as he came in, panting. 'Twenty-one laps just completed. Twenty-one's me age.'

'Like fook it is, Grandad,' the Monster snorted. 'Now, cut the fookin' crap, and let's get our heads down around this. We've got to get ten men upriver, to these two points, here and here. So let's get our fookin' brains in gear and focused on the job in hand, laddies.'

The Monster was Boat Troop's 2iC, and he was highly regarded by the other men of the Troop. While Jimmy might have had a sharper mind, he was seen as too much of a maverick to be put in a position of command. Which suited everyone in Boat Troop just fine: it meant that the dour Scottish Monster was the safe pair of hands, the slow but steady figure they could all rely on to get the job done.

'Right. Listen up. This is the fookin' gig,' the Monster continued, looking slowly around the faces of the other men as he did so. 'We use two inflatables. One takes the six-man obs team and drops them on the outskirts of Gberi Bana, in the forest, somewhere around here.' He indicated the rebel base on the northern river bank. 'They set up their OP as near as they can safely get to the fookin' rebel village. Second boat takes the four-man obs team and drops them in the forest on the outskirts of Magbeni, the rebel base on the opposite side of the river. That way, we get eyes on everything those bastards are up to. I reckon it looks like we can do the whole fookin' gig by boat, no problems – well, as much as ye can trust these fookin' maps. What do the rest of ye fookers reckon?'

''Ow long they going in for, the obs teams?' Jimmy asked.

'Dunno. The duration, laddie. As long as it fookin' takes,' the Monster replied, eyes still on the maps. 'Plan is they'll stay there until the assault proper goes in. Then they can do a CTR at first light, get the fookin' rebel village's visual, and guide the rest of us in to attack. Fookin' tally-ho! And up and at them. All that sort of shite.' Then, after a pause, 'So, I reckon we can get them in with full kit – food, comms, survival gear, weapons, ammo, explosives, the lot – by getting the fookin' boats right up to here. They take in everything they could fookin' wish for and we drop the fookers off here, and here.' He stabbed the map with a gnarled index finger to indicate the proposed drop-off points. 'From there, they can ferry the kit across the hundred yards or so to their obs points, in the forest around here. Any thoughts, laddies?'

'What 'appens if we have a fakin' nonsense?' said Jimmy. 'You know, like a fakin' waterfall 'arfway upriver or summit?'

'You see a fookin' waterfall marked on this map, laddie?' the Monster snorted. ''Cause I doon't. Does that say the fookin' Niagara Falls, laddie? Well, doos it? Now, I know I'm getting old and my eyesight's not what it was, but –'

'I'd trust these fakin' maps about as far as I could throw 'em,' Jimmy interrupted. 'Older than you by a long chalk they are, Monster me old mate, and that's fakin' saying somethin'. Na. Gotta get the obs teams in on 'ard routine, mate, real 'ard routine. Bare minimum. Gotta be. Ovverwise, what 'appens if we arse-end the boats over a waterfall or summit and they have to tab into the fakin' target? Across all that fakin' jungle? Carryin' all that fakin' kit. 'Ard routine, mate. Only way to do it.'

'Anyways, mate, the Niagara's in North America, mate –' the Kiwi added.

'Shut the fook up, Kiwi, ye fookin' smart-arse. I know where the fookin' Niagara fookin Falls is, mate, I was just making a fookin' point. If we do hit your fookin' imaginary waterfall, laddie, then they'll just have to leave the extra kit in the fookin' boats, won't they?'

'Na, mate. Won't work,' Jimmy persisted. 'What, an' unpack and repack their fakin' bergens in the middle of the fakin' jungle? Or worse still, in the pissing wet river? Na, mate. Won't work. Promise.'

'You just want to see those blokes suffer, isn't it, mate?' the Kiwi remarked, with a grin.

'Na, mate. 'Ard routine's the best,' Jimmy responded, with genuine enthusiasm. 'Fakin' luverly. I love it. Nothing better than a few days getting all jungly and covered in shite. Do 'em a power of good it will.'

For once, Jimmy meant what he was saying, too. He was renowned in D Squadron for his love of hard-routine obs work. He was a natural at it. He would have been one of those going in with the obs teams himself, only as one of Boat Troop, he was being kept back for the final river assault.

'Fair enough,' the Monster conceded. 'I take your point, Jimmy lad. You're not such a waste of space as ye like to make out, lad. As ye say, do the bastard obs teams good, a bit o' hard routine will.'

'What's the big hurry, anyways, mate?' the Kiwi asked. 'Why do we have to get them in tonight?'

'OC's worried the bastard rebels are gonna move the fakin' 'ostages,' Jimmy answered before the Monster could get a word in. 'Take 'em further into the jungle, like. Trouble is, wivout good obs we might never know 'bout it. Be like that fakin' Yank operation – in Vietnam I fink it was – parachuted into some POW camp to rescue some of their buddies, didn't they? Only trouble was, all the fakin' prisoners had already upped an' left. Camp was deserted, like. Typical of the Septics – they'd only used sat photos to plan the op. No local elements, no obs, no nuffin'. Sat photos were two days old, weren't they? In the meantime, the fakin' Nips 'ad moved 'em, the prisoners, like.'

'Yeah? Bummer, mate. Say, Nips are Japs, aren't they, mate?' the Kiwi said. 'You mean "Gooks", that's what the Yanks called the locals in Vietnam, mate.'

'Nips. Gooks. Slanty-eyed bastards. All the fakin' same to me, mate,' Jimmy came back at him. 'Na. OC's worried we might do a repeat performance of what the Yanks did in Nam. 'E's paranoid we'll 'it the fakin' rebel base, only to find the bastards 'ave moved 'em. Reckon he's right 'n' all, mate. Can't be too careful wiv these bastards.'

'Aye. Now, back to the job in hand, laddies,' the Scottish Monster said, pulling the team's focus back to the charts on the table. 'Now, which of ye fookers can tell me if the fookin' Rokel fookin' Creek is still tidal at this level, then? 'Cause fooked if I can.'

'What are we, a good forty miles inland is it, mate?' the Kiwi mused, poring over the maps. 'I'd say it's unlikely. But you just can't tell. Pretty flat country around there, isn't it, mate? So, it might be tidal. Hard to say, mate.'

'Fat lot of fakin' good you are, Kiwi,' Jimmy snorted. 'I thought you was dragged up on some fakin' farm in the middle of some fakin' mountains in the middle of fakin' nowhere, surrounded by sheep, mate? What was it? Fakin' goat hunting from 'elicopters, wasn't it? Highlight of your yoof, wasn't it, mate? Or was it takin' some poor fakin' sheep along to the local keg party or fakin' barn dance? What else did you 'ave to do all day long but fuck about in the fakin' rivers, mate? Me, I was dragged up in the East End of fakin' London, mate. How the 'eck should I know if the fakin' river's tidal or not up 'ere. What do we 'ave these flamin' Kiwis on the team for, if it's not this sort of shite?'

On paper, infiltrating the obs team looked like a straightforward mission. All in, it was no more than a fifty-mile boat journey from the Freetown Estuary up the Rokel Creek to Gberi Bana. The Rokel Creek and the Bankasok River were the two main water courses flowing into the Freetown harbour, so they were significant in terms of size (certainly more than large enough to accommodate a couple of inflatable boats). For most of its length, the Rokel was held by the British and the UN peacekeeping forces, not the West Side Boys. For the first thirty miles or so it wasn't unusual for the British military to be seen bobbing about on the river. The Paras had gone a good way up it during Operation Palliser, probing the territory for any signs of the RUF rebels.

So, the first thirty miles of the boat trip could be done on full throttle, that much was clear. And even at minimum revs – just puttering along at five miles an hour – the next five miles or so should take no more than an hour. For the last five they'd cut the engines and paddle in, so another hour or two for that. All in, they should have delivered the obs teams and be out again in six hours, eight at the very most. Having said that, no one had gone quite as high up the river as the West Side Boys' headquarters – so there was always potential for the unexpected.

The OC had already allocated which men should make up the obs teams. If he'd asked for volunteers, the whole Regiment would have wanted to go. No one would have wanted to miss the chance of getting in that close to the action. In addition to which, there had been a noticeable shift in the atmosphere now, a change in the sense and feel of things, a definite buzz around the camp. At last, things were happening. The fact that the obs teams were being sent in meant that D Squadron were that much closer to the whole thing kicking off. Part of the obs team's task was to establish the best route for the main body of the assault force's infil and to establish lay-up points and start lines. Come the day of the attack, the assault force would rest for the night at their lay-up points and then move on to their start lines in the morning, to launch the assault.

The two small craft – black rigid inflatables with outboards and camouflaged seats – set off at 11 p.m., and as predicted the first thirty miles proved fast and uneventful. But from there on in, it was to prove an entirely different matter. Throttled back to the minimum to kill the engines' noise, the two boats crept up the last ten miles or so of the river, shrouded in darkness. Faces blackened up to prevent any reflections in the moonlight, there was no talking or smoking allowed, as the teams had gone covert. Trouble was, the river was proving a lot harder to navigate than any of them had imagined. Some two hours into the journey and progress was down to a slow crawl, with frequent interruptions.

The problem was the sandbanks. Or rather mud banks, as it seemed to the men who had to clamber over and through them, dragging the heavily laden boats behind them. The river was certainly wide, on that the charts had been accurate. But what they hadn't shown were the vast sandbanks lying half submerged just below the water line. In fact, they were so low in the water that the men in the boats had little chance of spotting them in the darkness. NVGs helped a little, but even then flat water and flat sandbank looked pretty much indistinguishable from one another. In the eerie, mossy-green electronic glow of NVGs, the only way to tell the difference between the two was to catch the glitter of movement: the water had it, the sandbanks didn't. Both boats put a man out front scouring the way ahead with NVGs, and whispering directions. But even so, they still couldn't avoid all of the sandbanks. Suddenly, one or other boat would lurch to a halt, the prow riding up on the submerged obstruction, and they'd be forced to wade and drag the craft behind them again, until they were over it.

And the sandbanks were *everywhere*. What should have been a simple boat insertion was turning into a nightmare. Ever present in the back of the men's minds as they hauled the heavy craft over the muddy, boggy obstructions was the thought of crocodiles. Because they were moving so silently – like ghosts flitting across the darkened waters – they could be on top of a croc almost before the beast knew it. Several times, the men could have sworn they'd actually driven into one. To the left and right they would catch the swish of a tail, a dull flop and a flash of white water, as the startled reptiles scrabbled off a sandbank into the river. Somewhere around five miles short of the West Side Boys' base, the two boats' progress had slowed to little more than crawling pace.

'Nice 'ere, innit?' Jimmy whispered to no one in particular. He was crewing the lead inflatable, along with the Kiwi and the Big Scottish Monster. Together, the three of them were ferrying in the obs team going into Gberi Bana. 'Luverly. Crocs. Bogs. Bugs. Sandbanks. And fakin' boats. That lot don't mix, do they? I reckon we're fucked. Much more of this and we'll be too far committed upriver, too late, with too long to get back 'ome again. Then we'll 'ave to lie up all day hiding the fakin' boats – though 'ow the fuck we do that I don't know – in the middle of fakin' Injun country.'

'So what are you suggesting we do then, laddie?' the Scottish Monster growled softly. 'Fly the rest of the fookin' way in?'

'Well, we're goin' though the fakin' mixer 'ere, innit? Over one sandbank, into the river, stuck on another fakin' one in five minutes. No fakin' way can we get through all this shite right up to the rebel base. Not unless these fakin' inflatables can fly, or double as 'ovver-crafts, or summink. We're gonna have to drop the obs teams 'ere, innit, and leave 'em to beast it through the jungle. Nuffin' else for it, is there?'

'Ye think they'll fookin' get through all that shite', the Scottish Monster retorted, pointing at the wall of brooding forest on the near river bank, 'any easier than we'll get through this river shite, now do ye, laddie? By my reckoning it's five fookin' miles to the fookin' rebel base from here. Five fookin' miles through the fookin' jungle with all the fookin' kit they're carrying? They'll never fookin' make it, laddie.'

'No fakin' option is there, mate?' Jimmy hissed back. 'King Canute couldn't stop the fakin' sea, could 'e, just like we can't get any fakin' further up this river. At least wiv 'em they'll not be sticking out like a fakin' great big sore fumb in the morning, will they? Eh? They'll 'ave the fakin' jungle to 'ide in, won't they? Nice 'n' cosy an' all, wiv some trees over their 'eads. Not like a couple of big black rubber boats stuck out in the middle of a croc-infested swamp, is it? But you take your fakin' pick, mate.'

'The fookin' OC wants the obs teams in position tonight, laddie,' the Monster growled with frustration. '"Got to get eyes on the rebel base", he said, "in case they try to move the hostages." There'll be hell to pay, laddie, if the rebels fookin' move them, and our boys fookin' miss it all, because they're stuck in the fookin' jungle several clicks short of their positions.'

'I fakin' know all that, mate,' Jimmy hissed back, in exasperation. 'But you got a better idea? Course, we could just fakin' sit out 'ere all night fakin' talkin' about it. But I say fakin' drop the fakin' obs teams right 'ere, right now. Tell you fakin' what, mate, if I was on the obs team I'd 'ave no fakin' problem wiv beasting through the fakin' jungle. Fakin' five miles is a fakin' walk in the park, mate.'

Nosing the boats up on yet another vast sandbank, the men gathered in the darkness for a whispered Chinese parliament. It quickly became clear that there wasn't much to discuss. The men were knackered, soaked to the skin, covered in mud and filth from the river, and had been eaten alive by mosquitoes. The boat trip was clearly over. From here on in, the obs teams would be on their own. It was time to say their goodbyes.

'Take it easy, mate,' the Kiwi said softly, helping Lassie, one of the obs team, on with his bergen. 'And you guys go enjoy yourself in there, right.'

'No worries, mate,' Lassie replied, under his breath. 'We knew all that stuff about Boat Troop being able to walk on the water was bullshit. Just take us into the bank. We'll be seeing you.'

'Yeah. Complete pile of hogshit,' hissed Ginge, another of the obs-team men, as he struggled with his heavy rucksack. A real veteran of the Regiment, Ginge had become an SAS legend in his own lifetime. 'Fuckin' rely on Boat Troop to get you anywhere, you'd never fuckin' get there, innit, Jimmy mate? Bet you wish you was coming with us, eh, mate? Nice bit of fuckin' 'ard routine, be right up your street. Pity we can't 'ave you along, mate.'

'Yeah, well . . . thanks for the concern, mate,' Jimmy whispered. 'Anyways, reckon I spotted a nice little fakin' path back along with a greasy joe's caff at the end of it. If you put on a bit of speed, Ginge me old mate, reckon you'll make it there for breakfast. Looked like they did a fakin' good fry-up an' all.'

The six-man obs team was dropped on the northern river bank, the four-man team being dropped on the southern bank. The men of the obs teams were of necessity going in on extreme 'hard routine'. They were carrying their weapons, their comms equipment, some specialist spying gear and food. And that was it: no cooking equipment, no sleeping equipment, no hammocks or mosquito nets, no wet-weather gear and no change of clothing. It wasn't going to be pleasant. August and September were the months of the rainy season in Sierra Leone, and there was without fail a daily downpour of torrential tropical rain.

The obs teams were taking their waterproof Gore-Tex bivvy bags with them, but they weren't for sleeping in. They were for emergency use only, if a man was ill or injured. It was a golden rule of obs work that at all times each man kept all his kit packed, his clothes and boots on and was ready to move at a moment's notice, in case he was compromised (discovered by the enemy). That's why he could never risk getting caught inside his bivvy bag. He would only ever get out a piece of kit when he needed it, and repack it immediately afterwards.

As the assault planners weren't worried about radio intercepts – the West Side Boys had neither the technology nor the will to listen in on British communications – the men would be using standard, high-frequency radio kits (a PRC 319) to send their sitreps back to Waterloo Camp. And they were also carrying a satphone, as a back-up comms system and to use for longer-range communications. All of the sensitive comms and spying kit (which had been 'made rugged' in any case) was kept packed away in dry bags (waterproof, sealable rubber sacks). They would be eating cold food from the ration packs, and some chocolate, sweets or dried fruit which each man had brought with him. There could be no cooking food or brewing up: cooking smoke or even the smell of hot food or drink could easily give the game away. *Which meant that there would be no tea, for heaven's sake.* And for British soldiers, that was saying something.

For as long as it took, these ten men would remain in the same clothes that they were now standing up in – soaked to the skin, spattered in bog grime and covered in river mud as they were. As each man knew, the more dirt- and shit- and sweat-encrusted they became, the more all the smells and scents of civilised living – soap, deodorant, washing powder, cigarettes, frying fat, toothpaste – would be overtaken by those of the jungle. And the more that happened, the more effective they would be at remaining hidden and undetected. There would be monkeys and bush pigs and village dogs scavenging in the forest around the rebel base: a whiff of Imperial Leather or Colgate Extra could really give the game away. Ultimately, each man would take on the musky scent of an animal, something not unexpected in the forest shadows.

A rainforest canopy is like a thick overhead carpet, a dense roof of leaves, vines and branches spreading out a hundred feet above the forest floor. And below that, the forest is dark, very dark, and very sparsely vegetated. So little light penetrates through the canopy that very few plants are able to grow on the forest floor. Usually, this makes trekking through rainforest fairly easy, as there is little undergrowth to get in the way. However, where there are large breaks in the canopy, like wide stretches of water, the riot of vegetation spills right down to the forest floor and overflows in a thick wall of jungle – a wall spliced together with vines, strung with thick lianas, reinforced with tree trunks bearing cruel spines, and replete with vicious barbs and thorns.

And that was exactly the sort of place where the ten men of the two SAS obs teams found that the boat crews had now dropped them. On both sides of the Rokel Creek, they were hemmed in between the river waters and a towering wall of dense vegetation on the river banks. They had no choice but to try to prise a way through, and they had to resist using their machetes wherever possible. The fewer signs of their passing that the men left behind them, the fewer chances of their mission getting compromised. It was made all the more difficult by the fact that it was the pitch black of night, around 2 a.m., and they were not allowed to show any lights.

Once through that barrier, the two teams trudged their separate ways across the jungle to their OPs. But it was slow going: they were incredibly weighed down by all the weapons and ammo that they were carrying in their bergens. But whatever they might discover when they arrived at the West Side Boys' camp, whatever they might see or hear, however bad it might be for the hostages at Gberi Bana, there was no way they would ever be able to intervene on their own, no matter what amount of firepower they were carrying. That would be six guys up against two hundred or more; all it would serve to do was to get them – and the hostages – killed. The weapons and ammo that they were hauling in wasn't for that. It was in case they had to stay in their OPs until the very day of the assault itself – whereupon they would emerge from the jungle with guns blazing to join the main body of the assault force.

It took four, exhausting hours for the two teams to find a way through to their OP positions, and they arrived at them at around 5.30 a.m., just before first light. But the final few hundred yards of forest around the rebel base turned out to be dense, impenetrable, secondary jungle. And so they were forced to make do with lie-up points much further away from the targets than they had hoped for, some two hundred yards distant from the village. The men searched for the nastiest, most uninviting, impenetrable and thorny jungle thicket that they could find – the sort of place that no person in their right mind would ever think of crawling into – and then crawled right into it as far as they could go, using branches to brush away any signs of their passing. They would hunker down and stay put. This was it: home for the next few days.

The men wouldn't even risk letting the tell-tale signs of their bodily functions give them away: they would be urinating into bottles and defecating into plastic bags, all of which would be stowed in the side pockets of their bergens. After all, a bit of pink loo paper lying next to a freshly laid log was a dead giveaway.

For the time being at least, they could see no easy way of getting a line of sight into either Magbeni or Gberi Bana. So, they would have to rely on their ears – and some of their highly sensitive listening equipment – to keep tabs on goings-on in the villages. Immediately prior to the assault, both obs teams would move up to the very edge of the target villages at night, using established forest paths that they had already marked on their maps, based on the satellite photos back at Waterloo Camp. Just before first light, they would do a CTR. The team on the northern bank of the river would then get into a position where it had the village visual, and could guide in the main body of the assault force to Gberi Bana by radio. And the team of the southern bank would get into a similar position where it could call in the Paras for the assault on Magbeni.

Boat Troop and their SBS colleagues made it back to Waterloo Camp at around 5 a.m. just as the horizon over the Freetown Estuary was starting to show the first signs of the coming day. It had been a long night and everyone was in need of a good kip. But first things first, they would need to make a sitrep to the OC on what they had found out. That night's experiences on the waters of the Rokel Creek had changed things irrevocably for the men now assembled at Waterloo Camp: no assault force was going to get into Gberi Bana or Magbeni upriver, that much was certain. Any river-borne force would get no closer than five miles from the West Side Boys' HQ, at best, and five miles wasn't much good to anyone. It would leave the heavily laden men with a tough and exhausting trek through the forests ahead of them. And that was a no go.

A little later the two obs teams were able to radio in with their first sitreps, providing further vital intelligence: from the five-mile mark where they'd been dropped, the forest was impossible going. There was impenetrable jungle lining the banks of the Rokel Creek and dense thickets of secondary forest lying all around the villages of Gberi Bana and Magbeni. In short, and confirming Boat Troop's sitrep, the terrain was totally unsuited to a covert overland assault on the rebel bases.

By mid-morning it was clear to those in the Waterloo Camp ops tent that the riverine assault had no chance of succeeding. To make matters worse, the southern obs team were able to report that the Paras' favoured landing zone was pretty near impossible too. From the satellite photos, LZ2 – a large patch of terrain conveniently clear of jungle – had looked like the perfect place to drop the first of the Paras' Bayonets by Chinook. But on closer inspection, the SAS obs team had found out just why the area was clear of trees: it was a vast, waterlogged swamp. As they'd been unable to spend too much time investigating it, the obs team couldn't say for certain how deep it was. But from their experience of coming upriver, they knew that a soldier heavily laden with kit could easily sink up to his neck in one of those bogs. It was about as suitable an LZ as a swimming pool full of mushy-pea soup – and the Paras would have no guarantee that they weren't dropping in at the deep end.

Everyone knew that the success of Operation Barras depended on speed, secrecy and surprise. But it was now clear that the favoured plan of a staggered operation – the assault forces going in first by river and then through the jungle – was a non-starter: no clandestine assault force was getting into Gberi Bana or Magbeni along the river or through the forest. The only remotely feasible attack option now was the least covert and the least stealthy: the airborne assault. And even that had considerable problems in terms of the highly unsuitable LZ at Magbeni. The favoured attack plans that had been drawn up were now looking completely unworkable. Which left one question on everyone's mind.

Just how the hell was the Operation Barras assault force going to get in and hit its targets?

NO ESCAPE

Those who look upon other people's misery with indifference are the most miserable people of all.
– Paulo Coelho, *Manual of the Warrior of Light*

DAY ten of the hostage crisis was a Sunday, but no one in Gberi Bana was going to church. The West Side Boys believed in a bizarre fusion of black magic and voodoo – often called ju-ju in West African countries like Sierra Leone – so there was no special or regular day of worship for them. When practised traditionally in Sierra Leone, the belief system of a family, a village or tribe is rooted in reverence for their ancestors and in animistic beliefs (the worship of nature, the sky, trees and animals, all of which are believed to have souls). This is the ju-ju that is practised by the Kamajors in Sierra Leone. As such, it is supposed to provide the Kamajor warriors with unearthly powers in combat, and supernatural prowess in battle.

But the West Side Boys had taken this traditional belief system, and bastardised it. They had taken the ju-ju and turned it to the dark side, trying to use its powers to justify their cruel and inhuman behaviour, and to protect them against those who tried to rein in their depravities.

Much of their warped belief system seemed to be inspired by Foday Kallay's wife, their so-called Voodoo Queen. Mamma Kallay had an insatiable appetite for cruelty and evil. She took intense pleasure in killings and torture. Her speciality was summary executions. She would have prisoners tied up, place a pistol in their ear and pull the trigger, watching the brains spurt out the other side of the skull. She was addicted to heroin and crack cocaine, as was Foday Kallay himself, and regular supplies would be brought into the rebel base from Freetown, to feed their addictions.

The most popular time for the West Side Boys to have some heavy voodoo sessions with her was always just before they went into battle. The Voodoo Queen would gather the young warriors around her bulk, roll her eyes and jiggle her ample bosom, and mutter what the British hostages suspected was a load of complete gibberish. A chicken might be sacrificed, its entrails being 'read' to predict victory in a forthcoming battle. Feathers and bones would be handed out to the young fighters, as charms to ensure defeat for the enemy. Whatever, the rebels seemed to like it, and Mamma Kallay wasn't the one going off into battle with only a few chicken-feather charms to ward off the bullets.

Halfway through that quiet Sunday morning, the hostages noticed that there was a bit of a commotion down at the riverside. As they watched, a crowd gathered and shortly a group of thirty or so men and boys were hustled up the track towards the centre of the village. As they were frogmarched up the hill, they were being yelled at and hit around the head and generally intimidated by the West Side Boys. But in spite of their bad treatment, the group of captives – for that was clearly what they were – appeared shocked to discover six white soldiers sitting out on the veranda in the middle of the infamous rebels' base. Whoever the group of captives were, they obviously hadn't been spending enough time listening to the BBC, the Rangers thought to themselves, wryly.

The men and boys were lined up in front of Calm Down Fresh's house, and for a horrible moment the hostages feared that he was about to pull one of his crazed stunts – maybe a mass execution just for their benefit, a little taster of what he had in store for them later. Or maybe he was going to unleash the Voodoo Queen on them. The thirty captives appeared to be a group of Sierra Leonean rural folk, and they clearly didn't want to be there in that rebel base, any more than the British hostages did. There was a strong sense of an immediate bond of brotherhood between the British and the Sierra Leonean captives: it was instinctive and it spoke of shared injustices and fears. Taking advantage of the temporary lull in proceedings, the Major sidled up to the new arrivals to offer them a few words of encouragement and reassurance, in the simplest English he could muster.

While doing so, he managed to discover the basics of their story. Earlier that morning, the men had been on a bus together trundling along a dirt track through the jungle. Some of them had been going to an early-morning church service. Others were off to the local market or were visiting their relatives. The usual sort of stuff for a Sunday morning in the middle of the African bush. And then the West Side Boys had ambushed them. Stopping the bus, they had forced all the men and boys off at gunpoint and frogmarched them back to Gberi Bana. The terrified captives had been told that they were being taken to Gberi Bana to be forcibly trained as rebel 'recruits'. On the way, their gleeful captors had told them what their fellow rebels would be doing to the women and children left back on the bus.

The thirty men and boys were herded into the centre of the village clearing, and forced to wait in line while they each had their heads shaved. This, it seemed, was the first step in their transformation from African villager to West Side Boy warrior. And as for the next step, well, Calm Down Fresh had decided that here the British soldiers could be of great assistance. He strode over to the Major with a demented gleam in his eye, and proceeded to tell him that he expected the British soldiers to 'train the new recruits in British Army fighting techniques'. So there it was. That was Calm Down Fresh's cunning plan and tomorrow – Monday – would be training day.

'All right, lads,' the Major announced, wearily, when they were back in their room, 'it's training day tomorrow. I know you don't want to do this and neither do I. But look at it this way. First, it'll keep us on the good side of Calm Down Fresh and the other lunatics around here. Second, maybe we can make the training a little easier on those poor villagers. And third, anything's better than letting these bastards get their hands on them. So, no griping, eh, lads? Training's what they want and training's what we'll give 'em, OK?'

'Sure thing, sir.'

'Dead on, sir.'

'Now, Calm Down Fresh has asked for some "English Army rifle drill", whatever he means by that. So, I'm suggesting we start with a bit of square-bashing, just like we'd do with the SLA back at Benguema,' the Major continued. 'Make it look impressive and all that. After that, some basic rifle drill. Nothing fancy, just the basics. All right? Bloody hell, at least it'll give us something to *do*.'

'*Rifle* drill, sir? Youse mean to say these bastards are going to let us get our hands on some *weapons*?' Ranger Rowell queried. 'Because if they are, youse can guess what I'm thinking, so you can.'

'Well, I'm doubting they'll be giving us back our SA80s, lad, but you never know,' the Major replied. 'Best we remain on our toes just in case, eh? Now, I'll need Rangers Gaunt and Rowell to demo the rifle drill. Captain Flaherty, you can help with instruction. And Sergeant Smith, you can do stores.'

'Fair enough, sir. But just what stores exactly?' Sergeant Smith asked.

'Well, I'm presuming we'll use sticks for the rifle drill,' the Major responded, 'so handing them out, that sort of thing.'

The level of training that the Major had outlined would provide the 'recruits' with little that would be of any help in a real combat situation, but perhaps that was for the best. And at least it would give the Major a chance to talk to the recruits, and try to reassure them that all was not lost. In the back of his mind, the Major was hoping it would give him a chance to warn them, too. He needed to find a way to tell them about the British rescue assault, which he felt certain was coming very shortly now – to warn them that when they heard the choppers coming in low over the village they should keep their bloody heads down. And whatever else, they should not pick up a weapon, because if they did that it would very likely get them killed.

Around mid-morning the next day, the recruits were herded into the central clearing, each carrying a stick the vague shape and length of a gun. For a brief second one of the Rangers was struck by the thought that they should all join forces, club the nearest rebel to death with their sticks and grab his gun, and then the rebellion would be on. But only for a second, as the idea clearly had its shortcomings, not least of which was the difficulty in communicating with the recruits in English. Then, as the Major stood out front and began to instruct the villagers using the simplest language he could find to express himself, the two Rangers marched about before the recruits giving them practical demonstration, in a fraught attempt to get the Major's points across.

In any other circumstances, the Rangers would have felt like a couple of complete plonkers, marching about with a crooked branch each on their shoulder, in front of a bunch of bemused African villagers who could barely understand a word of what the OC was saying. It would have been utterly farcical were it not so tragic. But the British soldiers knew that they had to do their damnedest to try to make it look convincing. Calm Down Fresh and his henchmen were watching closely, and heaven forbid if they got any sense that the British soldiers were messing about or making fools out of them.

It was obvious that the forced recruits were very frightened. What the West Side Boys had got up to in the night with them didn't bear thinking about, and it was beholden upon the British soldiers to make this as easy as possible for them. After a good deal of milling about and some general confusion, they finally managed to get the 'trainees' formed up into three, reasonably straight ranks. After that, they had a little difficulty getting them to hold their 'rifles' properly, and keep them firmly on their shoulders as they moved about. But by around lunchtime, they had the 'trainees' marching to and fro in some sort of vaguely passable drill formation. Turning was a bit more difficult, but everything with time. *Hell, they were doing better than the flamin' SLA recruits had done at Benguema*, Ranger Gaunt found himself thinking, *and there was no hooch for them to be drinking, either.*

But in the back of the British soldiers' minds was the knowledge that these men were captives, just like themselves. They were training forced recruits, slave soldiers. And while this square-bashing was harmless enough and would be of little help in the chaotic jungle warfare that the West Side Boys excelled in, these captives *were* being prepared to fight and to die. Today they had sticks in their hands. Tomorrow, or the next day, it would be guns. And then, just who would they be sent to attack? It could be the UN, it could be British forces, it could be the SLA, it could be anyone. More than likely it could even be their own villages, or their own families. The rebels liked to traumatise new recruits by forcing them to carry out atrocities against their nearest and dearest. This served a double purpose: it hardened them to any further atrocities that they might be obliged to commit, while at the same time making it all but impossible for them ever to escape and return to their home communities.

As the British soldiers carried on with the square-bashing, it was difficult to tell just who was the more scruffy and dishevelled-looking – the instructors, or their Sierra Leonean trainees. The hostages were now eleven days into their ordeal, and they'd yet to have a chance to wash either themselves or their uniforms. In fact, they had been so concerned about keeping their combats on and not having them stolen that they'd barely spared a thought for personal hygiene. Survival, not smartness and cleanliness, was foremost in their minds. As the morning dragged on and the sun rose higher in the sky, Calm Down Fresh forced the British soldiers and the trainees to remain out there on the village clearing, square-bashing, without a break.

It wasn't so much the heat itself that was the problem, it was the humidity. Situated on the banks of a river in the midst of the jungle as it was, Gberi Bana suffered from 90 per cent-plus humidity. Which meant that the soldiers' sweat had nowhere to evaporate to, and clung to their clammy bodies. Sweat evaporation is the body's natural cooling system, but in this situation it wasn't able to function properly. Soon, the soldiers' dirty uniforms were soaked with sweat, and caked in the dust thrown up by thirty-two pairs of feet marching in something that was beginning to resemble unison.

By now, the hostages were getting bottled water brought in with their British Army rations, and they each drank five or six litres that day, under the blazing sun. But the village recruits were being allowed little to drink and they soon started dropping like flies. A crowd of rebels had gathered to watch the training, and as soon as one of the trainees fell to the ground, they would rush in and start kicking and rifle-butting him. He would then either drag himself to his feet and stumble on with the marching, or, if not, he would be hauled off to one side, where the dull thuds of the beating would continue. All the while, the Major kept talking to the recruits, trying to reassure them and urging them to keep moving. Calm Down Fresh was enjoying the whole spectacle immensely, and the beatings were clearly designed to further break the spirits of the captive villagers.

Calm Down Fresh kept them at it until late in the afternoon, when it was clear that the trainees could not continue. Then, and only then, did he come over and relieve the Major, congratulating him and his men on 'a job well done'. Turning to face those trainees who were still standing, he started to deliver a wild, jabbering speech, dancing and crawling around in front of them as he did so. The British soldiers couldn't understand a word, as it was all in the local lingo, but he was clearly giving them some sort of crazed fire and manoeuvre instruction, and acting it out in his own, unique fashion. As they watched, the British soldiers felt deeply sorry for the village trainees: sometime soon, they would be forced to put this half-baked training into action. The rebels were only ever a few days away from their next battle.

That morning, Corporal Mousa had overheard the rebels discussing who their next victims would be. From the darkness of the pit, he had heard their plans to attack the Nigerian UN peacekeepers. The problem was, their lack of ammunition. Mousa was already aware that the Jordanians UN 'peacekeepers' had been giving the West Side Boys food and alcohol, as he'd overheard the rebel soldiers talking about it. And as none of the rebels believed that Mousa would leave the pit alive, there was no way in which they could be saying these things just for his benefit. In fact, they probably weren't even aware that he could overhear them. But what he was about to hear now would shock and enrage the Sierra Leonean Corporal. He could hear Foday Kallay start giving orders to his men now.

'Listen, we no have enough ammunition to go attack de Nigerian dogs,' Kallay was saying. 'So, you go see my Jordanian friend, and you ask him for de dozen cases of bullets. And you go ask for some of dem boom-boom. You go say we go pay dem in de same same way, OK. De diamonds we go give dem, same-same as before.'

'Yes, sa. We go attack de Kamajor village on de return, sa?' Mousa overheard Mr Die asking Kallay. 'It be on de way back from de Jordanian friend-friend, sa. We go test de bullets dat way, sa.'

'Sure, sure. You go fuck dem up,' Kallay replied, enthusiastically. 'Kill kill dem Kamajor. But no use all de bullets, eh. We dem need for de Nigerian dogs.'

My God, Mousa was thinking to himself. *Some fucking Jordanian was giving the rebels ammunition, as well as food and booze. And 'boom-boom' were mortar shells. It must have been the rogue elements within the Jordanian army again – getting diamonds in exchange.* Despite his own injuries, Mousa could feel himself boiling with anger inside. *For fuck's sake, one of these bullets could even be used to execute him, or the British hostages.*

Mr Die and Foday Kallay's desire to assault the Kamajors made perfect sense in a way. British forces were rumoured to be preparing for an assault on the West Side Boys' base. That being the case, the Kamajors would already be acting as the eyes and ears of British forces in the jungles around Gberi Bana. Kallay was worried. If the rumours of the coming British assault were true, he would need an escape plan and he would need help. But first things first, he would deal with the troublesome Kamajors.

Later that afternoon, Mousa heard Mr Die and his men returning from the visit to the Jordanians. Gathering at Cambodia's place, they filled Foday Kallay in on what had happened.

'De Jordanian man he give us all de ammunition, sa. De village of de Kamajor it be very close to de Jordanian, so we de go dere first an attack de Kamajor. We use de new bullets to test dem, sa. Dey be very good. We kill many Kamajor and we capture dese weapons, sa. Den we cut off three dem heads and we carry dem here, sa. Look at dem heads on poles, sa, de proof we go kill de Kamajors. An we still got many many ammunition to go attack de Nigerians, sa.'

By now, Mousa had become like Foday Kallay's informal adviser.

He would often seek Mousa's advice, and if things were going well, Kallay would allow him out of the pit for a few hours. Kallay had even gone as far as getting his wife to cook Mousa a meal. But the Sierra Leonean Corporal was shocked to discover that the West Side Boys' leader had managed to develop such a close and mutually beneficial relationship with one of the Jordanians. Arms-for-diamonds deals. The Jordanian made the cash, the West Side Boys could wreak havoc and mayhem. And now they'd just turned up in the camp with some severed Kamajor heads, courtesy of the Jordanian bullets.

That evening, Sony came over and told the exhausted British soldiers about the attack against the Kamajors. But then Sony dropped his bombshell. Not content with just having shot up the Kamajor village, the West Side Boys had decided to escalate things still further. Using their machetes, they had hacked off the heads of several of their victims. Then, like some scene from the hostages' worst nightmare, they had proceeded to parade the heads through the jungle, mounted on poles. The rebels had gone along to that afternoon's face-to-face hostage-negotiation meeting, and had planted the heads on poles in the ground, ready to greet the British team upon their arrival. Needless to say, it hadn't turned out to be a very productive meeting.

Jesus! Fucking heads on poles! To the hostages, Sony's story was like the final scenes from the Vietnam War film *Apocalypse Now*, when a renegade US officer stumbles into a village of the dammed. Rotting corpses, humans in pits, and heads on poles: the rebel forces in that movie had had all the trappings of a mass descent into evil and horror, and so it seems did the West Side Boys. But there was more. Although Foday Kallay was claiming victory over the Kamajor warriors, at least one of the heads on poles had turned out to be that of *a little baby girl*. She was no warrior: she was a young, innocent, guiltless victim. While the British hostages had learned to steel themselves for at least one episode of horror a day at the hands of their captors, this was something else entirely. Instantly, it became like a symbol of everything that was so sick and warped and depraved in the world of the West Side Boys.

Yet perhaps even more worrying for the Rangers were their own, inner reactions to the whole heads-on-poles episode. Sure, they had been shocked and appalled. Who wouldn't have been? But as the evening wore on, they found their overriding emotion being one of a deep and residing concern: but it was a concern *not for the victims*, but for the effect this gruesome piece of theatre may have had on the outcome of the hostage negotiations and, by extension, *on their own fate*. A concern for how the heads-on-poles incident may have thrown any possible hostage-release deal off track. A concern for how it all might have impacted upon their own slender chances of getting out of there alive. *Concern, in short, for their own brute survival.*

Somehow, the West Side Boys were succeeding in rendering the most horrific, inhuman behaviour part of the banal rhythm of normal life. Torture, mutilation, kidnapping children, voodoo, drugs and alcohol. A chained-up gimp. Arbitrary executions. And now, a baby's head on a pole. It was all just another day in the land of the West Side Boys. The rebels had got this warped sense of the way of doing things down to a fine art with their own people. But the disturbing thing was that after so many days in their camp, the British hostages were finding that they, too, were becoming inured to the horror. In spite of their better instincts, they were starting to accept that unspeakably sick and depraved behaviour was the norm – that each day there would be at least one event that demonstrated the cheapness of human life here. They were expecting to witness cruelty, horror and insane behaviour masquerading as normal human existence on a daily basis. And they were expecting to witness their fellow human beings celebrating in and enjoying this collective psychosis.

They had been revolted by the incident, but life went on, and with it came the dominant fear that was eating away at them like acid corroding their insides: the fear that they were destined to end up facing a similar fate to that of the little Kamajor girl; the fear that they were already dead men. Perhaps the only redeeming feature of this whole gruesome incident was this: it had reawakened in the hostages a dreadful realisation of the urgency of escape.

At last light, the men were allowed down to the river for their first wash since being captured. This was Calm Down Fresh's idea of a reward for the training they'd carried out on the village recruits. Having stripped down to their boxers, a number of the men realised that they really did stink and that they really did need that wash. They left Calm Down Fresh's house and set off down to the river, taking their dirty shirts to dry themselves with. With no soap, they decided they would have to scoop up some sand from the river bed and use it to scrub their bodies clean. But at least the chance of a wash was lifting their spirits a little.

Down at the riverside, the Rangers began cracking jokes about where the washing facilities were worse, here in Gberi Bana or back at their base at Benguema. There, they'd been used to giving their dirty washing to some local women, who came up to the camp most mornings seeking work. After haggling over the price, they'd hand over a bundle of clothes in a laundry net, together with a box of soap. But they soon realised that the women were selling the soap powder at the local market and then beating the soldiers' clothes with rocks on the riverside to get the worst of the African mud out of them. Combats were returning worn and threadbare. Vest and shirts were coming back looking like an infestation of hungry moths had been at them.

'You'd never sort of know which feckin' clothes you'd get back again, either,' Ranger Gaunt said. 'Feckin' odd socks an' trousers like feckin' tents, or even some other bastard's skid-marked boxers.'

'Aye, Sandy, it was a flamin' lottery,' Ranger Rowell remarked. 'At times, yer feckin' combats just never came back at all. You'd be thinking to yerself: "Now I'm feckin' sure I gave her me combats, like. So where the feck are they? Meybe I'm mistaken, but . . ." Then a couple of days later you'd spot some fucker in the village wearing 'em. "There's me feckin' shirt," you'd be thinkin' to yerself, "on that bastard's back. The feckin' washer woman must've flogged it." Outrageous it was.'

'Aye. But there was sort of nothin' you could do about it, eh, Gav?' Ranger Gaunt added. 'At least here in Gberi feckin' Bana we get to do our own washing. There's no one about to beat our combats to a pulp with a feckin' great boulder, is there? Or flog them to the local rebel man about town. 'Tis a pity about the crocodiles, mind. We could meybe do without them.'

It was strange how such a little thing as the prospect of a good wash could lift the men's spirits so. Just then the Major glanced back up the track the two hundred yards or so to the village. As he did so, he realised that there was no one else around, other than the six hostages. Calm Down Fresh had forgotten to send any guards with them. *Right*, he thought to himself, *this is our chance*. Choosing two points on the river bank a set distance apart, he dropped a stick into the water and counted out the seconds it took to float past: one, two, three, four, five . . . From this, he was able to calculate that the river was flowing fast, around a hundred yards a minute. Which meant that within ten minutes they could be swept a thousand yards or more downstream. The rebels had warned them that the river was full of crocodiles, and to be careful while washing. But which was worse? To take their chances in the water with the crocs, or back on the land with the murderous reptiles who were holding them hostage?

'Listen, lads. Hold up a minute,' the Major hissed at the others. 'How about it? *The river*. Look, there's no guards around! In we go, keep low in the water, and let the current carry us down towards Freetown. Our boys can't be that far away. Twenty minutes, thirty maybe, of treading water, and we're home and dry.'

'Umm . . . crocs, sir. *Crocs*. Hows about them?' Ranger Gaunt ventured, nervously.

'And shouldn't we prepare for this first, sir?' Ranger Rowell added. 'I mean, check the maps an' stuff. See if there's not rapids and the like downstream?'

'And don't youse think those feckers'll sort of spot us, sir?' Ranger Gaunt said. 'I mean, the river runs past the other end of the village, so it does.'

The Major thought for a moment. It wasn't actually that dark yet, around 8 p.m., last light dwindling out of the sky. And they should check the maps, on that the Ranger was right. Maybe it was better to wait for another opportunity. Keep in the good books of Calm Down Fresh, come down later the next time, and slip away in the darkness. It would also give them a chance to prepare better. Make some water-bottle floats. Black up their faces maybe – that's if they could find something to blacken them with. That sort of thing. Just as these thoughts were flashing through the Major's mind, a couple of the rebels came ambling down the track towards them, with AK47s in their hands. Well, that decided it then. They'd postpone the escape attempt until their next wash, when they could be better prepared.

Back in their room, the chances for a riverine escape dominated the men's discussions. Escaping by *swimming* away was something that they'd just never really contemplated before. Stealing a canoe and heading off downriver – that had been an option they'd been looking at. But swimming away? They checked their maps. The Rokel Creek was shown as a large river flowing directly down to the Freetown Estuary, where they knew British troops were stationed. There didn't seem to be any gorges, or rapids or waterfalls marked on the map, either.

Maybe the river was full of crocodiles, as the rebels claimed. Unfortunately, none of the British soldiers had much of an idea of the sort of wildlife that inhabited Sierra Leone's forests or rivers. *Were there big cats in the jungles? Did the crocodiles in these parts eat people?* They just didn't know. One of the Rangers had a vague recollection of watching a BBC wildlife documentary, in which it said that only big crocs would tackle a human prey. The little ones were supposed to be pretty harmless. Whatever, they'd have to take their chances – because swimming down the river was looking increasingly like their best and only feasible route out of there. There was a general air of regret now that they hadn't gone for the riverine escape at the Major's initial urgings. Maybe they wouldn't get another chance. Maybe the rebels would remember to send guards with them from now on. Maybe they'd just blown their best and only chance.

'If we hadn't spent so long *talking* about it we could be aways by now, so we could,' Ranger Gaunt piped up, voicing the obvious. 'Couldn't we, sir?'

'Aye. Meybe Sandy's right, sir,' Ranger Rowell chipped in. 'Meybe we did have long enough before those two bastards appeared, to get aways?'

'Perhaps. But there's no point in thinking about maybes and might-haves now, lads,' the Major responded. 'You've seen the maps. It's looking good for the river. We'll get another chance, you mark my words. So, let's start getting our escape kit together, all right, lads?'

Each man proceeded to take the shoelaces out of his boots and cut them in two. One half he used to partially relace his boots, so he could keep wearing them. With the other, he lashed together two empty water bottles, leaving a loop in the middle of the shoelace to slip over his wrist and pull tight, using a special knot. This made a set of impro-vised floats that could help carry them downstream. Using the blades of the disposable tin openers from the British Army rations, each man then proceeded to cut a row of holes round the bottom of his boots to let the river water drain out. Not too big, mind you, in case the West Side Boys noticed them. If they had to leave the river and continue across land, the last thing they'd want to be doing is trekking with boots full of river water. Finally, they experimented with the soot from the Hexy stoves as paint to camouflage their skin. With soot-blackened faces, they'd be all but invisible once they were in the river.

The soot from the paraffin-wax fuel blocks had coated the bottom of the mess tins that Sergeant Smith was using to do the cooking. When the men tried it out, it made for perfect camouflage paint – thick, black and greasy, and completely impervious to water. But there was one, major problem. With no soap, the soot was all but impossible to wash off. If an escape attempt had to be aborted at the last minute and they had already blackened up, it would be all but impossible to clean it off before being discovered by their captors. They'd have a difficult job explaining that one away. In fact, having soot-blackened faces would be a dead giveaway. It was too big a risk, and so that part of the escape plan had to be abandoned. Instead, they'd rely on darkness and a bit of mud hastily slapped on at the river bank to conceal their getaway.

None of the British hostages – except the OC – had had any combat-after-capture training, the classic course that all Special Forces undergo, in case they are taken prisoner. Before departing for Sierra Leone, they'd had a basic verbal conduct-after-capture brief. But this was simply a set of instructions covering the 'big six', the six pieces of information a British soldier is permitted to give to an enemy if captured: name, rank, serial number, religion, blood group and date of birth. There was no practical element to it at all: no situation rehearsals, no role playing and no resistance training. The Major, having got them into this mess, would have to get them out again.

That night, the six British soldiers were on a real high – riding a wave of confidence that the river option would work. All they had to do was stay in Calm Down Fresh's good books, and with a little luck he'd allow them a second wash. As soon as it was dark, they'd head down to the river with their makeshift escape gear. They'd slap a little river mud on their faces and slip silently into the water, disappearing into the gathering darkness. Even if the rebels did spot them, they'd have a hard job shooting the men as they were carried away into the night: down low in the water, they would make for very difficult targets. They were all good swimmers, and they were fairly certain that none of the rebels could swim, so it wasn't as if they could jump in and follow. They'd love to see the look on Calm Down Fresh's face when he found out that his hostages had escaped. What that crazy bastard would do to the guards didn't bear thinking about.

It was a strange thing, but apart from having to cross the Rokel Creek in their canoes to get from Magbeni to Gberi Bana and vice versa, the West Side Boys seemed to avoid the river like the plague. It was almost as though they were scared of it. It was such a waste. The river was full of fish – the British soldiers had noticed as much when they'd been sent down there for their wash. In a place so short of food – and with what they did have so desperately lacking in protein – the rebels should have been spearing and netting and trapping the fish for all they were worth.

A couple of the soldiers were keen fishermen back at home, on the River Lagan and in Belfast Lough. They'd even been tempted to ask

Cambodia if he'd let them try their hand fishing in the Rokel Creek. It would keep their minds off their predicament, they'd reasoned, and might even be a chance to net some extra food. But after some of the more disturbing events of the past few days, the idea of going down to the river alone, or even in pairs, had lost its appeal. At least up at Cambodia's or even Calm Down Fresh's place, they felt they had a certain strength in numbers.

Maybe there was some heavy voodoo shit that prevented the West Side Boys from entering the water or eating the fish. After all, the rebels had said they wanted to drown Corporal Mousa, when they had suspected he was 'bulletproof'. Whatever, it didn't stop the British hostages from looking to the river as their new route to freedom. And they knew it could work. As their spirits lifted at the prospect of escape, they began talking about the Belfast pubs they'd hit first when they got back home, each man waxing lyrical about the quality of his own favourite boozer – Malone's, Madison's Bar or the Donegal Arms.

Soon, a light-hearted argument had begun about where to get the best pint of Guinness in Belfast. Each pull on the pint should leave a rim of creamy-white head around the side of the glass. At the end of the pint, the drinker should be able to count all the rings. If you couldn't, the pint wasn't worth the drinking. Everyone argued for their own local boozer, of course, and the men decided to hold off on making a final decision until they'd successfully escaped – then they could go on a crawl of all their favourite pubs, and thus the issue would be decided.

Generally speaking, the men hadn't talked about food or drink at all since being taken hostage. It was one of their unspoken rules. The same went for their families and for home; any talk about those sort of things and they'd start getting homesick, which would be bad for morale. They had also agreed that should they be offered the chance to speak to their families on the satphone, then they would refuse. The Major had argued that if their captors could hold that sort of thing over them, then it would start to break them down mentally. The rules that the hostages were now living by were like a secret pact they'd made with themselves, one designed to buoy up their spirits and retain their integrity as soldiers. There would be no talk about family, home, or food and drink – in the interests of collective sanity and survival.

That night, they had made an exception to those rules, and spent time fantasising about the perfect pint. Sergeant Smith had also allowed each man to smoke a whole cigarette, which was a real luxury by now. But their celebrations were to prove horribly premature. Around midnight, the door to their room burst open, and Calm Down Fresh came storming in. He was screaming and foaming at the mouth and making no sense whatsoever – which made it all the more terrifying for the hostages. Grabbing the Major and Ranger Rowell, he had them hauled out of the room. No explanations. No reasons. The door slammed shut behind them, leaving four stunned men. They had no idea what was going on. But of one thing they were certain: they knew that it was serious. They could tell what sort of mood Calm Down Fresh was in. This time, it was going to be real bad.

The sound of Calm Down Fresh's ranting and raving faded into the night, as the two hostages were dragged away. With the Major and Ranger Rowell now gone, the four men tried to work out what had happened. Calm Down Fresh must have been spying on them from the window and overheard something of the high spirits in their room. They'd kept the noise down low, to prevent anyone overhearing their river escape plans, so what exactly had that mad bastard seen or heard? If he'd realised that it was an escape committee he'd been spying on, it was going to be worse than bad for the Major and Ranger Rowell. Calm Down Fresh had been raging mad, that much was for sure.

It was no surprise that he'd chosen to pick on the Major: Calm Down Fresh clearly hated him with a vengeance way beyond any of the other hostages. Ever since the morning of their move from Cambodia's house, Calm Down Fresh had behaved towards the OC in a deeply aggressive and resentful way. Somewhere deep inside Calm Down Fresh's warped mind, there was obviously a real soldier still trying to get out. A man who wanted to distinguish himself through his courage, rather than his cowardice and cruelty. A man who wanted his men to follow him out of admiration and camaraderie, rather than fear. A man who wanted to lead with respect and honour. A man who was deeply jealous of the Royal Irish Rangers' OC.

Calm Down Fresh saw the man that he secretly wanted to be embodied in the British Major, and that only served to highlight his own inadequacies. And while the OC had real leadership skills, the Camp Commandant had none. He hated Major Martial with a corresponding intensity, and would love nothing more than to see him dead, of that the other soldiers were certain. Why Ranger Rowell had been taken away was less clear. But maybe Calm Down Fresh had taken one from the top and one from the bottom ranks, the men reasoned.

They strained their ears, trying to catch any sound that might give a clue as to what had happened to the two men. But there was nothing. The Major and Ranger Rowell must have been taken some distance away. So the four men waited in their room in silence for the gunshots that they feared would be coming.

Calm Down Fresh ordered the Major and Ranger Rowell to be blindfolded, and then had them dragged halfway around the village. Finally, at the edge of the forest (the two British soldiers could tell roughly where they were by all the forest noises) they were made to kneel with their heads bowed, as if facing a firing squad. Calm Down Fresh had left them like that for the best part of an hour. And every now and then, one or other of the rebels would put the muzzle of his gun to the back of the soldiers' heads. And then the threats and taunting would begin. Neither man knew what had made Calm Down Fresh fly into such a towering, murderous rage. But both of them knew that they were now the closest they had ever been to death in their whole lives.

Back in their room, the four remaining hostages were starting to panic. The OC and Ranger Rowell must have been gone for at least an hour now, and they had still heard nothing from outside. As the men lay there on the floor in the darkness – amid the rats and the cockroaches and the spiders, their regular night-time companions – they began imagining the worst. Each man started preparing himself mentally for the finality of gunshots and for the fact that then there would be four of them left alive. Captain Flaherty would then have to take over command, Ranger Gaunt reasoned to himself. But he had relied so heavily on the Major to help get him through.

'Where the feck d'you think he's taken them?' Ranger Gaunt whispered at last. No one wanted to say very much, in case Calm Down Fresh was still hiding outside, listening.

'They're away, and that's all we know,' Sergeant Smith whispered back. 'So youse best try to get some shut-eye, lad. There's nothing more we can do tonight.'

Neither the OC nor Ranger Rowell came back to rejoin the four men that night. There were no gunshots, but that didn't mean very much. The Boys had plenty of other choice ways in which to kill someone. And when an exhausted Ranger Gaunt did finally drop off into an uneasy sleep, he was racked by terrible dreams. From a distance, he could see Major Martial walking towards him. But the oddest thing was that they were no longer in Africa: the Major was approaching him along what looked like Belfast's Ormeau Road. And as he got closer, the Ranger could see what the Major was carrying: a head mounted on a pole.

Ranger Gaunt knew that the Major was already dead, but that didn't stop him from continuing to walk towards him with that dreadful thing in his hand. And as the Ranger watched, he realised with a growing sense of horror exactly whose severed head it was that the Major was carrying: *it was his own*. Ranger Gaunt woke with a start, jerking upright on the hard floor in a cold, cloying sweat, the dream still raw and screaming and tearing at his mind. *Oh my God. Maybe that's what the dream had meant: that there were six of them left, but they were already dead men.*

Ranger Gaunt sat there in the dark, his heart thumping, trying to calm himself down. If the assault force was out there preparing a rescue, it had better come damn quickly now, the Ranger thought to himself. Otherwise, all they might find of the hostages was six corpses.

Or maybe six heads mounted on poles.

OP CERTAIN DEATH

IT was to be 'Operation Certain Death' then, as the men of D Squadron had started calling the Operation Barras assault plan, now that their best-laid plans had failed. To have gone in by boat, lain up overnight and hit the rebel base hard, at first light, from the jungle, would have been pure poetry, and they knew it. The enemy would not have known a thing about it until it was all too late. D Squadron would have been on top of them so quickly, they'd have been hauling people out of their beds with no warning. The whole assault would have been far more predictable, intense, quicker, neater, easier and short-lived. It would have been stealth personified. Most importantly, it would have meant that the chances of getting to the hostages quickly and rescuing them safely would have been that much higher.

But now it was to be Operation Certain Death – roaring into the target on the choppers, all guns blazing and hoping beyond hope that they could get to the hostages before the rebels did. It was a plan born out of desperation. So be it. There was no other way. On a personal level, flying into the rebels' backyard really did jack up the tension and the fear factor. And the hostage-rescue team in particular knew that they were really up against it now. But overall, the men of the assault force had just one, overriding reaction to the new airborne assault plan: *let's do it*. Let's get in there, get it done, and get out again. In the Regiment as a whole there was no such word as 'can't'. No plan was ever seen as being too much – even Operation Certain Death. The only way to deal with it was to get the job done as quickly as possible, and be home for tea and medals.

Having said that, a lot of the men were convinced that the new plan would never get the go-ahead from the top brass. Certainly, had any of them presented a plan like Operation Certain Death during SAS selection, they'd have failed. There was nothing stealthy, subtle or covert about it, and it didn't jive with the ethos of the Regiment. But you never knew in this game. Stranger things had happened in the Regiment. And so the men of D Squadron went back to the taped-off area out the rear of the camp, and began to rehearse the assault all over again. Only this time, they were going in from their intended rope-down or drop-off points from the choppers. When they weren't doing rehearsals for the new assault plan, they were getting their weapons zeroed in out on the 'ranges' – a patch of semi-waterlogged ground out the rear of the camp, set in a curve of the jungle-clad Occra Hills.

And there were no fun and games any more. If this mission went ahead they knew that they were up against it; they knew that each and every one of them would be pushed to his limit and beyond.

Now that it was to be an airborne assault, the key planning decision to make concerned the hostage-rescue scenario itself. This would be the most difficult part of the whole operation. Timing was crucial. The hostage-rescue team would be first down the fast ropes into Gberi Bana, to hit the hostage house. But if they went in too early, they would have no back-up on the ground to repulse any rebel counter-attack, as the other fire teams would still be roping in. If they went in too late, the West Side Boys would have cottoned on to the assault, and put a bullet in the brain of each of the hostages. This was Air Troop's baby, and there were only two real options that they could foresee.

In the first, the hostage-rescue team would fast-rope down from the helicopter, enter the hostage house and clear all the rooms, killing or capturing their occupants: they would locate and secure the hostages as they did so. The bulk of the assault force would fast-rope in immediately behind them, to put down covering fire. In the second option, the hidden SAS obs team would move up from the forest into Gberi Bana just before the main, chopper-borne assault force came into target. The six men would move by stealth into the village, enter the target building, take out the occupants by lethal but silent means (knifes, garrottes), and secure the hostages. They would then wait for Air Troop to come in, secure the hostage house and effect the hostage extraction.

In the final analysis, it was judged that option two was too risky. If the obs team were discovered before they reached the hostages, it would be a disaster. All it would take was one pesky village dog, and the whole mission would be blown. The SAS obs team would then face a rebel force that outnumbered them some thirty to one. And that was suicide. The hostages would be either executed on the spot, or moved out of Gberi Bana to an unknown location. In the worst-case scenario, there could be six SAS casualties and six dead hostages. Alternatively, some of the SAS obs team might escape, and the six hostages might be split into two groups by the rebels and moved to separate locations. If that happened, there would be almost no hope of ever rescuing them. So it was decided: Air Troop's hostage-rescue team would be first into action, fast-roping in to secure the hostages. Once that decision was made, the rest of the assault could be designed around it.

The final plan that was drawn up for Operation Barras looked more like an emergency attack than a considered SAS assault. It was distinguished less by secrecy and stealth, and more by the sheer balls and audacity of the strike. The new plan involved putting the whole of D Squadron and their SBS colleagues on to two giant CH47 Chinook helicopters and flying them right into the heart of Gberi Bana village. As the first fire team – Air Troop's hostage-rescue team – hit the ground, they would head for the building dubbed the 'hostage house', while the hidden SAS obs team provided covering fire from the jungle. The rest of the fire teams would follow immediately after them, piling off the two Chinooks and hitting the rebels hard.

As there were only three Chinooks available for the operation, that left just one free to ferry the Paras on to target. Consequently, the first forty-five Paras (the maximum load per Chinook) would be choppered into Magbeni, on the southern river bank, at the same time as the SAS and SBS went into action at Gberi Bana. The first Chinook away from target would then turn round to pick up the remaining forty-five Paras at Waterloo Camp, and fly them in to join the assault on Magbeni – a round trip of some thirty minutes. Once the ninety-odd Para assault force were complete, they would advance through the forest to hit the main body of the West Side Boys. The two hidden SAS obs teams already on the ground would guide both chopper-borne assault forces (Special Forces and the Paras) in by radio.

In Gberi Bana, three potential landing zones had been identified. The first, LZ1, was the clearing out the front of the hostage house, in the southern half of the village. The second, LZ2, was the clearing out the front of Cambodia's house, in the northern part of the village. The third, and largest, LZ3, was the overgrown football pitch a little off to the western side of the village. When the Chinooks went into

Gberi Bana, one half of the assault force would be dropped into LZ1 in the south, while the other half would hit LZ2 in the north. LZ3 would be used to extract the assault force, when it was all over. Timing would be everything. The chopper hitting LZ1 had to put the first men – the six-man hostage-rescue team – down the fast ropes momentarily before the second chopper hit LZ2, giving them a few extra seconds to get to the hostage house and secure the six British captives, before the rebels woke up to the assault and tried to kill them.

At LZ1, all the men would be fast-roping in, as there was no area large enough to put the chopper down on the ground. The second chopper would go straight in to land at LZ2; the men had to be out of that chopper in record time, to minimise the chances of it getting hit while on the deck. The Chinooks are not armoured, and so neither the men of the assault force nor the chopper aircrews would have any protection while hovering over the village or touching down. Target times for getting both assault teams off the Chinooks were ninety seconds for all the men to have roped down at LZ1 (fifteen seconds per fire team), and twenty seconds for everyone to have piled off the second chopper as it touched down at LZ2. Each and every second longer could prove disastrous. And once the 'red mist' had come down – the animal aggression of combat – the men needed to be into the firefight as fast as humanly possible.

There would be two ropes dangling off the back ramp of the first chopper, and one in the middle going directly through a hatch in the floor. Each rope was about the size of an apple in diameter and the men would be fast-roping in from ninety feet, so everyone was supposed to be wearing thick, firemen's gloves to prevent rope burns. Each man would descend by taking the rope in both hands like a fireman's pole, and jumping out of the chopper with his feet free. He'd then stop himself by grabbing hold of the rope as hard as he could, as the ground rocketed up towards him. At least, that was the theory. In practice, they were going to have to break just about every rule in the book, if Operation Certain Death was to have a chance of succeeding.

It was impossible to hold a gun and fight while wearing thick gloves, and the few seconds spent fumbling to remove them could prove fatal. So everyone opted for a pair of thin leather gloves instead (and to hell with the rope burns). The rule book stipulated a maximum of two men on the rope at any one time, but each man would be jumping off the Chinook as soon as the man before him's head had disappeared. Sure, it meant there was the potential for a pile-up underneath the chopper – but any slower would keep the chopper in hover mode for too long. The rule book said that no one should take more than 25 lb of kit on the rope, but each man would be jumping into Gberi Bana carrying between 80 and 150 lb of gear, most of which was weapons and ammo. And while the rule book said that the men were supposed to fast-rope down from a reasonably stationary platform, in this case the chopper would be weaving and bobbing, to avoid presenting such an easy target.

There was no longer any room in the assault plan for fire-team support, either. Normally, one or two teams would take in some seriously big pieces of kit, like a couple of 50-cal HMGs. Once out of the choppers, they would set up on some pre-identified points of higher ground, and give covering fire to the main assault force. But every man on Operation Certain Death would be hitting the ground in one or other of the two landing zones located pretty much in the centre of the village, and there would be no chance to gain higher ground. So each fire team was going in as purely an assault team, and, so as to maximise mobility, taking light weapons only: 1 LMG (usually a GPMG or a Minimi – a light machine gun, with a shorter barrel and a retractable stock, ideal for jungle warfare) and five assault rifles (Diemacos – the re-engineered Canadian version of the M16) per team. The aim was to clear the village from the two central landing zones pushing outwards, forcing the rebels back into the jungle.

Each chopper would be carrying six fire teams – so a total of thirty-six men. Once on the ground, each fire team was responsible for clearing and making safe a number of specific, pre-identified targets in Gberi Bana. From LZ1, Fire Team 1 – the hostage-rescue team – was tasked with clearing the hostage house and checking if all hostages were present and correct. If any were missing they would act accordingly (i.e. find them before they got shot). Once in possession of the hostage house, half of the fire team would secure the back entrance while the other half would remain vigilant to the front. Once all hostages were reported present and correct, they were to remain in position and use lethal force to stop any of the enemy from advancing on or entering the building.

Fire Team 2 would fast-rope out of the chopper on to LZ1 some fifteen seconds after Fire Team 1, and start clearing buildings on the track running northwards from the hostage house towards Cambodia's. Fire Team 3, hitting the LZ next, would clear the buildings running south from the hostage house along the track down towards the upstream river bank. Fire Team 4 would go into action on the LZ next, clearing the hospital house and those buildings along the track running east down to the downstream river bank. And so on and so forth. At LZ2, Fire Teams 7–12 would be going into action tasked with similar roles, clearing the rebel forces out of Colonel Cambodia's end of Gberi Bana. Each fire team would be using standard forced-entry and building-clearance techniques, and there were an estimated two hundred rebels to take care of in Gberi Bana village.

Operation Certain Death had one, significant advantage over most normal assaults: because much of the village was made of mud buildings, the men would be able to fire through the thin walls, so killing or wounding the occupants. But by a similar token, anyone inside would also be able to fire back out at them.

On the night prior to the assault, the two obs teams would have moved up to do a CTR at Gberi Bana and Magbeni. At dawn the following morning, the obs team at Gberi Bana would have eyes on the hostage house as the assault force flew in. If they saw any rebels moving prior to the incoming air armada being audible to the naked ear, they would leave them unmolested, so as to avoid a compromise before the assault proper started. But as soon as the choppers could be heard coming in on the villages, any rebels that the obs team spotted up and about would be taken out, using a barrage of gunfire from their position hidden in the jungle.

While D Squadron had been busy drawing up the ground attack plan, the RAF and Royal Navy pilots had been working on their aerial assault profile. The choppers would be following the course of the Rokel Creek into target, sticking so low down on the river that they would remain below the tree line, masking the sound of their approach until the last possible moment. They might be audible to the naked ear a mile or more out of the village, but at the speed at which they were flying that was only thirty seconds to target.

The two rebel bases had been broken down into grids, for ease of aerial reference and assault planning. The three Chinooks would be supported by two Army AH7 Lynx attack helicopters, flown from HMS *Argyll*, along with one Royal Navy Lynx. A fast and agile aircraft, the Lynx has a top speed in excess of 200 mph, and is the British Army's primary battlefield all-purpose helicopter. Armed with eight TOW anti-armour missiles, and four 7.62mm GPMGs, it has a crew of two and can carry up to ten troops. In the air attack plan, as the Chinooks flared out over Gberi Bana and the first troops fast-roped down on to the target, the three Lynx helicopters would launch a blistering assault on the southern river bank, at Magbeni. This is where the bulk of the rebels' heavy weapons were known to be situated, and the helicopters were tasked with taking them out before they had a chance to fire in anger.

The Lynx pilots knew that their limit of exploitation in Gberi Bana was the tree line: they were to put down machine-gun fire and rocket salvos into the jungle only. The ground assault aimed to drive the rebels into the forest, where the air power could then deal with them. In Magbeni, the Lynx pilots had no initial LOE (except to avoid the Paras' landing zone), and so they were to hose down the rebel positions with everything they had. Once the Paras had signalled that they were going in, the Lynx pilots would revert to the same LOE as in Gberi Bana, namely the tree line. And once both ground forces were engaged with the enemy on both sides of the river, the Lynx pilots would rely on them to call in targeted air strikes on specific pockets of rebel resistance. In that way, they would minimise chances of any blue-on-blue incidents.

The pilots and aircrews who would fly the CH47 Chinooks were all from 7 and 9 Squadrons RAF, which are dedicated to Special Forces operations. And there was no doubt about it as far as the men of D Squadron were concerned, the men who flew their Chinooks were the best there were in the business. The crews of each giant, twin-rotor chopper consisted of a pilot and co-pilot/engineer (with the option of two 'loadies'/door gunners in the rear). The Chinook has a long, boxlike body, with twin twenty-metre rotor blades, mounted one above the nose and one above the tail section. Designed as troop transports and recovery aircraft, each can carry forty-five combat-equipped soldiers.

Though normally unarmed, the Chinooks had been rigged with door-mounted 12.7mm chain guns. While most automatic weapons operate using the gases produced by their projectiles to feed more bullets into the firing chamber, the operating cycle of the chain guns (load, fire, extract, eject) is driven by an electric motor utilising a chain (hence the name, 'chain gun', a generic term for any Hughes-designed weapon with his mechanism). This minimises stoppages (as misfired rounds will still be ejected by the chain-driven bolt action), and also allows for greater control over the rate of fire – from single shot to two thousand rounds per minute. Though relatively small in calibre, the 12.7mms mounted on the Chinooks packed a real punch, with an effective range of some two thousand yards.

While the ground forces were rehearsing the ground assaults, the

RAF crews were busy modifying their aircraft – doing the sort of things that would never have been allowed back in the UK. They were turning the Chinooks into DIY aerial-fire platforms. The glass in the portholes running along the sides of the Chinook could be pulled and rotated outwards so as to pop out the window completely (intended as an emergency escape exit if the chopper went down in the drink). All of these were now removed, so that once the Chinooks were over Gberi Bana, the men could take up positions at the windows and put down covering fire on to the village. The aircrews also removed the feed trays from the 12.7mm chain guns, as they had a tendency to get blocked and cause stoppages. This would mean that once the weapons were opened up over the target and were pushing out rounds at more than four thousand a minute, the spent casings would fly out all over the floor of the chopper and rain down on to the village below.

Royal Navy ships anchored off Freetown were also to play a significant role in the assault. In addition to the Lynx attack helicopters, the RFA ship *Sir Percival*, riding at anchor in Freetown harbour, was to be used as a hostage muster station and a hospital ship. Any casualties – and there were fears of significant numbers – would be choppered out directly to the *Sir Percival*, so as to avoid any unwelcome exposure to the press pack now gathered in Freetown.

But one of the greatest fears of the assault planners was that they still didn't have enough serious air cover. Even with the Paras going in alongside the men of the SAS and SBS, the assault force would be outnumbered some five to one – usually the sort of odds an attacking force would seek in its favour. Consequently, they would need all the air cover they could get. As the Nigerian UN forces were in Sierra Leone, there was the option of doing a deal with them so that their Alpha jets (a German jet aircraft, similar to the British Hawk trainer) could fly in support of the assault. But the timing and intent of Operation Barras had to be kept a complete secret from the West Side Boys. And for the British planners, this meant keeping it secret from all non-British forces, including those of the United Nations. The UN forces on the ground were seen as being leaky and unreliable. And as everyone in JFHQ Freetown was well aware, careless talk cost lives.

So, the British military would have to rely solely on their own air forces for the assault. The upside to this was that no information about the planned assault would be leaked to the rebels. The downside was that the British forces had no real top-notch helicopter gunships. The Chinook was basically a troop carrier, with a couple of very useful chain guns slung on its sides, and the Lynx was really a transport helicopter with an anti-tank capability. What Operation Barras needed was aerial firepower – and the answer, of course, lay in the ex-Executive Outcomes Air Wing.

Fearless Fred Marafono and Neall Ellis had already played a key role in the mission preparation, briefing up the British assault planners in JFHQ. They had made it clear that the choppers of the Air Wing and their crews – the de facto Sierra Leonean Air Force – were at the British force's disposal. And so it was that the Air Wing's Mi-24 gunship was written into the Operation Barras assault plan. The Mi-24 boasted a nose-mounted, four-barrelled 12.7mm Gatling gun turret (with a rate of fire of 4,000 rounds a minute), two 57mm rockets pods (carrying a total of 36 rockets) and titanium rotor heads capable of withstanding hits from 20mm cannons. And so, not for the first time in recent months, Fearless Fred and Neall Ellis and their Mi-24 were put under orders of the Commander of British Forces in Sierra Leone.

The one great advantage of the Air Wing – in addition to its Mi-24 gunship, of course, which packed just the sort of punch the British planners were looking for – was that it could be trusted. Fearless Fred Marafono was ex-Hereford, which in itself was enough for the British planners, and he was positively itching to go in alongside the men of his old regiment. And Nellis had more than proven his worth as a gunship pilot over the last six years in Sierra Leone. In fact, he was one of the most combat-experienced gunship pilots in the world. With their Mi-24 gunship now joining the three Lynx helicopters, the British planners felt much happier about things.

But it remained clear to JFHQ that a well-organised defending force in Gberi Bana could bring down one or even more of the British Chinooks. Some of the West Side Boys' weaponry was seriously top-notch – begging the question where they had got it from in the first place. The new assault plan was based on the premise that the West Side Boys did not constitute a well-organised defending force. In fact, it relied on them being caught totally by surprise. This was a major gamble for British forces to be taking, especially as the two SAS obs teams were already gathering evidence on the ground to the contrary. From everything they were hearing using their specialist listening equipment, the rebels were spoiling for a fight with British forces.

The SAS obs team also knew that the rebels had got the 50-cal HMG on the captured Royal Irish Rangers' WMIK Land-Rover up and running, because they kept hearing it firing off a single shot. So, the rebels were testing out their captured weaponry. In fact, before being hauled off his Land-Rover by the West Side Boys' mob, Ranger McVeigh had had the foresight to switch the 50-cal off automatic. It was a complex task to retime it to fire on auto again. This explained why the West Side Boys kept firing it off on single shot only; they were trying to work out how to get it back on to automatic. But even one, well-placed round from that gun could blast a Chinook out of the sky.

It stood to reason that the rebels could cause the British assault force some serious problems. Due to the density of the jungle surrounding Gberi Bana and the closeness of the trees to the actual village itself, there were really only two possible routes of approach for any airborne assault force. Both approaches were along the Rokel Creek, either from the upstream side or the downstream side of the village. All the rebels had to do to defend themselves effectively would be to place their best anti-aircraft weaponry in positions covering the two riverine approaches to their base. And then wait for the air armada to come thundering up the river from either one of the two directions, catch them coming in low over the village and open fire. The choppers would be sitting targets.

And the West Side Boys would be bound to put up a spirited defence. They were a battle-hardened bunch, many of them having seen years of combat in Sierra Leone. They were well armed and they had never before been beaten. So far, they had repulsed United Nations attacks on their territory, and they'd had great success in taking eleven British soldiers hostage. Without any sign of resistance, they had seized the British soldiers, the British vehicles and the heavy weapons that they carried. As far as the West Side Boys were concerned, no one could come down the dirt tracks leading into their territory, unless they allowed it. They ran their area and they were king of the jungle there. Or so they thought.

The men of D Squadron doubted that any government in the world would sign up to Operation Certain Death. When they had first been called together for a presentation of the new assault plan, the general consensus had been that it felt like a 'total fuck-up plan'. Flying in on choppers and fast-roping down on to the target were similar tactics to those used on the mission that had gone so badly wrong for US Special Forces in Mogadishu – in the so-called Black Hawk Down incident, or, as the Somalis call it, Malinti Rangers – the Day of the Rangers. None of the men now assembled at Waterloo Camp had forgotten those images of the naked corpses of US soldiers being hauled through the streets of Mogadishu by a victorious Somali militia. For better or for worse they were now committed to the plan: but they would do everything they possibly could to make sure it did not turn into another Somalia. In this game, however, there were never any guarantees.

If the whole op went pear-shaped – and there was every possibility that it might – it could spell disaster for Tony Blair's Labour government. Yet unbeknown to the men now making their final assault preparations, a decision had already been taken at the highest level that the six remaining Royal Irish hostages had to be rescued, and at any cost. If the men of the Operation Barras assault force ended up paying a heavy price for that freedom, then so be it. The rebels could not be allowed to defy and defeat the British military and the UN – for if they were to do so, that would be the end of the rule of law, and of peace, in Sierra Leone.

Tony Blair was receiving daily briefings on the hostage crisis. Both he and Robin Cook, the Foreign Secretary, held intensive discussions with General Sir Charles Guthrie, Chief of Defence Staff, concerning the military options open to them. Mission assessment was that in the worst-case scenario they would have to be willing to lose a Chinook and half a squadron. In other words, if Operation Barras went ahead, there was a very real possibility that some forty-odd British servicemen, including the flight crews, could be killed. And not just any old British servicemen: these would all be Special Forces, Britain's finest. The press would have a field day.

But there was more at stake than simply saving the rule of law, and the peace, in Sierra Leone, although that in itself was arguably reason enough to go in. There was now a very real prospect of the West Side Boys and the RUF joining forces over the British hostage crisis. And that was the ultimate nightmare scenario. The rebels could then outmanoeuvre and beat the best the British military had to throw at them, and could do with the six remaining hostages as they pleased. Ultimately, this would give the Libyan-backed, al-Qaeda-financed rebel coalition a real opportunity to succeed in their avowed aim of 'doing a Somalia' on British forces in Sierra Leone.

That was the real reason why the stakes were so high. And that was the reason why the assault forces waiting impatiently at Waterloo Camp for the green light might just get the go-ahead. With the hostage negotiations now running into their third week, relations between the rebels and the British negotiators seemed to be breaking down still further. Then, on Monday 4 September – day eleven of the hostage crisis – Foday Kallay decided to bring along the three decapitated Kamajor heads on poles (one, the little baby girl's) to the face-to-face hostage-negotiation meeting.

Perhaps he did this in an attempt to scare the British negotiating team into giving ground. But it had the reverse effect, filling the two Met officers and their SAS counterparts with utter revulsion. You clearly couldn't *negotiate* with these depraved bastards. You had to go in and deal with them on their own terms. And the men of the D Squadron reacted to this ghoulish incident with frustration and barely muted anger. *When are the fucking top brass going to wake up and smell the coffee?* they wondered.

Roll on Operation Certain Death and let's get up and at them.

16

THE KILLING GAME

With no great leap of imagination, Sierra Leone might serve as the ultimate African cliché. Everything political correctness forbids mentioning is there: indolence, poverty, natural wealth, voodoo, corruption, cannibalism and cruelty beyond measure. It is Kurtz's 'The horror! The horror!' in a modern 'Heart of Darkness'.

– Jim Hooper, *Bloodsong*

EARLY on the morning of day twelve of the hostage crisis, the four Royal Irish soldiers heard the door to their room being unlocked by the guards. They'd had a bad, bad night: patchy sleep disturbed by nightmares and evil visions. Already awake at first light, two hours or more ago, each man had been worrying himself sick about the fate of Major Martial and Ranger Rowell. Now, as the door creaked open, they braced themselves for what they thought was coming: a couple of bloodied corpses being thrown into the room on top of them. Instead, the two missing soldiers were shoved, sprawling, into the room – bloody and bruised and looking like death, but still very much alive. For all six captives this early-morning reunion was little short of a miracle.

After their night in front of the mock firing squad, the Major and Ranger Rowell looked physically and emotionally exhausted. They kept their explanations of what had happened to a bare minimum, avoiding the worst parts. They had been kept kneeling at the forest edge for an hour or more, blindfolded, their heads bowed, with the executioners' guns at their backs. The guards had taken great pleasure in telling them exactly what they were going to do to the two men, before killing them. Finally, Foday Kallay had materialised and, somehow, the Major had managed to talk him and his men out of their murderous intentions. The Major didn't go into how he'd done this exactly – he clearly didn't want to talk about it. After that, the two men had been taken to separate rooms and held there for the night, blindfolded and with their hands tied.

Once the Major had finished speaking, a grim silence descended on the room. All of the hostages were thinking the same thing: *how much more of this can we take?* They felt that death was but a hair's breadth away. They'd had no news about the hostage negotiations for several days, either: no new demands, no signs of progress. The talks seemed to have stagnated, and the option of a negotiated release was looking increasingly dead in the water. The one chink of light on the horizon was that the Major was still alive. As long as the men still had him leading them, all was not lost. There was still a chance of escape, or that they might be rescued. *Somehow, please God, they had to make it out of there.*

If the hostage negotiations had completely broken down, this raised a terrible question in each of the men's minds: *why were the West Side Boys still keeping them alive?* Each day, the hostages had hoped for some sort of progress as an incentive for the rebels not to kill them. But at what stage exactly would the bastards decide that they had outlived their usefulness – and so eliminate them? It wasn't as if the rebels were queasy about finishing off their captives, either. That morning, Sony had told the six hostages about the fate of some of the more unfortunate village 'recruits'. After the training was over, those recruits who had failed to do well were ordered to crawl around the village on their hands and knees. The rebels had then kicked the living daylights out of them, just for 'fun'. Sony doubted if one or two of the youngest recruits had survived.

For the rest of that day, Foday Kallay, Calm Down Fresh and Cambodia were nowhere to be seen, which only served to heighten the hostages' sense of unease. It probably meant that the three rebel leaders were ensconced in one of their houses, plotting. That evening, Calm Down Fresh refused the Major's request to let his men go to the river for a wash, and so the planned river-escape attempt was off too. As the men bedded down for another night on the bare concrete floor, a hollow hopelessness settled over them, the yawning void of despair. *But the following day, things were only to get worse.*

Day thirteen started off peacefully enough. But by mid-morning Calm Down Fresh and Cambodia had the BBC on the satphone out at the front of the house. As none of the hostages had taught the rebels how to operate the satphone, they presumed one of the British representatives on the hostage-negotiating team must have done so. Once he'd got a BBC reporter on the line, Calm Down Fresh started shouting for the Major to go over and speak on the satphone. He was to tell the BBC that everything was fine and that all the hostages were being treated well and in good health. But Major Martial refused to do so. After the horrible events of the previous night, the men feared that the Major's refusal was going to prove suicidal, and not only for him.

'Just go speak on it, sir,' Ranger Gaunt pleaded with the Major. The men could see Calm Down Fresh strutting about impatiently over by the satphone.

'Please, sir, he's not feckin' around,' Ranger Rowell urged. 'Just say a few words on the phone, sir.'

'Go on, sir,' Ranger Gaunt continued, '*go on.*'

'I can't, lads,' the Major retorted, through gritted teeth. 'I have to let them know that something's wrong.'

'But there's other ways, sir, sure to God there are.' Ranger Gaunt was convinced that the Major was badly misjudging things now.

'Come on, sir, surely it can't do no harm,' the other Ranger added.

'I'm sorry, lads,' the Major said, shaking his head. 'We have to get the right sort of message out. Things are in a bad way right now. This is the only way I can think of doing it.'

'But it's just a few *words*, sir. It won't sort of *hurt*,' Ranger Gaunt persisted. 'They're feckin' serious this time, sir. I can feel it. Just talk on the phone, sir. Youse have to.'

'You heard your men, Major,' Colonel Cambodia interrupted, having come over from his end of the village. 'The man from the BBC is now waiting for you, Major. 'We've even got three satellites showing and a very clear signal. So, like the young soldiers have said, it is just a few words on the satphone to the BBC, to let the world know that you are all OK. That is all we are asking.'

'I'm afraid I'm not able to do that, Colonel,' the Major replied, firmly. 'British Army rules state that no serving member of Her Majesty's Armed Forces can be made to speak with a member of the press while being held hostage or under duress. And that goes for all my men, not just myself.'

At the Major's words, Cambodia's face clouded over. 'All right, then,' he snapped, turning sharply away. 'But remember, you only have yourself to blame for what will happen now.'

Cambodia was clearly washing his hands of the situation, and there seemed to be nothing the Rangers could do to persuade the Major to speak. It wasn't as if they could try to convince Captain Flaherty or Sergeant Smith to speak, either. The Major had made it quite clear that *none* of the men were allowed to speak on the satphone. *But what'll I do if I'm ordered to speak*, a panicked Ranger Gaunt started thinking, his mind racing. *What'll I do if that mad bastard thrusts the receiver into my hand?* There was no doubt about it: despite the Major's warning, he knew that he would speak on the satphone if ordered to by their captors. It may have been a court-martial offence for all he knew, but rather that than face whatever the West Side Boys might now have in store for them.

Calm Down Fresh was now waving the satphone receiver about wildly, and yelling for the Major to speak, but he was stubbornly refusing to do so. Suddenly, Calm Down Fresh just flipped out, flying into a blind rage. Screaming at his men to cut off the live link to the BBC, he raced across to the British soldiers. Surrounding them with several of his men, Calm Down Fresh started yelling at two of the youngest boy rebels, ordering them to strip the hostages down to their boxer shorts. Each of the hostages was then hauled inside Calm Down Fresh's house, and subjected to a highly intrusive and degrading body search. The two boy rebels – one of whom was a cringing Assan – took everything off the British soldiers, including their precious escape maps.

Once all six men were back outside, Calm Down Fresh forced them to line up in their underwear, kneeling and with their heads bowed. He then started screaming orders at Assan and the other kid rebel to beat the British hostages. There was clear reluctance in the boys' eyes. Somewhere in the back of their minds, they knew that the British soldiers had shown them only friendship and respect. Assan, in particular, had perhaps begun to think of the hostages as something like his foreign friends. Yet at the same time, there was the far greater terror of Calm Down Fresh tearing into the boy soldiers' minds. After a split second's hesitation, the other boy stepped forward and cracked Ranger Gaunt around the head with the butt of his rifle. It wasn't a hard blow. But it meant that Assan was forced to follow suit.

'Good! Gooood! Again! AGAIN! Harder! HARDER!' Calm Down Fresh screamed, barely able to contain himself as the two young boys began laying into the hostages.

'Beat them. BEAT THEM! BEEAAT THEM!' he yelled. 'Beat them until dey go cry MERCY from de West Side *Niggas*.'

It seemed as if the whole camp was gathering to witness whatever fun and games Calm Down Fresh might have in store for the hostages. *What was it to be? Torture? Execution? Or something a little more unusual?* As the terrified British soldiers looked on, a carnival-like atmosphere descended on the village. In every direction, the kneeling hostages could see men and women and kid rebels dancing around in circles, singing and stomping their feet into the earth, pounding out a primeval rhythm. Then, taking their cue from Calm Down Fresh, they began yelling and shooting their guns into the air, as they closed in on the defenceless British soldiers. A savage free-for-all began, as a spitting, biting, screaming rebel mob bore down on the kneeling men.

Two women in particular tore at the men's hair, their faces contorted into masks of hate and fury. Then one grabbed a Ranger by his testicles, and began to scream obscenities at him, as she twisted and wrenched at his manhood. Men punched and kicked the hostages viciously. Enveloped in the stench of sweating bodies, and with the panting and cries of their attackers in their ears, the British soldiers went down under a hail of blows. All except Major Martial. The Major, bloodied yet unbowed, refused to buckle under the ferocious assault. But this just served to inflame the crowd yet further. As Calm Down Fresh goaded the mob to even greater violence, blows from boots and fists and rifle butts rained down on the OC.

Finally, the Major keeled over on to the ground, where the frenzied mob continued to kick and rifle-butt him for several seconds more. By now, Calm Down Fresh had started screaming just one, demented chant over and over again, as he danced about in front of the fallen British soldiers.

'Refuse to speak to de BBC! Refuse to speak to de BBC! Refuse to speak to de BBC!'

In one of their more private moments, one of the Rangers had reflected on how Calm Down Fresh was like 'Zebedee on bad drugs'. Now he sounded like some warped version of a Monty Python record being played at high speed. But the hostages knew that this situation was deadly serious. So far, they had relied on Colonel Cambodia to be the one, vaguely sane voice of rationality and reason among the rebel leadership. Now it seemed that even Colonel Cambodia had decided to turn on the hostages. And there was no contest as to which was the more terrifying: Calm Down Fresh's increasingly predictable madness, or the unexpected cold, hard steel that they heard in Cambodia's voice as he began speaking.

'So. It looks like we are going to have to treat you like the other prisoners, after all,' Cambodia observed, in a flat, matter-of-fact sort of way. It was almost as if he was speaking more to himself than to any of the hostages. 'And we have treated you soooo well. So veery, veery nicely. And yet you won't help us. So now we're going to have to show you our nasty side. We're going to have to start treating you like all the other prisoners. Which of you would like to be first, eh? Who would like to go in the pit? Join your friend, Mousa? And then, if you still won't cooperate, we will have to start killing you, like we do all the others. But which shall it be first? The pit, or perhaps a bullet? A bullet, I think. Maybe that will teach the rest of you to cooperate.'

Cambodia began calmly numbering off the hostages in the order in which they were to be dealt with. As he did so, Assan and the other boy soldier – not quite sure whether they'd done enough to satisfy Calm Down Fresh's blood lust – continued to punch and slap the six men sporadically. The rebel mob were leering over, while at the same time discussing in deliberately loud voices exactly what they were going to do to the British soldiers before killing them. As they proceeded to terrorise the soldiers, they were laughing and giving each other high fives.

'Yo, bro'! It go be him de first, then he go be next, then dat one, de small-small skinny one, he go be de last to be killed.'

'Yaaah! Give it der, nigga!'

'Yaah! High fives, bro'. Or why not go kill dem whiteboys de other way round? Start with de small-small one first. He no look like he go last that long, whatever we go do to him.'

'Yaah! Get him out of de way first, brother. Good thinkin', nigga!'

'Go put it dere, bro'!'

'Yaah! Which ever one's go be de last, bro', I want him to play wid. He go be mine, nigga, he go be mine.'

Oh please, God, don't let it happen, the Rangers were praying. *Don't let them fuck us like this.* I'm so fucking terrified, Lord. I'm so fucking scared. I feel like I'm going to shit or piss myself. God, please, *please* don't let me. Don't let them break me. Don't let me break down, not in front of the others. And not in front of these evil, evil bastards. Let me be strong, like the other men. Let me be like the Major. Let me be fucking BRAVE, Lord. Lord, give me strength. Lord, give me courage. Lord, let me take this like a *man*. Please, God. *Please*.

In the midst of all this mayhem, a terrified Ranger Gaunt was dragged off. He had no idea why he had been chosen or where he was being taken, but he feared the worst.

Sony went with the Ranger and kept trying to reassure him that it was all going to be all right.

'Don't worry, Jim,' Sony kept repeating. 'I'm with you. It's OK. It's going to be OK.'

What the feck d'youse mean, 'It's going to be OK,' the Ranger could hear a voice screaming inside his head. *These crazed feckin' bastards are taking me away alone up towards feckin' Foday feckin' Kallay's place. And youse know who lives there – the feckin' Voodoo feckin' Queen herself. Bollocks is it going to be OK.*

But somehow, just Sony's presence at his side made the Ranger feel less vulnerable, less abandoned. *Just keep on telling me it's going to be all right, Sony,* the voice inside the Ranger's head began pleading. *And whatever youse do, don't feckin' leave me.*

With a sick feeling in the pit of his stomach, the Ranger was shoved through the doorway of Kallay's house. Inside, there was a group of several women – including the voluptuous Voodoo Queen herself. The Ranger's mind started running riot, playing horrible scenes of a voodoo nightmare through his head, with himself as the central actor. But when Sony finally managed to work out just what the Voodoo Queen actually wanted of him, the Ranger all but collapsed with relief. All she needed was for him to fix her camera.

The rebels had taken a small, point-and-shoot camera out of one of the captured patrol's Land-Rovers. Now it seemed that the Voodoo Queen wanted to get some photographs of the hostages having their heads blown off, or whatever was about to happen to them. The problem was, in her haste to get the film into the camera she'd wound it on too far. As Ranger Gaunt fiddled with the winding mechanism, he noticed that his hands were shaking so much that he could barely keep hold of the camera. Sweat kept dripping into his eyes. The film was clearly fucked. But there was no way he was going to be the one to tell her that.

The Ranger did what he could, handed the camera back to its grinning 'owner', gave a shaky thumbs up, and was marched off back down the hill to rejoin the others. But by the time he got there, Calm Down Fresh and several of his goons had got hold of the Major and were dragging him off in the direction of the forest.

'So, we've changed our minds,' Cambodia was saying, in that same, terrifyingly dull monotone. 'Now it is your senior officer first. He is the one causing us all the trouble, so he is the one who's going to die . . .'

Cambodia then went to consult Foday Kallay, and they ordered Corporal Mousa to be fetched from the pit. By now, Kallay had given him a pair of underpants to wear, so at least the poor Sierra Leonean corporal wasn't completely naked any more.

'Mousa, we need you to go speak on de BBC,' Kallay told him. 'BBC need speak to one de hostages, but fuckin' Brittonian Major, he de refuse go speak, so we go big punish him now-now. You go say-say all de whiteboy soldiers dem be fine and treated well, na true.'

'Look, sa, if I go speak it go lessen your authority, sa,' Corporal Mousa responded. 'You think dey go treat you serious if you go speak and tell de BBC all de whiteboys they be OK? It go compromise you position. If Mousa go speak, the BBC go say: "Oh, nothing serious will happen to de British hostages, they all are being treated very well." Den dey go think you no threatening dem, no about to hurt dem or kill dem. You must go keep dem guessing. Keep dem worried. Keep dem scared if we really be OK. If dey convinced there be nothing to worry about, dey no treat you demands serious. Get Colonel Cambodia to speak to dem. He speak de good English, he tell them we go do bad things to de hostages if they no treat your demands as heavy-heavy serious.'

'Yes, yes. Mousa, dat be the best idea!' Foday Kallay enthused. 'Dis man he be clever-clever. We get Cambodia to make de threats to de BBC. That's what we go do.'

Now that the confrontation seemed over, the crowd started to lose interest and disperse. Once they had done so, the five exhausted hostages crawled back into their tiny room. They sat there, huddled together in shock, and waiting to see what would happen next. As they nursed their cuts and bruises, they knew with a sickening certainty that, this time, it was all over for the Major. And they knew that, sooner or later, they would be following their commanding officer to the execution ground. It had been going on for so long. *Too long*. This cruel game of life and death. And the men almost welcomed the idea of a certain, definitive end now. At least death offered them an escape.

At least then the nightmare would be over. At least then they would be able to rest in peace.

Yet two or three hours later – after their savage beating, the hostages had lost all track of time – Major Martial reappeared. He was thrown back into the hostages' room and collapsed on to the floor. He was unable to stand, but the wonder was that he was still alive. To the five other soldiers it was like a miraculous apparition, like a man coming back from the dead.

Barely able to muster the energy to speak, the Major explained as best he could what had happened. Calm Down Fresh and Cambodia had taken him to the edge of the forest, to a place they called the 'dead zone'. This was where they disposed of their prisoners when they decided they had no more use for them. They'd taken the Major there fully intending to kill him – of that, he had no doubt. The Major remained sketchy about what had then transpired, and how he'd managed to survive. There had been some sort of last-ditch negotiation with Foday Kallay. And, somehow, the Major had managed to do a deal with him – a deal that had saved not only his own life, but also the lives of his men. But of one thing Major Martial was adamant: he had not given in to their demands to speak on the satphone.

'I had to do what I did, lads,' the Major mumbled, exhaustedly, as if still trying to excuse himself for what had happened. 'I had to get a message out that something's wrong in the camp.'

'It's OK, sir, *we know*,' Ranger Gaunt tried to reassure him. 'We know.'

Jesus. The OC was still trying to apologise. For what? For taking the rap? For getting the message out that they were in real trouble? For taking the worst beating of any of them, and for whatever else had happened to him over at the forest? For cutting a deal with those fuckers that had saved them all from being shot, or worse? Jesus. Who else could have done all that? Today had been the worst yet. No doubt about it – a day of complete and utter terror. *The longest day*. The worst ever mob mentality since the moment of their capture. *But there was nothing to apologise for*. In retrospect, maybe the Major had even done the right thing, refusing to speak on the satphone. Either way, he'd ended up taking the rap and saving all of their lives in the process. *End of story*.

Major Martial may have felt that he had made the initial error of judgement in leading the vehicle patrol into the West Side Boys'

HQ in the first place. But in the minds of all eleven of the other hostages, it was he alone who had so far managed to keep them sane and keep them alive. He alone seemed to have the strength to stand up to the rebel leaders – to take them on at their own game. And even if his call over the satphone had seemed almost suicidal at the time, it was still a highly principled stand. And at the end of it all, he had won the day. He had beaten the rebels, defeated their plans and cheated death, all at the same time. In their eyes, Major Martial was a hero.

And the Major was not now behaving in a way that his training would have taught him to, certainly not if he valued his own survival. Classic conduct-after-capture training teaches a prisoner to behave like the 'grey man'. The quiet, unnoticed, unremarkable individual would always remain low on his captor's radar – and hence the last person they might think of executing. The Major was certainly not behaving like the grey man – in fact, quite the opposite. Here in the West Side Boys' base, the Major was deliberately offering himself up as the focus of the rebels' anger, aggression and violence. He had stood himself in the line of fire again and again and again.

The Major did seem to have specialist training in other areas that he was putting to good use. For example, he had a coded language by which he could communicate with the British negotiating team, either in person or via the radio, without the rebels realising. He was pretty cagey about all this cloak-and-dagger stuff with the other men. But a reference to the weather, for example, referred to the state of the hostages. 'A sunny day' meant that all was going well. If 'storms were gathering', then trouble was clearly on the horizon. On the day before the crisis over the satphone, the Major had managed to communicate some vital intel to the British negotiators. Via the rebels' radio he had told them that 'it was time for his wife Dawn to bring the boys down from Stirling'. In fact, the Major was unmarried and had no children. This was a coded message: 'dawn' was the best time for 'the boys from Stirling' – the SAS, then based at Stirling Lines – to launch their assault on the rebel base.

The Major was suggesting dawn as the best time for an assault because that was when the West Side Boys' hangovers were at their worst. For how long that would keep the rebels' heads down, he wasn't sure. A full-blown assault by the SAS might act as a pretty miraculous hangover cure. The Boys had already attacked the Kamajors, and they were clearly up for the fight. But they only ever seemed to go to war in the afternoons, when the drugs and alcohol were coursing through their veins. If faced with a dawn assault they should be caught at their very worst, bereft of the high that no doubt gave them their 'courage'.

When day fourteen dawned over Gberi Bana, it felt like it had been the longest two weeks any of the hostages had spent in their lives. It was a Thursday, which turned out to be as good a day as any for the West Side Boys to go to war again. Around lunchtime, the hostages saw them forming up into a drunken, drugged-up attack party, around some eighty men strong. Despite their own predicament, the British soldiers were sad to see that the captured, shaven-headed villagers were being forced to form up alongside the regular rebel crazies. As the rebel forces gathered, there was no visible sign of any sense of order or a military-style command structure. As far as the British soldiers could tell, it was just an anarchic, rabble mob – one fired up by home-made gin, home-grown drugs and the brute lust for war.

A couple of the rebels had fragmentation grenades strapped to their belts – the ones that they had stolen off the British patrol in the first place. But the men couldn't see any of their SA80 assault rifles anywhere. Before the rebels had begun to work themselves up into too much of a pre-battle frenzy, the Major decided that it would perhaps be best if they went inside, to get out of the way of things. It was impossible to know what Calm Down Fresh might dream up next, and there was always the fear that the British soldiers would be forced to join the attack party, or maybe even lead the village recruits on some real-life combat training. But before they disappeared inside, the Major asked one of the nearest rebels what all the fuss was about.

'De Ekomok!' one of them replied excitedly, rolling his eyes in mock delight. 'Yaaah – we go finish de Ekomok!'

'The Ekomok?' the Major queried.

'*E-CO-MOG*,' another of the rebels corrected him. 'ECOMOG. De Nigerians. *De UN*. We go attack de UN.'

The hostages knew that there was a Nigerian UN peacekeeping force not far from the West Side Boys' base. So, the attack party was off to hit them. To date, the rebels had kidnapped the British soldiers, ambushed the village buses and rounded up the forced recruits, attacked the Kamajors and mounted their heads on poles; now they were off to wage war on the forces of the United Nations. *Jesus*. And the Royal Irish Regiment had been briefed on their arrival in Sierra

Leone that these guys were 'friendlies'! *Well, with friends like these, who needs feckin' enemies?* the hostages wondered. It was the RUF that they had repeatedly been told to watch out for, not the West Side Boys.

For many months now, it was the British, the UN and the Kamajors who'd kept the present, democratically elected government in power in Sierra Leone. Now, the West Side Boys were waging total war on all of those forces. Whatever the rebels' claims to past allegiances, they obviously were no friends of the forces of law and order and justice in this country. That much should have been clear to anyone with half a brain cell. What the fuck had the intelligence boys been smoking, the hostages wondered, if they had seriously believed that these were the good guys?

As they prepared to leave, the rebels began bragging to the British hostages about what they were going to do to the Nigerian peace-keepers. It didn't sound very pleasant. They left brandishing their weapons – a mixture of assault rifles, machine guns and RPGs – but it was still impossible to see who was in command. As they made their way down to the river they started singing a war song, taking up a shuffling war dance, one moment bent double with heads bowed and guns thrust forward, the next jerking upright with weapons held high above their heads.

The West Side Boys had plundered fifty-odd canoes off the local fishing villages that lined the Rokel Creek. They used these to ferry their war parties into the jungle and to launch attacks up and down the river. The force that was now setting off to attack the Nigerians boarded canoes and paddled away down the Rokel Creek, their war song dying away into the forest as they went.

The West Side Boys' attack party would not return from their UN adventure until the following afternoon. And when they did so, it would be obvious that things had not gone to plan for them. Over the past two weeks, the British soldiers had heard rumours of some West Side Boys casualties. But the rebel leaders would never let the hostages catch sight of their wounded – almost as if they were trying to maintain their myth of voodoo-given invincibility. On a couple of occasions, however, Major Martial had been asked to go through the medical kit that their Land-Rovers had been carrying, and it had been obvious that the rebels were looking for dressings and antiseptics to treat their wounded. Although it was a basic first-aid kit, it was a treasure trove as far as the rebels were concerned. They had never set eyes on most of the medicines it contained. But those medical supplies were soon to be exhausted, once the rebel attack party struggled back into Gberi Bana.

The British soldiers spent the remainder of that afternoon sitting around listening to the radio. There'd been little of note in recent days, ever since the stagnation of the hostage negotiations, and they weren't expecting any major news. So they were somewhat shocked to hear the BBC reporter announce a breaking news story on the Sierra Leonean hostage crisis. With a feeling of deepening dread, they listened to the BBC reporter's unfolding story. It was about a contingent of '150 men of the Parachute Regiment that have landed in Senegal – but are believed to be on their way to Sierra Leone'.

Believed to be on their way to Sierra Leone. This was the one thing that the hostages had been dreading – hearing a BBC report about the gathering assault force. As they continued to listen, it got even worse, the BBC proceeding to add their own spin on the story, which was that the Paras were really coming after the West Side Boys. The unavoidable message of the BBC report was clear: a force of Paras was preparing to go in and rescue the six British and one Sierra Leonean hostages. The men knew that the West Side Boys' leaders would be listening to this report just as intently as they were. As it finished, it left them with a cold, burning anger against the BBC. *The bastards. Why not just go ahead and sign their fucking death warrants?*

Why hadn't the British government stopped them from broadcasting this? the men were thinking. Couldn't they see that announcing that British forces were preparing a rescue assault was highly dangerous, especially when put out on the *BBC*? They *knew* the rebels were paying great attention to the BBC broadcasts: it was the BBC that Cambodia was always calling on the satphone to give his interviews. *Jesus, wasn't it feckin' obvious how dangerous this was – for them, the British hostages, the very people being held at the mercy of the rebels?* The same rebels that the BBC had just said that the British forces were being sent to Sierra Leone to attack?

The hostages were deeply fearful of how the West Side Boys would react to the radio broadcast. But, the news that the Paras were on their way to Sierra Leone, and that they likely had the West Side Boys as their target, seemed only to hype them up into a more warlike frenzy than ever. A group of the rebels came swaggering over to the hostages and started mouthing off at them about how they were going to take on the British forces and give them a damn good hiding.

Bizarrely, rather than being angry at the hostages, the rebels just seemed to be completely up for it – as long as there was the prospect of some more fighting.

'Yaaah . . . Bri-tish whiteboy soldiers! Yo go hear de BBC! Yaaah . . . Dey do come fuck with us, do dey, de Bri-tish fighting men?'

Whenever the Boys were trying to be exceptionally intimidating, they elongated the word 'British', pronouncing it almost as two words – 'Bri-tish'. They appeared to have adopted most of their 'rebel talk' from a mixture of some very old Bob Marley reggae albums and some very bad US rap movies.

'They're not here for us, actually,' the Major tried. 'It's a different country. The BBC got it wrong, they're in Senegal . . .' But his words didn't seem to have much effect. The rebels had heard it on the BBC, so it had to be true. The Paras were coming for them.

'Come on! Yaaah! Yaah! Let yo Bri-tish soldiers dey dem come!' one of them mocked the Major. 'We go knock the shi-it out of dem!'

'Who de fuck are yo Pa-ras, anyway?' another sneered. 'Yaaah! WE ARE de West Side Niggas! NO ONE messes wid us. We go fuck with the SLA, the UN and the Ekomok. And if dey come, you no think we go fuck with yo British Army too?'

'Hey, Bri-tish whiteboys. Yo know if dey do come try get you, you gonna be DEAD MEN! Six dead whiteboys. Go try tell that to yo Bri-tish Army.'

A couple of the rebels then squatted down on the veranda with the hostages, to share some smokes with them. This time, even the CO accepted a cigarette – the first time the others had seen him do so – in an attempt to keep the rebels in a good humour. As he took his first drag on the tab, the Major started coughing his guts up – which would have been funny if it weren't for the delicate situation they were in. The Boys continued mouthing off about how they were going to kill the Bri-tish Army. The men could see that it wasn't just bravado, either. The West Side Boys were really up for the fight and clearly believed they would win: at last, after all the waiting and the talking and the useless hostage negotiations, it looked as though there was finally going to be some bang-bang.

Difficult though it was to have to sit there and listen to this bunch of thugs declare how they were going to mess with Her Majesty's finest, none of the hostages gave back any lip. As far as they were concerned, the BBC had already done enough damage. It didn't take much to flip the rebels over on to the dark side, and they didn't want to take any chances. Whenever the rebels started banging on about how invincible they were as a fighting force and how bullets just bounced off them, it was best just to agree with them.

That evening back in their room, the Major took the precaution of standing by the window, to block anyone who might be trying to spy on them. Then, in hushed whispers, they started to discuss the day's developments. They knew that if the Paras were in Senegal, then they must be coming for them. That made perfect sense, as Senegal was the FMB for all British military air operations into Sierra Leone. Just six weeks previously, the Royal Irish Regiment itself had passed through the FMB at Senegal's Dakar Airport. But what they couldn't work out was why this was being put out as news on the BBC. *Who needed a free press, if that's what the fuckers got up to?*

More worrying still – and thanks again to the BBC – the West Side Boys were now forewarned about the coming rescue operation, and forewarned is forearmed, as they say in the British Army. Any commander worth his salt would now double the vigilance of his men, triple his defences and quadruple the guard force put on the hostages. Foday Kallay may have looked like a flake, but he was proving himself to be a wily leader, of that there was no doubt. If Kallay now strengthened his defences in just one of those ways, it could make all the difference between the rescue force getting to the hostages before the West Side Boys killed them. Just one of those things could give the West Side Boys the edge, and if the Boys had the edge then the hostages were finished.

As the hostages tried to get to sleep that night, they were fired up by a raging, restless anger against the BBC. And, as always, they were deeply scared.

In fact, there had been a deal done between the Ministry of Defence (MOD) and the press over the whole hostage-crisis story. At a series of meetings in London with key elements of the press – including the BBC – the MOD had secured an agreement whereby they would brief the press on elements of the story that were safe to report, if the press agreed to lay off the hostage-rescue side of the story. And to be fair to the BBC, it had actually been the printed media that had first broken the press embargo. Several days earlier, and quoting unnamed military 'sources', a British broadsheet had run with an exclusive about a 'force package' of Paras being sent out for a 'hostage rescue' mission in Sierra Leone. The BBC had simply followed the newspaper's lead.

And by Wednesday 6 September – thirteen days into the hostage crisis, and one day prior to the BBC broadcast – the MOD would be forced into making a formal announcement of the Paras' deployment to Sierra Leone. Speaking to journalists in Freetown, the British forces spokesman, Lieutenant Colonel Tony Cramp, tried to play down the significance of their arrival: 'The deployment of the Paras in no way signifies an imminent military action. It is just a sensible contingency measure to place troops in the region. We have not ruled out any options for releasing the captives. But the talks are making progress and we are hopeful this can be ended peacefully.'

The difference was, of course, that the West Side Boys had no access to the British newspapers, or even press briefings in Freetown. By contrast, the BBC World Service was the rebels' window on to the wider world, their touchstone of all that was true and worthy of reporting. When they had heard one of their own commanding officers speaking on the BBC, they had been jubilant. It had meant that they had made it at last, that they were big, that they were happening. Likewise, when the BBC had broadcast its report on the Paras being on their way to attack the rebel bases, the West Side Boys had taken this as gospel too. It had been on the BBC. Therefore, it had to be true. So while the hostages couldn't see the wider picture, their anger at the BBC was still justified.

Most evenings, the men of the assault force preparing for action at Waterloo Camp had also been listening to the news on their short-wave radio sets. And they, too, had heard the BBC report with mounting consternation. To their minds, this was tantamount to broadcasting a warning message into the heart of the rebel base. '*WE ARE ABOUT TO ATTACK YOU,*' was what the BBC broadcast had said. '*Our soldiers are already in your country, so we will be coming to get you soon.*' To the soldiers poised to launch that rescue assault, this so-called public-service broadcaster had acted totally irresponsibly. *What the fuck did they pay their licence fee for*, the men of D Squadron wondered, *if the bastard BBC was going to broadcast stories like that directly to their enemies?*

Very, very early the following morning – day fifteen – Sony came over and woke the Major. He was looking worried, and he asked the Major to go for a stroll around the still deserted village. Once they were out of earshot, Sony started explaining in a hurried whisper that he didn't rate their chances of survival that highly any more. He'd overheard

Kallay, Calm Down Fresh and Cambodia discussing the contents of that previous evening's BBC report, and it wasn't looking good.

Calm Down Fresh was urging Kallay to kill all the British soldiers right away, so as to 'make Sierra Leone Britain's Somalia'. Kallay and Calm Down Fresh were very close, especially as Kallay liked to have people around him who advised him to kill, kill, kill. But Kallay was still arguing that they needed to keep the British soldiers alive. That was the only way they could force the British to give them all the logistics they needed – radios, food, medicines – in order to launch Operation Kill British and Operation Kill All Your Family. Kallay also argued that by keeping the British hostages alive they were assured of not being attacked by the British, as they would never risk the lives of the hostages. Kallay assured Calm Down Fresh that once they had got everything they wanted from the British, then the hostages would be the first to be killed under Op Kill British.

Cambodia was the only voice of reason. He was worried about British military reprisals if they did do anything to the soldiers. He was talking about moving them further into the jungle, away from any British forces who might try a rescue attempt. That would mean doing some sort of deal with the RUF, but as most of the leaders were ex-RUF anyway, that shouldn't present them with any major problems. But Kallay was paying little attention now to Cambodia's words of relative restraint.

They had clearly reached the endgame now, Sony explained to the Major. If a hostage-rescue attempt was forthcoming, the first reaction of the West Side Boys would be to kill the hostages, of that he was sure. Then Sony made an extraordinary offer. Over the past two weeks, he felt that they had become good friends, and he had decided that the time had come for him to help the British soldiers as best he could. He outlined his plan. On the next night of heavy monsoon rains, when the noise would mask the sound, he would creep around to the hostages' room and cut through the wooden bar holding the shutters across their window. Then it would be up to them to make a break for it. It was the best he could do. Any more than that would be almost certain suicide.

The Major thanked Sony as best he could for his offer and with genuine gratitude. He didn't quite understand who this enigmatic figure was or why he was risking his life to help them. But he'd been watching Sony closely, and over the past fifteen days he'd grown to like this well-spoken, clearly educated and gentle Sierra Leonean. And he'd grown to trust him. He believed that Sony was a good man. Before they parted, the Major decided to bring Sony into his confidence. It was a risk – but look at what this man was willing to risk in order to help them. He told Sony that he believed a British rescue party would be coming very shortly now, possibly within the next forty-eight hours. When he heard the helicopters coming in, Sony should take cover on the ground and stay down. Above all else, he must avoid picking up a gun – for if he did, the British soldiers would be bound to kill him.

'In the event of any rescue attempt, I'll do my best to make sure you're all right, Sony, of that you have my word,' the Major added. 'I'll keep my eyes peeled, and try and get you into our group, as a friendly.'

'Thank you, Major, but you needn't worry so much for me. If these men do come, I shall be all right,' Sony reassured him, gently. It seemed odd to the Major that Sony was so calm and confident, when he was supposedly in great danger. 'But are you so certain they *will* come for you? And that they will succeed? What about all these fighters and guns and bombs they have around this village?'

'They're coming all right, Sony,' the Major replied, grimly. 'And when they hit the ground, any West Side Boy who doesn't throw down his gun is a dead man. You haven't seen these people in action. *I have*. Believe me, if British forces have to come in and rescue us, this place is finished. There won't be a building left standing.'

The Major watched as Sony glanced around the village and shuddered, as if he were remembering past wrongs that had gone on there. Then he turned back to face his British friend.

'Then that, Major, will be a very good thing.'

Walking back towards the house, the Major continued to puzzle over Sony. Here was a cultured, decent man living in the heart of this lawless rebel village. A man who never carried a gun. *Just who the hell was he?* The Major remembered the note being pushed through the window – was that Sony's doing? Was he somehow working for the British? It would make sense that they'd try to have a local element on the inside of the rebel base. Perhaps he should have asked him. But the moment had passed. Sony just always seemed to be around at the right moment – helping, explaining, reassuring and calming things down.

Well, whoever he was, his escape plan was a sound one. The Major roused the others from their sleep and in hushed tones he began explaining Sony's offer to saw through the bar on their window. The men listened intently. They knew that things were on a knife-edge now and that this might be their last chance. It sounded simple enough. They could all fit through the window, so that wasn't an issue. And if the rain was heavy enough it would mask the sound of their escape. Once through the window, they would gather in the shadows against the outside wall, and when all six of them were there, they'd sneak off down to the river. It was a couple of hundred yards or so to the riverside. In the darkness and the rain, they should make it all right. And from there they would revert to plan A, the riverine escape. They would take their chances in the waters of the Rokel Creek and swim like the devil for Freetown.

'Sounds dead on to me, sir,' Ranger Gaunt said, nervously, once the Major had finished outlining the plan. 'Jesus. Flamin' Sony, eh? Just who the hell is he? Flamin' man of mystery, to be sure.'

'Yes, lad. But do we all trust him?' the Major asked.

'Well, he's sort of one of them,' the Ranger began slowly, 'but he isn't really, if youse know what I mean. I mean, it's partly thanks to him that we're all still sane, isn't it? *I* trust yer man. Dunno about the rest of youse, but I trust him.'

'Aye. For a Sierra Leonean and all, he's a good 'un,' Ranger Rowell added. 'Sure, he's been helping us from the very start. I've no idea who the feck he is, mind. But I reckon he's genuine.'

'Sergeant Smith? Captain Flaherty? Corporal? What are your thoughts?' said the Major.

'Aye, he's a good man,' Sergeant Smith remarked, quietly. 'That's enough for me. So sure, count me in.'

'I agree. Man of mystery is old Sony, but I'd trust him,' Captain Flaherty observed. 'He's been trying to help us ever since we first set eyes on him. It's a good plan, and maybe all we've got left.'

'Then it's agreed,' the Major concluded. 'I for one fail to see what he could possibly gain by not being genuine on this one. In fact, he's taking a huge personal risk. I'd wager they'll kill him outright if they catch him trying to help us escape.'

The last part of the Major's point was left unsaid. *They'll kill Sony, and then they'll deal with us too.*

That evening, the rebel force that had set off to attack the Nigerian UN base came limping back into Gberi Bana village. It was clear that things had gone horribly wrong. Somehow, the UN troops had had prior warning of the attack and had ambushed the West Side Boys' attack party. Keeping their fire disciplined, the Nigerian soldiers had managed to inflict serious casualties on the West Side Boys. There was no singing and dancing as what was left of the column snaked back into camp. Just as they came limping up the hill towards the village clearing, the heavens opened and there was a wall of rain thrown between the watching British hostages and the approaching column. Many of the rebels had black ponchos draped over them, to ward off the rain, and there were scores of walking wounded and a dozen or more on makeshift stretchers.

To the British soldiers it looked like a like a scene from some Vietnam War movie. As the attack force shuffled silently into the village clearing, the six men were hustled back inside their room. Clearly, the West Side Boys didn't want them to see the scale of their defeat at the hands of the UN forces. Later, the hostages would learn from Sony that of the hundred or so rebel fighters that had set out, fewer than sixty had returned. The rest had either been killed or captured or had run away. Most of the shaven-headed villagers had managed to escape – despite threats from the West Side Boys that they would shoot any of them who refused to fight.

In fact, the situation was far more dire than Sony would admit to the British soldiers. As Corporal Mousa was overhearing from his position in the dungeon, many of the West Side Boys themselves had refused to fight. These were the men of the Savage Group, and they were angry and disgruntled that Foday Kallay had arrested their leader and executed two of their men. Kallay was accusing Colonel Savage of using witchcraft to make a secret deal with the British, and other such crazed stuff. As the men of the Savage Group feared that they might be the next on Kallay's execution list, several of them – led by Colonel Faw Faw, one of the West Side Boys' chief executioners – had used the Nigerian attack as a cover to escape into the jungle.

But the oddest thing for the British hostages watching the return of the rebel attack force was that no one in the village seemed to be the remotest bit upset over what was clearly a major defeat. The women and children in particular just didn't seem to care. Presumably, some of the dead and wounded were their husbands or their fathers. The hostages had expected to see scenes of wailing wives and frightened children searching for the husband or father who had not returned. But there was nothing of the sort.

Thinking it over later, the hostages realised that many of the so-called 'wives' in the village had more than likely been captured in the first place, and then forced to marry their rebel 'husbands'. If that was the case, how many of the children would ultimately be the sons and daughters of rape, pillage and murder back in their home village? It dawned on the soldiers that none of the women and children really cared about whether their husbands and fathers had come back, about who had lived or who had died.

Such was the value of a human life in the land of the West Side Boys.

17

THE DEAD ZONE

The jungle is neutral.
                    – Lieutenant Colonel F. Spencer Chapman, 1949

On the morning of 6 September, thirteen days into the hostage crisis, the six-man SAS obs team secreted in the jungle shadows began to detect disturbing events unfolding in Gberi Bana. They couldn't get close enough to the rebel base for visual contact, due to the density of the jungle, but they were equipped with a hand-held listening device, which all but compensated for this visual deficit. It consisted of a foldable parabolic metal disc about the size and shape of a normal TV dish, with a unidirectional 'gun mike' sticking horizontally out of the front of it. With the mike pointed in the direction of the sound source, the dish would concentrate sound waves on to the receiver, so amplifying any sound source.

The operator would use a pair of all-enclosing earphones to block out all extraneous noise, so that he could focus on monitoring what he was hearing. And he could hear a great deal with this sort of specialist kit. The listening kit had adjustable sound levels for either ear, so that the operator could personalise it to suit his own needs, and dual microphones provided stereo sound, giving the most natural sense of hearing.

While it boosted sound, the listening device also had an automatic safety shut-off that kicked in at ninety-five decibels, to prevent any ear damage. So if, for example, the rebels started shooting, it would shut down to protect the operator's ears. It had a three-band equaliser, for tuning out any annoying background noise (the hum of the forest insects, the rustle of the wind in the trees), so that the operator could concentrate on picking up the specific sound he wanted to hear. The kit allowed the operator to record all that he was hearing on a separate sound-recording machine. And it wasn't heavy on the juice, either – one, nine-volt battery, providing forty hours' listening time. That Wednesday morning, the mike operator, Mat – a big Manchester lad – was detecting noises suggesting that the rebels were going crazy on the British hostages. The noise was confused, with many voices speaking all at once, but it sounded as if a large and hostile mob was gathering. And one, wild chant seemed to be dominating the cacophony of noise that Mat was picking up. '*Refuse to speak to the BBC!*' Over and over again, the same chant: '*Refuse to speak to the BBC!*' It sounded very much like the voice of that crazed rebel commander, the so-called 'Camp Commandant'.

The obs team had drawn up a rebel cast of characters, detailing each of the individual voices along with their distinguishing features (Colonel Cambodia – 'deep, quiet voice, low rumble'; Foday Kallay – 'feminine-sounding, stutter'; Camp Commandant – 'high-pitched whine – talks insane gibberish the whole time'). They were writing up accompanying character profiles as they went along (Camp Commandant – 'totally unpredictable psychopath'; Colonel Cambodia – 'better than most'; Foday Kallay – 'ineffectual, weak, but wily'; Colonel GS – 'nasty bastard, wants to be the boss'). From what Mat was now hearing, it seemed like the Camp Commandant had got the BBC on the satphone and was trying to get the hostages to speak to them. But the hostages, brave fuckers, seemed to be refusing to do so.

With growing anger, Mat listened as the six British soldiers were stripped to their underwear and savagely beaten by the mob – relating all that was happening to the rest of the obs team as he did so. They in turn would feed a sitrep back to Waterloo Camp as soon as it became clear where events were heading. By the time Mat heard the hostages being numbered off to be shot, he was consumed by a cold fury. At this moment, it was so tempting to pick up a weapon and charge into the rebel camp and waste some of the bastards. But that would do no good at all, the men of the obs team had to keep telling themselves. Far better that they remained where they were, feeding back their crucial pieces of intelligence to base.

From their jungle OP, their radio messages would go directly to the signals officer in the ops tent, and from there straight into the squadron OC's hands. If the sitrep had serious implications, the OC, Pete Cutgood, would call a briefing with the head sheds, who would in turn feed the information down to their specific troops. If things got really bad – say, if the rebels actually started the killing – then that would be the catalyst for an immediate airborne assault to be launched, to try to prevent any more hostages from being executed. The obs team was getting good intelligence now, which could provide the trigger. All going to plan, the men of the assault force could be on target within half an hour of being scrambled.

It was about time too, as this was not the most pleasant of OPs. On their very first night out in the bush, one of the soldiers had stuck his hand into his bergen to get a ration pack, when he'd noticed something odd, glistening inside. It hadn't been in there when he'd packed the rucksack, of that he was certain. Peering in, he'd realised it was an enormous silver grey spider, shimmering faintly in the moonlight. It was already rearing up on its hind legs to strike him. Wrenching his hand out of the bergen, he'd taken his combat knife and chopped the thing into several small pieces. Tipping the mashed-up arachnid out in disgust, he'd realised with a shock that the hairy monster had been as large as his own hand. *Welcome to the fucking jungle*, he'd thought.

After a couple days lying out in the densest jungle thicket ever, the men were now soaked to the skin and smelling worse than a badger's arse – to coin a popular phrase in the Regiment. They had also run into several snakes, rats, scorpions and other assorted jungle lowlife for whom this tangle of undergrowth had long been their home. And there were the mosquitoes, of course, who just couldn't keep away. The men were prevented from using any insect repellent, for fear that its tell-tale smell might give them away. And so they had resigned themselves to being eaten alive.

But the worst had been when Lassie had woken up in the night to find a motorway of driver ants going right across his chest. Lassie was a little bloke, around five foot six, and you'd never have known from looking at him that he was in the Regiment. But he could carry a house on his shoulders and just keep on going and going. He was quiet and conscientious, and was known as a stickler for order and discipline. With Lassie, everything had to be 100 per cent and just so.

The driver ant – also called the legionary or army ant – is a nomadic tropical ant that forages in large groups. As the name suggests, they migrate through the forest in dense roadways – a solid moving corridor of crawling legs and snapping mandibles. In Lassie's case, he had woken up to discover thousands of the inch-long black ants trundling up one side of his Gore-Tex smock, across his chest webbing and down the other side again. As he had lain there listening to the soft hissing and clicking of their legs and feelers, barely inches away from his face, Lassie had rapidly come to the conclusion that things were definitely not 100 per cent and just so.

Sometimes, the migration of a colony of driver ants can take several hours, the 'ant motorway' being a mile or more in length. Lassie knew that he had only two choices: the first, to lie there and wait for the whole colony to pass (but then he risked the fuckers discovering that he was edible; in the past, driver-ant colonies had been known to overrun a tethered domestic animal – one that couldn't run away – and start eating it alive, leaving only a heap of bones behind them); the second, to jump up, scattering the critters in all directions as he did so, and get the hell out of there before they regrouped and went on the attack. Choosing the later option, Lassie had leapt to his feet and bolted like a madman, to the utmost amusement of the five other men on the obs team. But then they had realised that the angry driver ants were on the warpath, and coming for them too. So they all had bolted, and regrouped at a safe distance from the enraged ant colony.

Mat now began hearing distinct changes in the goings-on in the rebel camp. The crowd had quietened down and was dispersing. But as he swept the microphone about, he detected a small group of rebels heading out of the village, in the direction of the nearby jungle. By the sound of things, they had at least one of the British soldiers with them. Mat could hear make out the distinct 'flip-flop' of the rebels' rubber sandals, and the heavier thud of a set of boots. *Bollocks*. Did this mean that the rebels were moving some of the hostages to a different location? If that was the case, there was no time to lose; the obs team would have to divide forces, so that one party could follow this smaller group and track their movements through the jungle, while the other continued to keep watch over Gberi Bana.

But what if the rebels were heading for the river, intending to move the hostages by canoe? If that was the case, there was no way that the obs team would be able to keep track of them. But on thinking this through, Mat decided it was unlikely. If anything, the rebels would be moving the hostages inland, towards the territory of the RUF rebels. Inland meant upstream, and he knew that the rebels didn't have any motorised canoes. And downstream, there were only British and UN forces. So that pretty much ruled out the river option. There was no way that the rebels would risk moving the hostages by road, either, as the British and the UN controlled all the routes out of there.

The unidirectional mike was picking up more details of what was happening now. Mat could hear the rebels ordering the British soldier to kneel; by the direction and intensity of the signal, he deduced it must be somewhere nearby, just on the edge of the forest. In briefings back at Waterloo Camp, the SAS soldiers had been told about a place the rebels called the 'dead zone' – this being a patch of jungle just outside the village where they carried out their executions. Mat had a distinct suspicion that this was where the British soldier had now been taken. From the way he was being spoken to, Mat also suspected that the lone hostage couldn't see, and so he was most probably blindfolded. It looked very much as it the rebels weren't relocating the hostage. They were preparing to kill him.

'I think the bastards are about to top one of our boys,' Mat remarked in a low voice, with urgency. He was giving a running commentary on everything he could hear as it happened, while Lassie was scribbling the occasional note. Sound recordings were all well and good, especially for Green Slime to analyse later on. But the obs team knew that they had no time to sift back through hours and hours of recordings, which was too slow a system for their purposes in any case. Their sitreps had to be immediate and bang up to date. It was far better to keep a written log as things developed.

'They've got one of the lads at the edge of the jungle, kneeling. I reckon blindfolded too,' Mat continued. 'Dunno which one it is yet. Can't tell. Several rebels with 'im. Maybe six or so.'

Mat was tensing himself for the gunshot that he feared was coming, and the dull thud of a body hitting the deck. 'I can hear a gun being cocked now. Sounds like an AK. One of the bastards is saying 'e's gonna shoot 'im. No response from the hostage. Hold on! The bastard's just pulled the trigger – with no round up the spout. Mock execution. They're all pissing themselves laughing. Oh yeah. Very funny. You fuckers.'

He took a second's break to wipe the sweat out of his eyes. By fuck, it was hot and humid in there. He'd been holding the bleeding mike still for so long, it felt as if his arm was about to drop off. There was a tripod mount for the mike to sit on, but it was next to useless in such a fluid situation, where you had to keep the mike moving to stick with the action. Hand-held was the only way to do it. In addition to which there was the ever present danger of being compromised, and having to make a very rapid getaway. If the men were discovered, they could not afford to waste precious seconds collapsing a tripod. *Steady now*, Mat told himself. Somehow, he knew that this little rebel game wasn't over by a long chalk. It was a game that they were all players in now – rebels, hostages and SAS soldiers alike – and it was a very nasty one at that.

He had to try to judge just how serious the rebels were. They'd lined the hostages up to shoot them before, yet backed off at the last minute. So this could all be yet another bluff. Or, the rebels might have finally lost patience and decided to start the killing. All six men of the obs team had to use their collective judgement on this, and it was a tough call. It was crucial to remain cool, keep things in perspective and stay detached: if the men got too involved with the hostages, then they'd end up flying off the handle and calling in the air strike too early. And that could get a lot of people killed. When all was said and done, unless and until one of the hostage's brains was hitting the sand, they couldn't really justify calling in the assault force.

'Now they're yelling for Foday Kallay,' Mat whispered, starting up his narration again. 'OK. He's on 'is way over – must be a couple of bodyguards with 'im, too. That makes nine or so of the fuckers. 'Old on – it's the bleedin' Major . . . Major Martial. I can hear it's 'im – 'e's started talking to Kallay now. "Came to see you to tell you to stop all the fighting," 'e's saying. "Didn't come with any bad intentions. If you kill us, it will be for no reason. Won't do you no good. Spare the 'ostages' lives, and I can get the British to start giving you what you want. If you kill us, they will know about it very quickly . . ." Sorry – fuck – can't get that bit. OK. Now . . . "Give me three or four days – that's all I ask. But you have to let me talk directly to the British hostage team."

'Now Kallay's replying. "All right. But we need to see some of the things we are asking for being given, Captain." He's a major, you fuckin' wanker, not a captain. "Need to know the British are serious. Otherwise . . ." Otherwise what, you motherfucker?' Mat snarled, under his breath. 'Otherwise we'll kick your fuckin' heads in, that's what. Sorry, lads, got carried away. Kallay's ordering them to take the Major back inside now. "Put 'im back with the others," 'e's saying. Fuck me, but that was a close one. The Major sounds on bleedin' good form, though. Voice firm. Not shaking. Wasn't begging, either. Just reasoning with 'em. I 'ope I could sound that cool with some cunt 'olding a gun to my 'ead and pulling the trigger on an empty chamber, that's all I can say.'

The obs team relayed all their information back to the ops tent at Waterloo Camp, whereupon it was passed on to JFHQ Freetown and on to London. The news of the threatened executions and the deadline – the Major's 'three or four days' – had an electrifying effect on those responsible for calling in the assault force. On the evening of Wednesday 6 September, an emergency meeting of the tri-service command structure came together at JFHQ, at which – and with a nod from London – it was decided that Operation Barras was now 90 per cent on. It would only take one further bad move by the West Side Boys to make it 100 per cent. One further breech of the negotiating process, one further assault on the hostages, and the mission would be green-lit.

The catalyst that would finally lead to Operation Barras getting the green light would take place two days later, on Friday 8 September. Once again, the vital intelligence would come in part from the SAS obs team at Gberi Bana, who had been in their OP now for four days. Often, of course, the West Side Boys would be speaking in their own language, which made it impossible for the British soldiers to eavesdrop effectively on their conversations. Although there were a couple of language specialists among the SAS men, Spanish and Arabic were of little help in Sierra Leone. The rebels were speaking a dialect of the Mende language – the native tongue of the country's dominant tribal group. But the SAS obs team had the good fortune of having a local Kamajor man join them in the OP. This man – one of the original Kamajor Hunter Force, trained by Executive Outcomes and subsequently the British – was proving an invaluable help. Whenever the rebels were speaking in their own language, the men would pass the headphones over to 'Hannibal the Cannibal', as they'd affectionately nicknamed the Kamajor man.

''Ere, 'Annibal, stick those on your 'ear'oles,' Mat would whisper, handing the headphones across to him. 'I can't understand a bloody word they're saying.'

On the Friday afternoon, Mat had detected what sounded like a large crowd of rebels gathering in the centre of the village. They were clearly drunk or drugged up, or both, which wasn't unusual. But they were also well tooled up, which was interesting, because it meant that this was a war party. It wasn't the first time that the obs team had heard the rebels preparing for an attack, but this was by far the largest yet. Who, the men wondered, might they be planning to have a go at this time? The UN again? The Kamajors? The Brits? Unfortunately, their Kamajor interpreter wasn't able to catch much of what was being said. He did manage to grasp that they were off to attack 'the British', but he couldn't pick up exactly who the rebels were targeting. An urgent sitrep went back to Waterloo Camp. It detailed the size of the rebel party, with their suspected intention of attacking a British force.

What had happened in the rebel village was this. A group of angry survivors from the disastrous attack on the Nigerian UN forces had decided to escalate matters still further. Incredibly, they had set off with the intention of ambushing the ongoing hostage negotiations, which were taking place at the UN/West Side Boys' checkpoint, out on the Masiaka–Freetown highway (on the West Side Boys' side of the checkpoint). The rebels were planning to capture the CO of the 1st Battalion, Royal Irish Rangers Lieutenant Colonel Simon Fordham, and everyone in his negotiating team. Luckily, the SAS obs team warning reached Waterloo Camp just in time.

Gerry Birt, one of the two SAS advisers on the British hostage-negotiating team, received the radio message while en route to their meeting with the rebels. It was a general warning of a suspected rebel attack on an unspecified British target. As their convoy of Land-Rovers had approached the checkpoint, his suspicions had been immediately raised. The rebels were far more numerous than usual, and they were all heavily armed.

The three captured Royal Irish Rangers Land-Rovers were there, with some of the West Side Boys manning the WMIK. As Gerry checked the rebels' positions, he realised the gunner on the WMIK was covering the approaching British convoy with the 50-cal and the HMG. There were also several rebel soldiers with RPGs on their shoulders, at the ready. It was obvious to the SAS man that the West Side Boys weren't there for a regular hostage-negotiation meeting this time. There was no doubt about it in his mind: the attack force had been sent out to ambush the British negotiating team.

'Turn the vehicles around!' he'd ordered. 'No questions. Just turn the fuckers round nice and slowly, and we head back the way we've come.'

And that had been that: the British party had pulled out of the meeting. Later that day, the 'local element' inside Gberi Bana had managed to get a message out to Waterloo Camp, confirming their suspicions. Clearly, there could now be no further face-to-face meetings with the West Side Boys. In fact, Gerry Birt was adamant: all options for a negotiated settlement were at an end. The rebels were not to be dealt with any longer, and it was time to call in the assault. A message to that effect was sent to PJHQ in London and on to Tony Blair in New York, where he was attending a United Nations summit. The stakes were high and the politicians and the British military planners knew it. But there was no other option. On the evening of Friday 8 September, a message came back from Blair: permission was finally been being granted for Operation Barras to proceed.

The attack would begin at first light on Sunday 10 September. This would give the British hostage-negotiating team some thirty-six hours in which to lull Foday Kallay and his men into a false sense of security. They were to do everything they could to convince the rebels that the British were giving in to their demands. The West Side Boys were to be told that all the boats, engines, vehicles and weapons that they had asked for were already being shipped out from the UK, and that the British authorities were in the final stages of negotiating their political demands with the Sierra Leonean government. In addition, they were to be told that the UN-brokered Lome peace agreement would be revisited on their behalf, with a view to the rebel leaders taking key positions in the government. In short, the rebels were to be led to believe that they had got everything they could have wished for and more out of the hostage crisis.

On the very eve of the assault itself, JFHQ Freetown came up with a cunning plan to further convince the West Side Boys that they had won their battle with the British. It had the added advantage that it would likely render the rebels a great deal less efficient as a fighting force the following morning, the time of the planned assault. A contingent of the Royal Irish Rangers was sent down to the nearest West Side Boys' checkpoint with a truck full of crates of beer and hard liquor. Handing over all the hooch to the rebels, the British soldiers told them that it was a surprise gift from the British Army, to celebrate the successful resolution of the hostage negotiations. Knowing the West Side Boys' predilection for booze, the plan was to get them well lashed the night before the assault went in.

At around 4 p.m. on Saturday 9 September, D Squadron and their SBS colleagues were called together at Waterloo Camp for the final mission briefing. The atmosphere was electric. Everyone taking part in the assault was in attendance: the men of D Squadron in their fire teams along with the SBS; the RAF, Army and Navy aircrews; and the men of the Air Wing. Although the Paras would be holding a separate mission briefing over on their side of camp, a number of them would be flying in alongside the Special Forces assault teams on to target. A dozen-odd Paras had been tasked to go on the Chinooks that would be assaulting Gberi Bana village. Their role was to put down covering fire from the choppers' windows as the fire teams piled into the village, to help keep the rebels' heads down.

D Squadron's OC stood up in front of the seventy-odd assembled men to present his address. 'Gentlemen, we are going in,' he began, pacing his words for maximum effect. 'Those are your final set of orders for the assault on Gberi Bana,' he continued, nodding towards a sheaf of papers pinned up on the ops noticeboard. The assembled men looked around at one another in disbelief. They'd never really believed the mission would get the go-ahead. *But now it had. Operation Certain Death was finally 100 per cent on.* 'Once you've read them you should each know exactly what you're tasked with. Pay careful attention. I want there to be no area in your mind that you are unclear on. You are going in at first light tomorrow morning. Good luck.' As the OC turned to leave, he hesitated for a moment, and then swung around to face his men again. 'And, gentlemen, I want you to be absolutely clear on one thing. Her Majesty's government has made it very clear: you are to go into those villages and give those bastards a bloody nose.'

Immediately after Pete Cutgood's address, there was an extraordinary buzz around camp. It was 5 p.m., and the assault would be going in at around 6 a.m. the following morning: thirteen hours until zero hour. Some of the men just couldn't believe that they'd got the green light. They were still convinced that the assault would get called off at the last minute. Nevertheless, it was time for one, final dress rehearsal. The whole of D Squadron and the SBS broke down into their Fire Teams again, got all their kit together and went out to the back of the camp for the final assault dummy run in the mock-up village. One last run-through, just to make sure they'd got it all clear in their hearts and minds.

As they did so, word went around that no one was to allow himself to be taken prisoner by the West Side Boys. It was pretty much standard operating procedure (SOP) really – each troop, each Fire Team, each soldier, coming to an agreement among themselves that they would finish each other off, if anyone was wounded and about to get captured. They knew what the rebels would do to any British prisoner they got their hands on: they would take his very soul. That person would face a slow, agonising death at the hands of someone who treated him as their plaything.

Each of the Fire Teams were free to choose their own weapons. Most men would take the Diemaco. Then there were those who took the GPMG or the Minimi. In addition, each man loaded himself up with a 66mm LAW, and there were also two 81mm mortars and two 60mm mortars being carried in. Each man carried on his person as much ammunition as he could stand up in (for example, a Minimi gunner would take in more than a thousand rounds, a Diemaco gunner some three hundred rounds in ten magazines), and strapped on half a dozen grenades (HE, smoke, WP and flash-bang stun grenades).

As a reserve back-up weapon, every man strapped a Sig Sauer P226 9mm pistol to his lower leg. Body armour was optional. But the men of D Squadron considered it too heavy and cumbersome for such an assault, and went for maximum ammo instead – prizing mobility and firepower above body protection. Each man also wore a Kevlar helmet, with radio earpiece and mouth mike, and carried a daypack on his back, full of plastic explosives, two water bottles, a brew kit and a bite to eat. In theory, the mission was to be very short-lived, an hour or so at most, and resupply by air was possible. But it was best to err on the safe side. The smokers were taking in eighty fags apiece, and each man also took plastic gloves for handling any bleeding casualties and plasticuffs for any prisoners. Finally, they were ordered to take in their bivvy bags to parcel up any dead, as the body bags that had been ordered for the assault had failed to arrive in time.

If the assault had been going in by river and from the jungle, as originally planned, the men would have loaded up special ammo: one tracer round for every two normal rounds, to be able to see if their shots were on target or not. But flying into the heart of the village like this, where all the fighting would be at such close quarters, there was little need for such niceties. No one would be in any doubt about whether a burst of fire was on target or not. Death would be taking place right before their very eyes.

Once the final assault dress rehearsal was completed, the men headed for the cookhouse tent for a brew and a scoff before bed. After the euphoria and elation of the news that they were going in, there were now some troubling last-minute thoughts crowding in on the men's minds. As they sat around drinking tea and chatting, some of the blokes got out their pads to scribble a last letter home. Just in case, they told themselves, with a grimace. *Just in case I cop it, like.* They wandered over to the ops tent, to leave a hastily penned note to their wives, girlfriends or their mothers with the radio operator or another of their mates – those men who would be remaining behind when the assault force hit the village at dawn the following morning.

'Nothing's gonna happen, like,' they'd say, sheepishly, as they handed the note over. 'But just in case, you know, pass this on to the missus for me, will you?'

One of the guys passing a note across for his girl was Brad Tinnion. He'd hardly had time to say goodbye to Anna, before leaving Hereford. He was sure as hell looking forward to seeing that baby of theirs on his return. Brad was going in as part of Fire Team 2, and there wasn't a finer Special Forces soldier to be fighting alongside, of that his fellow Boat Troop members were certain.

Brad, like the rest of the men of his troop, felt that he had a special reason to be going in on this assault. He'd never forgotten how two of his Boat Troop mates had been crushed in that road accident during training in Kenya. Those were two deaths that he and a lot of the other men put down to the West Side Boys. If those rebel bastards hadn't pulled the bloody hostage trick on the Royal Irish soldiers in the first place, then D Squadron would never have been pulled off Kenya training. In which case, Martie and Adie would still be alive. Whatever he did in the assault tomorrow, however well he performed, he'd be doing it in part for Martie and Adie – two good men who had died in a senseless accident a long way from home.

'What you gonna do, mate, if a kid comes at you tomorrow?' the Kiwi asked, quietly, addressing his question to no one in particular in the cookhouse tent. 'What d'you reckon? Will you shoot them, mate?'

'Does the Pope shit in the fakin' woods?' Jimmy snapped. 'Course I'll fakin' shoot 'em.'

'But what if it's just a young kid, mate?' the Kiwi persisted.

'What the fuck d'you mean, *a kid*?' Jimmy retorted, aggressively. 'They're all murderin' hostage-takin' fakin' rebel bastards, aren't they?'

'You know what I mean, mate,' the Kiwi came back, directing a steely gaze at the cockney. The Kiwi was a tough, wiry guy, without an ounce of fat on him. He was one of the fastest in the squadron at unarmed combat. Although he was gentle as a lamb most of the time, he had ice-blue eyes that could flash fire and murder when he was roused to anger. 'A fuckin' young kiddie, mate. They've got a lot of them in that camp. Young kids. You've got kids about the same age back at home, haven't you, mate?'

'What the fuck!?' Jimmy snorted, jumping to his feet. 'I'm not sittin' 'ere listenin' to this fakin' shite from a fakin' –'

'Laddies, settle doon, settle doon,' the Big Scottish Monster growled, butting in. 'No point beating around the fookin' bush, is there, Jimmy lad? We've all bin thinking the same thing, that's for sure. There's young laddies of ten and eleven and shite in that fookin' rebel camp, and there's no point pretending there isn't.'

'So what you fakin' suggestin', boyo?' Jimmy snapped back. 'One of 'em fakin' "kiddies" comes at me with an AK and he's gonna 'ave some, know what I mean? Those "laddies" don't play with fakin' Lego and Mechano sets no more, mate. They fuck around with the big toys.'

'Listen, mate, no offence intended,' the Kiwi said, trying to smooth things over. 'All I meant was we might have to take out kids and women in that village. So, we might as well face up to that now, mate, right.'

'An' no fakin' offence taken, Kiwi,' Jimmy replied. 'Take a lot more 'n that to get fakin' Jimmy Cockney riled. All I'm saying is a kid wiv' a gun is still a fakin' kid wiv' a gun, don't make no odds 'ow old the fucker is. An AK fires a fakin' big round, and it's still gonna hurt 'avin one of them up your arse no matter who's fakin' shootin' it.'

'I'm afraid Jimmy's right, Kiwi me lad,' the Scottish Monster added. 'Dis'ne matter if it's a wee kiddie or a wee women or whatever, if they're pointing a fookin' weapon at you you're gonna have to shoot them, and that's all there is to it. Different matter if they're unarmed of course, take the fooker prisoner, lad. But make abso-fookin'-lutely sure they're not packing a weapon before ye do so, all right, laddie?'

'Sure, mate. No worries,' the Kiwi replied, nodding his head. 'They're as good as dead, mate,' he added, after a few seconds' uncomfortable silence.

'Look, Kiwi mate . . . Sorry,' Jimmy ventured, uncertainly. 'I reckon I'm just as fakin' wound up about it as you are, otherwise I wouldn't 'ave flown off the fakin' 'andle, now would I? But there ain't no choice about it, is there? This op's going down. They've pulled the pin and we can't put the fucker back in again, now can we? An' in a fakin' country like this, there's more fakin' weapons than there are chickens for sale, innit? I mean, everyone's gonna be packin' a piece in that fakin' village, no matter who they are. Kid comes at you wiv a gun, and you're gonna 'ave to plaster the fucker all over the jungle, and that's the fakin' end of it, know what I mean.'

'No worries, mate,' Kiwi responded with a grin, reaching across the table and cuffing Jimmy across the head. 'At the moment of contact we treat the women and children like any other combatants, mate. If they've got a gun, then we shoot them in the head.'

'S'all right then, mate,' Jimmy replied, with a grin back at the Kiwi. 'You 'eard the OC. We're being sent in to finish 'em off, that's what 'e said. I mean, it's not like they don't deserve it, is it? A bunch of crazier, extremely nasty, evil bastards that need takin' out I ain't never 'eard of. Long past their sell-by date, aren't they? We'll do what we 'ave to do, an' that's the end of it.'

'Right then, that's settled, isn't it, laddies?' the Big Scottish Monster announced, bringing the discussion to a conclusion. Jimmy and the Kiwi had buried the hatchet, which was good news. You didn't want any niggling resentment between the men of your troop when the red mist of combat went down. 'Anyone fancy a fookin' good nosh-up, then?'

'Too right,' Jimmy remarked, enthusiastically. 'I'm 'Ank Marvin, mate.'

'Ank Marvin?' asked the Kiwi. 'What's Ank Marvin when it's at home, mate?'

'Ank Marvin – starvin'. You don't get the lingo in too much of an 'urry, do you, Kiwi mate? 'Ow long 'ave I been tryin' to teach you fakin' cockney rhymin' slang? Septic Tank – Yank. 'Ank Marvin – starvin'. Tiddlywink – drink. Jack Tar – bar. Pig's ear – beer. Pimple 'n' blotch – Scotch –'

'Aye, and fookin' fine and dandy is fookin' brandy, but you're boring us fookin' stupid, Jimmy lad,' the Scottish Monster interrupted. 'Let's get us a fookin' good feed, as there's work to be done on the morrow.'

'See, Kiwi mate? Simple, innit?' Jimmy added, with a grin. 'Oh yeah, an' Aristotle is bottle, just in case you fancy getting a round of tiddly-winks in after all this is over, mate.'

'Simple, mate? Not for a bloody Kiwi like me it ain't.'

'More sheep than brain cells, so I 'eard. Only joking, Kiwi mate. Come on. Let's be 'avin' us a bleedin' great fry-up. Gotta get a good feed down you, especially if it's gonna be your last. No one wants to cop it thinking they've missed a free scoff.'

'Fuck off, Jimmy, you morbid bastard,' the Kiwi retorted, racing to get to the food hatch before him. 'Got a breakfast there, Chef mate? Yeh. Everything. And nothing for the fat cockney bastard behind me, mate. Look at him, Chef. He's big enough as it is, without another flaming fry-up inside him. Never get him off the chopper, mate, the rate he's going. But no worries, eh, Chef, I'll have his portion too, mate.'

'Don't you worry, Cheffy me old mate, I'll be 'avin' a double portion,' Jimmy shouted over at the cook. 'See this Kiwi fucker 'ere, send a fakin' glass eye to sleep, 'e would. Same old jokes, an' they don't get any funnier, do they, Cheffy? Know what I mean?'

'No, sir . . . I mean, yes, sir. I mean, mate,' the chef called back. 'Will youse two be needing eggs, then? Take a few seconds if youse do, but I'm just on to it, so I am. Sure youse don't mind waiting a while?'

'Eggs? Only if they're white enough, mate,' Cockney Jimmy yelled back, rehashing the same joke from a few days before.

'Only if they're white . . . ?' the chef began, confusedly, before managing to stop himself. 'Ah, sure, you'll not be havin' me on that one again. They're just as white as the feckin' chicken can manage, will that do youse all right?'

'Perfick, mate,' said Jimmy, grinning. 'Or tell you what, tell your fakin' chicken I want 'em as white as the faces of those fakin' rebel bastards'll be when we 'it their village tomorrow mornin'. All right, mate?'

'Sure, I'll be seeing what I can do,' the chef replied, over the noise of the frying eggs. 'But it's up to the feckin' chickens, so no promises.'

There were a few seconds' silence as the two SAS men waited for their food, eventually broken by the young New Zealander. 'You reckon we'll get in there all right, mate?' he asked, lowering his voice a little. 'I mean the choppers, get us down on to target all right?'

'Don't take a fakin' genius, do it, Kiwi, to see the bastards gettin' lucky an' pullin' a chopper out of the sky,' Jimmy grunted, as the two men waited for their plates to be filled. 'I mean, they got fakin' GPMGs on mounts on the fakin' roofs, an' stuff, ain't they? Only takes one of the bastards wiv one of 'em up and at us and we're toast, like. Just the way it is, innit?'

'Yeah, mate. But the fire from the choppers'll keep their heads down, won't it, mate? I mean, long enough for us to get on the ground, right?'

'Yeah, you're right there, Kiwi. Nice to 'ave somethin' in the sky as back-up, innit? But tell you one thing, gunships or no gunships, if it was fakin' B Squadron defending that fakin' village, we'd all be fakin' dead before we even 'it the ground, mate. Na, we'll be all right. We'll just 'ave to 'ope we catch 'em nappin'. You pray, mate? If you fancy, I'll say some fakin' prayers wiv you, like.'

'Aw . . . cheers, mate. Don't mind if I do.'

'Na, mate, I'm not joking. I'm being fakin' serious. S'more a poem, really, mate, than a prayer. Me mother told us it at 'ome, those days she couldn't afford to put no food on the table. An' there was a lot of 'em, too, I can tell you. Any'ow, 'ere goes:

> If on a Spring night I went by,
> And God were standing there,
> What is the prayer that I would say
> To 'im? This is the prayer;
> O Lord of courage grave,
> O master of this night of Spring!
> Make firm in me an 'eart too brave
> To ask thee anything.

'Sweet, mate. Real sweet,' the Kiwi said, after a moment's awkward silence. There were hidden depths to Cockney Jimmy that he found hard to fathom, and the Kiwi was momentarily lost for words. Just then, the grinning chef thrust a plate piled high with fried breakfast towards him. 'Hey, take a look at that, mate,' the Kiwi enthused, showing Jimmy his plate. 'No doubt about it, mate, the chef here's a genius, right?'

'Yeah, nice scoff, mate. More importantly, where the fuck's mine?' Jimmy replied, with an appreciative look at Kiwi Mike's plate. 'You know what, mate? Know what those fuckers do to prisoners, don't you, if they catch you? Fakin' cook you and eat you, that's what they'll do. Oh yeah, and they give you a good buggerin' first – bit of stuffin', like. Worst case has the fakin' rebels parading through town with D Squadron's heads on fakin' poles, innit? Na, only jokin', mate – just trying to put you off your fakin' fry-up, like, so I can scoff it.'

There was a weird, wired atmosphere around Waterloo Camp as the minutes ticked by, and zero hour approached. Most couldn't sleep because of the adrenalin, so they sat around in groups, cleaning their weapons and chatting. The chef kept the breakfasts on all night long – a fried slice, eggs, growlers and baked beans – and some of the men would end up eating two or three before zero hour. Once the assault went in, they argued, you'd never know how long it would be before your next feed, and they sure as hell didn't want to be going hungry. Others weren't able to touch the food at all. Pre-operation nerves had tied their stomachs into tight knots. Jimmy, the Kiwi, the Big Scottish Monster and Brad, however, settled down to polish off their first breakfasts of the night – and they were all intending to have several.

'Brad. How you doin', mate?' Jimmy spluttered through a mouthful of food, as Brad carried his plate over. ''Ave a seat. Fakin' luverly scoff, fucked if it ain't.'

'Cheers, Jimmy, but I'll eat somewhere else,' Brad remarked quietly, taking a place on the bench further down. 'Seeing you eating is enough to put anyone off their food, mate.'

'Whatever,' Jimmy grunted. He was too intent on his food to get into a major verbal sparring match.

'Bit quiet, aren't you, mate?' the Kiwi said to Brad. 'What's on your mind, mate? Anything special?'

'Nothing much. Just the two guys that died in the Kenya training,' Brad replied. 'Martie and Adie. Reckon this is our chance to get even.'

'Sure thing, mate,' said the Kiwi. 'Reckon those bastards have got it coming to them, eh, mate?'

'Too fakin' right,' Jimmy interrupted, shoving back his empty plate as he did so. 'It's payback time. Reckon those West Side Fakers need some serious educatin'. An' we are not goin' to be takin' no prisoners.' With that Jimmy jumped to his feet, wiping his sleeve across an egg-stained mouth as he did so. 'For I will strike down with GREAT vengeance upon thee –'

'D'you fookin' MIND, lad?' the Scottish Monster roared, stopping Jimmy in full flow. The Monster took his food very seriously. 'You're fookin' gobbin' fookin' chewed-up growler and shite all over my fookin' plate. Sit yourself fookin' down. Or better still, go and get yourself another fookin' plateful. Ye finished that one in record fookin' time, lad. I don't reckon it even touched the fookin' sides.'

'S'good idea, Monster me old mate,' Jimmy retorted. 'Another round of scoff. Just what the fakin' doctor ordered.'

Over the far side of the camp, the Paras were also making their final preparations for the assault. But there would be a lot less eating going on among the men of the Parachute Regiment, that was for sure – a bunch of pimply youths next to the grizzled veterans of D Squadron. Major Lowe, the OC commanding the Paras' assault on the ground, would stay up half the night worrying. What would he do the following day if he had to tell any of the parents that their young son had been killed during the forthcoming action? It just didn't bear thinking about. And Captain Danny Matthews, his twenty-two-year-old 2iC, was painfully aware that he would be leading a lot of young men into their first time in combat. What a baptism of fire it would prove. It was an awe-inspiring responsibility.

Unbeknown to these men, a major drama was now playing out at sea on board HMS *Argyll*. The two Army Lynx attack helicopters that were spearheading the air assault had been shipped out to Freetown in the back of a Hercules C-130 transport aircraft. After being reassembled at Lungi Airport, they were flown out to HMS *Argyll*, the evening before the assault. But as the first chopper landed across deck, Flight Deck Officer Paul Philips had noticed that there was a problem with the chopper's starboard engine. It turned out that the aircraft had suffered a single engine failure. It was 9 p.m. by the time the problem was diagnosed, and the chopper was scheduled to head out to join the assault force at 5.30 a.m. the following morning.

Argyll's flight maintenance team realised that they had no choice but to change the whole engine. They began working feverishly to complete the job. But after removing the Army Lynx engine, they found that the spare engine they had on board ship – which was for a naval Lynx – was subtly different. The only option was to adapt and bastardise the spare naval Lynx engine in the hope that it would hold up during the following morning's assault. It was such an unorthodox operation that *Argyll*'s flight maintenance team had to seek special clearance from PJHQ London in order to be able to proceed. Precious minutes were lost waiting for permission. When clearance finally did come through, a second maintenance team was ferried across from the RFA *Sir Percival*, in *Argyll*'s sea boat, to lend a hand changing the engine. But it was a race against time, and the outcome at the end would be far from certain.

Working through the night, the engineers finally managed to fire up the refitted Lynx engine at 3 a.m. All they could do now was pray that it would keep the attack helicopter in the air long enough to play its part in the planned assault. But whatever happened, Lynx or no Lynx, Operation Certain Death was going in regardless.

PROOF OF LIFE

Be strong. A people that is not ready to die for its liberties loses them . . . Believe passionately in the ideas and in the way of life for which one is fighting. Liberty deserves to be served with more passion than tyranny.

— Andre Maurois, *Memoirs*

As the sun rose over the jungle on day sixteen of the hostage crisis, Calm Down Fresh and his henchmen could be seen setting up the satphone in the village clearing. Once he'd got a good signal and dialled up whoever it was that he wanted to talk to, he beckoned to Major Martial. *Oh Jesus, not again*, the British soldiers were thinking, with a sinking feeling. *Not the whole feckin' BBC-on-the-satphone nightmare again.* But this time, they needn't have worried. It turned out that it was Lieutenant Colonel Simon Fordham, the Royal Irish Rangers' Commanding Officer in Sierra Leone, on the other end of the satphone.

'Hello, Colonel. Good to hear your voice,' the Major began. 'Yes, we're all here. The weather? Bad, as it happens. Decidedly stormy. In fact, I'd say about as bad as it gets. The others? Of course, I'll call them over.'

The Major turned towards the veranda. 'It's the CO, lads. Speak to the CO. He just wants to say a few words.'

Ranger Gaunt was first to take the receiver. 'Hello, sir?'

'Hello, lad. Which one of you is it speaking?'

'Ranger James Gaunt, sir.'

'Ranger Jim Gaunt. Are you all right, lad?'

'Dead on, sir. No worries, like.'

'Good man, *James*. Just hang on in there, and we'll have you out soon. Now, pass me on to the next man.'

And so it went, the CO greeting each of the British soldiers in turn, a quick hello, and then on to the next one. For Calm Down Fresh to have allowed all six of them to speak to their CO like that, something must be going right at last, the hostages thought to themselves. Most likely, the hostage negotiations had been kick-started again. In any event, it was an incredible morale boost for the men. For several days now, they'd felt isolated and abandoned – and like they were on the verge of being got out of the way by the rebels. Now, all that had changed.

Unfortunately for Corporal Mousa, he hadn't been allowed out of the pit to speak to the British officer. And he'd been spending a lot of time in there recently, alone in the dark fetid waters, thinking about his own fate. Whatever happened to the British soldiers, Mousa was 99 per cent convinced he would never get out of there alive. His good offices with Foday Kallay were just buying him time, not a ticket out of there. The rebel rank and file had made it quite clear that he was never leaving the pit alive. Several times, Mr Die, the most evil of the lot, had stood there wearing only his shorts and belts of GPMG ammo slung around his bare torso, staring down through the trapdoor with cold, unblinking eyes. He was a man of very few words.

'When will dey let me go kill you, fuckin Mousa?' he'd growl. 'Dey keep you alive too long-long. Soon-soon now I go come finish you.'

The radio call with the Royal Irish Rangers' CO had clearly been a 'proof-of-life exercise', one designed to show the British high command that each of the hostages was actually there in the village, and in reasonably good shape. It wasn't enough for the Lieutenant Colonel just to ask Major Martial for confirmation that all the men were present and correct. For all he knew, the West Side Boys might be forcing the Major to say such things while at the same time holding a gun to his head. Hence the need for Lieutenant Colonel Fordham to speak to each of the men in turn. A decision had already been taken by the high command that any rescue attempt would now take place within the next forty-eight hours; this phone call would prove for sure that all of the men were still present in the rebel village.

Every single word of every satphone or radio conversation between the British forces and the West Side Boys was being faithfully recorded by a bank of machines set up for that purpose back in JFHQ Freetown, the nerve centre for Operation Barras. Invariably, it was Colonel Cambodia who would be doing the talking for the rebels – and there was now a growing body of tape recordings of his voice at JFHQ. The specialist hostage negotiators had been poring over these recordings, searching for clues to the state of mind of the rebel leaders. They would now use the recordings of this most recent satphone call to verify as best they could that the voices they had heard really were those of the six British hostages.

After the Major had finished speaking to Lieutenant Colonel Fordham, he seemed pensive and lost in thought. *What was going on? What had the CO been able to tell him?* The other men were desperate to know. But they knew that they shouldn't ask the Major such things while Calm Down Fresh was still around. Eventually, Ranger Gaunt's need to know got the better of him.

'So are things sort of looking up, like, sir?' he ventured.

'Erm . . . Oh, yes, very much so, lad,' the Major said, pulling himself back to the present. After a moment's silence he continued. 'The CO told me that the hostage negotiations are very much back on track again, just a few more details to be ironed out. And that's the best news we can have hoped for.'

'Dead on, sir,' the Ranger responded, enthusiastically. 'So, youse reckon we might sort of be gettin' out of here pretty quickly, like?'

'I think we will, Ranger, I think we will,' the Major replied.

Major Martial knew that the British negotiators had given the rebels every impression that the hostage-release deal was back on again, and that they would be getting everything they had asked for. As a result, the tension in the rebel camp had eased a little.

Over the past couple of days, the split between Colonel Savage and Foday Kallay had been festering badly. Kallay was backed by Colonel Cambodia, Changa Bulanga and Calm Down Fresh, who together commanded a lot of men. But even so, Foday Kallay had taken the precaution of disarming the Savage Group of all their heavy weapons – GPMGs, HMGs, RPGs and mortars – and storing them under heavy guard in his own house. Kallay was taking no chances.

But now that the deal seemed to have been reached with the British, Kallay decided to release Colonel Savage and his deputies – Mr Die, Cobra and Mr Murder. Over at the pit, Mousa watched as they were untied and given their weapons again. During the last few days, Mousa had repeatedly heard Colonel Savage moaning to his three deputies about the good treatment being given to the British soldiers. 'Dat Kallay he do treat dem whiteboys too damn fine. He should go look what de British did do to dis country dem. We should punish dem good-good for colonialism and now dat dey come back again to mess-mess wid us.' Mousa hoped that Kallay would be able to keep Colonel Savage and his rebel dogs on a tight leash. They even seemed to be blaming the British hostages for their arrest and incarceration in the dungeon.

Shortly after Savage's release from the pit, Corporal Mousa found himself being taken out of there too. He had started to develop pneumonia from lying in the water, and Foday Kallay didn't want Mousa dying on him just yet – not before the negotiations with the British were completed. Not before he felt ready to launch Operation Kill British and Operation Kill All Your Family. Mousa was brought over to Kallay's house and put out on the rear veranda. Although he was still tied up, Kallay assigned six guards to watch over him day and night. Mousa heard Kallay threaten the guards with death if he managed to escape. The rebel leader knew that Corporal Mousa was a well-trained soldier, skilled in the ways of the jungle; even in his present state, Kallay feared he might still manage to escape.

But if the truth be told, Mousa had already abandoned any thoughts of breakout. He knew that if he had managed to escape, he would have caused terrible suffering and perhaps even the death of the British hostages. Equally importantly, Mousa believed that he would be needed by the British soldiers if they did try to escape. On one of his recent walkabouts, the Major had briefly shared with Mousa his plans for a riverine escape. But Mousa had warned him of the dangers: rebel forces were positioned upstream and downstream from Gberi Bana. The West Side Boys kept permanent watch on the river. And Mousa knew that if he had escaped on his own, he would have been blamed for abandoning the British soldiers: he was after all the liaison officer assigned to the British patrol. Even if he had got the chance, Mousa was resigned to the fact that any solo escape attempt was not practicable.

That evening, the six hostages were sitting outside on the veranda with Calm Down Fresh, who seemed relatively sane and relaxed for once. The rebel commander's mood had brightened and it soon became clear why; he revealed that the British negotiators had agreed to give them everything they were asking for. They were being provided with the guns and boat engines and vehicles they had demanded. And a new deal was being put in place, granting the rebel leaders a prominent role in Sierra Leone's government. He himself might even end up with a ministerial position. Calm Down Fresh clearly believed that a new day was dawning for the West Side Boys.

He pointed up at various bright stars in the night sky, explaining to the hostages with a wide grin that they were allied satellites keeping watch on them all. He was chuckling away to himself, finding his conviction that they were collectively the focus of so much international attention highly amusing. None of the hostages could see anything looking remotely like a passing satellite in the night sky above them. Normally, they would appear as a moving dot of light, like a bright planet scooting across the heavens. But they smiled and nodded and laughed along with Calm Down Fresh anyway. They didn't give a damn. All they cared about was that he seemed to be in a sane mood for once.

'That one dere, go be de British satellite. That one, de American,' Calm Down Fresh said excitedly, pointing at the stars. 'And all of dem, go keep a watch on de West Side!'

'Aye. Sure, there's satellites up there all right,' Ranger Gaunt assured the rebel commander, throwing his head back and looking towards the heavens. It was a spectacularly clear evening, the black of the night sky speckled with bright clusters of galaxies. The Ranger felt as if he was so close to the constellations that he could almost reach up and touch them. But there were definitely no satellites moving up there, of that he was certain.

'Sure, lad, there's satellites, but none of them could find us among all this jungle,' the Major commented, gazing skywards himself. 'Too much tree cover to see anything. You've got nothing to worry about, Camp Commandant. They'll never find you here.'

'Aye, sir. Youse can say that again,' the Ranger agreed, catching the Major's drift. 'Not a hope in hell they'd have, with all this jungle around us. You're safe as houses, Calm Down – I mean, Camp Commandant, sir. Nothin' to worry yerself about up there at all.'

The Major took advantage of Calm Down Fresh's good mood to ask if they could go down to the river for a wash. To his surprise, the Camp Commandant agreed. By now, it was clearly dark enough to go for the escape, and all of the hostages were on for it. They set off down towards the Rokel Creek, with their makeshift water-bottle floats dangling casually in their hands, looking for all the world as though they were just taking them to help with the washing. But halfway down towards the river, they heard Calm Down Fresh ordering one of his guards to go with them. Their hearts sank, especially when they saw that it was Dennis the feckin' Menace. As they approached the river, the CO passed the word around that unless they could take Dennis the Menace out quietly, the escape was off. He would have liked nothing more than a good excuse to drill the British soldiers full of holes.

As feared, Dennis put a stop to any escape attempt, and as they were returning from their wash there was a commotion up in the village ahead of them. It turned out that the West Side Boys who had survived the recent, disastrous attack on the UN base had gathered together as a mob in the village clearing. They were preparing to kill their own CO, Colonel Mines, whom they were blaming for not planning the raid properly. Colonel Mines was lying before them, trussed up on the ground, as they argued over exactly what to do with him. But luckily for the rebel officer, a load of crates of beer and whisky had arrived in the camp that evening – a gift from the British military. And as the rebels proceeded to have a drink or two, they seemed to forget about their plans to polish off their own commanding officer.

What Major Martial hadn't told his men earlier that day – and felt that he still couldn't tell them – was the main message that he had received via the satphone call. The British assertion that they were giving in to the rebel demands was simply a ruse, one designed to lull them into a false sense of security. And the rebels were being fantastically naive in believing it. In fact, during the satphone call the CO had given the Major the code word, signifying that the hostage-rescue assault was going in. But if he told his other men this the Major was worried that their excited reactions might betray the fact to their captors. He feared that it might lift their spirits too much – as had happened previously, when they had first lighted upon the riverine escape plan – and that the rebels would notice something was up.

In addition to which, something could still go wrong, and if it did, the disappointment would be too much for the junior ranks to bear. The mission could be called off at the last minute for all sorts of reasons. An eleventh-hour rebel capitulation (although that seemed unlikely). Unforeseen logistical problems (a couple of the Chinooks going down with mechanical problems). Simple political expediency (the political taskmasters losing their bottle). Even the assault itself might prove problematic, to put it mildly. The assault force was *flying directly on to target*. Nothing quite like it had ever been tried before, and it had to make them highly vulnerable to ground fire from the rebel base. Such a mission was unprecedented in British Special Forces history, that much was clear. The Major was still coming to terms with the timing of the forthcoming assault himself, although he was trying his best to hide it.

The coded message had told him that the assault force would hit the village at first light the following morning.

(*Above*) Soldiers of the Pathfinder Platoon of the 16 Air Assault Brigade, Parachute Regiment, on board a CH47 (HC2) Chinook helicopter, deploying with the men of 1 Para to assault the West Side Boys' rebel base at Magbeni. (*Below*) British soldiers squeeze past a door gunner with L7 A2 7.62mm General Purpose Machine Gun (GPMG), prior to going on airborne patrol in Sierra Leone.

(*Above*) Door gunner mans a M134 mini-gun as an RAF CH47 (HC2) Chinook sweeps low over the jungles of Sierra Leone, carrying troops of the Pathfinder Platoon of the Parachute Regiment into action. (*Below*) Soldiers of the 1st Battalion, the Parachute Regiment, deploy from an RAF CH47 (HC2) Chinook onto a jungle landing zone in Sierra Leone.

(*Right*) Collapsible commercial parabolic listening device of the sort of type used in SAS/SBS jungle observation post for eavesdropping on rebel movements in Gberi Bana base.

(*Below*) Communication in use in observation post.

(*Left*) The remains of a UN truck base in the rebel base of Magbeni, after being blown up by the Paras. ECO stands for ECOMOG, part of the Nigerian forces drafted into Sierra Leone under the UN. It is now being used by local villagers as an improvised washing line.

(*Right*) Remains of rebel building in Magbeni base today, with roof still missing; it was blown off by the downdraft of the CH47 (HC2) Chinook helicopters, as they hovered to drop the British assault forces.

(*Left*) The walls of the ruined rebel buildings in Magbeni today – they remain peppered with gunfire.

(*Above*) The lead element of A Company, 1 Para, in full attack advancing through the rebel base at Magbeni. Smoke in the background denotes where forward elements of the Company have already cleared rebel buildings.

(*Above*) The men of A Company, 1 Para, advance through the rebel base at Magbeni, each soldier weighed down by additional ammo and their weapons, including SA80 assault rifles. (Below) Two men of A Company, 1 Para, inspect the impact of their fire on the rebel buildings in Magbeni.

An RAF CH47 (HC2) Chinook prepares to airlift the captured Land Rovers of the Royal Irish Rangers out of the rebel base at Magbeni.

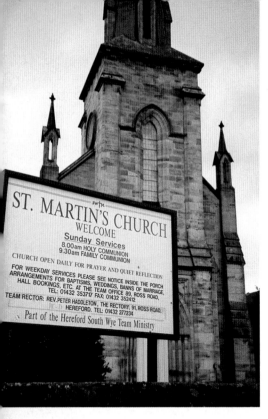

(*Above left*) St. Martin's Church, Hereford. (*Above right*) The gravestone of Lance Corporal Bradley 'Brad' Tinnion, who lost his life in Operation Barras, the hostage rescue assault on the rebel bases in Sierra Leone.
(*Below*) The cemetery at St Martin's Church, Hereford, hometown of the SAS.

DAWN RAIDERS

Victory at all costs, victory in spite of terror, victory however long and hard the road may be; for without victory there is no survival.
 – Sir Winston Churchill, 13 May 1940, in the House of Commons

I is 5.30 a.m. on the morning of Sunday 10 September. The seventy Special Forces men and the ninety men of 1 Para prepare to board their aircraft at Waterloo Camp. At the back of the base on a makeshift helipad – really no more than a boggy patch of flat ground – three giant Chinook helicopters of 7 Squadron, RAF, are waiting, engines running. The men of the Special Forces fire teams are wearing plain army camo fatigues and their warpaint, streaks of green and brown camo cream. They are weighed down with weapons, ammo and packs full of explosives, water, cigarettes and food. The assault force is scheduled to be on the ground no longer than an hour or so. But, just in case they are still holding the rebels' base come nightfall, a couple of the men in each of the fire teams have packed NVGs. They are prepared to last out the duration of this mission, no matter how long it may take.

As the men stride out to the waiting choppers, staggering under the weight of weapons and explosives, they glance down at their boots and notice that they are kicking through long grass that is soaking wet with glistening dew. The ground over this side of the camp is boggy, and with the load they are carrying they sink into it up to their ankles. For several of them, the bizarre thought suddenly comes into their heads that they will be going into combat with wet, muddy boots. *Shit, man,* they are telling themselves, angrily, *you are going into war. War. At the other end of that chopper ride lies fucking Armageddon. You are going to see your mates shot; you could yourself be badly injured;*

you might even die. What the fuck does it matter if you have wet boots or not?

Funny how the mind plays tricks like that, trying to keep the man from contemplating the stark reality of the job in hand, the need to look death calmly in the face and tell him not now, not yet, not this day.

They approach their winged chariots, and the whine of the chopper turbines is revving up to a fever pitch, like the roar of some angry beast, as the aircraft prepares to lift the men off the ground and into battle. They traipse past the base fence, coming in behind the rear of the helicopters, and as they do so they are hit by a hot gust of avgas exhaust – carrying with it that unmistakable smell that they have all come to know so well. How many times have they stood in the back blast from the choppers like this, about to be airlifted into an operation somewhere? Ten times? Fifty? Maybe more? But for these men there is one, overarching difference now: most of those had been training missions, a dummy run, a dress rehearsal. This time it is for real. And none of these men has ever been in on an assault of this magnitude before.

Joining the army, taking all the abuse that came with it, passing SAS selection, the years of training and training and training that had followed – all of that was leading up to this moment, this one moment where they will be tested to the full, pushed to the brink, forced to confront their true selves. Death, life, love, bravery, cowardice and survival – for each man the answer to these universal questions now lies at the end of this chopper ride. Most men never get to confront so starkly any of these eternal uncertainties, in their normal, humdrum lives. As they approach the choppers, the men of D Squadron feel a strange mixture of conflicting emotions: they are scared, daunted, confused and, somehow, honoured too, all at the same time.

Suddenly, to one side of them, Rod Bristol, the Regimental Sergeant Major (RSM), starts shouting – mouth wide open, cheeks bulging red – and as he does so he is punching the air. But the men can hardly hear him above the whine of the turbines and the roar of the chopper's downdraught. They strain their ears to catch the words, each man eager for some reassurance from their Sergeant Major, a soldier of so many years' experience, a regimental veteran if ever there was one, eager to catch something that will convince them that they will do their duty, and that they will not let their fellow soldiers down in the half-light of this damp African morning.

'Come on, D Squadron! COME ON! Fight, fight, fight, FIGHT and never stop fighting,' is what the RSM's words sound like, but none of the men can be really sure.

It still feels as if it isn't real yet, like being in a dream.

And then suddenly they are climbing up the rear ramp of the Chinook, up, up into the hot, stuffy interior, the piercing sound of the turbines all around them. The men line up inside, thirty-six to each aircraft, standing. They will fly in like this, on their feet, poised to leap out of that back ramp and into combat as soon as the chopper touches down. There is no point in trying to talk. The noise is deafening. They are in the belly of the beast now, and they can feel the giant aircraft shifting and groaning as it tries to lift off, the pitch of the straining turbines rising to a horrible scream. For a few seconds the Chinook remains there, stuck in the same clinging African mud that the men have plastered all over their boots, and then it breaks free, first one wheel, then another, as it hauls itself up, clawing at the sky, struggling with the awesome load that it is carrying.

Finally, they are airborne.

Thumbs up all round, a grinning and a nervous slapping of backs, as the aircraft gains height, banks and turns towards the east. But a growing sense of dread, now, heady and dizzying, as it surges up from the pit of the stomach on the heavy black wings of animal fear; this is the cloying dread of shrapnel shredding muscle and bullet exploding head and all of it being your own. That frailty, that vulnerability of the human body, that softness of human tissue, is suddenly so palpable in your mind.

Flesh and bone facing red-hot lead and fractured, razor-sharp steel.

You sense the Chinook put its head down now, and, true to its name – *a chinook, a dry warm gust that blows down the eastern slopes of the Rocky Mountains* – the aircraft starts to leap ahead like the wind. The raw terror passes, but it is replaced by a mind-numbing, suffo-cating foreboding. It is the fear of self and the fear of failure now, magnified 10,000-fold by the daunting mission before you. *Will I do well enough out there?* you ask yourself. *Will I perform? Should I even be here on this aircraft, alongside these men? Am I worthy?* You glance surreptitiously around at the faces of the other soldiers, but none of them is showing any visible signs of being afraid, and you feel guilty, uncertain that you should really be among them. *These men are true heroes*, you think to yourself. Glancing down at your leather-gloved fist grasping your weapon, you worry that your hands are shaking.

And you worry that it shows.

The chopper dives now, seeking the waters of the Freetown Estuary, which it will follow all the way across to the Rokel Creek – then taking the path of the river up towards Gberi Bana. And the anxiety is fading now, being replaced by a growing confidence and pride. There has been a devil on one shoulder saying you are not worthy, but an angel – your guardian angel – has just popped up on the other, and it is saying 'yes, you fucking are'.

Yes, you fucking are worthy. And yes, you fucking should be here.

An ultimate, total confidence floods through you, courses through your veins now, and suddenly, you feel honoured and *privileged* to be there. Privileged to bear arms on behalf of Her Majesty's government, on behalf of your country. A swelling, warm, glowing sense of pride in the mission surges through you, a pride in yourself like you have never ever come close to feeling before – because you know that you are going to do all right.

You are the man, the chosen one, the avenger, the warrior of light, *the Jedi*, and with your angel by your side you are going to get through this momentous day.

These men know that when they get off this chopper, all normal rules and values in life will have disappeared. There will be no one behind them from Safety checking that they're sticking to the rules, and they will do whatever is required to get the job done. Whatever it takes. From the moment they hit that target, they will be thinking about nothing else. Each man will exist in a totally new space, where if he does not do his job right he knows that he will end up dead. This is a unique moment in each of these men's lives: they have a single, absolute focus now, an all-consuming purpose. Nothing can get in its way. Nothing can stop them. These men are no longer just a group of individuals any more, a bunch of soldiers, a band of brothers even: they have become as one, a single fighting machine.

A living, breathing, deadly animal of war.

As the SAS assault force lifts off in the two Chinooks from Waterloo Camp, a further giant double-rotor Chinook crammed full of Paras is clawing skywards alongside them. The second half of the ninety-man Para assault force will have to await pickup by one of the returning Chinooks, some thirty minutes later, which will then turn round and fly them into target.

And elsewhere, other airborne forces are already streaking across the skies above the still-sleeping city of Freetown, on their way to join the air armada.

Five minutes before the Chinooks lift off, the three Lynx attack heli-copters leave the helipad on the rear of HMS *Argyll*, several miles out to sea. They are now heading in fast and low across the water to take up their positions to the rear of the Chinook troop transports. The Chinooks have to be first on to target, to maximise the chances of Fire Team 1 getting to the hostages before the rebels kill them. At the same time, Neall Ellis has fired up the turbines of the Mi-24, and Fred Marafono has checked the weapons pods one last time, before that chopper lifts off from the Air Wing's helipad, tearing full throttle into the skies above Freetown itself. Once past the city outskirts, Nellis puts the chopper's nose down and races eastwards, keen to take up his posi-tion in the aerial armada, leading the Lynx attack helicopters on to target.

It is 5.35 a.m. and there are now seven choppers thrashing through the skies towards the still-sleeping rebel target.

From his cockpit, Nellis is able to see the lush jungle canopy unrolling beneath the speeding Mi-24 as the pre-dawn light touches the treetops golden green. It is less than a fifteen-minute chopper ride inland to Gberi Bana, and the flat coastal plain quickly gives way to rolling, forested hills. Occasionally, a blunt pinnacle of rock poking through the treetops forces the Mi-24 to climb, before it dips down to treetop level again and races onwards. Gradually, the chopper gains altitude, hugging the hillside that rises up before it, until Nellis takes it up and over the crest of a spectacular forest-clad ridge. They begin their descent now across a pristine jungle, pierced here and there by granite outcrops – a descent which will end when Nellis levels out the chopper around thirty feet above the waters of the Rokel Creek. All going to plan, they will drop in just behind the speeding armada of CH47 Chinooks, joining the three Lynx helicopters to advance in formation upriver.

They will then be barely ten minutes to target – and it will almost be time to give the West Side Boys their wake-up call.

The jungles below them are some of the harshest on earth. During the course of Fearless Fred's twenty-two-year British military career – mostly spent with the SAS – he has been posted to some of the remotest forests in South and Central America and on the inhospitable Indonesian archipelago. Yet the West African theatre remains the most unforgiving. 'Impossible for us and impossible for them,' he maintains.

By *them* he means the rebels.

And now, radio contact has been established between the various elements of the air armada. There isn't much chatter in the pilots' headphones yet, just the occasional update from JFHQ Freetown. But as the choppers converge on the waters of the Rokel Creek, each aircraft starts to call in their position and their ready status, one by one, from the lead Chinooks back through the Lynx attack helicopters and the Mi-24 gunship. Although it is unlikely that the rebels are listening in on the radio traffic – in fact at this ungodly hour, they should still be in their beds sleeping soundly – the pilots use the prearranged code word to report they are ready in formation, the name of a peculiarly British relish.

'Sierra One is pickle.'

'Sierra Two is pickle.'

'Sierra Three is pickle. Sierra Four is pickle. Sierra Five . . . Sierra Six . . .'

And so on and so forth, until the lead Chinook is able to confirm: 'Sierra One, understand we are complete.'

United above the broad expanse of the Rokel Creek, the air assault force is in full formation now – even the Lynx helicopter with engine trouble has been ressurrected overnight, and is with them. It is 5.45 a.m., and the air armada begins its run-in towards target.

Nine minutes to go now, and then the fun and games will begin.

In the jungle fringes on the outskirts of Gberi Bana village, the six-man SAS obs team is waiting for the armada that they know is coming. (The four-man obs team on the southern river bank is doing likewise.) As the first streaks of dawn lightened the sky to the east of them, they have moved up from their hidden obs positions to do a close-target recce. Now, they are lying hidden among the palm trees at the very edge of the rebel village. Silent, alert, vigilant to the last man, they can see that no one is stirring in the pre-dawn mists and shadows. Everything is looking good for the assault. In their head-phones they are monitoring the air traffic; they hear the pilots of the seven choppers calling to each other, coordinating their flight paths so that they can converge on the Rokel Creek as planned. As they begin their attack run into the target, the airwaves go largely silent.

The calm before the storm.

Suddenly, Lassie can hear the faint, dull, thud-thud-thud of the approaching Chinooks' twin rotors chopping at the thick, moisture-laden air just above the river's surface. *Shit*, he thinks, *that's loud already*. He wishes he'd brought their listening kit with them, so he could have monitored the air armada's progress from way back. But it's too late for that now. *They're too fucking early*, he's thinking. *It's too dark. They can't go in yet. If they do, they won't be able to see to put the lads down properly.*

'Sierra One, this is Sierra Green Alpha, d'you copy?' Lassie calls softly into his radio mouthpiece, which is taped to his webbing just below his left shoulder.

'Sierra Green Alpha, this is Sierra One, hearing you loud and clear,' the reassuring reply comes back to him from the lead Chinook.

'You're too early, Sierra One. I have the target visual and it's too dark to hit the LZ. I can already hear you. Advise turn back, repeat turn back, and wait until we call you in again, over.'

'Roger that, Sierra Green Alpha. We'll go into a holding pattern over the estuary. Advise for how long, over.'

'Estimate fifteen minutes, over.'

'Roger that. Fifteen minutes. Sierra One, out.'

Breathing a sight of relief, Lassie hears the distant throb of the choppers fade away again as the air armada heads back downriver and out to sea. *Fifteen minutes should do it*, he says to himself, nervously. The chopper pilots just need to be able to see well enough to locate the LZs and hit them with their roping-in points. *If only the fucking mist would clear*, he thinks. *It is clinging to the fucking village like shit to a blanket.*

Gaining height and circling out above the vast expanse of the Freetown harbour, the seven aircraft go into a holding pattern now. It feels like an age to the men of D Squadron – tensed and poised and ready for action inside the choppers – although it can be little more than ten minutes. They all know the reason for the delay; they have been listening in on the radio net to the short exchange of words between the lead Chinook pilot and Lassie on the ground at the target. *If only the fucking sunrise would get a move on*, they're thinking. *If only the daylight were here.*

Despite the noise of the engines, it is eerily quiet as everyone waits for the mission proper to begin once more. This limbo does not exist in the minds of most of the men; they have put their very existence on hold until the assault is cleared to go in again. Then they feel the Chinooks turning, slipping, dipping down, losing altitude and gaining speed as they do so, and suddenly they are back in the reality of the moment with their hearts leaping.

It is 6.15 a.m., they are going in again and they are just ten minutes to target.

'This is it,' the loady yells back down the long body of the chopper. Most of the men cannot hear what he is saying above all the noise, but they know anyway. The expression on his face says it all.

'THIS IS IT. We're going in for real this time.'

No sooner has the loady finished speaking than the men on board the Chinooks start going crazy, pounding on the sides of the chopper with their fists, smashing their helmeted heads into the guy in front of them, yelling and screaming – all in an effort to relieve some of the tension and get the adrenalin really pumping for the assault.

'YEAH! YEAH! YEAH! YEAH! YAAAAAH! WE'RE GOIN' IN!'

'FUCKIN' A!'

'LET'S FUCKIN' GET IT ON!'

'GO, D SQUADRON, FUCKIN' GO!'

As the three Chinooks roar down the Rokel Creek at 160 mph in line abreast, their wheels are all but skimming the water's surface, scattering the river mists as they pass. There is the wild rush of wind through the open windows, with a blur of water, sky and trees all around them. The men are being thrown from side to side, as each giant chopper follows the contours of the river bed, hugging its twisting course through the trees.

The lead chopper has its rear ramp open now, and the men standing there in the pounding backdraught of the slipstream catch sight of reed beds flashing past directly below them, among the swirling river mists. There are crocodiles scrambling off sandbanks into the swamp at the river's edge, startled by the deafening roar of the airborne beasts above them. *It is like a sign for the coming mission*, the watching soldiers are thinking. *We are jumping into a crocodile-infested swamp. And woe betide any of the fuckers who don't get out of our way.*

The loady is counting down the time to target now, signalling each passing minute to the men behind him. As they reach the three-minute mark, he holds up three fingers, and the uproar in the chopper dies down, to be replaced by a silent, icy calm. Each man is preparing himself for the task before him, running through the assault plan one last time in his mind: his unit's overall objectives, his fire team's specific targets and LOE, and his own personal responsibilities.

This is it. No turning back now. They are going in.

They hit the two-minute mark, some five miles out from the rebels' base, and the first Chinook, Sierra One, starts to ease off on the throttle, the rest of the air armada following its lead. As the jungle clearing of the base comes into sight, straddling the Rokel Creek, Sierra One swerves hard left heading towards the northern end of Gberi Bana. The second Chinook comes roaring in directly after it, veering towards the southern end of the village. The third Chinook, packed with men from 1 Para, swings hard right across the water towards the opposite, southern river bank, where the Paras will be going into action at Magbeni. Suddenly, Sierra One and Sierra Two are over the scrub at the edge of the village and then flaring out over the buildings, as the pilots search for the LZs and the rope-down points. D Squadron are at the open windows now, guns at the ready, eyes searching in the mists below them for targets, as the first men prepare to jump.

As the leading two Chinooks swoop in low over the treetops, Lassie, Mat and the other men of the SAS obs team have the hostage house covered with their weapons, less than thirty yards away. Any sign of life, any movement from the West Side Boys, any hint of trouble, and they will be up and at them. Suddenly, there is the deafening howl of the belt-fed chain guns roaring into life above them, as the two Chinooks begin pounding the village with their machine-gun fire. The Chinooks' loadies are doubling as door gunners now, and they are targeting the rebels' HMG positions on the corners of the buildings – to stop them firing back at the choppers and blasting them out of the sky.

As the giant choppers flare to a hover, they let off spectacular clouds of chaff. This is normally used to confuse an enemy heat-seeking missile. But in this case, the pilots rain it down on the rebel village, to add a spectacular edge to the aerial assault. Now that the choppers are over the rebel positions there is nothing covert about the assault any more, and the aim is to hit the rebels hard with as much firepower and wizardry as possible, to cause maximum shock, confusion and fear. In doing so, they hope to make a coordinated, concerted rebel defence of the hostage house all but impossible.

The pilot of Sierra One, the southern chopper, searches for a stationary marker now, a reference point on the ground over which to hold his chopper steady while the first men rope down. But the only thing that he can spot in the long grass of the village clearing is a rebel soldier, the first to emerge from one of the buildings. He is staring up at the chopper open-mouthed and rooted to the spot with fear. The pilot manages to keep stationary on the rebel soldier for a few seconds, and the men of Fire Team 1 – the hostage-rescue team – go down the fast ropes at exactly 6.25 a.m.

As they do so, their fellow soldiers in the Chinook above them spot half a dozen rebels come charging out of the White House – the assault forces' code name for Foday Kallay's house. They are racing across the clear ground to get to the hostage house before Fire Team 1 can do so. From the open windows of the chopper there is a series of muzzle flashes, and at the same time the hidden SAS obs team opens up on the rebels from the jungle. Before they can get to the hostage house, all six of the rebels go down – and none will be getting up again.

Taking aim from the Chinook's open window, Frank Ray, one of the SBS lads, fires three 40mm grenades through the front veranda of the White House, to deter any more rebels from making a run for the hostages. It disappears in a gout of smoke and flame, concrete supports collapsing under the force of the explosions, bringing the veranda roof crashing down with them. As two rebels come tearing out of the smoking ruins, he puts another 40mm grenade into the ground at their feet, and both men are blown into the air by the force of the explosion.

Fire Team 1 hits the ground running now, and the six men race the thirty yards or so across to the hostage house, yelling and kicking in the front door as they do so. In seconds, they're inside the building. There is a series of flashes and loud explosions from the corridor and the side rooms, smoke billowing from the shattered doorway and the windows, followed by the controlled *crack-crack-crack* of gunfire.

But as Fire Team 2 prepares to rope in, the rebel soldier that the pilot is using as his marker suddenly goes down, disappearing from view in the long grass. *Fuck*, the pilot curses. Some silly bastard has shot him, and so he has lost his marker. As he fights to keep the aircraft steady while searching for an alternative marker, the massive downdraught from the two straining rotors starts tearing the roofs off the nearby buildings. Sheets of corrugated iron go spinning through the air, along with billowing clouds of grass thatch, and beams and planks go crashing down on to the rebel occupants still inside. Without some reference point over which to hold his aircraft stationary, the chopper will be skewing about like crazy, the ropes dragging and jerking around, making it all but impossible for the remaining fire teams to get safely down on to the ground. Finally, he locates a blackened tree stump in the centre of the village clearing, and the rest of the fire teams are given the Go! Go! Go!

Barely twenty seconds after the hostage-rescue team have hit the ground, a breathless voice comes over the radio net.

'Sierra One Zero. Hostage safe! Repeat, hostage safe.' It is Captain Dan Temper, the leader of the hostage-rescue team, and he is sounding elated but calm.

'Sierra One Zero, this is Sierra Control, how many safe, over?' It is the unflappable voice of the OC, Pete Cutgood, radioing in from HQ at Waterloo Camp.

'Six British safe. One Sierra Leonean still to locate, over.'

'Good work, Sierra One Zero. Stay with them.'

The SAS obs team spots more rebels stumbling forth from their buildings now, dressed in nothing but their underpants. Half a dozen of them start firing wildly at the Chinooks with their AK47s – emptying whole magazines skywards, with no attempt to aim – but most are just gazing dumbly at the two massive aircraft suspended in the sky above them. And then suddenly, they are hit by a wall of fire from the obs team in the jungle, and from Fire Team 2 as they hit the ground and engage the enemy.

For the two-hundred-odd wakening rebels, this is shock and awe now: the pilot struggling to keep the huge aircraft stationary, as it bucks and skews about above them, turbines whining and screaming like some terrible animal hunting them down; the massive rotor blades blasting a suffocating downdraught on to the village huts – iron roofs, doors, windows being blown in and torn away by the furious wind – like the fiery breath of some avenging beast of the air; the chaff firing off a hundred blinding flares in some dizzying, bewitching firework display, a miracle of the white man's rage and retribution; chain guns roaring and spitting and chewing up the village in front of them, a clattering cloud of spent shells spinning into the air like a dark swarm of avenging locusts; screaming killers leaning out of every window, guns spitting fire, raining down death on the village below them. It is as if the vengeance of some terrible, alien God is being visited on Gberi Bana, and the West Side Boys – stumbling from their sleep in shock and terror – have nowhere that they can see to run to, and to hide.

Less than half a mile away across the waters of the Rokel Creek, the fleet of four gunships are pounding the West Side Boys' positions at Magbeni. As the Mi-24 roars back in for its second attack run, Nellis catches sight of a brilliant yellow stab of Christmas tree-shaped flame below him – the rebels' ZPU-2 is spitting fire skywards, searching, groping for a target. A twin-barrelled Soviet anti-aircraft gun, the ZPU is a serious threat to the gunship. To the left of him, there are the pink, pencil-thin lines of flame from 14.5mm anti-aircraft guns cutting through the early-morning mists, also seeking their aerial kill. The rebel gunners have well and truly woken up to the assault; but their gunfire has also betrayed their location to the hunting gunships.

As tracer loops up towards him, Nellis tears the aircraft round in a screaming turn, and zeroes in on to the target. Levelling out, he fires a salvo of eight 57mm rockets, and the building next to the

ZPU disappears in a sheet of flame. As debris is hurled into the air by the force of the explosion, Nellis can see rebel soldiers scattering in all directions, silhouetted against the flames. The chopper roars in low over Magbeni, the rear gunners going into action on the targets below them, their GPMGs chewing into the village. To the left and right of his Mi-24, the Lynx attack helicopters are also pounding their targets now.

But one of those choppers is already in serious trouble.

Sierra Seven, one of the two army Lynx MK7, has led the air assault over Magbeni. However, even as it made its attack run up the Rokel Creek, Sierra Seven suffered complete communications failure. The pilot had no choice but to pull back and give Sierra Six, his fellow Lynx attack helicopter, the lead.

With complete communications failure, the pilot is now faced with a horrible dilemma. If his aircraft remains in the assault, then it will do so blind of all communications – from the ground forces, from the other six choppers in the air armada, and from all elements of command and control. To remain flying risks great danger of a blue-on-blue incident on the ground, or even an air collision between the various choppers of the air assault. To pull out of the assault deprives the Paras of this attack chopper's vital suppressing firepower.

Making a snap decision, the pilot of Sierra Seven decides to keep flying. He passes word around his aircrew to keep vigilant for all other aircraft, and friendly forces on the ground.

It is less than two minutes into the assault now, and in both Gberi Bana and Magbeni, battle has truly been joined.

A RUDE AWAKENING

Far better is it to dare mighty things, to win glorious triumphs, even though chequered by failure, than to rank with those poor spirits who neither enjoy much nor suffer much, because they live in the grey twilight that knows no victory nor defeat.

– Theodore Roosevelt

DAY seventeen would be the hostages' third Sunday in captivity. But very early in the morning, they are jerked awake in the grey pre-dawn light by what sounds like the faint throb of helicopters. The men haven't been sleeping that deeply anyway, for understandable reasons. As they strain their ears, there is definitely the distant thud-thud-thud of rotor blades reaching them on the chill jungle air. It sounds like several helicopters bearing fast upriver towards the village. The initial fear of the men is that it must be the forces of the UN coming in with their gunships for a revenge attack on the West Side Boys. There is no way they can conceive that this might be the SAS assault force: flying in with guns blazing on to target is just not the way they do things. And if it *is* a UN attack it is a fearful prospect: either they'll get gunned down by the choppers, or the West Side Boys will take things out on them, once the attack is over.

'Any of youse hear what I hear?' Ranger Gaunt croaks, almost too scared to make any noise in case he wakes their captors.

'Choppers,' comes a muttered reply.

'Who the feck d'you think it is?' The Ranger's voice is laced with fear.

'Keep it down, lads,' the Major hisses under his breath. 'It sounds like helis coming upriver. More than one, that's for sure. Keep your heads down, lads. We don't know who they are, yet, but we need to be ready for anything.'

'But who it is, sir?' Ranger Gaunt hisses back, with rising panic. 'The feckin' UN? After revenge on these fuckers? Whatever, it's bad news for us, isn't it, sir?'

'Look, lad, just stay calm,' the Major reassures him, quietly. 'All we know for sure is that it sounds like a bunch of choppers inbound. It could even be just an overflight, not even headed here. We'll just have to cool it, lad, and wait and see what happens.'

'What time d'you reckon it is, sir?' Ranger Rowell asks, anxiously.

'Not sure exactly, lad. But it's bloody early. Pre-dawn, I'd say.'

'Maybe it's a dawn assault, sir,' Ranger Gaunt cuts in, in an excited whisper. 'You know, by *our boys*. Couldn't it be, sir? A dawn assault, sir?'

'Could be, lad, but there's no guarantees,' the Major replies, evenly. 'My guess is it's going to be good news for us – that it's going to be our boys on a rescue mission – but just keep it down, lad, and stay calm. All right?'

As the six men strain their ears, trying to work out just where the airborne force is headed, they hear the noise of the choppers growing first louder and then gradually fading away into the distance. Eventually, the faint throb of their rotors disappears altogether. The choppers must have approached so far up the river, and then turned around and left in the direction in which they've come. None of the men can make any sense of it at all.

'Well, what the feck was that all about, then?' Ranger Rowell grunts under his breath.

'Maybe it was the UN, and they sort of lost their bottle, like,' Ranger Gaunt whispers, grinning nervously at his mate. 'It wouldn't be the first time, now would it?'

'At least none of those bastards seem to have woken up,' remarks the Major, jerking his thumb over his shoulder in the direction of the guards outside the door. 'That's one good thing.'

'Aye . . . Sentry? What's a sentry?' quips Ranger Gaunt.

'Like I said, lad, couldn't organise a piss-up in a brewery,' the Major replies, a wry smile playing across his face.

The six men settle down to rest again. It is so early that even the bloody camp cockerel – which normally wakes them regular as clockwork at 6:30 a.m. – has yet to start making its dreadful early-morning racket. But no sooner have they put their heads down than they become aware of a similar noise of a force of choppers, which seems to be coming back again. Only this time, the dull *thud-thud* of their rotors it is getting rapidly louder, as the unidentified air armada races upriver towards the village.

'*Jesus!*' hisses one of Rangers, propping himself up on one elbow. 'They're coming back in again, and feckin' fast this time. *Oh shite.* Those fuckers are bound to wake up this time.'

'Shall we get ready at the door, sir? Just in case they try and come for us?'

'There's no time, lads,' the Major replies, with urgency, already straining his voice to make himself heard above the thunderous noise of the approaching air armada. 'Just get your bloody heads down and stay on the floor.'

As the six men take cover in the corners of the room, they hear the first chopper roar in low over the rooftops. Suddenly, there is the deafening high-pitched whine of its turboprops right above them and the blast of the downdraught, and then all hell breaks loose, as the heavy machine guns on the chopper start opening up and chewing into the village. The six men press their faces down into the dirt floor, with their hands over their heads. It doesn't sound like a rescue attempt: it sounds like a full-blooded attack. They are so worried it is the UN gunships on a revenge mission that they don't even recognise the noise of their own, giant Chinook helicopters.

'Oh for feck's sake, don't let the feckin' thing come over here,' a terrified Ranger Gaunt starts yelling above all the noise.

'Fuck off out of here, why don't youse just FUCK OFF!' Ranger Rowell screams up at the chopper.

But the Rangers' voices are all but lost in the ear-splitting roar of gunfire. A fearsome barrage is coming down on the village now, and the six men are desperately trying to take cover and hide. Incredibly, there still seems to have been no answering fire from the West Side Boys.

The men can hear one of the choppers flaring out now, as it prepares to land nearby. Almost simultaneously, there is a deafening tearing of metal and a splintering of wood above them, as the downdraught from the Chinook rips the roof right off their hut and whisks it away. Suddenly, the six hostages are lying with their heads pressed into the dirt trying to take cover, but with their roof open to the sky above them. They are sitting ducks for any of the gunmen in the choppers above them now.

All of this takes place in just a few, frenzied seconds. But in the minds of the Rangers everything is playing in slow motion, as if they are in a dream. They see mothers, brothers, the friendly streets of Belfast, scenes from childhood, their passing-out parade as cadets for the Royal Irish Rangers – the whole of life is flashing before their eyes. They are cringing, flinching, trying to shrink away from the shattering impact of gunfire from above that they are certain is coming, expecting at any moment to feel bullets drilling into their exposed backs. Or if not that, then to see their deranged captors come bursting into their room, with murder smouldering in their eyes.

But instead, the men hear the distinct *crack-crack-crack* of gunshots *inside* the house now, very close to them, and in a split second there is a boot smashing at their door. *Oh shite, shite, shite, SHITE. THIS IS IT. Oh, make it the feckin' SAS, Lord. Make it THE BOYS.*

There is a sharp splintering of wood, as the door caves in on its hinges, and suddenly the Major is yelling at the top of his voice: 'BRITISH SOLDIERS! BRITISH SOLDIERS! BRITISH SOLDIERS!'

And then there is a familiar, authorative answering cry from a figure standing silhouetted in the doorway. 'British Army! British Army! Stay down! Stay down! Stay on the floor.'

The man, the saviour, the knight, the warrior, takes a step into their room now, and glances round at the men. 'Right. Listen up,' he says, in a voice laced with urgency, straining to be heard over the din of battle. 'Are you all here?'

'All six British,' the Major replies. 'All except the Sierra Leonean, Corporal Mousa.'

'Where the hell is your Corporal Mousa, then?'

'Out the front door. Turn left. Large white building.'

'Right. *The White House.* Stay down. And here, take this,' the man orders, handing the Major a pistol. 'But no heroics. Only use it if you have to. And if you see any of our guys, keep it hidden. You don't want to be seen with a weapon, OK? Now, I'll be back in a jiffy with your Mousa.'

And then he is gone.

'Feckin' A! Feckin' A! FECKIN' A!' the Rangers are screaming inside their heads. 'It's *THE BOYS*.'

Nothing has ever sounded so sweet to the six hostages as those few words spoken by that British Special Forces soldier as he crashed through the splintered remains of their door to rescue them.

While all six hostages have Belfast accents, this guy is definitely a true Brit. Officer class, by the sounds of things. He is a cool customer too, seeming completely unruffled by whatever combat he's just been through in order to get to their room. But the noise of the firefight outside is reaching deafening proportions now. The West Side Boys have clearly woken up to the British assault at last, and the fightback has begun.

One vital (and totally unexpected) advantage that the assault force now has is the blown-in-roof factor: scores of sleeping rebels have been trapped inside their huts, as the powerful downdraught of the descending Chinooks has caved the roofs in on top of them. Over the thump of grenades and the juddering clatter and roar of machine-gun fire, the hostages can now hear their Special Forces man at the front door to their building, shouting orders to what must be the rest of his fire team.

'Grey! How far down are you? One missing, the Sierra Leonean, Mousa. He's in the White House. Take Geordie and go fetch.'

The hostages hear him race back down the central corridor of their building to the back entrance.

'Gaza, mate! All present but one. Geordie and Grey are on it. Next building up, the White House. Watch it. And if you see any of those bastards, put a bullet in their brains.'

CHICKEN RUN

People sleep peaceably in their beds at night only because rough men stand ready to do violence on their behalf.

> – George Orwell, in Tom Clancy's *The Teeth of the Tiger*

THERE is tracer coming up at the choppers now, as Sierra Two, the Chinook in the north of Gberi Bana, flares out to let off its assault force. The downdraught from the Chinook's giant twin rotor blades blasts into the village huts, collapsing walls and blowing more roofs clean off, making the rebels easy targets for the soldiers on the chopper above them. A few rounds of rebel gunfire slam into the side of the Chinook, but no serious damage is done. It is mostly light machine-gun fire only: the rebels have been caught so totally by surprise that they've failed to fire up any of their heavy machine guns, before the Chinook's chain guns blast them to oblivion.

As the Chinook touches down and the first fire team piles off, the small force of Paras left on board the chopper is putting down a barrage of covering fire from the open windows. Ten seconds later the last fire team hits the deck, and the Chinook lifts off, leaving these soldiers facing an unknown destiny. But this is the point in the operation where dog sees rabbit, and dog is most definitely going to go for it. It is at this moment that Operation Certain Death has become Judgement Day for the West Side Boys.

For a moment, Sierra Two struggles to gain altitude, the giant aircraft tearing full throttle skywards, and then it puts its head down, turning towards the west. It is 6.27 a.m. as the chopper starts speeding back out towards Freetown.

As the two Chinooks had come flying in over Gberi Bana, the SAS obs team on the ground had kept up a running commentary on the radio net, guiding the chopper crews down on to their targets. It wasn't until they had flared out over their landing zones that the first West Side Boys had been spotted, running from their huts. As the chain guns on the sides of the choppers had kicked into action, tearing up the ground and knocking some of the smaller trees in half, they had spread terror among the village. While a dozen-odd rebels had stood their ground to fight, most had made a run for what they thought was the safety of the forest. But then the hidden SAS obs team had opened up on them from their position in the jungle – and so the rebels were suddenly being hit from all sides.

All seventy men of the assault force are safely on the ground now, and the mind of each and every one of them is crystal clear. There is no fear now, no doubt any more, and there is nothing to live for other than killing the other guy first and staying alive. The training is kicking in and all the assault rehearsals are paying off, and thoughts of being wounded or dying just don't figure. But there is one hell of a lot of fire being directed at them now, far more than expected, either coming from village buildings or the jungle nearby (to where scores of the rebels have already fled).

This group of rebels is now regrouping in the jungle just to the east of the village, and they are coming back at the assault force with everything they've got. For several minutes, the northern assault force is pinned down on its LZ. The men burrow on their stomachs into the long, emerald-green bush grass on the clearing outside Cambodia's house. But grass doesn't stop bullets. There is no real cover to be had, and the rebels have a clear territorial advantage – the shelter of the jungles. The assault force is in a badly exposed position now, and the rebels should be able to make mincemeat out of them, picking off the British soldiers one by one. There are around two hundred rebel fighters in the village. Between the obs team and the gunfire from the Chinooks, maybe a dozen or so have already been taken care of. But the remainder have now woken up to the attack and grabbed their guns – which means the men of the assault force pinned down in the bush grass are heavily outnumbered.

But they concentrate their minds – blocking out any feelings of being horribly exposed and vulnerable – and focus on spotting the enemy muzzle flashes in the jungle. They take careful aim at just below the flash, in the darkness beneath the jungle canopy, and squeeze the trigger. A short burst of three rounds – 'one, two – stop' they are counting – and the muzzle of the rebel gunner is silenced. Each man wastes no time now; he presumes the rebel has taken a bullet and gone down. He takes his focus off that target and searches for the next, among the early-morning mists still clinging to the trees. The enemy has no face yet; he cannot see the man behind the gun spurting jagged flashes of fire in the forest shadows, and that makes it all the easier to kill him.

The braver – or more foolhardy – of the rebels start stepping out of the jungle with their AK47s held above their heads, letting off on automatic, and spraying whole magazines in the direction of the British soldiers. And then they duck back into the trees again, but only if they're lucky and don't get shot first. It is loud and dramatic and there is one hell of a lot of ordnance flying about, but hardly any of it is on target. The rebels must be panicked, totally spooked, the men of the assault force are thinking, or maybe this is just how they always fight, in such a chaotic, badly targeted way.

As the rebels spray off whole magazines like this, it gives the men of D Squadron ample time to locate them, sight the individual target and fire. Several of the West Side Boys are hit, spinning round and keeling over, their weapons still firing on automatic as they go down. The rebels are acting as if they think they are Rambo or something, but they are just being torn apart. A dozen or more never even make it back into the cover of the trees. And yet individual rebel fighters keep on attacking in this way, seeming unable to believe that they too will be hit and taken down.

Somewhere in the back of the British soldiers' minds – amid the red mist of combat, and the smell and the speed and the raw noise of battle – these men know that they are in a certain state of bliss now. For once in their lives, they feel liberated from all other worldly concerns, apart from the pure kill or be killed of combat. And in that sense this is the single, most intense experience of living that these men have ever known. The men of D Squadron feel cleansed, reborn almost, momentarily washed clean of all their sins.

The sixteen grand's worth of debt, the grinding mortgage, the recent fight with the wife, the daughter's missed birthday – none of this matters a damn any more. Faced with the pure white fury of the raging assault, the animal aggression of mortal combat, even a suitcase full of a million dollars would be totally worthless. The very essence of existence has been distilled into one simple, relentless priority: winning this duel with death. And until it is over, fathers, mothers, wives and children simply do not figure any more.

These men will make the most of this pure feeling: it is likely to be the one and only time in their lives that they feel this way. They will rescue the hostages; they will kill the rebels; they will waste this village; and they will fight the good fight, the hardest fight ever in their lives, shoulder to shoulder with their brothers in arms, and they will win through.

There is a momentary lull in the fighting in the northern end of the village. Maybe the rebels are pausing to reload, as they've certainly been firing off enough rounds to need to do so. And suddenly, Fire Team 7 are up and charging through the elephant grass towards Cambodia's house. Within seconds, they have kicked their way into the hostages' old residence. As Gerry Birt leads his team through the front doorway, he spots the unmistakable figure of Colonel GS trying to make a getaway out the back entrance. That bastard gave him such shit at the hostage-negotiation meetings that Gerry would recognise him anywhere.

And Gerry's on to him. *It's payback time*, Gerry thinks, as he races after the rebel Colonel.

At the back entrance to the house, he drops to one knee and takes aim with his assault rifle, only to notice that GS is wearing one of the Rangers' flak jackets. So he can't put a bullet in his torso, to drop him, Gerry thinks, grimly. *It's three to the head then.* He squeezes the trigger and watches Colonel GS's skull explode, before he does a somersault into the bush and stays down. Gerry makes a mental note to return later, if there's time, to retrieve the Ranger's flak jacket. Those young lads have been through enough shit as it is, he's thinking: the least they deserve is to get some of their kit back.

In the southern end of the village, Fire Team 2, led by the Scottish Monster, have hit the ground off the fast ropes and sprinted across the short distance to the White House, their key first target. Suddenly, there is a boot smashing at the door, flash-bang stun grenades hurled in as the wood splinters, and two men are piling inside, one, the Kiwi with his Diemaco at the shoulder, ready, primed to kill. Jimmy, with a Minimi light machine gun (capable of putting out a thousand rounds per minute – although at that rate of fire the weapon would probably melt the barrel!), follows, staying back, giving cover to his mate, searching in the smoke and the noise and the confusion for signs of rebel resistance, for targets, for the enemy.

There, in a corner of the first room, a figure crouches with an arm raising an AK47, half hidden by a line of washing strung from one corner of the room to the other. And suddenly the Kiwi is on to it, a double tap, two bullets to the body and one to the head, and the figure drops to the floor. Behind him in the corridor now, a deafening burst from Jimmy's Minimi, as two rebels – stumbling in shock from a room further down the building – are taken out before they can decide either to flee or to open fire. On, on, on into the next room, a splintering of wood and a screaming of raw aggression, with doors ripped off their hinges and a rebel fighter, gun muzzle blasting at the British soldiers, is taken down in the pre-dawn shadows before he can find his target.

The men are one minute into the assault now, and yet still the West Side Boys are barely awake. As the rebels stumble about in shock and confusion, it is clear that there has been no formal sentry or lookout system in place at Gberi Bana. Those caught in the White House come staggering from their beds, groping for their weapons in the darkness, desperately trying to shake off the smog of sleep as they do so. As they lurch into the corridor from their rooms, they seem shocked and disorientated – almost as if they cannot believe what is happening. Almost as if they never really believed that the British Forces might be coming for them. And by then it is too late: Fire Team 2 are already on to them.

But the strangest thing of all is the chicken.

As the Monster, the Kiwi and the others fight their way into the White House, Jimmy can't help noticing that a white chicken is running in after them, on their very heels, almost like it is part of the fire team. Each of the men in Boat Troop carries a little plastic rubber duck with him – sort of the troop talisman, for obvious reasons (Boat Troop = inflatables on water = rubber duck). So Jimmy, of course, notices the chicken. And as each of the rooms is cleared in turn, the chicken runs in after then, as if it's checking whether they've done a good job or not. Quick look round the smoking remains of the first room and then the chicken is off again, down the corridor and into the next. And then the next and the next, and so on and so forth, close on Brad and the Kiwi's heels.

Fakin' Chicken Run or what, Jimmy is thinking to himself, grinning.

He's keeping one eye on the corridor inside the hostage house and the other out front, sweeping the ground with his Minimi, in case any more rebels should appear. Yet at the same time, he can't help watching the fucking chicken. *What's Chicken Run doing?* he's thinking to himself – for as soon as that name came into his head it has stuck. *What's she after, a place on the fucking chopper? Someone, get Chicken Run a gun!* Rubber duck as their talisman, and now they've got a fucking white chicken going into action alongside them.

No doubt about it, this is weird.

What does it all mean? Jimmy's thinking. Is it a good sign? A bad omen? Or is it some spooky, voodoo shit? He knows that white chickens mean heavy magic in the temples of the voodoo gods. A live chicken is sacrificed, cut open so the voodoo priest can read the future in its entrails. Something like that, anyways. Jimmy decides that it is a good sign, and that whatever else happens, he'll find that fuckin' chicken at the end of the mission – *when it's all over* – and she'll be coming out on the chopper with the rest of them. Any chicken that's brave enough to go into action alongside his fire team is good enough to be an honorary member of the squadron. *Fuck it, he might even take her back to Hereford.* After all, the Regiment has a goat for a mascot, living up at the camp.

So why not Chicken Run, too?

Barely two minutes into the assault, and the White House has been declared secure. Three rebels are confirmed dead, and Mamma Kallay, the Voodoo Queen, is trussed up like a fat sow on the floor. She has been slightly injured in the assault, and taken prisoner by Fire Team 2. But her husband, the elusive rebel leader, is nowhere to be seen. The hostage house has also been declared secure, with Fire Team 1 holding firm there. After clearing the White House, Fire Team 2 starts pushing north, aiming for the buildings and the huts on the track leading up towards Colonel Cambodia's house. And Fire Team 3 have been moving east, taking out the hospital house and on. But as the teams try to advance further into the village, they start meeting fierce resistance.

Only Fire Team 4 has a fairly easy run of things, moving south through the scattering of huts leading down towards the river, the six men racing in to clear the buildings as they do so. They push as far as the banks of the Rokel Creek, leaving several injured rebels behind them. Their mission is to secure and hold the area now, keeping careful watch on the opposite river bank, in case the rebels try to sneak any reinforcements across the Rokel Creek to Gberi Bana. They will remain in position here, taking cover along the river bank, unless called to do otherwise.

From their defensive points on the north bank of the Rokel Creek, Fire Team 4 watches with grim satisfaction as the Lynx attack helicopters rake the ground across the other side of the river with their heavy machine guns, following up with TOW anti-tank missiles. As there are no British hostages being held in Magbeni, the assault plan calls for as much fury and firepower as possible to be unleashed on the rebel positions there.

The Mi-24 gunship is weaving and swooping just above the jungle canopy, flying so low at times that it disappears from the watching fire team's line of sight. The low, throaty roar of its Gatling guns carries clearly across the water, followed by the spectacular blast of a salvo of eight 57mm rockets being fired from the chopper's weapons pods. A split second later, fire and smoke erupts from the jungle, as chunks of debris and sheets of torn metal are thrown into the air by the force of the explosions. Smoke from the burning village begins to drift across the water, mingling with the early-morning mist still clinging to the river.

Neall Ellis's Mi-24 gunship quickly settles into a rhythm of hunting and attack, as he keeps the aircraft flying at barely above treetop level. Either the nose gunner will spot rebel movement below, or one of the side gunners will report something similar on the intercom. Nellis then takes a bearing, levels out on to target, and hits it with either a 57mm rocket salvo, or the Gatling gun – depending on target priorities. With thirty-two rockets per pod, Nellis is capable of eight salvos, before having to return to Freetown to rearm (it would take him the best part of forty-five minutes to do so, by which time most of the action at Magbeni should be over). As the chopper turns across the target, the side gunners follow up, raking the ground with bursts from their GPMGs.

Flying at 160 knots (around 185 mph) and roughly thirty feet above the jungle canopy, terrain flashes past at dizzying speed. It takes all of Nellis's concentration and flying skill to keep the aircraft airborne, process radio messages incoming on his earphones, and act accordingly to engage with enemy targets and aim and fire the rocket salvos. And as the jungle canopy is dotted with the odd 'emergent' tree – a forest giant that towers some thirty to forty feet above the surrounding treetops – one missed call, a split second's lack of concentration, can so easily prove fatal.

There are two, compelling reasons for such low-level flying tactics. Firstly, Sierra Leone's rebels are known to have acquired several SAM7s (Soviet shoulder-held surface-to-air-missiles). There is no reason why the West Side Boys shouldn't have got their hands on a couple of them. Although the Mi-24 is supposed to have anti-missile jamming equipment, all the controls in the aircraft are marked in Russian Cyrillic script, and it is never that easy to tell which switch turns the system on and off. It is far better to keep low and fast, so as to avoid the missile operators acquiring a firm target. On the ground below them, the tree cover keeps the low-flying chopper hidden until the last possible moment. It emerges out of the trees as a blur, flying fast and low across the patch of sky above, providing little or no time to locate the target and fire.

And the second reason to keep low and fast is to avoid the sort of heavy ordnance that the rebels' ZPU can put up at them. There are also scores of RPG7s in the hands of the rebels – a weapon whose dramatic noise and smoke makes it one of their favourites. A few weeks earlier, Nellis had received a report that an Indian Air Force Alouette helicopter gunship – unarmed and in distinctive white UN livery – had been targeted by RPG fire. It was on a recce flight over rebel territory and had spotted a column of rebel troops moving through the jungle. The rebels had stopped and put down their weapons to wave at the helicopter, and the Alouette had paused to hover, so the UN crew could wave back at them. As they did so, three RPGs had shot out of the bush, heading straight for the tiny French chopper. The rebels – very likely high on their afternoon drugs and alcohol – had missed. But even so, it had demonstrated that RPGs were a real threat. By sticking low and fast, the aircrews know that the rebels will find it almost impossible to target them.

Nevertheless, one of the choppers now in action over Magbeni is already in serious trouble, although it hasn't been hit by ground fire. Sierra Six, one of the three Lynx helicopters, has lost one of its twin turbines. This is the Lynx that underwent the overnight engine refit on HMS *Argyll*, and it is that turbine that seems to have failed. The pilot is painfully aware of what will happen if his other engine malfunctions or is hit: his chopper will go down either in the jungles around Magbeni or into the Rokel Creek itself, the two main attack runs that they are making over the rebel positions.

Needing a snap decision, the pilot of Sierra Six chooses to keep the Lynx gunship flying and remain in combat, despite the obvious dangers of doing so. By the end of this day's fighting, he will somehow have completed his mission and coaxed his chopper back to Freetown. The pilot and aircrew of this helicopter will be hailed as some of the true heroes of the assault over Magbeni.

In the southern end of Gberi Bana, the fire teams are pinned down now, finding it hard to advance beyond the limits of the village clearing. Heavy firing is coming from a patch of forest some fifty yards to the north-east of them. Long bursts of AK47 fire are raking the ground all around the beleaguered fire teams, punctuated by the *whoosh-crash* of incoming RPG7s. None of the rebel fire seems particularly accurate, but it is heavy and sustained. There must be some sixty or seventy rebels holed up in the jungle there, to account for all the incoming. Fire Teams 2 and 3 have taken cover as best they can, feeling particularly exposed, and they are unable to advance to secure their objectives.

All together, there are about forty-eight men of the SAS on the ground now, along with twenty-four of their SBS colleagues – some seventy men in all. Half that number is in the northern part of the village, half in the southern sector. As soon as the northern assault force had piled off their Chinook, they had been pinned down by rebel gunfire. But now they are able to report on the radio net that they are less tied down, more mobile. They agree to make a fighting advance from the clearing outside Cambodia's house, down the village track in the direction of the river, to link up with the southern assault force. Between the northern and southern halves of the assault force there lies the patch of forest from where the West Side Boys are now mounting their stiffest resistance. The plan is to trap the rebels in a pincer movement, hitting them from both sides.

The jungle from where the rebels are counter-attacking is on the opposite side of the track to the village football pitch. After the six British hostages, this is the second most vital objective for the assault. It is crucial that the football ground be made safe as a landing area for the choppers. It had been ruled out as a LZ for the assault force to go in on, because it is too far from both the hostage house and the main body of the rebels. But it is an ideal LZ for the hostage extraction and any casevacs that might be necessary.

Bringing the giant Chinooks in to land in the middle of the firefight is going to be tough enough as it is. The assault force needs to take possession of the football pitch and clear the surrounding forest, in order to make it a reasonably secure LZ. The rebels now counter-attacking from the jungle will have to be dealt with. Darting from house to house, as the other members of their fire teams give covering fire, the men from Fire Teams 2 and 3 push north and east towards the patch of jungle sheltering the rebels.

Rob, one of Fire Team 3's GPMG gunners, is down on his belly on the ground now, concentrating on putting down covering fire as his mates advance. Suddenly, there is the instinctive pricking of fear in the nape of his neck. Twisting his head around, Rob finds a rebel soldier behind him with an AK47 levelled at him. *Oh fuck.* They must have missed one of the bastards among the buildings they have just cleared. The rebel is only young, and Rob reads a mixture of shock and hatred in the kid soldier's bloodshot eyes.

Lying prone as he is with the GPMG under his shoulder, Rob knows that there is no way that he can spin round in time and shoot. As the rebel boy soldier and the D Squadron veteran lock eyes, Rob is resigned to die, if that's what fate holds in store for him. But there is fear in the rebel's eyes too, real raging full-blooded terror. *Why terror?* Rob thinks. *He's the one holding the gun to my head, so why's he afraid?*

Why hasn't the silly bastard just pulled the fuckin' trigger?

Their stare holds for what seems like a lifetime – though it can only be a split second – and then the rebel thrusts his gun right into the small of Rob's back and pulls the trigger. But all that happens is an answering click. *Click.* Only click. There is no explosion, no burst of hot gases and roaring lead, no shattering of the bones at the base of the spine and splintering of vital organs. Just a dull, silent click. Maybe that's why he has been standing there for so long, with his gun levelled, but not shooting.

The silly bastard has no round in the chamber. He's out of ammo.

The look in the eyes the young West Side Boy fighter says it all now; he knows that he is out of ammo and facing a white soldier with eyes like blue fire whose gun is loaded and primed and ready. A man that he has just tried to kill. As Rob swings the big machine gun round, twisting his body as he does so, the boy rebel crumples, his body collapsing, imploding with the certainty of what is coming. He lifts his arms up, up to shield his face, to plead for the bullets not to harm him, to push death away.

But there is no answering 'click' from the GPMG.

As Rob squeezes the trigger the gun roars, once, twice, three times – each roar throwing the small hunched figure backwards and upwards as flesh tears, and blood spurts from the ragged rents torn in the body of the young rebel who didn't want to die. 'You are invincible,' Mamma Kallay had told him, as she had handed out her voodoo charms and spells. 'The bullets will run off you like water.' *Oh no they won't*, the boy soldier is thinking, as he falls to the earth in slow motion, his body hitting the ground with a soft thud. *Not when the bullets come from the avenging wrath of the gun of the white man.*

Some of the blood of the dying kid splatters on to Rob's uniform.

They had a job to do Rob told himself, *and he was sure as hell going to do it.* But this time the enemy had a face, fear and sweat and flesh and blood, a life before him that now would never be led. But there is no time to think about this, no time to dwell on it, no time to wonder what might have been. It was kill or be killed, and the silly fucker was out of ammo. Otherwise, it would now be him, Rob, lying there with his lifeblood draining into the damp sand. He had no choice. And the firefight is still raging all around him.

And the men of his troop need him.

Rob turns away from the dead kid soldier, pulls the reassuring bulk of the GPMG back into his shoulder again, aims for the flashes under the trees and starts firing. So much easier to shoot them when there are no faces to the enemy, so much more like a harmless video game, so much less real than the intimacy of point-blank killing. By now, there are the bodies of several dead rebels on the ground in Gberi Bana, but a lot more must have gone down in the forest.

And one of those corpses is the boy that Rob has just killed.

The haunting memory of the frightened kid crumpling before him will be with Rob for the rest of his days. And the dull, hollow thud of his lacerated body hitting the damp earth. What hell had that kid already lived through? What sort of life had he had up until now? What sort of childhood? What horrors, what traumas, what sick perverse machinations of human minds, had been visited on him by the rebels, by adults, by people who should have known far better? At night, had the boy soldier cried for a long-lost family?

Had he wept over sweet dreams of home?

It is Rob's first, definite kill. *Ever.* After several years in D Squadron. He knows that he should feel elated, transfixed by the glory of the moment, by the knowledge that he has been blooded and can join that exclusive club of men who have killed. Instead, he just feels sickened. Instead, he just wants to pack up his guns and go home. He pulls the GPMG closer to his torso now, and the hot barrel bucks and spits fire as he aims for the targets in the trees. It is reassuring. *It helps blank the doubt from his mind.* But at the same time there is an agonised dialogue going on inside his head, one of accusal and counter-accusal, and Rob can't seem to get it to stop, or to find a way to make it leave him alone.

All he wants is to do his duty and keep fighting, but the voice won't let him.

It was a fuckin' kid, the voice keeps screaming in his head. *Yeah, but the fuckin' kid had a gun*, comes Rob's reply. *One day your son will be that old*, comes the voice again. *Yeah, but when he is he won't be a motherfuckin' gun-toting rebel hostage-taking bastard, will he?* comes the reply. *Did the kid choose that life then, or was he just another defenceless rebel kidnap victim?* comes the voice, accusingly. *I don't know. But the kid had a gun*, comes Rob's reply again. *Yeah, and if your boy follows in his dad's footsteps he may end up packing a gun too. And then maybe someone, someday, will pump bullets into him at point-blank range*, comes the voice inside his head again. *Fuck off, just fuck off and die, fuck off and die and let me do my job*, Rob pleads with the voice. *We can talk about this later, after the battle, but not now.* And the voice comes again: *Later? You want to talk about it later? Sure. There's going to be all the time in the world. You're going to have this in your head for the rest of your existence*, it says, with finality.

It always seems to need to have the last word.

As the Chinooks had begun their second attack run on Gberi Bana, a trussed-up Corporal Mousa had woken to the noise of the approaching air armada. At first, the six rebels standing guard over him had carried on chatting among themselves. But as the noise grew louder, a worried Mousa had started thinking to himself: 'Oh fuck, what the hell's going on? These guys have threatened to kill us, so who the fuck's flying these choppers in?' Finally, the rebel guards had noticed the thud-thud-thud of the approaching choppers, and one of them, the notorious Mr Die, had gone to fetch Foday Kallay.

'Sa, we go hearing de sound of chop-chop helicopters downstream,' Mousa had heard Mr Die say.

Immediately, there had been was a commotion inside Kallay's house, with people shouting and yelling all at once. Then Foday Kallay had come out of his room to listen.

'Oh, if dese people do think they can come-come and attack us we will den kill all de whiteboy hostages and kill dese people too!' Kallay had begun to rage. 'Kill, kill, kill – kill dem all!'

As the noise of the choppers had grown louder, Corporal Mousa heard Kallay instruct his men to go tie up the British hostages and bring them to him. Half a dozen men, under the command of Mr Die, rushed off to the hostage house. But just at that moment, the skies above Gberi Bana had exploded with rolling, thunderous gunfire. A terrified Mousa could hear it chewing up Kallay's house just behind him, heavy-calibre bullets punching through the walls. Convinced that he was about to die, Mousa heard a deafening screeching sound of tearing metal, as the roof of Foday Kallay's house was literally ripped off by the chopper's downdraught. It had come crashing down behind the house, covering the veranda as it did so. But miraculously, Mousa had found that he was still alive, as the roof had landed more or less intact, trapping him underneath it.

He lay there for what felt like the best part of fifteen minutes, listening to the sounds of the Chinooks raining down death from above. Then he had heard the choppers withdrawing, after which there was only shooting on the ground. At this moment, Mousa thought that the British attack had failed and that the gunfire was the West Side Boys shooting up at the retreating choppers.

Convinced that he was now about to be executed, the Corporal struggled to free himself from his binds. He got his hands behind his back up against a piece of torn galvanised roofing, and began to saw backwards and forwards on the rope binds. The stabbing pain in his arms and shoulders was all but unbearable, but he knew this was his last chance to escape into the nearby jungle. As he struggled to be free, Mousa wondered about the fate of the British hostages. But in his heart of hearts he knew that they would have stood no chance at the hands of Mr Die and his men.

Just then, the Sierra Leonean corporal heard the faint shouts of 'Mousa! Mousa!' But his hearing was so dulled by the noise of the shooting that the shouts were barely audible. 'Mousa, Mousa!' he heard again, this time nearer and louder.

At first he feared it was the West Side Boys trying to find him. *Oh my God, this is the final onslaught*, Mousa thought to himself, as he tried to stay hidden. *They've come to finish me off.*

But when those searching for him got close enough, Mousa could tell that these were white people's voices. The way they were calling 'Mousa! Mousa!' it was British voices.

At this moment, Major Martial's advice to him of a few days before flashed into Mousa's mind. *'When our boys come in, Corporal, you're to yell as loud as you bloody well can: "British soldier! British soldier!" Strictly speaking it's not true of course, but at least that way you'll escape getting shot.'*

Remembering those words, Corporal Mousa started yelling at the top of his voice: 'British soldier! Yes, I'm here! British soldier! Mousa is here!'

At that, the calling soldiers went silent, then suddenly there was a tearing at the galvanised sheeting above him.

'Don't fucking move, or I shoot!' Mousa heard the soldier yelling as he towered above him. His white face was daubed in black and green camo warpaint, his eyes raw red with the aggression and the heat of combat. It was Grey, one of the soldiers from the hostage-rescue team, and he had his gun sticking in Mousa's face. He had a torch attached to his rifle, and he switched it on so it shone in the Sierra Leonean corporal's eyes.

'Right. What's your fuckin' NAME!' Grey demands.

'It's Mousa. Don't shoot. It's me, Mousa.'

With that, Grey grabbed Mousa by the scruff of the neck. 'AGAIN! What's your FUCKIN' NAME?' he yells, his face inches from the terrified Corporal's face.

'Mousa. I'm Mousa . . . I'm Corporal Mousa. I . . . I'm one of the hostages.'

'A'right, Corporal, on your fuckin' legs and follow me,' Grey ordered, as he turned on his heel and started kicking his way back through the debris, heading out towards the door of the building. 'And look smart now. I'm not fuckin' waiting.'

'I . . . I can't move . . .' Mousa replied, pleading. 'My legs . . . my arms . . . I can't move.'

Crouching down, Grey inspected the Corporal's binds. 'Jesus,' he muttered to himself, 'the evil bastards. They've give you a fuckin' hard time, haven't they, mate?' he added, softening his tone. 'Come on, let's get you free, and get you out of 'ere.'

Taking a knife from his belt, Grey sliced through the Corporal's binds. Then he lifted Mousa up, slung him over his shoulder, resting the Corporal's weight half on his bergen and the LAW that he had strapped to it, and grabbed his GPMG with his one free hand.

'Geordie, cover me, mate. 'E's in a real bad way. I'm gonna 'ave to carry 'im down there.'

'Righto, mate. Off you fookin' go then.'

With that, Grey set off at a run with Mousa on his shoulders, Geordie putting down covering fire. As he did so, Mousa caught sight of two rebel corpses among the debris of Foday Kallay's house. One had been crushed under a fall of masonry where he lay on his bed; he had a white bloodstained sheet over him and a huge concrete block on his chest. All he could see of the other is a green blanket, and a rigid arm sticking out of a pile of debris and dust and mangled sheets of galvanised iron.

As Mousa was carried across the forty-odd yards to the hostage house, he noticed rebel bodies scattered around in the long grass. A quick *crack-crack-crack* from Gerodie's Diemaco, and Mousa saw another of the rebels go down. *Fuck, he thought to himself, these guys are good. Each time they fire they find a target. Each time, one or another of the West Side Boys goes down.* A few seconds later, and they were in through the back door of Calm Down Fresh's house and Grey dumped Corporal Mousa in the room with the rest of the hostages.

'There you go, Mousa,' he remarked with a grin. 'Safe as 'ouses now, mate. Back with your old buddies, eh?'

Suddenly the British hostages are all around Mousa, embracing him, the relief clearly showing on their faces. Until now, all of them were convinced that Mousa had been killed in the assault on Foday Kallay's house.

'You see, Mousa,' says a grinning Major Martial. 'Didn't I tell you you'd be freed. It's all over. Time to be happy.'

'We're off back to the UK, Mousa. We're going home,' adds a smiling Ranger Gaunt. 'Get to see me mum and dad. And youse – youse can forget about any more shite from those feckin' West Side bastards. They're feckin' history.'

It is 6.35 a.m., barely ten minutes into the assault, when Corporal Mousa is reunited with his fellow hostages. After greeting the Corporal, the men get back down prone on the floor, as chunks of shrapnel and bullets are still cutting through the air above them. With no roof and flimsy mud walls, theirs is not the best of locations in which to sit out a full-blooded, all-guns-blazing, SAS assault. But they have little choice.

'Youse hear that? Feckin' A!' Ranger Gaunt keeps shouting, above all the noise of combat. 'We're feckin' getting out of here!'

'Aye, that we are,' his fellow Ranger is yelling back again. 'Those fuckers are finished.'

'But . . . but you've come right in and attacked their base,' a shocked Corporal Mousa remarks, more to himself that the other hostages. 'The West Side Boys will be very angry now. They're going to come back and attack. If they do we will never get out of this alive.'

'Ah, put a sock in it, will youse, Mousa?' Ranger Rowell calls over at him. 'You've never seen our boys in action before, now have you? The feckin' West Side Boys are *history*.'

The SAS fire team leader, Captain Dan Temper no less, is still charging up and down the corridor outside their room, directing the action to the front and back of the hostage house. They can hear him calling out instructions to the rest of his team – five men who have thrown a ring of steel around the hostage house, in order to stop any of the rebels getting at them, taking cover in doorways, windows and behind the concrete pillars of Calm Down Fresh's veranda. He is shouting his commands from both the doors and the windows of the house, his team members yelling back confirmation of those orders. And for the listening hostages, this is music to their ears.

Whenever they hear an extra loud burst of gunfire close by, they look around at each other and wonder which of their captors is getting it this time. *Could it be Cambodia? Colonel GS? Mad Dennis? Calm Down Fresh would be best of all.* They don't know what has happened to the rebel guards who shared the other rooms in the house with them, but they presume they have been taken out before they've even had a chance to pick up their weapons and fire. Do they spare a thought for the boy soldier, Assan? Not really. This is the endgame now being played out before them. And if Assan had a gun and refused to drop it, then the assault force will have shot him in the head.

Now that the battle is well and truly underway, an order goes out from JFHQ Freetown to the various UN peacekeeping troops and the SLA: they are to seal off the area around Gberi Bana and Magbeni, so that the West Side Boys cannot call in any of their reinforcements by road. And if any forces of the RUF rebels are spotted trying to come to their fellow rebels' aid, then the UN forces and the SLA are to use all necessary measures to prevent them from doing so.

The six men of the SAS obs team now emerge from the jungle and prepare to rejoin the main assault. They are covered in insect bites and rashes, and they are gaunt and drawn from their seven days camped out in the jungle. While in the OP, they have plastered themselves in mud and leaves and vines as camouflage. As they charge out of the trees and thunder across the hundred yards of open ground into the centre of the village, they look more like the haunted and ghostly spirits of the jungle, rather than the crack Special Forces troops that they are.

Once the worst of the fire from the jungle has been suppressed, the main body of the assault force goes back to its task of clearing the village buildings. In the southern end of the village, Fire Team 2 bursts into a room crammed full of men whom they presume are the enemy. The Scottish Monster is just about to lob a grenade in through the doorway, when he realises that none of the men appear to be armed.

With his hand poised on the pin of the grenade, there is a split second's indecision, as he glances around the room at the group of cowering bodies. All of the men seem to have the same shaven heads, which must mark them out as *prisoners*, he reasons. The Monster makes a snap decision, and he and the Kiwi round the terrified men up at gunpoint instead. They are plasticuffed and bagged: plenty of time to work out who on earth they are later. Fire Team 2 then advances north through the village to secure the 'radio shack' – the rebels' communications hut, where the squadron plans to set up its temporary HQ.

The six fire teams in the northern sector of the village are clearing the buildings that run north-east along the track towards the wall of jungle at the end of the village, and south down towards the river. They are meeting less resistance now, as most of the rebels have retreated into the surrounding jungle. In that sense, the assault is going to plan: take the village and force the rebels back into the tree line, where the air power can deal with them more effectively. Once the men of the fire teams have secured their key targets and reached their LOEs, they will get down and find themselves some cover. Some fifteen buildings have been cleared now – including those of Colonel Cambodia, Calm Down Fresh and Foday Kallay.

Ideally, they will scoop out a shell scrape at least, a body-sized hole in which to get down from any rebel fire. But with all the incoming, few of the men think that this will be possible. The best they will be able to do is use the cover provided by the buildings and the natural terrain: walls, tress, ditches, mud banks and the like. And then they will prepare to stay put, as it becomes more of a waiting game.

But in the meantime, there are still scores of rebels out there in the forest with their hearts set on 'doing a Somalia' on the British assault forces.

IN FOR THE KILL

This was one of the most complicated operations I have ever been involved in. We were not playing some stupid arcade game. The West Side Boys were no pushover. They fought very hard. We did not want to have to do this, but the clock had started ticking.
— General Sir Charles Guthrie, Chief of Defence Staff

ON the southern river bank, the four-man SAS obs team is having a busy morning of it, too. Like their fellow D Squadron members on the northern bank, they have first heard and then watched the air armada come swooping up the Rokel Creek, the two leading Chinooks peeling right into Gberi Bana, the third left towards Magbeni. Their task is to talk that third Chinook, Sierra Three, into its pre-identified landing zone – for which they have already provided the pilots with GPS coordinates and grid references. The LZ is on the west side of Magbeni, some five hundred yards from the village itself.

As that huge chopper comes flaring in to land, the obs team is providing a thin line of security. The four men are hidden among the fringes of the jungle and ready to put down covering fire, should any of the rebels appear. They know that this landing is going to be problematic, to put it mildly. The one area of vaguely firm ground that they have been able to identify anywhere on this waterlogged LZ is a small patch of bog grass, which is only slightly less treacherous than the rest of this vast swamp. The chopper pilot is going to have to keep his giant aircraft in a stationary hover just a few feet off the ground, while the forty-five Paras pile out of the rear ramp. They will be jumping the several feet, weighed down with all their kit. The obs team just have to hope that the swamp doesn't swallow the whole damn Para assault force without trace.

The pilot of Sierra Three is searching for the pre-identified LZ now. As he eases the aircraft down over the boggy stretch of land, he spots the lone figure of an SAS soldier waving him in. God, he is glad these guys are there on the ground. *He wouldn't do their job for anything.* The SAS man is talking him in over the radio now – a calm voice, '*Sierra Three, I have you visual*' – as the pilot struggles to keep the chopper level, and moving forward, just a few yards above the surface. The downdraught of the giant twin rotors is whipping up a storm of spray, beating the long grass flat to the ground, revealing large patches of watery terrain as it does so.

My God, it looks boggy down there, the pilot thinks to himself.

Glancing through the cockpit windscreen, he gets a double thumbs up from his SAS man on the ground, and holding the aircraft in a steady hover, he hits the signal for the first man to go. *Pity that first bugger down.* One Para will jump first, and if he goes in over his head, none of his fellow soldiers will follow. It will then be *his* job, the pilot's, to search for another patch of the LZ where he might be able to put the men down. If he fails to find a drop-off point, they will need to hop across to check out the other, alternative LZ.

And all of this will take precious time.

The first Para off the back ramp of the Chinook hits the swamp's surface and goes straight down, disappearing in an eruption of mud and slime and rotting vegetation. Seconds later, he reappears with his head and shoulders just above the filth-speckled surface. They've picked one of the biggest blokes to go in first, and the rest of the Paras can just make out his white toothy grin through a face covered in black swamp mud, as he squints back up at the hovering aircraft above him. He's standing there, *grinning* up at them.

And he's giving the thumbs up for the rest of the men to follow.

Suddenly, the loady's giving them the 'GO, GO, GO', the red jump light's blinking and they're piling off the back of the chopper, one after the other down the ramp and then there's an explosion of stinking filth and slimy water all around them. With all the weight they're carrying, the force of the impact sends their legs plunging into the swamp, torsos getting sucked in after them, the men struggling not to go under, and above all else to keep their weapons, their radios and the rest of their more sensitive fighting gear up above their heads and out of the bog water. A second later, arms extended, rocking back and forth in the filth, each man stabilises himself, catching his breath and searching, groping for a solid foothold. As soon as his feet have found the bottom of the swamp, he starts wading towards the nearby line of jungle.

Behind it lies Magbeni, the rebel target.

But it is hard and exhausting work, struggling through this neck-deep shit soup and every few seconds a man in front or to the side goes down a hole, disappearing from view entirely, until his mate lunges over, digs deep and helps haul his fellow soldier up again. *The smell is unbearable.* But more importantly, the Paras feel completely exposed, trapped in this cloying swamp and unable to move or fight properly. Every man in painfully aware that if they get caught out here, in the midst of this quagmire, they'll be taken apart by the West Side Boys. And all that now stands between them and the rebels are the four SAS soldiers, ahead of them in the thin line of trees.

Then suddenly, there is the thud-thud-thud of approaching choppers.

As the men glance skywards through mud-caked eyes, they catch sight of the air armada flashing past above them, the choppers seeming to clip the treetops as they pass. The Mi-24 is leading now – sleek, cruel, like some avenging bird of prey – with the three, squatter Lynx gunships following in its wake. As the choppers streak overhead the Paras feel like cheering – GO, AIRBORNE! GO! – but their mouths are gummed up with mud and filth and swamp dirt. And then all conscious thought is lost in the rush of sound and the awesome, sucking blast as the choppers unleash a salvo of rockets just beyond the tree line ahead of them. An eruption of fire and debris rips through the air, the shock waves bending and shaking the tallest palm trees – as if a tropical hurricane were tearing through the rebel village. The very sight and sound of it all urges the Paras on to even greater efforts to extricate themselves from this gutter of a bog that they have been dropped in.

So they can follow the choppers up and into battle.

During the last few minutes of their chopper ride, many of these young men, like their Special Forces comrades, have also felt the fear monster tearing at their soul. The fear monster, paralysing all coura-geous thoughts and action. The fear monster, trapping them in the blank void of indecision. Will they go into action, jump off that chopper, fight and fight and kill? Or will they crumple and fold and fall like a rag doll, once they hit the battlefield? Most of these men are an unknown quantity; this is their first time to war. But now, as they haul themselves out of this swamp, they have something tangible and immediate to struggle against, to fight against, to focus the mind. It is an enemy real enough to eclipse the dread in their hearts.

And to force the fear monster back into its lair.

As the airborne forces roar into action against their enemy over Magbeni village, the Paras want to be in there, now, getting in among the rebels. But they feel *so heavy*. Unlike their Special Forces brothers in arms, they are all burdened with body armour. Their assault planners have judged that the level of rebel firepower they're up against demands such protection, in spite of the extra weight. In each section there are two Paras weighed down with GPMGs and belts of ammunition, and the others all have SA80s. There are even several men who have jumped into that swamp carrying base plates, tubes and crates of shells for 61 and 81mm mortars. Each man is weighed down with some 80–170 lb of gear. It is an exhausting struggle, and as the men finally heave themselves out on to firm land, they are stinking and dripping with filth, and panting to catch their breath.

Yet they have still not fired a single shot in anger.

Moving into the tree line, the first Paras out of the swamp throw a protective cordon around the LZ. But, as one of the young lads struggles out of the quagmire, he trips over a slimy tree root and takes a fall, and as he goes down he inadvertently tenses his hand around his rifle. There is the sharp *crack!* of a bullet leaving his SA80, and a millisecond later a cry from the jungle, as one of the four men of the SAS obs team goes down. He has been hit in the back by the bullet, and at this range, it strikes him like an express train, and he hits the deck hard. The man down is Ginge, one of the Hereford lads, and a living SAS legend.

The young Para struggles to his feat in panic, fearing the worst. For a moment the poor sod thinks he's killed him. There is a split second's deathly silence, and then a booming voice comes out of the bush from the direction of the fallen man.

'Steady on there, lads!' Ginge roars, as he struggles to extricate himself from the undergrowth. 'There's enough to go round without 'aving to 'ave a go at one of your own.'

Ginge hauls himself to his feet, grinning, and straightens out the back plate of his body armour. The SA80 round has hit him fair and square in the centre of his rear armour plate, and apart from being winded, Ginge is fine. Unlike his Special Forces mates now going into action at Gberi Bana, Ginge and his three fellow members of the obs team have – luckily – opted to wear body armour for the assault on Magbeni.

'Which one of you young guns was it, then, eh?' he adds, amicably. 'You? Nice shot, mate. But wrong side. It's them you need to be malleting, mate, not us. All right?'

Major Lowe now musters his forces for the assault. Under the command of the Para CSM, 1 Platoon are left behind to guard the LZ, while 2 and 3 Platoons advance eastwards three hundred yards through the jungle, with Captain Matthews in control. Once they reach the break-in point for the rebel village, they take cover, and await confirmation that the second half of the Para assault force has been dropped safely at the LZ. It will take the best part of half an hour for the Paras to be choppered in to join them. Until then, there are forty-five of them up against some three hundred rebels in Magbeni.

With guns levelled at the rebel positions, the men hold their fire – alert for any movement or sign that the enemy has discovered them. As they wait for the signal that the assault force is complete and that they can attack, each minute seems to last a lifetime. The adrenalin is pumping, and the heavy thud of combat is just up ahead of them, as the air armada continues to pound the rebel village.

At any moment the men of 2 and 3 Platoons are expecting the West Side Boys to counter-attack from the near end of the village, using their heavy weapons to chew up the jungle where they are hiding. As the minutes drag by and no rebel counter-attack comes, it occurs to these men that the West Side Boys may have mistaken their Chinook for one of the roving gunships. It would be quite possible, among all the rocket salvos and machine-gun fire coming at them from the air, and the resulting chaos and confusion. In which case, the rebels may not yet have realised that the Paras have landed, which means that they still have surprise on their side. If only the second half of the attack force were here, now, on the ground and ready to roll, they could capitalise on that and attack.

Come on, the men are thinking, *where the fuck are you?*

Chinook Sierra Three dropped the first forty-five Paras at the swamp LZ at around 6.25 a.m., the same time that D Squadron were hitting Gberi Bana on the northern river bank. The first Chinook away from the West Side Boys positions then did a thirty-minute turnaround and dropped the remaining forty-five Paras on to the same, swampy LZ at around 6.55 a.m. As a call went out from the Chinook pilot that the second contingent of Paras had been dropped on to target, the gunships began to ease off their attack runs on Magbeni.

It is at this stage that Major Lowe gives the signal for the Para assault force to go in proper.

The first up on their feet and into action on the ground are 3 Platoon, advancing – hearts pumping and aggression surging – through the crumbling, one-storey buildings at the start of the rebel village. The walls are peppered with bullet holes from the helicopter attacks, and burning and smoke-blackened from their missile salvos. Moving forward from the cover of building to scattered building, 3 Platoon can see a wide track up ahead of them running down the centre of the village. The track runs for a thousand-odd yards, from one end of the village to the other. There are several rebel corpses scattered along it already, so clearly the gunships have been doing good work. As 3 Platoon take up covering positions in wrecked buildings and behind walls, 2 Platoon advance past them, sticking to the northern side of the track, closest to the river bank. If the rebels do try to send reinforcements across river to Gberi Bana, this is the side of the village from which they will do so.

But as 2 Platoon push steadily forward, the rebels finally catch sight of the British ground assault force. Suddenly, the leading Paras come under heavy machine-gun fire from rebel positions up ahead. The men take cover as best they can among the burned-out buildings and the coconut groves, using the drainage ditches, the corners of buildings, concrete pillars and walls and doorways. Huge jagged holes have been rent in the buildings by the heavy machine-gun fire from the attack helicopters. In some, the walls are peppered with holes like a sieve, the early-morning sunlight streaming through into the darkened rooms inside.

The advance of 2 Platoon is effectively halted. With 3 Platoon providing covering fire from the rear, the Para command unit (their mobile HQ), consisting of Major Lowe and his senior NCOs, moves forward now. But as they do so, an enemy mortar unit that has survived the air blitz starts opening up on the Paras' positions. As the deafening boom of exploding shells creeps closer to 2 and 3 Platoons' cover, disaster strikes. A single mortar round plunges into a tree just above the advancing Para command unit. Exploding in the branches, the shell acts like an air burst, the blast throwing the men off their feet and showering red-hot, jagged metal fragments in all directions.

In an instant, Major Lowe, the overall CO of the Para assault force, goes down, his legs torn up by chunks of shrapnel. The OC of 2 Platoon, two signallers, and two of the Paras' headquarters staff are also badly wounded. One man has had his buttocks all but ripped off by the force of the blast. At a stroke, the Paras' command and control structure, and their signals, have been put out of action. From being on the offensive and pushing forward, the assault force is now reeling under the impact of this one mortar strike. Suddenly, this ace fighting force, with air power in support, is midway through a fiercely contested battle where speed and mobility are key, and yet it has lost the most crucial elements for effective attack: commanders empowered to give orders and keep their men moving forward, and communications to coordinate all parts of the assault. And perhaps most crucially of all, they have lost their ability to communicate properly with the air cover. Minus their weapons, ammo and radios – which have been taken by others in the platoon – the badly wounded men are dragged back towards the LZ. The radios go haywire now as Sergeant Fitzwalter, one of the uninjured NCOs of 2 Platoon, calls for an urgent casevac chopper for the six men who have been fragged.

Back out over the forests east of Freetown, Sierra Two is heading fast up the Rokel Creek on a mission to extract the six Royal Irish hostages from Gberi Bana. When the Chinook pilot hears Para Sergeant Fitzwalter's urgent request for a casevac, he figures that the hostages can wait a little while longer for their pickup.

They've been seventeen days without rescue, so another few minutes won't hurt them.

The pilot of Sierra Two puts out a response call, saying that he is diverting towards the Paras' positions at Magbeni. Over at the swamp LZ, 1 Platoon prepare to load the six Para stretcher cases on to a Chinook that cannot land, hovering over a waterlogged bog in the middle of a raging firefight. It will not be the easiest of casualty evacuations. Some twenty minutes later – and after a particularly hair-raising casevac – the wounded Paras are being treated in the medical bay on the RFA ship *Sir Percival*, back in Freetown harbour. All of them will recover from their wounds and survive to fight another day.

But that one, 'lucky' mortar round has effectively paralysed the whole Para assault. With their OC out of action, 2 Platoon are pinned down at the eastern end of the village, taking heavy machine-gun and mortar fire. Unless they do something, and pretty smartish, there will be further Para casualties, and they may even lose the battle for Magbeni village. If they do, the consequences for Operation Barras as a whole do not bear thinking about.

Suddenly, the assault on Magbeni is this close to becoming a defeat.

SALVATION

This is a war of the unknown warriors; but let us all strive without failing in faith or in duty.

– Winston Churchill

DESPITE the fact that it feels like a good twenty minutes since the hostages first heard the choppers coming in low over Gberi Bana, the din of the battle outside their room keeps rolling in on them – waves of crashing sound denoting the ongoing tumult of war. They can still feel the occasional dirt thrown up by the explosions falling through the open roof of their room, as the firefight thunders on out there, further off now, more into the village periphery and the jungle. And just as they are wondering what will happen to them next, their Special Forces man is back at their door. As usual, he is cool as a cucumber.

'OK, listen up,' he shouts above all the noise. 'Everyone line up behind me. When I say GO, you move it like shit off a bloody shovel, following my lead. We're headed for the rebels' radio shack. OK? You all know where that is? You all clear?'

'Aye, clear as day, sir,' says a grinning Ranger Gaunt, from his position prone on the floor.

'Dead on, sir,' the other Ranger adds.

It is 6.40 a.m., barely fifteen minutes into the assault, when the six British – and one Sierra Leonean – hostages pick themselves up off the floor and brush themselves down. Pumped up with adrenalin, hearts pounding, blood thumping in their heads – they line up in the corridor outside and prepare to run for their lives. Major Martial takes the lead, followed by Captain Flaherty and the two Rangers, with Corporals Mousa and Mackenzie and Sergeant Smith to the rear. Captain Dan Temper goes ahead of the Major, while three of his men take up positions to either flank and to the rear of the seven hostages. Then Captain Temper turns round and gives the thumbs up to the men behind him.

'You chaps all ready?'

There is a chorus of 'Aye, sir' and 'Dead on' in reply, as the seven men give the thumbs up back. They are full of the confidence of men plucked from the very jaws of death.

'Then on me, let's GO!' the SF officer yells, as he tears down the corridor, with the seven hostages and his three fellow SAS men following him.

They burst out of the house going like the clappers, straight into the firefight outside. The SF officer tears right, straight up the track leading towards Cambodia's place, and the hostages follow him, close on his heels. Almost immediately they hit the village track, and race past a corpse, bloodied and slumped in the long grass to the side. It looks like Colonel Mines, one of Calm Down Fresh's sidekicks, but the hostages can't be sure. *It is good to see that the SAS boys may have got that evil bastard.* Yet there is no time to stop and stare and gloat, as the men keep muscles pumping and hearts pounding on, on up the track before them. It is two hundred yards or so from the hostage house to the radio shack, but to the hostages it feels like they are running a marathon.

Yet after only a few paces more, Mousa's legs just seem to give out and fold beneath him, and he collapses in a heap on the track.

It is hardly surprising that Mousa has gone down. If the British hostages have been having a tough time of it, Corporal Mousa has just been through a living hell. And the poor man is still consumed by the fear that they are all going to get wasted by the West Side Boys.

'ONE MAN DOWN!' Sergeant Smith starts yelling from the back, the Rangers picking up his cry. 'Feckin' Mousa! Mousa's down! MOUSA'S DOWN!'

'WELL, GET HIM FUCKING UP,' yells the SF officer, as the men grind to a halt. 'COME ON! Get him fucking up and GET MOVING.'

The four men of the hostage-rescue team spread out and form a defensive circle – their weapons covering the forest fifty yards to the right of them, from where the majority of the gunfire is coming – as the Major and Captain Flaherty haul Mousa to his feet. Half carrying the Sierra Leonean Corporal draped over their shoulders, they hammer on to their destination.

As they reach the radio shack, the first men hurl themselves in through the doorway. This is the heart of D Squadron's operation in Gberi Bana now, the nerve centre of the UKSF assault, and the safest place to be in the whole of the village. *Sanctuary. Feckin' sanctuary.* At long last, they have found sanctuary from the rebels.

Thankfully, none of the seven hostages has been hit during the mad dash up here. Captain Temper herds the men into a side room, to keep them out of the way. As they pass inside they catch sight of another dead body, slumped on the floor in the room next door, broken and bloodied among a pile of old car batteries. They cannot tell exactly who it is, because the body is lying at an odd angle, but it looks like it could be Dennis the Menace. That evil bastard always did used to like hanging about in the radio shack. *They can always live in hope that it's him, anyway.*

'What the feck, Mousa?' Ranger Gaunt splutters, turning a grinning face towards the Sierra Leonean Corporal once they are inside their room. 'Youse trying to get us all killed, is it?'

'I can't believe it . . . I just can't believe . . .' Mousa keeps repeating to himself, looking white as a sheet and slumped in one corner.

'Can't believe what, Mousa?' says the Ranger, trying to banter with him and lift his spirits. 'It's like we said, these boys'll be getting us out of here pretty sharpish now, so they will.'

The radio shack has been chosen by the British assault force as their makeshift HQ for some very good reasons. First, it is of sounder construction than just about all the other buildings in the village, lending a bit of security and cover to anyone inside. Second, it is bang in the centre of the village, so as good a place as any from which to control the action. Third, it has some sort of comms set up already, which the Special Forces sparks might find useful. And fourth, and most important of all, it is right next door to the village football pitch – the largest area of cleared forest in the whole of Gberi Bana. If you need to put a couple of big choppers down in the village, this is obviously the best place to do so.

After the hostages have had a few minutes to catch their breath, Captain Temper comes in with some flasks of water for the men. In all the adrenalin and excitement, they have forgotten how thirsty they are, and they drain the bottles to the last drop. Captain Temper then tells Major Martial that he needs his help outside, identifying some of the prisoners. He instructs the rest of the men to wait there for the chopper, which will be airlifting them out of there pretty shortly now.

Left to themselves, the six men take stock of their surroundings. There is an old mattress at one end of the room and a couple of self-loading rifles propped in one corner. For a moment, they consider picking up the guns to defend themselves with, just in case anything happens. But they know in their heart of hearts that it is unnecessary, that they won't be needing them now. Just then, Mat, one of the men from the obs team that kept watch on Gberi Bana, pops his head round the door to the soldiers' room.

'Fookin' hell then, you all right, lads?' he asks, with a grin.

'Aye. Dead on, like. Now that youse all have taken care of them bastards,' Ranger Gaunt replies.

'You'll never guess, Mousa,' Mat continues, turning to the Sierra Leonean Corporal, 'but I was watching you take a piss a couple of days ago. They took you round the back of that fooker Cambodia's place. All tied up you was. I was about forty yards away, in the bush, and could see you clear as day, lad. Took a photo of you, I did. I'll send it to you if you like, after this little caper's over. Catch you on the *Sir Percival*, a'right? Give me your address, and I'll pop it in the fookin' post. Little memento of your stay in Gberi Bana, like.'

Out at the front of the building, the Major is looking at a large group of prisoners lying face down on the village track, arms plasticuffed behind their backs. One or two of them are the shaven-headed village 'recruits', and as he steps forth from the radio shack, they raise their faces off the dirt, eyes opening wide, pleading for the Major to recognise them. The prisoners are clearly in deep shock, their faces a mask of blank fear. They have stopped functioning properly and gone into total shutdown mode. The Major can see it in their glazed, expressionless eyes: they are on trauma- and terror-induced autopilot. *I cannot do anything for myself any more*, the expression on the faces of the rebel prisoners is saying. *My brain has stopped functioning. Order me what to do and I will do it, because my free will has been completely paralysed by panic and shock and fear.*

There are fifteen or more prisoners, a mixture of the 'recruits' and surrendered rebels (four of whom are women). It is easy for the Major to tell the difference. After seventeen days as their hostage, the Major is able to recognise most if not all of the West Side Boys on sight. And the shaven-headed villagers have barely had the time to grow any stubble on their bald skulls. As he walks up the line pointing out the village 'recruits', a Special Forces soldier makes a note of what each is wearing. The Major explains to Captain Temper the simple difference between the recruits and the rebels – that all the former have their heads shaved bare. Unless any of the West Side Boys have been up very early this morning, shaving their heads, it is a foolproof method of separating out the innocent villagers from the rebels. So there is no mistaking them now.

But the one figure that the Major can't seem to find anywhere is Sony and, somehow, he isn't overly surprised. The Major is glad that Sony isn't among them. He feels certain that Sony would have slipped away from Gberi Bana unnoticed, the night before the assault came in.

'They've got several of the bastards held prisoner out there,' the Major announces, as he comes back to join the other men. 'Oh, and some of the shaven-headed recruits, too. They'll be all right. I've ID'd them. They'll be getting out of here OK, that's for sure.'

Hardly has the Major finished speaking, when they hear Captain Dan Temper calling up one of the choppers on the radio.

'Sierra Two, this is West Side One Control, do you read me, over?' (West Side One is the code name for Gberi Bana, with West Side One Control being the assault force HQ on the ground.)

'Sierra Two here, reading you loud and clear, over.'

'What's you current locstat, over?'

'Inbound towards West Side One, over.'

'Roger. All hostages ready for exfil, I repeat, seven ready for exfil, from LZ3, over.'

'Roger. Inbound for exfil now from LZ3. Expect five, repeat five minutes to LZ. Sierra Two out.'

Once he's got the extraction chopper booked to get the hostages out of there, Captain Temper tells one of his men to put out a smoke grenade on the football field, to mark the LZ from the air. Twice Sierra Two tries to come in for a landing on that marker, but both times the Captain has to warn the pilot off by radio: he is coming in too close to the jungle from where the West Side Boys are still mounting their sporadic counter-attacks. Earlier, an RPG7 fired from out of the forest narrowly missed one of the choppers, and Captain Temper doesn't want to give the rebels any second chances. The third time the Chinook makes its run-in, he is about to warn it off again, but then changes his mind. The damn thing has to come down at some stage and brave the firefight.

'Oh, bugger it,' the Captain says. 'Let's put her down, Sierra Two, quick as you can on the LZ.' Then he turns to the seven hostages. 'Come on then! On your feet and ready to go. You're getting the hell out of here!'

Jesus, the hostages are thinking to themselves, *what a difference a day makes.*

TEN MEN DOWN

Death is not forgetting, it is remembering. Comfort comes from the sharing of grief, but more especially from the sharing of gratitude. The spirit of someone who dies lives on, through gratitude, in the hearts of those left behind.

– Don McClen, *The Heart of Things*

THERE is the whoosh-crash of an RPG7 impacting nearby, and the Kiwi hits the deck, raising his head slowly from the dirt to take stock of any damage. The RPG came out of a nearby building, of that much he is sure, two up from the rebels' hospital house. Glancing over, he realises with a shock like a blow to the stomach that Billy – the big, invincible Scottish Monster – has been hit. As Billy spins and staggers with the impact of a big grenade frag, the Kiwi watches, open-mouthed in disbelief, as a red rose of blood blooms like a flower on the big man's chest and he is going down. In an instant, this big dour man of iron is rolling around in agony and fear and squealing like a crying baby.

The Kiwi knows that his orders are not to stop to help any man down but to carry on fighting and to leave it to the medics to patch up the wounded. But that is the theory and this is the practice, and the Big Scottish Monster looks to be in a bad, bad way. The Kiwi goes for his throat mike, to radio for a paramedic. But just as he's about to hit send, he hears Cockney Jimmy's voice coming up over the net. He sounds calm and collected, and there's less of an east-London twang to his voice now, as he yells for a medic to attend to the big man, their fire team leader, who's gone down bad.

'This is Sierra Two Zero, Sierra Two Zero, one man down and badly wounded, I repeat badly wounded. Shrapnel frag to the chest an' bleeding heavily. We're in need of a medic. An' get a chopper called in 'ere pronto, 'cause this boy needs evacuatin'.'

'Sierra Two Zero, this is Sierra Control, roger that,' comes back the voice of the OC on the net.

The radio chatter fades away into the background, as they leave it to the squadron OC to sort out the casevac details. The Kiwi carries on firing, but he is still racked by guilt, the guilt of leaving his buddy, the Big Man, lying there on the deck in pain and fear, and in a pool of his own lifeblood. The Kiwi concentrates his guilt into a cold, icy rage and searches for the enemy, for just one of the rebel bastards who might have done this to his man. Reaching behind his head, he grabs his 66mm LAW from where it's strapped to the top of his rucksack. He flips up the sight, extends the barrel (from its 1-metre carry mode to 1.5-metre fire mode), and takes aim on the window of the building he guesses the RPG came from. Nestling the weapon into his shoulder, he squeezes the trigger, gently but firmly, until the rocket fires, flame and smoke bursting out twenty yards or more behind him.

The rocket leaps forward some forty yards or so, a cheetah sensing its prey, and disappears through the open window – the building in the Kiwi's sights disappearing in a sheet of flame. *That's one for the Big Scot*, the Kiwi yells inside his head. A rebel soldier comes stumbling out of the gutted building, screaming, his clothes on fire. *Burn in hell, you motherfucker, burn in hell*, the Kiwi is thinking, grimly. He grabs his Diemaco and takes aim. But before he can pull the trigger, there's a quick *crack-crack-crack* of gunfire from the right of him, and Jimmy has taken the rebel soldier down. A 'double tap', two to the body and one to the head. Professional. Neat. Terminal.

Then the Kiwi spots movement, a figure trying to escape through a side window of the smoking building, a person for whom the fear of death by burning is now greater than the fear of being shot by the foreign soldiers waiting outside. As one bare leg is thrust over the windowsill, and the torso follows, the Kiwi takes aim and fires, two to the body to stop him and one to the head to make sure he's dead. Only . . . there's something wrong here, the Kiwi suddenly realises. As the second leg joins the first and the figure falls from the window, he can see that it is wearing a cheap dress – a dress that is already stained crimson with blood from the three bullets that he has just fired.

It's not a he, the Kiwi realises. *It's a she*. He's just shot dead a woman.

He saw the head explode in his gun sights as he made that third shot, so he knows that she is dead. *This is what I have dreaded*, the Kiwi is thinking to himself, *killing kids and women*.

But strangely, he feels no remorse now, only cold rage and anger. Billy, the invincible team leader, is lying close by, still screaming for the medic, and the Kiwi is mad, mad like a raging bull, and he has no regrets. Who knows, she could have been the bitch who fired the RPG that took out the Big Scot. *The rebel women carry weapons and fight*, he tells himself. *So she got what she had coming.* Yes, he's just shot dead a woman. But any guilt, any regret, is now subsumed by his concern for his fellow soldier.

Where the fuck is the medic? he's thinking, as he searches for another of the rebels to kill.

Ten members of the assault force are seriously wounded in the initial twenty minutes of the battle – five of whom (the Big Scot included) will need air evacuation. All of them are hit in the first stages of the firefight, when the rebels regroup and counter-attack from the jungle. Many more are hit by stray battlefield ordnance, which causes minor wounds, but these men will carry on fighting anyway. By the end of the day, almost all the seventy-odd men of the assault force will end up with a stray piece of shrapnel embedded somewhere in them, there is so much flying around.

Most of the wounds that the men suffer are from RPGs. In answer, the British assault force come back at the rebels firing salvos of 40mm grenades into the jungle, from the M204 grenade launchers they have slung beneath the barrels of their Diemaco assault rifles. Of the ten soldiers seriously wounded, the five with flesh wounds only will remain in Gberi Bana for the duration of the assault, and carry on fighting. They will patch up their own injuries themselves – deep gashes rent in thighs, forearms torn to the bone by chunks of shrapnel – using the emergency medical packs that each man carries on his person.

And then they will hunker down in a position of good cover and, gritting their teeth against the pain, they will last out the assault as best they can, giving whatever covering fire possible to the rest of their team. Each of these men could have opted for a casevac: their wounds are serious enough to justify doing so, and they have lost a lot of blood. But each chooses instead to stay behind and fight, to stick with their brothers in arms and see the assault through to its bloody end – because that is what they know their mates would have done for them, had things been the other way round.

The West Side Boys are loosing off anywhere and everywhere they can. The rebel gunfire is too inaccurate to be very effective, but even stray bullets aimed at no one in particular can still find a target and kill. It is one of these stray rounds that finds Brad Tinnion. The 7.62mm AK47 round hits him in the leg, but the bullet slews off the bone up into his body. The round has struck Brad from behind – from the opposite side of the assault force to where the rebels are now counter-attacking. So it must have been a ricochet, a stray bullet rebounding from a building. Brad had taken cover and hunkered down, like the rest of his fire team, but that has done nothing to stop a wayward bullet coming from behind.

Within minutes, the men of the assault force know that Brad is in a bad way, because the medic attending to him starts screaming for a chopper to come in for a casevac.

Of the five wounded soldiers who need immediate evacuation by air, there are two whose cases are really worrying. It is difficult to know if they will make it. One of those is the Big Scot, with the serious shrapnel wound to his chest cavity, his breath coming heaving and gurgling through clotted blood. Shock affects the wounded in different ways, and at first Brad seems alert and is still able to talk. But appearances can be deceptive. The quicker the casevac chopper can get in there, the greater chance these men have of making it out of there alive. Sierra One is five minutes away from Gberi Bana, and closing fast.

'West Side One Control, this is Sierra One, inbound now towards West Side One,' comes the voice of the Chinook pilot over the net. 'Estimate five, repeat five minutes to casevac.'

'Sierra One, the is West Side One Control, the LZ is hot, over,' comes the voice of Captain Dan Temper, speaking from the radio shack, warning the pilot that the landing will be under fire.

'Roger that,' the pilot of Sierra One replies, calmly.

Minutes later and the big Chinook comes swooping in fast in a tight turn from the southern end of Gberi Bana, flaring out over LZ1. It is an outstanding piece of flying to put the chopper down in the midst of the firefight in the centre of the rebel base, and the men of the assault force know that the pilot is coming in far too early for his own safety. No one has planned for such a large number of seriously wounded at this stage in the assault, and it takes a courageous pilot to bring in his aircraft to take the stretcher cases out to safety. But the pilot knows that the lives of these men depend on his flying into the teeth of this battle, and he does so with a cool head and a strong heart.

For several seconds the Chinook waits, poised, wheels barely touching the beaten earth, rotors spitting and turbines screaming, shifting its mass from side to side as the big aircraft strains to be airbone again and free. The men of D Squadron take their five stretcher cases and rush them up into the belly of the beast. Bullets and shrapnel and smoke and debris are spinning past the chopper, but still the pilot keeps his cool and holds his position.

But a rebel fighter has found his target now, and above the screaming of the straining turbines there is the sound of bullets smacking, tearing into the side and front of the aircraft. One bullet through a hydraulic line, one bullet through a vital electric lead, one bullet through *the pilot's heart*, and that chopper is going nowhere fast . . . Yet still the pilot holds steady until the last wounded man is aboard, and then he slams the throttle to full, the big machine leaping, lurching forward and upwards and away across the roofs of the village, a giant beast of the air reaching for the sky, the clouds, for safety, impatient to be leaving the treacherous, bullet-scarred battlefield behind.

Together with the Big Scot and the three other badly wounded men, Brad is flown straight out to the *Sir Percival*. One of the Special Forces paramedics, Stan, goes out with the injured, to try to keep them alive on the flight. He just needs these five men to hold on long enough to reach the hospital ship. But halfway through the chopper ride, Brad knows that he isn't going to make it.

'I'm fucked, mate. I'm not going to be able to hold on.'

'Listen, man, shut up, for Chrissake,' Stan tries to reassure him. 'You're going to make it. You'll be fucking fine.'

'Fuck that, Stan. I know what I'm saying. I just felt one lung collapse, mate. I'm a gonner. Just shut up and listen . . . Just tell Anna I love her. That's all . . .'

The Special Forces wounded are choppered on to the dockside, adjacent to the *Sir Percival*, at around 7 a.m. HMS *Argyll*'s medical officer, Surgeon Lieutenant Jon Carty, has been relocated to the *Sir Percival* to act as the triage officer for any casualties and walking wounded. As such he is the first point of contact, charged with assessing which are the most serious and should be treated first. He's set up a casualty clearing station in a sea freight container, on the jetty adjacent to the *Sir Percival*'s mooring.

Now, as the five soldiers are rushed down the rear ramp of the Chinook, the Surgeon Lieutenant has no doubts as to his first priority. Brad Tinnion is hurried on board the ship and down to the medical deck.

It is 6.55 a.m., thirty minutes into the assault, and Pete Cutgood, D Squadron's OC, together with the squadron RSM have flown in from Waterloo Camp to Gberi Bana, on the casevac chopper. They are doing a quick tour of the assault forces' positions, to assess the status of the battle and to give their men a morale boost. Cutgood takes word around that of their badly wounded, one man, Brad Tinnion, is in a very bad way. While Billy the Scot and the other D Squadron wounded will probably be all right, the OC tells the men, Brad Tinnion will be unlikely to make it. Boat Troop have lost two men to casevacs. And one of them is very likely not going to live.

Brad's D Squadron mates are consumed with anger and pain at the OC's news. *Brad. Fucking surfer-boy Brad, the perfect dresser and the natural soldier, how could those bastards possibly have got Brad?*

He should have shone on the catwalk, not taken a bullet in some godforsaken rebel base in the jungle. He should have lived to see his young daughter and hold her close to his still-beating heart, not felt his life force drain away as he lay on a stretcher among the spent shell cases and the field dressings. He should have lived to bounce his grand-children on his knee, not coughed his heart out on the floor of a Chinook as it clawed its way through the muggy air, speeding him onwards towards Freetown. He should have lived, not drifted away into the cold grey half-light as the medic desperately tried to keep him breathing, and willed him to stay with us and never leave.

What a senseless, senseless waste. And all because some evil bastards took eleven innocent British soldiers hostage.

Several of the men are actually crying in reaction to the news – their camo cream-, dirt- and cordite-streaked faces now smeared with tears, too – though whether it's tears of rage or of sorrow no one is quite sure. And then a shout goes out from one of the men, one of many in the squadron who see themselves as kindred spirits of Brad's.

'*The bastards!* The bastards got Brad!' It is Jimmy's voice that is yelling, and the pain and the trauma reverberates around Gberi Bana like a war cry of the bereaved and the bereft.

'YOU BASTARDS! YOU BASTARDS! YOU BASTARDS! Get me a knife so I can slice one of these FUCKERS up! He was worth more than this WHOLE STINKIN' VILLAGE.'

Jimmy has kept his radio on send, and his war cry is a cathartic call to arms, a signal to the other men of the assault force to unleash havoc and mayhem on the rebel base. As 66mm rockets are fired into buildings, and 40mm grenades go plummeting through windows, a series of massive explosions shake the very foundations of the village – rows of huts and concrete-block houses disappearing in a wall of fire. Gouts of flame burst forth, as smoke from the burning buildings belches skywards, rising high above the tree line of the surrounding jungle.

Down at the White House, the men of the mortar team set up their four 81mm mortars and send a barrage of shells crashing into the bush all around the village. There is a series of pops as the mortar tubes fire, followed seconds later by a massive *boom!* as they mortar in a 360-degree section all around the forested outskirts of the rebel base. This is where the West Side Boys have been hiding, and launching their sporadic counter-attacks – and this is from where the AK round will have been fired that got Brad. The mortar team aim to set up a no man's land around the village perimeter, so that no more aberrant rebel machine-gun fire can cause the assault force further casualties.

It is at this point that Pete Cutgood decides to bring in the big guns. The rebels have been beaten back into the forest, where the air power can really have a go at them. He puts out a call on the radio, and the Mi-24 gunship comes roaring across the river and swooping in low over Gberi Bana, Fred Marafono waving down at his D Squadron mates as it does so. The OC has given Nellis the coordinates of the patch of forest where the bulk of the rebels are holed up, with instructions that he should unleash everything he has on them.

As the Mi-24 gains altitude and then dives on to target, it delivers eight rockets into the bush around the north-eastern village perimeter. Gouts of flame erupt from the trees as the salvo strikes, explosions shaking the ground. As the chopper passes above target, Fred Marafono and his fellow door gunner are pouring fire from their GPMGs down into the jungle below them, chasing the terrified rebels through the trees. By the time the Mi-24 has turned for a follow-up attack run with its Gatling gun, the West Side Boys' positions have fallen silent. The rebels are terrified of anything that comes out of the air at them. They seem to believe that the power that swoops out of the sky is invincible – the wrath of the foreigner transformed into a fire-spitting monster of the air.

25

TIME FOR A BREW

I decided the most sensible thing to do was to get a brew on because it looked like it was going to be a very long day. Stopping in mid-battle and having a brew was met with complete amazement by the blokes.
– Major Phil Neame, in Max Arthur's *Above All, Courage*

As the seven hostages line up for the air extraction, Captain Dan Temper explains the form to them: it will be a repeat performance of the exit from the hostage building. Only this time, no falling over please, remarks the Captain, looking over at Corporal Mousa with an encouraging grin. What with all the adrenalin and the excitement of the morning, the seven soldiers find themselves desperate for a pre-departure piss. They decide to urinate on the old mattress in the corner of their room, as a parting gift to the West Side Boys. That done, they form up in line once more, this time in the radio shack, and rush out of the back of the building in a straight sprint across the football field, with a covering escort as before.

As they do so, Chinook Sierra One is just touching down, the downdraught of its rotors sending clouds of bright purple smoke from the spotter grenade billowing towards them. The chopper's wheels hit the dirt, and four, heavily armed men pile out of the rear ramp. They are covered in the mud and leaves and grime of more than half a dozen days living in the jungle, and they look more like scarecrows than British soldiers. It is the SAS obs team from Magbeni, who have been flown across river to rejoin their squadron. They hurry off, eager to lend a hand in the clearance of the last of the rebels from Gberi Bana.

In a second, the seven hostages are up inside the belly of the chopper, and with the screaming of straining turbines it lifts off again. In moments, they are airborne, the Chinook clawing its way skywards, hurrying the men up and away, away from the last seventeen days during which their lives became a living nightmare in the village of Gberi Bana.

It is 7 a.m. as the Chinook sets a course for Freetown. There is still one hell of a firefight going down below, although none of it is directed at the chopper any more – as the West Side Boys have their hands full fighting the ground forces. Despite the firepower unleashed by the assault force in the blind fury upon rage on hearing of Brad's likely death, the rebels have not given up. They keep popping up in the bush and loosing off a magazine or lobbing a grenade over.

It isn't the concerted counter-attack that the men of D Squadron had planned for: they had expected the rebels to reorganise and regroup in the jungle and come back at them with accurate, targeted mortar fire and sniping. But that is the way in which *they* would have defended the village, and it is becoming increasingly obvious that they cannot judge the rebels on their own terms. The West Side Boys have a completely different concept of combat, a totally unique *esprit de corps*. And one thing they do not seem to do is give up: it is almost as if they have no instinct for self-preservation and survival.

The signals team at the Gberi Bana HQ decide it is now time to set up a proper radio antennae, stringing a transmitter wire between the radio shack and an adjacent building. But there is a dead body of one of the West Side Boys lying on top of a pile of old car batteries that the rebels had used to power their radios, and it is in the way.

'Better get that guy off of there,' the RSM remarks, 'or he'll ruin his clothes.'

The OC has a bodyguard for his own protection, and with comms up and running he heads outside the radio shack to make a sitrep to Operational Command in Freetown. As he is making the radio call he takes cover behind one of the buildings. At this moment, a rebel soldier jumps out from his hiding place behind a wall barely fifteen yards away, bringing his AK47 to bear on the OC. Firing over the shoulder of the OC, his bodyguard takes the rebel soldier out with a short burst, before he can open fire.

'Is there any need for that?' remarks Pete Cutgood, with a grin. 'Can't you keep the noise down? I'm trying to make a radio call here.'

On board the Chinook, the freed hostages are ordered up to the front of the aircraft. A paramedic is tending to the six wounded Paras, who have been air-lifted out of Magbeni and take up the bulk of the floor space. On the ten-minute flight to Freetown, the paramedic calls

each man back again, and, one by one, he gives them a task to help
with the wounded Paras. Mostly they have shrapnel wounds to the
arms and upper torso, and the medic has them pretty much under
control. While the other hostages hold up drips and the like, Captain
Flaherty applies field dressings to flesh wounds. The paramedic yells
above the noise of the chopper that he wants the hostages to keep the
Paras talking. They've been given hefty doses of morphine and he wants
them kept awake until they reach the makeshift hospital facilities at
Freetown. This is the only way to stop the wounded Paras from going
into shock, and drifting off into unconsciousness.

'How's it been, like, sort of on yer side of the river, then?' Ranger
Gaunt asks one of the injured men.

'Pretty heavy. Awesome firefight,' he replies, sounding groggy with
the fog of morphine. 'You all got out all right then, lads?'

'Aye. We're all here,' says the Ranger.

'It's all good then,' the wounded Para grins. 'Did we get all of the
fuckers our side, d'you know?'

'Aye, by the sounds of things I'd reckon youse did.'

'Bet the Hereford boys are giving them a right fuckin' kicking, eh?'

'Aye. You can bet your feckin' life they are. Never seen anything like
it in me life before. Now youse just sort of keep talkin' to me, like, and
we'll be there soon enough.'

At the front of the chopper, a grinning Corporal Mousa just keeps
repeating to himself over and over again: 'I can't believe it. *You beat
the West Side Boys.* Came right into their camp and chased them out
of it. I just can't believe you did it.'

'*We* didn't do it, Mousa,' a grinning Ranger Gaunt yells over, above
the noise of the chopper. 'Yer SAS man did, and all the rest of the boys.
That's the feckin' *SAS* for youse. Flamin' magic, that's what they are.'

'Aye, you're a lucky man, Mousa, that's for sure,' Ranger Rowell
adds. 'There's not another army in the world could do what those
feckin' boys did, you mark my words.'

The big Chinook finally puts down on the Freeport dockside, screened
from the banks of TV camera crews and press photographers by a wall
of shipping containers that have been piled up there for that very purpose.
As soon as the rear ramp is lowered, the freed hostages go into
stretcher-bearer mode, rushing the Paras off the chopper and across
towards the RFA *Sir Percival*. Here, the ship's medics take over and the
wounded are lain out so the process of triage can begin – the most
serious being taken on board first and down to the ship's dressing station.

The rescued hostages have hardly had time to put down the stretchers, when several familiar faces emerge from the crowd, take them firmly by the arm and lead them towards the *Sir Percival*. It's a bunch of their mates from the Royal Irish Regiment, who've formed an impromptu reception party. They all seem to begin speaking at once.

'Haven't seen youse around for a while, Ranger. Where the feck've youse been all this time?'

'No ways was we going to let those bastards keep a hold of youse.'

'Beers are in the fridge, lads. No Guinness though . . . only shite lager.'

There will be no beers for Corporal Mousa, however. He is rushed down to the sick bay, where he will be kept for four days' intensive medical treatment. He has head injuries, back injuries, and his arms, legs and hands are practically paralysed from being bound so tightly for sixteen days. As the medics begin to wash and bandage his wounds, they joke with the Sierra Leonean corporal that they may as well just wrap him like a mummy in bandages from head to toe, as there is no part of his body that has escaped unscathed.

It is 7.15 a.m. in Sierra Leone as the freed hostages walk up the gangplank into the RFA *Sir Percival*. It is 6.15 a.m. back in London, and the mood in the PJHQ has changed dramatically. The tension and stress of the first thirty minutes of the assault have been relieved by the news that the hostages are safely out of Gberi Bana, and that there are no choppers down. But at the same time, the British high command know that the assault force has suffered significant casualities, and that one man, Brad Tinnion, has been fatally wounded. And it isn't over yet, by a long chalk.

As soon as the hostages have been got out of Gberi Bana, the call goes out over the net: 'Hostages evacuated. Hostages evacuated.'

Just at that moment, D Squadron's Garry is in the White House – a building that has supposedly already been secured – souvenir hunting (typical thieving Scouser that he is). But when he looks under one of the beds, he finds a small, frightened man in a pair of polka-dot cycling shorts. *It's that fookin' bastard Foday fookin' Kallay,* Garry thinks to himself, as he drags him out by the scruff of his neck. By this time the men know there are a number of their own men down, and that Brad Tinnion is unlikely to live. Needless to say, tempers are running high, as is the adrenalin.

When Garry realises that Foday Kallay has his fingers stuffed with the Royal Irish soldiers' wedding rings, he just loses it. He hauls Kallay outside, fully intending to put a bullet in the back of his head and finish him off there and then. Here is the leader of the West Side Boys, the single person responsible for all this unnecessary, unwanted and unlooked-for death and destruction – and all for a couple of Land-Rovers and a few wedding rings.

But just as Garry is about to shoot the rebel leader in the head, he is spotted by Captain Dan Temper.

'Good man, you've got Kallay,' the Captain shouts over. 'Let's get him lined up for the chopper, then. There's more than a few questions we want to ask that bastard.'

Shoving a gun in Kallay's back, Garry frogmarches the rebel leader up towards the radio shack, where the prisoners are being mustered. 'If I had my way, you bastard, I'd fookin' splatter yer brains across the fookin' sand,' he snarls. 'Now get fookin' walkin'.' Upon arrival at the radio shack, Garry shoves Kallay on to his knees, and starts frisking him. But rather than finding any weapons on him, he discovers the rebel leader's webbing is stuffed with bundles of dirty, pinkish notes – a few million leones or more. What Garry fails to detect are the sixty-odd diamonds that Kallay has sown into the lining of his webbing – which are worth a small fortune. These will only be discovered later, back in Benguema Camp, by which time it is far too late for Garry – or any of the other soldiers for that matter – to walk away with them.

By 7.25 a.m. the men have gone firm on the village. All fire teams have reached their LOE, and taken cover in their pre-established positions. Spread out with interlocking arcs of fire, there is no avenue of approach to the village that isn't covered. The rebels have been forced into the jungle, and any counter-attack from any direction will now run into D Squadron's defensive positions. But it's been one hell of a fight to get to this point in the assault, and none of the men has had time to dig in or make any proper cover.

In the original assault plan, they should have been in and out of Gberi Bana in under an hour. They have been on the ground for over an hour now, and still their extraction is nowhere in sight. The rebels have been caught by surprise, that much of the assault plan working like clockwork, and the hostages have been rescued more or less unopposed. But after that, they have encountered far stiffer resistance than they had planned for. Inaccurate and ill-disciplined though the rebels have proven in combat, they have demonstrated immense – some would say foolhardy – resistance, time and time again coming back at the assault force from the jungle. The density of the surrounding bush means that the rebels can creep up more or less unnoticed on the assault force, and so the men have had to remain alert and focused at all times.

Out of the original seventy men that have gone in on the assault, sixty-five remain – the others have gone out wounded. Of those, five have serious flesh wounds, and are hardly mobile or operating at 100 per cent. Luckily, the SAS obs team at Gberi Bana has come in to reinforce their numbers in the initial stages of the firefight, and then the other SAS obs team from Magbeni has been choppered across the river to join them. That has added ten men to the strength of the able-bodied assault force now holding Gberi Bana, bringing it back up to around the seventy mark.

But the battle is far from over. British intelligence reports had it that a unit of the SLA Special Forces, calling themselves 'the Scorpions', had recently defected to the West Side Boys. They were supposedly holed up in the jungle to the north of Gberi Bana. It was feared that the Scorpions would organise the rebels to regroup and come back at the village in an organised and sustained counter-attack. Hence the original plan of attack had called for the assault force to follow the rebels into the jungle on 'hot pursuits', so pushing them back still further from the village, and giving them no chance to regroup. In reality, the assault force may have enough men to hold the village perimeter, but there is clearly no way in which they are going to be chasing the rebels further into the jungle.

The upside of this is that they can remain in the cover of their defensive positions, and not have to show themselves too much. The downside is that the rebels can linger in the jungle on the fringes of Gberi Bana, and keep coming back at them. And somehow, the assault force still has to ensure that the surrounding terrain is secure enough to get the choppers in safely for the exfil. Although air cover should be able to deal with the surviving rebel forces, the choppers have been airborne and in the full flow of combat for well over an hour now, and they must be very close to returning to base to refuel and rearm. Either way, a mission that was originally scheduled to last an hour at the most, is looking very much like dragging on for several hours more.

Disturbing images are flashing through the minds of the men of the assault force now – they are of scores of US Delta Force and Rangers pinned down in Mogadishu, in 1993. The nature of that US operation had been so similar to their own: crack US forces had been flown by helicopter into the heart of the enemy stronghold, to 'snatch' a group of Somalis from a known location. But once on the ground, many of those US troops were killed or seriously wounded as the Somali militias, seemingly heedless of their own casualties, surrounded and tried to annihilate the US Special Forces. As the hot afternoon faded into a muggy Somali night, the US soldiers found themselves running desperately short of medical supplies, water, ammo and food, and with no obvious escape route out of there.

Don't let's make Sierra Leone another fuckin' Somalia, the men are thinking.

It is 7.40 a.m., the men are hunkered down in their positions of cover, and they go quiet on the mission now. This is standard operating procedure (SOP) – to go silent on an operation, once the defensive points have been secured. Most, if not all, of the SAS and SBS men are smoking, in an effort to calm their nerves. Even those who aren't regular smokers are cadging cigarettes off their mates. It is now that Lassie – only recently arrived from guiding in the assault choppers from his jungle OP – gets the first brew of the day on, using a Hexy stove.

'You've got to have a brew on these things,' Lassie says to no one in particular, as he fires up the tiny stove. 'Can't go killing all these bastards without a tea break.'

The tea is hot and sweet – being heavily laced with sugar – and it provides a much needed energy boost for the men. But it does prove a bit of a pain, crabbing over to the next man in line trying not to spill the cup of tea, while dodging any incoming rounds at the same time.

Taking advantage of a slight break in the firefight, Lassie belly-crawls over to Jimmy, who is down in a ditch beside one of the buildings. Jimmy has taken over command of Fire Team 2, now that the Scottish Monster has been evacuated to the *Sir Percival*, and Lassie has come in to reinforce the depleted numbers of his team. Together, the two men are keeping a watch on the clump of jungle to the north-east of the village hospital house, which is now just a smoking, blasted ruin. This is where most of the rebel resistance is still coming from.

''Ave a brew, mate,' Lassie whispers, handing Jimmy a tin mug of steaming tea.

'Grand 'ere, innit?' Jimmy grunts back at him, grinning. Carefully, he takes hold of the tea. 'Luverly. Perfick place for a cuppa.'

'Always time for a tea break, mate,' Lassie replies, scrabbling down beside him in the ditch to take cover against the wall.

For a few minutes, the two men lie there in silence passing the cup of tea between them, neither soldier taking his eyes off the village track up ahead of them, running past the wall of ragged forest. Suddenly, Lassie becomes aware of a fiery, stinging sensation running up his right leg. Glancing down, he realises that his combats are crawling with fire ants, and the little critters aren't looking very happy.

'What the fuck?' he hisses, wriggling his leg about to try to shake them off. But this only serves to make the ants all the more angry, and the stinging just gets worse.

'Fakin' 'ell, Lassie, matey, stay still, will you? If you ain't careful, I'll spill the fakin' tea,' Jimmy remarks, trying not to crack up laughing. 'What's going on? You got fakin' ants in your pants or summit?'

'This place is fuckin' infested with 'em!' Lassie hisses back.

'Join the club, mate. An' I've got them fakin' everywhere, so I 'ave,' Jimmy replies. 'Fakin' ants in me pants, fakin' savages trying to fakin' kill us, and lying 'ere in this fakin' ditch that stinks of shit and piss and God only knows what else. Welcome to Gberi fakin' Bana, mate. What did you expect? Fakin' Butlins?'

'What I didn't expect, mate, was to risk me life crawling across 'ere to give a fucker like you a cup of tea, only to get eaten alive,' Lassie grunts, as he resigns himself to letting the ants do whatever they will with his leg.

''Old on a minute,' Jimmy remarks, nudging Lassie in the ribs. 'Wakey, wakey, Lassie me old mate. Looks like the fuckers are coming back for some more, like. This'll be for Brad, this will. You fuckers may 'ave got lucky once, but it won't be 'appenin again, like.'

Lassie looks in the direction that Jimmy is indicating with his eyes. Sure enough, a couple of rebels have just stuck their heads out of the jungle, and are glancing nervously all about them. With the men of the assault force having gone quiet on the mission, the village appears completely deserted. As the rebels can see no sign of movement anywhere, they must think that the British enemy have already left. A couple of Chinooks have been in and out of there by now – to carry out the hostage and casualty evacuations – so it isn't too much of an irrational conclusion for them to have reached. The two British soldiers keep silent watch as the rebels keep nudging each other in the ribs, and egging each other on to go further in towards the village.

'Careful now, me old mate,' Jimmy whispers, as he takes aim with his Minimi on the advancing figures. 'You set, Lassie? We'll open up on 'em when they reach that bit of mangled galvanised, to the right front of the fuckers. Give 'em a fakin' good malleting, all right?'

'Got it, mate,' Lassie whispers, bringing his Diemaco to bear on the distant figures now creeping towards the village.

'Sierra Two Zero, callin' all units,' Jimmy whispers over the net. 'Several enemy at three o'clock, repeat three o'clock, advancin' from tree line towards the White House. On me, fire at will, over.'

'Sierra Three Zero here, we have them visual. Ready when you are, over.'

'Sierra Four Zero here. Nothing moving our end. They're all yours.'

'Roger that, Sierra Two Zero out.'

By the time the first rebel soldiers come level with the sheet of galvanised iron – which has come off one of the roofs blown in by the choppers – there are now eight of them out in the open. Jimmy begins the count down to the moment when they will open fire.

'OK, Lassie, 'ere goes. Ready, ready, ready, ready, ready, ready, NOW!'

Jimmy's last words are lost in an eruption of gunfire, as he and Lassie open up on the advancing figures. A split second later, their fellow soldiers to the right and left of them open fire, too. Several of the rebels are blown clean off their feet by the hail of bullets coming at them from the fire teams' hidden positions. Of the eight rebels who have advanced out of the tree line, none makes it back to the safety of the jungle shadows. This becomes a pattern of the battle for the next two hours or more: the assault force going quiet on the village, the rebels emerging from the forest and then getting blasted again. No matter how many times they are hit in this way, the West Side Boys never seem to learn their lesson, and they just keep coming back for more.

After this first episode, sporadic bursts of answering AK fire come back at Lassie, Jimmy and the others from the cover of the jungle, but the men are well hunkered down now. At this range, the rebels would need heavy machine guns, or better still mortars, to have any real chance of causing the British soldiers problems. And while they have abandoned most of their heavy kit in the village, they also seem to have run out of RPG rounds by now. But just as the firefight starts to die down, Jimmy spots Chicken Run – the white chicken from their assault on the White House – coming wandering up the track towards them.

'Bugger! Oi! It's the flamin' chicken! Getoutatheway, Chicken Run!' Jimmy hisses at the chicken, which is completely oblivious to the danger.

'Don't go that ways, you silly feathered fucker. You'll 'ave a right nonsense if you do.'

'What the fuck're you on, mate?' Lassie asks, shaking his head. '*Chicken Run*? You're off your fuckin' head, aren't you? You trying to talk to the fuckin' animals, now is it . . . What the fuck's goin' on between you and that bird, anyways? Didn't know you was into the feathered kind.'

'Lassie, r'you just plain *stupid* or summink?' Jimmy asks, incredulously. 'That is fakin' *Chicken Run*, that is. An 'eroic bird if ever there was one. Chicken Run came in wiv' us on the assault on the White 'Ouse, didn't she? Bravest fuckin' bird I ever seen. Oh fuck it. You wouldn't understand, you dozy bastard. Only, I was gonna take 'er back wiv us on the chopper, like, you know, sort of Regimental mascot, an' all.'

Lassie is shaking his head in disbelief. 'How the hell was you going to catch it, then, you fuckin' lunatic? Thought of that one, 'ave you, you big fuckin' softie?'

'Easy, innit? Fate would have sorted it out. It was good voodoo an' all that brought Chicken Run into the White 'Ouse wiv us in the first place, an' good fakin' voodoo was gonna sort it all out.'

But just as Jimmy is finishing speaking, Chicken Run takes a fatal step too far and disappears in a puff of white feathers and a splattering of blood. She had been caught in one of the long bursts of machine-gun fire coming from the West Side Boys' positions, and her remains are now splattered across the track in front of the two British soldiers.

'Na, fuck it,' says Jimmy, visibly upset. 'I did warn you, Chicken Run, you silly fucker, didn't I? I said, "You go any further and you're a fuckin' dead chicken." Now look what's gorn an' 'appened. First they got the Big fakin' Scot and now they got Chicken Run. Who the fuck's it gonna be next? Rest in peace, Chicken Run . . . Rest in peace . . . Best we give 'er a minute's silence, eh, Lassie mate?'

Suddenly, as Lassie and Jimmy are mourning the untimely death of Chicken Run, the comparative quiet is broken by the sound of a heavy firefight breaking out in the jungle to the northern end of the village. The two men exchange glances. After the slight lull in the battle, it is obviously kicking off again. The rebels, it seems, still want their village back. Smoke from grenades begins drifting across to them, carrying with it the distinctive, peppery tang of cordite. The smell of burning buildings and of gunfire mingles with the musty stench emanating from the ditch.

'Sounds like someone's hit the jackpot, mate,' Lassie remarks, once the minute is up, jerking his head in the direction of the firefight behind them.

'Yeah, mate. Lucky bastards.' Jimmy replies. 'You know what, mate,' he continues, wrinkling his nose, 'it stinks around here, don't it? Know what that smell is? It's the stench of death. *Theirs*. Not ours. After the Big Scot, Chicken Run and the others, they ain't fakin' gettin' no more of us. *This is a village full of fakin' dead men*. Dunno which smells worse, mate. You after a fakin' week in the jungle, or this fakin' village.'

As the SAS fire teams are getting their first brew on in Gberi Bana, the rescued British hostages are doing the same on the RFA *Sir Percival*. After tea and a few hasty cigarettes, they are sent below decks to see the Royal Irish Rangers' Quartermaster. He has a change of uniform and other kit for them. Then they head off for a good shit, shave, shower and shampoo. They have two weeks of facial growth to get rid of, and teeth that haven't had a good scrubbing, or even so much as seen a dollop of toothpaste, for seventeen days. Before they can hit the ship's canteen, they are sent for a medical, and then there is a debrief to go through with the officers. As well as their CO, Simon Fordham, and the Regiment's Padre, the two Met hostage-negotiating officers are also waiting to have a word with them, along with some of the top brass. It isn't a formal debrief as such, more just a chat with the assembled men.

'You're out now, lads,' the top brass are saying, trying to be reassuring. 'It's certainly been one hell of an ordeal, I'm sure, but you're safe as houses now.'

The men from the Met are keen to know exactly how successful the various hostage-negotiation tactics have been – from the perspective of the hostages themselves. Small details of the drama are picked over in detail, including the fact that the Met officers tried to smuggle cigarettes into the men, hidden inside the Hexy burners. None of the cigarettes got through to the hostages themselves of course; they must all have ended up in the hands of the West Side Boys. They were top-brand ciggies, too, the Met officers point out, Marlboros and the like, not the nasty local lung rot that the rebels – and increasingly the hostages – had been smoking.

A bergen stuffed full of letters, chocolates and other goodies had also been sent over from the Royal Irish Regiment, but none of that had got through to the hostages – not that the men can think what the fuck the West Side Boys might have wanted with their letters. The heads-on-poles incident is mentioned, of course; it has become like a symbol of the worst depravities of the rebels. Then the two Met officers lend the ex-hostages their flash mobile phones – ones that work even here in West Africa – so they can put a call through to their folks back at home.

'You put a 00 44 before your normal number, and drop the first 0 off the start of that,' one of the officers tells them, helpfully. 'And don't worry, your parents shouldn't be too surprised to hear from you. They were told last night that the assault was going in, and so to expect a call.'

And so, in pairs, the free men walk out to the back of the ship, where the press can't see them, and dial home.

By now it is 8 a.m. British time, and General Sir Charles Guthrie, Chief of Defence Staff, has been given the news that all the hostages have been rescued safely. Months earlier, he had been booked to appear that morning on BBC1's *Breakfast with Frost*, and Major Tom Thornycroft is able to whisper the news to him in the wings of the BBC studio. Sir Charles then breaks the news to the nation that an operation is underway in West Africa and that all the hostages have been rescued.

RETURN OF THE JEDI

I am afraid the war will end very soon now, but I suppose all good things come to an end sooner or later, so we mustn't grumble.
– Captain (later Field Marshal) Earl Alexander, 1917,
in a letter to his mother

WITH their command unit having been taken out by the rebel mortar, the Paras are still pinned down in Magbeni. But luckily, there is one senior Para officer who has survived that air-burst mortar – Captain Danny Matthews, Major Lowe's 2iC. As Major Lowe was evacuated by Chinook, he called up his Captain on the radio and ordered him to take over command of the assault.

Thinking fast and on his feet – as this eventuality, the taking out of the whole Para command unit, has hardly been planned for – the young Captain considers his options. Unable now to communicate properly with the air cover (the radios have been pretty much put out of action in the enemy mortar attack), he cannot call in an air strike. At the same time, he has no mortar back-up of his own, with which to pound the enemy positions: the men of the Paras' mortar unit have been unable to find a patch of firm ground to set up their mortars, back on the swampy landing zone. So Captain Matthews decides that there is but one option left him: pure, aggressive soldiering.

He will order all units into a full-frontal assault against the rebel positions, in order to silence the enemy mortars . . . before the mortars silence *them*. It will be a charge of the Bayonets. *And, please Lord, it better bloody well work.*

Ordering 1 Platoon to move up from the LZ into the rear of his position, Captain Matthews calls for smoke to be put down on to the track running through the centre of the village, to provide cover for the advance. As the Paras' mortars cannot be used to lay down the smokescreen, 3 Platoon move towards the village track and throw red phosphorous grenades instead. Captain Matthews then orders the men of the lead units, 2 and 3 Platoons, 'up and at' the rebel defences: they are to advance through the cover of the jungle and the buildings on the northern edge of the village, some eight hundred yards or so, hitting that flank of the rebel mortar position. At the same time, 1 Platoon is to move up from behind 2 and 3 Platoons' positions to cross the village track under the cover of smoke, in order to hit the rebels' southern flank. This will require them to do a fighting advance a thousand-odd yards or more through the village.

With Paras attacking from both sides, Captain Matthews intends to trap the rebels in a pincer movement and force them to abandon their mortar positions. As the Bayonets advance from the west, hitting the northern and southern flanks of the rebel positions, there will be left just one avenue of escape to the rebels – to fall back into the jungles at the eastern end of the village. There is nothing overly subtle about the Captain's plan of attack; basically, it is designed to retake the offensive and win the day. The Captain knows that if it fails, the whole assault may be defeated in the process.

It is 7.30 a.m. when Captain Matthews orders his men to advance. Having first been dumped neck-deep into a swamp and now having had six of their most senior ranks, *including their* CO, taken out by a lucky rebel mortar, the men of 1 Para are seething, burning, fired up with anger and fury. Breaking cover on the Captain's order and driving ahead with screams of enmity, the Bayonets thrust forward, aggression forcing them on. They are met by a hail of bullets coming at them from the rebel positions, yet they keep pushing forward. Employing classic fire-and-manoeuvre tactics, half a section of men advancing while the others put down a barrage of covering fire, they thrust ahead. Darting from patch of jungle to patch of jungle, and building to building, and weaving among the dense smoke, the Bayonets put down a blistering wall of fire, as they bear down remorselessly on the enemy.

Several of the Paras put their hand-held 66mm LAWs into use now on the buildings at the far edge of the village. While walls might stop bullets, the LAWs pound into them, pulverising concrete blocks into dust and throwing galvanised roofing skywards. Under such accurate and devastating firepower, the rebel front starts to falter in the face of this lightning assault. As fear takes hold and the West Side Boys realise

RETURN OF THE JEDI 369

that their positions are about to be overrun by these 'white devils', their resistance crumbles. Suddenly, all the fight goes out of them, and is replaced by blind terror and the urge for flight. In a split second the battle turns in the Paras' favour, the rebel retreat becoming a rout.

The West Side Boys are falling back now, back into the jungle towards the eastern end of the village – the Golden Bridge of escape that the young Para Captain has deliberately left open for them in his assault plan. As 1 Platoon make a fighting advance towards the river, they seize one of the key targets of the assault: the rebel ammunition dump, an underground storage pit covered by a tarpaulin. It is stuffed full of 61mm mortar shells, RPG rounds, and cases of heavy machine-gun ammo. The Bayonets from 3 Platoon continue to advance east, cutting the track leading to the Laia Junction as they do so. Here, they set up a roadblock to stop any rebel reinforcements being driven down into Magbeni.

Meanwhile, 2 Platoon have taken possession of the burned-out village itself. The whole of Magbeni has now been seized by the Paras, and all terrain has been secured by brute soldiering, raw aggression and military professionalism – with little help from the air power overhead, and no mortar support. The blood of the Paras is well and truly up now, and the Bayonets fan out into the jungle surrounding the village in hot pursuit of the enemy. It is all that Captain Matthews can do to stop his men chasing the rebels all the way back to Freetown itself. Nevertheless, he calls them in, regroups them, and sends separate fire teams out to secure the area and retrieve the three captured Royal Irish Land-Rovers.

The Paras' mortar team is picked up by chopper from the swamp LZ and flown across to firmer ground. From here, they put down harassing mortar fire on to the enemy. But smoke-spotter rounds fired into the jungle fail to show, owing to the density of the vegetation. So Captain Matthews requests that one of the orbiting gunships provides mortar fire control (MFC) (by spotting the exploding mortar rounds from the air and radioing in adjustments). But the ongoing problems with their radio sets make effective comms between the air and ground forces all but impossible, and so the aerial MFC is abandoned. Instead, the mortar fire has to be adjusted by ear, which is a pretty inexact science – an experienced mortar operator listening to the explosions, guessing distance and trajectory from the sound, and adjusting fire accordingly. In this way, a 61 and 81mm mortar barrage pounds the jungle in an arc towards the eastern end of the village.

There are some two to three hundred West Side Boys fighters hiding out in that jungle, and the battle for Magbeni will splutter on for a further thirty minutes or so, before the Paras are finally able to declare the area clear of hostile forces.

By 8 a.m., the village of Magbeni is certified secure. The centre of the village has been completely shot to pieces by the helicopter gunships. The occupying forces are surrounded by the smoking ruins of buildings and the remains of destroyed gun emplacements. Many of the rebels must have fled before the aerial assault, but the place is still littered with the wounded and the dying. The rebel Bedford truck with the twin 14.5mm ZPU guns is still intact, although all the rebel technicals (machine-gun-mounted Toyota pickups) have been hit by the gunships and reduced to smoking, twisted heaps of metal.

The three original Land-Rovers of the Royal Irish patrol are largely unharmed and still drivable. Spare keys for the vehicles have been flown in from Freetown, and so they are driven down into the centre of the village. Here, they are rigged with massive harnesses for air carriage, and each of the three vehicles is slung beneath one of the three giant Chinooks, to be flown back to Waterloo Camp. As the massive choppers lift off and haul the Land-Rovers skywards, there is a sense of closure to the whole mission now, as if another of the rebels' wrongs has finally been put to right.

While the main body of the Para assault force withdraws to the central landing zone – *on dry, firm ground* – a thirteen-man demolition team goes into action in the village. The ZPU-mounted Bedford requires a massive charge of plastic explosives to render it unusable, the force of the explosion lifting the truck bodily from the ground, and leaving it a twisted, burning wreck. There is also a large quantity of mortar shells, RPG rounds, mines, ammunition and other weaponry left scattered around the village by the retreating rebels – all of which is doused in petrol and set alight using red phosphorous grenades.

It is just 9.30 a.m. when the entire Para assault force finally lifts off in the three Chinooks. As they climb skywards, they look back on a massive firework display below them in Magbeni, a series of timed detonation charges going off and sending the rebel ammo dump up in smoke. The battle for Magbeni is already over. As the chopper-borne force gains height, the waters of the Rokel Creek roll away beneath them, glistening in the early-morning sun.

And to the north of them, the battle for Gberi Bana rages on.

*   *   *

Some of the Paras who have pulled out of Magbeni are flown over to reinforce the assault teams in Gberi Bana. These young lads are incredibly pumped up from all the fighting on their side of the river. But in Gberi Bana, they find a bunch of blokes lying around drinking their tea and having their sarnies. This is what really shocks the Paras. They just can't believe it. In the midst of this firefight, the men of the Regiment look like they are enjoying an early-morning tea party.

'Got to 'ave a brew an' some scoff on the job,' Lassie remarks, to a bemused young Para.

They're either the coolest motherfuckers that ever served in Her Majesty's Armed Forces, or they are completely barking, the Paras are thinking to themselves. *Probably a bit of both. Who in their right mind wouldn't want to join them?*

Some three hours into the operation and the men of the assault force have gone through all the buildings, and there are piles of captured weapons in the village: AK47s, RPGs, SLRs, grenades and mortar rounds. And then there are the stashes of captured drugs to be burned – both grass and the white powder (which does turn out to be heroin). By mid-morning, the drugs and the damaged small arms have been piled up into a single heap in the centre of the village, doused in petrol, and set alight – the burning pyre throwing a pillar of flame and oily black smoke high into the sky. Some of the hostages' personal effects, those that the West Side Boys had taken off them, have also been recovered.

Now that the Special Forces HQ at the radio shack has got a friendly security fence of fire teams stationed around the village perimeter, they can get work parties out, collecting up the wounded and the dead. Pulling on white rubber surgical gloves to protect themselves from infection, the men start checking if the rebels who have gone down really are dead, or just badly wounded, and that none of the rebel corpses are booby-trapped in any way. Once they've done that, they start taking them away. They have been ordered to clear up as many corpses from the battle scene as possible.

With one man on either arm, the soldiers drag the dead bodies through the village to a collection point adjacent to LZ3, leaving shallow drag marks in the damp ground behind them. Soon, there is a long line of corpses lying in the mud and the long grass. All of them are barefoot; none has had the time to pull their boots on this morning before going to war. One, a man in a white singlet, mouth half open and disbelieving, staring blankly skywards; another in a combat shirt and purple Y-fronts, face down in the earth; a third, younger, in bright yellow shorts, fingers grasping, clawlike, at the air; a fourth corpse, a woman, incongruous in a white brassiere and light-blue-and-white checked shorts; a fifth, a man in full combats and a black T-shirt, with *The New Legend* emblazoned across the front of it.

The men of the assault force will now have to check their reserves of ammo, and radio in resupply if necessary. And they will have to call in extra water, because the two bottles that each man has carried in with him are nowhere near sufficient. In the tropical heat and humidity, and laden down as they are, the body needs several litres of fluid to keep functioning properly. Before completing a successful exfil, the men will dynamite Gberi Bana's mortar and HMG emplacements with charges of plastic explosives, just to make sure that they can never be made serviceable again.

Among the rebel prisoners now gathered at the radio shack HQ, there are several wounded – including Foday Kallay's wife. No voodoo spells or charms were able to protect the rebels' Voodoo Queen when D Squadron hit the village. The wounded are being patched up as best they can be by the paramedics, the shaven-headed village 'recruits' in particular getting priority treatment. A number of them have been wounded in the crossfire, and – after being positively identified by Major Martial – the medics are now doing their best to help them.

One of the Chinooks, Sierra One, is called back in to the LZ at the village football field, to evacuate the prisoners – the stretcher cases, the walking wounded, the captured rebels and the villagers. The chopper waits on the ground as the dead bodies of the rebels, some twenty-five in all, are collected up and piled on board. In the absence of body bags, they have been ordered to stuff the dead bodies into their bivvy bags. But it is proving all but impossible to do so, because they are the type with only a small head hole at the top. After struggling for a few minutes, most just give up and throw the corpses into the chopper as they are, with plasticuffs around them to hold their arms and feet together.

There are at least two young children and several women among the rebel dead loaded on to the chopper that morning, along with the eighteen rebel prisoners. Finally, they throw Foday Kallay, in plasticuffs, on to the floor of the chopper – which by now is running in blood – and then they pile the bodies of the rebel dead on top of him. A couple of the lads shoves a partially severed head into Kallay's face, just to keep him company on the chopper ride. *This is for Brad*, the men of D-squadron are thinking.

Sierra One ferries the dead bodies over to the Jordanian UN base, and dumps them out on the ground. That'll give the UN peacekeepers something to be getting on with. It then flies on to the Royal Irish base at Benguema, to drop Kallay off and the other rebel prisoners. But as soon as Kallay is booted off the chopper, the Royal Irish soldiers realise that he is wearing several of their mates' wedding rings. It is now that Kallay gets his second beating of the morning, as the enraged British soldiers tear the rings off the rebel leader's fingers.

All together, the men of the assault force will end up being on the ground for four hours at Gberi Bana. This indicates the level of resistance put up by the West Side Boys. True to type, once they had woken up to the fact of the assault, the rebels had decided to stand and fight – all be it in their own peculiar way. Despite all the mortar rounds and rocket fire and the helicopter gunship attacks levelled at them, the main body of the West Side Boys only ever retreated as far as the cover of the jungle. Rather than running away, they repeatedly counter-attacked from the forest.

At 10.25 a.m. it is time for the exfil main to go out – two Chinooks flying out with all the remaining Special Forces men and the handful of Paras. The floors of the choppers are thick with blood and gore by now, most of it from the dead and injured rebels. Both Chinooks will be coming in to land on the village football field – LZ3 – for the final, defensive exfil. The men of the assault force have retreated to that LZ, using a defensive fire-and-manoeuvre technique – half of the men from each fire team covering as the other half pull back from their positions in the village, and then vice versa, all the way back to the clearing at LZ3. Here the assault force has gathered together, with its defensive perimeter pulled back to the boundary of the football field itself.

''Ear that, mate?' Jimmy asks, as Lassie and the Kiwi line up with him for the chopper ride out. 'Silence. Fakin' silence. Music to your ears, mate. Listen. Even the fakin' monkeys 'ave shut up their racket. Even the birds 'ave stopped singin'.'

The three men stand there for a few seconds, listening. Sure enough, apart from the distant throb of the incoming choppers, Gberi Bana is totally, deathly quiet.

'Sounds like we've done a good job, eh, mate?' the Kiwi remarks.

'Too right. Pity we can't leave some fakin' booby traps for the evil bastards, though,' Jimmy muses, as he glances around the shattered, smoking ruins of the rebel base. 'Give 'em a nice surprise it would, when they fakin' come back into it, like. Anyways, at least we've fakin' trashed the joint, innit?'

'Yeah, mate,' the Kiwi replies, with an exhausted grin. 'I left a big turdy on one of the beds for the bastards. What about you, mate?'

'Biggest fakin' log I ever laid in me life, mate. Right in the middle of the fakin' White 'Ouse an' all. Tell you what though, I was dying to leave some fakin' graffiti – you know, tellin' the bastards what we really think of the fakin' West Side Boys now. Trouble is, what if the fakin' press was to come in an' film it all, or summink? Cause a right nonsense, wouldn't it? Can't be 'avin' that, now can we?'

'Pity about the chicken, though, eh?' Lassie remarks, sarcastically. 'Fuckin' Chicken Run, wasn't it? Could have scraped up the pieces, couldn't you, Jimmy mate, and brought 'em along, like, just for good luck. Could've glued 'em back together at Hereford, and made yourself a stuffed mascot instead of a living one. Damn sight easier to look after and keep fed, mate.'

'*What fakin' chicken?*' Jimmy counters, looking over at Lassie incredulously, as if he's gone completely insane. 'You cracked or summink? 'Ere we are after four hours of not fakin' around at all with these bastards – they presented their arse to us and we fakin' kicked it, like – an' all you can think of is a fakin' *chicken*. What you on about a fakin' chicken for, Lassie, mate? You fucked in the 'ead, or summink? All the action done your 'ead in, 'as it?'

'This bloody great softie wanted to take this fuckin' white chicken out with him, Kiwi,' says Lassie, defensively. 'Honest he did. Said it had been with your fire team all round the White House when you cleared it. Sort of Regimental talisman, he said. Talk about cracked, that takes the fuckin' biscuit, that does. Then it was hit by a stray round. Poof! Cloud of feathers and it was history. Only a fuckin' chicken, mind, but this bloke was acting like his own mother had just copped it. Called it fuckin' Chicken Run, he did.'

'Yeah, mate,' the Kiwi replies, pensively. 'Well, it was a bloody amazing bird. Not always you get to go into action with a bloody chicken for company, right? Is it a bird, is it a plane, no – it's Chicken Run. But no wonder Jimmy there wanted to take it home with him, mate. Take a look at him. Chicken Run there was about the only bird he's likely to get his hands on this side of Christmas, mate.'

'You're 'avin' a fakin' nonsense, aren't you, Kiwi mate?' Jimmy retorts, raising his eyebrows. 'As everyone knows, I'm fakin' awesome with the birds. Don't matter what you looks like, Kiwi mate, the winged-dagger cap badge just sends 'em weak at the knees. Every time, mate. You can be ugly as sin – just like me, mate – but the cap badge does it every time, for the birds, like. Only reason I stay in the fakin' Regiment, mate. Can't be no other, can there, not when I 'ave to put up with a couple of fakin' frobbers like you two. And as to the feathered variety, I'm fakin' allergical to 'em . . .'

Jimmy's last words are lost in the howl of the approaching choppers. As the first Chinook, Sierra One, comes in to land, Sierra Two holds off with a fire team of Paras on board and the loadies manning the chain guns. They are ready to give covering fire, just in case there are any rebels still in the vicinity feeling like they may get lucky. Once Sierra One has taken on board a little over half the squadron, it lifts off to hover over the LZ and give covering fire for Sierra Two, which puts down and picks up the remaining thirty-odd men.

It is 10.45 a.m. by the time the second chopper lifts off with the last of the assault force on board – and it is leaving behind a gutted, deserted camp, with fires burning in many areas. As the Chinook climbs into the air the full extent of the devastation becomes clear, with thick, oily columns of black smoke rising from both sides of the Rokel Creek. There is no doubt about it to the exhausted men of Her Majesty's Special Forces on board the two Chinooks: they are leaving behind a job well done.

On the chopper ride out, the men are buzzing, high, exhausted, blown away by it all. But the sense of victory is overshadowed by Brad and the other casualties – the Big Scottish Monster among them – whose fate is still hanging in the balance. Yet there is also the strong feeling of having made history, of having taken part in something momentous that will be talked about and written about for many years to come. This is an intensely personal thing: each man has made his mark and he knows that he will never be able to fully share that feeling with anyone other than the men on board the chopper with him right now. And he doesn't need to, either. These men are enough. It will be their own private, personal experience. The events of this morning will be talked about, sifted over and relived between them for many years to come.

The first scheduled stop for the two Chinooks is the Royal Irish camp at Benguema, where D Squadron has been promised a post-op booze-up with the Royal Irish Rangers. But it turns out that the world's press and their dog are camped out at the site gates, just waiting for the story. So, after dropping off the last of the captured weapons, the two choppers press on to the outskirts of Freetown and Waterloo Camp. In addition to the seriously injured that have already gone out, there are one hell of a lot of walking wounded on those two exfil flights. Few if any of the men have escaped without being hit by some piece of ordnance or other. The OC, Pete Cutgood, is on the very last chopper out, and on that flight he is able to get final confirmation that Brad Tinnion is certified dead.

Back at Waterloo Camp, the men of D Squadron and their SBS colleagues hurry to strip down their weapons and hand in any unused ammo and explosives to stores. They have their own personal kit to pack, and that of any of the casualties who are unable to carry their own gear out of there. The priority has now become one of getting out of Waterloo before the press get a sniff of where the assault force is holed up, and come looking for them.

They gather for a short breather around mugs of tea in the mess tent, as all the stories start coming out. At the same time, the medics are doing the rounds to tidy them up a bit, as there are small pieces of shrapnel that need taking out of arms and legs and the like. At first, there is a lot of laughter and high spirits, because they've pulled it off and got out of there alive. But there is also a sombre atmosphere, because Brad Tinnion hasn't made it.

It takes a real man to admit that he was scared, now – after the mission, after they have all done their duty and more. It takes a real man to sit down with his mates in the mess tent and discuss all this, coming clean, sharing the moment when the blind fear took hold, and the fog of terror came down. But there are a number of such discussions in the mess tent that lunchtime – because all of these men have done their duty, and none of them has failed, and they feel that they will never be closer to their fellow soldiers than they are right now, in the immediate afterglow of mortal combat.

Now is the time for talking, for honesty, to lay bare the soul; for in one month, one week, one day or even just one hour, the moment will have passed and the shutters and the walls will have come down again.

'I reckon I've been through just about every fakin' last emotion it's possible to 'ave,' Jimmy remarks, exhaustedly. 'You know, like I was shitting myself at first light; then there was the madness and uproar as we choppered in along the river; then ice-cold anger on the ground as we went into action; then the rage and murder in my 'eart when I 'eard that Brad had gone down bad; the sense of relief when I knew we were out of there OK; and then the feeling of really missing me family in the immediate aftermarf, when I knew I'd made it through, like. Any one of you fakers know what I'm on about? Or am I just' talkin' to me fakin' self, like?'

'Sure, mate,' observes the Kiwi, quietly. 'I know exactly what you're on about, mate. I felt the same bloody way, right.'

'Well, thank fuck for that,' says Jimmy, with obvious relief. 'I thought I was the only mad fucker among the lot of us.'

'No worries, mate. You're all right,' the Kiwi says, laughing. 'It's those fuckers back in that village you need to say your prayers for, mate.'

'Too right. Say, you 'eard anything about the Big Scot?' Jimmy asks, anxiously. 'I mean, 'e was pretty fakin' bad when they choppered 'im out of there, innit. Don't make fakin' sense, do it. Built like a brick shithouse . . . 'E's fakin' indestructible, that big Scottish bastard.'

'No, mate, I haven't heard,' the Kiwi replied, quietly. 'Sure as hell he'll be all right though, mate. Nothing could put the Big Scot down for long, right.'

'Yeah, I reckon . . .' Jimmy says, not completing his sentence, clearly lost in thought, concerned for his wounded mate. 'You see those fakin' chain guns, mate?' he continues, pulling himself back to the present. He is feeling weird, one moment really up because they've made it through all right, the next minute really down because of Brad, and his wounded friends. 'Awesome, wannit? Just a circular set of barrels that spun and spun and spun the bullets out at an awesome rate of death. There's no way you'd want to be on the wrong end of that, know what I mean?'

'Take a look at this, you hairy-arsed bunch of bastards,' Gerry Birt butts in, holding up a set of webbing. 'Got it off that fucker GS. Set of the Rangers' webbing, see? Same that he stole off 'em when he kidnapped 'em. Reckon I'll return it to the lads when I see 'em on the boat, so I will. And look, how sad is that? 'E's even stuck a pathetic little set of colonel's pips on the front. That fucker was no more a colonel than my grandmother. Stupid bastard.'

'You got the bastard, then?' Jimmy asks.

'Too right. Fat lot of good fuckin' body armour did 'im,' Gerry answers. 'Not when 'e's got the fuckin' Regiment on his tail. Three to the 'ead, it was.'

Of the seventy Special Forces men that had set out at dawn that morning from Waterloo Camp, sixty have returned more or less intact. One is certified dead already. Nine are injured and are being treated on the RFA *Sir Percival*. And there are also nine badly wounded on the

Paras' side – six of whom were hit in the mortar attack and the rest in the battle for Magbeni. With it being a dawn raid, the men are back in time for lunch at Waterloo Camp. By late afternoon, they are flown on the Chinooks across to the *Sir Percival*, where they are allowed a couple of cans of lager each. Then, all two-hundred-odd men involved in Operation Barras are herded into the ship's huge mess hall, so that Brigadier Simon Chadwell, the Commander of UK Special Forces, can say a few words.

'I'm very pleased to say that all the objectives of Operation Barras were achieved successfully,' he begins. 'As you will know, the six British and one Sierra Leonean hostages were rescued unharmed and brought out to safety. Gberi Bana was successfully held for four hours, despite stiff resistance from the West Side Boys. On the southern river bank, the Paras drove out the enemy and we retrieved our three captured vehicles intact, which were airlifted out by Chinook. Around twenty-five bodies of the enemy were recovered from the northern river bank, though many more are likely to have perished in the jungle. We anticipate the final casualty figure on the enemy side at Gberi Bana being far higher, over a hundred or more dead. And at Magbeni, the Paras may have accounted for a similar number. Our forces suffered some twenty-odd wounded, though none of those appears life-threatening. I am sad to say that D Squadron lost Brad Tinnion in the first few minutes of the firefight. I'd like to thank both the SAS and the Paras for a very successful mission.'

The Shakyboats who'd taken part in Operation Barras are not happy that the SBS has received no special mention in the CO's debrief. But that traditional rivalry with their SAS colleagues is gradually being forgotten. That morning, they had fought integrated into D Squadron's fire teams, and so they don't feel too short-changed. As the men of D Squadron and the SBS pass through the boat on their way out, there is just time for a brief chat with the rescued hostages.

The six Royal Irish soldiers have settled down to their first cooked meal on-board ship, and the chefs have prepared a special feast for them: roast beef with huge chunks of chocolate cake for pudding. But the men can hardly eat anything, their stomachs have shrunk so much over the past seventeen days. As they try to force the food down them, they look up to see the SAS and SBS boys passing through the ship's mess, on the way out of their post-op debriefing.

'How you doing then, lads?' one of the men from the Regiment calls over. 'Get it down you, mind. You'll be needing a good feed.'

'Cheers. But we're dead on, like,' one of the Rangers calls back.

'Sure, it's all thanks to youse lot,' the other Ranger adds.

'We hammered the bastards good an' proper, like,' another of the passing SF soldiers shouts over.

'Aye, we know youse did. And thanks for that.'

From the RFA *Sir Percival* the men of the SAS and SBS are ferried back across the Freetown Estuary to Lungi Airport, and put straight on to a C-130 Hercules transport aircraft, which flies them directly back to RAF Brize Norton in the UK. Within twenty-four hours of the start of Operation Barras, the men of D Squadron are having a brew back in their base in Hereford. The Big Scottish Monster and the other three seriously wounded men of the Special Forces assault force will follow on in due course, once their conditions have been stabilised in the *Sir Percival* sick bay. None of their wounds will prove life-threatening and all will return to active service after a short recovery period.

Tony Blair had spent much of the weekend of the assault at Chequers, approving the last details of the Operation Barras plan. After receiving a call from Sir Charles Guthrie, informing him of the initial assault success, Blair returned to London, to make a statement to television cameras in front of Number 10 Downing Street.

'The operation was authorised once it became clear to us that the negotiations for their release were not being carried out in good faith and the lives of the hostages were in danger,' the Prime Minister told the assembled media. 'I cannot pay high enough tribute to the skill, professionalism and the courage of the armed forces involved. Inevitably in such an operation there are casualties. Our thoughts and prayers are with the families. British personnel are in Sierra Leone in order to save that country from dictatorship, from armed gangs who are already responsible for thousands of deaths.

'We can be proud of those armed forces,' Blair continued, after a slight pause. 'There really are no finer armed forces anywhere in the world.'

D Squadron had been ordered to go in and give the West Side Boys a bloody nose, and that's what they had done. A lot of the rebels had been finished off at close range, and there were women and children among the dead. D Squadron had been ordered to clear up the bodies because headquarters didn't want the press crawling all over the village after the assault, and recording what they had been up to. If the men of the assault force had been carrying out the same sort of operation in the centre of London – like the Iranian Embassy siege had been – they would have faced all sorts of forensic questions afterwards. That was one of the key factors that had made Operation Barras so much simpler and easier to put into action: no one was ever going to be brought to book for what they had done out there on the ground.

As one member of D Squadron put it: 'We'd been sent in to eliminate a rebel base in the morning. That's what we did. And we were back in time for tea in Hereford by the next evening.'

ENDGAME

When the enemy escapes, we harass.
When he retreats, we pursue.
When he is tired, we attack.
When he burns, we put out the fire.
When he loots, we attack.
When he pursues, we hide.
When he retreats, we return.

– Mao Tse-tung (1893–1976)

ON the morning of the assault, the noise of the last retreating Chinook faded away into the forest at around 11 a.m., Sierra Leonean time. Shortly thereafter, the first of the West Side Boys' survivors emerged from the jungle into the smoking ruins of the village. Many of them were just teenage boys, and they wandered around in a state of shock. Never before had they seen such massive destructive power as the British assault force had unleashed on Gberi Bana and Magbeni. Their headquarters were left a smoking, shattered ruin. Shrapnel and spent munitions lay everywhere.

Not all the rebel dead had been removed by the British forces. In fact, the majority lay scattered amid the jungle, lying where they had fallen. And there were also scores of wounded, moaning and crying. There were corpses floating in the shallows of the Rokel Creek, where some of the rebel wounded had tried to crawl away from the firefight, and ended up drowning instead. Among the dead there were a handful of the shaven-headed village 'recruits' – those who had panicked, ignored Major Martial's advice, and run into the firefight. For several days after Operation Barras, half-eaten and decomposing rebel corpses would keep washing up downstream of Gberi Bana, on the beaches of the Freetown Estuary.

With so many dead, seriously wounded and captured, the West Side Boys had lost a huge number of their men. Somewhere in the region of 150 had been killed or mortally wounded in the assault. The surviving rebel commanders ordered their men to collect up the badly wounded – those judged unlikely to survive – and throw them into the river. There were no medical supplies to treat them, and even if there had been, the village hospital building was now a smoking ruin. There were an even greater number of walking wounded who might not live through the coming days, as wounds festered untreated in the steaming jungle. Without specialist treatment, any major wound to the torso would result in septicaemia (a disease caused by toxic micro organisms in the blood-stream, where the whole circulatory system literally turns septic). And in the tropics, septicaemia would kill someone in a matter of hours.

As they surveyed the carnage, the West Side Boys realised that they had paid a very heavy price indeed for taking those eleven British and one Sierra Leonean soldiers hostage. They had lost all of their communications equipment, all of their heavy machine guns and mortars, and all of their vehicles. The rebels' technicals, the Bedford mounted with the ZPU and all the four-wheel-drives that the rebels had looted off the aid agencies were now just hunks of twisted, smoking metal lying around Magbeni. And they had lost their commander-in-chief, Foday Kallay, along with most of the other high command. As a fighting force, the West Side Boys had been struck a mortal blow.

One of the only surviving senior officers was Colonel Changa Bulanga – the rebel commander who had orchestrated the first savage beatings of Corporal Mousa. He promptly declared himself the new leader of the West Side Boys, and began threatening his surviving men with execution if they tried to leave the jungle and surrender. Captain T.T. Kamara had also survived the assault, and he joined Changa Bulanga in mustering the surviving men at their ruined Gberi Bana base. A hard core of some two hundred surviving West Side Boys regrouped under their command.

Colonel Changa Bulanga was determined to launch a revenge attack on Freetown. But late in the afternoon of the day of the assault a joint force of British troops and the SLA were massing out on the main Freetown–Masiaka highway, at Songo-Mabontoso, where the Jordanians controlled the UN checkpoint marking the border of the West Side Boys' territory. These forces were planning a sweep through all the territory, to mop up any remnant rebel forces. Colonel Changa Bulanga had also heard Nellis's Mi-24 gunship patrolling the skies above Magbeni and Gberi Bana, and it was clearly hunting for any West Side Boys stragglers.

Deciding that discretion was now the better part of valour, Changa Bulanga ordered his force of two hundred men to abandon their bases at Magbeni and Gberi Bana and head deeper inland. That evening, a ragged column of West Side Boys survivors disappeared into the jungle, taking with them only what weapons and supplies they could carry on their person.

Meanwhile, one brigade of SLA troops had assembled at Songo-Mabontoso. The first they had heard of Operation Barras was when they were given their orders that afternoon to deploy to mount the moping-up operation. Op Barras had been kept a complete secret from all but a few of the Sierra Leonean Army top brass. The SLA Brigade would be deploying alongside 'the Poachers', the men of the Parachute Regiment who had been drafted into Sierra Leone as part of Operation Palliser. The Poachers would spearhead the advance on Magbeni, while the SLA inserted blocker groups into the jungle to cut off any routes of retreat. Songo-Mabontoso was to be the start line of the operation.

At least that was the plan. Unfortunately, the British and SLA troops were stopped at Mabonsonto by the Jordanian UN forces who manned the checkpoint into the West Side Boys' territory. The Jordanians were opposing any further advance of the British–SLA force. After Operation Barras, the West Side Boys had to be given a chance to surrender voluntarily, the Jordanians maintained. A heated confrontation ensued, but the Jordanians relied on their UN mandate to block any further advance. For two days, the attack force waited, as the frustration mounted and tempers boiled over. The SLA troops were particularly angry: they wanted to put into practice their IMATT training and demonstrate that they could operate effectively alongside the British forces.

Finally, the joint British–SLA forces were allowed to move forward, and the Paras' advanced on Magbeni on 13 September. At the same time, the SLA forces headed into the interior of the country, pushing out foot patrols on either side of the road. Two days were spent probing the West Side Boys' terrain in this fashion. But despite recent signs of their presence, no West Side Boys fighters were tracked down or engaged. There was ample evidence of the rebels having left the area in a great hurry: abandoned positions strewn with weapons and kit deemed too heavy or cumbersome to carry.

The SLA forces were then retasked to cross the Rokel Creek inland of Gberi Bana, and set up blocking positions in the jungle. This would cut off the West Side Boys' escape route, should the Poachers be able to flush any of the rebels out of the jungles around their bases. As the SLA did not have the boats to cross the Rokel Creek, they opted instead to drive east towards Port Loko, cross the river on the road bridge, and then deploy on foot into the jungles. They then began to sweep back through the West Side Boys' territory in the direction of Gberi Bana. Keeping a Battalion HQ element based at Port Loko, one company of men, broken down into recce and combat patrols, fanned out from either side of the road. They moved forward for several miles, checked the area was clear, regrouped on the road and advanced again. They advanced like this for three days, before they reached the outskirts of Gberi Bana.

As they approached the rebel HQ, the SLA soldiers started to find signs of the British operation, including the OP that Lassie, Mat and the others of the six-man SAS obs team had used. When they reached Gberi Bana itself, the place was completely deserted. Empty shells of all types littered the ground, as did the remains of the rebel weaponry that had been destroyed. To one side of the village at the forest's edge, the SLA troops discovered a mass grave. It contained the partially decomposed bodies of around a dozen men, most of whom had been killed by a shot to the head. These were some of the prisoners that the West Side Boys had executed in the days and weeks prior to the assault.

The SLA forces now linked up with the Poachers, who came across river by boat to Gberi Bana. By now, the entire West Side Boys' territory had been combed by either British or SLA forces and no West Side boys had been found. The delay caused by the Jordanian UN soldiers holding up the advance of the British and SLA troops must have given the rebels the time to make their getaway. There was only one place they could have fled to – the jungles further inland.

So the regrouped British–SLA forces headed further inland themselves, to the SLA headquarters at Port Loko. From there, they would carry out similar operations, combing the jungle to the north and east, towards the Kabatta Junction and Kambia, right up on the border with Guinea. On arrival at Port Loko, they discovered that more than 150 of the retreating West Side Boys had surrendered to UNAMSIL forces there. But the hard core of West Side Boys, lead by Colonel Changa Bulanga and Captain T.T. Kamarra, had moved further inland to join up with the RUF rebels.

The British–SLA forces advanced after them, pushing the joint force of RUF–West Side Boys further north-east, until they spilled over the border into neighbouring Guinea. There, the rebels caused havoc in the border villages and refugee camps, going on a looting, burning and raping spree. The Guinean government reacted with fury at the rebel incursions, sending in heavy battle tanks and a squadron of helicopter gunships. Over the coming weeks, these last remnants of the West Side Boys found themselves squeezed between a vengeful Guinean military on one side, and the British–SLA forces on the other. There was nowhere left to retreat to, and a further 150-odd West Side Boys surrendered, accounting for most if not all of the rebels that hadn't already been killed.

The town of Kambia was completely levelled in the fighting. It was to be the first place that the UN would move into big time once peace was restored in the country. And that peace was not short in coming. Considering what had happened to the West Side Boys, the RUF realised it was game over for the rebels in Sierra Leone. Operation Barras, a show of awesome military strength and professionalism by the British military, was the beginning of the end for the rebels. Within months, they had sued for peace, and to all intents and purposes the war was over in Sierra Leone. And the rebuilding of Kambia was used as a model for the UN-led post-war recovery.

The men of the Operation Barras assault force had done more than simply rescue the British and Sierra Leonean hostages. They had, in effect, brought about an end to ten years of terrible civil war and appalling suffering in Sierra Leone. One mindless, murderous rebel group had been removed from the scene, and then the others had basically surrendered. Which meant that the people of that suffering country could finally breathe a little more easily. There would be no more lopping off of the limbs of babies, no more gang rapes of children, no more rebel Russian roulette or 'sex the child' games. Those British soldiers who had risked their lives – *and sacrificed their lives* – on Operation Certain Death had not done so in vain.

POSTSCRIPT

It is always a bad sign in an army when scapegoats are habitually sought out and brought to sacrifice for every conceivable mistake. It usually shows something is very wrong in the highest command.

– Field Marshal Erwin Rommel

IN Britain, word had got out among the D Squadron wives around lunchtime on the Sunday of the assault that the men of D Squadron had experienced a serious casualty. But Brad Tinnion's partner, Anna Homsi, would not hear of his tragic death until much later that day. In his personal documents, Brad Tinnion had nominated his brother as his next of kin – and thus the first person to be informed in the event of his death or serious injury. Unfortunately, his brother, also a serviceman, was on exercises in Belize at the time, and so alerting him to his Brad's death was less than straightforward. As a result, certain details about the outcome of Operation Barras were effectively suppressed for several hours until a confirmation message was received back from Belize: 'NOK INFORMED'.

Anna Homsi issued a press statement later that week, in which she described Brad Tinnion as 'the man of my dreams. We are deeply shocked and devastated by Brad's death,' she continued, 'but enormously proud he died doing the job he loved.' Charles Tinnion, Brad's Father, spoke from his home in Harrogate, North Yorkshire, of his grief. 'It's a very upsetting time for the family and at the moment we are trying to come to terms with what happened.' 'We are distraught,' Brad's mother, Phyllis Collins, said. 'We had a lovely son and now we have lost him for ever. Now we would like to get on and grieve.' 'Brad Tinnion died bravely doing the job he loved, helping to rescue those hostages,' Brigadier Jonathan Bailey, the CO of Brad's parent unit, the Royal Artillery Regiment, remarked. 'We will always remember him with great pride. I would now ask that the family are left alone to mourn in private.'

From the Sunday of their rescue through to the following Tuesday, the six Royal Irish soldiers would stay on board the RFA *Sir Percival*, drinking, winding down and getting shipshape again. When the men finally got to the bar on that first evening, they discovered that they were no more able to drink than they had been able to eat. Three or four cans of beer, and the men were unable to get another drop down them, their stomachs had shrunk so much. And by then they were already so drunk that it would have been embarrassing, if it wasn't so funny. For the next two days, the ex-hostages had little else to do but sleep, eat and drink.

They had been offered critical incident counselling by the ship's medical officer, but most turned it down. Instead, the men talked about what had happened among themselves; they felt they had to do so now, while they still had the chance as a group to get it out of their systems. In the immediate aftermath of their ordeal, they felt they could open up to each other about how terrified they'd been at times in Gberi Bana – far more so than they had been able to while they were still being held captive, and trying to put a brave face on things. But it was all done with black humour and laughter, because they were alive and free and they had made it through, and were determined to have a good time of things.

They talked especially about the morning of the assault and the rescue. Each of them had a different sense of the exact detail of what had happened. It had all been so quick that they were still reeling from the shock and surprise. They wondered just how close-run a thing the assault had really been. One fatality. Scores of wounded. There were rumours running around the ship that it had been that close to a total disaster, that the top brass had got the threat assessment all wrong. But at the time, the hostages had never believed for a minute that the SAS and SBS were anything other than totally in control. The West Side Boys had fought back, but at no stage were they ever winning. And on the southern river bank, the Paras had just seemed to wipe the table with them.

On the morning of the attack itself, several of their fellow soldiers from the Royal Irish Regiment had been sent up to reinforce the nearest UN checkpoint. From there, they had had a direct line of sight to the air assault going in over Gberi Bana and Magbeni, some six miles away. One of those soldiers came and found the ex-hostages on board the ship. 'It was awesome,' he told them, commenting on the air assault. 'I've never seen anything like before in my life. It's a wonder any one of the rebels survived.' None of the ex-hostages had any regrets about the large number of West Side Boys who had been killed. None. In fact, they felt as if the rebels had got exactly what they deserved. The only person that they were keen had got away was Sony – and somehow they were certain that he would have got out of there unscathed.

On day two, the questions were already starting to be asked about why the patrol had driven down into the West Side Boys' headquarters in the first place. Major Martial and Captain Flaherty were called up to the captain's cabin, where a brigadier asked them for a full account of what had taken place on the afternoon of their capture. Both men outlined their conversation with the Jordanian UN contingent over lunch, and the mentioning of the location of the rebel headquarters. Both explained how this had seemed like a rare opportunity to gather some valuable intel on the West Side Boys' strength and positions, and so the patrol had taken an unscheduled detour down into their area. The report that he would go on to write would place some blame for the patrol's capture on Major Martial.

By Wednesday, the eleven men were back at their Canterbury base in the south-east of England. Their first duty was then a deeply personal and emotional one: to attend the funeral of Brad Tinnion, a man who had died while doing his duty and fighting to save their lives. Brad's funeral was held at St Martin's Church, Hereford, at 1 p.m. on 15 September, twenty-two days almost to the hour after the Royal Irish soldiers had been taken hostage. Everyone from Operation Barras was at the funeral: all the men from D Squadron and the SBS who'd gone in on the assault; the RAF, Army and Navy pilots who'd repeatedly flown their choppers into the teeth of a raging firefight; and everyone that could be mustered from the other three squadrons of 22 SAS. In fact, the only glaring absence were the men of 1 Para, and Neall Ellis and Fred Marafono and their aircrews – all of whom had played such vital roles in the assault.

The funeral was a difficult affair, especially as the eleven men were to meet Brad Tinnion's mother and his partner, Anna Homsi. They found themselves tongue-tied and emotional, as they struggled to find the words to express what they wanted to say. The only one of them who didn't seem fazed by it all was the Major Martial – which was astonishing, considering the way in which the press had treated him. Over the past few days of a media-feeding frenzy, the press had eaten the Major alive, portraying him as the main person responsible for the patrol being captured.

Although the MOD issued an official denial that Brad was a member of the SAS (as is their blanket policy on all UK Special Forces personnel) his funeral service proved otherwise: it displayed the famous winger dagger and motto of the SAS, 'who dares wins', alongside the crest of his parent Regiment – the Royal Artillery – a crown and a cannon with the motto, '*quo fas et gloria ducunt*', 'where duty and glory lead'. The CO of 22 SAS gave a reading, and there were hymns chosen by Anna Homsi and Brad's parents. The service was followed by the volley salute, the playing of the last post, the minute's silence and then reveille, as the RAF did the traditional fly-past.

The funeral took place less than a month after D Squadron had buried Martie and Adie – the two men of Boat Troop who had died while on exercises in Kenya. Among the other readings given at Brad's funeral by fellow soldiers of D Squadron, which included the SAS Regimental Collect, were lines from *The Golden Journey to Samarkand*, by J.E. Flecker. These perhaps best sum up the Regiment's ethos, as embodied in the life and achievements of Martie and Adie and Trooper Tinnion, and all of those who had fought in Operation Barras.

> We are the pilgrims, master we shall go
> Always a little further, it may be
> Beyond that last blue mountain barred with snow
> Across the angry or that glimmering sea.

Unfortunately, the funeral was marred by one ugly incident, due to the press having got wind of it beforehand. The night prior to the funeral, some of the men from D Squadron had discovered that the paparazzi had set up shop in one of the houses opposite the church, hoping to get shots of the funeral service itself. One of the local residents had rented out an upstairs front bedroom to them, with a picture-perfect view of the churchyard.

It was bad enough having a bank of paparazzi camped outside Anna Homsi's house, but this was too much for the men of D Squadron. They were so angry that they were about go down there and give the paparazzi a good beating – along with the person who'd rented out the room to them. But instead, they took a couple of high-sided trucks from the base and went and parked them right outside the house, completely blocking any view the paparazzi might have of the funeral. Once again, rather than using their brawn the men had used their brains – and doing so had won them the day.

Brad Tinnion's death was also surrounded by another form of controversy – not the interest of a vicarious and avaricious media, but speculation as to exactly who had shot him. There were rumours of friendly fire circulating around Hereford, that Brad had been a victim of a blue-on-blue incident. There were even rumours that no medals were going to be given out to the men of D Squadron who had undertaken the assault, because of a woeful lack of fire discipline on the ground (which could have been the cause of Brad's death, if indeed it had been due to a friendly-fire incident).

As it was, Operation Barras turned out to be one of the most highly decorated UK Special Forces missions since the Second World War. And the final coroner's report into Brad's death recorded a wound from a 7.62mm round, which is AK47 calibre. The entry point of the bullet and its trajectory also supported the contention that it was a stray round, probably an unlucky ricochet. In all likelihood, the bullet was one of the many thousands sprayed indiscriminately by the rebels at the men of the Special Forces as they attacked the West Side Boys' positions.

In fact, the firefight had been so intense around Gberi Bana that several of the men from D Squadron hadn't realised that they had been hit until they got sent back to their homes for a few days' leave. Two or three days after their return, a cut or a gash on an arm or leg had started itching and smelling bad, and the men would discover from their doctor that there was a nasty chunk of shrapnel still inside.

Back in Belfast, Major Martial took it upon himself to visit and talk to the rescued hostages' parents. The families had been very well cared for by the Royal Irish Regiment – with regular visits and briefings from the HQ staff at Malone Army Barracks, in south Belfast. And in Canterbury, the UK mainland HQ for the Regiment, the partners of the married men had been brought into the base for daily briefings. But some of the family members were still openly angry with Major Martial. The Major had been fingered in the press for taking the patrol down into the West Side Boys' headquarters in the first place, and the parents wanted some answers. Why had he taken their boys down that road in the first place? The press had blamed him for a serious lapse of judgement. But had the Major really acted totally independently? On his own accord? If so, why? Was that the full story? But no matter what was asked of him, the Major refused to be drawn on these points. 'There's always two sides to every story,' was all that Major Martial would say. 'And I'm afraid for security reasons I'm not able to tell you mine.'

By November 2000, two months after Operation Barras, Julius Spencer, Sierra Leone's Information Minister, was able to declare that the West Side Boys were 'finished as a military threat'. Freetown's biggest-selling daily newspaper, the *Democrats*, came out with the screaming headline, 'Brits Kicked Ass in West Side'.

The British Foreign Secretary, Robin Cook, remarked that 'the West Side Boys leadership is now behind bars. Their headquarters have been destroyed. But the people of Sierra Leone still live under the threat of brutal rebels lopping off the arms and legs of women and children.' Those West Side Boys who were being held and would eventually face trial included Foday Kallay, Colonel Savage and Colonel Bomblast. While it was confirmed that Colonel GS and Calm Down Fresh had been killed in the assault, Colonel Changa Bulanga remained unaccounted for, and was probably still at large. And in a bizarre twist of fate, Colonel Cambodia was being rehabilitated back into the Sierra Leonean Army, where he was kept under close watch.

'We wanted rid of the West Side Boys for a long time,' the Director of one of the Sierra Leonean military agencies told me, when I visited Freetown to research this book in 2003. 'It was our luck that you British came in and did it for us. It was unfortunate that one of your soldiers died. But you know what it meant for Sierra Leone, that military action of yours? It was the beginning of the end for the rebels. After Barras, the rebels all knew that if they carried on fighting, they'd go the same way as the West Side. So, they gave up the fight. And now we have peace, thanks to your British soldiers.'

Foday Kallay was imprisoned in Pendema Road jail, but on his first day there a riot almost broke out, because he had so many enemies. Kallay was then moved to an isolation unit. Interviewed in his jail cell two weeks after the conclusion of Operation Barras, Kallay appeared bewildered, confused and hard done by. 'I was alone, asleep in my house, when I heard a terrible noise,' he said of the morning of the assault. 'The heavy pressure of the wind from the British helicopters blew in the roof of my house and I was trapped.'

Kallay had then lain there listening to the deafening noise of the battle between the British forces and his men, before being pulled out of the house by one of the SAS soldiers. 'It was a surprise attack,'

Kallay added, with some indignation. 'We had no warning. They came in with so much firepower. We never experienced anything like it before. We were negotiating with the British and then they attacked us. I ask the British government and people to accept that I feel sorrow for capturing the hostages. I ask them to forgive and forget.' Kallay's pleas for clemency were unlikely to be heard, as he faced the prospect of standing trial for war crimes and crimes against humanity.

Foday Kallay's wife Mamma Kallay, the so-called 'Voodoo Queen', is now living in Freetown as a free, but broken, woman – wandering around the streets in rags and soiling her own clothes. Insanity appears to be her only sanctuary from past wrongs. Bentu Sessay, Calm Down Fresh's wife, survived the assault and immediately gave birth to a son. Several women who came with their rebel 'husbands' to surrender at the UN Disarmament, Demobilisation and Reintegration (DDR) camps, turned out to have been abducted by the West Side Boys and forced to 'marry' them. 'You are automatically married to the man who abducted you,' said Ulimata, aged seventeen. 'You have no choice. If you refuse, you will be killed.'

And what of Sony, the enigmatic figure who had done so much to try to help the British hostages? It seems almost beyond doubt that Sony was the 'local element' that the British forces had inside the West Side Boy's base. On every analysis, he fits the bill. However, he was a far more ambivalent figure than the British hostages imagined. Sony was actually Foday Kallay's linkman into Freetown. He ran drugs into the rebel camp, and did a trade in information too. Corporal Mousa Bangura learned all this while incarcerated in the dungeon – from what he overheard the rebels discussing. They were always waiting for Sony and his next shipment of drugs. As such he was an untouchable figure in the rebel camp.

He never actually stayed in the camp, as he lived in Freetown and would travel in to 'deal' with Foday Kallay. According to Corporal Mousa, he was treated pretty much like royalty by the West Side Boys. But Mousa also pointed out that Sony was basically a good, reasonable, decent man. This picture of Sony fits more closely with him being the key local element that the British had in the rebel camp, and he had every opportunity to pass information to the British, on his frequent journeys in and out of the base from Freetown.

Interestingly, in 1995–6, Executive Outcomes had also used a Sony-like figure in their operations in Sierra Leone. Jonathan (not his real name) was a young, Sierra Leonean man who had had some education in the UK. He spoke excellent English, and could translate the local languages for the EO operatives. He was able to understand how both the 'white mercenaries' and the Sierra Leonean rebels thought and behaved. EO used Jonathan for their intelligence-gathering and interrogation purposes. After his stint with EO, Jonathan was granted twelve months' military training in the UK, by the British High Commission. So perhaps 'Sony' and 'Jonathan' are one in the same person. Either way, it is highly likely that Sony was warned off the night before the assault went in on Gberi Bana, and that he made his escape.

As word spread throughout Sierra Leone of the annihilation of the West Side Boys by British forces, the other rebel units also started losing their heart for the fight. The men of the SAS, the SBS and the Paras, aided by the RAF and Sierra Leone's own Air Wing, had spoken the only language that the rebels understood: the language of lethal force and brute power. RUF rebels began surrendering en masse across the country, and the interminable civil war that had claimed so many innocent lives finally looked to be drawing to a close.

If that was indeed the outcome, then the British forces and their political taskmasters had scored a crucial psychological, as well as a military, victory with Operation Barras. They had sent a powerful, unmistakable message that British and allied policy in Sierra Leone would not be allowed to fail; that the UN-brokered peace deal would be respected and the rule of law upheld; that the unspeakable, demented brutality of the rebels would no longer be tolerated; and that Libyan-backed and al-Qaeda-financed forces could not take over West African countries at their will, and in defiance of the international community. In short, that the day of the rebels was over.

Operation Barras itself was hailed as a resounding military success, one that achieved all its objectives. The hostages had been rescued unharmed. No helicopters had been shot down. None of the assault teams had been captured or routed, and the three patrol Land-Rovers had been recovered intact. There had been only one British fatality. Rebel leader Foday Kallay had been taken prisoner and his plans for Operation Kill British and Operation Kill All Your Family – which would have seen him take over as Sierra Leone's President – were dead and buried. His hopes to 'do a Somalia' on British forces were never realised.

Anything but a major victory could well have led to British forces pulling out of Sierra Leone – rather like US forces pulled out of Somalia, after the infamous 'Day of the Ranger' incident. Giving the British Army a black eye would have raised the notoriety of the West Side

Boys and their power too – which would have meant more drugs, more diamonds, and more raping and maiming of civilians for them. A major defeat for the British forces could quite conceivably have brought down the Blair New Labour government.

But the British forces hadn't had it all their own way. Their success had come at a price. The Paras suffered one in ten wounded, the UK Special Forces more. It was luck, some would argue, that they didn't take far greater casualties. 'Who the fuck did they think these West Side Boys were?' asked one of the Operation Barras Paras, quoted in the *Observer* newspaper, immediately after the assault. 'Someone was being very overconfident thinking they would just leg it when they heard the fire. You have got to ask yourself why we took so many hits. Taking one in ten casualties is fairly serious. It was, as they say, a damn close-run thing. It was just that far from being a total fuck-up.'

Certainly, the men of D Squadron were on the ground for over four hours, far longer than the original mission plan had allowed for. 'We thought we would be in and out,' said an MOD source immediately after the attack. 'But the whole operation lasted for close to five hours.' British forces were obliged to stay on the ground for so long to deal with the ferocious rebel resistance. The West Side Boys just kept coming back at the assault force, regardless of the consequences.

'No one had ever explained to these young fighters the rules,' remarked another of the Paras. 'No one had ever explained to them that war is not like a *Rambo* video, about how soldiers should behave in a firefight, about when to be scared. They mostly just stood there and blasted away at us, and must have been surprised as hell when they got hit.' Operation Barras was a gamble that paid off in the end. It is not a gamble that many of the men would ever want to repeat.

Shortly after Operation Barras and the mopping-up operation that followed it, the Jordanian UN contingent left Sierra Leone. There were several articles in the Sierra Leonean press alluding to the unhealthy alliance with some of the Jordanians formed with the West Side Boys. The Jordanians were replaced in due course by a Pakistani UN peace-keeping contingent, who by all accounts have been doing a remark-ably good job since then.

This is Corporal Mousa Bangura on the behaviour of the Jordanian 'peacekeeping' forces in Sierra Leone: 'What the Jordanians did to the British forces – to their allies – was unbelievable, outrageous. *It was sabotage*. You cannot treat friendly forces like that. We didn't know the West Side Boys were down the road to Magbeni – the Jordanians advised us to go down there. The rebel bases on the main highway are fairly static, but inside the jungle like that, in their own territory, they move them around – so we didn't know they would be down there. But what the Jordanians did while we were there was far, far worse: they gave the rebels *ammunition*, which they used to kill innocent Kamajor villagers and to attack fellow UN peacekeepers, the Nigerians. The Jordanian UN forces betrayed the British, they betrayed the Nigerians and they betrayed the people of Sierra Leone. Did they have no shame? Thank God they were removed from our country.'

The success of Operation Barras was also marred by two factors after the event. The first was the treatment of Anna Homsi. Before joining the SAS, Brad Tinnion had served with distinction in the Royal Artillery. At his death, Anna was denied a service widow's pension and other benefits, because they were unmarried – this despite the fact that they had lived together for eight years, and had a little daughter, Georgia.

Anna was forced to threaten to sue the MOD. 'I was so proud of Brad and what he did and I understood that one day I might lose him,' she said as the time. 'All I want to do now is to be able to bring up our child well. At the moment I just can't afford that.' After her case was taken up by Paul Keetch, MP for Hereford, the MOD paid her a sum in compensation.

The second was the treatment of Major Martial, a flawed hero, but a hero all the same. By the end of the week of 11 September – the week that the hostages were rescued – the official report into Major Martial's conduct accused the Major of having made a 'grave mistake' in taking the decision to drive down into the West Side Boys' headquarters. But the wider implications of the hostage crisis were now also beginning to surface. Questions arose as to whether the Major alone was to blame. Or had the world's most professional armed forces badly underestimated the fighting capabilities and threat posed by an unruly, but battle-hardened, rebel force? If this was the case, they had done so with tragic consequences. On the ground in Sierra Leone, it had always been the Major's call. But British military intelligence had been woefully lacking, if, as seems to be the case, Major Martial had been led to believe that the West Side Boys were 'friendlies'.

Colleagues within the military were not overly surprised that Major Martial took the initiative – and attendant risk – of 'pushing out' towards the rebel headquarters. 'Officers are taught at staff college to gather intelligence at every opportunity,' said one military commentator at the time, quoted in the *Observer*. 'One would have expected Martial to test the information he had received. But a prudent officer would always make sure he had an escape route and certainly not allow himself to be surrounded. Perhaps he thought the West Side Boys were friendlies. Big mistake.'

In the final analysis, senior British military officials were impressed by the way in which Major Martial dealt with the rebels during his captivity and attempted to safeguard his men, sustaining savage beatings in the process. They were also impressed that he did not seek to avoid blame for what had happened, telling the investigating officer that he alone was responsible for the patrol's capture. Perhaps the British military felt that Major Martial's 'naming and shaming' by the British press was enough of a punishment, as no further disciplinary action appears to have been taken against him.

All the members of the captured patrol are unanimous in one thing: Major Martial demonstrated true bravery and fortitude during their seventeen-day ordeal. Without his leadership, they do not believe they would have made it through alive. Part of his mission as a British forces commander in Sierra Leone had been to gather intelligence on potentially hostile units in the region. In a sense, he had done nothing wrong. For the eleven other men of the Royal Irish patrol – and for the Sierra Leonean hostages held by the West Side Boys at the time – it is right and fitting that no action was taken against Major Martial. After their rescue, several of the village captives spoke of their admiration for the courage the British Major displayed.

The most outspoken in his defence was Corporal Mousa Bangura. 'He should have had many years of brilliant work ahead of him as a professional soldier,' the Corporal told the international press at the time. He had only agreed to speak to the media in an attempt to save the Major's good name and professional reputation. 'Now it looks as though his career is over. There were times when we were certain we would be killed, but he did not let us despair. He was kind and courageous and never complained about his own suffering. I thank Alex Martial for saving my life. I would like to think that one day I could be as good a soldier as he is.'

As to the others, some months after their return to the UK Captain Flaherty and Ranger Rowell left the army. The other eight soldiers stayed in.

At the approach of the second Gulf War, the Royal Irish Regiment were mobilised for duty in Iraq. On hearing the news that his mates would be going back into combat, Ranger Rowell volunteered to rejoin his unit so he could accompany them into battle stations in Kuwait. There, the Royal Irish Regiment would be serving under the direct command of the US 7th Air Cavalry Assault Brigade. Captain Flaherty also rejoined the royal Irish Regiment in time to serve with the Rangers in their deployment to the Gulf.

And what of Corporal Mousa? A week after he had been let out of the RFA *Sir Percival* sickbay, Corporal Mousa was invited to visit the leaders of Sierra Leone. He went to the President's residence and met President Kabbah and several of his ministers. They congratulated him on his courage and fortitude and for speaking out on behalf of the British Major. But Corporal Mousa received no compensation at all for his injuries, and he even had to pay for his own medical care costs once he had been released from the *Sir Percival*'s sickbay. A few days after Operation Barras, Major Martial did a whip-round and sent Mousa $70 as a contribution from the Royal Irish Rangers. As the Major knew Corporal Mousa loved reading so much, he also sent him ten books, including a couple of John Grisham novels (Mousa's favourite author) and a history of the Royal Irish Rangers. It was one month before Mousa could stretch his arms out properly, and for many months he feared his hands would be paralysed. One week after leaving the sickbay, Mousa volunteered for duty again and rejoined the IMATT training team to resume his duties as Liaison Officer to the British at Benguema.

It wasn't until some time after their return to the UK that the majority of the British hostages heard about the rebels' wider aspirations in Sierra Leone. At the time, few of them had heard about the two recent UN-led attacks on the West Side Boys' base (one of which, Operation Thunderbolt, had been supported by the Mi-24 gunships). Few of the men had known about the West Side Boys' history of hostage-taking, including other British soldiers. Few of them had heard that the rebels had wanted to make Sierra Leone 'Britain's Somalia'. Yet all of this rang so true to these men after they had escaped from their seventeen-day ordeal. The men shivered at the thought of what might have happened, had the West Side Boys succeeded in handing them over to the RUF rebels, as was clearly their intention during the final days of their incarceration.

'If we'd known all that back then,' one of the Rangers remarked, 'we'd have been far more up for the fight when we were captured.

Trouble is, the West Side Boys were in the "friendly forces" section of the written brief passed down to us every evening. We got that from the Section Commander, who took it from the Platoon Commander, who took it from his superior officer, and so on and so forth, so the info came pretty much from the top. How they can have put the feckin' West Side Boys in the friendlies section beats me. When we drove down to their HQ, we were still thinking they were friendly – youse would, wouldn't youse, if that's what you'd been told? If the West Side Boys had gotten us into the hands of the RUF, maybe then they would have done a feckin' Somalia on us after all. And then we wouldn't be here now.'

Military commentators have argued that the British Army should have better known the volatility of the area and the reputation of the West Side Boys. The rebel group should certainly not have been classed as 'friendlies' in the on-the-ground briefings to the UK-led IMATT forces, especially considering the long military and intelligence involvement of British forces in the region. This fact was picked up on almost immediately following the patrol's capture, by the local Sierra Leonean press.

The *Expo Times* wrote of the abduction of the eleven British soldiers: 'This did not come as any surprise to many Sierra Leoneans. This may well be the West Side Boys' revenge for Operation Thunderbolt – the UN helicopter gunship attack on the rebels' base a few days earlier.' And an editorial in the *Sierra News* drew attention to Barras being the last two syllables of *embarrass*, although it was unclear at the time exactly who would end up suffering the ultimate ignominy – the rebels or the British forces.

The key questions that remain unanswered for the British soldiers held hostage by the West Side Boys are these: Why did they drive down that road into the rebel HQ in the first place? And why were they told the rebels were 'friendlies'? The answer to the latter question may have something to do with Operation Palliser, the British Army's May 2000 military intervention in Sierra Leone (i.e. just prior to Operation Barras). During Op Palliser, the West Side Boys 'joined' a pro-government coalition that fought against the RUF (i.e. they fought on the pro-British side). However, this in no way accounts for them having been classed as 'friendlies': ever since their creation in 1997, the defining feature of the West Side Boys was their ability to form a totally unpredictable, shifting miasma of allegiances with whoever benefited them at the time. The defining features of the West Side

Boys were disloyalty and self-interest. And British forces should have known that they were never to be trusted.

This being so, a further question has to be asked by any enquiring mind. Was there in fact some hidden agenda for the patrol to take that fatal turning down into the rebel village? In doing so, was some sort of secret, British military-political plot being served? Was the patrol allowed to take that turning for reasons that go to the heart of the nature of the British military intervention in Sierra Leone? And if so, why? The conspiracy scenario that has been voiced in some quarters is that the British patrol was used as bait in a trap, a trap into which the rebels walked eyes wide shut. In the final analysis, the hostage crisis ended with the rebels being annihilated – and in so doing the British military broadcast a powerful warning to the RUF and other hostile forces in Sierra Leone. Mess with us at your peril.

Plausible though this conspiracy theory might at first appear, on reflection it is unlikely and lacks credibility. There were far easier and less risky ways for the British forces to take on the West Side Boys. After all, the UN had already launched two assaults against them (Operation Thunderbolt being one of them) in the weeks just prior to the Royal Irish patrol's capture. It was hardly as if the British forces needed to cook up some dramatic excuse – like the hostage crisis – to do so themselves. And once the British soldiers were held hostage, so much could so easily have gone wrong. In fact, it was a public relations disaster in the making. If Op Barras had failed, it could have meant the end of the Blair government. When all is said and done, cock-up rather than conspiracy is by far the more likely scenario.

But such a cock-up remains unacceptable. After all, one soldier of the SAS died in rescuing the hostages (and many of the men of D squadron argue that two more men – Martie and Adie – also died as an indirect result of the operation, when they were recalled from exercises in Kenya). Several score British soldiers were injured, over a dozen seriously so. And the British casualty toll could so easily have been far, far higher. And on the rebel side, the death toll alone must have been well in excess of a hundred (among whom there would be several adolescents, young children, and a number of women).

When all is said and done, the grim legacy of the Royal Irish soldiers' time spent as hostages in Sierra Leone is one that will be with them for the rest of their lives. In the weeks and months that followed their rescue, the nightmares started in earnest. Every night, without fail, they would dream of something springing from their experiences in the rebel camp. Some nights the dreams would be terrifying enough to wrest them from their sleep, minds racked by treacherous memories. That trauma, those memories, are something that will fade with time, but never completely disappear. As one of the soldiers recently described it, he may not have thought about the hostage ordeal for months, and then, suddenly, a smell or a sound or a word will trigger the memories, and the horror will come flooding back in again.

At the time of the hostage crisis, an editorial in *The Times* had thundered: 'They had better be rescued fast, by negotiation or by force, if the government is not to be held culpably reckless of the safety of Britain's armed forces.' After the successful completion of Operation Barras, Britain's Defence Secretary, Geoff Hoon, addressed the UK press on the outcome of the mission. 'We only embarked upon this mission very reluctantly. It has been at great cost. But obviously, we constantly review our involvement in what is clearly a dangerous environment like Sierra Leone. The six former hostages . . . are expected to be questioned by senior officers about the circumstances of their kidnap and what they were doing in rebel-held territory. British forces are in Sierra Leone to help train the government army in the fight against the rebel militia.'

The Tory opposition had already begun to use the hostage crisis as a means to criticise the whole of the British military intervention in Sierra Leone (the IMATT initiative). They spoke of 'muddle and mission creep' putting the lives of British soldiers in danger. Francis Maude, then shadow foreign affairs spokesman, said: 'Our view has always been that the whole mission has always been very ill-defined from the start and a lot of these problems arise out of that. The government has been adamant that our troops are not part of the UN-peacekeeping force, and then they have some not very clear role involving the UN. The whole thing is a muddle and muddle means danger.'

The Labour government's concern had surfaced openly in the UK press on 3 September – barely eleven days into the seventeen-day hostage crisis – when it demanded a full-scale inquiry into the kidnappings. Defence ministers, apparently embarrassed that no one on the ground in Sierra Leone could explain why the patrol had gone down into the West Side Boys' base in the first place, had made it clear that senior heads would roll. But there were concerns over the government raising this issue publicly when the patrol were still being held hostage.

'They appear to be looking for a scapegoat,' an army source told the *Daily Telegraph*. 'It is obvious that something has gone very wrong here but it's the whole concept that is flawed. There aren't enough of our guys there to defend themselves against the rebels, and the UN is next to useless.'

The findings of the inquiry into the hostage crisis did point one finger of blame at Brigadier Gordon Hughes, the then Commander of British Forces in Sierra Leone. 'The Commander of British Forces has been reminded that Sierra Leone remains an unstable and volatile environment, that the deployment of forces is to be strictly controlled; and that the Commander is to take all necessary measures to ensure UK forces do not find themselves in a position that may lead to their capture.' However, again, by far the lion's share of the blame fell on Major Martial's shoulders. 'The commander of the patrol, Major Alex Martial, made an error of professional judgement in diverting from a planned and authorised journey so as to make an unauthorised visit to the village of Magbeni on the banks of the Rokel Creek.'

As it would turn out, Major Martial's was not the first British patrol ever to drive down the jungle track towards Magbeni. His error was to do so when the rebels were in the midst of their afternoon drugs-and-drink binge, and in the immediate aftermath of some bruising confrontations between the rebels and UN forces. Arguably, he was also caught with his guard down.

There is some disagreement over one element of the Paras' role in the assault on the rebel base at Magbeni. Although the Paras deny this, credible reports have it that the Paras actually mortared themselves, rather than having been hit by an enemy mortar round. This is how the story is told by one Operation Barras soldier. 'Trouble was, the Paras had been dropped in the midst of a waist-deep swamp. It was the only flat area the choppers could find to put them down. As the main assault force tried to extricate itself from the swamp, the artillery teams set up their 81mm mortars on the one dry bit of river bank. But as they began putting down a barrage of mortar fire on to rebel positions, one mortar shell went up into the forest canopy, exploded, and took out seven of the Paras. One of those wounded and put out of action was their CO.'

Officially, however, the Paras maintain that their command unit was hit by an enemy mortar round, and that is the most likely and credible version of events. But whatever the truth of the matter, the Paras succeeded in carrying out a blistering assault on the rebel base at Magbeni, against considerable odds. On 20 September, barely a week after the assault itself, Geoff Hoon, called upon 1 Para in their barracks in Dover, south-east England. 'I have no doubt that many years from now, it will be held up as an example of how things ought to be done,' he told the assembled men, speaking of Operation Barras and their assault on rebel positions at Magbeni. 'You should be proud of the part you played in it.'

There were questions raised within the British military at the time as to why 1 Para had been given Operation Barras (alongside the SAS and SBS). Strictly speaking, their part of the operation should have gone to the quick-reaction Spearhead Battalion, at that time the 1st Battalion of the Grenadier Guards. There is also a long-standing British military tradition that when a British regiment finds its men being held hostage, honour requires that regiment to rescue its own men. Indeed, the previous Royal Irish IMATT contingent could have been recalled to Sierra Leone, to carry out the Magbeni side of the rescue operation. After 1 Para's high-profile role in first Kosovo and then Operation Palliser, their involvement in Operation Barras did give rise to some cries of 'favouritism' and 'specialism' within the British Army.

Similar, but greater, disagreement (some would say controversy) surrounds the role that the SAS and the SBS played in Operation Barras. Most press reports at the time had the Paras playing the lead role in the assault, and many do not even mention the role British Special Forces played. In fact, in many quarters, Operation Barras was construed as a Para mission. Which is hardly surprising, seeing as the official policy of the MOD is to deny all Special Forces involvement in operations. Those media reports that did mention Special Forces have the SAS playing the key, lead role in the assault. There is little if any mention of the role the SBS played alongside them. But one-third of the Operation Barras assault force consisted of SBS men.

Such SAS–SBS rivalry is supposed to be fading – with the integration of the two units into one, homogenised UK Special Forces entity. But where high-profile and successful missions like Operation Barras are concerned, the SBS remain distinctly rankled by all the media credit being given to the SAS. Even the British Army's own glossy magazine – *Soldier* – reported that SAS went into action in Operation Barras – making no mention of the role played by the SBS. In the eyes of the SBS, positive media exposure amounts to profile, and profile ups the chances of that unit getting the more interesting, challenging missions next time around.

As is always the case with UK Special Forces operations, the Ministry of Defence had no comment to make at the time on the press reports of UKSF involvement in Operation Barras. But in an extraordinary show of military secrecy, the MOD subsequently ordered the pulping of 90,000 copies *Soldier*, after an article about the success of Operation Barras broke MOD rules by publicly mentioning the role that the SAS had played. The original article, headlined 'Tight Security Key to Jungle Rescue Success', had reported that the SAS had swooped by helicopter on to the rebel base, and that one SAS soldier, Trooper Brad Tinnion, had been killed in the raid. All the details in the magazine had already appeared in the national press reports over the preceding month. Truckloads of *Soldier* – subtitled *'the magazine of the British Army'* – bound for such outlets as WHSmiths, were recalled and destroyed, at a cost of some £70,000. A censored version of the magazine was then published, with no mention of the role played by Special Forces.

The MOD maintained that it ordered the magazine destroyed to prevent confusion over its policy on the role UKSF play in operations. 'We don't comment on our Special Forces activities or personnel for fear of compromising their safety,' an MOD spokesman said. 'It was an editorial oversight and the magazine was reprinted with the offending paragraphs removed.'

But this was seen as being excessively cautious by many in the army, who were proud of the success of Operation Barras, and wanted to see UKSF getting the public recognition that they deserved. One former military officer told the *Daily Telegraph*: 'I see no problem in confirming that Special Forces took part in Operation Barras once the rescue was over and the unit concerned had pulled out. I also think it is an insult to the SAS and the family of the trooper who died not to give him credit as being a member of the Regiment. Surely, in death there is no problem in stating he was a member of the SAS.'

Overall, Operation Barras ended up being a highly decorated mission. The majority of the decorations went to the Special Forces observation teams, those men who spent a week in the jungle on the fringes of the rebel bases, keeping watch. The success of their mission proved crucial to the eventual success of the assault. Two members of the UKSF were to receive the Conspicuous Gallantry Cross, second only to the Victoria Cross in terms of British military honours. In addition, four Military Crosses (MCs) were awarded to the men of the Operation Barras assault force, three to the SAS and SBS, and one to the Parachute Regiment. There were a number of 'MiMs' – Mentioned in Dispatches – on both the SAS and SBS sides.

Not surprisingly, 1 Para's Captain Daniel Matthews received an MC, for his bravery in taking over command of the assault after his CO had been injured in the rebel mortar attack, and leading the Paras to final victory. Five of the RAF helicopter crew received Distinguished Flying Crosses (DFC) for the extraordinary part they played in the mission, and their remarkable courage flying into the teeth of enemy fire. The pilot of Sierra Seven – the army Lynx attack helicopter that kept flying despite single-engine failure – was not one of those who received a DFC. For his sacrifice during Operation Barras, Brad Tinnion was to receive little posthumous recognition, although he was 'Mentioned in Dispatches'.

Today, Gberi Bana and Magbeni villages have been rebuilt – with the assistance of money provided by Britain's own Department for International Development (DFID). They have been resettled by families who were originally from that area, or whose villages were destroyed in the civil war. There is now a bustling new school, attended by obedient kids wearing smart blue uniforms. The main street is full of chickens pecking at the dirt, kids on bikes and women sat braiding each other's hair. There are no guns to be seen. The only evidence of Operation Barras is the odd bullet case lying half buried in the dirt and one or two shot-up buildings. The twisted debris of the West Side Boys' vehicles has been bulldozed into obscurity in the bush or in the river – all apart from a captured UN truck, the chassis of which has been turned into the village washing line.

But there are signs that some of the West Side Boys' foot soldiers are still active in West Africa's internecine civil wars. In the spring and summer of 2003, British cameraman James Brabazon filmed some quite extraordinarily graphic and powerful footage of the civil war in Liberia, Sierra Leone's eastern neighbour. Liberia had been the rebels' key ally in their war to seize power in Sierra Leone – Liberia's President Charles Taylor shipping weapons to the rebels in return for their 'conflict diamonds' (diamonds sourced illegally from conflict areas). Many international experts have accused Charles Taylor of being the single greatest source of the conflict that had ravaged this part of West Africa for the best part of a decade. As a result, Taylor has been portrayed as 'Africa's Hitler' and 'West Africa's Milošović'.

James Brabazon had been filming the civil war that was then raging across the country to topple Charles Taylor, and rid the region of his malevolent presence once and for all. Brabazon is English-educated and lives in London, but he's half-Irish. When filming in decidedly dodgy environments like Liberia, James usually chooses to describe himself as Irish, as it can have a lower profile than English nationality. But to the (ex) West Side Boys that he met in Liberia, the fact that he was Irish wasn't to be well received at all.

The Boys were leaving their graffiti all over the bombed-out buildings in Liberia: *DEMOLISHUN BY THE WEST SIDE NIGGAS*. And three years down the road, the memories of the Royal Irish hostage-taking and the British assault under Operation Barras were still raw in the rebels' minds. One afternoon during a lull in the fighting, Brabazon was sat around with a bunch of the rebels. They introduced themselves as being from the 'West Side Niggas'.

'Did you say West Side "*Niggers*"?' Brabazon asked.

'Yo. Niggas. That's what we call ourselves – the West Side Niggas.'

'Niggers? Are you the same as the West Side Boys, then?'

'Same-same. We known as the West Side *Boys* in UK and places. But we have always called us as the West Side Niggas.'

'Why d'you call yourself Niggers? You know what it means . . . ?'

'We've always said Niggas. It's who we are.'

Brabazon realised the conversation wasn't really getting him anywhere. He decided to try to change the subject.

'So, you're from Sierra Leone then?'

'Yah, yo got it. Where're you from?'

'I'm from Ireland,' he replied, without thinking.

'From *where*? Yo said Ireland?'

'Yeah.'

'You fucking Irish then?' The tone of the conversation had quickly changed. It had been bored curiosity before. Now there was anger and raw aggression. 'We came across some of yo Irish bros couple of years ago. Bunch of soldiers doubled-crossed us . . . Didn't turn out too good for us in de end. Maybe you heard 'bout it?'

'Not really,' Brabazon lied. He knew the West Side Boys couldn't touch him out in the open like this and get away with it. He and his mates were there at the invitation of the leaders of the Liberian rebels, so he had powerful friends. But it was clearly time to be leaving.

The West Side Boys that Brabazon found in Liberia were still packing weapons in a civil war, the only difference being that they had moved across the border from Sierra Leone to Liberia to do their fighting. Brabazon filmed some highly disturbing scenes of cannibalism in that civil war, the climax of his shoot showing a group of rebel fighters disembowelling a captured Liberian Army soldier. They cut out his heart and his liver while the soldier was still alive and then ate them raw. The spirit of the West Side Boys lives on it seems – together with their belief that eating the body parts of a captured enemy warrior will transfer his strength and bravery to those doing the eating.

When I visited Sierra Leone in October 2003 to research this book, ex-RUF/West Side Boys commanders told me that Mr Murder, one of Colonel Savage's lieutenants, had gone on to fight for Charles Taylor in Freetown, as had a number of other ex-Boys. More worryingly still, there was a grand plan being put in place, which would see the rule of the rebels return to Sierra Leone. From his jail cell, Foday Kallay was plotting to return to power by violent means. Ex-RUF and West Side Boys fighters would first win the war for Charles Taylor in Liberia, then they would launch a new rebel movement, backed by Liberia, to take the war back into Sierra Leone.

Today, Foday Kallay even claims that his eventual rise to power in Sierra Leone has been preordained, that it had been foretold. One of the so-called 'Revolutionary Reverends' – Christian priest-cum-voodoo man-cum-rebel clairvoyant – had read Foday Kallay's future for him. Kallay had been told that there would be two major battles with 'outside forces' (i.e. the British). The first would end in failure and defeat. But the second would see Foday Kallay leading a victorious rebel uprising to seize power in Freetown. When I was there in the autumn of 2003, dark forces were certainly active in Sierra Leone trying to make this a reality. The defeat of Charles Taylor in Liberia and his exile to Nigeria will help ensure that these forces will not be able to bring the rule of chaos, terror and evil back to this suffering land.

AFTERWORD

Gold and diamond smuggling, an endless guerrilla war between soldiers, rebels and foreign mercenaries, all makes Sierra Leone one of the poorest, most corrupt, dangerous . . . and exciting countries in the world.
                              – Will Scully, *Once a Pilgrim*

MANY people wanted this story to be told. First and foremost were the men of the Operation Barras assault force. The SAS and SBS assault teams, who had received little or no public recognition for the role they played in the operation. The men of the Parachute Regiment, whose 1 Para played such a key support role in the assault. The British Army, Navy and RAF pilots, who flew on to the rebel targets in the teeth of a raging firefight. To a man, they maintained that if there was one British military story, one Special Forces rescue mission, that really needed to be written about, then it was Operation Barras – for it is the most extraordinary story of British military fortitude, ingenuity and heroism in action for many a year. And the men of the Royal Irish Rangers who were taken hostage by the rebels in Sierra Leone – they also wanted this story to be told (at least all those that I had contact with). As far as they are concerned, no shame attaches to their side of the story. The miracle is that they all survived their terrible ordeal relatively unscathed; they too are the heroes of this story. The mercenaries and those who ran the private military companies that operated in Sierra Leone also wanted the wider nature of their role to be put on the record. And so many Sierra Leoneans wanted this story to be told, especially if it could help bring the suffering of that nation to a wider audience, and highlight the ongoing struggle of the people of that country for a future worth living. I received help not only from those

Sierra Leoneans involved in the British military operations, but also from many who were not. I hope I have done this story justice, for I was given the generous help, assistance and raw materials from so many quarters in order that I might do so. If not, the fault is entirely my own.

APPENDIX 1: ANALYSIS

Everything changed with the end of the Cold War. Up to then we knew what we had to do and we knew who the potential enemy was and we could train and prepare accordingly. Now it's all guesswork.
   – General Sir Peter Inge, Chief of Defence Staff, 1996

THE Sierra Leonean hostage crisis and Operation Barras was a huge media story at the time. But when starved of material to report, the press can be fickle, and the attention of the world media soon moved on to other events. It was hardly surprising. In the aftermath of the assault, none of the eleven British hostages was at any time presented to the news-hungry press pack. And few, if any, of the British soldiers who comprised the Operation Barras assault force were inclined to talk to the media, either. The journalists reporting the story at the time secured their 'eyewitness accounts' of the assault on Gberi Bana either from the West Side Boys' survivors (even Foday Kallay himself, speaking from prison), or from other Sierra Leoneans – namely Corporal Mousa and the village 'recruits'. No press access was given to the British side of the story. In this world of instant news the attention span of the public is increasingly short-lived, and the press soon lost interest. And that, it seemed, was to be the end of the story.

The hostage-taking and subsequent rescue placed the British establishment on the horns of a dilemma: it was a daring and audacious assault by Britain's finest troops that showed the British military at its best; but at the same time the capture of eleven, heavily armed British soldiers by a renegade band of rebels did quite the opposite. At the time, the British establishment's position on the hostage crisis and rescue assault appeared confused. Was this to be a chapter in British military history to be celebrated, or shunned? Was it something of which the British people should be proud, or somewhat ashamed? Did the 'Barras' of Operation Barras stand for the em*barrass*ment of the West Side Boys, or of the British forces taken hostage (as a Sierra Leone newspaper had suggested)? When the furore of the capture and rescue had died down, the story looked set to fade away into obscurity. And the British soldiers involved – hostages and rescuers alike – went quietly back to their regiments to continue to do their duty.

The press reports at the time were often, and somewhat understandably, inaccurate. Newspaper articles had 'SBS frogmen emerging out of the river to attack the rebel base', 'the SAS abseiling through the roof of the hostage building', and Foday Kallay 'strutting about in the captured British soldiers' uniform'. In the research that I have carried out for the writing of this book, I have come across just one, authoritative account of the assault, written a year after the event. Richard Connaughton, formerly the British Army's Head of Defence Studies and now a security consultant, wrote a short article entitled 'Operation Barras' in the academic journal *Small Wars & Insurgencies*. It is a brief and somewhat dry account of what he describes as 'an audacious and brilliantly executed joint operation'. At the same time, he points to the 'serious and embarrassing setback when 11 British soldiers and their Sierra Leonean liaison officer were taken hostage by a bandit group'. Other than that far from widely read publication, the story of the hostage crisis and Operation Barras seemed to have disappeared without trace.

Which is a pity, because this is a story that needs to be told. In fact, it demands to be shouted from the rooftops, not just because it is a compelling human tale, but because men risked their lives and were injured – and died – doing their duty. Clearly, there were acts of great and exceptional fortitude and heroism among the men of the British assault force, who went into the rebel base heavily outnumbered and succeeded in rescuing the hostages. But the real courage that emerges from the pages of this book lies as much with the hostages themselves – ordinary soldiers thrown into a horrific situation, who rose to the terrible challenges they faced with a dignity and integrity of which they should feel proud.

There are perhaps two types of 'courage' in this world: physical courage and moral courage. Whereas the men who assaulted the rebel base did what they had been trained to do, and exhibited immense and extraordinary physical courage in the process, the British soldiers taken hostage were thrown into a completely alien environment for which their training could never have prepared them. As such, they had the choice to proceed with moral cowardice or moral courage, and almost without exception they chose to do the latter. Despite the powerlessness of their situation, despite the depravity and terror they faced from the rebels on a daily, almost hourly, basis, they retained their principles, their values, their solidarity and their beliefs, even when they could have been killed for doing so. Not for one moment did they ever allow their actions or behaviour to sink to the same level of meaningless horror and evil as the rebels. And it would have been so easy for them to have done so. That is what saw them through their terrible ordeal, and that is what helped save them.

In the telling of their story there is also the opportunity, *indeed the need*, to discuss the wider issues thrown up by this short chapter on the history of suffering in a country like Sierra Leone. That discussion in part concerns our response to the demands of international peacekeeping in strife-torn regions across Africa and in the wider, conflict-torn world. In fact, the story of the British military intervention in Sierra Leone has many lessons to offer us in an increasingly insecure world.

Many of those to whom I have spoken about the story of the Sierra Leonean hostage crisis and Operation Barras cannot help but make comparisons with the 1993 mission in Somalia – the US-led Operation Restore Hope and the catastrophic Day of the Ranger that followed. In Sierra Leone, the British military won the trust of the majority of the Sierra Leonean people, and defeated a recalcitrant and murderous rebel minority. The hostage crisis was just one of the most high-profile and dramatic chapters in the much longer story of British military intervention in that country. The greatest success of the British military appears to have been that, while waging war in Sierra Leone, they succeeded in convincing the people of that country that they were there to stop the conflict and win the peace.

By contrast, in its 1993 Somali adventure, the US military seems to have quickly lost the trust of the Somali people. Rather than demonstrating to them that it was on a war-terminating, peace-building mission, the US military appears to have done the opposite. And it behaved with a degree of arrogance and insensitivity that fuelled a growing sense of Somali alienation. This is not to disrespect the heroic sacrifices of the seventy-odd US servicemen who died or were injured on that day of infamy in the Black Sea district of Mogadishu, doing their duty and following their orders. In fact, the US military maintains that its political taskmasters sent American troops into Somalia against their advice, with little or no accurate intelligence or understanding of the situation on the ground, and with an unworkable, unachievable mission. And the US military could not refuse their political taskmasters.

The very popularity of British troops in Sierra Leone demonstrated the wholehearted support that the people gave to the British military intervention. It is this popularity, this winning of the battle for hearts and minds, which goes some of the way to explaining why British forces succeeded in Sierra Leone, whereas US forces failed so badly in Somalia. In Somalia, the US military managed to turn an enthusiastic welcome from the Somali people into outright bloodlust and hatred of US forces in a little under six months. Heavy-handed military strategies, and an over-reliance on technology are some of the factors that lay behind this US failure.

Had British forces behaved in the same way in Sierra Leone as US forces did in Somalia, Operation Barras might arguably have ended up going as disastrously wrong as the infamous Day of the Ranger incident did for US forces in Somalia. This is a lesson that US forces will have to learn better in future if they are to successfully intervene militarily outside of their own borders. Recent events in Afghanistan and now Iraq also demonstrate this to be so.

In fact, the contrasts and similarities between the Somali and Sierra Leonean missions go further still – and likewise the lessons to be learned. Somalia was a nation torn apart by warlords, clans and the power of the gun. At the time of the US military intervention, it was also a nation ravaged by famine – the mass starvation of the Somali people being the initial reason for intervention by the international community. Sierra Leone was a country that had been destroyed by a rebel insurgency employing a degree of senseless brutality and evil that is hard to convey. Only the Khmer Rouge in the time of Cambodia's killing fields appear to have equalled the RUF, the West Side Boys and the renegade military in the levels of horror visited on a people. At the time of the British military intervention, Sierra Leone was once again being plunged into anarchy and mayhem, and facing the total collapse of the rule of law. It was this that prompted the first British military intervention, under Operation Palliser. Both the Somali clans and the Sierra Leonean rebels used drugs to fuel their fighters' courage: khat in Somalia and alcohol, cannabis and crack cocaine in Sierra Leone.

But that is where the similarities stop. In Somalia, the failure of the US-led military intervention led to the collapse of the international effort to bring peace and security to that suffering country. In the wake of the withdrawal of US forces, the UN mission to Somalia all but collapsed. Over a decade later, Somalia remains a state where little has changed; it is still riven by warlordism and is ranked as one of the 'failed states' among the international community. As a nation and a people, Somalia has been branded a disaster. And the Americans – who posses the world's most powerful armed forces and remain the single, greatest funding source of the UN – walked away from Somalia humiliated and badly burned – since then they have been loath to set foot back in Africa.

Ever since Somalia, the US administration has sought not to cross the so-called 'Mogadishu line' as far as policy to Africa goes. But how long can that continue? The events of September 11 and the so-called war on terrorism are beginning to force a change in the US stance, as the needs of international security become paramount. As evidence, see the US's limited intervention in the Liberian civil war. And Africa's growing strategic importance post-9/11 should not be ignored. US imports of oil from Africa stand at around 15 per cent, and are growing. Soon, they may have reached strategic levels to rival those of the Middle East – giving the US administration an alternative source of supplies to those from largely Islamic regimes.

In Sierra Leone, by contrast to the US in Somalia, Britain stood by its military commitment, by not withdrawing its troops in the aftermath of the hostage crisis. As academic and security expert Paul Williams points out: 'Such a withdrawal would have been foolish, because it would have signalled to the world that the British Army is as casualty-shy as its US counterpart, and would simply encourage groups in other parts of the world to ensure they surpass the necessary casualty threshold.' The success of the British-led military intervention led in turn to the re-inforcing of the UN's mandate in that country. After Operations Palliser and Barras, and with the British military's ongoing commitment to train and equip the Sierra Leonean armed forces, the RUF and the West Side Boys were quickly brought to heel. As a result, the UN-led international initiative to bring peace and security to the nation was consolidated. Less than half a decade later, much of what was promised to the suffering people of Sierra Leone has been achieved.

In Sierra Leone, Britain achieved proof of concept, a test case exempli-fying how war-termination and peace-enforcement can be successfully achieved. Sierra Leone had suffered over a decade of terrible trauma and pain at the hands of a wily, well-armed and entrenched group of rebels. Against all the odds, it has effectively been brought back into the community of peaceful nations. In May 2003, the head of the UN refugee agency was able to call post-war Sierra Leone 'an island of stability' in a largely chaotic region. 'There is an enormous difference now,' the UN High Commissioner for Refugees, Ruud Lubbers, said of the country, 'and I commend Sierra Leone, as compared to twenty-seven months ago, when it was a refugee-producing country.'

Britain's success in Sierra Leone has been achieved only with the tacit and real support of its foremost ally, the US. At all stages of the British military intervention, the US was privy to British policy and plans. This relationship was not without its conflicts, but in the wider analysis, it worked tolerably well. And since the events of May and August 2000, and the last-ditch UN rescue mission led by the British, the level of real US support to Sierra Leone has greatly increased. The Clinton administration's African Crisis Response Initiative (ACRI) ploughed some $110 million into supporting the Nigerian military's peacekeeping efforts in Sierra Leone and Liberia, providing 'non-lethal' military equipment. After the near collapse of UNAMSIL in May 2000 (the catalyst for Operation Palliser), hundreds of US troops were sent out to Nigeria to train five Nigerian battalions, and one each from Senegal and Ghana, for deployment to Sierra Leone, at a cost of some $260 million.

This deployment was arguably the US's single largest and most direct involvement of US troops in an African conflict since Somalia. Short of crossing the Mogadishu line, it represented a relatively robust response to events in Sierra Leone, training African soldiers to do the peacekeeping job that US (and European) nations are loath to do. 'Sierra Leone is a test case of America's commitment to democracy,' Susan Rice, the Clinton administration's Assistant Secretary for African Affairs said. 'Either we support democratic governments, institutions and peacekeeping efforts, or we risk allowing insurgents to spread terror throughout the region.'

As part of the international effort to win the peace in Sierra Leone, the UN Special Court has been set up to try the leaders of the rebel groups and rogue army officers for war crimes – with the strong backing of the UK and the US. 'We hope that the people who have consistently violated all the rules of international and national behaviour, who have committed such gross violations of human rights, will understand that the noose continues to tighten around them as we move forwards,' said the US Permanent Representative to the United Nations, Richard Holbrooke. 'The concept of bringing all parties in Sierra Leone together in a peaceful way should continue. But the RUF [and other rebel] leadership has written itself out of any legitimate role in this process.'

The Special Court's work is ongoing in Sierra Leone, and complemented by a South Africa-style Truth and Reconciliation Commission (TRC). President Kabbah testified at the TRC in July 2003 on the role senior SLA officers played in the May 1997 coup, which brought the AFRC to power – in effect ushering in months of murder and mayhem under the rule of the RUF, the West Side Boys and renegade SLA officers.

One of the key sponsors of the Special Court is the USA, and the Bush administration may now be waking up to the importance of this whole region in the fight against international terrorism. The US is also the largest financial contributor to the ongoing work of the UN peacekeeping forces in the country. Bush has noted the 'close, friendly ties' between the two nations and has praised the country's efforts to recover from a decade of civil war. And Bush paid tribute to the work of the Truth and Reconciliation Commission, the Special Court, and the government's Anti-Corruption Commission in bringing a sense of closure to the conflict and of normality back to the war-ravaged country.

To better understand the lessons of the British military intervention in Sierra Leone, one has to first understand the roots of that country's troubles. The level of human suffering in Sierra Leone has to be seen to be believed. A visit to a Freetown amputee camp is a harrowing experience to which no statistics can do justice. Yet the statistics are uniquely horrible in themselves and do require pause for thought. The country is about the size of Ireland, with a similar population of some 5 million people. Yet life expectancy hovers at around half that of the Irish at just forty years, and child mortality rates are the highest in the world. Out of every thousand children born in Sierra Leone, three hundred will be dead by the age of four. Imagine what that means. If you lived in Sierra Leone your child would have a one-in-three chance of being dead by the time it reached its fourth birthday.

During the decade of war, somewhere in the order of 100,000 people were senselessly, brutally maimed in Sierra Leone – the chopping off of hands and feet with old axes and machetes making these people an added burden on a country that was already on the very brink of collapse. Because of the internecine war waged by the various rebel factions over the years, a staggering two-thirds of the population fled from the fighting – this tiny country spawning one of the largest refugee crises in the world.

In its January 2003 report, entitled 'We Kill You If You Cry', Human Rights Watch writes of a nation 'haunted by silent war crimes'. Sexual violence was the single biggest war crime, the report stated, far more widespread than the highly visible amputees. Although the war was officially declared over on 18 January 2002, 'an unknown number of women and girls still remain with their rebel "husbands" who abducted them'. Survivors of rape – boys as well as thousands of women and girls – were in desperate need of counselling, health care and basic education. The Human Rights Watch report named the RUF rebels, the West Side Boys and the AFRC as being the main groups responsible (plus Liberian forces sent in by Charles Taylor to fight alongside the RUF). The report points out that due to a lack of funding and its limited scope, the UN Special Court will try only a very few of the leaders responsible for such crimes, while the vast number of the perpetrators will go unpunished.

'Child combatants were forced to rape women old enough to be their grandmothers,' the report continued. 'Rebels raped pregnant women and breastfeeding mothers, and fathers were forced to watch their daughters being raped. The rebels targeted young women and girls they thought were virgins. Women were raped so violently that they sometimes bled to death, or suffered from tearing in the genital area. Many victims who were pregnant at the time miscarried. Thousands of women and girls were abducted by the rebels and forced into sexual slavery. Their "husbands" deliberately carved the name of their rebel faction on to the breasts of the abducted women and girls.'

In Sierra Leone, the principal targets of the war were civilians, as opposed to the combatants. The normal rules of war were turned on their heads. In his 1999 report for the Canadian government, David Pratt, Canada's Special Envoy to Sierra Leone, wrote:

The conventional 'Rules for Armed Combat' have disappeared. Civilian populations, rather than being afforded protection, became the targets and tools of war. Murder, rape, mutilation, looting, abductions, human shields, child soldiers, land-mines, property destruction; Sierra Leone is rife with such issues. Of particular note is the plight of women and children, who have borne the worst of the atrocities inflicted by the rebels. Refugee camps and hospitals are full of victims who have had one or more limbs amputated, the youngest being just a few years old. Approximately 3,000 kidnapped children are still unaccounted for, and for those who survived, there are no schools.

The scope of the humanitarian tragedy is staggering. A decade of war has resulted in 75,000 dead. The country has been traumatized by violence, human rights abuses and atrocities on a massive scale. The rebels have two calling cards; dead civilians, and hundreds of living civilians with their hands, feet, ears or genitals crudely amputated. The latter served as a living and constant warning to anyone in their path, and rumours of an RUF attack were often enough to clear entire towns and villages. The children of Sierra Leone have born the brunt of the conflict. In many cases, children were forced by the rebels at gunpoint to kill family members or neighbors. By committing acts of violence against those close to them, not only are they traumatized, but they cannot go back to their families or their communities.

Somehow, a ragtag group of rebels who espoused no coherent political or social doctrine and had little popular support, was able to force Sierra Leone to its very knees. How was this possible? And how did it come about? How did the RUF, the West Side Boys and the renegades of the SLA (the so-called 'sobels' – soldiers by day, rebels by night) come into being? As Sierra Leone's President Kabbah himself pointed out: 'While we unreservedly condemn the junta and its rebel allies, we must not forget to ask ourselves why this happened in the first place.' The answer has much to do with poverty, social exclusion, corruption and the abuse of power by successive civilian and military governments in Sierra Leone. After decades of such abuse, the people of Sierra Leone finally turned on themselves in an orgy of violence and self-destruction that had its roots deep in their frustration and a desperate thirst for money and power.

During the seventies and eighties, Sierra Leone was saddled with a series of corrupt, dictatorial regimes (often with the tacit support of the West) that bankrupted the nation, and its people ended up with no effective means of redress for their grievances. With the nation's wealth ending up concentrated in the hands of a tiny and obscenely wealthy elite, the ordinary people of Sierra Leone felt powerless and marginalised. The battle for the 'ownership' of Sierra Leone's wealth – at its simplest, the diamond mines – was increasingly being determined by force of arms. Those who fought that battle included corrupt politicians, miners, rebels and 'sobels'. For some, the resort to violence brought considerable and immediate profit. According to security expert Paul Williams, Sierra Leone's war was largely a desperate struggle over resources located within a country at the very bottom of the global economy.

By the early eighties, disaffected youth with no prospects for education and employment in Sierra Leone had begun talking of revolution. Under the influence of Libyan leader Colonel Gaddafi's *Green Book* – a socialist treatise and supposed cure for all Africa's ills – many of these budding revolutionaries adopted anti-imperialist and anti-Western views. Rather than examine the nation's corrupt and rotten ruling system, the ills of the nation were laid at the door of the old colonial powers, and Libya began to fan the flames of discontent. By the late eighties, it was providing money and military training to angry young men who had no prospects in their own country. Libya was busy setting up an African revolutionary army, and the young unemployed Sierra Leoneans were eager recruits. In the folklore of the revolution-to-be, armed struggle was the way these men would seize power, and with it the status that for so long had eluded them.

Initially, the RUF, the mother of all rebel movements in Sierra Leone, did espouse some political aims to overthrow '*de system*'. The only document ever produced by the RUF, *Footpaths to Democracy: Towards a New Sierra Leone*, called for an overthrowing of 'colonial-style' rule, a socialist-style redistribution of resources, and reform of the education system and the economy – all of which was to be achieved by the armed struggle.

But when, on 23 March 1991, the RUF launched its first major attack at Bomaru, in Kailahun District, Foday Sankoh had already risen to become its leader. Sankoh was first and foremost a military man. He purged the RUF top ranks of any educated, thinking individuals, and replaced them with uneducated, angry youths. Under his leadership, the so-called revolutionary movement began to slaughter and terrorise the very people that it was supposed to be 'liberating'. The RUF's *Footpaths to Democracy* is peppered with phrases from Mao and other socialist thinkers. But it quotes most widely from the RUF's chief ideologue, Foday Sankoh himself, the architect of the RUF's violence and evil. For example, this is from an early, and chilling, RUF lecture to forced recruits: 'There is no fairness and transparency in the system in Sierra Leone. Despite mineral riches, there is no development of roads, schools and health centres in rural areas. No one in government is listening. Thus the time for talking is past. Violence is now the only option. Your people have been abducted for guerrilla training to regain their birthright.'

The initial RUF recruits were predominantly the rural unemployed, and included a fair number of criminals, drug addicts and thieves. From the very start, then, the RUF hardly had the makings of a principled revolutionary movement – and it quickly degenerated into a bandit movement that visited extreme violence and brutality on the ordinary people of Sierra Leone. At the same time, decades of corrupt misrule had rendered the SLA little better than the RUF: it too had recruited its numbers from street children, drug users and criminals. It was hardly surprising, then, that the rebel RUF, the rebel West Side Boys and the renegade Sierra Leonean Army joined forces to seize power. They shared one, collective ideology: the lust for power and the wealth that would come with it. Under their AFRC, they seized power in 1997 and the rule of law collapsed into total anarchy.

So while some of the rebels in Sierra Leone perhaps deserved some sympathy – many were brutalised as children or forced recruits – that does not mean that they should have been given any quarter during the war. Not while they still possessed large amounts of weaponry and the will to wreak havoc and terror on the civilian population, turning yet more innocent children into killers.

The rebels in Sierra Leone were no Che Guevaras, no romantic Robin Hoods fighting for the people, no freedom fighters in Sudan, no pro-democracy guerrilla forces in Burma: these were terrorist bandits with no political or ideological aims, who had turned the most horrific and terrible acts imaginable into their own brand of fun and games. As such, they possessed no sense of justice; they had no understanding of peace; they held nothing sacrosanct; no level of bestiality escaped them; they knew only war and they deserved no sympathy. As such, they elevated terror to a religion, hatred to a creed, cruelty to an art form, and oppression and evil had become their gods.

The only way to deal with such people at the time was to disarm and dispossess them of their territory by force. And that, in short, meant waging war against them. And that is what the United Nations – with all its massive funding and resources – a force of 13,000 rising to some 20,000 peacekeeping troops in 2002 – failed spectacularly to do. And that is what the 'mercenaries' of Executive Outcomes and then the British forces of the Parachute Regiment, the Marines and the UK Special Forces did so successfully and so well. For in each case, with only a few hundred crack troops, these forces spoke the only language that the rebels were willing to understand – that of war. Any residual sympathy for the rebels could come later. After they had been stopped. After an end to the reign of carnage and terror. Then and only then could the brutalised child soldiers, the tortured adolescent torturers and the orphaned killers be put into demobilisation camps and the process of rehabilitation begun.

But for the leaders of the rebel groups – for the agitators and the torture chiefs and the controllers of these legions of horror – there should be only war-crimes tribunals and the implacable rule of law. The carrot and the stick – the promise of assistance and the military deterrent – both had to be employed to bring an end to the rebel nightmare. It is not just the military and the governments of countries like the UK who believe this; after witnessing the dark years of rebel mayhem in Sierra Leone, most if not all of the aid and humanitarian groups working in the country had reached the same, stark conclusion. They had accepted that first and foremost, the rebels had to be crushed militarily – before any political and humanitarian solution to the nation's problems could be found.

Writing in April 2001, William Shawcross of the International Crisis Group (ICG) – a world-renowned think tank – is absolutely clear on this point. 'If the RUF does not surrender, Britain, with the UN's backing, should support the Sierra Leone Army to defeat it. British forces are popular in Sierra Leone. They are training the ragtag SLA for an eventual showdown with the rebels. Remarkably, a mass rally at the end of last year called for Britain to re-establish colonial rule. British officers should now be placed in the chain of command of the SLA.' Shawcross is clear on another point too: that the UN's peacekeeping efforts in Sierra Leone were an abject failure. 'Why were the UN not up to doing the job? Because they did not have an adequate mandate and their performance was woeful. The UN's failures reflect the bitter realities of peacekeeping today. Western countries would rather pay third world nations than send in their own troops.'

The ICG's own April 2000 report on the options for Sierra Leone concluded that: 'The world community must help Sierra Leone take decisive military action against the RUF. The military option could be spearheaded by UK trained and led SLA forces, with the UN securing the areas regained. The UK should provide military and intelligence backup to guarantee the safety of UN forces. The Kamajors could provide additional security for local villages and settlements.' The ICG called for an immediate UN Security Council resolution demanding that the RUF surrender, followed by military action against those who refused, led by British forces.

But why did Britain eventually take the risk of intervening in Sierra Leone? What were the key British interests there that led to the will being found to intervene on such a dramatic level? What made the Blair government willing to put British troops in harm's way in some obscure country in West Africa that most of the British public had never even heard of? Sierra Leone has some strategic value: it possesses West Africa's only deep-sea port, at Freetown. Twice it served the British well, once as a port for naval operations during the Second World War, and once as a naval base during the Falklands War. But this in itself is hardly reason enough to explain the British military interventions of recent years. A popular rumour doing the rounds among British troops at the time of the first major military initiative – Operation Palliser – was that Blair had a special affection for Sierra Leone, as his father was once a schoolteacher there. Possibly. But that hardly explains why Blair, himself a shrewd political operator, was willing to risk so much in the killing fields of this ex-colony in a remote corner of Africa.

At its simplest, Blair had pinned his colours to the mast as early as April 1999, when, writing in a *Newsweek* article, he called for a 'new internationalism' that would not tolerate those who 'visit horrific punishments on their own people to stay in power'. In his so-called Chicago speech of the same month, Blair spoke of 'the most pressing foreign policy problem we face being to identify the circumstances in which we should get actively involved in other people's conflicts'. In this speech, Blair identified five criteria by which to judge whether British forces should be sent to intervene overseas. 'First, are we sure of our case? Second, have we exhausted all diplomatic options? Third, on the basis of a practical assessment of the situation, are there military options we can sensibly and prudently undertake? Fourth, are we prepared for the long term? And finally, do we have national interests involved?'

In making such pronouncements, Blair was sending a powerful signal to the US administration in particular: the UK would no longer follow the hands-off approach to Africa of a US military which had been badly mauled in Somalia. For the New Labour government the proof of concept for this 'new internationalism' would be Sierra Leone. 'Britain's use of force in Sierra Leone follows similar instances of military interventions in Iraq (1998), East Timor (1999) and the Balkans (1999)', argues Paul Williams, 'that have been waged by the

New Labour government purportedly in defence of values rather than territorial ambitions.'

Williams identifies five reasons behind the Labour government's intervention in Sierra Leone. First, a concern to protect British citizens. Second, a humanitarian impulse to do something as Sierra Leone teetered on the brink of the abyss yet again. Third, the defence of democracy via military means, reflecting a decision to back up the government of President Kabbah. Fourth, a way to translate the Labour government's ethical foreign policy imperatives into practice on the ground – promoting peace, prosperity and democracy on the African continent. And fifth, the urgent need to intervene to bolster the credibility of UN peacekeeping operations.

Blair's new doctrine of Western involvement in the developing world has most recently seen itself played out in the high-profile British military role in Gulf War Two – in the so-called 'raid and aid' policies of the British forces around Basra. At its simplest, it rests upon the precept that no amount of aid and humanitarian assistance can help a country ruled by anarchy and chaos – and that first and foremost security must be imposed. That security can be imposed only by a competent military force – one mandated to use lethal means wherever necessary. In the wake of military action, aid agencies and humanitarian groups can move in to help the civilian population, and peace deals and political settlements can be drawn up. In a post-9/11 world, that policy sees itself being played out in the UK's ongoing military role in Sierra Leone, in the Australian military intervention in the Solomon Islands, and the US military's (limited) intervention in Liberia – where Western powers recognise that far-off conflicts left to fester can rebound in terms of international terrorism.

After the successful rescue of the Royal Irish hostages in September 2000, the British military intervention continued in Sierra Leone. Soon after, the Royal Irish contingent at Benguema was replaced by some three hundred further British troops who took over their activities. By the end of 2000, some three thousand SLA troops would have completed the IMATT training course. In fact, IMATT was mandated for a three-year contract to sort out the situation in Sierra Leone, with a budget in excess of some £30 million. The British military continued to operate in Sierra Leone, doing by default what the UN had proven itself incapable of – enabling the SLA to operate effectively against the rebels and bring about an end to the country's internecine civil war.

IMATT was and remains a British-led initiative, which is not under the UN. It uses only experienced military personnel: in addition to the Royal Irish Regiment, the Royal Gurkha Rifles, the Royal Anglian Regiment and several other units have served under IMATT in Sierra Leone. There are also smaller allied contingents, including several Canadian and American troops. In 2000, the Canadians deployed military personnel under Operation Sculpture, and they worked alongside the British forces training the SLA. Between August 1999 and March 2000, IMATT cost the British taxpayer some £7.4 million – and that was prior to the massive military interventions of Operation Palliser and Operation Barras. The price tag for the British military intervention in Sierra Leone is not inconsiderable.

At the start of 2001 – several months after Operations Palliser and Barras – three scenarios were facing IMATT. Under the first, 'golden scenario', the rebel forces would disband in the face of British forces and a newly revamped SLA. In the second, 'silver scenario', the 13,000-strong peacekeeping forces of UNAMSIL would move into the rebel areas, and oversee a nationwide rebel disarmament programme. It was the third, 'bronze scenario', that IMATT were training the SLA for – a massive offensive to sweep the RUF and associated rebels out of their jungle bases once and for all. The SLA's elite Force Recce Unit – one hundred of its best troops, trained by UK Special Forces – were already combing the jungles of the interior to locate the main rebel bases.

Colonel Mike Dent, IMATT's CO, was pretty clear about the British forces' mandate against the rebels. 'We need to orchestrate success and ensure that when we attack, we can take our objective completely. This is to build up confidence within the Sierra Leonean ranks, to test what our training teams have taught them, and to send a message to the RUF and quite possibly other forces in . . . Liberia as well.'

The British IMATT initiative involved far more than just the rank and file of the SLA. Senior commanders and Defence Ministry civil servants were also receiving training. The plan for IMATT took a year to put together, with a civil servant and an army colonel working in Freetown with Sierra Leonean government representatives. In addition to training the rank-and-file SLA out of Benguema, SLA officers were flown to Ghana for officer training at the Ghanaian military staff college. The end result would be a completely new armed force of some 8,500 men, renamed the Republic of Sierra Leone Armed Forces

(RSLAF). In short, the British intervention in Sierra Leone probably represents the single biggest British involvement in an African nation's affairs since colonial times.

The issues facing Sierra Leone cut across many traditional British political enmities. Though IMATT was a Labour government initiative, it enjoyed a large groundswell of Conservative support – despite concerns about 'mission creep'. In a House of Commons debate on Sierra Leone on 25 May – just as Operation Palliser was really getting to grips with the RUF in Sierra Leone – Crispin Blunt MP, a Tory, spoke approvingly of the British military actions.

The RUF is a bunch of terrorist gangsters, which supports itself in power through the supply of money that it gets from Sierra Leone's diamond mines and its relationship with Liberia, where the diamonds are marketed. The key military objective must be to destroy the RUF by taking control of ground that is vital to them – that is the diamond-producing areas. I believe that is achievable, given that the RUF has no cultural basis of support and no tribal loyalty. The operation should be properly followed up by retraining the Sierra Leone Army, training the police force and the civil service and putting in place civil institutions.

For his unstinting support over the last four years in Sierra Leone, Tony Blair received the personal thanks of President Kabbah. In an open letter Kabbah expressed profound thanks for 'the principled and ethical position' that Britain has taken on the conflict in his country. Blair himself certainly sees Sierra Leone as a success story, one demonstrating the efficacy of his policies on international intervention in troubled nations: 'When people say that they run an ethical foreign policy, I say Sierra Leone was an example of that.'

During an October 2002 visit to the charities she supports in Sierra Leone, the Duchess of York was taken to the Freetown Milton Margai School for the Blind. In a country that sees itself owing so much to the UK (and in particular the British armed forces) this was the nearest the people of Sierra Leone had come to a British royal visit. The school is for young children either born blind, or for the many who lost their sight in the war. In attendance with her was Brigadier Patrick Davidson-Houston, then Commander of British Forces in Sierra Leone. The kids said they had a song they wanted the visitors to hear, and they proceeded to sing of how 'we cannot see but we will conquer'. As the song came to its rousing chorus, it became an anthem for the depth of affection people in Sierra Leone feel towards the British military.

'We thank the Brigadier, and those who look after us,
In the Army and the Royal Air Force,
And also the Royal Navy!
Helping bring peace to the people of Sierra Leone,
And happiness to the children of Milton Margai
School for the Blind!'

One of the greatest difficulties now facing the country is the numbers of those who in one way or another have been involved in the fighting – either as rebels, militia, Kamajor or SLA. There are an estimated 50,000 such combatants, and only eight-thousand-odd of those could be integrated back into the IMATT-trained RSLAF. The rest – some 40,000 – were destined for the UN-operated Disarmament, Demobilization and Reintegration programme, which aims to provide some training and civilian jobs for the new non-combatants.

The enemies of IMATT went far beyond the borders of Sierra Leone. Consider the wider scenario. It was one in which Liberia's Charles Taylor helped the RUF by taking their conflict diamonds, selling them internationally, and providing weapons in return. That was the way by which the RUF converted diamonds into money and arms. By extension, any enemy of IMATT's was also a friend of Liberia's. And as the RUF was initially trained and backed by Libya, there were even wider international implications. Add into that the recent diamond deals that the RUF have done with al-Qaeda operatives (conflict diamonds being an untraceable and unfreezable form of almost ready cash), then IMATT was in effect taking on the minions of Osama bin Laden and his world-terror network as well. All the more reason, therefore, for the British government's serious commitment to getting the job done in Sierra Leone.

In May 2000, President Taylor attacked the role British forces were playing in Sierra Leone. 'The British government has been among the collaborating governments which have posed a direct threat to the security of Liberia by rearming a non-restructured Sierra Leone Army, and the Kamajors . . . which include special forces of Liberian dissidents in Sierra Leone.' Turning up the heat on its war with Britain and the US, Liberia accused the two nations of supporting Liberian rebels and backing a plot to assassinate Charles Taylor himself. In interviews with the BBC, Taylor denied charges that he was aiding the RUF, and went on the counter-attack. 'Isn't it easy for the great United States to confront this little country with evidence, so that everyone will say, "Yes, you are wrong"?' Taylor went on to claim that the US had sent

American assassins into the country to kill him, posing as missionaries and diplomats. The US was supposedly paying $2 million for the killing of Charles Taylor.

In the spring of 2003, David Crane, the Chief Prosecutor of the UN Special Court in Sierra Leone, revealed growing evidence of an al-Qaeda link to the civil wars in both Sierra Leone and Liberia. President Taylor was allegedly harbouring al-Qaeda operatives. 'We know that they are moving about. We know that they are trading in diamonds, laundering money and being protected by Charles Taylor,' David Crane told the Reuters news agency. It was high time to examine the region's terrorist links, Crane said, before the world community would come to rue the day that it had ignored the area for so long. 'Charles Taylor is harbouring terrorists from the Middle East, including al-Qaeda and Hezbollah, and has been doing so for years. Taylor is a player in the world of terror and what he does affects the lives of those living in the United States and Europe.' Interestingly, the US is the world's single biggest market for diamonds, accounting for some 50 per cent of the global trade.

The growing trend in warfare around the globe has shifted radically as we enter the twenty-first century. In the classic military combat of history, two opposing sides fought each other until one side was defeated and the other claimed victory. In its place, modern wars tend to disdain direct combat between opposing forces and concentrate on targeting the civilian population in order to destroy the ethnic power base and support structure of rival forces. There are often more than two parties to the war, with shifting allegiances. In the former Yugoslavia, Rwanda, Sudan, the Congo, Burundi, Algeria, Liberia, Central African Republic, Burma and a host of other countries, this 'terroristic' approach to warfare has turned conflict into human tragedies for the civilian population, as opposed to focusing on battlefield victories and military casualties. The end of the Cold War effectively ushered in a new era of 'Hot Peace', wherein Western powers like the UK have to deploy forces in firefighting operations around the world. Sierra Leone is a prime example of this new-style warfare.

Whereas peacekeeping may have worked in the past – the old UN style of the blue helmets keeping two sides apart – it does not necessarily do so now. In the past there were clearly defined sides to a conflict, wars were largely fought between two foreign powers through their military forces. Examples of such ongoing UN peacekeeping initiatives are the Eritrea–Ethiopia conflict, the India–Pakistan conflict and in

Cyprus (Turkey versus Greece). In all these cases, the war is defined by being waged between two, easily identifiable sides – the armies of the nations involved. In these cases, 'old-style' UN peacekeeping does still seem to fit the bill.

But in the complex mix of civil wars and rebel factions and guerrilla insurgencies, old-style peacekeeping doesn't always fit the bill. In Sierra Leone, for example, there simply was no peace to keep. This is what the UN failed to realise when it sent 13,000 peacekeeping troops to that country – and it learned its lessons there the hard way. At the time, UNAMSIL was the largest United Nations peacekeeping effort in the world – yet its role in Sierra Leone was to prove an embarrassing debacle.

At worst, the UN should at least have been on a peace-enforcing mandate, as opposed to a peacekeeping one – empowered to use lethal force against recalcitrant rebels. At best, the UN needed an aggressive and professional fighting force to take the war to the rebels and finish them once and for all. This is what Executive Outcomes had achieved with 150-odd mercenaries over nineteen months in 1995–6, at a cost of under $2 million a month. After EO's intervention, and for the first time that decade, Sierra Leone witnessed an end to the civil war and the rebels were forced to the peace table. Four years later, 13,000 UN peacekeepers arrived, at a cost of some $600 million a year. Within months of their arrival the civil war was back on again, and UN forces stood by impotently as the RUF advanced on Freetown, threatening to plunge the country back into a living nightmare. In short, in Sierra Leone the UN lost the peace.

As Hugo Young wrote in the *Guardian*, in May 2000:

The force in Sierra Leone is the largest UN peacekeeping army in the world. Yet it is pathetically failing. It has become hostage to the armed gangs of the rebel forces who are destabilising the regime it should be defending . . . If this massive UN presence is incapable of sustaining peace against a disorderly and largely untrained rabble, one must ask what future there can ever be for the entire principle of humanitarian peacekeeping intervention by the UN.

It was in May 2000 that the British took unilateral action and sent its toughest armed forces into the fray. This was no peacekeeping mission and the British government were careful not to get bogged down in the UN operation. This was a separate and complementary force to the chaotic and malfunctioning UNAMSIL, and it did not share the UN's peacekeeping mandate. The British went to Sierra Leone with a similar set of objectives to Executive Outcomes before them: to go on the offensive and take the war to the rebels. In a matter of weeks, the concerted action of a five-hundred-strong force of Paras rolled the rebels back into the jungle and defeated their offensive.

In Sierra Leone peacekeeping failed on every level and cost a fortune. Peace-enforcement would probably have fared little better. What Sierra Leone needed was a military force capable of waging warfare against rebel forces in order to protect a vulnerable and traumatised civilian population. Sadly, peace just wasn't in it.

And what of the UN's own position on its woeful performance in Sierra Leone? In effect, the UN Secretary-General, Kofi Annan, damned the British military role with faint praise. While lauding the 'big psychological boost' the arrival of the British Rapid Reaction Force under Operation Palliser gave to the then 13,000 UN forces in-country, he went on to say that 'it would have been preferable if they would have been under the UN'. That misses the whole point. It goes against the very reasons the British were successful. The soldiers that the British sent in were not UN peacekeeping forces. These were men sent in to wage war on the rebels of Sierra Leone, to take the battle to the jungles and chase the rebels back to their lair.

In truth, the arrival of a few hundred British Paras under Operation Palliser prevented UN forces that outnumbered them some thirty to one from collapsing completely, and at the same time stopped the RUF rebels from taking Freetown. As the Paras flew into Lungi Airport in May 2000, the people of Freetown were poised to turn on the UN blue helmets and literally rip their throats out. As far as they could see, the 13,000 UN 'peacekeepers' appeared unable and unwilling to keep the peace, or even to stop the rebels from seizing the nation's capital city. The murderous rebels were poised to run amok in Freetown once again, and the forces of the United Nations had clearly failed them. When the Operation Barras assault forces hit the West Side Boys three months later, this sent out yet another powerful message to the rebels in Sierra Leone: the rule of international law was not to be flouted, however absurd and ineffective the UN had proved up until then.

But where the UN fails, are Western armies like Britain's always going to be willing to intervene? So many examples – Bosnia, the Congo, Rwanda, to name but a few – suggest otherwise. And one of the unique lessons of Sierra Leone is perhaps that of the role mercenaries can play in such situations – rebranded as Private Military Companies (PMCs). Not once, but twice, PMCs waged war in Sierra Leone to stop the massacre of the innocents by faceless, soulless, evil killers. Where 13,000 UN peacekeepers with an annual budget of over half a billion dollars failed dismally in 2000, a force of just 150 mercenaries deployed by Executive Outcomes succeeded four years earlier with an annual budget of $20 million.

Yet the international community reacted at the time with outrage that a group of mercenaries could be used in such a way. Why? Does political correctness make it acceptable that countless innocent men, women and children be raped and maimed and abused and murdered by psychopathic killers while the UN stands by and does nothing, but unacceptable for mercenaries to step in and stop the slaughter? Does some refined sense of political correctness somehow make it all right for the slaughter to continue as long as mercenaries are not involved, even when those mercenaries are there by invitation of the legitimate ruling government?

A year after EO were forced out of the country, Colonel Tim Spicer's Sandline, a British PMC, stepped in to play a further, key role in vanquishing Sierra Leone's rebels. But like EO before them, Sandline's reward was to be vilified in the media and disowned by British politicians. Sandline became embroiled in the so-called 'Arms-to-Africa' affair, a sorry scandal of distasteful political expediency and pointless buck-passing that saw the FCO pilloried in the press and Sandline hauled over the coals for the role it played in shipping arms to Sierra Leone – when all Spicer's men had done was to help reinstate a democratically elected African president to his rightful place as the leader of his country. Again, the question has to be asked, why? Sandline, like EO, helped drive a bunch of murderous, evil killers out of Freetown and return the President of Sierra Leone to power. And for their efforts they were pilloried. Does this make any sense to anyone, anywhere?

As Andrew Rowbathan MP stated in the House of Commons (around the time of the May 2000 launch of Operation Palliser), when commenting on the abject failure of UNAMSIL:

A 150-strong deployment by a private military company [EO] in 1995–6 is widely acknowledged, even among the critics of 'mercenaries', as having created the conditions that brought the rebels to the negotiating table and brought about the first democratic elections for many years. The later crisis in Sierra

Leone would never have arisen if the contract with Executive Outcomes had not been prematurely terminated in 1996 (contrary to advice given to the Sierra Leone government at the time).

That contract was terminated because of international pressure from Western governments uncomfortable at mercenary involvement in the country. Just who is making sense here? The PMCs and those who support them, or their politically correct detractors? And all of this in spite of the clear wishes of the people of Sierra Leone themselves, who treated the soldiers of EO and Sandline (and later, of Her Majesty's Armed Forces) as avenging heroes delivering them from evil incarnate.

As James R. Davis, a Canadian security consultant, writes of the EO Sierra Leone operations: 'I have to respect a group of soldiers who have had the courage to put their lives at risk when the rest of the international community just stood by and watched. In Sierra Leone they fulfilled their contracts and won these dirty wars for their paymasters.' Or Michael Grunberg, an adviser to Sandline: 'If the indigenous population of a country like Sierra Leone – the very people who will be able to go through life with both hands as opposed to having them chopped off with a blunt axe by the rebels – want a company like Executive Outcomes to maintain the peace, who should blame them in the absence of any other help?'

Or Colonel Tim Spicer, late of Sandline:

Since the end of the Cold War, smouldering ethnic conflicts have broken out all over the globe. In the old days, one or other of the superpowers would have snuffed them out. Now, the forces of the traditional 'policemen' are depleted. Most have neither the resources nor the political will to involve themselves in faraway conflicts, particularly if it is not nationally significant. So how can countries create a safe, stable environment for peaceful existence and economic growth? Often they can't and are left on their own with catastrophic results. That's where private military companies come in. Could things have been different in Burundi or Rwanda if an effective military force had been deployed quickly? The answer is yes. Thousands of lives could have been saved, but nobody went.

Speaking of Rwanda, Paul Williams makes the following point:

PMCs can deploy rapidly, can risk the lives of their soldiers more readily than states, and can avoid the political entanglements that tend to haunt complex UN operations. After exploring whether it had the capacity to react to the 1994 Rwandan genocide, Executive Outcomes concluded that not only did it have the capacity to rapidly deploy 1,500 soldiers with air support within six weeks, but it could have done so for $150 million for a six-month operation. Compare this to the UN operation [UNAMIR II], which deployed after the genocide and ended up costing $3 million a day (or $547 million for a six-month period). Executive Outcomes were welcomed in Freetown and would no doubt have been lauded in Rwanda, had the $150 million be found to pay for them to halt the genocide.

With US forces loath to intervene in Africa and British forces over-stretched, PMCs may remain the most attractive option. But there is still the question of who would pay for them to intervene in a crisis like Sierra Leone. The soldiers who populate PMCs are professionals and they work for money. In fact, most soldiers, most peacekeepers – most aid workers and human-rights monitors for that matter – work for money and have to be paid. If the money can be found to pay for the inflated budgets of disastrous UN 'peacekeeping' efforts, then the international community can afford the more reasonable budgets of the PMCs. At present there are only two options open to world leaders, other than sending in a PMC. The first is the UN, which as the case of Sierra Leone shows (along with many other examples) is prohibitively expensive and tragically ineffective. The second is the army of an effective military power, but political will and public inertia often go against such unilateral military interventions in far-distant conflicts.

The British military did a peerless job in Sierra Leone, but you only have to look as far as the disastrous US military intervention in Somalia, to show how 'Operation Restore Hope' quickly became 'Operation Never Send US Troops To Africa Ever Again'. Or take the more recent example of Liberia. In the summer of 2003, rebel forces were poised to topple Charles Taylor. But the British – already committed to neighbouring Sierra Leone – were reluctant to intervene, while the Americans, under whose influence Liberia falls (being a nation created for freed US slaves) were refusing to send troops. Meanwhile, the rebels and Taylor's militia slogged it out as the capital Monrovia burned and the people of the country suffered. Eventually, a small US force was sent to Liberia, but not before massive suffering among the civilian population. With the proper funding and mandate, PMCs would have been in there to sort it out like a shot – as a war-termination task force – just as they had done twice in Sierra Leone and in Angola before that.

If a mechanism can be found to fund the PMCs, there are significant advantages to their role in spearheading any international intervention. PMCs are not better than professional national armies, but they do risk less of the unpalatable spin-offs that make military interventions difficult for Western governments. Most importantly, casualties are a fact of life among the men who work for PMCs, and they do not have the same emotive impact or media interest as do those from national forces. And PMCs can move quickly. While presidents and world leaders vacillate, PMCs can get men and equipment in-country efficiently and rapidly to intervene where needed.

These PMCs are not the old 'dogs of war'. These are no casual mercenaries. In Sierra Leone, Executive Outcomes had its own air force for international medical flights and logistics, its own training teams to drill some fighting discipline into the SLA, its own intelligence-gathering and operational planning facilities, its own attack and transport helicopters. EO's operatives briefed international governments and led national armies of several countries in the war against the rebels. If PMCs are to take on some of this international conflict-termination role, that will be because they are uniquely placed to deploy a large number of highly trained and disciplined former army personnel more quickly and more cheaply and with none of the associated PR risks of either the United Nations or national governments. To do so, they will need to observe a form of military hierarchy and associated discipline, respect the laws and customs of the host nation, and adhere to the international rules of war. In a world of increasing uncertainty, the lessons of Sierra Leone surely point to PMCs having a vital role to play in ensuring security in the world conflicts. Working alongside national armies, they have considerable potential to make a genuine contribution to world peace.

Which is not to say that the UN is redundant. Far from it. But it should be used appropriately and where it can be effective and provide good value for money, which certainly was not the case in Sierra Leone. In a sense, the UN itself is not even to blame for its abysmal record on peacekeeping in Africa. The UN has no standing army of its own, no United Nations Armed Forces (you can imagine the acronym even now, but 'UNAF' doesn't, sadly, exist). When the UN sent 13,000 peacekeeping troops to Sierra Leone it had to beg its member states to provide them from within their own armed forces. And whereas the UK and the US were reluctant to send troops, Bangladesh, Ghana, Guinea, Kenya, Jordan, Zambia, Nigeria, India and Russia were not. The UN Mission in Sierra Leone ended up with 13,000 troops from nine different countries speaking several different languages. The best troops were undoubtedly the Indians, but even their overall commander in Sierra Leone, General Vijay Muar Jetley, was unequivocal about the UN's failings there. In an ABC interview in Freetown, in August 2000, he stated:

It is time to take stock of the manner in which we conduct peacekeeping operations. Firstly, the mental preparedness to do this is lacking with most countries who contribute to UN forces. There's a misconception that peace-keeping means being very well turned out, wearing a nice blue helmet or cap and being in a white vehicle with a blue flag fluttering around and marching up and down, and that that's peacekeeping. It is not. At the moment the international community must understand that I need troops who are going to neither question nor dither. What I need is troops who can deliver.

Equipped with several different and incompatible radio communications systems, the various UN contingents were often unable even to communicate with each other. They were hardly the best-quality, most highly motivated soldiers in the first place. But parachuted into Sierra Leone's civil war with an inadequate mandate (they had to have really, really good reasons to shoot any of the rebels), incompatible comms equipment and a defunct command-and-control structure, is it any wonder the UN mission imploded? The UN is not to blame – its member governments are. The UN invariably ends up being provided with the world's least competent soldiers to carry out the world's most difficult peace missions, a guaranteed recipe for failure. All too often, the will within the member states and their armed forces is, quite simply, lacking.

Following the near collapse of the UNAMSIL in May 2000, the army chiefs of staff from the nine different countries providing troops met in New York to discuss a change in their mandate from 'peacekeeping' to 'peace enforcement'. Yet they refused to endorse this – arguing that it would be tantamount to a declaration of war against the RUF, which was not what their forces had originally signed up for.

But while the UN is not to blame for the failures in its peacekeeping per se, it is to blame if it persists, as a body, in refusing to see the writing on the wall, and continues deliberately to stand in the way of any other, more effective alternatives. And in Africa, in particular, that writing says very clearly that the blue helmets have pretty much had their day (at least in their traditionally constituted role). It is time to give something else a go. And that something else will, most likely, include the PMCs.

'It is a question of deciding what kind of world we want. People wrung their hands over the genocide of Rwanda, but who did anything about it?' says Colonel Tim Spicer, in justifying the role of the PMCs. 'Yes, we expect to be paid, but we are a lot less costly than a sovereign or UN military force and may be far more effective. Yes, we apply commercial values, but what if we do? Surely it is better to prevent death, destruction and hardship than turn your back on it, especially if a private military company is the last and only resort?'

Or, put somewhat more directly by Canadian Brigadier General Ian Douglas, speaking of the conflict in Sierra Leone: 'You have to stop the violence before you can start the peace negotiations. Sometimes the only way to stop it is to go in with a bigger bunch of guys and guns than the bad guys have. Executive Outcomes did that in Sierra Leone. They literally stopped the war.'

Brigadier General Douglas, an adviser on UN peacekeeping operations, is not alone in being an advocate for PMCs to be given a greater role around the world. He recently briefed UN officials on the role PMCs can play, and the argument is achieving increased currency in international peacekeeping and political circles. There are many detractors still, but the Brigadier General believes it is only a matter of time before PMCs are widely in use with UN operations. In perhaps the first case of its kind, Brigadier General Douglas helped organise an $8 million UN contract to hire 1,500 troops in Zaire to provide security for the UN refugee camps. It would have cost the UN $80 million to have paid traditional peacekeeping troops to have done the same job. Every time the argument is made for greater use of PMCs in such operations, the example of EO (and Sandline) in Sierra Leone is used as justification for such an expanded role.

Dr Kevin A. O'Brien, an expert on international security issues, argues that the twenty-first century may witness the rise of a new type of PMC, one that overturns the stereotypes of old-style 'mercenaries'. In fact, he argues that the new model PMC had already begun to emerge out of the last decade of the twentieth century.

In many cases, but not all, PMCs were much more effective in resolving conflicts in many African countries than the international community; they took a much more direct interest in the well-being of the populations in the countries in which they brought a halt to the conflicts than did the international community; and – in the largest number of cases – it has not been the fault of the PMCs that long-lasting stability and peace did not come to the countries in which they have operated, but of the international community which failed to step in to secure that peace, as in Sierra Leone in 1997.

There is presently a Green Paper before the British Parliament to establish a formal licensing system for PMCs, seen by many as the first step towards legitimising mercenary work and bringing them in out of the cold. The Green Paper itself states that: 'The relative stability achieved following Executive Outcomes' operations [in Sierra Leone] enabled elections to be held.' It goes on: 'It is at least possible that if the UNAMSIL-style tasks were put out to tender, private companies would be able to do the job more cheaply and more effectively. It is also possible that such forces might be available more quickly than the UN and they would be more willing to integrate under a single command than is the case with such [UN] national contingents.'

The very real option of the UK government utilising the services of PMCs can be seen in some of the submissions to that Green Paper. The UK Select Committee on Foreign Affairs wrote that: 'Rather than force the industry offshore, the Government needs to regulate, and where possible, utilise PMCs to pursue its overseas objectives in support of the nation's armed forces.' The British Department for International Development (DFID) points out that it has already used PMCs in non-combatant roles on contract in the past, and continues to do so. In an astute observation, DFID states: 'Perhaps the greatest difficulty in employing PMCs is the type of message this sends to the rest of the world.' The British military is fairly unambiguous on the matter: 'It is almost unanimously accepted by military personnel that PMCs can offer significant advantages over national armies in terms of speed of response and are able to fulfil such roles as the security of aid agencies if so wished. In the current operational climate, British forces will inevitably end up operating alongside PMCs contracted by local governments and multinational companies in most African and some Asian theatres.'

Of course, there are caveats to the use of PMCs. First, PMCs would need to adhere to the laws of war and deliver on a specific contract and mandate as agreed with their paymaster (the UN or other world body). To help ensure this, their operations could be placed under the jurisdiction of the International Criminal Court, as part of the terms of their employment. Second, as Paul Williams points out, there is a danger that in privatising peacekeeping, states may turn their backs on their responsibility to maintain international peace and security in general. The divide between rich-world peacekeeping and poor-world peacekeeping could become even more stark – there being a willing-ness to intervene in our own backyard and a lack of will to do so elsewhere. But as the lessons from Rwanda and the Balkans (to name but two examples) amply demonstrate, that international will to inter-vene is all too often lacking.

Paul Williams also notes that private military forces are one of the major causes of the dilemmas now affecting continents like Africa – where wayward mercenaries will work for the highest bidder, regardless of their legitimacy. And he points out that EO are largely the exception, rather than the rule. Few other PMCs have organised and run combat missions on a level that EO did in first Angola and then Sierra Leone. This may have been the case historically, but there are presently around a dozen PMCs who are actively seeking work on a scale similar to that carried out by EO in Sierra Leone. They claim to have the human resources and the capacity to intervene rapidly, if contracted to do so.

Williams cautions that peacekeeping operations of whatever nature ought to aim to encourage non-violent forms of conflict resolution. 'Dispersing military force to a greater number of actors only compli-cates already complex emergencies. Privatised peacekeeping may lead to less regulation and less democratic scrutiny.' Other risks include the fact that PMCs could withdraw from an operation if the factors changed on the ground and it became unprofitable for them. And that PMCs recruit effective soldiers first and foremost, whose experience of peace operations and respect for human rights may leave some-thing to be desired. There is also the issue of exactly who should have the power to hire the private peacekeepers. But the answers to such questions surely lie in proper regulation, control and accountability. As Paul Williams points out: 'Ultimately, those hiring PMCs must be morally responsible for their actions.'

Despite such arguments, persuasively made, and the evidence from the field, the UN still appears to be implacably opposed to the use of PMCs. In its 1997 UN Human Rights report, 'On the Question of the Use of Mercenaries as a Means of Violating Human Rights and Impeding the Rights of People to Self-Determination', UN Special Rapporteur, Enrique Bernales Ballesteros, called for UN member states to immediately ratify a UN convention designed to outlaw the activi-ties of mercenary companies. This UN convention, adopted by the UN General Assembly in December 1989, has yet to gain enough signatories to become international law. It requires just twenty-two signatories from the 185 members of the UN, and so far only sixteen have signed it, indicative of the dearth of support UN member states have for the UN's supposed official position seeking to ban mercenary operations. While member states may not particularly like the work that PMCs do, the majority clearly recognise the need for them in the twenty-first century.

In fact, the UN position appears somewhat schizophrenic. Speaking at the annual Ditchley Foundation lecture recently, the UN Secretary-General spoke up in support of the work of PMCs, even suggesting they may be the answer to some of the UN's ills.

Some have even suggested that private security firms, like the one which recently helped restore the elected President to power in Sierra Leone, might play a role in providing the United Nations with the rapid reaction capability it needs. When we had need of skilled soldiers to separate fighters from refugees in the Rwandan refugee camps in Goma [during the 1994 Rwandan genocide] I even considered the possibility of engaging a private firm. But the world may not yet be ready to privatise peace.

Speaking on ABC *Lateline* in 2000, Sir Brian Urquhart, who is considered the founding father of UN peacekeeping and who spent fifteen years directing such UN efforts, was even more direct.

The problem is the UN is using an old technique of peacekeeping between sovereign governments to try to deal with civil wars in one country and, of course, it doesn't work. The UN itself should have a small rapid reaction force, trained along the lines of Special Forces with a UN slant, which could get in at the beginning and really try to nip the crisis in the bud. If the UN could get its act together on the new problems it's facing and get a new technique to deal with them, it does seem to me that some of these private [military] companies could play an extremely useful role.

US academic Doug Brooks has recently carried out a study to ascertain how much it would cost the UN to contract PMCs to end all of Africa's internecine civil wars. He asked Sandline to come up with an informal tender bid for the task. The price tag? Just $750 million, or only a little over the cost of one year's disastrous 'peacekeeping' efforts of the UNAMSIL in Sierra Leone. Brooks, a specialist on African security issues, argues that PMCs would do the work far more effectively. He believes that it is time the UN contracted out its peacekeeping, peace-enforcement and humanitarian efforts in Africa, because no one else is willing to do the job properly. Brooks writes: in a 2001 article in *African Analysis*:

The very real stumbling block to utilising PMCs for peace operations comes from the very organisation charged with bringing about world peace. The UN has the ultimate legitimacy but not the capability or the resolve to do peace operations. Lacking any military arm of its own, it is forced to rely on soldiers proffered by its member states. Unable to see any direct threat to their own national interests, developed countries with the best militaries rarely offer their own troops to UN peace-keeping missions, leaving the least capable soldiers doing the most difficult missions. PMCs could change all that, offering professional soldiers, most of whom previously served in the best militaries in the world.

Recently, a consortium of PMCs calling themselves the International Peace Operations Association (IPOA) has proposed that it be hired to work on behalf of the largely ineffectual UN peacekeeping operations in eastern Congo. The PMCs making up IPOA, which range from aerial surveillance operators to a company of Gurkha veterans, have offered to create a 'security curtain' (a thirty-mile demilitarised zone) in one of the most lawless areas of the African continent. The IPOA's charge would be between $100–200 million, dependent on the scale of the operation. So far, it has found no buyers for the plan, but the level of violence in the area continues to escalate. In the US, however, the use of PMCs is already becoming very much of a reality: Dyncorp are training the police force in Iraq; Vinnell have for many years trained the National Guard in Saudi Arabia; Kellog Brown and Root are involved with security in Iraq for Halliburton.

As international security expert P.W. Singer writes:

It is only a matter of time before the next humanitarian crisis occurs in an area that falls outside the interests of the leading states. Whenever it happens, there is a strong possibility that the UN will have to stomach its concerns about the unseemliness of privatized peacekeeping or face the prospect of watching thousands of men, women, and children die when the market could have saved them. The onus is on to deal with these issues now, before the next crisis brings this quandary to the fore.
 The decision to watch genocide and do nothing is not only morally unaccepta-ble, but is also untenable in a world of ever-present media attention. So, if the international community is unwilling to pay the costs of providing its own capable peacekeeping forces, then it is better that it now begins finding ways to mitigate the underlying concerns with contracting out humanitarian

intervention . . . From passenger planes serving as cruise missiles to private companies trading in armies, we live in a time of immense flux. A mere 10 years ago, the very notion of private firms taking over the responsibilities of peacekeeping would have been absurd. It is now a real prospect. These firms are not altruistic by any measure . . . But if the public sector is unwilling to get its house in order, the private sector offers a new way to protect those who would otherwise be defenceless.

Singer presents a theoretical scenario that appears all too real:

Violence breaks out in a small African state. The local government collapses and reports emerge that civilians are being massacred by the tens of thousands. Refugees stream out in pitiable columns. As scenes reminiscent of the Rwanda genocide are played out on the world's television screens, pressure mounts to do something. The UN's calls for action fall upon deaf ears. In the US, the leadership remains busy with the war on terrorism and Iraq and decides that the political risks of doing nothing are far less than the risks of losing any American soldiers' lives in what is essentially a mission of charity. Other nations follow its lead, and none are willing to risk their own troops. As the international community dithers, innocent men, women, and children die.

. . . It is at this point that a private company steps forward with a novel offer. Using its own hired troops, the firm will establish protected safe havens where civilians can take refuge and receive assistance . . . Thousands of lives might be saved. All the company asks for is a check for $150 million. What would the international community do when faced with such a choice? Would it allow peacekeeping to become a profit-making exercise? Or would it choose to spurn the firm's offer, but at the risk of the lives on the ground? It is certainly a fascinating dilemma, but one that sounds almost too implausible to consider seriously. It is not.

The time is fast approaching when this scenario will likely become reality. The community of nations had better have its act together before then, and have worked out an appropriate response. Otherwise, a new evil akin to that which overtook Sierra Leone may rise to power again, and this time we may have no effective means to drive away the darkness.

If the same set of factors were to re-emerge in Sierra Leone as existed in the eighties and nineties – the poverty and social exclusion that spawned that country's rebel movements – there could quite conceivably be a new West Side Boys or RUF rise to power in the nation's jungles. And there are, sadly, shortfalls in the funding of the rehabilitation efforts for ex-combatants in Sierra Leone. Likewise, the Truth and Reconciliation Commission has received only $1.6 million of a required $6 million funding, and its work is in jeopardy. 'It is striking that an initiative invested with such importance may not be funded,' warns the Conflict, Security and Development Group, of King's College London, in a March 2003 report on peacekeeping in Sierra Leone. 'The danger is that the lack of opportunity that drove young people into the ranks of the RUF is likely to persist, and the frustration that it generates may boil over once again,' the report concludes. 'The durability of the peace will ultimately be tied to the health of the country's economy, the even-handedness of its political culture and the opportunities the two provide for the average Sierra Leonean.' The UN peacekeeping force, presently at some 17,000 troops, is costing $700 million a year. The UN plans to reduce the size of that force to 5,000 troops by the end of 2004, dropping to some 2,000 and then eventual UN withdrawal. Heaven forbid that upon the pull-out of UN forces, disaffected ex-rebels pick up their weapons and head into the jungles again.

That nightmare scenario is not beyond the realms of possibility. And Sierra Leone is but one nation among many in Africa and beyond where such a prospect of ongoing, internecine conflict is quite possible. It is the responsibility of the international community to try to ensure that the factors that breed such conflict are addressed. We owe it to ourselves, because, in a world beset by international insecurity and menaced by terrorism, we cannot afford to allow such conflicts to fester and become the breeding grounds for further terror. If nothing else in Sierra Leone, the few millions now required to build the peace must be found, or the international community will be found woefully lacking.

Yet if and when such a situation does arise again, in whatever insecure, poverty-stricken country – and surely it is only a matter of time before it does – then the world community should have mechanisms in place to intervene. And to intervene quickly, efficiently and effectively. The mechanisms that presently exist within the structure of the United Nations do not work. Unilateral military interventions by the militaries of the UK and the US can be highly effective, but cannot be relied upon to sort out all the world's ills. A new modus operandi is called for, and it will be one that doubtless embraces the role that PMCs can play.

When all is said and done, the British military were forced to intervene in Sierra Leone because the UN failed. If the UN's 13,000 peacekeepers had been doing their job properly, IMATT, Operation

Palliser and Operation Barras would not have been necessary. In the final analysis, the eleven British soldiers of the Royal Irish Rangers were kidnapped and held hostage as an indirect result of UN failings in Sierra Leone. And the British soldiers who were wounded and killed in the hostage-rescue mission were the victims of those same failings. Finally, Sierra Leone was pulled back from the brink of becoming another Somalia, but not as a result of the actions of the UN peacekeeping forces at the time. It was due to a robust and aggressive engagement of British troops on a search-and-destroy – and ultimately, also, a rescue – mission.

They may not be ready, willing and available next time round.

APPENDIX 2: CALL SIGNS

Call Sign	Which Assault Element
Air Assault	
Sierra One	Chinook into southern Gberi Bana LZ1
Sierra Two	Chinook into northern Gberi Bana LZ2
Sierra Three	Chinook into Magbeni with Paras
Sierra Four	Air Wing Mi-24 Gunship
Sierra Five	Navy Lynx Attack Helicopter
Sierra Six	Army Lynx Mk7 Attack Helicopter
Sierra Seven	Army Lynx Mk7 Attack Helicopter
Ground Assault	
Sierra One Zero	UKSF Fire Team 1 – hostage-rescue team – into LZ1 Gberi Bana
Sierra Two Zero	UKSF Fire Team 2 into LZ1 Gberi Bana
Sierra Three Zero	UKSF Fire Team 3 into LZ1 Gberi Bana
Sierra Four Zero	UKSF Fire Team 4 into LZ1 Gberi Bana
Sierra Five Zero	UKSF Fire Team 5 into LZ1 Gberi Bana
Sierra Six Zero	UKSF Fire Team 6 into LZ1 Gberi Bana
Sierra Seven Zero	UKSF Fire Team 7 into LZ2 Gberi Bana
Sierra Eight Zero	UKSF Fire Team 8 into LZ2 Gberi Bana
Sierra Nine Zero	UKSF Fire Team 9 into LZ2 Gberi Bana
Sierra Ten Zero	UKSF Fire Team 10 into LZ2 Gberi Bana
Sierra Blue One	UKSF Fire Team 11 into LZ2 Gberi Bana
Sierra Blue Two	UKSF Fire Team 12 into LZ2 Gberi Bana
Sierra Green Alpha	UKSF Observation Team in Gberi Bana
Sierra Green Beta	UKSF Observation Team in Magbeni

Command and Control

West Side One Control	UKSF HQ in Gberi Bana, situated in the rebels' radio shack
West Side Two Control	Paras HQ in Magbeni
Sierra Control	UKSF HQ in Waterloo Camp

Landing Zones

LZ1 (UKSF)	South Gberi Bana, on clearing outside Calm Down Fresh's house
LZ2 (UKSF)	North Gberi Bana, on clearing outside Colonel Cambodia's house
LZ3 (UKSF)	West Gberi Bana, on overgrown village football field
LZ1 (Paras)	Clearing in centre of Magbeni village
LZ2 (Paras)	Swampy clearing on western side of Magbeni village

APPENDIX 3: CHRONOLOGY OF THE HOSTAGE CRISIS

Date	Event
Friday 25 August	Day 1 of the Sierra Leonean hostage crisis. Twelve-man Royal Irish Rangers patrol is captured by the West Side Boys. Corporal Mousa Bangura is put into the rebels' 'pit'.
Saturday 26 August	Day 2 Corporal Mousa Bangura is tortured outside hostages' rooms during the night.
Sunday 27 August	Day 3 Rebel leader Foday Kallay puts in his first appearance.
Monday 28 August	Day 4 Rebel Colonel GS threatens to execute all hostages unless rebel demands are met.
Tuesday 29 August	Day 5 Major Martial and Captain Flaherty are taken to hostage-negotiation meeting. Rebels demand satphone so they can speak with world's media. Six-man SAS advance party flies back from Kenya to UK to prepare Martie's and Adie's funerals.

Wednesday 30 August   Day 6
Five of hostages are released by the West Side
Boys.
RUF rebels express interest in British hostages
to press.
West Side Boys are given satphone.
Delegation of West Side Boys' mothers visits
rebel base to plead with their sons to give up
the hostages.
All of D Squadron arrive back in UK from
Kenya for funerals and to prepare for deploy-
ment on Operation Barras.
Paras are warned off for a deployment to
Sierra Leone as part of Operation Barras.

Thursday 31 August   Day 7
'Gimp' goes crazy with rebel boy soldier's AK47.
Hostages abortive effort to escape into jungle
around Gberi Bana.
Paras warned off for possible hostage-rescue
mission in Sierra Leone.
SAS/SBS advance party arrives at Senegal's
international airport en route to Sierra Leone.

Friday 1 September   Day 8
Hostages are moved from Colonel Cambodia's
house down to Camp Commandant's house.
SAS/SBS main assault force heads out by RAF
Hercules to Senegal, the forward mounting
base for the mission.
Paras move to operational mounting centre
for deployment from UK to Senegal/Sierra
Leone.

Saturday 2 September   Day 9
SAS/SBS assault force flies into Sierra Leone
in three C-130 Hercules aircraft, establish HQ
at Waterloo Camp.
Paras advance party flies out to Senegal's international airport, en route to Sierra Leone.
Story of Paras' deployment to Sierra Leone for
a hostage-rescue mission is leaked to the press.

Sunday 3 September   Day 10
Note is put through the hostages' window at
night, referring to seeing the 'boys from
Stirling soon'.
Camp Commandant tries to shoot boy soldier
Assan.
Buses full of villagers hijacked by West Side
Boys. Colonel Savage thrown in pit.
Villager forced recruits brought to Gberi Bana
at gunpoint for 'training'.

Monday 4 September   Day 11
Para advance party flies into Sierra Leone.
British soldiers held hostage are forced to train
village 'recruits' in drill and basic combat.
West Side Boys launch attack on Kamajor
village.
Three severed Kamajor heads mounted on
poles and taken to hostage negotiations by
West Side Boys.
British hostages get first wash of captivity, and
abort riverine escape attempt.
Rebel leaders take Major Martial and Ranger
Rowell out to 'dead zone' to kill them.

Tuesday 5 September   Day 12
Major Martial and Ranger Rowell are
reunited with four other hostages.
SAS/SBS obs teams are taken in upriver by
inflatables and establish OPs at Gberi Bana
and Magbeni.
Paras main assault force flies into Sierra Leone
and establish base at Waterloo Camp.

Wednesday 6 September   Day 13
Rebel leaders try to force Major Martial to
give an interview to BBC on satphone.
All hostages given savage beatings when
Major Martial refuses to do so.
Rebel leaders carry out mock executions of
Major Martial after his refusal to speak on
satphone.

SAS/SBS obs team report satphone drama and mock executions to operational headquarters. Operation planners put Operation Barras on 90 per cent to proceed.
MOD are forced to give press briefing in Freetown on Paras' deployment to Sierra Leone.

Thursday 7 September Day 14
West Side Boys set out to attack Nigerian UN peacekeepers.
BBC reports Paras on their way to Sierra Leone to launch an assault on the West Side Boys.
'Operation Certain Death' becomes plan of assault for the forces at Waterloo Camp.

Friday 8 September Day 15
Sony warns Major Martial that rebel leaders are planning either to kill them or move them into more remote jungle, and proposes his escape plan to saw through hostages' window.
West Side Boys return from disastrous attack on UN Nigerian forces.
West Side Boys set off to ambush ongoing hostage negotiations and capture British negotiators.
Blair sends message giving Op Barras green light.

Saturday 9 September Day 16
Royal Irish Rangers commander makes 'proof of life' phone call to six hostages.
Final assault briefing for SAS, SBS and the Paras.
Army Mk7 Lynx attack helicopter undergoes emergency overnight engine refit on HMS *Argyll*.

Sunday 10 September Day 17
Operation Barras assault force launches pre-dawn air assault on rebel bases at Gberi Bana and Magbeni.
All British hostages rescued safely.
Brad Tinnion is killed by rebel fire.

APPENDIX 4: CHRONOLOGY OF SIERRA LEONE

Date	Event
March 1991	RUF launch first rebel attacks into Sierra Leone from bases in Liberia.
May 1995	Executive Outcomes' first forces arrive in Sierra Leone.
January 1997	Executive Outcomes withdraw from Sierra Leone.
April 1997	Sierra Leone Army sign agreement with UK on training first two SLA battalions (start of IMATT).
May 1997	Coup led by Major Johnny Paul Koroma brings the AFRC to power, a coalition of the RUF, West Side Boys and SLA renegades.
July 1997	RUF leader Foday Sankoh becomes vice-chairman of the AFRC.
August 1997	Kamajor start offensive to liberate Freetown.
October 1997	UN Security Council imposes Resolution SCR1132, an embargo on arms, ammunition and fuel to Sierra Leone. Representative of Sandline meets with President Kabbah to discuss military options.

February 1998	Forces of ECOMOG, the Kamajors, supported by Sandline, gain control of the Freetown Peninsula.
March 1998	President Kabbah is reinstated in Freetown. UN Security Council lifts arms embargo, places travel ban on the RUF and AFRC.
July 1998	UN Security Council establishes (UNOMSIL) – 70 observers sent.
August 1998	RUF and others announce nationwide 'terror campaign'.
October 1998	34 army officers charged with treason and 24 executed (the AFRC plotters).
6 January 1999	Freetown retaken by AFRC/West Side Boys/RUF, and Operation No Living Thing imposed – 7,000 killed.
26 January 1999	Kamajors and police force rebels/AFRC out of Freetown.
February 1999	Publication in UK of Foreign Office's 'Arms to Africa' affair report.
May 1999	Ceasefire deal signed between Foday Sankoh of the RUF and President Kabbah.
August 1999	Lome Peace Accord signed by President Kabbah and Foday Sankoh, giving blanket amnesty to rebels and power sharing.
August 1999	UK government pledges $7.1 million for training Sierra Leone Army.
August 1999	Ten UNOMSIL and twenty ECOMOG soldiers kidnapped by rebels.
October 1999	UN Security Council Resolution 1270 establishes UNAMSIL, mandated for 6,000 peace keeping troops.
November 1999	Indian General Vijay Kumar Jetley appointed to lead UNAMSIL.

January 2000	Staff of Médicines sans Frontières (MSF) kidnapped by RUF's Sam Maskita Bockerie.
February 2000	UN Security Council Resolution 1289 increases forces of UNAMSIL to 11,000 troops.
April 2000	UNAMSIL peacekeeping troops deployed to nine of their twelve districts in Sierra Leone.
May 2000	UN hostages taken, four killed, UN helicopter shot down – all by RUF.
May 2000	30,000 people march on the streets of Freetown against RUF.
May 2000	Operation Palliser goes into effect, with the Paras landing at Lungi Airport, and the ARG setting sail for Freetown.
May 2000	UN Security Council increases UNAMSIL strength to 16,500 troops.
June 2000	Foday Sankoh arrested and held in Freetown.
July 2000	UK military training under IMATT begins in earnest.
August 2000	UN Secretary-General recommends increasing UNAMSIL strength to 20,500 troops.
August 2000	Twelve-man Royal Irish Rangers patrol kidnapped by West Side Boys.
September 2000	Operation Barras goes into action – hostages rescued and West Side Boys defeated.
April 2001	UN Security Council Resolution 1346 increases UNAMSIL strength to 17,500 troops with strengthened mandate.

GLOSSARY

AFRC Armed Forces Revolutionary Council, the Sierra Leonean rebel-military junta that ruled for several months during 1997.

Air Wing the Sierra Leonean helicopter force, flown by ex-mercenaries.

AK47 Soviet-designed 7.62mm Kalashnikov assault rifle.

ALARP air-landing airborne-refuelling platform, a mobile facility full of aviation fuel, usually for refuelling helicopters near to the battlefield.

APC armoured personnel carrier.

ARG Amphibious Ready Group, the amphibious element of the British military's Joint Rapid Reaction Force.

AWOL absent without leave, but also used as slang for someone going crazy.

Bergen army backpack containing mess kit, sleeping bag, etc.

BMP a Soviet bloc light-armoured vehicle, mounted with a 30mm cannon.

Casevac casualty evacuation (by air).

CB-MRE-B Coke-bottle meals-ready-to-eat bomb.

Chaff radar-reflecting tinsel and heat-seeking missile confusing flares used by aircraft to deter homing missiles.

CHASL Christian Health Association of Sierra Leone, a charity giving medical aid.

Chinook a large, twin-rotor transport helicopter with a lifting capability of ten tons, with door-mounted chain guns.

CMHQ Cockerill Military Headquarters, the headquarters of the Sierra Leone military in Freetown.

CO Commanding Officer.

Conflict diamonds diamonds that originate from areas under the control of forces in opposition to elected and internationally recognised governments.

CSM Company Sergeant Major.

CT counter-terrorism.

CTR close-target reconnaissance.

Cyalumes transparent plastic tubes filled with a light-producing chemical liquid.

DDR demobilisation, disarmament and reintegration.

Delta Force supposedly ultra-secret US Special Forces, recruited from the US Army and with very similar functions to the SAS.

DRC Democratic Republic of Congo, a central African country.

ECOMOG Economic Community of West African States Ceasefire Monitoring Group, West Africa's own peacekeeping force, dominated by the Nigerian military.

EHC evacuation handling cell.

EO Executive Outcomes, a South African-based private military company.

EP evacuation point.

Exfil exfiltration, leaving battle scene or area of operations at end of mission.

Fablon a plastic-based waterproofing film.

FAC forward air control, the ability to call in air strikes to specific enemy targets.

1st NZ SAS Group New Zealand SAS.

Flare out term for a helicopter slowing down to a hover or for a landing.

FMB forward mounting base, a forward position from which to prepare for deployment into action.

Fragged Paras' slang for injured or killed by a fragment of artillery.

Frobbers British soldiers' slang for idiots.

GPMG general purpose machine gun.

Green Slime British soldiers' slang for British intelligence.

Harrier British-made vertical take-off and landing-strike aircraft.

HE heavy explosives.

Hercules (C-130) American-built C-130 transport aircraft, used by British military, commonly known as a 'Herc'.

Hexy stove a tiny, collapsible metal stove, which burns solid, white paraffin-based fuel blocks.

HMG heavy machine gun.

Humint human intelligence sources.

IAF Indian Air Force.

IMATT International Military Advisory and Training Team.

Infil infiltration.

IPOA International Peace Operations Association.

JFHO Freetown Joint Force Headquarters, the tri-service command HQ for British military operations in Sierra Leone.

JRRF Joint Rapid Reaction Force, the tri-service rapid-reaction capability of the British military, developed as a result of the 1998 Strategic Defence Review.

Koevoet the South-West African Police counter-insurgency unit.

LAW light anti-armour weapon, an American-made 66 or 94mm disposable, one-man-portable rocket system with a 500-metre range.

LOE limit of exploitation, the agreed extent to which a military unit will advance on the battlefield.

LRDG Long Range Desert Group, the Second World War forerunners to the SAS.

Lynx British-built attack helicopter.

LZ landing zone.

MAD mutually assured destruction.

Malleting slang for shooting or blowing up the enemy, as in 'give them a good malleting'.

MAMS Military Air Management System, a British military air-traffic control team.

MFC Mortar fire control.

Mi-17 Soviet bloc transport helicopter.

Mi-24 Soviet bloc helicopter gunship.

MP5 A Hechler and Koch short machine gun, ideal for Special Forces use.

MRE meals ready to eat, US Army ration packs.

NAF Nigerian Air Force.

NCO non-commissioned officer.

NEO non-combatant evacuation operation.

NOK next of kin.

NVG night-vision goggles.

OG orders group, a meeting at which a unit's officers are briefed by the commander.

OC Officer Commanding.

OMC operational mounting centre, the departure point for British forces being deployed out of the UK.

OP observation post, a position from where to spy on enemy movements.

Op operation.

Operation Agricola the Paras' deployment to Kosovo, in 1999.

Operation Barras code name for the Sierra Leonean hostage-rescue assault, September 2000.

Operation Kukri code name for the British–UN raid to free hundreds of UN hostages from rebels in Sierra Leone, June 2000.

Operation Nimrod 1980 Iranian Embassy siege in London, ended by an SAS assault.

Operation Palliser code name for the British military intervention in Sierra Leone in May 2000.

Operation Restore Hope the United Nations mission to Somalia, in 1993.

Operation Sand Storm the 1998 Nigerian military-led ECOMOG mission to retake the capital of Sierra Leone from the forces of the AFRC.

Operation Thunderbolt code name for the UN attack on the West Side Boys in Sierra Leone, August 2000.

Opsec operational security.

Paras the men of the Parachute Regiment.

PJHQ Permanent Joint Headquarters, the UK military tri-service command centre.

PMC private military company.

Prepped prepared for a mission.

Psyops psychological operations.

PT Physical Training.

Recce Commandos South African Defence Force Special Forces unit.

RFA Royal Fleet Auxiliary.

RFL restricted fire line.

RPG rocket-propelled grenade.

RSLAF Republic of Sierra Leone Armed Forces, the name for the Sierra Leonean armed forces, post-2000.

RSLMF Republic of Sierra Leone Military Forces, the name for the Sierra Leonean armed forces, pre-1997.

RSO Regimental Signals Officer.

RUF Revolutionary United Front, Sierra Leone's largest rebel force.

SADF South African Defence Force.

SAM surface-to-air missile.

SAS Special Air Service, the UK's foremost Special Forces unit.

SASR Australian SAS.

SBS Special Boat Service, the UK's smaller, sister Special Forces unit to the SAS, with a marine-riverine specialism.

SBU Small Boys Unit, a rebel force of boys between eight and fourteen years old.

Scoff slang for prepare food, get a meal ready, eat.

Sea Harriers Harrier version fitted with Blue Fox radar.

Sea King naval anti-submarine helicopter, capable of carrying twenty men.

SEAL Sea Air Land Team, Special Forces recruited from within the US Navy and Marine Corps, and tasked with direct action missions and amphibious operations.

SF Special Forces.

Shakyboats slang for the men of the Special Boat Service.

Sitrep situation report.

SLA Sierra Leonean Army.

Slabbering slang for giving the new recruits a good verbal dressing-down.

SLE Spearhead Lead Element of the Parachute Regiment.

SLR self-loading rifle.

Sobels Sierra Leone soldiers by day, rebels by night.

SOP standard operating procedure, the normal way of doing things in any given military situation.

Tabs slang for cigarettes.

32nd 'Buffalo' Battalion a South African Special Forces unit, which used a lot of foreign fighters.

TOW tube-launched, optically tracked, wire-guided anti-tank missiles.

TRC Truth and Reconciliation Commission.

Tristars passenger airliners used by British military as troop transports.

2iC second in command.

UKSF United Kingdom Special Forces (the SAS and the SBS) including support elements.

UNAMSIL the United Nations Mission to Sierra Leone.

Warned off British military phrase meaning to be given first warning of an impending deployment.

WMIK weapons mount installation kit, a Land-Rover-mounted heavy machine gun set-up, including a GPMG and a 50-cal.

WP white phosphorous, an incendiary shell.

ZPU Soviet bloc twin 14.5mm heavy machine gun, designed for anti-aircraft use.

QUOTATION ACKNOWLEDGEMENTS

Chapter 6: The Nightmare Begins
From the *Breviary of a Medieval Knight*

Chapter 7: Get the Brits
Copyright © Major General John Frost 1983, *A Drop Too Many*
Extracted from *A Drop Too Many* published by Pen & Sword Books
Ltd 2002.

Chapter 8: Dances with Death
Excerpt from *War As I Knew It* by General George S Patton. Copyright
© 1947 by Beatrice Patton Walters, Ruth Patton Totten and George
Smith Totten. Copyright © renewed 1975 by Major George Patton,
Ruth Patton Totten, John K. Waters, Jr. and George P. Waters.
Reprinted by Permission of Houghton Mifflin Co. All rights reserved.

Chapter 9: This Means War
Copyright © Paulo Coelho, Manual of the Warrior of Light
HarperCollins Publishers Ltd.

Chapter 10: Lottery of Freedom
Brigadier David Richards, Commander of British Forces in Sierra Leone.
Quoted in the *Daily Telegraph* 24 May 2000.

Chapter 11: Virgin Warriors
General Wesley K. Clark, *Winning Modern Wars*
Reprinted by permission of PublicAffairs, a member of Perseus Books
Group LLC, From Winning Modern Wars by General Wesley Clark,
Copyright © 2003.

Chapter 12: The Siege of the Gimp
Chinese proverb

Chapter 13: Riverine Assault
Sun Tzu, *The Art of War* circa 500 BC.

Chapter 14: No Escape
Copyright © Paulo Coelho, *Manual of the Warrior of Light*
HarperCollins Publishers Ltd.

Chapter 16: The Killing Game
Bloodsong
HarperCollins Publishers Ltd. Copyright © Jim Hooper 2003

Chapter 17: The Dead Zone
Lieutenant Colonel F Spencer Chapman, 1949
The Jungle is Neutral, Chatto and Windus.

Chapter 18: Proof of Life
Andre Maurois, *Memoirs*, 1970, Harper and Row.

Chapter 19: Dawn Raiders
Winston Churchill 13 May 1940, to the House of Commons in his first address as Prime Minister.

Chapter 20: A Rude Awakening
Theodore Roosevelt, 10 April 1899, excerpt from a speech given before the Hamilton Club, Chicago, Illinois.

Chapter 21: Chicken Run
George Orwell
© George Orwell reproduced by permission of Bill Hamilton as the Literary Executor of the Estate of the Late Sonia Brownell Orwell and Secker and Warburg Ltd.

Chapter 22: In For The Kill
General Sir Charles Guthrie, Chief of Defence Staff in a statement to the press, 10 May 2000.

Chapter 23: Salvation
Winston Churchill, excerpt from article, 'Shall We All Commit Suicide?' *Nash's Pall Mall*, 24 September 1924.

Chapter 24: Ten Men Down
Don McClen, *The Heart of Things*
reproduced by kind permission of the author.

Chapter 25: Time for a Brew
Major Phil Neame, in Max Arthur's *Above All, Courage*
Copyright © Max Arthur 1985
Macmillan 1985.

Chapter 26: Return of the Jedi
Captain (later Field Marshall) Earl Alexander, 1917, in a letter to his mother.

Chapter 27: Endgame
Mao Tse-Tung

Postscript
Field Marshall Erwin Rommel

Appendix 1: Analysis
General Sir Peter Inge, Chief of Defence Staff, 1996.

Afterword
Extract from Once a Pilgrim © Will Scully 1998,
Headline
Reproduced by permission of Headline Book Publishing Ltd.